W9-CND-902

QuickBooks 2013

the missing manual®

The book that should have been in the box®

Bonnie Biafore

O'REILLY®

Beijing | Cambridge | Farnham | Köln | Sebastopol | Tokyo

QuickBooks 2013: The Missing Manual

by Bonnie Biafore

Published by O'Reilly Media, Inc.,
1005 Gravenstein Highway North, Sebastopol, CA 95472.

O'Reilly books may be purchased for educational, business, or sales promotional use. Online editions are also available for most titles (*http://my.safaribooksonline.com*). For more information, contact our corporate/institutional sales department: (800) 998-9938 or *corporate@oreilly.com*.

October 2012:   First Edition.

Revision History for the First Edition:

2012-10-10   First release

See *http://oreilly.com/catalog/errata.csp?isbn=9781449316112* for release details.

ISBN-13: 978-1-449-31611-2

[LSI]

Contents

Part One: Getting Started

Part Two: **Bookkeeping**

Part Three: Managing Your Business

Part Four: QuickBooks Power

Part Five: **Appendixes**

> **NOTE** You can find three bonus appendixes online at *www.missingmanuals.com/cds*: "Keyboard Shortcuts," "Tracking Time with the Standalone Timer," and "Advanced Form Customization."

The Missing Credits

ABOUT THE AUTHOR

 **Bonnie Biafore** has always been fascinated with math in its practical and more esoteric forms. As an engineer and project manager, she's thorough and steadfastly attentive to detail but redeems herself by using her sick sense of humor to transform these drool-inducing subjects into entertaining reading. She writes about personal finance, investing, accounting, and project management. Her *NAIC Stock Selection Handbook* and *Successful Project Management* won major awards from the Society of Technical Communication and APEX Awards for Publication Excellence (but the raves she receives from beginning investors mean much more to her).

Bonnie is also the author of O'Reilly's *Microsoft Project 2010: The Missing Manual*, *Personal Finance: The Missing Manual*, *Quicken 2009: The Missing Manual*, and *Online Investing Hacks*. She writes a monthly column called "WebWatch" for *Better Investing* magazine and is a regular contributor to *www.interest.com*. Applying her humor to another genre, she has published a novel, *Fresh Squeezed*, a crime comedy. As a consultant, she manages projects for clients, provides training, and wins accolades for her ability to herd cats.

When not chained to her computer, she hikes and cycles in the mountains, walks her dogs, takes aerial dance classes, and cooks gourmet meals. You can learn more at Bonnie's website, *www.bonniebiafore.com*, or email her at *bonnie.biafore@gmail.com*.

ABOUT THE CREATIVE TEAM

Dawn Mann (editor) is associate editor for the Missing Manual series. When not reading about QuickBooks, she beads, plays soccer, and causes trouble. Email: *dawn@oreilly.com*.

Melanie Yarbrough (production editor) lives, works, and does pretty much everything else in Cambridge, MA. When she's not ushering books through production, she's writing and baking up whatever she can imagine. Email: *myarbrough@oreilly.com*.

Brad White (technical reviewer) is COO of Real World Training and has been teaching and consulting on QuickBooks since 1998. When he isn't fixing someone else's computer problems, he enjoys listening to audio books, eating sushi, and thinking about golfing. Website: *www.QuickBooksTraining.com*.

Michael Cobb (technical reviewer) is an Information Designer with Real World Training and enjoys paying way too much for tech gadgetry, cooking insanely spicy food, and traveling to exotic lands like California. Email: *michael_cobb@realworldtraining.com*.

Nan Reinhardt (proofreader) lives in the Midwest, where she enjoys summer weekends at the lake, boating, swimming, and reading voraciously. Nan is not only a freelance copyeditor and proofreader, but she's also a published romance novelist. Check out her work at *www.nanreinhardt.com*. Email: *nanleigh1@gmail.com*.

Ron Strauss (indexer) lives and works in Northern California. He moonlights as a classically trained violist. Email: *rstrauss@mchsi.com*.

ACKNOWLEDGEMENTS

Behind the scenes, a horde of hard-working folks help make this book (and me) look as good as we do. I am always grateful for the improvements that people make to my writing. My words (and bookkeeping) are better for it. Dawn Mann raised the bar this year to make the book as clear as possible and the process of producing it *almost* painless. Special thanks to Ron Strauss for building an index that helps you find all the information you want (especially important given the absence of an index in QuickBooks Help). And for making me look good—literally—I'd like to thank Garrett Hacking, my friend and professional photographer extraordinaire, for the best author photo ever.

I also want to thank the technical reviewers, Brad White and Michael Cobb, whose encyclopedic knowledge of QuickBooks was a much appreciated gift. And, as always, I thank my agent, Neil Salkind, for helping me turn my writing into a second career.

—*Bonnie Biafore*

THE MISSING MANUAL SERIES

Missing Manuals are witty, superbly written guides to computer products that don't come with printed manuals (which is just about all of them). Each book features a handcrafted index and cross-references to specific pages (not just chapters). Recent and upcoming titles include:

Access 2010: The Missing Manual by Matthew MacDonald

Adobe Edge Preview 7: The Missing Manual by Chris Grover

Buying a Home: The Missing Manual by Nancy Conner

Creating a Website: The Missing Manual, Third Edition, by Matthew MacDonald

CSS: The Missing Manual, Second Edition, by David Sawyer McFarland

David Pogue's Digital Photography: The Missing Manual by David Pogue

Dreamweaver CS6: The Missing Manual by David Sawyer McFarland

Droid 2: The Missing Manual by Preston Gralla

Droid X2: The Missing Manual by Preston Gralla

Excel 2010: The Missing Manual by Matthew MacDonald

FileMaker Pro 12: The Missing Manual by Susan Prosser and Stuart Gripman

Flash CS6: The Missing Manual by Chris Grover

Galaxy S II: The Missing Manual by Preston Gralla

Galaxy Tab: The Missing Manual by Preston Gralla

Google+: The Missing Manual by Kevin Purdy

HTML5: The Missing Manual by Matthew MacDonald

iMovie '11 & iDVD: The Missing Manual by David Pogue and Aaron Miller

iPad: The Missing Manual, Fourth Edition by J.D. Biersdorfer

iPhone: The Missing Manual, Fifth Edition by David Pogue

iPhone App Development: The Missing Manual by Craig Hockenberry

iPhoto '11: The Missing Manual by David Pogue and Lesa Snider

iPod: The Missing Manual, Tenth Edition by J.D. Biersdorfer and David Pogue

JavaScript & jQuery: The Missing Manual, Second Edition by David Sawyer McFarland

Kindle Fire: The Missing Manual by Peter Meyers

Living Green: The Missing Manual by Nancy Conner

Mac OS X Mountain Lion: The Missing Manual by David Pogue

Microsoft Project 2010: The Missing Manual by Bonnie Biafore

Motorola Xoom: The Missing Manual by Preston Gralla

Netbooks: The Missing Manual by J.D. Biersdorfer

NOOK Tablet: The Missing Manual by Preston Gralla

Office 2010: The Missing Manual by Nancy Connor, Chris Grover, and Matthew MacDonald

Office 2011 for Macintosh: The Missing Manual by Chris Grover

Personal Investing: The Missing Manual by Bonnie Biafore

Photoshop CS6: The Missing Manual by Lesa Snider

Photoshop Elements 10: The Missing Manual by Barbara Brundage

PHP & MySQL: The Missing Manual by Brett McLaughlin

Switching to the Mac: The Missing Manual, Mountain Lion Edition by David Pogue

Windows 7: The Missing Manual by David Pogue

Windows 8: The Missing Manual by David Pogue

Your Body: The Missing Manual by Matthew MacDonald

Your Brain: The Missing Manual by Matthew MacDonald

Your Money: The Missing Manual by J.D. Roth

For a full list of all Missing Manuals in print, go to *www.missingmanuals.com/library.html*.

Introduction

Thousands of small companies and nonprofit organizations turn to QuickBooks to keep their finances on track. And over the years, Intuit has introduced various editions of the program to satisfy the needs of different types of companies. Back when milk was simply milk, you either used QuickBooks or you didn't. But now, when you can choose milk from soybeans and rice as well as cows, and with five different levels of fat, it's no surprise that QuickBooks comes in a variety of editions (which, in some cases, are dramatically different from their siblings), as well as six industry-specific editions. From the smallest of sole proprietorships to burgeoning enterprises, one of these editions is likely to meet your organization's needs *and* budget.

QuickBooks isn't hard to learn. Many of the features that you're familiar with from other programs work the same way in QuickBooks—windows, dialog boxes, drop-down lists, and keyboard shortcuts, to name a few. And with each new version, Intuit has added enhancements and new features to make your workflow smoother and faster. The challenge is knowing what to do according to accounting rules, and how to do it in QuickBooks. This book teaches you how to use QuickBooks and explains the accounting concepts behind what you're doing.

▇ What's New in QuickBooks 2013

Despite the fluctuating size of the tax code, accounting and bookkeeping practices don't change much each year. The changes in QuickBooks 2013 are mostly small tweaks and subtle improvements, but some of them might be just what you've been waiting for:

- QuickBooks 2013 sports a **brand-new look** that simplifies the interface, removes clutter, and presents features and options in a much more organized and consistent way. The new color scheme is designed to help you focus on the task at hand: Navigation areas like the top and left icon bars are darker and monochromatic with silver icons so they recede into the background while the areas where you do your work stand out; blue, green, and yellow icons represent other features that relate to the work you do; the button that's clicked when you press Enter is also blue so it's easy to identify. Font sizes also vary to reinforce the hierarchy of information. The rows in transaction windows' tables are taller and overall spacing is more ample to make data easier to read. One downside to this new look is that windows take up more space on your screen—but the feature described in the next bullet point can help with that.

NOTE The changes to the user interface are bound to generate a swell of feedback. Don't be surprised if you see tweaks to the interface when Intuit distributes intermediate releases of the software.

- **Supermax view** (page 38) enlarges a single window, such as Create Invoices, to fill the entire QuickBooks window. It also minimizes the window's *ribbon* (described later in this list) so you can see more data, such as more lines in an invoice table.

- QuickBooks Centers (Vendor, Customer, Employee—and Inventory if you use QuickBooks Premier and Enterprise) now include **tabs for transactions, contacts, to-dos, and notes** (page 75). When you choose a name in a center—for example, a customer in the Customer Center—the panel at the window's bottom-right provides the full scoop about that customer. The Transactions tab displays all the transactions for that customer, and you can filter those transactions by type (invoices, credit memos, payments, and so on), status (such as open or all), and date. When you click the Contacts tab, you can create and manage multiple contacts, from the president to the accounting manager to the receptionist who knows where to find everyone. The To Do's tab lets you create and manage to-dos you have to perform. Similarly, the Notes tab is where you create and manage notes you record.

- Using the Notes tabs in the QuickBooks Centers, QuickBooks 2013 lets you **create multiple notes for each name** (page 83). In previous versions, you could add as many notes as you wanted, but they all resided in one field in the Edit Note dialog box. On the Notes tabs, you can scan the list of individual notes, create new ones, or edit and delete existing ones.

- You can **set preferences to make QuickBooks mark all your time and expenses as billable or non-billable.** In the Preferences dialog box's Time & Expenses category, you can turn on the "Mark all time entries as billable" checkbox so that QuickBooks automatically turns on the Billable checkbox for every time record you create. (If you bill time only once in a while, turn this checkbox off so that time records are marked as non-billable unless you make them billable.) Similarly, if most of your expenses are billable, you can turn on the "Mark all Expenses as billable" checkbox. Then, in windows such as Enter Bills and Write Checks, expenses you add are automatically marked as billable. (If you bill only a few of your expenses, turn this checkbox off.)

- Similar to Microsoft programs, QuickBooks now uses **a ribbon** (a panel that contains buttons and drop-down menus to access the program's features) across the top of many of its windows, such as Create Invoices. Features that used to be scattered over the window's toolbar, the form itself, and shortcut menus are now gathered at the top of the window. (If you're a fan of right-clicking to open shortcut menus, those are still available.)

- The **left icon bar** (page 36) is a new option that helps you access a variety of QuickBooks elements, including shortcuts to your favorite features, the Quick-Books windows that are open, applications you use, and to-dos that are on the horizon. If you haven't graduated to a widescreen monitor, you can still use the top icon bar or hide both icon bars.

- The **Find button at the top-left of QuickBooks transaction windows** (page 356) makes it easy to find specific transactions you're looking for. When you click this button, a compact version of the Find dialog box opens so you can specify search criteria, such as customer name, date, bill number, or amount.

▦ When QuickBooks May Not Be the Answer

When you run a business (or a nonprofit), you track company finances for two reasons: to keep your business running smoothly and to generate the reports required by the IRS, SEC, and anyone else you have to answer to. QuickBooks helps you perform basic financial tasks, track your financial situation, and manage your business to make it even better. But before you read any further, here are a few things you *shouldn't* try to do with QuickBooks:

- **Work with more than 14,500 unique inventory items or 14,500 contact names.** QuickBooks Pro and Premier company files can hold up to 14,500 inventory items and a combined total of up to 14,500 customer, vendor, employee, and other (Other Names List) names. (The QuickBooks Enterprise Solutions version makes the number of names virtually unlimited.)

- **Track personal finances.** Even if you're a company of one, keeping your personal finances separate from your business finances is a good move, particularly when it comes to tax reporting. In addition to opening a separate checking account for your business, track your personal finances somewhere else (like in Quicken). If you do decide to use QuickBooks, at least create a separate company file for your personal financial info.

- **Track the performance of stocks and bonds.** QuickBooks isn't meant to keep track of the capital gains and dividends you earn from investments such as stocks and bonds. But companies have investments, too, of course. A machine that costs hundreds of thousands of dollars is an investment that you hope will generate lots of income, and you should track it in QuickBooks. However, in QuickBooks, these types of investments show up as *assets* of the company (page 163).

- **Manage specialized details about customer relationships.** Lots of information goes into keeping customers happy. With QuickBooks, you can stay on top of customer activities with features like To Do items, Notes, Reminders, and Memorized Transactions. You can also keep track of leads before they turn into customers. But if you need to track details for thousands of members or customers, items sold on consignment, project progress, or tasks related to managing projects, a customer-management program or program like Microsoft Excel or Access might be a better solution.

NOTE Some third-party customer-management programs integrate with QuickBooks (page 85).

Choosing the Right Edition

QuickBooks comes in a gamut of editions, offering options for organizations at both ends of the small-business spectrum. QuickBooks Pro handles the basic needs of most businesses, whereas Enterprise Solutions (the most robust and powerful edition of QuickBooks) boasts enhanced features and speed for the biggest of small businesses. On the other hand, the online editions of QuickBooks offer features that are available any time you're online.

WARNING QuickBooks for Mac differs *significantly* from the Windows version, so this book isn't meant to be a guide to the Mac version of the program. Likewise, features vary in the editions for different countries; this book focuses on the U.S. version.

This book focuses on QuickBooks Pro because its balance of features and price make it the most popular edition. Throughout this book, you'll also find notes about features offered in the Premier edition, which is one step up from Pro. (Whether you're willing to pay for these additional features is up to you.) Here's an overview of what each edition can do:

- **QuickBooks Online Simple Start** is a low-cost online option for small businesses with very simple accounting needs and only one person running QuickBooks at a time. It's easy to set up and use, but it doesn't offer features like entering bills, inventory, tracking time, or sharing your company file with your accountant. You can download transactions from only one bank (or credit card) account.

- **QuickBooks Online Essentials** allows up to three people to run QuickBooks at a time and lets you connect to as many bank or credit card accounts as you want. As its name suggests, it offers essential features like automated invoicing, creating estimates, and entering bills.

- **QuickBooks Online Plus** has most of the features of QuickBooks Pro, but you access the program via the Web instead of running it on your PC.

> **NOTE** These online editions let you use QuickBooks anywhere, on any computer, so they're ideal for someone who's always on the go. However, the online editions are subscription-based, so you pay a monthly fee to use the software. A year's subscription adds up to more than what you'd typically pay to buy a license of QuickBooks Pro, but with a subscription, your software is always up-to-date—you don't have to upgrade it or convert your company files to the new versions you installed.

- **QuickBooks Pro** is the workhorse edition. It lets up to three people work on a company file at a time. QuickBooks Pro includes features for tasks such as invoicing; entering and paying bills; job costing; creating estimates; saving and distributing reports and forms as email attachments; creating budgets; projecting cash flow; tracking mileage; customizing forms; customizing prices with price levels; printing shipping labels; and integrating with Word, Excel, and hundreds of other programs. QuickBooks Pro's name lists—customers, vendors, employees, and so on—can include up to a combined total of 14,500 entries. Other lists, like the Chart of Accounts, can have up to 10,000 entries each.

> **NOTE** QuickBooks Pro Plus is a subscription product that costs a little more than the one-time license fee you pay for QuickBooks Pro, but QuickBooks Pro Plus offers mobile access, unlimited phone support, and always-up-to-date software. Similarly, QuickBooks Premier Plus is the premier version of the subscription product.

- **QuickBooks Premier** is another multiuser edition. It can handle inventory items assembled from other items and components, generate purchase orders from sales orders and estimates, apply price levels to individual items, export report templates, produce budgets and forecasts, work with different units of measure for items, and it offers enhanced invoicing for time and expenses. This edition also includes a few extra features like reversing general journal entries. When you purchase QuickBooks Premier, you can choose from six different industry-specific flavors (see the next section). Like the Pro edition, Premier can handle a combined total of up to 14,500 list entries.

- **Enterprise Solutions** is the edition for larger operations. It's faster, bigger, and more robust than its siblings. Up to 30 people can access a company file at the same time, and this simultaneous access is at least twice as fast as in the Pro or Premier edition. The database can handle lots more names in its customer, vendor, employee, and other name lists (1 *million* versus 14,500 for Pro and Premier). You can handle inventory in multiple warehouses or stores, and produce combined reports for those companies and locations. And because more people can be in your company file, this edition has features such as an enhanced audit trail, more options for assigning or limiting user permissions, and the ability to delegate administrative functions to the other people using the program. And if you subscribe to Advanced Inventory, you can value inventory by using first-in first-out (FIFO) inventory valuation.

TIP You don't have to pay list price for QuickBooks. Your local office supply store, Amazon.com, and any number of other retail outlets usually offer the program at a discount. (If you buy QuickBooks from Intuit, you pay full price, but you also have 60 days to return the program for a full refund.) In addition, accountants can resell QuickBooks to clients, so it's worth asking yours about purchase and upgrade pricing. QuickBooks ProAdvisors can get you up to a 30 percent discount on QuickBooks Pro or Premier, and you'll still have 60 days to return the program for a refund.

FREQUENTLY ASKED QUESTION

Nonprofit Dilemma

I'm doing the books for a tiny nonprofit corporation. I'd really like to avoid spending any of our hard-raised funds on a special edition of QuickBooks. Can't I just use QuickBooks Pro?

You may be tempted to save some money by using QuickBooks Pro instead of the more expensive QuickBooks Nonprofit edition, and you can—if you're willing to live with some limitations. As long as funding comes primarily from unrestricted sources, the Pro edition will work reasonably well. You'll have to accept using the term "customer" when you mean donor or member, or the term "job" for grants you receive. Throughout this book, you'll find notes and tips about tracking nonprofit

finances with QuickBooks Pro or QuickBooks Premier (the general business edition—not the nonprofit edition).

However, if you receive restricted funds or track funds by program, you'll have to manually post them to equity accounts and allocate them to accounts in your chart of accounts, since QuickBooks Pro doesn't automatically perform these staples of nonprofit accounting. Likewise, the program doesn't generate all the reports you need to satisfy your grant providers or the government, although you can export reports (page 651) and then modify them as necessary in a spreadsheet program. In that case, QuickBooks Premier Nonprofit might be a real timesaver.

The QuickBooks Premier Choices

If you work in one of the industries covered by QuickBooks Premier, you can get additional features unique to your industry. (When you install QuickBooks Premier, you choose the industry version you want to run. If your business is in an industry other than one of the five options, choose General Business.) Some people swear that these customizations are worth every extra penny, while others say the additional features don't warrant the Premier price. On the QuickBooks website (*http://quickbooks.intuit.com/premier*), you can tour the Premier features to decide for yourself. Or you can purchase QuickBooks Accountant, which can run any QuickBooks edition, from QuickBooks Pro to the gamut of Premier's industry-specific versions.

NOTE The Accountant edition is designed to help professional accountants and bookkeepers deliver services to their clients. It lets you run any QuickBooks edition (Pro or any of the Premier versions). In addition to being compatible with all other editions, it lets you review your clients' data and easily correct mistakes you find, transfer an accountant's copy to your client, design financial statements and other documents, process payroll for clients, reconcile clients' bank accounts, calculate depreciation, and prepare clients' tax returns. In mid-2012, Intuit introduced QuickBooks Professional Bookkeeper, which is somewhere between the QuickBooks Pro and QuickBooks Accountant editions. It lets you work on two company files at a time, manage client passwords, and create new company files based on existing files, but it doesn't offer many of the Accountant edition's advanced features, such as reclassifying transaction, calculating depreciation, and creating reversing journal entries.

Here are the industries that have their own Premier editions:

- The **General Business** edition has Premier goodies like per-item price levels, sales orders, and so on. It also has more built-in reports than QuickBooks Pro, sales and expense forecasting, the Inventory Center, and a business plan feature (although, if you're using QuickBooks to keep your books, you may already have a business plan).

- The **Contractor** edition includes special features near and dear to construction contractors' hearts: job-cost and other contractor-specific reports, the ability to set different billing rates by employee, and tools for managing change orders.

- **Manufacturing & Wholesale** is targeted at companies that manufacture products. Its chart of accounts and menus are customized for manufacturing and wholesale operations. You can use it to manage inventory assembled from components and to track customer return materials authorizations (RMAs) and damaged goods.

- If you run a nonprofit organization, you know that several things work differently in the nonprofit world, as the box on the previous page details. The **Nonprofit** edition of QuickBooks includes features such as a chart of accounts customized for nonprofits, forms and letters targeted to donors and pledges, info about using the program for nonprofits, and the ability to generate Statement of Functional Expenses 990 forms.

- The **Professional Services** edition (not to be confused with QuickBooks Pro) is designed for companies that deliver services to their clients. Unique features include project-costing reports, templates for proposals and invoices, billing rates that you can customize by client or employee, and professional service-specific reports and help.

- The **Retail** edition is customized to work for retail businesses. It includes specialized menus, reports, forms, and help, as well as a custom chart of accounts. Intuit offers companion products that you can integrate with this edition to support all aspects of your retail operation. For example, QuickBooks Point of Sale tracks sales, customers, and inventory as you ring up sales, and it shoots the information over to your QuickBooks company file.

Learning More about Accounting

If you need to learn a lot about QuickBooks and a little something about accounting, you're holding the right book. But if bookkeeping and accounting are unfamiliar territory, some background training (page 715) may help you use QuickBooks better and more easily (without calling your accountant for help five times a day).

The Accounting and Business School of the Rockies offers an accounting and bookkeeping self-study course that you can play on a VCR or DVD player. The course presents real-life accounting situations, so you'll learn to solve common small-business accounting challenges, and it includes hands-on exercises to help you master the material. It doesn't take long to complete, so you'll be up and accounting in no time. To contact the school, visit *www.absrschool.com* or call 1-303-755-6885.

Real World Training offers "Mastering Accounting Basics for QuickBooks," an Intuit-endorsed product that teaches basic accounting concepts using QuickBooks in its examples. It's available online, on CD, and on DVD. Check it out at *http://tinyurl.com/rwaccounting*.

■ Accounting Basics: The Important Stuff

QuickBooks helps people who don't have a degree in accounting handle most accounting tasks. However, you'll be more productive *and* have more accurate books if you understand the following concepts and terms:

- **Double-entry accounting** is the standard method for tracking where your money comes from and where it goes. Following the old saw that money doesn't grow on trees, money always comes from somewhere when you use double-entry accounting. For example, as shown in Table I-1, when you sell something to a customer, the money on your invoice comes in as income and goes into your Accounts Receivable account. Then, when you deposit the payment, the money comes out of the Accounts Receivable account and goes into your checking account. (See Chapter 16 for more about double-entry accounting and journal entries.)

NOTE Each side of a double-entry transaction is either a debit or a credit. As you can see in Table I-1, when you sell products or services, you credit your income account (since your income increases when you sell something), but debit the Accounts Receivable account (because selling something also increases how much customers owe you). You'll see examples throughout the book of how transactions translate to account debits and credits.

TABLE I-1 *Following the money through accounts*

TRANSACTION	ACCOUNT	DEBIT	CREDIT
Sell products or services	Accounts Receivable	$1,000	
Sell products or services	Service Income		$1,000
Receive payment	Checking Account	$1,000	
Receive payment	Accounts Receivable		$1,000
Pay for expense	Office Supplies	$500	
Pay for expense	Checking Account		$500

- **Chart of accounts.** In bookkeeping, an *account* is a place to store money, just like your checking account is a place to store your ready cash. The difference is that you need an account for each kind of income, expense, asset, and liability you have. (See Chapter 3 to learn about all the different types of accounts you might use.) The *chart of accounts* is simply a list of all the accounts you use to keep track of your company's money.

- **Cash vs. accrual accounting.** Cash and accrual are the two different ways companies can document how much they make and spend. Cash accounting is the choice of many small businesses because it's easy: You don't show income until you've received a payment (regardless of when that happens), and you don't show expenses until you've paid your bills.

  The accrual method, on the other hand, follows something known as the *matching principle*, which matches revenue with the corresponding expenses. This approach keeps income and expenses linked to the period in which they happened, no matter when cash comes in or goes out. The advantage of this method is that it provides a better picture of profitability because income and its corresponding expenses appear in the same period. With accrual accounting, you recognize income as soon as you record an invoice, even if you'll receive payment during the next fiscal year. For example, if you pay employees in January for work they did in December, those wages are part of the previous fiscal year.

- **Financial reports.** You need three reports to evaluate the health of your company (described in detail in Chapter 17):

  - The *income statement*, which QuickBooks calls a *Profit & Loss* report, shows how much income you've brought in and how much you've spent over a period of time. This QuickBooks report gets its name from the difference between the income and expenses, which results in your profit (or loss) for that period.

- The *balance sheet* is a snapshot of how much you own and how much you owe. Assets are things you own that have value, such as buildings, equipment, and brand names. Liabilities are the money you owe to others (like money you borrowed to buy one of your assets, say). The difference between your assets and liabilities is the *equity* in the company—like the equity you have in your house when the house is worth more than you owe on the mortgage.

- The *statement of cash flows* tells you how much hard cash you have. You might think that a Profit & Loss report would tell you that, but noncash transactions—such as depreciation—prevent it from doing so. The statement of cash flows removes all noncash transactions and shows the money generated or spent operating the company, investing in the company, or financing.

About This Book

QuickBooks Help provides a healthy dose of accounting background and trouble-shooting tips. If you don't find the answer you need in the "Have a Question?" window (page 707), the Intuit Community—which lets you ask your peers and experts for answers (page 709)—or by searching with keywords, where do you turn next?

This book provides lots of real-world examples and you can search for topics in its index. In addition, with this book, you can mark your place, underline key points, jot notes in the margin, or read about QuickBooks while sitting in the sun—stuff that's hard to do onscreen.

This book applies to the U.S. *Windows* version of QuickBooks Pro and Premier. (Because the Mac version of the program differs significantly from the Windows one, this book won't be of much help if you have QuickBooks for Mac. Versions for other countries differ from the U.S. version, too, although primarily in how you work with payroll and taxes.)

In these pages, you'll find step-by-step instructions for using every QuickBooks Pro feature, including those you might not quite understand: progress invoicing (page 315), making general journal entries (page 451), customizing forms (page 669), writing off losses (page 424), and so on. If you're just starting out with QuickBooks, read the first few chapters as you set up your company file. After that, go ahead and jump from topic to topic depending on the bookkeeping task at hand. As mentioned earlier, you'll learn about some of the extra bells and whistles in the QuickBooks Premier edition, as well. (All the features in QuickBooks Pro—and in this book—are also in Premier.) To keep you productive, this book also includes evaluations of features to help you figure out which ones are most useful and when to use them.

NOTE Although each version of QuickBooks introduces new features and enhancements, you can still use this book if you're using an earlier version. Of course, the older your version of the program, the more discrepancies you'll run across.

QuickBooks 2013: The Missing Manual is designed to accommodate readers at every technical level. The primary discussions are written for people with beginner or intermediate QuickBooks skills. But if you're using QuickBooks for the first time, special boxes titled "Up To Speed" provide the introductory info you need to understand the current topic. On the other hand, people with advanced skills should watch for similar boxes labeled "Power Users' Clinic," which cover more technical tips, tricks, and shortcuts for experienced QuickBooks wranglers.

About the Outline

This book is divided into five parts, each containing several chapters:

- **Part One: Getting Started** explains how to set up QuickBooks based on your organization's needs. These chapters cover creating and managing a company file; setting up accounts, customers, jobs, invoice items, and other lists; and managing QuickBooks files.

- **Part Two: Bookkeeping** follows the money from the moment you rack up time and expenses for your customers and add charges to a customer's invoice to the tasks you have to perform at the end of the year to satisfy the IRS and other interested parties. These chapters describe how to track time and expenses, pay for things you buy, bill customers, manage the money that customers owe you, pay for expenses, run payroll, manage your bank accounts, and perform other bookkeeping tasks.

- **Part Three: Managing Your Business** delves into the features that can help you make your company a success—or even more successful than it already is. These chapters explain how to keep your inventory at just the right level, build budgets, and use QuickBooks reports to evaluate every aspect of your enterprise.

- **Part Four: QuickBooks Power** helps you take your copy of the program to the next level. You'll learn how to save time and prevent errors by downloading transactions electronically; boost your productivity by setting the program's preferences to match the way you like to work and integrating QuickBooks with other programs; customize the program's components to look the way you want; and—most important—set up QuickBooks so your financial data is secure.

- **Part Five: Appendixes** provides a guide to installing and upgrading QuickBooks, and a reference to helpful resources.

NOTE You can find three bonus appendixes online at *www.missingmanuals.com/cds*: "Keyboard Shortcuts," "Tracking Time with the Standalone Timer," and "Advanced Form Customization."

◼ The Very Basics

To use this book (and QuickBooks), you need to know a few basics. This book assumes that you're familiar with the following terms and concepts:

- **Clicking.** This book includes instructions that require you to use your computer's mouse or trackpad. To *click* means to point your cursor (the arrow pointer) at something on the screen and then—without moving the cursor—press and release the left button on the mouse (or laptop trackpad). To *right-click* means the same thing, but you press the *right* mouse button instead. (Usually, clicking selects an onscreen element or presses an onscreen button, whereas right-clicking typically reveals a *shortcut menu*, which lists some common tasks specific to whatever you're right-clicking.) To *double-click*, of course, means to click the left button twice in rapid succession, again without moving the pointer at all. And to *drag* means to move the cursor while holding down the left mouse button the entire time.

  When you're told to *Shift-click* something, you click while pressing the Shift key. Related procedures, like *Ctrl-clicking*, work the same way—just click while pressing the corresponding key.

- **Menus.** The *menus* are the words at the top of your screen: File, Edit, and so on. Click one to make a list of commands appear, as though they're written on a window shade you've just pulled down. Some people click to open a menu and then release the mouse button; after reading the menu choices, they click the option they want. Other people like to press the mouse button continuously as they click the menu title and drag down the list to the desired command; only then do they release the mouse button. Both methods work, so use whichever one you prefer.

- **Keyboard shortcuts.** Nothing is faster than keeping your fingers on your keyboard to enter data, choose names, trigger commands, and so on—without losing time by grabbing the mouse, carefully positioning it, and then choosing a command or list entry. That's why many experienced QuickBooks fans use keyboard shortcuts to accomplish most tasks. In this book, when you read an instruction like "Press Ctrl+A to open the Chart of Accounts window," start by pressing the Ctrl key; while it's down, type the letter A; and then release both keys.

◼ About→These→Arrows

Throughout this book, and throughout the Missing Manual series, you'll find sentences like this one: "Choose Lists→Customer & Vendor Profile Lists→Customer Type List." That's shorthand for a much longer instruction that directs you to navigate three nested menus in sequence, like this: "At the top of your screen, click the Lists menu. On the Lists menu, point to the Customer & Vendor Profile Lists menu item. On the submenu that appears, choose Customer Type List." Figure I-1 shows the menus this sequence opens.

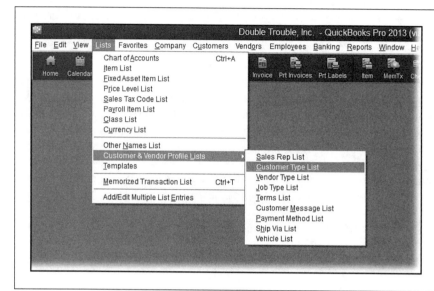

FIGURE I-1.

Instead of filling pages with long and hard-to-follow instructions for navigating through nested menus and nested folders, the arrow notation is concise but just as informative. For example, choosing Lists→Customer & Vendor Profile Lists→Customer Type List takes you to the menu item shown here.

Similarly, this arrow shorthand also simplifies the instructions for opening nested folders, such as Program Files→QuickBooks→Export Files.

◼ About the Online Resources

As the owner of a Missing Manual, you've got more than just a book to read. Online, you'll find example files so you can get some hands-on experience, as well as tips, articles, and maybe even a video or two. You can also communicate with the Missing Manual team and tell us what you love (or hate) about the book. Head over to *www.missingmanuals.com*, or go directly to one of the following sections.

Missing CD

This book doesn't have a CD pasted inside the back cover, but you're not missing out on anything. Go to *www.missingmanuals.com/cds* and click the "Missing CD-ROM" link for this book to download a sample company file that includes an opening balance general journal entry, as well as three additional appendixes to this book. And so you don't wear down your fingers typing long web addresses, the Missing CD page also offers a list of clickable links to the websites mentioned in this book.

Registration

If you register this book at oreilly.com, you'll be eligible for special offers—like discounts on future editions of *QuickBooks: The Missing Manual*. Registering takes only a few clicks. To get started, type *http://oreilly.com/register* into your browser to hop directly to the Registration page.

Feedback

Got questions? Need more information? Fancy yourself a book reviewer? On our Feedback page, you can get expert answers to questions that come to you while reading, and you can share your thoughts on this Missing Manual. To have your say, go to *www.missingmanuals.com/feedback*.

Errata

In an effort to keep this book as up-to-date and accurate as possible, each time we print more copies, we'll make any confirmed corrections you've suggested. We also note such changes on the book's website, so you can mark important corrections into your own copy of the book, if you like. Go to *http://tinyurl.com/9l5h5ks* to report an error and view existing corrections.

■ Safari® Books Online

Safari® Books Online (*http://my.safaribooksonline.com*) is an on-demand digital library that lets you easily search over 7,500 technology and creative reference books and videos to find the answers you need quickly.

With a subscription, you can read any page and watch any video from our library online. Read books on your cell phone and mobile devices. Access new titles before they are available for print, and get exclusive access to manuscripts in development and post feedback for the authors. Copy and paste code samples, organize your favorites, download chapters, bookmark key sections, create notes, print out pages, and benefit from tons of other time-saving features.

Creating a Company File

A *company file* is where you store your company's financial records in Quick-Books, so it's the first thing you need to work on in the program. You can create a company file from scratch or convert records previously kept in a small-business accounting program or Quicken. Another approach is to use a file that *someone else* created. For example, if you've worked with an accountant to set up your company, she might provide you with a QuickBooks company file already configured for your business so you can hit the ground running.

This chapter starts by explaining how to launch your copy of QuickBooks. Then, if you need to create your own company file, you'll learn how to use the QuickBooks Setup dialog box and the EasyStep Interview to get started (and find out which other chapters explain how to finish the job). Finally, you'll learn how to open a company file, update one to a new version of QuickBooks, and modify basic company information.

■ Opening QuickBooks

Here are the easiest ways to open QuickBooks:

- **Desktop icon**. Double-click the desktop shortcut that QuickBooks created during installation to launch the program.

- **Windows taskbar**. The fastest way to open QuickBooks is to click its icon on the Windows taskbar—but first you have to put it there. In Windows 7, right-drag (that's dragging while holding down the right mouse button) the program's desktop shortcut onto the taskbar, as shown in Figure 1-1. (The right-drag technique also works for copying or moving a shortcut from Windows Explorer or from the Start menu.)

FIGURE 1-1

Windows' taskbar keeps your desktop tidy. It's easy to reach, because program windows don't hide it the way they do desktop shortcuts.

- **Start menu**. Without a desktop icon, you can launch QuickBooks from the Start menu. Click Start→QuickBooks Pro 2013 (or QuickBooks Premier 2013). If QuickBooks isn't already listed on the Start menu, choose Start→All Programs→QuickBooks→QuickBooks Pro 2013 (or QuickBooks Premier 2013).

The first time you launch QuickBooks, you're greeted by the QuickBooks Setup dialog box, whose sole purpose is to help you create a company file in one way or another. The rest of this chapter explains how to create a company file and then how to open company files you create. After that, you'll be ready to dive into bookkeeping.

> **TIP** If you're running QuickBooks Accountant edition, the Accountant Center opens every time you launch the program. The Tools section at the top of this center includes shortcuts to features that accountants use all the time: the Chart of Accounts window, the Fixed Asset Item List (for entering depreciation), Make General Journal Entries, Client Data Review for checking the data your client entered, Reclassify Transactions for correcting transactions that were assigned to the wrong accounts, and so on. However, if you don't want this window to open automatically, turn off the "Show Accountant Center when opening a company file" checkbox at the bottom-left of the center. (You can open the Accountant Center anytime by choosing Accountant→Accountant Center.)

■ Before You Create a Company File

If you've just started a business and want to inaugurate your books with QuickBooks, your prep work will be a snap. If, on the other hand, you have existing records for your business, you have a few small tasks to complete before you jump into QuickBooks' setup. Whether your books are paper ledgers or electronic files in another program, gather your company information *before* you open QuickBooks. That way, you can hunker down in front of your computer and crank out a company file in record time. This section explains what you need to create a company file in QuickBooks.

Choosing a Start Date

To keep your entire financial history at your fingertips, you need to put every transaction and speck of financial information in your QuickBooks company file. But you have better things to do than enter years' worth of checks, invoices, and deposits, so the comprehensive approach is practical only if you just recently started your company.

The more realistic approach is to enter your financial data into QuickBooks starting as of a specific date and, from then on, add all *new* transactions to QuickBooks. The date you choose is called the *start date*. (The start date isn't something that you enter in a field in QuickBooks; it's simply the earliest transaction date in your company file.) You shouldn't choose it randomly. Here are your start date options and the ramifications of each one:

- **The last day of the previous fiscal year**. The best choice is to fill in your records for the entire year. Choose the last day of your company's previous fiscal year as the company file start date. That way, the account balances on your start date are like the ending balances on a bank statement, and you're ready to start bookkeeping fresh on the first day of the fiscal year.

  Yes, you have to enter checks, credit card charges, invoices, payments, and other transactions that have happened since the beginning of the year, but that won't take as much time as you think. And you'll regain those hours when tax time rolls around, as you nimbly generate the reports you need to complete your tax returns.

  If more than half of the year has already passed, the best approach is to be patient and postpone your QuickBooks setup until the next fiscal year. (Intuit releases new versions of QuickBooks in October or November each year for just that reason.) But waiting until next year isn't always an option. In cases like that, go with the next option in this list.

TIP   For practice, you can decide to start entering transactions that occur after the closing date of one of your bank statements. Then you can enter transactions for the month and try reconciling your QuickBooks records with your bank statement (page 426).

- **The last day of the previous fiscal period**. The next best start date is the last day of the previous fiscal quarter (or fiscal month at the very least). Since your company file doesn't contain a full year's worth of detail, you'll have to switch between QuickBooks and your old filing cabinets to prepare your tax returns and look up financial information. Starting just before a fiscal period reduces this hassle but doesn't eliminate it.

Account Balances and Transactions

Unless you begin using QuickBooks when you start your business, you need to know your account balances as of your selected start date to get things rolling. For example, if your checking account has $342 at the end of the year, that value goes into QuickBooks during setup. You also need every transaction that's happened since the start date—sales you've made, expenses you've incurred, payroll and tax transactions, and so on—to establish your asset, liability, equity, income, and expense accounts. So dig that information out of your existing accounting system (or shoebox). Here are the balances and transactions you need and where you can find them in your records:

- **Cash balances**. For each bank account you use in your business (checking, savings, money market, and so on), find the bank statements with statement dates as close to—but *earlier* than—the start date of your QuickBooks company file. Gather deposit slips and your checkbook register to identify the transactions that haven't yet cleared; you'll need them to enter transactions, unless you download transactions from your bank (page 579). If you have petty cash lying around, count it and use that number to set up your petty cash account (page 448).

TIP For Subchapter C corporations, Subchapter S corporations, and partnerships, the balance sheet that you included with your previous year's tax return is a great starting point for account balances. Your tax return also shows your federal tax ID number, which you'll need, too.

- **Customer balances**. If customers owe you money, pull the paper copy of every *unpaid* invoice or statement out of your filing cabinet so you can give QuickBooks what it needs to calculate your Accounts Receivable balance. If you didn't keep copies, you can ask your customers for copies of the invoices they haven't paid or simply create invoices in QuickBooks to match the payments you receive.

- **Vendor balances**. If your company thinks handing out cash before you have to is more painful than data entry, find the bills you haven't yet paid and get ready to enter them in QuickBooks so you can generate your Accounts Payable balance. (Or, to reduce the number of transactions you have to enter, simply pay those outstanding bills and record the payments in QuickBooks.)

- **Asset values**. When you own assets such as buildings or equipment, their value depreciates over time. If you included a balance sheet with the tax return you filed for your company, you can find asset values and accumulated depreciation on your most recent tax return (yet another reason to start using QuickBooks at the beginning of the year). If you haven't filed a tax return for your company yet, an asset's value is typically the price you paid for it.

- **Liability balances**. Find the current balances you owe on any business loans or mortgages.

- **Inventory**. If you stock products that you sell and track as inventory, you need to know how many items you had in stock as of the start date, how much you paid for them, and what you expect to sell them for.

- **Payroll**. Payroll services are a great value for the money, which you'll grow to appreciate as you collect the info you need for payroll (including salaries and wages, tax deductions, benefits, pensions, 401(k) deductions, and other stray payroll deductions you might have). You also need to know who receives withholdings, such as tax agencies or the company handling your 401(k) plan. Oh, yeah—and you also need payroll details for each employee. Chapter 14 explains the payroll options that are available inside and outside of QuickBooks.

> **TIP** If you have outstanding payroll withholdings such as employee payroll taxes, send in the payments so you don't have to enter those open transactions in QuickBooks.

Creating a Company File

Keeping books requires accuracy, attention to detail, and persistence—hence the customary image of spectacled accountants scanning row after row of numbers. QuickBooks can help you keep your books without ruining your eyesight—as long as you start your company file with good information. If you want to practice with QuickBooks, you can experiment with a sample file, as the box on page 6 explains.

QuickBooks makes it easy to create a company file from scratch. (The box on page 6 tells you how to find someone who can help you create one.) You can opt for a short and sweet process, which asks you for the bare minimum of info before it creates your file. Or you can use a wizard that guides you through the process with a series of questions that takes about 30 minutes to answer. The questions cover the basics of creating and customizing a company file to fit your business. The program wants to know some company information, the industry you're in, and the features you want to use. QuickBooks then sets your preferences and creates a few accounts (like basic income and expense accounts and your checking account). Of course, you have to do the bulk of the setup work later, which you learn in the section "What's Next?" on page 18.

Getting Help Creating a New Company File

The proud owners of brand-new businesses face a dilemma: They have more important things to do than muddle through setting up a company file in QuickBooks, but money is usually as short as free time. If you don't know much about bookkeeping or accounting, a few hours of an accountant's time is a worthwhile investment when you're getting started in QuickBooks. You'll not only save untold hours, but also know that your books are set up properly. Accountants well versed in QuickBooks can create a flawless company file without breaking a sweat.

If you plan to do without an accountant but you want some help setting up your company file, you can choose Help→Find A Local QuickBooks Expert. By answering a few questions on the Local QuickBooks Expert website (*http://tinyurl.com/find-qbadvisor*), you can locate someone in your area who can help you get started.

Options for Creating a Company File

You can create a company file in several ways, and the QuickBooks Setup dialog box—which opens automatically the very first time you start QuickBooks—is your ticket to all of them. If you don't see this dialog box, choose File→New Company (or click "Create a new company" in the No Company Open window). The dialog box takes up most of the screen, so you can stay focused on creating your company file.

Experimenting with a Sample File

You don't have to use your real company file to test out QuickBooks features you've never used. The program comes with a couple of sample files: one for a basic product-based business, another for a basic service-based business. And if you use QuickBooks Premier, you can experiment with several other sample files for more specialized pursuits like contracting, consulting, manufacturing, and so on.

To experiment with QuickBooks features before you put them in production, in the No Company Open window, click "Open a sample file" and choose the one you want. (To display the No Company Open window, you have to close any open company files by choosing File→Close Company (or File→Close Company/Logoff if there's more than one user set up for the file). If the QuickBooks Setup dialog box is open, close it, too.) Another handy use for a sample file is to test the latest software

update from Intuit. If QuickBooks asks whether you want to install a software update, close your company file and open one of the sample files. Then install the software update. If you don't spot any issues with the update, go ahead and reopen your company file.

Don't try to use one of these sample files as your company file. They come with accounts, customers, vendors, and transactions (such as checks, invoices, and purchase orders). Besides, QuickBooks sets "today's" date in these files to 12/15/2016, which makes transactions later than you or your vendors would like (although you can edit the values in date boxes).

If you botch your experiment with sample files, you can always retrieve them from the QuickBooks CD. (If you downloaded QuickBooks, you can call Intuit Customer Support and request an installation CD for a small fee.)

The three basic approaches to creating a company file are covered by the QuickBooks Setup dialog box's three buttons:

- **Express Start**. This button is in pole position because it's the best option if this is your first time creating a company file. QuickBooks holds your hand and asks for a few bits of info at a time before moving to each new screen. If you stop filling in information before QuickBooks creates your company file, the program won't save any of the values you entered. So make sure you have at least 15 minutes to complete the first set of steps. The instructions for Express Start begin below.

- **Advanced Setup**. If you've been around the QuickBooks block before, this option launches the EasyStep Interview window, which asks for more information on each screen than Express Start does. If you need help during the process, you can always click the "Get answers" link at the top right of the window. You can also use Advanced Setup to go back and modify info you entered previously, whether you entered it using Express Start or the EasyStep Interview. (The instructions for the EasyStep Interview begin on page 10. If you're unsure what to put in any of the fields you're supposed to fill in, they're described in the Express Start section, because you fill in much of the same information regardless which approach you use.)

- **Other Options**. This button covers the rest of the bases. You can use it to open an existing company file or to convert existing records that are in Quicken or another accounting program (page 23) for use in QuickBooks.

> **NOTE** If you use the QuickBooks Accountant Edition, you can create a company file from an existing file. Choose File→New Company from Existing Company File.

Whether you use Express Start or the EasyStep Interview, you tell QuickBooks the basic 411 about your company, such as its name and tax ID. (If any of the fields confuse you, try clicking the "Need help? Give us a call" button in the QuickBooks Setup dialog box or the "Get answers" link in the upper-right corner of the EasyStep Interview dialog box.) The next section provides the full scoop on the information you need to provide.

Using Express Start

As its name implies, Express Start gets you going as quickly as possible by asking for the minimum amount of info (you can go back later to fill in the details). To use it, choose File→New Company and then, in the QuickBooks Setup dialog box, click Express Start. The "Tell us about your business" screen appears, and you can start entering info. The following sections explain what the program needs to know to create your company file.

■ COMPANY INFORMATION

In the "Tell us about your business" screen, shown in Figure 1-2, you need to cough up only three answers, but these responses are the foundation of many of the preferences that QuickBooks sets:

- **Company Name**. Type the name you want to appear on invoices, reports, and other forms. Later on, you can specify your company's legal name (page 9).

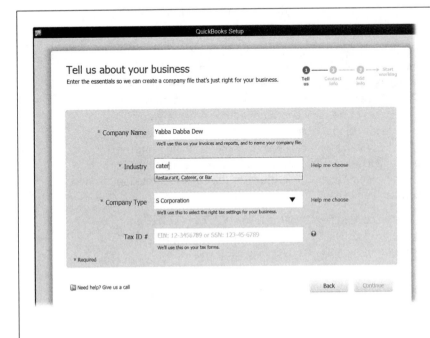

FIGURE 1-2

QuickBooks' list of industries is robust, so chances are good you'll find one that's close to what your company does. You can start typing an industry and the program will display options that match what you've typed so far, such as "cater" to display the industry "Restaurant, Caterer, or Bar" shown here. Or you can click the "Help me choose" link to see all the industries the program offers. The Tax ID box is for the federal tax ID number you use when you file your taxes—your Social Security number or Federal Employer Identification Number.

- **Industry**. Choose your industry carefully. Based on your choice, QuickBooks adjusts its settings and chart of accounts to match how your business operates. For example, the program creates income and expense accounts for your type of business and automatically turns on features like sales tax and inventory if your industry typically uses them. If QuickBooks makes assumptions you don't like, you can alter your preferences (page 595) and accounts (page 51) later.

  If you don't see an obvious choice in the Industry list, scroll to the bottom and choose either General Product-based Business or General Service-based Business.

- **Company Type**. The tax form you use depends on the type of business entity you have. This drop-down list contains the most common types, from sole proprietorships and partnerships to corporations and nonprofits. When you select a type, QuickBooks assigns the corresponding tax form to your company file. After you finish creating your company file, you can see the tax form the program selected by choosing Company→Company Information, which brings up the Company Information window shown in Figure 1-7 (page 18). The Income Tax Form Used box at the bottom of that window lists the tax form for your company type.

- **Tax ID**. This box is for the federal tax ID number you use when you file taxes. You don't have to enter it now, but you'll need it come tax time. You'll use a Federal Employer Identification Number (EIN) if your company is a corporation or partnership, you have employees, or fit a few other criteria (go to *www.irs. gov* to see if you need an EIN). Otherwise, your tax ID is your Social Security number or Individual Tax Identification Number (ITIN).

When you finish filling out the first screen, click Continue.

■ BUSINESS CONTACT INFORMATION

Next, you can enter your basic contact info. If you're itching to start printing and emailing invoices, bills, and other forms, fill in the following fields:

- **Legal Name**. This is the name you use on contracts and other legal documents. Your company name and legal name are usually the same unless you use a DBA (doing business as) company name. If you own a corporation, the legal name is what appears on your Certificate of Incorporation.

- **Contact info**. Enter your mailing address, telephone number, email address, and website address, if you have one. The Zip and Phone fields are the only ones that are required.

Click Preview Your Settings to see which features QuickBooks selected for you based on the industry and company type you provided (Figure 1-3), and to specify the accounts you want to use and where you store your company file. Here's what you can do on each tab in this dialog box:

- **Features Selected**. This tab is purely informational. You can't modify the features that QuickBooks chooses for your company in this dialog box, but once you've used QuickBooks for a while, you can change the program's preferences (Chapter 23) to suit your needs.

- **Chart of Accounts**. This tab lists accounts typically used in your industry. The accounts that the program chose have checkmarks next to their names. You can include or exclude accounts in your chart of accounts by turning their checkmarks on or off.

- **Company File Location**. This tab shows the path on your computer where the program plans to save your company file. To choose a different spot, click Change Location and then select the folder you want. If the folder doesn't exist, in the Browse For Folder dialog box, click Make New Folder. Click OK to close the Browse For Folder dialog box.

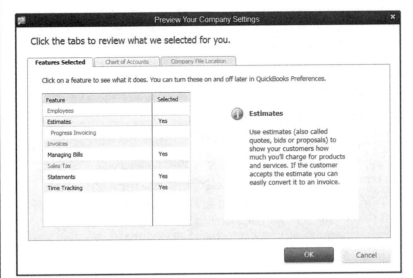

FIGURE 1-3

You can't use this dialog box to change the features listed on the Features Selected tab. However, you can adjust those settings later in the Preferences dialog box (page 608). To modify the accounts in your company file or where the file is stored, click the Chart of Accounts or Company File Location tabs, respectively.

When you've made the changes you want to your company settings, in the Preview Your Company Settings dialog box, click OK to return to the main QuickBooks Setup dialog box.

■ CREATING YOUR COMPANY FILE

Once everything is the way you want it, click Create Company File. A Working message box appears to show QuickBooks' progress in creating your file. You know it's finished when the "You've got a company file! Now add your info" screen appears. If you have time, you can add your customers, vendors, and employees; the products and services you sell; and your bank accounts. To learn how to do these tasks, jump to "Beginning to Use QuickBooks" on page 15.

Using the EasyStep Interview

The EasyStep Interview also guides you through the setup process, but it gives you more control over setting up your company file than Express Start does. For example, you can provide more info about your company up front and choose which features to turn on.

To access the EasyStep Interview, choose File→New Company and then, in the QuickBooks Setup dialog box, click Advanced Setup. The "Enter your company information" screen appears. As you enter the following info, click Next to proceed to each new screen:

- **Name and contact info**. The first screen wants to know the name of your company, its legal name, tax ID, and your contact info. The "Company name" field is the only one that's required—you can fill in the other fields later on by choosing Company→Company Information.

- **Industry**. On the "Select your industry" screen, choose the industry closest to yours. That way, most of the settings the program chooses will be what you want.

- **Type of company**. On the "How is your company organized?" screen, select the option for your company type. This setting determines which tax form, accounts, and tax form lines you'll use to prepare your business tax return.

- **First month of fiscal year**. When you start a company, you choose a fiscal year. On the "Select the first month of your fiscal year" screen, QuickBooks automatically sets the "My fiscal year starts in" box to January because so many businesses stick with the calendar year for simplicity. If you start your fiscal year in another month, choose it from the drop-down list.

- **Administrator password**. The administrator can do absolutely anything in your company file: set up other users, log in as other users, and access any area of the company file. Although QuickBooks lets you click Next and skip right past the "Set up your administrator password" screen, this is no time for shortcuts, as the box on page 12 explains. Type the password you want to use in both the "Administrator password" and "Retype password" boxes, and then keep the password in a safe but memorable place. (Page 684 explains how to change the administrator name and password.)

■ CREATING YOUR COMPANY FILE

After you set the administrator password and click Next, the "Create your company file" screen appears. (If you're new to QuickBooks, click the "Where should I save my company file?" link, which opens a Help Article dialog box that explains the pros and cons of storing company files in different places.) When you're ready to create the file, on the "Create your company screen," click Next to specify the filename and location.

Safe Login Practices

Don't even *think* about having everyone who works with a company file share one login. You don't want everyone to have access to payroll data, and you wouldn't know which person to fire if you found any less-than-legal transactions in the file. Even if you run a small business from home, an administrator password prevents the chimney sweep from swiping your business credit card number. Chapter 26 has much more about keeping your QuickBooks files secure, but here are some password basics:

- Set a password that's at least eight characters long and is a combination of letters and numbers.

- Passwords are case sensitive, so make sure that Caps Lock

isn't turned on by mistake.

- *Type* the password in both the "Administrator password" and "Retype password" boxes. If you copy and paste the password from the "Administrator password" box into the "Retype password" box, you could copy a typo and not be able to access the company file you just created.

If you forget the administrator login and password or lose the piece of paper they're written on, you won't be able to open your company file without some fancy footwork, so keep a record of them someplace safe. If you've tried everything and your administrator password is still missing in action, see page 686 to learn how to reset it.

QuickBooks opens the Filename for New Company dialog box, which is really just a Save As dialog box. Navigate to the folder where you want to store your company file. QuickBooks automatically sets the "File name" box to the company name you entered, and the "Save as type" box to "QuickBooks Files (*.QBW, *.QBA)." Here are some guidelines for naming and saving your company file:

- If you want to call the file something other than the company name you entered earlier in the interview, simply type a new name in the "File name" box. For example, you may want one that's shorter or that better identifies the company's records within.

- Consider storing your company file in a folder with the rest of your company data so that it gets backed up along with everything else. For example, if you're the only person who uses QuickBooks, you could create a Company Files folder inside your My Documents folder. See page 703 for more about choosing a location for company files.

When you click Save in the Filename for New Company dialog box, QuickBooks may take a minute or so to create the new file. In the meantime, a message box with a progress bar appears. When the company file is ready, the EasyStep Interview displays the "Customizing QuickBooks for your business" screen. Click Next to dig in.

TIP At this point, the progress bar in the left margin of the EasyStep Interview window is depressingly short because you still have to do the bulk of the company file setup. If you need a break before continuing, click Leave. The next time you open that company file, the EasyStep Interview continues where you left off.

■ CUSTOMIZING YOUR COMPANY FILE

After you click Next on the "Customizing QuickBooks for your business screen,"
the next several screens of the EasyStep Interview ask questions about your business to help QuickBooks decide which features to turn on, what to include on your
QuickBooks Home page, and so on. The interview displays "(recommended for your
business)" next to the options that are typical for a company in your industry, as
shown in Figure 1-4.

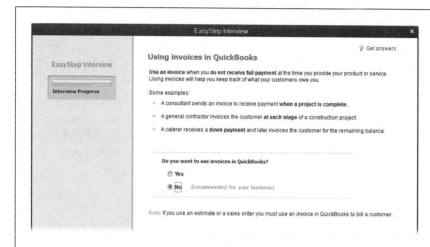

FIGURE 1-4

*The EasyStep Interview
sticks to the basics, so
you'll have more setup
to do later. As you step
through the screens in this
section, make a list of the
features you're turning
on (and the correspond-
ing page numbers in this
book) for reference. If
you decide to change any
of these settings later,
Chapter 23 tells you how.*

Here are some guidelines for answering the questions on the screens that follow:

- The **What do you sell?** screen is where you tell QuickBooks whether you offer
  services, products, or both. When you choose one of these options, the program
  figures out which types of income accounts you need. If you select "Products
  only" or "Both services and products," another screen later in the interview asks
  whether you want to track inventory.

- The **Do you charge sales tax?** screen has only two options: Yes and No. If you're
  one of the unfortunate souls who has to navigate the rocky shoals of sales tax,
  select Yes. If you don't charge sales tax, select No. For detailed instructions on
  dealing with sales tax in QuickBooks, see page 140.

- On the **Do you want to create estimates in QuickBooks?** screen, select Yes or
  No to turn the estimate feature on or off. If you prepare quotes, bids, or estimates
  for your customers and want to do so in QuickBooks (page 310), select Yes.

> **NOTE** If you use QuickBooks Premier, the "Tracking customer orders in QuickBooks" screen appears, asking
> whether you want to use sales orders to track backorders (page 305) or other orders that you plan to fill at a later
> date. QuickBooks Pro doesn't include this sales order feature.

- The **Using statements in QuickBooks** screen is where you tell the program whether you generate statements to send to customers (page 328). For example, your wine-of-the-month club might send monthly statements to its members. Or a consultant could send invoices for work performed and then send a statement that summarizes the fees, payments, and outstanding balance.

- On the **Using invoices in QuickBooks** screen, select Yes to tell the program that you want to use invoices, which you probably do because invoices are the most flexible sales forms (page 272). If you answer No (if, for example, you own a restaurant), QuickBooks jumps to the "Managing bills you owe" screen.

- If you answer Yes on the "Using invoices in QuickBooks" screen, the **Using progress invoicing** screen asks whether you invoice customers based on the percentage you've completed on a job. To learn why (and how) you might use this feature, see page 315.

- The **Managing bills you owe** screen asks whether you plan to write checks to pay bills immediately (select No) or enter bills in QuickBooks and then pay them later (select Yes). You can read about bill preferences on page 600 and payment preferences on page 618.

TIP   Entering bills in QuickBooks (page 219) requires more steps than simply writing checks *without* entering the bills in QuickBooks, but there's a benefit to the extra effort: the program can remind you when bills are due or qualify for timely payment discounts, and keep track of the total you owe.

- **Tracking inventory in QuickBooks** is the screen where you tell the program whether you keep track of the products you have in stock. This screen provides a few examples of when to track or bypass inventory, and page 113 has more about how to decide whether tracking inventory makes sense for your business.

- **Tracking time in QuickBooks** is ideal if you bill by the hour. In that case, select Yes on this screen to track the hours people work and create invoices for their time. Chapter 8 explains how to set up time tracking.

- The **Do you have employees?** screen is where you specify whether you want to use QuickBooks' payroll and 1099 features (select Yes). If you use non-Intuit services to run payroll or generate contractors' 1099s, select No.

When you click Next on the "Do you have employees?" screen, you see the "Using accounts in QuickBooks" screen, and the progress bar indicates that you're almost done with the interview. Click Next to set up these final things:

- The **Select a date to start tracking your finances** screen summarizes what you learned about start dates on page 3. To start at the beginning of this fiscal year (which QuickBooks can figure out using the current calendar year and the starting month you select), choose the "Beginning of this fiscal year: 01/01/13" option. (The year you see listed depends on the current calendar year.) If you've decided to start on a different date, select the "Use today's date or the first day of the quarter or month" option instead. You can then type or choose any date you want in the box, such as the last day of the previous fiscal period.

- The **Review income and expense accounts** screen lists the accounts typically used by companies in your industry, as shown in Figure 1-5.

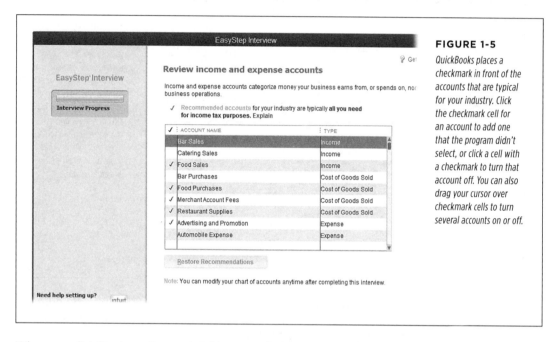

FIGURE 1-5

QuickBooks places a checkmark in front of the accounts that are typical for your industry. Click the checkmark cell for an account to add one that the program didn't select, or click a cell with a checkmark to turn that account off. You can also drag your cursor over checkmark cells to turn several accounts on or off.

When you click Next, you'll see a bright orange, but premature, "Congratulations!" You still have a few more steps to complete before you can open your company file. Click Go to Setup and then read the next section.

Beginning to Use QuickBooks

After you create your company file with Express Start or the EasyStep Interview, you'll see the "You've got a company file!" screen, which is where you perform the additional steps you have to complete, such as adding bank accounts and items you sell. If you want step-by-step guidance through these processes, click one of the Add buttons in these sections:

- **Add the people you do business with**. Adding people you do business with is a snap. Click the first Add button and you can import names from your email program (Outlook, Yahoo, or Gmail), paste data from an Excel workbook, or enter info manually. If you select one of the import options and click Continue, you'll see a table with the names from your email program, as shown in Figure 1-6.

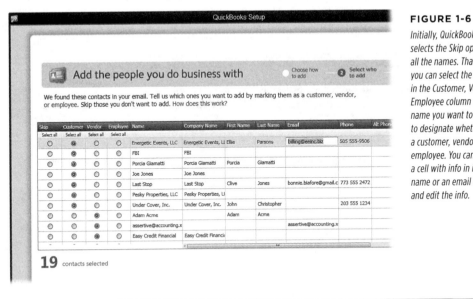

FIGURE 1-6

Initially, QuickBooks selects the Skip option for all the names. That way, you can select the option in the Customer, Vendor, or Employee column for each name you want to import to designate whether it's a customer, vendor, or employee. You can select a cell with info in it (like a name or an email address) and edit the info.

- **Add the products and services you sell**. When you click the Add button in this section, you first choose either the Service or Non-inventory part option, because you fill in different fields for each type of item. Select the Service option to set up services you sell, or select the Non-inventory part option to create products you sell (see page 129 to learn about products you keep in inventory), and then click Continue. Fill in the names, description, and prices, and click Continue again to save your items.

- **Add your bank accounts**. For bank accounts, you fill in the account name, account number, opening balance, and opening balance date.

> **TIP** If you're in the middle of entering names, products and services, or bank accounts, and want to get back to the "You've got a company file!" screen, click Cancel.

After you finish these additional steps, click Start Working to open the Quick Start Center window. You can click icons and links in this window to open the corresponding features, click "Return to Add Info" to reopen the QuickBooks Setup dialog box, or click the X at the top right of the window to close it so you can work directly in the program.

TIP If you'd rather perform these tasks later or want more control over setup, click the Close button (the X at the top-right corner of the Quick Start Center dialog box). Page 18 tells you where to turn in this book for more detailed instructions on the rest of the setup you need.

After you close the QuickBooks Setup dialog box or Quick Start Center window, you see the QuickBooks Home page (page 26), which includes icons for the features you turned on during the EasyStep Interview.

NOTE You may also see the QuickBooks Learning Center window (you can open this window anytime by choosing Help→Learning Center Tutorials), which includes links to tutorials (page 714). In the window, click a link (blue text) to watch a video on that topic.

▇ REOPENING THE QUICKBOOKS SETUP DIALOG BOX

As you've learned in the previous sections, the QuickBooks Setup dialog box offers shortcuts for adding info to your company file. If your data-entry session was cut short by other pressing tasks, you can jump back to this dialog box later to finish the job. Here's how:

1. **Choose Help→Quick Start Center.** At the top right of the Quick Start Center, click "Return to Add Info."

   The QuickBooks Setup dialog box opens to the "You've got a company file!" screen.

2. **Click the Add button for the type of info you want to enter and then jump back to the instructions on page 15.**

When you're done, click the Close button (the X) at the top right of the QuickBooks Setup dialog box to close it and get to work.

▇ Modifying Company Info

In Express Start and the EasyStep Interview, QuickBooks gets the basic facts about your company in small chunks spread over several screens. But after you create your company file, you can edit any of this information in one dialog box, shown in Figure 1-7. To open it, choose Company→Company Information. Remember, your company's legal name and address are the ones you use on federal and state tax forms.

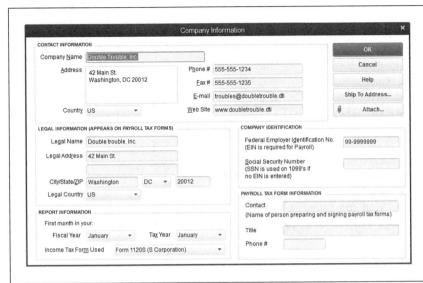

FIGURE 1-7

Some bits of company information change more often than others. For instance, you might relocate your office or change your phone number, email address, or website address. But stuff like your company's legal name and address, Federal Employer Identification Number, and business type (corporation, sole proprietor, and so on) usually stays the same.

What's Next?

Whether you used Express Start or the EasyStep Interview, quite a bit of setup is complete, but you may need guidance for the rest. Look no further than the book in your hands. Here are the ways you can flesh out your company file:

- **Set up your users and passwords**. See "Assigning the Administrator User Name and Password" on page 684.

- **Review and/or change the preferences that QuickBooks set**. See "Preferences: The Basics" on page 596.

- **Set up or edit the accounts in your chart of accounts**. If you didn't set up all your accounts yet, you can create them now. See "Creating Accounts and Subaccounts" on page 51.

- **Create a journal entry to specify accounts' opening balances**. See "Creating General Journal Entries" on page 454.

NOTE See "Recording Owners' Contributions" to learn how to record your initial contribution of cash or assets to your company.

- **Create items for the products and services you sell**. See "What Items Do" on page 111.

- **Set up sales tax codes**. See "Setting Up Sales Tax" on page 140.

- **Set up your 1099 tracking**. See "Tax: 1099" on page 632.

- **Sign up for Intuit Payroll Service**. See "Using an Intuit Payroll Service" on page 409.

- **Enter your historical transactions**. For invoices, see "Creating Invoices" on page 276; for bills, see "Entering Bills" on page 219.

Opening an Existing Company File

After you've opened a company file in one QuickBooks session, the next time you launch the program, it opens that same company file automatically. If you keep the books for only one company, you might never have to manually open a QuickBooks company file again.

But if you're an irrepressible entrepreneur or a bookkeeper who works on several companies' books, you don't have to close one company file before you open another. You can open another company file in QuickBooks anytime you want and the program automatically closes the previous one. (Because QuickBooks stores data in a database, you don't have to save a company file before you close it. And if you use QuickBooks Accountant or Professional Bookkeeper editions, you can have two company files open at the same time, as the Tip below explains.) The following sections describe the different ways to open a company file.

TIP With QuickBooks Accountant, QuickBooks Professional Bookkeeper, and QuickBooks Enterprise, you can have two company files open at the same time. Choose File→Open Second Company, and your computer launches a new instance of QuickBooks. In the new window, double-click the name of the file you want to open. The second company file opens with the text "(Secondary)" after the company name in the QuickBooks window's title bar. (In the first QuickBooks window, the company name is followed by the text "(Primary).") There are some restrictions when you open two files, mostly on the secondary file. To learn about these restrictions, search QuickBooks Help for "second company."

Opening a Recently Opened Company File

If you work on more than one company file, you may frequently switch between them. The easiest way to open a recent file is to choose File→Open Previous Company, and then choose the file you want to open, as shown in Figure 1-8. If the Open Previous Company submenu doesn't list the file you want, follow the steps in the next section instead.

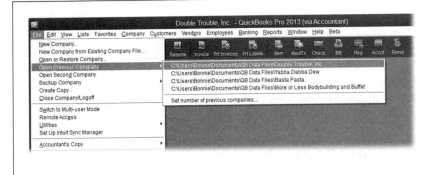

Opening Any Company File

Sometimes, a company file you want to open falls off the recent-file list. (The box
on page 21 explains how to tell QuickBooks how many files to include on the Open
Previous Company submenu.) Say your bookkeeping business is booming and you
work on dozens of company files every month. Or maybe you want to update a file
from a previous version (see the box on page 22). Here's how to open any company
file, no matter how long it's been since you last used it:

1. **Choose File→Open or Restore Company.**

   If the No Company Open window is visible, you can click "Open or restore an
   existing company" instead.

2. **In the Open or Restore Company dialog box, select the "Open a company
   file" option and then click Next.**

   The Open a Company dialog box appears.

3. **Navigate to the folder with the company file you want and double-click
   the file's name.**

   You can also click the filename and then click Open.

4. **If the QuickBooks Login window appears (which it will if you've assigned a
   password to the Administrator user account or set up multiple users), type
   your user name and password.**

   If the Administrator is the only user, the Password box is the only one that appears. But if you have more than one user for the company file, both the User
   Name and Password boxes appear.

5. **Click OK.**

QuickBooks opens the company file, and you're ready to keep the books.

Restoring a Backup File

Backup files are the answer to the adrenaline rush you get when you do something dumb with your company file, your hard drive crashes, or a plume of smoke wafts up from your computer. To restore a backup file, choose File→Open or Restore Company. In the Open or Restore Company dialog box, select the "Restore a backup copy" option, click Next, and then choose the file you want. (To learn how to create backup files, as well as the details on restoring them, see "Backing Up Files" on page 175.)

ORGANIZATION STATION

Fast Access to Several Companies

If you work on several sets of company books at the same time, choosing File→Open Previous Company is the quickest way to hop between company files. Out of the box, QuickBooks lists up to four companies on the Open Previous Company submenu.

If you work with fewer companies, the submenu may have company files that you'd rather forget. You can change the number of companies QuickBooks lists on this submenu to match the number of companies you work with. With a clever workaround, you can also clear out old entries that you don't want to see.

Here's how to change the number of companies on the Open Previous Company submenu:

1. Make sure you have a company file open, and then choose File→Open Previous Company→"Set number of previous companies."

2. In the Set Number of Previous Companies dialog box, type the maximum number of companies you want to see on the submenu, and then click OK. QuickBooks can show up to 20, which it lists starting with the most recent.

3. To clear old entries off the menu, change the number of entries to 1 and then click OK. After you do so, QuickBooks lists only the most recent company file, clearing all the others off the list.

4. If you want to see more than one company, reset the number of entries again, this time to a higher number. Now, when you open another company file, it will appear on the list.

Opening a Portable Company File

A *portable file* is a special type of file that makes QuickBooks company files compact so you can email them more easily. Opening a portable file is similar to opening a regular file:

1. **Choose File→Open or Restore Company.**

   The Open or Restore Company dialog box opens.

2. **Select the "Restore a portable file" option and then click Next.**

   The Open Portable Company File dialog box appears. QuickBooks automatically changes the "Files of type" box to "QuickBooks Portable Company Files (*.QBM)."

3. Navigate to the folder with the portable file and double-click its name.

QuickBooks opens the file.

Updating a QuickBooks File

How do I update a company file to the newest version of QuickBooks?

If you've used a previous version of QuickBooks, your company file is set up to work with that version of the program. When you upgrade to QuickBooks 2013, the program has to make some changes to your company file.

Once you update a company file, your coworkers won't be able to open it until you upgrade their computers to QuickBooks 2013. So to prevent work disruptions, plan to upgrade all copies of QuickBooks and the company file during downtime.

Fortunately, updating a company file is easy: All you have to do is open it in the new version of QuickBooks and follow the onscreen instructions. Here are the steps:

1. In your new version of QuickBooks, choose File→"Open or Restore Company."

2. In the Open or Restore Company dialog box, select the "Open a company file" option, and then click Next.

3. In the Open a Company dialog box, double-click the company file you want to update. If you see the Password box, enter your password.

4. In the Update Company File for New Version dialog box, turn on the "I understand that my company file will be updated to this new version of QuickBooks" checkbox, and then click Update Now.

5. Click OK to create a backup before you upgrade. Follow the steps to create a backup copy of your company file (page 179).

6. When the Update Company message box appears, click Yes to start the update. Keep in mind that the process could take a while if your company file is large or if you're updating from several QuickBooks versions back.

■ Converting from Another Program to QuickBooks

If you launched your small business from your basement and kept your records with Quicken Home & Business, your accountant has probably recommended that you make the leap to QuickBooks. On the other hand, you may have used another accounting program like Peachtree or Small Business Accounting and have decided to move to QuickBooks. Regardless of which other program you used, the command to convert your records to QuickBooks is the same: File→Utilities→Convert. Then choose From Quicken, From Peachtree, From Microsoft Small Business Accounting, or From Microsoft Office Accounting. (You can also convert a file from the QuickBooks Setup dialog box: Click Other Options and then choose Convert Quicken Data or Convert Other Accounting Software Data.) The rest of this section explains what else you need to know.

Converting from Quicken Home & Business

Quicken doesn't report your business performance in the way that most accountants want to see, nor does it store your business transactions the way QuickBooks does. So if you want the conversion to proceed as smoothly as possible, do some cleanup in your Quicken file first.

For example, record overdue scheduled transactions and send online payments before you convert your Quicken file. Also, while you're in Quicken, delete accounts you no longer need, because once they're in QuickBooks, you can't delete them if they contain any transactions. And make sure that customer names are consistent and unique. QuickBooks doesn't support repeating online payments, so you also have to tell Quicken to delete any repeating online payments you've set up. In addition, you need complete reports of your past payrolls because Quicken payroll transactions don't convert to QuickBooks.

> **WARNING** When you convert from Quicken to QuickBooks, all the names that are converted are added to the Other Names List. You can then change which list the names belong to (page 158 but if your Quicken data file has tons of names, it's easier to export those names to a spreadsheet and then import them by using QuickBooks' Add/Edit Multiple List Entries feature (page 94).

Intuit publishes a detailed guide to help you prepare for a Quicken conversion. Go to *http://tinyurl.com/2af78q5* and follow the instructions there.

> **NOTE** If you've already cleaned up your Quicken file and run into conversion problems in QuickBooks, check the QuickBooks company file for errors by choosing File→Utilities→Verify Data, as described on page 190. Another potential solution is to remove transactions prior to the current fiscal year before converting the file. If nothing you try works *and* you're willing to send your Quicken file to Intuit, contact QuickBooks technical support by choosing Help→Support. (A browser window opens to the Intuit QuickBooks Support page. In the horizontal navigation bar, click Contact Us.) They may agree to convert the file for you (for a fee).

When your Quicken file is ready for conversion to QuickBooks, you have two options in QuickBooks:

- **Choose File→New Company**. In the QuickBooks Setup dialog box, click Other Options and then choose Convert Quicken Data.

- **Choose File→Utilities→Convert→From Quicken**.

Converting from a Non-Intuit Program

To convert files created in other accounting programs, like Peachtree or Small Business Accounting, you have to download a conversion tool from the QuickBooks website. Choose File→Utilities→Convert and then choose the program you want to convert from. In the browser window that opens, fill in the boxes for your name, company name, and email address, and then click Submit.

Getting Around in QuickBooks

You have more than enough to do running your business, so you don't want bookkeeping to take any more time than necessary. The QuickBooks Home page is your command center for all things financial; it helps you get your accounting done quickly and efficiently. The page not only provides a visual roadmap of the bookkeeping tasks you perform regularly, but it also gives you quick access to tasks and information related to vendors, customers, and employees, along with the features and overall financial info you use most often. Click an icon, and the corresponding window or dialog box appears. The Home page also includes Company and Banking panels with icons that open windows like the Chart of Accounts, Item List, Write Checks, and everyone's favorite—Make Deposits.

This chapter explains how to use the workflow icons on the Home page, as well as the Vendor, Customer, and Employees Centers that open when you click the corresponding buttons in the Home page's panels. (The Inventory Center, which is available in QuickBooks Premier and Enterprise, is described on page 506.) You'll also see how to review your company's finances in the Company Snapshot window and keep track of upcoming or overdue to-dos and transactions with the QuickBooks Calendar.

If you typically work with more than one window open in QuickBooks, the Home page might be buried beneath a mosaic of transaction windows, such as Create Invoices and Enter Bills. If that's the case, the top icon bar or the left icon bar (new in QuickBooks 2013) both offer shortcuts to your favorite features. Each icon bar has its pros and cons, so you have to decide which one you prefer (or you can turn them off completely). This chapter shows you how to access QuickBooks features from the menu bar and icon bars, and how to work with all the windows you open during a rousing bookkeeping session.

The Home Page

The QuickBooks Home page (Figure 2-1, background) is a slick way to work through your company's bookkeeping tasks. (If it isn't visible, choose Company→Home Page or click Home in the QuickBooks icon bar to display it.) When you create your company file (page 13), the settings you choose determine what appears on the Home page. Depending on what choices you made during setup, you'll see several *panels*—Vendors, Customers, Employees, Company, and Banking—that each contain various icons. For example, if you tell the Setup wizard that you invoice customers and send statements, the Customers panel includes icons for invoicing and preparing statements. Or if you run a one-person shop with no employees, you won't see the Employees panel.

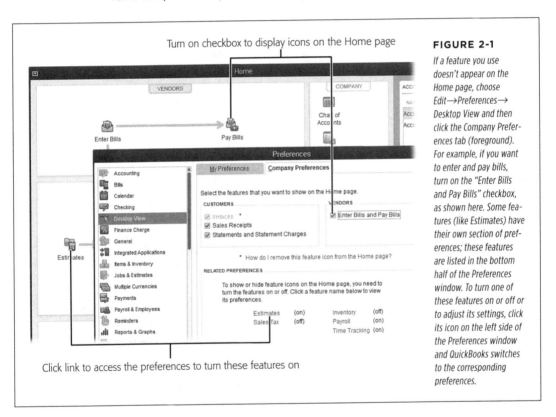

Turn on checkbox to display icons on the Home page

Click link to access the preferences to turn these features on

FIGURE 2-1

If a feature you use doesn't appear on the Home page, choose Edit→Preferences→ Desktop View and then click the Company Preferences tab (foreground). For example, if you want to enter and pay bills, turn on the "Enter Bills and Pay Bills" checkbox, as shown here. Some features (like Estimates) have their own section of preferences; these features are listed in the bottom half of the Preferences window. To turn one of these features on or off or to adjust its settings, click its icon on the left side of the Preferences window and QuickBooks switches to the corresponding preferences.

The Home page also has icons for other important features, like the Chart of Accounts icon in the Company panel, which opens the Chart of Accounts window, and the Check Register icon in the Banking panel, which opens your checking account register window. This section shows you how to use the Home page to best advantage.

TIP The Home page appears each time you log into a company file. If you prefer to keep the Home page hidden, choose Edit→Preferences→Desktop View, click the My Preferences tab, and then turn off the "Show Home page when opening a company file" checkbox. Then, when you want to see the Home page, simply choose Company→Home Page.

The arrows on the Home page show how bookkeeping tasks fit together so you can follow your money from start to finish. Vendors, customers, and employees each have their own panel on the Home page. The bookkeeping tasks for each group are laid out like breadcrumbs you can follow. Each company is different, so you don't *have* to use every icon you see. This section outlines the tasks you can perform from each panel and where to find detailed instructions elsewhere in this book.

Vendors

Whether you purchase products and services to run your company or to sell to your customers, the Vendors panel steps you through purchasing and paying for the goods and services you use; these steps are described in detail in Chapter 9.

Click the Vendors button at the top of the panel (or choose Vendors→Vendor Center) to open the Vendor Center shown in Figure 2-2, where you can set up and edit vendors, and check the status of purchase orders, bills, and other vendor transactions. The Vendor Center is the best place to create, edit, and view what's going on with your vendors. Here's what you can do there:

- **Create a new vendor**. In the Vendor Center toolbar at the top of the window, click New Vendor→New Vendor and the New Vendor window opens so you can create a new vendor record, as described on page 91. If you click New Vendor→Add Multiple Vendors instead, QuickBooks lets you create several vendors in one window (page 94).

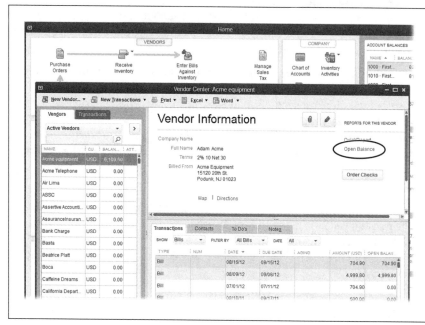

FIGURE 2-2

The Vendor Center puts all vendor-related tasks in a single window. When you choose a vendor in the list on the left, the Vendor Information pane on the right displays info about that vendor and its transactions. Click the Open Balance link (circled) to see how much you owe that vendor. You can even click the Map or Directions link to find out how to get to your vendor.

- **Find a vendor**. If you have a bazillion vendors, you can shorten the vendor list that you see in the Vendors tab on the left side of the center. The tab's unlabeled drop-down list is initially set to Active Vendors. If you want to see active and inactive vendors alike, click the field and choose All Vendors instead. If you'd rather see only the vendors you owe money to, choose Vendors with Open Balances. Choose Custom Filter to specify exactly the criteria you want.

  To do a quick search of vendor records, type part of a vendor's name in the Vendors tab's *second* unlabeled box and then click the Find button, which has a magnifying glass on it. (The Find button changes to a red X, which you can click to clear the value in the Find box and redisplay the full list.)

- **Review a vendor's record**. When you select a vendor on the Vendors tab (shown in Figure 2-2), basic info about that vendor appears at the top right of the window.

- **Edit an existing vendor's record**. To change a vendor's record, on the Vendors tab, right-click the vendor's name and then choose Edit Vendor; or, on the right side of the Vendor Center, click the Edit button (it looks like a pencil). Either way, the Edit Vendor window opens with the same fields you filled in when you created the record (page 91).

- **Attach an electronic document to a vendor record**. You can add attachments to a vendor's record as described on page 344.

- **Create transactions for a vendor**. In the Vendor Center toolbar, click New Transactions to display a drop-down menu of vendor-related features like Enter Bills, Pay Bills, and Receive Items. (These do the same thing as the icons in the Home page's Vendors panel.)

- **Review and manage transactions, contacts, to-dos, and notes for a vendor**. When the Vendors tab is displayed, the bottom-right part of the Vendor Center displays tabs for transactions, contacts, to-dos, and notes. When you select a vendor in the Vendors tab, the Transactions tab at the bottom right of the Center lists that vendor's transactions. By filtering these transactions, you can find out which purchase orders are still open, whether any bills are overdue, and what payments you've made. To see a specific kind of transaction, in the Show drop-down list, choose a type, like Bills or Bill Payments.

  The Filter By drop-down list lets you restrict the transactions in the table by their status, such as Open Bills or Overdue Bills. To track down transactions within a specific date range, choose a date range from the Date drop-down list. (The options in this menu are the same as the ones available in report windows; see page 553.)

  Click the Contacts, To Do's, or Notes tab to create, edit, or view contacts, to-dos, or notes for the selected vendor.

TIP To view a transaction in its corresponding window, double-click the transaction in the list.

- **Review transactions for all vendors**. When you click the Transactions tab on the left side of the window (*not* the bottom right) and then click a type of transaction, such as Bills or Bill Payments, you'll see transactions of that type for all vendors on the right side of the window. You can filter these transactions by status (such as open or overdue), by date, and, if you use multiple currencies, by currency.

- **Print or export vendor information**. In the Vendor Center toolbar, click Print to print vendor lists, vendor info, or vendor transactions. Click Excel to paste, import, or export vendor info and transactions (page 651).

- **Prepare vendor letters**. In the Vendor Center toolbar, click Word to create letters to vendors (page 638).

Customers

The Customers panel has icons for customer-oriented features like creating invoices, statements, sales receipts, and so on. (Chapter 10 describes how to work with invoices, estimates, sales orders, refunds, and customer credits. Chapter 11 covers creating statement charges and statements. Receiving payments and sales receipts for cash sales are both described in Chapter 13.) Click the Customers button at the top of the panel (or choose Customers→Customer Center) to open the Customer Center, where you can perform the following tasks:

- **Create a new customer or job**. In the Customer Center toolbar at the top of the window, click New Customer & Job. In the drop-down menu, choose New Customer to create a new customer record (page 66), or choose Add Multiple Customer:Jobs to add several customers. If you want to add a job to an existing customer, first select the customer in the Customers & Jobs tab on the left side of the Customer Center, and then click New Customer & Job→Add Job (page 76).

- **Find a customer**. You can filter the list in the Customers & Jobs tab list to show active customers, only customers who owe you money (customers with open balances), and so on, simply by choosing an option in the tab's unlabeled drop-down list (it's initially set to Active Customers). Choose Custom Filter to specify criteria for the customers you want to see. To search for a specific customer, type part of the customer's name in the tab's second unlabeled box, and then click the Find button (it has a magnifying glass on it). The Find button changes to a red X, which you can click to clear the value in the Find box and redisplay the complete list.

- **Review a customer record**. When you select a customer in the Customers & Jobs tab, the right side of the center displays the basic 411 about that customer. In the Customer Information section, shown in Figure 2-3, you can get directions to its location, look at key information like the customer's open balance, attach electronic documents to the record, or run reports about the customer.

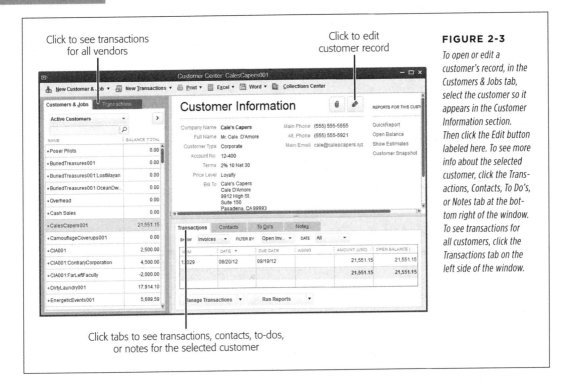

Click to see transactions
for all vendors

Click to edit
customer record

Click tabs to see transactions, contacts, to-dos,
or notes for the selected customer

FIGURE 2-3

*To open or edit a
customer's record, in the
Customers & Jobs tab,
select the customer so it
appears in the Customer
Information section.
Then click the Edit button
labeled here. To see more
info about the selected
customer, click the Transactions, Contacts, To Do's,
or Notes tab at the bot-
tom right of the window.
To see transactions for
all customers, click the
Transactions tab on the
left side of the window.*

- **Review a customer's status**. On the right side of the Customer Center, click the Customer Snapshot link to open the Company Snapshot window (page 32) to the Customer tab. There, you can quickly scan the customer's recent invoices and payments, look at a bar graph of sales you've made to the customer by time period, and review the items that customer buys the most.

- **Edit an existing customer's record**. To open the Edit Customer window, in the Customers & Jobs tab, either right-click a customer's name and then choose Edit Customer, or select a customer and then click the Edit button that's labeled in Figure 2-3.

- **Attach an electronic document to a customer record**. You can add attachments to a customer's record or scan an image of them into QuickBooks, as described on page 344.

- **Create transactions for a customer**. In the Customer Center toolbar, click New Transactions and then choose a transaction type from the drop-down menu, such as Estimates, Invoices, or Receive Payments. The items in this menu are the same as the icons in the Home page's Customers panel and open the cor-responding window to record that type of transaction.

- **Review and manage transactions, contacts, to-dos, and notes for a customer.**
When the Customers & Jobs tab is displayed on the left side of the window, the
bottom right of the Customer Center includes tabs for transactions, contacts,
to-dos, and notes. If you click the Transactions tab, you'll see a table at the
bottom right of the Center with the transactions for the customer you select in
the Customers & Jobs tab. You can filter these transactions by type (estimates
or invoices, for example), status, and date. Double-click a transaction in the list
to open a window with details about it. Click the Contacts, To Do's, or Notes
tab to create, edit, or view contacts, to-dos, or notes for the selected customer.

- **Review transactions for all customers.** When you select the Transactions
tab on the left side of the window and then click a type of transaction (such as
Estimate, Invoices, or Received Payments), you'll see transactions of that type
for all customers on the right side of the window. Depending on the type you
choose, you can filter these transactions by status (such as open or overdue),
payment method, date, and, if you use multiple currencies, by currency.

- **Print or export customer information.** In the Center's toolbar, click Print to print
customer information (page 169) or click Excel to import or export customer
and job info (page 651).

- **Prepare customer letters.** In the Customer Center toolbar, click Word to create
letters to customers (page 638).

Employees

The Employees panel has only a few icons. The devilish details arise when you click
one of these icons to enter time, set up paychecks, or pay payroll tax liabilities. The
Employee Center works the same way as the Vendor and Customer centers you just
learned about. To open it, click Employees in the Employees panel of the Home page
or choose Employees→Employee Center. (See Chapter 8 to learn how to record the
time that employees work. Chapter 14 introduces the process for paying employees
and other payroll expenses.)

In the Employee Center, you can create new records for employees, update info for
existing employees, and view transactions like paychecks. On the Employees tab on
the left side of the Center, you can filter the list to view active employees, released
employees (ones who no longer work for you), or all employees.

Company

The Company panel is on the right side of the Home page. The two icons in this panel
that you'll probably click most often are Chart of Accounts and Items & Services,
which open the Chart of Accounts (page 51) and Item List (page 119) windows, respectively. If you track inventory, click the Inventory Activities icon and then choose
a feature, such as Adjust Quantity On Hand, which lets you change the quantity and
value of your inventory (page 513). If you use QuickBooks Premier or Enterprise,
choose Inventory Center to open a window similar to the Customer Center, except
that it focuses on the status of and transactions involving your inventory items
(page 506).

Banking

The Home page's Banking panel is a one-stop shop for banking tasks. Whether you visit this panel frequently or almost never depends on how you like to record transactions. For example, you can click the Write Checks icon to open the Write Checks window (page 257) or simply press Ctrl+W to do the same thing. (Or, if you like to record checks in a check register window, you might prefer to double-click your bank account in the Chart of Accounts window instead.) Similarly, clicking the Enter Credit Card Charges icon opens the Enter Credit Card Charges window (page 262), though you can also record credit card charges directly in a credit card account's register (page 414).

Clicking the Record Deposits icon opens the Payments to Deposit dialog box so you can record bank deposits (page 397 The Reconcile icon opens the Begin Reconciliation dialog box so you can reconcile your QuickBooks records to your bank's (page 426). And the Print Checks icon opens the Select Checks to Print dialog box so you can choose the ones you want to print and send them to a printer loaded with blank checks.

> **NOTE** If you use the top icon bar (View→Top Icon Bar), the far-right side of the Home page shows account balances at the top and a link to display reminders at the bottom. In between are a few links to additional services that Intuit offers. You also see a Backup Status section that tells you when your last backup ran and includes info about the Intuit Data Protect backup service (page 180). If any of these sections are collapsed, click the panel's down arrow to expand it. Click a section's up arrow to collapse it.
>
> If you use the left icon bar (View→Left Icon Bar), you can see your account balances by clicking View Balances in the middle section of the bar. See page 662 to learn more about the icon bars.

■ The Company Snapshot

The Company Snapshot window (choose Company→Company Snapshot or click the Snapshots icon on the icon bar to open it) is a dashboard that shows important aspects of your company's financial state, like account balances, income breakdown (by top-level income accounts), customers who owe money, best-selling items, and reminders, as you can see in Figure 2-4. You can choose from 12 different views (page 667) to see the information you care about most.

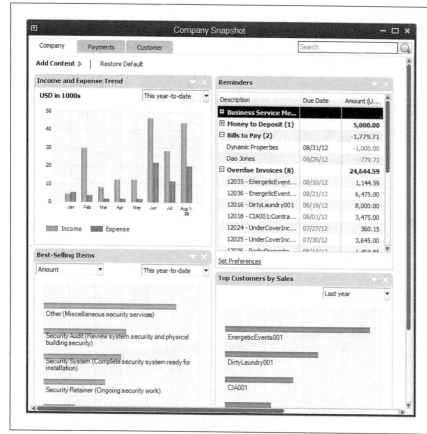

FIGURE 2-4

Not only can you quickly scan your company's financial status in this window, but you can also double-click entries here to dig into the details. You can even add or remove items from the Snapshot window or drag items to rearrange them, as described on page 667.

Your Financial Calendar

Paying a bill late can result in a whopping late fee. Conversely, you can leave money on the table if you don't take advantage of early payment discounts. And it's bad form to forget to do things like call people or send them info. The Calendar window (Figure 2-5) acts as a dashboard that shows when transactions and to-dos are due. To open it, choose Company→Calendar, or click the Calendar icon on the icon bar.

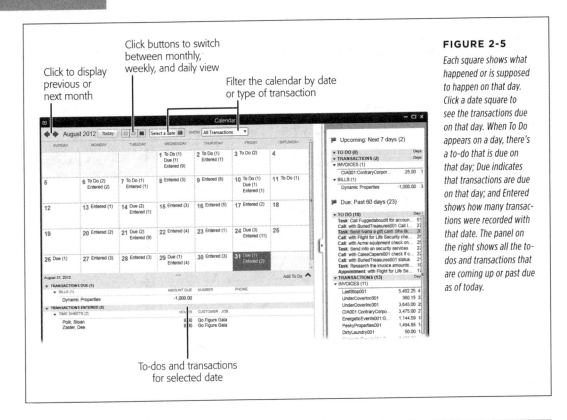

Click to display
previous or
next month

Click buttons to switch
between monthly,
weekly, and daily view

Filter the calendar by date
or type of transaction

FIGURE 2-5

*Each square shows what
happened or is supposed
to happen on that day.
Click a date square to
see the transactions due
on that day. When To Do
appears on a day, there's
a to-do that is due on
that day; Due indicates
that transactions are due
on that day; and Entered
shows how many transac-
tions were recorded with
that date. The panel on
the right shows all the to-
dos and transactions that
are coming up or past due
as of today.*

To-dos and transactions
for selected date

NOTE The Calendar window's toolbar includes icons and boxes for controlling your view. Here's what they do from left to right: Click a blue arrow to move to the previous or next time period. Click Today to select the square for today's date. Click the icons to display one day, one week, or one month, respectively. Use the Show drop-down list to pick the transactions you want to see in the calendar.

Out of the box, the Calendar window has three panes:

- The **calendar** displays an entire month initially. Each day in the calendar sum-marizes the transactions and to-dos for that day, as shown in Figure 2-5.

TIP If you want to see more detail in the calendar, switch to a weekly or even a daily view. To the right of the Today button, click the first button to display a single day in the calendar pane. The daily view shows transac-tions and to-dos for a day, similar to what you see in the bottom pane of the Calendar. Click the second button to display a weekly view.

- The **Upcoming and Due pane** on the right lists the to-dos and transactions that are on deck or past due as of today, which is incredibly handy for staying on top of your bookkeeping and business activities. Double-click a to-do to open the Edit To Do dialog box with the details about what you're supposed to do and when. Double-click a transaction to open it in its corresponding window (such as Create Invoices for an invoice).

- The **activity pane** at the bottom of the window lists the to-dos and transactions for the date you select in the calendar. The customer's telephone number is listed for invoices, which is handy if you want to call and find out when you can expect a payment. If a day is particularly busy, you can expand this bottom pane by pointing your cursor at the three blue dots at the top of the pane and then dragging.

NOTE To hide the "Upcoming and Due" pane, click the right arrow on its left edge; to restore this pane, click the left arrow on the Calendar pane's right edge. To collapse the activity pane, click the up arrow at its top right; to expand the pane, click the down arrow. If you click Daily View, the calendar disappears; to restore the calendar, click the Weekly View or Monthly View button.

Menus and the Icon Bars

Although the Home page guides you through bookkeeping tasks, QuickBooks veterans may still prefer to use the menu bar at the very top of the QuickBooks window (Figure 2-6) to launch different activities. The menu bar is handy because it's always visible and serves up every feature QuickBooks has to offer.

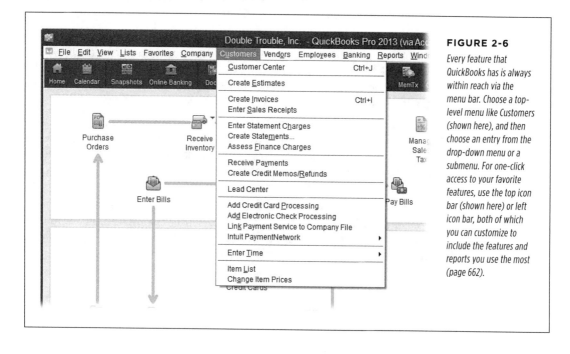

FIGURE 2-6

Every feature that QuickBooks has is always within reach via the menu bar. Choose a top-level menu like Customers (shown here), and then choose an entry from the drop-down menu or a submenu. For one-click access to your favorite features, use the top icon bar (shown here) or left icon bar, both of which you can customize to include the features and reports you use the most (page 662).

In QuickBooks 2013, you can use the View menu to choose between two icon bars: the top icon bar and the left icon bar. The top icon bar has been around for years. It sits just below the QuickBooks menu bar and displays your favorite features as icons with brief identifying labels. Click an icon, such as Home, Calendar, or Customers, and the corresponding feature launches. If you haven't graduated to a large widescreen monitor, this icon bar is both convenient and space-saving. (If you *really* need more space, you can hide the icon bar by choosing View→Hide Icon Bar.)

The left icon bar (see Figure 2-7) is new in QuickBooks 2013 and offers access to more features than the top icon bar. Here's what the entries in the middle section of the left icon bar do:

- **My Shortcuts**. This entry is selected initially. It displays your favorite shortcuts at the top of the left icon bar. These shortcuts are the same ones you see on the top icon bar, such as Home, Calendar, Snapshots, Reports, and so on.

- **My Apps**. If you use add-on programs, click this entry to access those programs or find new ones.

- **Do Today**. Unsurprisingly, when you click this entry, the top section of the left icon bar lists transactions and to-dos that are due today.

- **View Balances**. When you use the left icon bar, the Home page doesn't display account balances on the right side as it does when you use the top icon bar. To see your account balances at the top of the left icon bar, click this entry.

- **Run Favorite Reports**. Clicking this entry lists the reports that you've flagged as your favorites (page 544). The reports you see are the same ones that appear on the Favorites tab of the Report Center.

- **Open Windows**. If you turn on the preference to use multiple windows (page 605), you can click this entry to see a list of the open windows at the top of the left icon bar. Click a window's name to make it active. This entry displays the same windows you see if you choose View→Open Window List when you use the top icon bar, as described in the next section.

> **TIP** The left icon bar takes up a couple of inches on the left side of the main QuickBooks window, so it's more useful if you use a widescreen monitor. With older and smaller monitors, you'll have trouble fitting the left icon bar and your transactions windows onscreen at the same time.

After shortcut menus and keyboard shortcuts (see Appendix C, online at *www.missing-manuals.com/cds*), icon bars are the fastest way to launch your favorite features. You can add features, memorized reports, and windows you open often to them—and remove features you don't use. Page 662 tells you how to customize the icon bars.

▇ Switching Among Open Windows

If you tend to work on one bookkeeping task for hours on end, you can set Quick-Books up to display one full-size window at a time (page 605). That way, when you open additional windows, they get stacked on top of each other so you see only the last one you opened. If you go with the one-window approach, you can choose the window you want to see in several ways:

- Click Open Windows in the left icon bar, shown in Figure 2-7. Then, click the name of the window you want in the list at the top of the left icon bar.

- If you use the top icon bar, you can see a list of open windows by choosing View→Open Window List. Then, in the list, simply click the name of the window you want to work with.

- On the menu bar, choose Window, and then choose the name of the one you want to see.

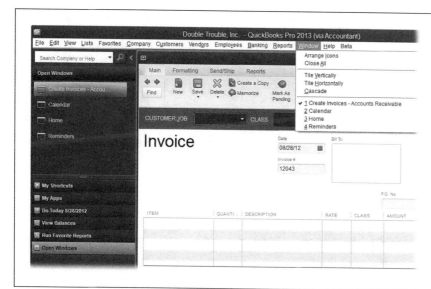

FIGURE 2-7

If you focus on one window, you can switch to another window by clicking the Window menu at the top of the screen and choosing the window you want to display. When you have multiple windows open, the Window menu includes entries for arranging them, such as Cascade and Tile Vertically.

If, on the other hand, you flit between bookkeeping tasks like a honeybee in an alfalfa field, you probably want to display several windows at a time. QuickBooks can do that. Like windows in other programs, simply click a window to bring it to the front, or use the buttons in its upper right to minimize, maximize, or close it. You can reposition windows by dragging their title bars, or resize them by dragging their edges and corners.

To learn how to tell QuickBooks which window setup you prefer, see page 605.

Supermax View

New in QuickBooks 2013, you can expand transaction windows, such as Create Invoices, to Supermax view, which is perfect when you want to see more information in a transaction window, as shown in Figure 2-8.

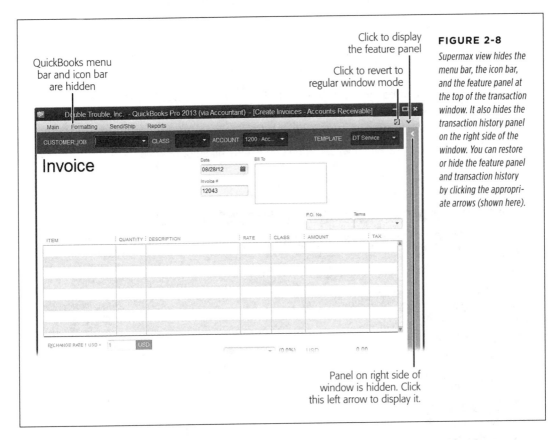

FIGURE 2-8

Supermax view hides the menu bar, the icon bar, and the feature panel at the top of the transaction window. It also hides the transaction history panel on the right side of the window. You can restore or hide the feature panel and transaction history by clicking the appropriate arrows (shown here).

Click to display the feature panel

Click to revert to regular window mode

QuickBooks menu bar and icon bar are hidden

Panel on right side of window is hidden. Click this left arrow to display it.

This view does several things so you can see more of the data entry lines:

- Hides the QuickBooks menu bar and icon bar (if you use one)

- Minimizes the feature panel (a.k.a. the ribbon, if you're familiar with Microsoft's ribbon) at the top of the window

- Fills the entire QuickBooks window with the transaction window you Supermaxed

- Hides the transaction history panel on the right side of the window

To switch a transaction window to Supermax mode, at the top right of the window, click the icon that looks like a four-headed arrow. To revert to regular window mode, click the icon again. (When the window is in Supermax mode, the icon looks like a square with an arrow pointing to its bottom-left.)

NOTE When you revert to regular window mode, the QuickBooks menu bar, icon bar, and feature panel at the top of the transaction window all reappear. However, the transaction window is maximized to fill the rest of the QuickBooks main window. If you want to restore the window to its previous size, click the Maximize button (it looks like two offset windows) at the top right of the main QuickBooks window.

Setting Up a Chart of Accounts

I f you've just started running a business and keeping your company's books, all this talk of accounts, credits, and debits might have you flummoxed. Accounting is a cross between mathematics and the mystical arts; its goal is to record and report the financial performance of an organization. The end result of bookkeeping and accounting is a set of financial statements (page 467), but the starting point is the chart of accounts.

In accounting, an *account* is more than a real-world account you have at a financial institution; it's like a bucket for holding money used for a specific purpose. When you earn money, you document those earnings in an income account, just as you might toss the change from a day's take at the lemonade stand into the jar on your desk. When you buy supplies for your business, that expense shows up in an expense account that works a lot like the shoebox you throw receipts into. If you buy a building, its value ends up in an asset account. And if you borrow money to buy that building, the mortgage owed shows up in a liability account.

Accounts come in a variety of types to reflect whether you've earned or spent money, whether you own something or owe money to someone else, as well as a few other financial situations. Your *chart of accounts* is a list of all the accounts you use to track money in your business.

Neophytes and experienced business folks alike will be relieved to know that you don't have to build a chart of accounts from scratch in QuickBooks. This chapter explains how to get a ready-made chart of accounts for your business and what to do with it once you've got it. If you want to add or modify accounts in your chart of accounts, you'll learn how to do that, too.

NOTE Industry-specific Premier editions of QuickBooks include a chart of accounts, an Item list, payroll items, and preferences already tuned to your industry (such as construction, manufacturing, nonprofit, professional services, or retail). The industry-specific editions also have features unique to each industry, like enhanced job costing in the Contractor edition. These features may save you time during setup and your day-to-day bookkeeping, but you have to decide whether you want to spend a few hundred dollars more than the QuickBooks Pro price tag (page xx) to get them.

Acquiring a Chart of Accounts

When you create a new QuickBooks company file and choose an industry (page 8), the program automatically sets up the chart of accounts with accounts that are typical for that industry. For example, if you choose a product-oriented industry, you'll see an income account for product or parts income, while a service-oriented business gets an income account for labor income. If your company is like many small businesses, the chart of accounts that QuickBooks creates includes everything you need.

However, if you want to customize your chart of accounts to mirror your company's needs, the easiest—although probably not the cheapest—way to get a chart of accounts is from your accountant. Accountants understand the accounting guidelines set by the Financial Accounting Standards Board (FASB—pronounced "faz bee"), a private-sector organization that sets standards with the SEC's blessing. When your accountant builds a QuickBooks chart of accounts for you, you can be reasonably sure that you have the accounts you need to track your business and that those accounts conform to accounting standards. If you're a business owner and want a specific account or want to see your business financials in a particular way, ask your accountant to set that up for you.

NOTE Don't worry—getting an accountant to build a chart of accounts for you probably won't bust your budget, since the accountant won't start from scratch. Many financial professionals maintain spreadsheets of accounts and build a chart of accounts by importing a customized account list into QuickBooks. Or, they may keep QuickBooks company files around to use as templates for new files.

Importing a Chart of Accounts

If you don't want to pay an accountant to create a chart of accounts for you, how about finding one built by experts and available at no charge? A quick search on the Web for "QuickBooks chart of accounts" returns links to sites with predefined charts of accounts. For example, if you run a restaurant, you can go to *www.rrgconsulting.com/restaurant_coa.htm* and download a free .iif file with a restaurant-oriented chart of accounts that you can import into QuickBooks, as explained in the next section.

In the not-for-profit world, the National Center for Charitable Statistics website (*http://nccs.urban.org/projects/ucoa.cfm*) includes downloadable QuickBooks files that contain the Unified Chart of Accounts for nonprofits (known as the UCOA). You can download a QuickBooks backup file of a nonprofit company file, complete with a chart of accounts (see page 184 to learn how to restore a backup file), an .iif file that you can import into QuickBooks, or a backup file for the Mac version of QuickBooks.

■ IMPORTING ACCOUNTS FROM EXCEL

If you have an Excel spreadsheet with your company account information, you can import that info directly into your company file. The full story on importing from Excel is on page 654, but here are the basic steps:

1. **Open the QuickBooks Chart of Accounts window.**

   Press Ctrl+A or, at the top right of the Home page, in the Company panel, click Chart of Accounts.

2. **At the bottom of the Chart of Accounts window, click Account→Import from Excel.**

   The "Import a file" dialog box opens.

3. **Click Browse and locate the file that contains the accounts you want to import; click its filename and then click Open.**

   The filename appears in the File box.

4. **If necessary, in the "Choose a sheet in this Excel workbook" drop-down list, select the worksheet with the data, as shown in Figure 3-1.**

   Keep the "This data file has header rows" checkbox turned on if the Excel worksheet includes a row with the names of the fields you're importing.

5. **In the "Choose a mapping" drop-down list, pick < Add New >. In the Mappings dialog box that appears, type a name in the "Mapping name" box, such as Imported Accounts.**

   A *mapping* is when you designate which fields from one program match up with fields in another program so you can transfer data between the programs. The left side of the Mapping dialog box lists the fields for accounts.

6. **For each QuickBooks account field, click the cell in the corresponding "Import data" column and choose the matching spreadsheet header name or column.**

   If the spreadsheet doesn't have a header row, you have to choose Column A, Column B, and so on.

7. **When you've completed your choices, click Save to close the Mappings dialog box, and then click Import in the "Import a file" dialog box to create accounts from the imported data.**

   QuickBooks displays a message box that recommends that you back up your company file first. Click Yes. Then, when the backup and import are done, you'll see a message telling you whether the import was successful.

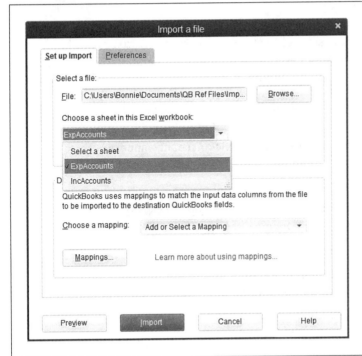

FIGURE 3-1

If the Excel workbook contains more than one worksheet, choose the one you want to use. For example, if your workbook has worksheets for income and expense accounts, you can import only the expense accounts by choosing the worksheet for those accounts.

■ IMPORTING A DOWNLOADED CHART OF ACCOUNTS

If you download an .iif file with a chart of accounts, you can import that file into a QuickBooks company file. Because you're importing a chart of accounts, you want to create your company file with basic info about your company and as few accounts as possible in the Chart of Accounts list. Here's how you create a QuickBooks company file with bare-bones information so you can import a chart of accounts from an .iif file:

1. **Choose File→New Company; in the QuickBooks Setup window that appears, click Express Start.**

2. **On the "Tell us about your business" screen, enter your company's name, type, and Tax ID. In the Industry box, type Other/None, and then click Continue.**

3. **On the "Enter your business contact information" screen, do just that.**

   See Chapter 1 for details. If you click Preview Your Settings and then click the "Chart of Accounts" tab, you see that the accounts list is empty. Click OK to close the preview window.

4. **After you finish filling in your contact info, click Create Company File.**

   QuickBooks creates your company file and then displays the "You've got a company file! Now add your info" screen in the QuickBooks Setup window.

5. **To close the QuickBooks Setup window, click Start Working.**

   You can also close the QuickBooks Setup window by clicking the X at the window's upper right.

6. **Choose File→Utilities→Import→IIF Files.**

   QuickBooks opens the Import dialog box to the folder where you stored your company file and sets the "Files of type" box to "IIF Files (*.IIF)."

7. **Navigate to the folder that contains the .iif file you want to import, select the file, and then click Open.**

   A message box appears that shows how the import is progressing. If all goes well, QuickBooks then displays a message box that tells you that it imported the data successfully. Click OK. If QuickBooks ran into problems with the data in the .iif file, it tells you that it didn't import the data successfully. In that case, you have to open the .iif file in a text editor or Excel and correct the account info. (You can see what information QuickBooks expects by exporting an account list, as described on page 649.)

To admire your new chart of accounts, in the QuickBooks Home page's Company panel, click Chart of Accounts (or press Ctrl+A). Now that your chart of accounts is in place, you can add more accounts, hide accounts you don't need, merge accounts, or edit the accounts on the list. The rest of this chapter explains how to do all these things.

◼ Planning the Chart of Accounts

A chart of accounts is a tool for tracking your company's finances at a relatively high level—it helps you produce financial statements (see page 467) and prepare your business tax returns. When setting up your chart of accounts, bear in mind that it will be easier to work with if you keep the number of accounts to a minimum. (Even the income statements for ginormous global corporations typically fit on a single page.) This section helps you figure out which accounts you need and provides guidelines for naming and numbering them.

Do You Need Another Account?

QuickBooks offers several features—including items, jobs, and classes—that can provide details about your company's performance without you having to add additional accounts. So before you create an account, think about whether another feature can track the information you want instead. Here's a brief description of what each feature does and when to use it:

- **Accounts**. When you create transactions in QuickBooks, the program allocates money to accounts in your chart of accounts. Then, when you run a Profit & Loss report (page 468), you see financial results by account. So create a new account if you want to see a particular pool of money broken out in your financial reports. For example, add an income account for services you're offering in addition to your product sales.

NOTE Subaccounts (page 54) are an option if you want to break one category into several smaller pieces, such as divvying travel expenses up into airfare, lodging, transportation, and meals.

- **Items.** In QuickBooks, items track details about what you buy and sell. For example, you might create dozens of items for each specific service you provide, such as cutting down trees, cutting logs, chipping wood, splitting wood, and hauling trash. However, each of those items can be assigned to the same services income account. Chapter 5 provides the full story on items.

- **Jobs.** If you work on different projects for the same customer, you can create jobs in QuickBooks (page 76). That way, you can assign invoices to specific jobs and track income by job. You can also make bills or other expenses billable to specific jobs to track job expenses.

- **Classes.** If your business is broken into segments, such as regions, business units, or partners in a partnership, you can turn to classes (page 598). You can assign a class to each transaction, such as an invoice or bill, which lets you track income and expenses across accounts, customers, and vendors. For example, if you create a class for each business unit, you can assign the appropriate class to each transaction you record. Then, a Profit & Loss report by class (page 474) will produce an income statement for each business unit in the company.

Naming and Numbering Accounts

Account names and numbers make it easy for accountants, bookkeepers, and company employees to find the accounts they need. In addition, with standardized naming and numbering, you can compare your company's financial performance to others in your industry. This section suggests some rules to follow as you set up naming and numbering conventions.

If you accept the accounts that QuickBooks recommends when you set up your company file, then they already have assigned names and numbers, as shown in Figure 3-2. You might think that lets you off the hook. But by taking the time to learn standard account numbers and names, you'll find working with accounts more logical, and you'll understand more of what your accountant and bookkeeper say.

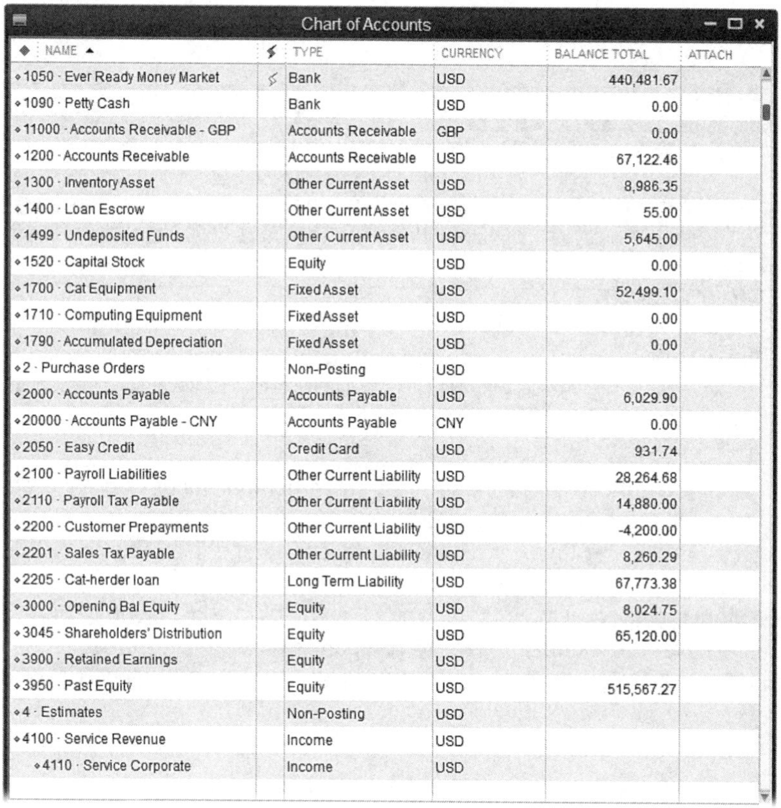

Chart of Accounts

NAME		TYPE	CURRENCY	BALANCE TOTAL	ATTACH
1050 · Ever Ready Money Market	⚡	Bank	USD	440,481.67	
1090 · Petty Cash		Bank	USD	0.00	
11000 · Accounts Receivable - GBP		Accounts Receivable	GBP	0.00	
1200 · Accounts Receivable		Accounts Receivable	USD	67,122.46	
1300 · Inventory Asset		Other Current Asset	USD	8,986.35	
1400 · Loan Escrow		Other Current Asset	USD	55.00	
1499 · Undeposited Funds		Other Current Asset	USD	5,645.00	
1520 · Capital Stock		Equity	USD	0.00	
1700 · Cat Equipment		Fixed Asset	USD	52,499.10	
1710 · Computing Equipment		Fixed Asset	USD	0.00	
1790 · Accumulated Depreciation		Fixed Asset	USD	0.00	
2 · Purchase Orders		Non-Posting	USD		
2000 · Accounts Payable		Accounts Payable	USD	6,029.90	
20000 · Accounts Payable - CNY		Accounts Payable	CNY	0.00	
2050 · Easy Credit		Credit Card	USD	931.74	
2100 · Payroll Liabilities		Other Current Liability	USD	28,264.68	
2110 · Payroll Tax Payable		Other Current Liability	USD	14,880.00	
2200 · Customer Prepayments		Other Current Liability	USD	-4,200.00	
2201 · Sales Tax Payable		Other Current Liability	USD	8,260.29	
2205 · Cat-herder loan		Long Term Liability	USD	67,773.38	
3000 · Opening Bal Equity		Equity	USD	8,024.75	
3045 · Shareholders' Distribution		Equity	USD	65,120.00	
3900 · Retained Earnings		Equity	USD		
3950 · Past Equity		Equity	USD	515,567.27	
4 · Estimates		Non-Posting	USD		
4100 · Service Revenue		Income	USD		
4110 · Service Corporate		Income	USD		

FIGURE 3-2

Accounts that QuickBooks adds to your chart of accounts during setup come with assigned names and numbers. If you don't see account numbers in the Chart of Accounts window (open it by pressing Ctrl+A), page 598 tells you how to display them.

ORGANIZING ACCOUNT NUMBERS

Account numbers are initially turned off when you create a new company file in QuickBooks (page 598 explains how to display them), and you don't have to use them. However, account numbers make it easier for your bookkeeper or accountant to work with your financial records. This section explains the typical numbering convention that financial folks use.

Companies reserve ranges of numbers for different types of accounts, so they can identify the *type* of account by its number alone. Business models vary, so you'll find account numbers carved up in different ways depending on the business. Think about your personal finances: You spend money on lots of different things, but your income derives from a precious few sources. Businesses and nonprofits are no different. So you might find income accounts numbered from 4000 to 4999 and expense accounts using numbers anywhere from 5000 through 9999 (see Table 3-1).

TABLE 3-1 *Typical ranges for account numbers*

RANGE	ACCOUNT TYPE
1000–1999	Assets
2000–2999	Liabilities
3000–3999	Equity
4000–4999	Income
5000–5999	Cost of goods sold, cost of sales, job costs, or general expenses
6000–7999	Expenses, overhead costs, or other income
8000–9999	Expenses or other expenses

NOTE Most businesses use the same account-numbering scheme up until the number 4999. After that, things can differ because some companies require more income accounts, but in most businesses, expense accounts are the most numerous.

Account numbering conventions don't just carve number ranges up for account types. If you read annual reports as a hobby, you know that companies further compartmentalize their finances. For example, assets and liabilities get split into *current* and *long-term* categories. (Current means something that's expected to happen within the next 12 months, such as a loan that's due in 3 months; long-term is anything beyond 12 months.) Typically, companies show assets and liabilities progressing from the shortest to the longest term, and the asset and liability account numbers follow suit. Here's one way to allocate account numbers for current and progressively longer-term assets:

- **1000–1099.** Immediately available cash, such as a checking account, savings account, or petty cash.

- **1100–1499.** Assets you can convert into cash within a few months to a year, including accounts receivable, inventory assets, and other current assets.

- **1500–1799.** Long-term assets, such as land, buildings, furniture, and other fixed assets.

- **1800–1999.** Other assets.

Companies also break expenses down into smaller categories. For example, many companies keep an eye on whether their sales team is doing its job by tracking sales expenses separately and monitoring the ratio of sales to sales expenses. Sales expenses often appear in the 5000–5999 range. QuickBooks reinforces this standard by automatically creating a Cost of Goods Sold account numbered 5001. (In fact, you can create as many Cost of Goods Sold accounts as you need to track expenses that relate directly to your income, such as the cost of purchasing products you sell, as well as what you pay your salespeople.) Other companies assign overhead expenses to accounts in the 7000–7999 range, so they can assign a portion of those expenses to each job performed.

> **TIP** When you add new accounts to your chart of accounts, increment the account number by 5 or 10 to leave room in the numbering scheme for similar accounts you might need in the future. For example, if your checking account number is 1000, assign 1010 or 1015 to your new savings account rather than 1001.

In QuickBooks, an account number can be up to seven digits long, but the program sorts numbers beginning with the leftmost digit. So if you want to categorize in excruciating detail, slice your number ranges into sets of 10,000. For example, assets range from 10000 to 19999; income accounts span 40000 to 49999, and so on.

> **NOTE** QuickBooks sorts accounts by type and then by number, beginning with the leftmost digit. For example, account 4100020 appears before account 4101.

■ VIEWING ACCOUNT NUMBERS

If you want to see or hide account numbers in QuickBooks, here's how to turn them on or off:

1. **Choose Edit→Preferences.**

   The Preferences dialog box opens.

2. **On the left side of the dialog box, click the Accounting icon, and then in the middle, click the Company Preferences tab.**

   You have to be a QuickBooks administrator (page 684) to open the Company Preferences tab.

3. **Turn on the "Use account numbers" checkbox to show account numbers.**

   To hide them, turn *off* this checkbox.

4. **Click OK to close the Preferences dialog box.**

With this setting turned on, account numbers appear in the Chart of Accounts window, account drop-down lists, and account fields. In addition, the Add New Account and Edit Account windows display the Number box, so you can add or modify an account's number.

> **NOTE** Turning off the "Use account numbers" checkbox doesn't remove account numbers you've already added; it simply hides them in the spots mentioned above. You can see them again by simply turning the checkbox back on. However, you can't *add* account numbers to any accounts you create while the checkbox is turned off. If you create an account anyway, you can edit it (page 57) to add an account number.

■ CHOOSING GOOD ACCOUNT NAMES

Account names should be meaningful, both to you and your accountant (or book-keeper). In addition, your accounts should be unique in name and function because you don't need two accounts for the same type of income, expense, or financial bucket. For example, if you consider advertising and marketing two distinctly differ-ent activities, then create an account for each. But if advertising and marketing blur in your mind, then create one account with a name like "Marketing & Advertising."

> **NOTE** Because accounts represent high-level categories, stick to names that summarize the income or expense, such as Service Income and Product Income. If your account names are something like Tom's Consult-ing, Dick's Consulting, and Harry's Consulting, your accounts and their names are too specific—and might cause confusion if Rosie takes over Harry's work.

QuickBooks does its part to enforce unique account names. Say you try to create a new expense account named "Postage," but an account by that name already exists. QuickBooks displays the message, "This name is already in use. Please use another name." What QuickBooks *can't* do is ensure that each account represents a unique category of money. Without a naming standard, you could end up with multiple accounts with unique names, each representing the same category, as shown by the following names for an account used to track postage:

Expense-postage

Postage

Postage and delivery

Shipping

If you haven't used QuickBooks before, here are some rules you can apply to help make your account names consistent:

- **Word order**. If you include the account type in the name, then append it to the end of the name. You'll spot "Postage Expense" more easily than "Expense Postage."

- **Consistent punctuation**. Choose "and" or "&" for accounts that cover more than one item, like "Dues and Subscriptions." And decide whether to include apostrophes, as in "Owners Draw" or "Owners' Draw."

- **Spaces**. Decide whether to include spaces for readability or to eliminate them for brevity; for example, "Dues & Subscriptions" vs. "Dues&Subscriptions."

- **Abbreviation**. If you abbreviate words in account names, then choose a standard abbreviation length. If you go with four-letter abbreviations, for example, "Post-age" would become "Post." For a three-letter abbreviation, you might use "Pst."

WARNING QuickBooks won't enforce your naming standards. So after you set the rules for account names, write them down so you don't forget them. A consistent written standard encourages everyone (yourself included) to trust and follow the naming rules. Also, urge everyone to display inactive accounts (page 60) and scan the chart of accounts for synonyms to see if such an account already exists *before* creating a new one. These rules are easier to enforce if you limit the number of people who can create and edit accounts (page 693).

Creating Accounts and Subaccounts

Different types of accounts represent dramatically different financial animals, as described in the box on page 52. The good news is that every type of account in QuickBooks shares most of the same fields, so you need to learn only one account-creation procedure.

If you look closely at the chart of accounts list in Figure 3-2, you'll notice that accounts fall into two main categories: those with balances and those without. If you're really on your toes, you might also notice that accounts with balances are the ones that appear on the Balance Sheet report. (Accounts without balances appear on the Profit & Loss report.) To learn more about financial statements and the accounts they reference, see Chapter 17.

Creating an Account

After you've had your business for a while, you won't add new accounts very often. However, you might need one if you start up a new line of income, take on a mortgage for your new office building, or want a new expense account for the subcontractors you hire to manage your workload.

Creating accounts in QuickBooks is simple, which is a refreshing change from many accounting tasks. Before you can create an account, you have to open the Chart of Accounts window. Because the chart of accounts is central to accounting, you have several ways to open this window:

- Press Ctrl+A (which you can do from anywhere in the program).

- At the top right of the Home page, in the Company panel, click Chart of Accounts.

- In the menu bar, choose Lists→Chart of Accounts.

The Chart of Accounts window works much like other list windows. For example, you can sort the account list by different columns or drag accounts in the list to different locations. (See page 168 to learn how to sort and rearrange lists.)

Making Sense of Account Types

QuickBooks' account types are standard ones used in finance. Here's a quick introduction to the different types and what they represent:

- **Bank**. Accounts that you hold at a financial institution, such as a checking, savings, money market, or petty cash account.

- **Accounts Receivable**. The money that your customers owe you, like outstanding invoices and goods purchased on credit.

- **Other Current Asset**. Things you own that you'll use or convert to cash within 12 months, such as prepaid expenses.

- **Fixed Asset**. Things your company owns that decrease in value over time (depreciate), like equipment that wears out or becomes obsolete.

- **Other Asset**. If you won't convert an asset to cash in the next 12 months and it isn't a depreciable asset, then it's—you guessed it—an other asset. A long-term note receivable is one example.

- **Accounts Payable**. This is a special type of current liability account (money you owe in the next 12 months) that represents what you owe to vendors.

- **Credit Card**. Just what it sounds like: a credit card account.

- **Other Current Liability**. Money you owe in the next 12 months, such as sales tax and short-term loans.

- **Long Term Liability**. Money you owe *after* the next 12 months, like mortgage payments you'll pay over several years.

- **Equity**. The owners' equity in the company, including the original capital invested in the company and retained earnings. (Money that owners withdraw from the company also shows up in an equity account, but reduces the value of the account.)

- **Income**. The revenue you generate through your main business functions, like sales or consulting services.

- **Cost of Goods Sold**. The cost of products and materials that you held originally in inventory but then sold. You can also use this type of account to track other expenses related to your sales, such as commissions and what you pay subcontractors to do work for your customers.

- **Expense**. The money you spend to run your company.

- **Other Income**. Money you receive from sources other than business operations, such as interest income.

- **Other Expense**. Money you pay out for things other than business operations, like interest.

- **Non-posting Account**. QuickBooks creates non-posting accounts automatically when you use features such as estimates and purchase orders. For example, when you create an estimate (page 310), you don't want that money to appear on your financial reports, so QuickBooks stores those values in non-posting accounts.

TIP You can create accounts on the fly by clicking < Add New > in any Account drop-down list. Suppose you create a new service item (in the Item List window, press Ctrl+N) and want a new income account to track revenue for that service. In the New Item dialog box, scroll to the top of the Account drop-down list and then choose < Add New >. Fill in the info and then click Save & Close. QuickBooks fills in the Account box with the new account, and you can finish creating your item.

Once you've opened the Chart of Accounts window, here's how to create an account:

1. **Press Ctrl+N to open the Add New Account window.**

   Alternatively, on the menu bar at the bottom of the Chart of Accounts window, you can click Account→New. Or, right-click anywhere in the Chart of Accounts window, and then choose New from the shortcut menu.

   No matter which method you use, QuickBooks opens the Add New Account window, shown in Figure 3-3.

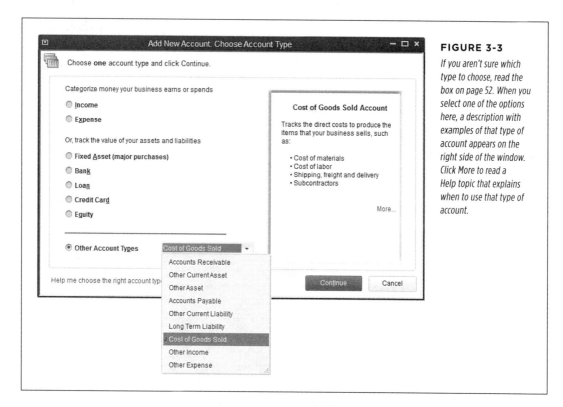

FIGURE 3-3

If you aren't sure which type to choose, read the box on page 52. When you select one of the options here, a description with examples of that type of account appears on the right side of the window. Click More to read a Help topic that explains when to use that type of account.

2. **Select the type of account you want to create, and then click Continue.**

   The Add New Account window lists the most common kinds of accounts. If you don't see the type you want—Other Current Liability, for example—select the Other Account Types option, and then choose from the drop-down menu (Figure 3-3).

3. **In the Number box in the upper right of the Add New Account window (Figure 3-4), type the chart of accounts account number you want to use. (If you don't see the Number box, flip to page 598 to learn how to display it.)**

If you keep the Chart of Accounts window in view while creating new accounts, you can review the account numbers for similar types of accounts. That way, you can increment the new account number by 5 or 10 higher than an existing account number, so that the new one snuggles in nicely with its compatriots in the chart of accounts.

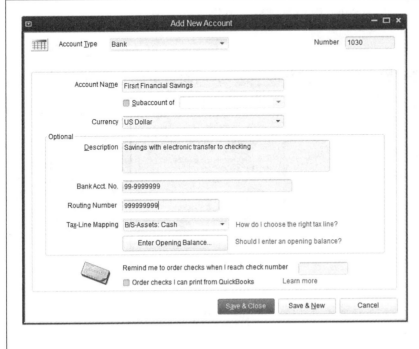

FIGURE 3-4

The Bank account type includes every account field except for the Note field. It also includes one field that you won't find in any other account type: If you want QuickBooks to remind you to order checks, in the "Remind me to order checks when I reach check number" field, type the check number you want to use as a trigger. If you want the program to open a browser window to an Intuit site where you can order supplies, turn on "Order checks I can print from QuickBooks." If you get checks from somewhere else, just reorder checks the way you normally do.

4. **In the Account Name box, type a name for the account.**

   See page 50 for tips on standardizing account names.

   > **NOTE** If you create an account and don't see one of the fields mentioned here, it simply doesn't apply to that account type.

5. **If you want the account to be a subaccount, then turn on the "Subaccount of" checkbox. Then, in the drop-down list, choose the account that you want to act as the parent.**

   Subaccounts are a good way to track your finances in more detail, as the box on page 55 explains. In the chart of accounts, subaccounts are indented below their parent accounts to make the hierarchy easy to see, as shown at the bottom of Figure 3-2 on page 47).

TIP When you use subaccounts, QuickBooks displays both the parent account's name and the subaccount's name in the Account fields found throughout the program, which often makes it impossible to tell which account a transaction uses, as you can see in Figure 3-5 (top). If you want to see only the lowest-level subaccount in Account fields, head to the Accounting section of the Preferences dialog box and turn on the "Show lowest subaccount only" checkbox, which is on the same tab as the "Use account numbers" checkbox described on page 598.

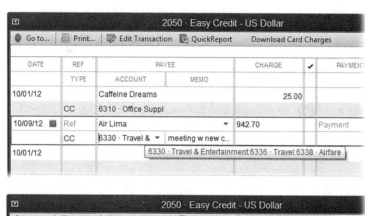

FIGURE 3-5

Top: QuickBooks combines the names of parent accounts and their subaccounts into one long name in Account fields and drop-down lists, like the travel example shown here. In many instances, only the top-level account is visible unless you scroll within the Account field.

Bottom: When you turn on the "Show lowest subaccount only" checkbox, the Account field shows the subaccount number and name instead, which is exactly what you need to identify the assigned account (in this case, Airfare).

Adding Detail with Subaccounts

Say your company's travel expenses are sky-high and you want to start tracking what you spend on different types of travel, such as airfare, lodging, and limousine services. Subaccounts make it easy to track details like these. Subaccounts are nothing more than partitions within a higher-level account (called the *parent* account).

When you post transactions to subaccounts only (not the parent account), your reports show the subtotals for the subaccounts and a grand total for the parent account, such as the Travel account (number 6336, say) and its subaccounts Airfare (6338), Lodging (6340), and Transportation (6342), for example.

Subaccounts also come in handy for assigning similar expenses to different lines on a tax form. For example, the IRS doesn't treat all travel expenses the same: You can deduct only half of your meal and entertainment expenses, while other travel expenses are fully deductible. Meals and Entertainment are separate subaccounts from Travel for this very reason.

6. **If you've turned on QuickBooks' multiple currency preference, the Currency box appears below the "Subaccount of" checkbox. If the currency for the account is different from the one listed there, choose the right currency in the drop-down list.**

   If you do business in more than one currency, see page 617 to learn how to set up multiple currencies in QuickBooks.

7. **To add a description of the account, fill in the Description box.**

   For instance, you can define whether a bank account is linked to another account or give examples of the types of expenses that apply to a particular expense account. The Description field can hold up to 256 characters, which should be more than enough.

8. **If you see a field for an account number—such as Bank Acct. No., Credit Card Acct. No., or simply Account No.—type in the number for your real-world account at your financial institution (checking account, savings account, loan, and so on).**

   If the account type you chose in step 2 doesn't include a field for an account number, you see the Note field instead, which you can use to store any additional information you want to document about the account.

9. **For a bank account, in the Routing Number box, type the routing number for your bank.**

   A routing number is the nine-digit number in a funny-looking font that's at the bottom of your checks.

10. **To associate the account with a tax form and a specific line on that tax form, in the Tax-Line Mapping drop-down list, choose the entry for the appropriate tax form and tax line.**

    The Tax-Line Mapping field is set to < Unassigned > if you haven't specified the tax form that your company files with the IRS. See page 8 to learn how to choose a tax form for your company.

    If QuickBooks hasn't assigned a tax line for you, you can scan the entries in the drop-down list for a likely match. If you don't find an entry that seems right or if QuickBooks tells you the one you chose isn't compatible with the account type, your best bet is to call your accountant or the IRS. You can also get a hint for an appropriate tax line for the account you're creating by examining one of QuickBooks' sample files (page 6).

    To remove a tax line from an account, in the drop-down list, choose < Unassigned >.

NOTE Below the Tax-Line Mapping field, you may see the Enter Opening Balance button. It's easy to figure out the opening balance for a brand-new account—it's zero—so you can ignore this button. But if you're setting up QuickBooks with accounts that existed prior to your QuickBooks start date, those accounts *do* have opening balances. Even so, clicking the Enter Opening Balance button isn't the best way to specify an opening balance for an account you're adding to your company file. The box on page 58 explains how to specify opening balances for all your accounts in just a few steps.

11. **Click the Save & New button to save the current account and create another one.**

    If you want to save the account you just created and close the Add New Account window, then click Save & Close instead. Or click Cancel to discard the account-in-progress and close the Add New Account window.

12. **If the Set Up Online Services dialog box appears, click Yes if you want to set up a bank account for online services.**

    When you click Yes, QuickBooks' windows close while you go through the setup. (See Chapter 22 to learn about online services and QuickBooks.) If you want to set up the account for online banking later—or never—click No.

■ Modifying Accounts

If you stick to your account numbering and naming conventions, you'll have few reasons to edit accounts. But the Edit Account window lets you tweak an account's name or description, adjust its number to make room for new accounts, or change its level in the chart of accounts hierarchy.

You're not likely to change an account's type unless you chose the wrong one when you created the account. If you do need to change the account type, back up your QuickBooks file first (see page 179) in case the change has effects that you didn't anticipate. Also, note that QuickBooks has several restrictions on changing account types. You can't change an account's type if:

- It has subaccounts.

- It's an Accounts Receivable or Accounts Payable account. (You also can't change other types of accounts to AR or AP accounts.)

- QuickBooks automatically created the account, like Undeposited Funds.

To modify an account, in the Chart of Accounts window, select the account you want to edit and then press Ctrl+E or click Account→Edit Account. In the Edit Account window that appears, make the changes you want, and then click OK.

Hiding and Deleting Accounts

If you create an account by mistake, you can delete it. However, because QuickBooks drops your financial transactions into account buckets and you don't want to throw away historical information, you'll usually want to *hide* accounts that you don't use anymore instead of deleting them. The records of past transactions are important, whether you want to review the amount of business you've received from a customer or the IRS is asking unsettling questions. For example, you wouldn't delete your Nutrition Service income account just because you've discontinued your nutrition consulting service to focus on selling your new book, *The See Food Diet*. The income you earned from that service in the past needs to stay in your records.

Doing Opening Balances Right

When I add an account to my company file, can I just click the Enter Opening Balance button and type the balance I want to start with in the Opening Balance field? That seems the most logical place for it.

You can, but your accountant may not be too happy about it. Filling in the Opening Balance field from the Add New Account window (or in the Edit Account window, for that matter) automatically adds that balance to the Opening Bal Equity account, which accountants consider sloppy bookkeeping. Instead, they usually recommend creating a general journal entry from your trial balance for most of your accounts. The three exceptions are your Accounts Receivable (AR), Accounts Payable (AP), and bank accounts. Because QuickBooks requires customer names and vendor names in journal entries that contain AR and AP accounts, you're better off creating invoices and bills to define your AR and AP opening balances. With bank accounts, you can enter your previous reconciled balance in the Opening Balance field and then bring the account up-to-date by recording all the transactions since your last reconciliation. If you work with an accountant, ask her how she'd like you to enter opening balances—or better yet, have her do it.

Whoa! What's a general journal entry? What's a trial balance?

Here's the deal: *General journal entries* (page 451) are mechanisms for moving money between accounts—on paper, that is. A *trial balance* (page 484) is a report (from your accountant or your old accounting system) that lists all your accounts with their balances in either the Debit or Credit column. In the days of paper-based ledgers, bean counters totaled the Debit and Credit columns. If the totals weren't equal, the accountant had to track down the arithmetic error. Happily, QuickBooks' digital brain does the math for you, without errors. But it's up to you to set up the journal entry properly in the first place.

If you look at the trial balance on the first day of your fiscal year, it's quite simple—it includes balances only for your balance sheet accounts, not income and expense accounts. You can use these values to fill in a general journal entry to assign all your accounts' opening balances: First, set the journal entry's date to the last day of the previous fiscal year; that way, you can start fresh for your current fiscal year. Next, for each account, add a line in the general journal entry with the account name and the balance from your trial balance report in either the Debit or Credit column. Finally, omit your AR and AP accounts from the general journal entry; instead, create invoices and bills to define the opening balances for those accounts. If you didn't use the Opening Balance field to set your bank account balances, you can include your bank accounts in the general journal entry.

To see this in action, you can download from *www.missing manuals.com/cds* a sample company file that includes an opening balance general journal entry from.

Hiding Accounts

Hiding accounts doesn't mean withholding key financial info from prying eyes. When you hide an account in QuickBooks, the account continues to hold your historical transactions, but it doesn't appear in account lists, so you can't choose it by mistake with a misplaced mouse click.

Hiding and reactivating accounts (Figure 3-6) also comes in handy when QuickBooks creates a chart of accounts based on the industry you choose during setup (page 8). If QuickBooks overwhelms you with accounts you don't think you need, simply hide those accounts for the time being. That way, if you find yourself saying, "Gosh, I wish I had an account for the accumulated depreciation of vehicles," the solution might be as simple as reactivating a hidden account.

Deleting Accounts

You can delete an account only if nothing in QuickBooks references it in any way. An account with references is a red flag that deleting it might not be the right choice. If you try to delete such an account, QuickBooks displays a message box telling you it can't delete the account and recommends making it inactive instead. If that isn't enough to deter you, the sheer tedium of removing references to an account should nudge you toward hiding the account instead. If you *insist* on deleting an account, here are the conditions that prevent you from doing so and what you have to do to remove the constraints:

- **An item uses the account**. If you create any items that use the account as an income account, expense account, cost of goods sold account, or inventory asset account, you can't delete it. You have to edit the items to use other accounts first, as described on page 146.

- **The account has subaccounts**. You have to delete all subaccounts before you can delete the parent account.

- **Payroll uses the account**. You can't delete an account if your payroll setup uses it.

- **At least one transaction references the account**. If you created a transaction that uses the account, either edit that transaction to use a different account or hide the account if you want to keep the transaction the way it is.

- **The account has a balance**. An account balance comes from either an opening balance transaction or other transactions that reference the account. You remove an account balance by deleting all the transactions in the account (or reassigning them to another account).

To delete transactions, in the Chart of Accounts window, double-click the account's name. For accounts with balances, QuickBooks opens a register window where you can select a transaction and then press Ctrl+D to delete it. For accounts without balances, QuickBooks opens an Account QuickReport window. To delete a transaction that appears in the report, double-click the transaction. Quick-Books then opens a window related to that transaction (for instance, the Write Checks window appears if the transaction is a check). Right-click anywhere in that window and choose Delete Check or the corresponding delete command for the type of transaction.

After you've deleted all references to the account, in the Chart of Accounts window, select the account you want to delete, and then press Ctrl+D or choose Account→Delete Account. QuickBooks asks you to confirm that you want to delete the account; click OK.

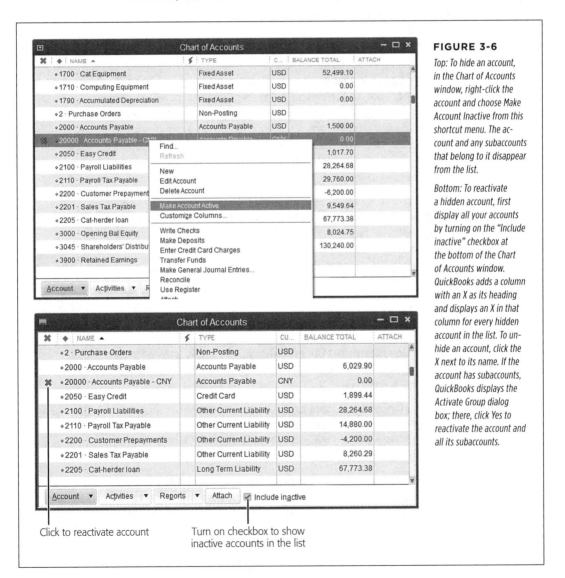

FIGURE 3-6

Top: To hide an account, in the Chart of Accounts window, right-click the account and choose Make Account Inactive from this shortcut menu. The account and any subaccounts that belong to it disappear from the list.

Bottom: To reactivate a hidden account, first display all your accounts by turning on the "Include inactive" checkbox at the bottom of the Chart of Accounts window. QuickBooks adds a column with an X as its heading and displays an X in that column for every hidden account in the list. To unhide an account, click the X next to its name. If the account has subaccounts, QuickBooks displays the Activate Group dialog box; there, click Yes to reactivate the account and all its subaccounts.

Click to reactivate account

Turn on checkbox to show inactive accounts in the list

■ Merging Accounts

Suppose you find multiple accounts for the same purpose—Postage and Mail Expense, say—lurking in your chart of accounts. No problem! You can merge the accounts into one and then remind everyone who creates accounts in QuickBooks about your naming conventions. (If you haven't gotten around to setting up naming conventions, see page 50 for some guidelines.)

> **TIP** Before you merge accounts, see what your accountant thinks. There's no going back once you've merged two accounts—they're combined for good. And the QuickBooks audit trail (page 694) doesn't keep track of this kind of change.

QuickBooks sweeps all the transactions from the account you merge into the account you keep, so you can merge accounts only if they're the same type. (As an experienced manager, you can imagine the havoc that merging income and expense accounts would cause in your financial statements.) In addition, accounts must be at the same level in the chart of accounts list. To move an account to another level, position your cursor over the small diamond to the left of the account's name. When the cursor turns into a four-headed arrow, drag to the left or right so that the account is indented the same amount as the other account.

> **NOTE** If you find two accounts with similar names but different types, those accounts might not represent the same thing. For instance, a Telephone Ex. expense account probably represents your monthly telephone service, while the Telephone Eq. asset account might represent the big telephone switch that your mega-corporation owns. In this situation, the accounts are different types and should be separate, although more meaningful names and descriptions would help differentiate them.

Here's how to eliminate an extraneous account:

1. **Switch to single-user mode, as described on page 173.**

   You have to be in single-user mode to merge accounts. Be nice to your fellow QuickBooks users by making these changes outside of working hours. If you have to merge accounts during the workday, remember to tell your coworkers they can log into the program after you've switched the company file back to multiuser mode.

2. **Press Ctrl+A to open the Chart of Accounts window. Then, in the chart of accounts list, select the name of the account you want to *eliminate* and then press Ctrl+E.**

   The Edit Account window opens.

3. **In the Edit Account window, change the account number and name to match the values for the account you want to *keep*.**

   As long as you get the letters and numbers right, QuickBooks takes care of matching uppercase and lowercase for you.

   If you don't remember the number and name of the account you're keeping, drag the Chart of Accounts window and the Edit Account window so you can see both at the same time. (If QuickBooks won't let you do that, you might have the One Window preference turned on; see page 605 to learn how to change your settings to display multiple windows.)

4. **Click Save & Close, read the message informing you that the name is in use and asking if you want to merge the accounts, and then click Yes.**

   In the chart of accounts list, the account you renamed disappears, and any transactions for that account now appear in the account you kept.

Setting Up Customers, Jobs, and Vendors

You may be fond of strutting around your sales department proclaiming, "Nothing happens until somebody *sells* something!" As it turns out, you can quote that tired adage in your accounting department, too. Whether you sell products or services, the first sale to a new customer can initiate a flurry of activity, including creating a new *customer* in QuickBooks, assigning a *job* for the work, and the ultimate goal of all this effort—*invoicing* your customer (sending a bill for your services and products that states how much the customer owes) to collect some income.

The people who buy what you sell have plenty of nicknames: customers, clients, consumers, patrons, patients, purchasers, donors, members, shoppers, and so on. QuickBooks throws out the thesaurus and applies one term to every person or organization that buys from you: customer. In QuickBooks, a *customer* is a record of information about your real-life customer. The program takes the data you enter about customers and fills in invoices and other sales forms with your customers' names, addresses, payment terms, and other info.

Real-world customers are essential to your success, but do you need customers in QuickBooks? Even if you run a primarily cash business, creating customers in QuickBooks could still be a good idea. For example, setting up QuickBooks records for the repeat customers at your store saves you time by automatically filling in their information on each new sales receipt.

If, on the other hand, your business revolves around projects, you can create a job in QuickBooks for each project you do for a customer. To QuickBooks, a *job* is a record of a real-life project that you agreed (or perhaps begged) to perform for a customer—remodeling a kitchen, designing an ad campaign, or whatever. Suppose you're a plumber and you regularly do work for a general contractor. You could create several jobs, one for each place you plumb: Smith house, Jones house, and Winfrey house. In QuickBooks, you can then track income and expenses by job and gauge each one's profitability. However, if your company doesn't take on jobs, you don't have to create them in QuickBooks. For example, retail stores sell products, not projects. If you don't need jobs, you can simply create your customers in QuickBooks and then move on to invoicing them or creating sales receipts for their purchases.

In addition to customers, you're going to do business with vendors and pay them for their services and products. The telephone company, your accountant, and the subcontractor who installs Venetian plaster in your spec houses are all vendors. The information you fill in for vendors isn't all that different from what you specify for customers.

This chapter guides you through creating customers, jobs, and vendors in Quick-Books. It also helps you decide how to apply the program's customer, job, and vendor fields to your business. And you'll learn how to manage the customer, job, and vendor records you create in QuickBooks.

Creating Customers in QuickBooks

Alas, you first have to persuade customers to work with your company. But once you've cleared *that* hurdle, creating those customers in QuickBooks is easy. The box on page 66 provides some hints on keeping customers straight in QuickBooks. The program offers several methods for creating customer records:

- **QuickBooks Setup**. When you're getting started with the program, you can use the QuickBooks Setup window to quickly import piles of customer information (as well as vendor and employee info) from your email program or by copying and pasting data from Excel, as described on page 15. You can return to the QuickBooks Setup window at any time (page 17) to add more records.

- **One at a time**. The New Customer window lets you create one customer at a time, although you can create several records in a row without closing the window. The section "Creating a New Customer" on page 66 describes how to create customers with this window and explains what each customer field represents.

TIP   If you don't add customers very often, you can create a customer record when you create that customer's first invoice. The handy < Add New > entry in every drop-down list of customers and jobs is your ticket to just-in-time customer and job creation.

- **Copying data**. You can also create customers in batches. With the Add/Edit Multiple List Entries feature (page 94), you can paste data from Microsoft Excel or copy values from customer to customer.

TIP QuickBooks doesn't care if you create customers and jobs without any forethought, but it pays to take the time to set them up properly. For example, you can create customers and jobs without classifying them in any way, but you might want to categorize them so you can send customized communications to each type or determine which types are the most profitable. If you want to categorize customers from the get-go, turn to page 79 to learn how to set up customer and job types and different ways to use them.

The Customer Center (Figure 4-1) is a one-stop shop for customers and jobs: creating, modifying, and viewing their records, and creating transactions for them. QuickBooks gives you four easy ways to open the Customer Center window:

- From anywhere in the program, press Ctrl+J.

- At the top of the Customers panel on the QuickBooks Home page, click Customers.

- On the icon bar, click Customers. (If you don't see a Customers item on the icon bar, flip to page 663 to learn how to add it.)

- On the QuickBooks menu bar, choose Customers→Customer Center.

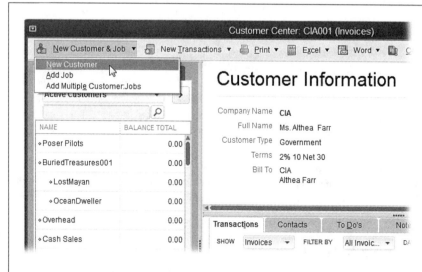

FIGURE 4-1

To create a new customer in the Customer Center, click New Customer & Job and then choose New Customer. To view a customer's details and transactions, click the customer's name in the Customers & Jobs list on the left side of this window. If the Transactions tab is selected instead of the Customers & Jobs tab, you'll see the New Customer feature on the Customer Center menu bar; clicking it opens the New Customer window immediately.

Making Customers Easy to Identify

In QuickBooks, the Customer Name and Vendor Name fields don't show the names that appear on invoices or bills. Instead, they display a code that uniquely identifies each customer or vendor so it's easy to tell them apart.

If you own a small company, you're not likely to mistakenly create multiple records for the same customer or vendor. Your Customer and Vendor lists are short, so you probably remember which ones you've created. Even so, it's a good idea to define a standard for names.

Consistent naming can help you avoid having multiple records for the same customer or vendor by preventing you from creating slightly different values in the Customer Name or Vendor Name field. For example, you could end up with three customer records in QuickBooks all representing the same real-world customer, such as Cales's Capers, Cales Capers, and CalesCapers. The same holds true for vendors.

QuickBooks doesn't enforce naming conventions. After you define rules that work for your business, you have to be disciplined and apply those rules each time you create a new customer or vendor. You're free to use alphanumeric characters and punctuation in names. Here are a few of the more common naming conventions:

- **The first few letters of the customer's or vendor's company name, followed by a unique numeric identifier**. This standard is easy to apply and differentiates customers or vendors as long as their names don't all begin with the same words. For example, if the companies you do business with aren't imaginative, your names could

end up as Wine001, Wine002, and Wine003. But if the companies are Zinfandels To Go, Merlot Mania, and Cabernet Cabinet, this system works nicely.

- **For individuals, the last name followed by the first name and a numeric ID to make the name unique**. Although unusual names such as Zaphod Beeblebrox render a numeric ID unnecessary, using this standard ensures that all names are unique.

- **The actual company name with any punctuation and spaces omitted**. Removing spaces and punctuation from company names helps eliminate multiple versions of the same name. If you choose this convention, using capital letters at the beginning of each word (called *camel caps*) makes the name more readable. For instance, Icantbelieveitsyogurt is a headache waiting to happen, but ICantBelieveItsYogurt looks more like its spaced and punctuated counterpart.

- **A unique alphanumeric code**. Customer:Job drop-down menus and reports sort entries by the values in the Customer Name field of customer records. (Vendor drop-down menus and reports sort by the Vendor Name field.) Codes like X123Y4JQ use only a few characters to produce unique identifiers, but they're also so cryptic that they make it difficult to pick out the name you want in drop-down lists, or to sort reports in a meaningful way. Stick with using part of the company name (at the beginning of the name, since names appear alphabetically) unless you have hundreds or thousands of customers or vendors.

Creating a New Customer

Here's the short and sweet method of creating a customer in QuickBooks:

1. **In the Customer Center toolbar, click New Customer & Job→New Customer or press Ctrl+N.**

   The New Customer window opens (Figure 4-2).

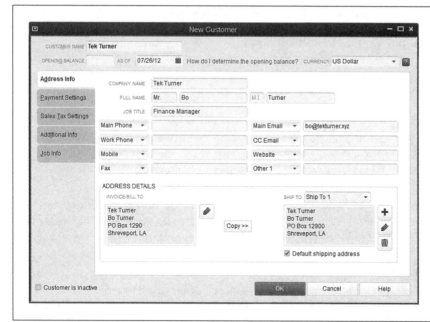

FIGURE 4-2

Although the Opening Balance box beckons from below the Customer Name field in the New Customer window, it's better to leave it blank. The box on page 58 explains the best way to define a customer's opening balance, and the following sections explain what's on each of this window's tabs (Address Info, Payment Settings, and so on).

2. **In the Customer Name field, type a unique name or code for this customer, following the naming convention you've chosen (see the box on page 66).**

   The Customer Name field is the only field you *have* to fill in—the rest are optional.

3. **To save that customer's record and close the New Customer window, click OK.**

   To discard what you entered and close the window, click Cancel instead.

> **TIP** To create a job for a customer, you have to close the New Customer window and open the New Job window. So it's a lot faster to create all your customers first and *then* add the jobs for each one.

The box on page 66 tells you how to prevent your QuickBooks Customer List from growing out of control.

If you've turned on QuickBooks' multiple currency option (page 610), a Currency box appears in the New Customer window in the row below the Customer Name box, as shown in Figure 4-2. QuickBooks automatically fills in this box with your home currency, so you usually don't have to change this value. But if the customer pays in a foreign currency, choose it in the Currency drop-down list. QuickBooks creates a separate Accounts Receivable account (page 52) for each currency you use.

NOTE In QuickBooks 2013, the organization of tabs and fields in the New Customer (and Edit Customer) windows is much improved. The contact and address info is all on the first tab, Address Info. All the fields related to payments are now on the Payment Settings tab. The Sales Tax Settings tab contains fields for sales tax, so you can skip it entirely if you don't sell taxable goods. The Additional Info tab, which used to be a jumble of different types of fields, now holds a few miscellaneous fields like customer type, sales rep, and custom fields you've created. You'll learn about the Job Info tab on page 77.

TROUBLESHOOTING MOMENT

How Many Names?

If you're a big fish in the small-business pond, you might bump up against limitations on the number of names you can add to QuickBooks. In QuickBooks Pro and Premier editions, the maximum number of *total* names you can have (including customers, vendors, employees, and other names) is 14,500, and the maximum number of each *type* of name is 10,000. Here are a few techniques you can use to avoid maxing out your name lists:

- **Conserve names**. Be frugal with names by creating one customer or vendor to represent many individual sales or purchases. For example, you can aggregate all your cash sales under a single customer named Cash Sales. Or you can combine all your meal expenses by using a single vendor named Meals. Just keep in mind that, by

doing so, you can't produce reports by individual names. However, you can store a customer's name in the Bill To field in sales forms or in the Memo field in a bill, check, or credit card charge.

- **Keep an eye on how many names you have**. Press F2 anytime to call up the Product Information window so you can view the number of entries you have in each list. They appear in the List Information box on the right side of the window.

- **Upgrade**. If there's no getting around your company's gluttony for names, QuickBooks Enterprise Solutions lets you add more than 100,000 names, although Intuit warns you that the program might not run as quickly as the number of names increases.

■ ENTERING CONTACT INFORMATION

If you plan to bill your customers, ship them products, or call them to make them feel appreciated, address and contact information is important. You record this info on the New Customer window's Address Info tab. Here's a guide to what you enter on this tab:

- **Company Name**. Unlike Customer Name, which acts as an identifier, the Company Name field is the customer's name as you want it to appear on invoices and other forms you create. QuickBooks automatically copies what you type here into the Invoice/Bill To box below.

- **Contact**. To address invoices, letters, and other company communications, enter the primary contact's salutation or title, first name, middle initial, and last name in the appropriate fields. QuickBooks automatically copies the information you type in these fields into the Invoice/Bill To fields. You can also fill in the Job Title box with the contact's title.

NOTE After you create a customer, you can add additional contacts for that customer in the Customer Center. Page 75 tells you how.

FREQUENTLY ASKED QUESTION

Opening Act

Should I add an opening balance for new customers?

Since the Opening Balance field is always visible at the top of the New Customer window (Figure 4-2), you might think you should fill it in. But you're actually better off skipping it altogether.

Entering an opening balance as of a specific date is a shortcut that eliminates having to create the invoices that generate the customer's current balance. But that shortcut comes at a price: If customers haven't paid, then you might have a hard time collecting the money, especially if you can't tell them what

services and products you delivered, how much they cost, the invoice numbers, and when the invoices were due. In addition, when your customers *do* pay, you can't accept those payments against specific invoices to track your accounts receivable.

The best way to record a customer's balance is to create QuickBooks invoices for the invoices the customer hasn't paid yet (called "open invoices"). That way, you'll have complete documentation of those sales and the corresponding balance in your Accounts Receivable account. Also, you can then apply the payments that come in to settle those invoices. See Chapter 10 to learn all about invoicing.

TIP The Address Info tab has more fields for contact information, including four phone numbers, two email addresses, the company's website, and a field labeled "Other 1." If you look closely, you'll notice that the labels for these eight fields have down arrows on them, so you can set these fields to any of 16 contact-related fields, such as LinkedIn, Facebook, and Skype ID.

- **Invoice/Bill To**. QuickBooks uses the address you enter in this box on invoices. To edit the address at any time, click the Edit button (its icon looks like a pencil). Then, in the Edit Address Information dialog box, fill in the street address, city, state, country, and postal code, or paste that info from another program. QuickBooks automatically turns on the "Show this window again when address is incomplete or unclear" checkbox, which tells the program to notify you when you forget a field like the city or when the address is ambiguous. For example, if the address of your biggest toy customer is Santa Claus, North Pole, then QuickBooks opens the Edit Address Information dialog box so you can flesh out the address with a street, city, and arctic postal code.

TIP You can quickly enter addresses and contact info for all your customers by importing data from another program (page 654 or by using QuickBooks' Add/Edit Multiple List Entries feature (page 94).

- **Ship To** If you don't ship products to this customer, you can skip the Ship To field altogether. If the billing and shipping addresses are the same, click "Copy>>" to replicate the contents of the Invoice/Bill To field in the Ship To field. (The greater-than symbols on the button indicate the direction that QuickBooks copies the address—left to right.) Otherwise, type the shipping address in the Ship To box.

TIP You can define more than one ship-to address for a single customer, which is perfect if that customer has multiple locations. To add another ship-to address, click the + button to the field's right and fill in the Add Shipping Address Information dialog box. Once you've added shipping addresses, you can choose the one you want in the Ship To drop-down list. When the shipping address you use most often is visible, turn on the "Default shipping address" checkbox below the Ship To field to tell QuickBooks to pick that address automatically. Click the Edit button (the pencil icon) or Delete button (the trash can icon) to modify or remove a shipping address, respectively.

■ ENTERING PAYMENT INFORMATION

The Payment Settings tab, shown in Figure 4-3, is the place to indicate how the customer pays and how much credit you're willing to extend.

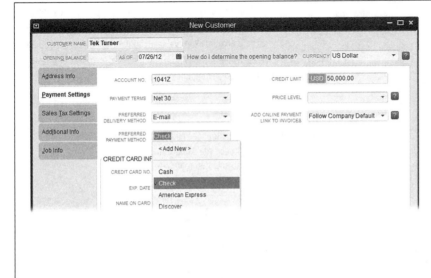

FIGURE 4-3

Several of the fields on the Payment Settings tab use QuickBooks' lists. To jump directly to the entry you want in long lists, in any text box with a drop-down list, type the first few characters of that entry. QuickBooks selects the first entry that matches the characters you've typed and continues to reselect the best match as you continue typing. You can also scroll to the entry in the list and click to select it. If the entry you want doesn't exist, click <Add New> to create it.

You can use the following fields to specify the customer's payment info:

- **Account No**. Account numbers are optional in QuickBooks. Large accounting programs often assign unique account numbers to customers, which greatly reduces the time it takes to locate a customer's record. In QuickBooks, the Customer Name field works like an identifier, so you're best off reserving the Account No. field for an account number generated by one of your other business systems.

- **Payment Terms**. What you select here represents the payment terms the customer has agreed to. The entries you see in this drop-down list come from the Terms List (page 160), which QuickBooks uses for both payment terms for your customers *and* the ones you accept from your vendors. This list includes several of the most common payment terms, such as "Due on receipt" and Net 30, but you can choose

<Add New> at the top of the drop-down list to define additional payment terms in the Terms List. If you leave this field blank in a customer's record, you have to choose the payment terms every time you create an invoice for that customer.

- **Preferred Delivery Method**. Choose E-mail, Mail, or None to identify the method that your customer prefers for receiving information. If you choose E-mail, QuickBooks automatically turns on the E-mail checkbox when you create forms (such as invoices) for this customer. The Mail method uses an add-on QuickBooks service to mail invoices (additional fees apply). Choose None if you typically print documents and mail them the old-fashioned way. You can't add a new entry to the Preferred Delivery Method list, so if you use carrier pigeons to correspond with your incarcerated customers, you'll just have to choose None and remember that preference.

- **Preferred Payment Method**. Choose the form of payment that the customer uses most frequently. This drop-down list includes several common ones such as Cash, Check, and Visa, but you can add others by choosing <Add New>. The payment method you specify appears automatically in the Receive Payments window (page 374) when you choose this customer. If a regular customer pays with a method different than the one you chose here, you can simply select that method in the Receive Payments window.

- **Credit card information**. For credit card payments (see page 350 to learn about QuickBooks' credit card processing service), you can specify the customer's card number, the name on the card, the billing address, the Zip/postal code, and the expiration date. (You can enter only one credit card number for each customer.)

NOTE   If you store customer credit card numbers in QuickBooks, turn on the Customer Credit Card Protection feature (choose Company→Customer Credit Card Protection and then click Enable Protection). That way, the program helps you comply with credit card industry security requirements (page 687). For example, any user who views complete credit card information must create a complex password. In addition, QuickBooks doesn't let you store the card's security code (the three-digit code on the back of the card) because doing so violates your merchant account agreement and PCI (Payment Card Industry) standards.

- **Credit Limit**. You can specify the amount of credit that you're willing to extend to the customer. If you do, QuickBooks warns you when an order or invoice exceeds this customer's credit limit, but that's as far as it goes—it's up to you to reject the order or ship your products COD. If you don't plan to enforce the credit limits you assign, don't bother entering a value in this field.

- **Price Level**. More often than not, customers pay different prices for the same product. Just think about the labyrinth of pricing options for seats on airplanes, for instance. In QuickBooks, price levels represent discounts or markups that you apply to transactions. For example, you might have one price level called Top20, which applies a 20 percent discount for your best customers, and another price level called AuntMabel that extends a 50 percent discount to your

Aunt Mabel because she fronted you the money to start your business. Page 153 explains how to define price levels. Once you create a price level, you can apply it to every transaction for a customer by choosing that price level in this box.

- **Add Online Payment Link to Invoices**. Online payment links on invoices allow your customers to pay you through the Intuit PaymentNetwork either by making a payment directly from their bank accounts into yours or by credit card. (The fees you pay vary based on how the customers pay). However, setting up this feature requires a couple of steps. First, be sure to sign up for the Intuit PaymentNetwork service. If you don't sign up and your customers click an online payment link, they'll see a message telling them that you haven't signed up for the service yet. Choose Customers→Intuit PaymentNetwork→About Payment-Network to learn about the service and how to enroll. Page 290 describes how online payment links work.)

On the Payment Settings tab, you can use this field to tell QuickBooks which online payment option to use for this customer. "Follow Company Default" applies the setting that you selected in QuickBooks preferences (page 619). Choosing "Always ON (bank only)" means the customer can only pay through their bank account regardless of your company preference. With "Always ON (bank or credit card)," the customer can pay by bank account or credit card. "Always OFF for this customer" means QuickBooks doesn't display the online payment link on this customer's invoices.

■ SPECIFYING SALES TAX INFORMATION

The Sales Tax Settings tab appears whether or not you turn on QuickBooks' Sales Tax preference (page 628). However, if sales tax isn't turned on, the fields on this tab are grayed out. If the customer pays sales tax, choose "Tax" in the Tax Code drop-down list. Then, in the Tax Item drop-down list, choose the tax item that specifies the tax rate the customer pays. (See page 140 for instructions on setting up sales tax items and page 287 for the full scoop on charging sales tax.)

Customers who buy products for resale usually don't pay sales tax because that would tax the products twice. (Who says tax authorities don't have hearts?) To bypass sales tax for a customer, choose Non (for "nontaxable sales") in the Tax Code drop-down list, and then type the customer's resale number in the Resale Number field. That way, if tax auditors pay you a visit, the resale number tells them where the sales-tax burden should fall.

■ SPECIFYING ADDITIONAL CUSTOMER INFORMATION

The New Customer window's Additional Info tab serves up a few fields that categorize your customers. Here are the fields you can fill in and some ways to use them:

- **Customer Type**. Categorize this customer (see page 79) by choosing from this drop-down list, which displays the entries from your Customer Type List, such as government, health insurance, or private pay, if you run a healthcare company.

- **Rep**. Choosing a name in this field links a customer to a sales representative, which is helpful if you want to track sales reps' results. But reps don't have to be *sales* representatives: One of the best ways to provide good customer service is to assign a customer service rep to a customer. When you choose <Add New> here to create a new Rep entry (page 157), you can select existing names from the Employee List, Vendor List, and the Other Names List, or even add a new name to one of those lists to use as a rep.

- **Custom Fields**. QuickBooks offers 15 custom fields, which you can use to store important info that QuickBooks doesn't include fields for out of the box. Because custom fields don't use drop-down lists, you have to type your entries and take care to enter values consistently. The box below has more about custom fields.

GEM IN THE ROUGH

Defining Custom Fields for Lists

QuickBooks' customer, vendor, employee, and item records include lots of fields you can fill in, but those fields may not cover all the information you need. For example, you might add a custom field for the branch office that services a customer. Or for employees, you could set up a custom field to track whether they make charitable contributions that your company matches.

QuickBooks' answer to this issue is custom fields. After you create a custom field and apply it to a list, QuickBooks adds the custom field's label and a text box to the Additional Info tab (Figure 4-4, background). You have to type your entries each time; there's no drop-down list or a way to compare it to text you entered in other records. It's up to you to make sure that your data entry is correct and consistent.

To set up a custom field, follow these steps:

1. In the appropriate New or Edit window (New Customer or Edit Vendor, for example), click the Additional Info tab.

2. Click the Define Fields button. The "Set up Custom Fields for Names" dialog box (Figure 4-4, foreground) opens.

3. In one of the 15 Label cells, type a name for the field.

4. If you're associating a custom field with a customer, vendor, or employee record, click the cell for the appropriate list (Cust, Vend, or Empl) and QuickBooks puts a checkmark there. For example, the Region custom field could apply to both the Customer:Job List and the Vendors List, so you'd want checkmarks in both the Cust and Vend columns.

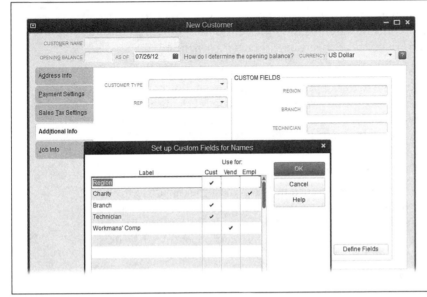

FIGURE 4-4

The "Set up Custom Fields for Names" dialog box (which opens when you click Define Fields in a New or Edit window for customers, vendors, or employees) lets you create up to 15 custom fields. To associate a custom field with a customer, vendor, or employee, click the corresponding cell in the field's row in the table. You can associate a custom field with one or more types of names; for example, with both customers and employees.

NOTE The New Customer window also includes a Job Info tab, which (not surprisingly) has fields for job-related information. If you don't track jobs, you could use this tab's Job Status field to store the overall status of your work for the customer, although a contact-management or project-management program is probably more useful. And if a customer hires you to do more than one job, skip the Job Info tab, since you'll create separate jobs to track the info, as described on page 76.

ALTERNATE REALITY

Tracking Donors for Nonprofits

For nonprofit organizations, any individual or organization that sends money is a *donor*, but the term "donor" doesn't appear in most QuickBooks editions. The Premier Nonprofit edition of the program mentions donors, pledges, and other nonprofit terms, but QuickBooks Pro and other Premier editions focus single-mindedly on customers, so you may have to get used to thinking "donor" whenever you see "customer" in QuickBooks.

Likewise, a job in QuickBooks is the equivalent of a contract or grant. If you need to report on a grant or contract, add a separate job for it to the customer (er, donor) who donated the funds.

Entering members or individual donors as separate customers can max out QuickBooks' customer name limit or make the program run slowly. The Enterprise Solutions edition of QuickBooks can handle a larger number of customers, but most nonprofits would choke at that edition's price tag.

To solve this dilemma, create customers in QuickBooks to represent generic pools, such as donors and members. For example, create a customer called Unrestricted and then post all unrestricted donations to that customer. Then, keep the details of your donor and member names in a separate donor database, spreadsheet, or program designed specifically for nonprofits.

Adding More Customer Contacts

When you create a customer, you can specify information about a contact on the Address Info tab of the New Customer window (page 68). However, you can then add more contacts to a customer's record. For example, you might add contacts for the person who handles day-to-day billing questions, the employee who resolves shipping issues, as well as the owner in case you need to escalate a problem. You can also edit or delete contacts as the people you deal with change offices or transfer to new jobs.

When you select a customer in the Customer Center's Customers & Jobs list, you see contact info for that customer on the right side of the window. To add more contacts to the customer's record, click the Contacts tab in the Center's lower-right pane (Figure 4-5). The Contacts tab doesn't list the contact you specified in the Address Info tab of the New Customer or Edit Customer window.

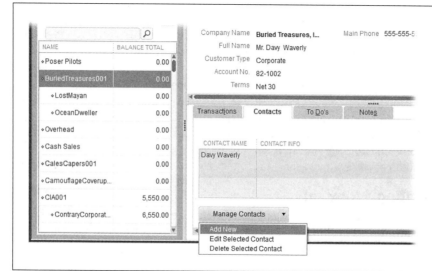

FIGURE 4-5

Any time you want to see information about one of the additional contacts you've created, select the contact in the Contacts tab shown here, click Manage Contacts, and then choose Edit Selected Contact from the drop-down menu. To delete the contact, select the contact, click Manage Contacts, and then choose Delete Selected Contact. Or choose Add New to add another contact.

To add a new contact, click Manage Contacts at the bottom of the pane (if you don't see this button, drag a corner of the Customer Center window to make it taller), and then choose Add New to open the Contacts window. Then, start filling in the boxes, such as Job Title, First Name, Last Name, and so on.

In the Contacts dialog box, you can select any contact for that customer if, for example, you want to edit or delete the contact. Click the down arrow to the right of the Contact box to see a drop-down list that includes all the contacts for that customer sorted by first and last name.

The fields in the Contacts dialog box are a subset of those on the Address Info tab in the New Customer window. They include Job Title and name fields, as well as five other fields that are initially set to Work Phone, Work Fax, Mobile, Main Email, and Additional Email, respectively. However, if you contact the person via Skype or

LinkedIn, click the down arrow on the right end of a field label and then choose the appropriate type of contact info from the drop-down list. Click "Save and New" to add another contact or "Save and Close" to close the window.

Creating Jobs in QuickBooks

Project-based work means that your current effort for a customer has a beginning and an end (even if it sometimes feels like the project will last forever). Whether you build custom computer programs or rustic cabins, you can use QuickBooks' job-tracking features to analyze financial performance by project. Suppose you want to know whether you're making more money on the mansion you're building or on the bungalow remodel, and the percentage of profit you made on each project. As long as you create jobs for each project you want to track, QuickBooks can calculate these financial measures.

NOTE If you sell products and don't give a hoot about job tracking, you can simply invoice customers for the products you sell without ever creating a job in QuickBooks.

In QuickBooks, jobs cling to customers like baby possums to their mothers. A Quick-Books job *always* belongs to a customer. In fact, if you try to choose the Add Job feature before you create a customer, you'll see a message box telling you to create a customer first. Both the New Customer and Edit Customer windows include tabs for customer info *and* job info. So when you create a customer, in effect, you create one job automatically, but you can add as many as you need. This section explains how.

Creating a New Job

Because jobs belong to customers, you have to create a customer (page 66) before you can create any of that customer's jobs. Once the customer exists, follow these steps to add a job to the customer's record:

1. **In the Customer Center's Customers & Jobs tab, right-click the customer you want to create a job for, and then choose Add Job from the shortcut menu.**

    You can also select the customer in the Customers & Jobs tab, and then, in the Customer Center toolbar, choose New Customer & Job→Add Job. Either way, the New Job window appears.

2. **In the Job Name box, type a name for the job.**

    This name will appear on invoices and other customer documents. You can type up to 41 characters in the box. The best names are short but easily recognizable by both you *and* the customer.

    QuickBooks fills in most of the remaining job fields with the information you entered for the customer associated with this job. The only time you have to edit the fields on the Address Info, Payment Settings, and Additional Info tabs is when the information on these tabs is different for this job. For example, if materials for the job go to a different shipping address than the customer's, type the address in the fields on the Address Info tab.

3. **If you want to add info about the job type, dates, or status, click the Job Info tab and enter values in the appropriate fields.**

   If you add job types (page 159), you can analyze jobs with similar characteristics, no matter which customer hired you to do the work. Filling in the Job Status field lets you see what's going on by scanning the Customer Center, as shown in Figure 4-6. If you want to see whether you're going to finish the work on schedule, you can document your estimated and actual dates for the job in the Date fields (the box on page 78 has more about these fields).

NOTE To change the values you can choose in the Job Status field, modify the status text in QuickBooks' preferences (see page 616).

4. **After you've filled in the job fields, click OK to save the job and close the New Job window.**

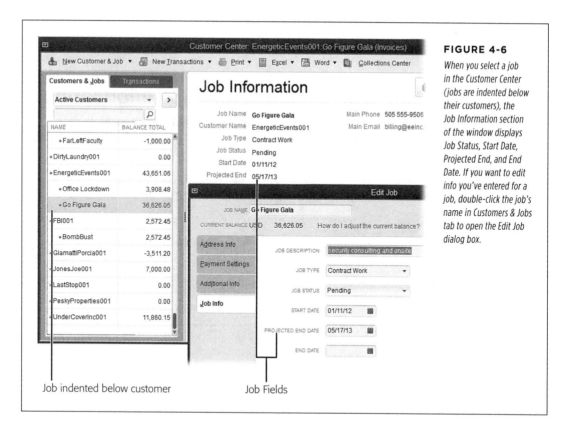

FIGURE 4-6

When you select a job in the Customer Center (jobs are indented below their customers), the Job Information section of the window displays Job Status, Start Date, Projected End, and End Date. If you want to edit info you've entered for a job, double-click the job's name in Customers & Jobs tab to open the Edit Job dialog box.

Job indented below customer   Job Fields

Specifying Job Information

The fields on the New Job (and Edit Job) window's Job Info tab are optional—you can invoice a customer even if every one is blank. However, the Job Status and Job Type fields can both help you analyze your business performance, past and future. You don't even have to use the terms that QuickBooks provides in the Job Status drop-down list; you can customize the list by adjusting the Jobs and Estimates preferences described on page 616.

Here's a guide to the Job Info tab's fields and how you can put them to use:

- **Job description**. Here's where you can type a detailed description to remind you about the work in case the job's name doesn't ring any bells.

- **Job type**. If you categorize your jobs, choose the job type (page 82) from this drop-down menu.

- **Job status**. This field can indicate trends in your business. If several jobs are set to Pending status, for example, a resource crunch might be in your future.

- **Start date**. Set this field to the date you started the job.

- **Projected end**. If you've estimated when you'll complete the job, select that date here.

- **End date**. When you complete the job, set this field to the date you actually finished up. By comparing the actual end date with your projection, you can improve future estimates or change how you work in order to finish jobs on time.

Modifying Customer and Job Information

You can edit a customer's record at any time to add more data or change what's already there. Similarly, you can create a job with only the job name and then come back later to edit it or add details.

QuickBooks gives you a few ways to open the Edit Customer or Edit Job window when the Customer Center window is open. On the Customers & Jobs tab:

- Double-click the customer or job you want to tweak.

- Select the customer or job you want to edit and then press Ctrl+E or, on the right side of the Customer Center, click the Edit button (its icon looks like a pencil).

- Right-click the customer or job and then choose Edit Customer:Job from the shortcut menu.

NOTE You can also modify multiple customer and job records at once, as described on page 94.

In the Edit Customer window, you can make changes to all the fields except Current Balance. QuickBooks calculates the customer's balance from the opening balance (if you provide one) and any unpaid invoices for that customer. Once a customer exists, you modify the customer's balance by creating invoices (page 276), credit memos (page 321), journal entries (page 451), or payment discounts (page 378).

Similarly, all the fields in the Edit Job window are editable except for Current Balance. Remember that the changes you make to fields on the Address Info, Additional Info, Payment Info, and Job Info tabs apply only to that job, not to the customer.

You can't change the currency assigned to a customer if you've recorded a transaction for that customer. So if the customer moves from Florida to France and starts using euros, you'll need to close that customer's current balance (by receiving payments for outstanding invoices). Then you can create a new customer in QuickBooks and assign the new currency to it. After the customer's new record is ready to go, you can make the old record inactive (page 88).

WARNING Unless you've revamped your naming standard for customers (page 66), don't edit the value in a customer's Customer Name field. Why? Because doing so can mess up things like customized reports you've created that are filtered by a specific customer name. Such reports aren't smart enough to automatically use the new customer name. So if you do modify a Customer Name field, make sure to modify any customizations to use the new name.

Categorizing Customers and Jobs

If you want to report and analyze your financial performance to see where your business comes from and which type is most profitable, categorizing your QuickBooks customers and jobs is the way to go. For example, customer and job types can help you produce a report of kitchen remodel jobs that you're working on for residential customers. With that report, you can order catered dinners to treat those clients to customer service they'll brag about to their friends. If you run a construction company, knowing that your commercial customers cause fewer headaches *and* that doing work for them is more profitable than residential jobs is a strong motivator to focus future marketing efforts on commercial work. The box on page 80 explains how you can analyze your business in other ways.

If you take the time to plan your QuickBooks customers and jobs in advance, you'll save yourself hours of effort later, when you need information about your business. You can add customer and job *types* (as well as customers and jobs) anytime. If you don't have time to add types now, come back to this section when you're ready to learn how.

Categorizing with Classes

The Class Tracking feature explained on page 150 is a powerful and often misunderstood way to categorize a business. Classes are powerful because of their ability to cross income, expense, account, customer, and job boundaries.

Say you want to track how much each sales region actually sells to figure out who gets to host your annual sales shindig. Your income accounts show sales by products and services, even if each region sells all those items. Customer types won't help if some large customers buy products from several regions. The same goes if a job requires a smorgasbord of what you sell. To solve this sales-by-region dilemma, you can create a class for each region.

When you turn on Class Tracking, every transaction includes a Class field. Unlike the Customer Type and Job Type fields, which you assign when you create a customer or job, a transaction's Class field starts out blank. For each invoice, sales receipt, and so on, simply choose the class for the region that made the sale. That way, you can produce a report sorted by class that shows each region's performance.

As you'll learn on page 154, classes can track information that spans multiple customers and jobs, such as business unit, company division, and office location. But don't expect miracles—classes work best when you stick to using them to track only one thing. If you want to apply classes for different purposes, such as both business units *and* locations, you can create subclasses to further categorize your data. For example, you could create top-level classes for your locations, and then create subclasses for the business units in each location.

Understanding Customer Types

Business owners often like to look at the performance of different segments of their businesses. Say your building-supply company has expanded over the years to include sales to homeowners, and you want to know how much you sell to homeowners versus professional contractors. In that case, you can use customer types to designate each customer as a homeowner or a contractor to make this comparison, and then total sales by Customer Type, as shown in Figure 4-7. As you'll learn on page 73, categorizing a customer is as easy as choosing from the Customer Types list.

Customer types are yours to mold into whatever categories help you analyze your business. A healthcare provider might classify customers by their insurance, because reimbursement levels depend on whether a patient has Medicare, uses major medical insurance, or pays privately. A clothing maker might classify customers as custom, retail, or wholesale, because the markup percentages are different for each. And a training company could categorize customers by how they learned about the company's services.

NOTE As you'll see throughout this book, QuickBooks' lists make it easy to fill in information in most QuickBooks dialog boxes by choosing from a list instead of typing.

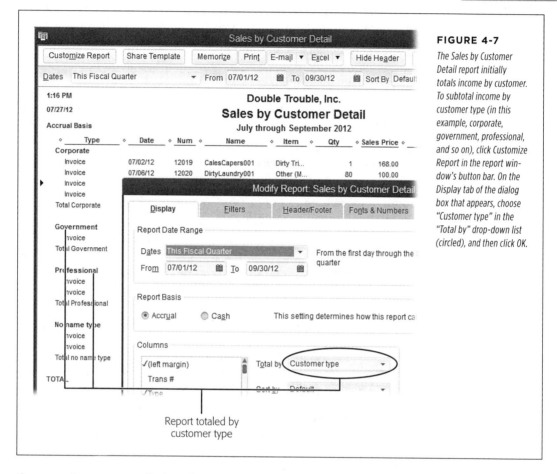

Report totaled by
customer type

FIGURE 4-7

The Sales by Customer Detail report initially totals income by customer. To subtotal income by customer type (in this example, corporate, government, professional, and so on), click Customize Report in the report window's button bar. On the Display tab of the dialog box that appears, choose "Customer type" in the "Total by" drop-down list (circled), and then click OK.

If you create a company file by using an industry-specific edition of QuickBooks or you select an industry when creating your company file (page 8), QuickBooks fills in the Customer Type List with a few kinds of customers that are typical for your industry. If your business sense is eccentric, you can delete QuickBooks' suggestions and replace them with your own entries. If you're a landscaper, you might include customer types such as Green Thumb, Means Well, or Lethal, so you can decide whether orchids, cacti, or Astroturf are most appropriate.

TIP A common mistake is creating customer types that don't relate to customer characteristics. For example, if you provide several kinds of services—like financial forecasting, investment advice, and reading fortunes—your customers might hire you to perform any or all of those services. So if you classify your customers by the services you offer, you'll wonder which customer type to choose when someone hires you for two different services. Instead, go with customer types that describe the customer in some way, like Economics, Investments, and Gambler.

Here are some suggestions for using customer types and other QuickBooks features to analyze your business in different ways:

- **Customer business type.** Use customer types to classify your customers by their business sector, such as Corporate, Government, and Small Business.

- **Nonprofit "customers."** For nonprofit organizations, customer types such as Member, Individual, Corporation, Foundation, and Government Agency can help you target fundraising efforts.

- **Location or region.** Customer types or classes can help track business performance if your company spans multiple regions, offices, or business units.

- **Services.** To track how much business you do for each type of service you offer, set up separate income accounts or subaccounts in your chart of accounts, as outlined on page 45.

- **Products.** To track product sales, create one or more income accounts or subaccounts in your chart of accounts.

TIP   Create income accounts for broad categories of income, such as services and products. Don't create separate accounts for each service or product you sell; you can use items to track sales for each service and product instead, as described in Chapter 5.

- **Marketing.** To identify the income you earned based on how customers learned about your services, create classes such as Referral, Web, Newspaper, and Blimp, or enter this info in a custom field (page 73). That way, you can create a report that shows the revenue you've earned from different marketing efforts—and figure out whether each one is worth the money.

Creating a Customer Type

You can create customer types when you set up your QuickBooks company file or at any time after setup. If you want, you can even set up a customer type as a subtype of another type. To see the list of customer types, choose Lists→Customer & Vendor Profile Lists→Customer Type List. See page 158 to learn how to create customer types and subtypes.

Categorizing Jobs

Jobs are optional in QuickBooks, so job types matter only if you track your work by the job. If your sole source of income is selling organic chicken-fat ripple ice cream, jobs and job types don't matter—your relationship with your customers is one long run of selling and delivering products. But for project-based businesses, job types add another level of filtering to the reports you produce. If you're a writer, then you can use job types to track the kinds of documents you produce (Manual, White Paper, and Marketing Propaganda, for instance) and filter the Job Profitability Report by job type to see which forms of writing are the most lucrative. (Page 559 describes how to filter reports.)

Creating a job type is similar to creating a customer type (page 158): Choose Lists→Customer & Vendor Profile Lists→Job Type List. When the Job Type List window opens, press Ctrl+N to open the New Job Type window, and then enter a name for the job type. If you want to create a subtype, turn on the "Subtype of" checkbox and choose the job type this subtype belongs to.

◼ Adding Notes

Attention to detail. Follow-through. These are a couple of the things that keep customers coming back for more. Following up on promises or calling to check that an issue was resolved successfully is good business. But sending reorder brochures after customers have made purchases can just make them mad. If you use another program for managing customer relationships, you can track these types of details there. But if you prefer to use as few programs as possible, QuickBooks' notes feature can help you stay in customers' good graces by tracking what's been going on, and the to-do items that still need to be done.

In earlier versions of QuickBooks, there was only one note box for all the notes you added to a customer's or job's record. But in QuickBooks 2013, you can add as many separate notes as you want. To view them, simply open the Customer Center, select a customer or job in the Customers & Jobs tab, and then click the Notes tab on the right side of the window. All the notes for the selected customer or job appear, as shown in Figure 4-8 (background). On the Notes tab, you can add, edit, and delete notes in the same way you work with contacts (page 75):

- **Add a note**. With a customer or job selected, click Manage Notes→Add New. The Notepad dialog box opens with the customer's contact information filled in as shown in Figure 4-8 (foreground).

- **Edit a note**. Select the note you want to edit, and then click Manage Notes→Edit Selected Note.

- **Delete a note**. Select the note you want to delete, and then click Manage Notes→Delete Selected Note.

The Notes tab displays all the notes you've added for the selected customer or job. To limit the notes to a date range, click the down arrow to the right of the Date box and choose the time period you want, such as This Month-to-date. To keep track of when conversations happen, click Date Stamp before you start typing. If you're adding a note about something that happened on a day other than today, you have to type in the date.

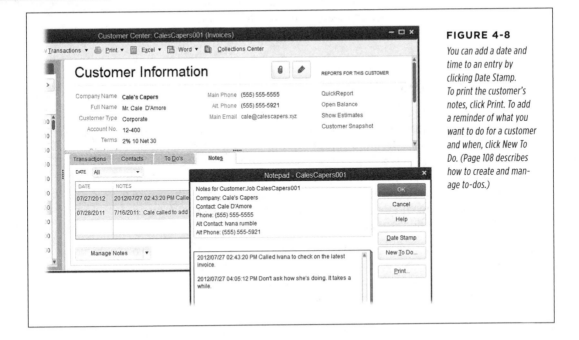

FIGURE 4-8

You can add a date and time to an entry by clicking Date Stamp. To print the customer's notes, click Print. To add a reminder of what you want to do for a customer and when, click New To Do. (Page 108 describes how to create and manage to-dos.)

Working with Leads

Suppose you attend a tradeshow and return to your office with a stack of leads. If you want to turn those leads into new sales, you usually have a host of to-dos, like following up on the questions that prospects asked, sending out more info about your products and services, or simply taking the next step in your sales process. The information you collect about leads is similar to that for customers, but leads aren't customers—yet. If your lead-tracking needs are simple, the Lead Center can help you track prospects while you're trying to turn them into customers. Then, if your persuasion pays off, you can transform leads into customers in QuickBooks.

To work with leads, open the Lead Center by choosing Customers→Lead Center. The Lead Center looks a lot like the Customer Center with a few exceptions. The Leads list on the left shows the lead's name and status. And because leads don't have transactions, the tabs at the bottom of the Lead Center focus on to-dos, contacts, locations, and notes you can use to try to convert the leads into customers.

NOTE The Lead Center's features aren't as powerful as the ones you find in market-leading customer relationship management (CRM) programs. For example, you can't send an email to a lead from the Lead Center or create an estimate for a lead. But if your leads are scribbled in a notebook or listed in a spreadsheet, the Lead Center can help you organize them—and because it's built into QuickBooks, it doesn't cost extra. If you need more sophisticated tracking tools, skip the Lead Center and check out CRM programs that integrate with QuickBooks. You can find a few dozen listed at the Intuit marketplace (*http://tinyurl.com/7xntgpe*). QuickBooks also integrates with Salesforce, a major CRM provider. You can learn about this program in the Lead Center window by clicking the "Learn about Salesforce" button to the right of the Lead Information heading.

Here are some of the actions you can perform with leads:

- **Create a new lead**. In the Lead Center toolbar, click New Lead. In the Add Lead dialog box, name the lead. The Status field lets you classify leads as Hot, Warm, or Cold, so you know which ones to focus on first. The Company tab contains fields for info such as company name, telephone number, email address, website, and main address. (You can add other addresses if the company has several locations.) The Contacts tab lets you add contact information for people in the company. The first contact you enter is designated the Primary Contact, but you can add other contacts by clicking the Add Another Contacts button.

NOTE After you create a lead, you can add more contacts or locations to it by selecting it on the left side of the Lead Center and then clicking either the Contacts or Locations tab at the bottom of the window.

- **View leads**. Like the Customer Center, the Lead Center lists your leads on the left side of the window. The list shows the lead's name and status. You can filter the list by choosing an entry in the View drop-down list. For example, choose Active Leads to see all the leads you're working on, or choose Hot to filter the list for all your most promising leads.

- **Search leads**. If your sales team is prolific, your lead list could be quite long. You can search for specific leads by typing part of the lead's name in the Find box on the left side of the Lead Center and then clicking the magnifying glass icon. QuickBooks filters the list to show all the leads that contain the text you typed.

- **Edit a lead**. After you create a lead, you can view its information and edit it. Simply double-click the lead in the Leads list on the left side of the Lead Center.

- **Create a to-do**. To add a to-do for a lead, select the lead in the Leads list. Next, click the To Do's tab at the bottom of the Lead Center, click To Do at the bottom of the tab, and then choose New To Do. (See page 108 to learn how to create different types of to-dos.) The To Do's tab shows info about that lead's to-dos, including the type of to-do, its priority, when it's due, and whether it's complete.

- **Add notes**. To add notes about a lead, first select the lead in the Leads list. Next, click the Notes tab at the bottom of the Lead Center, and then click Add Notes. In the "Note For <customer>" dialog box, type the information you want to record. For example, you might specify the particular services or products that lead is interested in or her budget. When you add a note, QuickBooks automatically records the date you wrote it. To filter the notes by date, choose a time period in the Notes tab's Date drop-down list.

- **Convert a lead to a customer**. Leads are stored in a separate list from your customers. When you turn a lead into a customer in real life, you can easily do the same in QuickBooks. Right-click the lead in the Leads list and choose "Convert to a Customer" in the shortcut menu. (Or click the "Convert this Lead to a Customer" button in the Lead Center's upper right.) QuickBooks asks you to confirm this action, because you can't undo it. When you click OK, the lead disappears from the Active Leads list. You can see the leads you've converted to customers by choosing Converted Leads in the View drop-down list. Although you can still view these converted leads in the Lead Center, you can no longer *edit* them there. They appear as customers in the Customer Center, and you can edit them there as you do other customers (page 78).

- **Import leads**. To import information about several leads, in the Lead Center toolbar, click Import Multiple Leads. The Import Leads dialog box that appears lets you type values into a table, but you can also copy and paste information from an Excel spreadsheet like you do in the Add/Edit Multiple List Entries window (page 94).

Merging Customer Records

Suppose you remodeled buildings for two companies run by brothers: Morey's City Diner and Les's Exercise Studio. Morey and Les conclude that their businesses have a lot of synergy—people are either eating or trying to lose weight, and usually doing both. To smooth out their cash flow, they decide to merge their companies into More or Less Body Building and All You Can Eat Buffet. Your challenge: to create one customer in QuickBooks from the two businesses, while retaining the jobs, invoices, and other transactions that you created when the companies were separate. The solution: QuickBooks' merge feature.

> **TIP** Here's another instance when merging can come in handy: If you don't use a standard naming convention as recommended on page 66, you could end up with multiple customer records representing one real-life customer, such as "Les's Exercise Studio" and "LesEx." You can merge these doppelgangers into one customer just as you can merge two truly separate companies into one.

When you merge customer records in QuickBooks, one customer retains the entire transaction history for the two original customers. In other words, you don't so much merge two customers as turn one customer's records into those of another.

QuickBooks doesn't have a Merge Customer button. If you want to merge two customers' records into one, the secret is to rename one customer to the same name as another. Sounds simple, right? But there's a catch: The customer you rename can't have any jobs associated with it. So if the customer you want to rename has jobs associated with it, you have to move all those jobs to the customer you intend to keep *before* you start the merge. Your best bet: Subsume the customer with fewer jobs so you don't have to move very many. (If you don't use jobs, then subsume whichever customer you want.)

NOTE If you work in multiuser mode, you have to switch to single-user mode for the duration of the merging operation. See page 173 to learn how to switch to single-user mode and back again after the merge is complete.

To merge customers with a minimum of frustrated outbursts, follow these steps:

1. **Open the Customer Center.**

   In QuickBooks' icon bar, click Customers, or in the Customers panel of the Home page, click Customers.

2. **If the customer you're going to subsume has jobs associated with it, on the Customers & Jobs tab, position your cursor over the diamond to the left of the job you want to reassign.**

   Jobs are indented beneath the customer to which they belong.

3. **When the cursor changes to a four-headed arrow, drag the job under the customer you plan to keep, as shown in Figure 4-9, left.**

4. **Repeat steps 2 and 3 for each job that belongs to the customer you're going to subsume.**

   If you have hundreds of jobs for the customer, moving them is tedious at best—but move them you must.

5. **On the Customers & Jobs tab, right-click the name of the customer you want to subsume and, from the shortcut menu, choose Edit Customer:Job.**

   You can also edit the customer by selecting its name on the Customer & Jobs tab and then, when the customer's info appears on the right side of the Customer Center, clicking the Edit button (the pencil icon). Either way, the Edit Customer dialog box opens.

6. **In the Edit Customer dialog box, edit the Customer Name field to match the name of the customer you intend to keep, and then click OK.**

   QuickBooks displays a message letting you know that the name is in use and asking if you want to merge the customers.

7. **Click Yes to complete the merge.**

   In the Customer Center, the customer you renamed disappears and any balances it had now belong to the remaining customer, as shown in Figure 4-9, right.

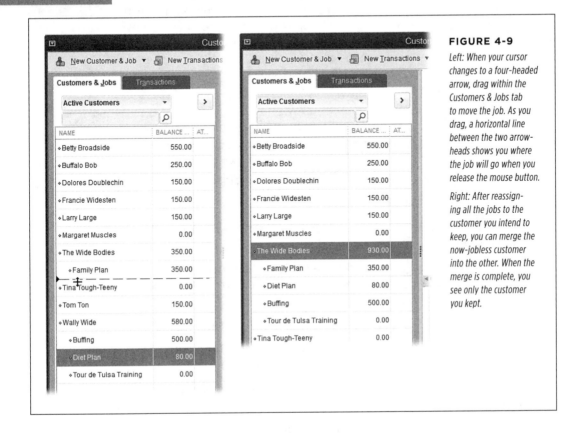

FIGURE 4-9

Left: When your cursor changes to a four-headed arrow, drag within the Customers & Jobs tab to move the job. As you drag, a horizontal line between the two arrow-heads shows you where the job will go when you release the mouse button.

Right: After reassigning all the jobs to the customer you intend to keep, you can merge the now-jobless customer into the other. When the merge is complete, you see only the customer you kept.

Hiding and Deleting Customers

Hiding customers isn't about barricading them in a conference room when the competition shows up to talk to you. Because QuickBooks lets you delete customers only in very limited circumstances, hiding customers helps keep your list of customers manageable and your financial history intact. This section explains your options.

Hiding and Restoring Customers

Although your work with a customer might be over, you still have to keep records about your past relationship. But old customers can clutter up the Customer Center, making it difficult to select active customers. The solution is to hide old customers, which also removes those customers' names from all the lists that appear in transaction windows so you can't select them by mistake. Hiding old customers is a better solution than deleting them, because QuickBooks retains the historical transactions for those customers so you can reactivate them if they decide to work with you again.

To hide a customer, in the Customer Center's Customers & Jobs tab, right-click the customer and then, from the shortcut menu, choose Make Customer:Job Inactive. The customer and any associated jobs disappear from the list. Figure 4-10 shows you how to unhide (reactivate) customers.

FIGURE 4-10

To make hidden customers visible again and reactivate their records, set the drop-down list at the top of the Customers & Jobs tab to All Customers as shown here. QuickBooks displays an X to the left of every inactive customer in the list. Simply click that X to restore the customer to active duty.

Deleting Customers

You can delete a customer only if there's no activity for that customer in your QuickBooks file. If you try to delete a customer that has even one transaction, QuickBooks tells you that you can't delete that record.

If you create a customer by mistake, you can remove it, as long as you first remove any associated transactions—which are likely to be mistakes as well. But QuickBooks doesn't tell you which transactions are preventing you from deleting this customer. To find and delete transactions that prevent you from deleting a customer, follow these steps:

1. **View all the transactions for the customer by selecting that customer in the Customer Center's Customers & Jobs tab, and then, in the Transactions pane, setting the Show box to All Transactions and the Date box to All, as shown in Figure 4-11.**

   You can also view transactions by running the "Transaction List by Customer" report (Reports→Customers & Receivables→Transaction List by Customer).

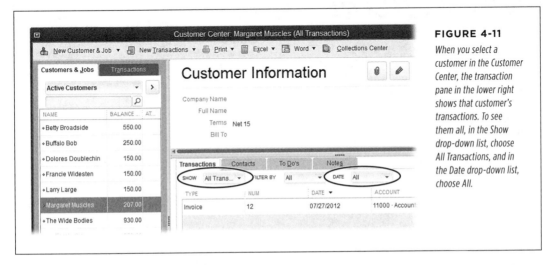

FIGURE 4-11

When you select a customer in the Customer Center, the transaction pane in the lower right shows that customer's transactions. To see them all, in the Show drop-down list, choose All Transactions, and in the Date drop-down list, choose All.

2. **In the Customer Center or the report, open the transaction you want to delete by double-clicking it.**

   The Create Invoices window (or the corresponding transaction window) opens to the transaction you double-clicked.

3. **Right-click the Create Invoices window and choose Delete Invoice from the shortcut menu (or choose Edit→Delete Invoice, Edit→Delete Check, or the corresponding delete command).**

   In the message box that appears, click OK to confirm that you want to delete the transaction.

4. **Repeat steps 2 and 3 for every transaction for that customer.**

5. **Back on the Customers & Jobs tab, select the customer you want to delete, and then press Ctrl+D or choose Edit→Delete Customer:Job.**

   If the customer has no transactions, QuickBooks asks you to confirm that you want to delete the customer; click OK. If you see a message stating that you can't delete the customer, go back to steps 2 and 3 to delete any remaining transactions.

■ Setting Up Vendors

Creating and editing vendors is similar to creating and editing customers: You can add them one at a time or create them all at once. The New Vendor window lets you create one vendor at a time. The next section describes how to use that window and explains the fields that are unique to vendors.

> **TIP** You can create a vendor record when you create that vendor's first bill (page 220). Simply choose <Add New> in the Enter Bills window's Vendor drop-down list.

You can use the QuickBooks Setup window to import vendor information from your email program or copy and paste data from Microsoft Excel, as described on page 15. And the Add/Edit Multiple List Entries feature lets you paste data from Excel or copy values from vendor to vendor; you can read how to use it on page 94.

Importing vendor information into QuickBooks is another fast way to create oodles of vendor records. After you create a map between QuickBooks' fields and fields in another program, you can transfer all your vendor info, as described on page 654.

The Vendor Center makes creating, editing, and reviewing vendors in QuickBooks a breeze. Like the Customer Center (page 29), the Vendor Center lists the details of your vendors and their transactions in one easy-to-use dashboard. To open the Vendor Center window, use any of the following methods:

- Choose Vendors→Vendor Center.

- In the Vendors panel of the QuickBooks Home page, click Vendors.

- In the icon bar, click Vendors.

Creating a Vendor

You create a new vendor from the Vendor Center window by pressing Ctrl+N or, in the Vendor Center menu bar, by clicking New Vendor→New Vendor. Either way, the New Vendor window opens.

Many of the fields you see should be familiar from creating customers in Quick-Books. For example, the Vendor Name field corresponds to the Customer Name field, which you might remember is actually more of a code than a name (page 67). Use the same sort of naming convention for vendors that you use for customers (see the box on page 66). As with customer records, you're better off leaving the Opening Balance field blank and building your current vendor balance by entering the invoices or bills they send.

The following sections explain how to fill out the rest of the fields in a vendor record.

ENTERING ADDRESS INFORMATION

If you print checks and envelopes to pay your bills, you'll need address and contact information for your vendors. The Address Info tab in the New Vendor window has fields for the vendor's address and contact info, which are almost identical to customer address and contact fields, so see page 68 if you need help filling them in.

PAYMENT SETTINGS

In QuickBooks 2013, the fields related to payments reside on the Payment Settings tab. Here are the fields and how you fill them in:

- **Account No**. When you create customers, you can assign account numbers to them; when it's your turn to be a customer, your vendors return the favor and assign an account number to *your* company. If you fill in this box with the account number that the vendor gave you, QuickBooks prints it in the memo field of checks you print. Even if you don't print checks, keeping your account number in QuickBooks is handy if a question arises about one of your payments.

- **Payment Terms**. Choose the payment terms that the vendor extended to your company. The entries in this drop-down list (page 70) are the same as for customers.

- **Print Name On Check As**. QuickBooks automatically fills in this box with whatever you enter in the vendor's Company Name field on the Address Info tab. When you print checks, QuickBooks fills in the payee with the contents of this field, so to print a different name, simply edit what's in this box.

- **Credit Limit**. If the vendor has set a credit limit for your company (like $30,000 from a building supply store), type that value in this box. That way, QuickBooks warns you when you create a purchase order that pushes your credit balance above this limit.

- **Billing Rate Level**. If you use the Contractor, Professional Services, or Accountant edition of QuickBooks, this is another list that lets you set up custom billing rates for employees and vendors. Billing rates let you price the *services* you sell the same way a Price Level helps you adjust the prices of products you sell. Say you have three carpenters: a newbie, an old-timer, and a finish carpenter. You can set up a Billing Rate Level for each one based on experience. Then, when you create an invoice for your carpenters' billable time, QuickBooks automatically applies the correct rate to each carpenter's hours.

SALES TAX SETTINGS

QuickBooks 2013 keeps the two sales tax–related fields on the Sales Tax Settings tab. Here's what they do:

- **Vendor ID**. You have to put the vendor's Employer Identification Number (EIN) or Social Security number in this field *only if* you plan to create a 1099 for this vendor.

- **Vendor eligible for 1099**. Turn on this checkbox if you're going to create a 1099 for this vendor (page 497).

NOTE When you hire subcontractors to do work for you, you have them fill out a W-9 form, which tells you the subcontractor's taxpayer identification number. Then, at the end of the year, you fill out a 1099 tax form that indicates how much you paid them, which they use to prepare their tax returns. See page 497 to learn how QuickBooks can help with 1099s.

■ FILLING IN EXPENSE ACCOUNTS AUTOMATICALLY

When you write checks, record credit card charges, or enter bills for a vendor, you have to indicate the expense account to which you want to assign the payment. The Account Settings tab in the New Vendor or Edit Vendor window lets you tell QuickBooks which accounts you typically use. However, the easiest approach to filling in expense accounts is to tell QuickBooks to automatically recall your previous transactions. That way, when you record a bill, check, or credit card charge for a vendor, the program creates a new bill using the total amount and the accounts you chose on the previous transaction. Page 612 explains how to set the "Automatically recall last transaction for this name" preference.

■ ADDITIONAL INFO

With all the New Vendor window's new tabs in QuickBooks 2013, the Additional Info tab is rather sparse, which is probably why it's the last tab in the list. Here are its fields and what you can do with them:

- **Vendor Type**. If you want to classify vendors or generate reports based on their types, choose an entry in this drop-down list or create a new type in the Vendor Type List (page 159) by choosing <Add New>. For example, if you assign a Tax type to all the tax agencies you remit taxes to, you can easily prepare a report of your tax liabilities and payments.

- **Custom Fields**. If you want to track vendor information that isn't handled by the fields that QuickBooks provides, you can add several custom fields (see the box on page 73). Say your subcontractors are supposed to have current certificates for workers' comp insurance, and you could be in big trouble if you hire one whose certificate has expired. If you create a custom field to hold the expiration date for each subcontractor's certificate, you can generate a report of these dates.

■ Data Entry Shortcuts

If you frequently add or edit more than one customer or vendor a time, filling in the New Customer or New Vendor window isn't only tedious, it also takes up time you should spend on more important tasks, like selling, managing cash flow, or finding out who has the incriminating pictures from the last company party.

When you set up your company file, the QuickBooks Setup window helps you bring information in from an email program or Excel (page 15), and you can use that same window anytime you want to add more customers or vendors. Another option is the Add/Edit Multiple List Entries feature. When you're creating customers, vendors, or items, you can use the Add/Edit Multiple List Entries window to paste data from Excel into QuickBooks. Or, to edit existing records, you can filter or search the list in that window to show just the customers (or vendors, or items) you want to update and then paste Excel data, type in values, or copy values between records.

Then again, you might store info about customers and vendors in other programs such as a database or word-processing program where you create mailing labels. If your other programs can create *Excel-compatible files* or *delimited text files*, you can avoid data-entry grunt work by transferring data to or from QuickBooks. (Delimited text files are nothing more than files that separate each piece of data with a comma, space, tab, or other character.) In both types of files, the same kind of info appears in the same position in each line or row, so QuickBooks (as well as other programs) can pull the information into the right places. When you want to transfer a *ton* of customer information between QuickBooks and other programs, importing and exporting is the way to go. By mapping QuickBooks fields to the fields in the other program, you can quickly transfer hundreds or even thousands of records.

This section covers it all: working with multiple entries, importing, and exporting.

Adding and Editing Multiple Records

The Add/Edit Multiple List Entries feature is a great tool for adding or updating values in the Customer, Vendor, and Item Lists. If you have data in an Excel spreadsheet, you can paste it directly into a table in the Add/Edit Multiple List Entries window. Features for copying or duplicating values between records come in handy with changes like updating the billing address for a customer who sends you job after job. (Typing values into cells works, too, if you notice a typo in one of the records in the list.) And you can customize the window's table to show only the customers, vendors, or items you want to edit and the fields you want to modify.

This feature goes by different names depending on where you find it in QuickBooks. Choose it in any of these locations to open the Add/Edit Multiple List Entries window:

- **In the Lists menu, choose Add/Edit Multiple List Entries.** When you go this route, QuickBooks sets the window's List box to Customers.

- **In the Customer Center toolbar, click New Customer & Job→Add Multiple Customer:Jobs or Excel→Paste from Excel.** QuickBooks sets the List box to Customers.

- **In the Vendor Center toolbar, click New Vendor→Add Multiple Vendors or Excel→Paste from Excel.** QuickBooks sets the List box to Vendors.

- **At the bottom of the Item List window (page 119), click Excel→Paste from Excel.** QuickBooks sets the List box to Service Items.

■ SELECTING A LIST TO WORK WITH

As mentioned above, if you open the Add/Edit Multiple List Entries window from the Customer Center, Vendor Center, or Item List window, it automatically selects the appropriate list in the List drop-down menu. You can switch lists by choosing Customers, Vendors, Service Items, Inventory Parts, or Non-Inventory Parts from this drop-down menu.

TIP If you set up jobs for customers, the Add/Edit Multiple List Entries window's table includes rows for both customers and jobs. The Name column contains the customer's name for a customer row and the job's name for a job row. Usually, you can spot job rows by looking at the Company Name field, since all jobs for that customer will have the same value listed here.

To make it easier to edit existing list entries, you can display only the ones you want to change. Here are some ways to control what you see in the table:

- **Filter the entries**. The View drop-down list includes several choices for filtering the list. Choose Active Customers if you want to make changes to only active customers in your company file. Choosing Inactive Customers displays only customers that you've set to inactive status (page 88). You can filter for active or inactive vendors and items, too.

  Because QuickBooks doesn't save the changes you make in the Add/Edit Multiple List Entries window until you click Save Changes, you can filter by Unsaved Customers (or Unsaved Vendors or Unsaved Items) to see all the entries you've edited but haven't yet saved. Choosing the entry that ends in "with errors" displays only entries that contain invalid values, like a vendor type or tax code that doesn't exist in your company file. In fact, if you click Save Changes when there are records with errors, the window automatically filters the list to the "with errors" view so you can see what you need to correct before you can save your changes. Page 100 explains how to spot and fix errors.

  To filter the list to your exact specifications, choose Custom Filter and then fill in the dialog box shown in Figure 4-12. For example, if you want to divide your government customers into local, state, and federal groups, you can filter the list to show only records with "Government" in their customer fields. Note that QuickBooks displays only list entries that *exactly* match what you filter for, so if you type *(555)* to look for the 555 area code, records that don't have parentheses around the area code won't show up.

- **Find entries**. Typing a word, value, or phrase in the Find box is similar to applying a custom filter to the list, except that QuickBooks searches *all* fields. For example, if you type *555* in the Find box and then click the Search button (which looks like a magnifying glass), QuickBooks will display records that contain 555 anywhere, whether it's in the company name, telephone number, address, or account number field.

TIP To clear a custom filter or the search criteria you typed in the Find box, simply click the button to the right of the Find box (which has a red X on it when you've applied a filter or find criteria to the list).

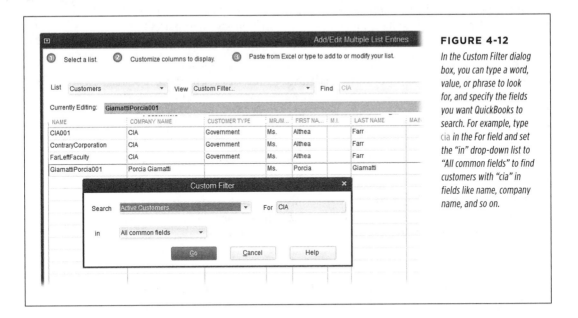

FIGURE 4-12

In the Custom Filter dialog box, you can type a word, value, or phrase to look for, and specify the fields you want QuickBooks to search. For example, type cia *in the For field and set the "in" drop-down list to "All common fields" to find customers with "cia" in fields like name, company name, and so on.*

NOTE QuickBooks is quite literal in its searches, so the entries you see in your search results exactly match what you typed in the Find box. For example, if you type *New York*, QuickBooks displays customer records that contain that exact phrase, but not ones that use the abbreviation NY.

- **Customize the columns that appear in the table**. To paste data from Excel in a jiffy, you can customize the table's columns to match your Excel spreadsheet. (If you're an Excel whiz, you may prefer to rearrange the columns in your spreadsheet before pasting data.) Click Customize Columns to open the Customize Columns dialog box. The tools for customizing columns are straightforward, as Figure 4-13 illustrates. To add a column, select the field you want in the Available Columns list and then click Add. To remove a column, select it in the Chosen Columns list and then click Remove.

- **Sort the list entries**. To sort the entries in the table, click the column heading for the field you want to sort by, and QuickBooks sorts the records in ascending order (from A to Z or from low to high numbers). Click again to sort in descending order.

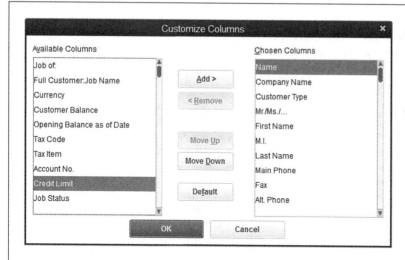

FIGURE 4-13

In addition to adding and removing columns, you can change the position of a column by selecting it in the Chosen Columns list and then clicking Move Up or Move Down. If you completely mangle the columns, click Default to restore the original ones.

■ ADDING OR EDITING LIST ENTRIES

Whether you want to add new entries or edit existing ones, you can paste data from Excel, type in values, or use features like Copy Down to copy values between records. (When you want to add a new record, you have to click the first empty row at the bottom of the list before you can enter any data.) Here are the various ways to enter values in records:

- **Type values in cells**. This method is straightforward: Click a cell and make your changes.

- **Copy and paste values from Excel**. If you're a fan of copying and pasting (and who isn't?), you can copy data from an Excel spreadsheet (a single cell, a range of cells, one or more rows, or one or more columns) and paste it into the table. The only requirement is that the rows and columns in the table and in the spreadsheet have to contain the same information in the same order. You can rearrange the rows and columns either in the Add/Edit Multiple List Entries window or in the spreadsheet, whichever you prefer.

  If you want to copy and paste customers and jobs (or items with subitems), you first have to create the top-level entries, as shown in Figure 4-14. That's because jobs or subitems you paste include the name of the customer in the Company Name field (a parent item's name appears in the "Subitem of" field). Once the parent entries exist, you can use the Add/Edit Multiple List Entries window again to paste jobs or subitems.

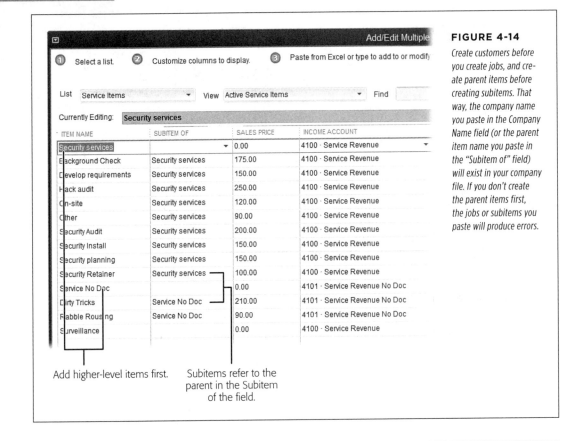

FIGURE 4-14

Create customers before you create jobs, and create parent items before creating subitems. That way, the company name you paste in the Company Name field (or the parent item name you paste in the "Subitem of" field) will exist in your company file. If you don't create the parent items first, the jobs or subitems you paste will produce errors.

Add higher-level items first.

Subitems refer to the parent in the Subitem of the field.

NOTE To prevent errors when you copy and paste data, make sure the values you reference, such as accounts, tax codes, and so on, already exist in your company file.

When you paste Excel data into existing records in the Add/Edit Multiple List Entries window, QuickBooks overwrites the existing values in the cells. To paste Excel data into *new* records, be sure to select the first empty row in the window before pasting the data.

- **Copy and paste data within the table**. You can also copy and paste data from one cell in the table to another. For example, if a customer with several jobs has relocated its main office, you can copy values from Bill To cells and paste them into the cells for the customer's jobs. When you copy and paste data within the table, you can copy only one cell at a time.

TIP If you want to copy several cells in the Add/Edit Multiple List Entries table, it's quicker to make the changes in your Excel spreadsheet and then paste the data from Excel into the Add/Edit Multiple List Entries table.

- **Duplicate a row**. To create a new record that has many of the same values as an existing record, right-click a cell in the row you want to duplicate and then choose Duplicate Row from the shortcut menu. The new record appears in the row below the original and contains all the same values as the original record, except that the value in the first field begins with "DUP" to differentiate it from the original. Edit the cells in the row that have different values. Then edit the Name cell to reflect the new name.

- **Copy values down a column**. You can quickly fill in several cells in a column by using the Copy Down feature. Because this feature copies data into *all* cells below the one you select, it's important to filter the list (page 95) to show only the records you want to change. Then right-click the cell you want to copy down the column and choose Copy Down from the shortcut menu. QuickBooks copies the value in the selected cell to all the cells below it in the column, overwriting any existing data. For example, if you want to change the contact name for all the jobs for a particular customer, filter the list to show just the records for that customer (in the Find box, type the customer's name, and then click the magnifying glass icon). Next, type the new contact into the first Contact cell. Then, right-click the cell and choose Copy Down.

NOTE If a cell is selected, right-clicking it doesn't display the shortcut menu. Click a different cell and then right-click the cell you want to copy so you can choose the editing entries on the shortcut menu.

- **Insert a row**. If you want to insert a blank line in the table (to create a new job for a customer, for example), right-click the row that's currently where you want the blank line, and then choose Insert Line from the shortcut menu (or press Ctrl+Insert).

- **Delete a row**. If you created a record by mistake, you can get rid of it by right-clicking anywhere in its row and then choosing Delete Line. (This entry is grayed out if the entry is used in a transaction or other record, because you can't delete a record if it's referenced somewhere else in your company file.)

- **Clear a column**. To clear all the values in a column, right-click in the column and then choose Clear Column from the shortcut menu; QuickBooks immediately removes all the values in the column. If you chose this feature by mistake, you can undo the deletion by clicking Close, and then, in the Unsaved Customer message box, click No.

■ SAVING CHANGES

After you've completed the additions and modifications you want in the Add/Edit Multiple List Entries window, click Save Changes to save your work. QuickBooks saves all the entries that have no errors and tells you how many records it saved.

■ CORRECTING ERRORS

If you try to save changes and QuickBooks finds any errors, like a value that doesn't exist in the Terms list, it displays those entries in the Add/Edit Multiple List Entries window's table and changes the incorrect values to red text. Point your cursor at a cell to see a hint about the error. For example, if you typed a letter in a price field, QuickBooks tells you that the field contains an invalid character. If the problem is a list entry that doesn't exist, the "<list name> Not Found" dialog box opens (where "<list name>" is a list like Terms) and tells you the value isn't in the list. Click Set Up to add the entry to the list. Fix the errors and then click Save Changes again.

> **TIP** If you don't know what the problem is, you can select the incorrect value and delete it by pressing Delete or Backspace. When you figure out what the value *should* be, you can edit that record in the Add/Edit Multiple List Entries window or the corresponding Edit dialog box.

Importing Customer or Vendor Information

If you have hundreds of customer or vendor records to stuff into QuickBooks, even copying and pasting can be tedious. If you can produce a delimited text file or a spreadsheet of customer or vendor info in the program where you currently store it (page 657), then you can match up your source data with QuickBooks' fields and import all your records in one fell swoop.

Delimited files and spreadsheets compartmentalize data by separating each piece of info with a comma or a tab, or by cubbyholing them into columns and rows in a spreadsheet file. An exported delimited file isn't necessarily ready to import into QuickBooks, though. Headings in the delimited file or spreadsheet might identify the field names in the program that originally held the information, but QuickBooks has no way of knowing the correlation between those fields and its own.

But don't worry: You can help QuickBooks understand the data you're importing. QuickBooks looks for keywords in the file you're importing to figure out what to do, as shown in Figure 4-15. So you'll need to rename some headings to transform the file produced by the other program into an import file that QuickBooks can read. QuickBooks' customer keywords and the fields they represent are listed in Table 4-1, and vendor keywords and fields are listed in Table 4-2. Fortunately, it's easy to edit headings in Excel and other spreadsheet programs. When your exported file looks something like the one in Figure 4-15, save it in Excel 2010 by clicking that program's File tab and then choosing Save (if you're using Excel 2007, click the Office button and then choose Save). The box on page 105 describes how to use spreadsheets for other data tasks.

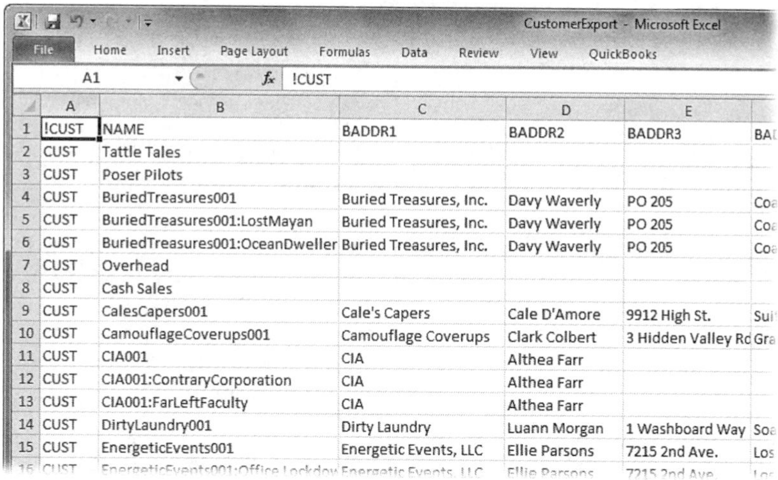

FIGURE 4-15

A file you import has to use field names that match QuickBooks'. For example, replace a Street_Address heading with BADDR1, which is the keyword for the first address line field in QuickBooks, and a Last_Name heading with LASTNAME. The first column has to include the keywords QuickBooks uses to identify customer (CUST) or vendor (VEND) records. And the first cell in the first row of a customer import file has to contain the text "!CUST," as shown here. (The first cell in the first row of a vendor import file has to contain "!VEND" instead.)

TIP   To see how QuickBooks wants a delimited file to look, export your current QuickBooks Customer List to an .iif file (page 649) and then open it in Excel and check out the field names it uses.

TABLE 4-1 *Customer keywords and their respective fields in the order that QuickBooks exports them*

KEYWORD	FIELD CONTENTS
NAME	(Required) The Customer Name field, which specifies the name or code you use to identify the customer.
BADDR1 – BADDR5	Up to five lines of the customer's billing address.
SADDR1 – SADDR5	Up to five lines of the customer's shipping address.
PHONE1	The number stored in the Phone Number field.
PHONE2	The customer's alternate phone number.
FAXNUM	The customer's fax number.

KEYWORD	FIELD CONTENTS
EMAIL	The customer's email address.
NOTE	Despite its confusing keyword, this field is the name or number of the account stored in the Account No. field. (To set up a customer as an online payee, you have to assign it an account number.) The NOTEPAD keyword explained below, on the other hand, represents the notes you enter about a customer.
CONT1	The name of the customer's primary contact.
CONT2	The name of an alternate contact for the customer.
CTYPE	The customer's type. If you import a customer type that doesn't exist in your Customer Type List, QuickBooks adds the new type to the list.
TERMS	The payment terms by which the customer abides.
TAXABLE	Y or N in this field indicates whether you charge the customer sales tax.
SALESTAXCODE	The code that identifies the type of sales tax to charge.
LIMIT	The dollar amount of the customer's credit limit with your company.
RESALENUM	The customer's resale number.
REP	The representative who works with the customer. The format for a rep entry is *name:list ID:initials*, such as "Saul Lafite:2:SEL." *Name* represents the rep's name; *list ID* equals 1 if the rep's name belongs to the Vendor List, 2 for the Employee List, or 3 for the Other Names List; and *initials* are the rep's initials.
TAXITEM	The name of the type of tax you charge this customer. What you enter has to correspond to one of the sales tax items in your Item List (on page 142).

KEYWORD	FIELD CONTENTS
NOTEPAD	This field is where you can wax poetic about your customer's merits or simply document details you want to remember. To see this imported data in QuickBooks, in the Customer Center, select the customer's name, and then click the Notes tab.
SALUTATION	The title to include before the contact's name, such as Mr., Ms., or Dr.
COMPANYNAME	The name of the customer's company as you want it to appear on invoices or other documents.
FIRSTNAME	The primary contact's first name.
MIDINIT	The primary contact's middle initial.
LASTNAME	The primary contact's last name.
CUSTFLD1-CUSTFLD15	Custom field entries for the customer, if you've defined any. (Page 73 explains how to create custom fields.)
HIDDEN	This field is set to N if the customer is active in your QuickBooks file, or Y if he's inactive.
PRICELEVEL	The customer's price level (page 71).

NOTE QuickBooks also exports the fields for job information into six columns with the keywords JOBDESC, JOBTYPE, JOBSTATUS, JOBSTART, JOBPROJEND, and JOBEND.

TABLE 4-2 *Vendor keywords and their respective fields in the order that QuickBooks exports them*

KEYWORD	FIELD CONTENTS
NAME	(Required) The Vendor Name field, which specifies the name or code that you use to identify the vendor.
PRINTAS	The name you want to appear as the payee when you print a check for the vendor.
ADDR1–ADDR5	Up to five lines of the vendor's billing address.
VTYPE	The vendor's type. If you import a vendor type that doesn't exist in your Vendor Type List, QuickBooks adds the new type to the list.

KEYWORD	FIELD CONTENTS
CONT1	The name of the vendor's primary contact.
CONT2	The name of an alternate contact for the vendor.
PHONE1	The number stored in the Phone Number field.
PHONE2	The vendor's alternate phone number.
FAXNUM	The vendor's fax number.
EMAIL	The vendor's email address.
NOTE	This mislabeled field is the name or number of the account stored in the vendor's Account No. field. (To set up a vendor as an online payee, you have to assign an account number.)
TAXID	The vendor's tax ID, which you need to produce a 1099 for the vendor at the end of the year.
LIMIT	The dollar amount of your credit limit with the vendor.
TERMS	The payment terms the vendor requires.
NOTEPAD	This field is your opportunity to document details you want to remember. The data you import into this field appears when you select a vendor in the Vendor Center and then click the Notes tab.
SALUTATION	The title that goes before the contact's name, such as Mr., Ms., or Dr.
COMPANYNAME	The name of the vendor's company as you want it to appear on documents and transactions.
FIRSTNAME	The primary contact's first name.
MIDINIT	The primary contact's middle initial.
LASTNAME	The primary contact's last name.
CUSTFLD1–CUSTFLD15	Custom field entries for the vendor, if you've defined any. (Page 73 explains how to create custom fields.)
1099	Y or N to indicate whether you produce a 1099 for the vendor at the end of the year.
HIDDEN	This field is set to N if the vendor is active in your QuickBooks file, or Y if it's inactive.

The Easy Way to View Data

Data is easier to examine when you view an export or import file with a spreadsheet program like Excel, as described in Chapter 24. Most programs can open or import delimited text files, but Excel is a master at reading the records stored in these text files and displaying them clearly.

When you export data to a delimited text file and then open it in Excel, the program puts the data into cells in a spreadsheet. Because records and fields appear in neat rows and columns, respectively, you can quickly identify, select, and edit the data you want. Furthermore, you can eliminate entire rows or columns with a few deft clicks or keystrokes.

Here's how to open a delimited text file with Excel:

1. In Excel 2010, click the File tab and then choose Open. In Excel 2007, click the Office button and then choose Open.

2. The delimited text files won't appear in the Open dialog box at first because they're not Excel files. Delimited text files come with a range of *file extensions* (the three characters that follow the last period in the filename), so choose All Files in the file-type drop-down list to make sure you'll see your delimited file listed.

3. To open the file, navigate to the folder where it's saved, and then double-click the file's name. The Text Import Wizard dialog box appears. (A *wizard* is a series of question-and-answer screens that walk you through a particular process.)

4. As you tell the wizard which characters act as delimiters and what type of data appears in each column, it shows you what the data will look like after it's imported into Excel. When its interpretation of the data is correct, click Finish.

Now, you can use Excel to rename column headings or to delete the columns or rows you don't want to import.

Exporting Customer or Vendor Information

QuickBooks lets you do lots of cool things with customer or vendor info, but say you already have a mail merge set up in FileMaker Pro, or you want to transfer all your records to Microsoft Access to track product support. In cases like that, you have to export your customer or vendor data out of QuickBooks into a file that the other program can read and import.

You have three ways of extracting customer or vendor info from QuickBooks:

- **Export the information directly to Excel** if you're not sure what info you need and you'd rather delete and rearrange columns in a spreadsheet program. Quick-Books exports every customer or vendor field. You can then edit the spreadsheet all you want and transfer the data to yet another program when you're done.

- **Create a report** when you want control over exactly which fields QuickBooks exports. By creating a customized version of the Customer Contact List report or Vendor Contact List report, for example, you can export the same set of records repeatedly, creating delimited files, spreadsheets, and so on. (Chapter 21 covers QuickBooks' reports in detail.)

- **Export a text file** of your data if you need a delimited text file to load into another program. The delimited file lists each customer or vendor in its own row with each field separated by tabs.

The following sections explain all your options.

■ EXPORTING TO EXCEL

Exporting QuickBooks' Customer List or Vendor List to Excel is a snap. To export all the customer data stored in QuickBooks to an Excel file, in the Customer Center toolbar, click Excel, and then choose Export Customer List to open the Export dialog box (Figure 4-16). To export vendors, in the Vendor Center toolbar, click Excel, and then choose Export Vendor List. The Excel menus in both centers also contain features for exporting transactions, and for importing and pasting spreadsheet data into QuickBooks.

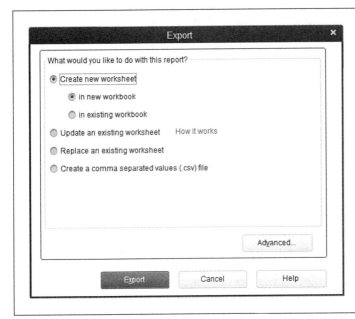

FIGURE 4-16

The Export dialog box that appears is already set up to create a new spreadsheet. Click the Export button, and you'll be looking at you customer or Vendor List in Excel in mere seconds. If you'd rather give QuickBooks more guidance on creating the spreadsheet, click the Advanced button and then adjust options like AutoFit (which sets the column width so you can see all your data) before clicking Export.

■ CUSTOMIZED EXPORTS USING CONTACT LIST REPORTS

By modifying the settings in the Customer Contact List report or the Vendor Contact List report, you can export exactly the fields you want for specific customers or vendors. For example, storing email addresses in QuickBooks is perfect when you email invoices to customers, but you probably also want these addresses in your email program so you can communicate with customers about the work you're doing for them. Exporting the entire Customer or Vendor List is overkill when all you want are the contacts' name and email address; that's where exporting a report shines.

Out of the box, QuickBooks' Customer Contact List report includes Customer, Bill to, Contact, Main Phone, Fax, and Balance Total columns. The Vendor Contact List report includes Vendor, Account No., Bill from, Contact, Main Phone, Fax, and Balance Total columns. Here's how you transform these reports into an export tool, using the Customer Contact List as an example:

1. **Choose Reports→Customers & Receivables→Customer Contact List.**

    The Customer Contact List report window opens. (For the Vendor Contact List, choose Reports→Vendors & Payables→Vendor Contact List instead.)

2. **In the report window's toolbar, click Customize Report.**

    The "Modify Report: Customer Contact List" dialog box that appears lets you adjust the report to filter the data that you'll export. (See page 551 to learn about other ways of customizing reports.)

3. **Click the dialog box's Display tab (if you're not already on it) and, in the Columns section, choose the fields you want to export.**

    The Customer, Contact, Main Phone, and Fax fields might be good ones to export. Then again, they might not. You can add or remove whichever fields you want by clicking a field's name in the Columns list to toggle that field on or off. If there's a checkmark in front of the field's name, the report will include a column for that field.

4. **To produce a report for only the customers you want, click the dialog box's Filters tab. In the Filter list, choose Customer. In the Customer drop-down list that appears, choose "Multiple customers/jobs" to select the customers you want to export.**

    QuickBooks displays the Select Customer:Job dialog box with the Manual option selected; that's what you want. In the list of customer names on the right side of this dialog box, click each customer you want to export, and then click OK. Then, in the Modify Report dialog box, click OK.

    You see the report with the modifications you've made.

TIP Saving the modified report you just created reduces the number of steps you have to take the next time you export. Page 563 explains how to make QuickBooks memorize a report.

---

5. **In the Customer Contact List window's toolbar, click Excel→Create New Worksheet.**

    The "Send Report to Excel" dialog box opens. To create a new Excel workbook, keep the "Create new worksheet" option selected and click Export. Your computer launches Excel and displays the report in a workbook.

■ EXPORTING A TEXT FILE

To create a delimited text file of the entire Customers & Jobs List (or any other QuickBooks list), choose File→Utilities→Export→Lists to IIF Files. The first Export dialog box that appears includes checkboxes for each QuickBooks list, described in detail on page 649. Turn on the checkboxes for the ones you want to export, and then click OK.

TIP If you want to export *only* names and addresses to a tab-delimited file, choose File→Utilities→Export→Addresses to Text File. In the "Select Names for Export Addresses" dialog box, you can choose to export all names, all customer names, all vendor names, or other subsets of names.

▊ Tracking To-Dos

QuickBooks lets you track your business to-dos in your company file. QuickBooks' to-dos are preferable to papering the edges of your computer monitor with sticky notes, although you might prefer to keep to-dos in a program that you keep running constantly, like your email or calendar program, so that you see reminders when you need them.

You can create to-dos for customers, leads who aren't yet customers, vendors, and employees. You can manage all your to-dos in the To Do List window, which lets you filter by type, status, date, customer, lead, or vendor.

Creating a To-Do

QuickBooks gives you several ways to create to-dos:

- **In the Customer or Vendor Center**. Select a customer or vendor, and then click the To Do's tab at the bottom of the center. Then, click the Manage To Dos button and choose Create New on the drop-down menu.

- **In the Lead Center**. Select a lead and then, on the To Do's tab at the bottom of the center, click To Do (or click the down arrow and choose New To Do).

- **In the To Do List window**. Open the global To Do List by choosing Company→To Do List. Then, at the bottom of the window, click To Do (or click the down arrow and choose New To Do).

Once the Add To Do dialog box is open, follow these steps:

1. **In the Type drop-down list, choose the kind of to-do you want to create.**

   To-dos can be calls, faxes, emails, meetings, appointments, or tasks.

2. **In the Priority box, choose High, Medium, or Low.**

   You can sort the to-dos in the To Do List by any field including Priority.

3. **If the to-do is associated with someone, turn on the With checkbox. Next, in the drop-down list below the checkbox, choose Lead, Customer, Vendor, or Employee. Then, in the drop-down list below *that*, choose the specific customer, lead, vendor, or employee associated with the to-do, as shown in Figure 4-17.**

4. **Specify the due date and time.**

   QuickBooks automatically selects the current date, so be sure to choose the date by which you want to complete this to-do. To specify a time, turn on the checkbox to the left of the first Time box, and then set the time.

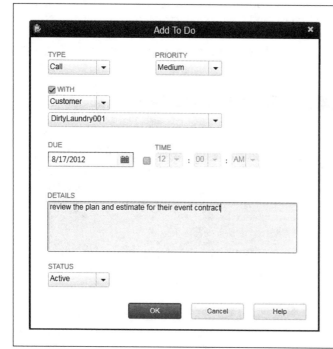

FIGURE 4-17

A to-do doesn't have to be associated with someone. For example, you may just want a reminder to submit your quarterly income tax form. In a situation like that, simply turn off the With checkbox. However, if a to-do is a task or communication with someone, turn on the checkbox, and then specify the person or company it's connected to.

5. **In the Details box, type information about the to-do.**

   By filling in the Details box, you can remind yourself what you want to do or delegate the to-do to someone else.

6. **In the Status box, choose Active.**

   Active represents to-dos that aren't complete yet. Later on, you can edit the to-do and change its status to Done when the task is complete, or Inactive if you no longer need to perform the task.

7. **Click OK to save the to-do.**

   It appears in the To Do List window.

TIP The global To Do List includes all the to-dos for customers, leads, vendors, and employees. To see just the to-dos for a specific person or company, in the Customer, Lead, Vendor, or Employee Center, select the customer, lead, vendor, or employee and then click the To Do's tab at the bottom of the center.

Editing a To-Do

The To Do List window (Figure 4-18) is your one-stop shop for editing to-dos, whether you created them for customers, leads, vendors, or employees. Open this window by choosing Company→To Do List, and then double-click the to-do you want to edit. The fields in the Edit To Do dialog box that opens are the same as the ones in the Add To Do dialog box. Simply make whatever changes you want, and then click OK.

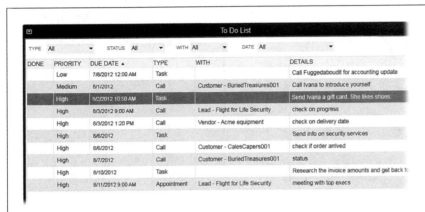

FIGURE 4-18

You can view or edit to-dos in this window. Double-click a to-do to edit it, or view specific to-dos by choosing a value from the Type, Status, With, or Date drop-down list.

NOTE To-dos that you created in QuickBooks 2011 or earlier are automatically set to the Task type, so they aren't associated with a customer, lead, or vendor. If you want to add an association like that, double-click the to-do to open the Edit To Do dialog box, and then choose a type other than Task. Then turn on the With checkbox, and in the drop-down list below it, choose Lead, Customer, or Vendor. In the drop-down list below that, choose the specific customer, lead, or vendor.

Viewing To-Dos

The To Do List window shows all the to-dos that you've created. You can sort them by clicking a column heading, such as Priority, or filter the list by choosing entries in the drop-down lists at the top of the window:

- Choose a **Type** to see only a specific kind of to-do, such as calls you need to make.

- To focus on tasks that aren't complete yet, in the **Status** drop-down list, choose Active.

- To see to-dos for just leads, customers, vendors, or employees, choose a category in the **With** drop-down list.

- To see to-dos that are due during a specific time period, choose the period in the **Date** drop-down list.

NOTE To-dos also appear in the QuickBooks Calendar (page 33). And, if you display the left icon bar (View→Left Icon Bar), you can see any to-dos that are due today by clicking the Do Today shortcut.

Setting Up Items

Whether you build houses, sell gardening tools, or tell fortunes on the Internet, you'll probably use *items* in QuickBooks to represent the products and services you sell. But to QuickBooks, things like subtotals, discounts, and sales tax are items, too. In fact, *nothing* appears in the body of a QuickBooks sales form (such as an invoice) unless it's an item.

Put another way, to create invoices (which you'll learn how to do in Chapter 10), sales receipts, or other sales forms in QuickBooks, you need customers *and* items. So, now that you've got your chart of accounts and customers set up in QuickBooks, it's time to dive into items.

This chapter begins by helping you decide whether your business is one of the few that doesn't need items at all. But if your organization is like most and uses business forms like invoices, sales receipts, and so on, the rest of the chapter will teach you how to create, name, edit, and manage the items you add to forms. You'll learn how to use items in invoices and other forms in the remaining chapters of this book.

What Items Do

For your day-to-day work with QuickBooks, items save time and increase consistency on sales forms. Here's the deal: Items form the link between what you sell (and buy) and the income, expense, and other types of accounts in your chart of accounts. When you create an item, you describe what the item is, how much you pay for it, how much you sell it for, and the accounts to which you post the corresponding income, expense, cost of goods sold, and asset value. For example, say you charge $75 an hour for the bookkeeping service you provide, and you want that income to show up in your Financial Services income account. So you create an item for bookkeeping and associate it with your income account. That way, when you add the item to a sales form, QuickBooks automatically multiplies the price per hour by the number of hours to calculate the full charge, and then posts the income to your Financial Services account. You also create items for other stuff you add to sales forms, like discounts, shipping charges, and subtotals.

Items also make it easy to look at your company's finances from different perspectives. You can set up your chart of accounts to cover what you show on your financial statements (page 467), which are usually summarized to include only what your bankers or other interested parties need to know. At the same time, items (and classes, which you'll learn about on page 150) let you track income and expenses to the level of detail you want. For example, you might set up two income accounts: one for services and one for products. However, you can create items for every type of service and product you sell.

When it's time to analyze how your business is doing, items shine. QuickBooks has built-in reports based on items, which show the dollar value of sales or the number of inventory units you've sold. (To learn how to use inventory reports, see page 507.) Other item-based reports are described throughout this book. You can work out which accounts to assign items to on your own or with the help of your accountant (a good idea if you're new to bookkeeping), and then specify those accounts in your items, as shown in Figure 5-1. QuickBooks remembers these assignments from then on.

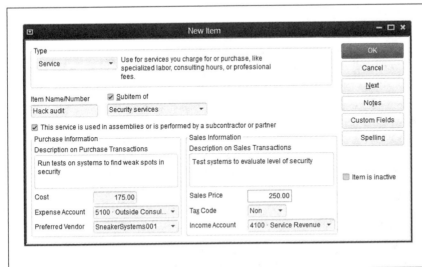

FIGURE 5-1

You'd be bound to make mistakes if you had to enter item details each time you added an entry to an invoice. By setting up an item in the New Item window, you can make sure you use the same information on sales forms each time you sell or buy that item. When the inevitable exception to the rule arises, you can edit the item info that QuickBooks fills in on the sales form.

When You Don't Need Items

Without items, you can't create any type of sales form in QuickBooks, including invoices, statements, sales receipts, credit memos, and estimates. But if you don't use sales forms, you don't need items. Not many organizations operate without sales forms, but here are a few examples of ones that do:

- Old Stuff Antiques sells junk—er, antiques—on consignment. Kate, the owner, doesn't pay for the pieces; she just displays them in her store. When she sells a consignment item, she writes paper sales receipts. When she receives her cut from the seller, she deposits the money in her checking account.

- Tony owns a tattoo parlor specializing in gang insignias. He doesn't care how many tattoos he creates and—for safety's sake—he doesn't want to know his customers' names. All Tony does is deposit the cash he receives upon completing each masterpiece.

- Dominic keeps the books for his charity for iceberg-less penguins. The charity accepts donations of money and fish, and it doesn't sell any products or perform services to earn additional income. He deposits the monetary donations into the charity's checking account and enters each deposit in QuickBooks. He keeps track of the donors' contributions and fish inventory in a spreadsheet.

Should You Track Inventory with Items?

If your business is based solely on selling services, you can skip this section entirely. But if you sell products, it'll help you understand your options.

You can handle products in two ways: by stocking and tracking inventory or by buying products only when work for your customers requires them. The system you use affects the types of items you create in QuickBooks.

When you buy products specifically for customers, you need items, but you don't have to track the quantity on hand. In this case, you create *Non-inventory Part items*, which you'll learn about shortly. For example, general contractors work on various types of projects, so they usually purchase the materials they need for a specific job and charge the customer for those materials. Because general contractors don't keep materials in stock, they don't have to track inventory and can use Non-inventory Part items.

On the other hand, specialized contractors like plumbers install the same kinds of pipes and fittings over and over. These contractors often purchase parts and store them in a warehouse, selling them to their customers as they perform jobs. These warehoused parts should be set up as *Inventory Part items* (page 129) in QuickBooks. When you use QuickBooks' inventory feature, the program keeps track of how many products you have on hand, increasing the number as you purchase them and decreasing the number when you sell them to customers.

Because tracking inventory requires more effort than buying only the materials you need, use the following guidelines to determine whether your business should track inventory:

- **Track inventory if you keep products in stock to resell to customers**. If your company stocks faux pony bar stools to resell to customers, those stools are inventory. By tracking inventory, you know how many units you have on hand, how much they're worth, and how much money you made on the stools you've sold.

  On the other hand, the faux pony mouse pads you keep in the storage closet for your employees are business supplies. Most companies don't bother tracking inventory for supplies like these, which they consume in the course of running their business.

- **Track inventory if you want to know when to reorder products so you don't run out**. If you sell the same items over and over, keeping your shelves stocked means more sales (because the products are ready to ship out as soon as an order comes in). QuickBooks can remind you when it's time to reorder a product.

- **Don't track inventory if you purchase products specifically for jobs or customers**. If you special-order products for customers or buy products for specific jobs, you don't need to track inventory. After you deliver the special order or complete the job, your customer has taken and paid for products, and you simply have to account for the income and expenses you incurred.

- **Don't track inventory if you rent equipment to customers**. For leases and rentals, you receive income for the rental or lease of assets you own. In this case, you can show the value of the for-rent products as an asset in QuickBooks and the rental income as a Service item (page 123), so you don't need Inventory Part items.

Your business model might dictate that you track inventory. However, QuickBooks' inventory-tracking feature has some limitations. For example, it lets you store only up to 14,500 items. If you answer yes to any of the following questions, QuickBooks isn't the program to use to handle the products you sell:

- **Do you sell products that are unique?** In the business world, tracking inventory is meant for businesses that sell commodity products, such as electronic equipment, and stock numerous units of each product. If you sell unique items, such as fine art or compromising Polaroid photos, you'd eventually hit QuickBooks' 14,500 item limit. For such items, consider using a spreadsheet to track the products you have on hand.

TIP Here's one way to track unique products using QuickBooks: When you sell your unique handicrafts, record the sales in QuickBooks using generic Non-inventory Part items. For example, use an item called Oil Painting on the sales receipts for the artwork you sell and fill in more specific information about the painting in the sales receipt's Description field.

- **Do you manufacture the products you sell out of raw materials?** QuickBooks inventory can't follow materials as they wend through a manufacturing process or track inventory in various stages of completion.

> **NOTE** QuickBooks Premier and Enterprise editions can track inventory for products that require *some* assembly. For instance, if you create Wines from Around the World gift baskets using the wine bottles in your store, you can build an Inventory Assembly item (page 130) out of wine and basket Inventory Part items. The box on page 133 explains another way to track assembled inventory.

- **Do you value your inventory by using a method other than average cost?** QuickBooks Pro and Premier calculate inventory value by average cost. If you want to use other methods—like last in, first out (LIFO) or first in, first out (FIFO)—you can export inventory data to a spreadsheet program and then calculate inventory cost there (page 651). Or you can upgrade to QuickBooks Enterprise and subscribe to Intuit's Advanced Inventory add-on service (which costs extra.)

- **Do you use a point-of-sale system to track inventory?** Point-of-sale inventory systems often blow QuickBooks' inventory tracking out of the water. If you forgo QuickBooks' inventory feature, you can periodically update your QuickBooks file with the value of your inventory from the point-of-sale system.

> **NOTE** If you like the point-of-sale idea but don't have a system yet, consider Intuit's QuickBooks Point of Sale, an integrated, add-on product for retail operations that tracks store sales, customer info, and inventory. Head to *http://pointofsale.intuit.com* for more info.

You don't have to use QuickBooks' inventory feature at all if you don't want to. For example, if you perform light manufacturing, you can track the value of your manufactured inventory in a database or other program. You can then periodically add journal entries (page 451) to QuickBooks to show the value of in-progress and completed inventory.

> **TIP** The answer to your inventory dilemma could be an add-on program that tracks inventory *and* keeps QuickBooks informed. One of the best is FishBowl Inventory (*www.fishbowlinventory.com*).

Planning Your Items

Setting up items in QuickBooks is a lot like shopping at a grocery store. If you need only a few things, you can shop without a list. Similarly, if you're going to use just a few QuickBooks items, you don't need to write them down before you start creating them. But if you use dozens or even hundreds of items, planning your Item List can save you lots of frustration.

If you jumped straight to this section, now's the time to go back and read "Should You Track Inventory with Items?" on page 113, which helps you with your first decision: whether to use items that represent services, inventory, or non-inventory products.

By deciding how to name and organize your items before you create them, you won't waste time editing and reworking existing items to fit your new naming scheme. Read on to learn what you should consider before creating items in QuickBooks.

Generic or Specific?

Conservation can be as important with QuickBooks' items as it is for the environment. QuickBooks Pro and Premier can hold no more than 14,500 items, which is a problem if you sell unique products, such as antiques, or products that change frequently, such as current clothing styles for teenagers. Once you use an item in a transaction, you can't delete that item, so you could end up with lots of items you no longer use (see page 145). By planning how specific your items will be, you can keep your Item List lean.

For instance, a generic item such as Top can represent a girl's black Goth T-shirt one season and a white, poplin button-down shirt the next. Generic items have their limitations, though, so use them only if necessary. For example, you can't track inventory properly when you use generic items. QuickBooks might show that you have 100 tops in stock, but that doesn't help when your customers are clamoring for white button-downs and you have 97 black Goth T-shirts. In addition, the information you store with a generic item won't match the specifics of each product you sell. So, when you add generic items to an invoice or a sales form, you'll have to edit a few fields, such as Description or Price, as shown in Figure 5-2.

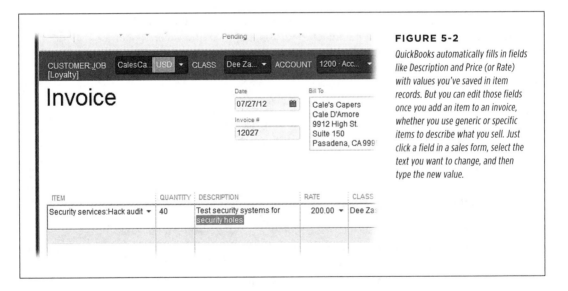

FIGURE 5-2

QuickBooks automatically fills in fields like Description and Price (or Rate) with values you've saved in item records. But you can edit those fields once you add an item to an invoice, whether you use generic or specific items to describe what you sell. Just click a field in a sales form, select the text you want to change, and then type the new value.

Naming Items

Brevity and recognizability are equally desirable characteristics in item names. Short names are easier to type and manage, but they can be unintelligible. Longer names take more effort to type and manage but are easier to decipher. Decide ahead of time which type of name you prefer, and stick with it as you create items.

QuickBooks encourages brevity because an item's name can be no more than 31 characters. If you sell only a handful of services, you can name your items the same things you call them. For instance, for a tree service company, names like Cut, Limb, Trim, Chip, and Haul work just fine. But if your Item List runs into the hundreds or thousands, some planning is in order. Here are some factors to consider when naming items:

- **Aliases**. Create a pseudonym to represent the item. For a carpet company, "Install standard" could represent the installation along with vacuuming and hauling waste, while "Install deluxe" could include the standard installation *plus* moving and replacing furniture. You can include the details in the item description.

- **Sort order**. In the Item List window (to open it, on the Home page, click Items & Services), QuickBooks sorts items first by type and then in alphabetical order. If you want your items to appear in some logical order in drop-down lists (like an invoice item table, for instance), pay attention to the order of characteristics in your item names. Other Service items beginning with the intervening letters of the alphabet would separate "Deluxe install" and "Standard install." By naming your installation items "Install deluxe" and "Install standard" instead, they'll show up in your Item List one after the other.

- **Abbreviation**. If you have to compress a great deal of information into an item name, you'll have to abbreviate. For example, suppose you want to convey all the things you do when you install a carpet, including installing tack strips, padding, and carpet; trimming carpet; vacuuming; and hauling waste. That's more than the 31 characters (including spaces) you have to work with. Poetic won't describe it, but something like "inst trim vac haul" says it all in very few characters. The box on page 118 suggests two other ways to identify complicated items.

Other Ways to Identify Items

If you want to keep item names lean but still include detailed information, look to these two item features:

- **Descriptions**. Items have fields for both names and descriptions. When you create an invoice, you choose the item's name from a drop-down list, but the invoice that the customer sees shows the item's description. You can keep your item names brief by putting the details in the Description field, which, for all practical purposes, can hold an unlimited amount of text.

- **Group**. Instead of creating one item that represents several phases of a job, you can create separate items for each phase and then create a *Group item* (page 136) to include those phases on an invoice. For instance, create one item for installing tack strips, padding, and carpet, and then create additional items for vacuuming, hauling, and moving and replacing furniture. Then create a Group item that contains all the individual service items included in a carpet-installation job. That way, when you add that Group item to an invoice, QuickBooks adds each item to a line on the invoice.

NOTE Construction companies in particular can forgo long hours of item data entry by using third-party estimating programs. Construction-estimating programs usually include thousands of entries for standard construction services and products. If you build an estimate with a program that integrates with QuickBooks, you can import that estimate into QuickBooks and then sit back and watch as it automatically adds all the items in the estimate to your Item List. To find such QuickBooks-integrated programs, go to *http://marketplace.intuit. com*. On the menu bar, click Find Software→Find Solutions by Industry. Then, on the By Industry tab, choose Construction/Contractors.

Subitems

If you keep all your personal papers in one big stack, you probably have a hard time finding everything from birth certificates to tax forms to bills and receipts. If you've got one big list of items in QuickBooks, you're in no better shape. To locate items more easily, consider designing a hierarchy of higher-level items (*parents*) and one or more levels of subitems, as shown in Figure 5-3. The box on page 119 explains how to make sure you have items for every purpose.

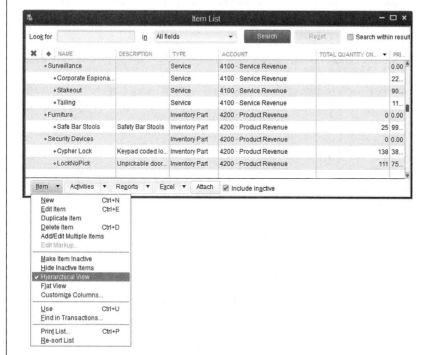

FIGURE 5-3

The Item List window's Hierarchical View (shown here) indents subitems, making it easy to differentiate the items that you use to categorize the list from the items you actually sell. To check which view you're seeing, click the Item button at the bottom of the window to display the menu shown here. If you work with long lists of subitems, the parent item might end up off the screen. To keep the hierarchy of items visible at all times, choose Flat View, wherein QuickBooks uses colons to separate the names of each level of item and subitem.

For example, a landscaping business might create top-level items for trees, shrubbery, cacti, and flower bulbs. Within the top-level tree item, the landscaper might create subitems for several species: maple, oak, elm, sycamore, and dogwood. Additional levels of subitems can represent categories such as size (seedling, established, and mature, say).

WORD TO THE WISE

Catchall Items

When you develop a hierarchy of parent items and subitems, eventually someone in your company will run across a service or product that doesn't fit any of the existing subitems. The solution? A catchall subitem to give these outcasts a home. If you assign a transaction to the parent item, QuickBooks automatically creates a subitem called "Other" for these catch basins. For example, if you have a parent item called Security Services, you'd get a subitem like Security Services-Other.

Catchall items can act as holding pens while you figure out which item you should use. They're also an easy way to look for transactions that should be reassigned to a different subitem. For instance, you can create a transaction by using the Security Services-Other item, and then change the item in the transaction later (page 325) when you've identified (or created) the correct item.

◼ Creating Items

The best time to create items is *after* you've created your accounts but *before* you start billing customers. Each item links to an account in your chart of accounts, so creating items goes quicker if you don't have to stop to create accounts as well.

Similarly, you can create items while you're in the midst of creating an invoice, but you'll find that creating items goes much faster when you create several at once. How long it takes to create items depends on how many you need. If you sell only a few services, a few minutes should do it. On the other hand, construction companies that need thousands of items often forgo hours of data entry by importing items from third-party programs (see page 646).

Creating Multiple Items

The Add/Edit Multiple List Entries feature is a real time-saver when you want to populate your Item List. If you're comfortable working with Excel, you can set up an Excel spreadsheet and fill in values for all your items by using that program's tools and shortcuts. Then you can paste that data from Excel into the table in the Add/Edit Multiple List Entries window. This feature works for Customer, Vendor, Employee, and Item lists; page 94 gives you the full scoop on how to use it.

Here's how you get started with using Add/Edit Multiple List Entries to fill in items:

1. **On the QuickBooks Home page, in the Company panel, click Items & Services.**

   The Item List window opens.

2. **Right-click the Item List window, and then choose Add/Edit Multiple Items from the shortcut menu. (Alternatively, at the bottom of the window, click Item→Add/Edit Multiple Items.)**

   The Add/Edit Multiple List Entries window opens. The List box is set to Service Items or the type of item you selected the last time you used this feature. The table initially displays the active items for the type selected in the List box (Figure 5-4), which makes sense because you typically want to add or edit items that you're currently using. To filter the list (page 95) to show specific kinds of items, in the View drop-down menu, choose the kind you want.

3. **If you want to work with a different type of item, in the List drop-down menu, choose Service Items, Inventory Parts, or Non-inventory Parts.**

   The columns that you see in the table vary depending on the type of item you select and the preferences you've turned on. For example, for Service items, the table includes Item Name, Subitem of, Sales Price, Income Account columns, and Sales Tax Code if you've turned on the sales tax preference (page 628.) If you've turned on the preference for inventory (page 615) and choose Inventory Parts, you see a COGS Account column, among others. If you want to change the columns that appear in the table or their order, click the Customize Columns button on the right side of the window.

4. **Switch to Excel and copy the data you want from your spreadsheet.**

   The order of the columns in the Add/Edit Multiple List Entries table and your Excel spreadsheet have to match or you'll see errors when you paste the data (which you'll do in the next step). To fix that, you can reorder the columns in either Excel or QuickBooks. To reorder them in QuickBooks, click the Customize Columns button to insert or remove columns, or change their order to match that of your Excel spreadsheet. See page 96 to learn how. When the programs' columns match, in Excel, select the information you want to paste into Quick-Books and then press Ctrl+C to copy it.

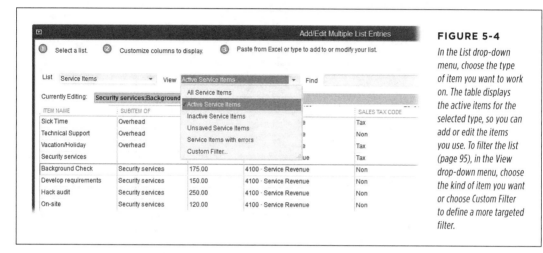

FIGURE 5-4

In the List drop-down menu, choose the type of item you want to work on. The table displays the active items for the selected type, so you can add or edit the items you use. To filter the list (page 95), in the View drop-down menu, choose the kind of item you want or choose Custom Filter to define a more targeted filter.

5. **Back in the Add/Edit Multiple List Entries window, click the first blank Item Name cell and then press Ctrl+V (or choose Edit→Paste).**

   QuickBooks pastes the copied data into the selected cell and then continues pasting into the cells below and to the right of the selected cell. Cells that contain data with errors, such as invalid values or list entries that don't exist in Quick-Books, appear in red text. See page 100 to learn how to correct these errors.

TIP If you want to paste parent and subitems into the Add/Edit Multiple List Entries table, paste the top-level items first, followed by a separate paste pass for each subsequent level of your Item List. That way, the parent items you need will already exist so the new entries will paste in without errors.

Creating Individual Items

Each type of item has its own assortment of fields, but the overall process of creating an item is the same for every type. With the following procedure under your belt, you'll find that you can create many of your items without further instruction. (If you *do* need help with fields for a specific type of item, read the sections that follow to learn what each field does.)

1. **On the QuickBooks Home page, click Items & Services (or, choose Lists→Item List) to open the Item List window.**

   When you first display the Item List, QuickBooks sorts the entries by type. The sort order for the item types isn't alphabetical—it's the order that types appear in the Type drop-down list, as shown in Figure 5-5. You can change the list's sort order by clicking a column header.

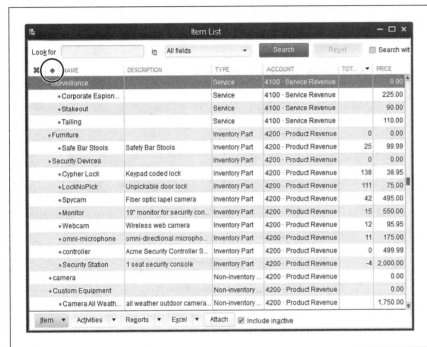

FIGURE 5-5

QuickBooks lists items in alphabetical order within each item type. You can change the sort order of the list by clicking a column heading. If you click the heading again, QuickBooks toggles the list between ascending and descending order. To return the list to being sorted by item type, click the diamond to the left of the column headings (circled), which appears anytime the list is sorted by a column other than Type.

2. **Open the New Item window by pressing Ctrl+N or clicking Item→New.**

   QuickBooks opens the New Item window and selects the Service item type (page 123) in the Type drop-down list.

3. **To create a Service item, just press Tab to proceed with naming the item. To create any other type of item, choose it in the Type drop-down list.**

   Some item types won't appear in the list if you haven't turned on the corresponding feature. For example, the Inventory Item type doesn't appear unless you've turned on inventory tracking, as described on page 615.

4. **In the Item Name/Number box, type a unique identifier for the item.**

   For example, if you opt for long and meaningful names, you might type *Install carpet and vacuum*. For a short name, you might type *Inst Carpt*. See page 117 for guidelines on naming items.

5. **To make this item a subitem, turn on the "Subitem of" checkbox and then choose the item that you want to act as the parent.**

If the parent item already exists, simply choose it from the "Subitem of" drop-down list. To create the parent *while* creating the subitem, choose <Add New> at the top of the "Subitem of" list, and then jump back to step 3 to begin the parent-creation process.

> **NOTE** Subitems and parents have to be the same type, and you can't create subitems for Subtotal, Group, or Payment items.

6. **Complete the other fields as described in the following sections for the type of item you're creating (page 123, page 129, and so on).**

QuickBooks will use the info you enter to fill in fields on sales forms. For example, it uses the sales price you enter on an invoice when you sell some units. If the sales price changes each time, simply leave the item's sales price field (which is labeled Rate, Price, or Sales Price depending on the type of item and the item's settings) set to zero. That way, QuickBooks doesn't fill in a price so you can type one in each time you sell the item. (Even if you set up a value for an item, you can overwrite it whenever you use the item on a sales form.)

> **NOTE** You have to assign an account to every item, whether it's a parent or not.

7. **If you have additional items to create, click Next to save the current item and start another.** If you want to save the item you just created and close the New Item window, click OK.

If you've made mistakes in several fields or need more information before you can complete an item, click Cancel to throw away the current item and close the New Item window.

Service Items

Services are intangible things that you sell, like time or the output of your brain. For example, you might sell consulting services, Internet connection time, haircuts, or Tarot card readings. In construction, services represent phases of construction, which makes it easy to bill customers based on progress and to compare actual values to estimates.

Suppose you run a telephone answering service. You earn income when your customers pay you for the service. You pay salaries to the people who answer the phones, regardless of whether you have two service contracts or 20. For this business, you earn income with your service, but your costs don't link to the income from specific customers or jobs.

In some companies, such as law practices, the partners get paid based on the hours they bill, so the partners' compensation is an expense associated directly with the firm's income. Services that you farm out to a subcontractor work similarly. If you offer a 900 number for gardening advice, you might have a group of freelancers who field the calls and whom you pay only for their time on the phone. You still earn income for the service you sell, but you also have to pay the law-practice partners or the subcontractors to do the work. The partners' or subcontractors' cost relates to the income for that service. Conveniently, QuickBooks displays different fields depending on whether a service has costs associated with income.

The mighty Service item single-handedly manages *all* types of services, whether you charge by the hour or by the service, with associated expenses or without. This section describes the fields you fill in when creating Service items.

Service Items Without Associated Costs

Here's how the fields in the New Item (or Edit Item) window work when you're creating a Service item that *doesn't* include purchasing services from someone else (that is, when you leave the "This service is used in assemblies or is performed by a subcontractor or partner" checkbox turned off, as shown in Figure 5-6):

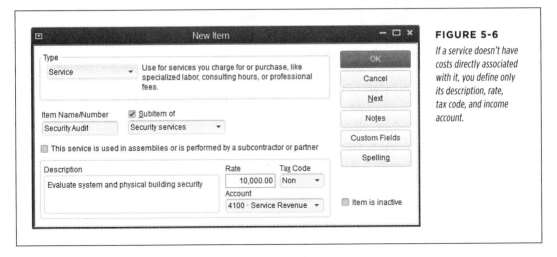

FIGURE 5-6

If a service doesn't have costs directly associated with it, you define only its description, rate, tax code, and income account.

- **Description.** Type a detailed explanation of the service in this box. This text appears on invoices and sales forms, so use terms that your customers will understand.

- **Rate.** Type how much you charge customers for the service. You can enter a flat fee or a charge per unit of time. For example, you might charge $9.95 for unlimited gardening advice per call, charge by the minute, or charge $200 for unlimited calls each month.

When you add the item to an invoice, QuickBooks multiplies the quantity by the sales price to calculate the total charge. If the cost varies, leave the Rate or Sales Price field set to 0; you can then enter the price when you create an invoice or other sales form. If the rate or price is often the same, fill in the most common rate. Then, when you add the item to an invoice, you can modify the rate whenever you want to use a different amount. For services that carry a flat fee, use a quantity of *1* on your invoices.

NOTE QuickBooks multiplies the cost and sales prices by the quantities you add to sales forms. Be sure to define the cost and sales price in the same units (by hour or carton, for example) so that QuickBooks calculates your income and expenses correctly.

- **Tax Code.** Most Service items are nontaxable, so you'll choose *Non* here more often than not. (This field appears only if you've turned on the sales tax feature, as described on page 628.)

- **Account.** Choose the income account to which you want to post the income for this service, whether it's a catchall income account for all your services or one you created specifically for this service.

Service Items with Associated Costs

If you sell services that have associated costs, such as when you purchase services from someone else, you have to set up the service item to include those costs. The key to displaying the fields you need to fill in when you purchase services from someone else is the "This service is used in assemblies or is performed by a sub-contractor or partner" checkbox, shown in Figure 5-7. In addition to the basics like Item Name/Number and "Subitem of," here are the fields you fill in when an item *does* have associated costs:

- **Description on Purchase Transactions.** Type in the description that you want to appear on the bills or purchase orders you issue to subcontractors.

- **Cost.** Enter what you pay for the service, which can be an hourly rate or a flat fee. For example, if a subcontractor performs the service and receives $175 for each hour of work, type *175* in this field. If the cost varies, leave this field set to 0; you can then enter the actual cost when you create a purchase order.

- **Expense Account.** Choose the account to which you want to post what you pay for the service. If a subcontractor does the work, choose a Cost of Goods Sold account or an expense account for subcontractor or outside consultants' fees. If a partner or owner performs the work, choose a Cost of Goods Sold account or an expense account for service-related costs.

- **Preferred Vendor.** If you almost always use the same vendor for a service, choose that vendor in this drop-down list. That way, if you don't select a vendor when you first create a purchase order, QuickBooks selects that vendor when you add this Service item. However, if you purchase the item from several vendors, leave this field blank.

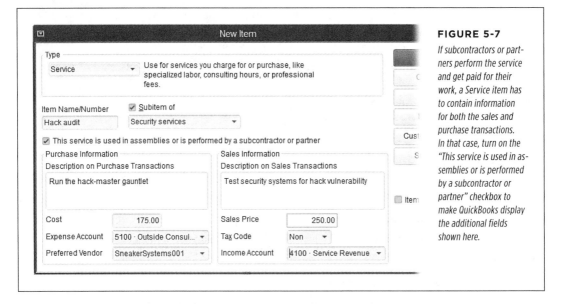

FIGURE 5-7

If subcontractors or partners perform the service and get paid for their work, a Service item has to contain information for both the sales and purchase transactions. In that case, turn on the "This service is used in assemblies or is performed by a subcontractor or partner" checkbox to make QuickBooks display the additional fields shown here.

- **Description on Sales Transactions.** This field appears on sales forms like invoices and sales receipts. QuickBooks copies the text from the Description on Purchase Transactions box into this field. However, if your vendors use technical jargon that your customers wouldn't recognize, you can change the text in this box to something more meaningful.

- **Sales Price.** Type in how much you charge customers for the service, as you would in the Rate field for a Service item that you don't purchase from someone else (page 124).

- **Tax Code.** Most Service items are nontaxable, so you'll choose *Non* here most of the time. (This field appears only if you've turned on QuickBooks' sales tax feature, as described on page 628.)

- **Income Account.** Choose the income account to which you want to post the income for this service, whether it's a catchall income account for all services or one you created specifically for this service.

Subitems for Nonprofits

Service items are the workhorses of nonprofit organizations. Donations, dues, grants, and money donated in exchange for services all fall into the Service-item bucket. The only time you'll need another type of item is if you raise money by selling products from inventory (calendars and notecards, for instance).

For nonprofits without heavy reporting requirements, you can make do with one item for each type of revenue you receive (grants, donations, dues, fundraising campaigns), with a link to the corresponding income account. For example, a Service subitem called Donation would link to an income account called Donations.

But subitems also come in handy for categorizing the money you receive for different types of services, particularly when donors give money and want to see detailed financial reports in return. You don't make the big subitem-related decision yourself—the organizations that contribute do. If your organization receives money from the government or a foundation

with specific reporting requirements, you can set up subitems and classes (see page 150) to track the details you need for the reports they require. Here's an example of an Item List that differentiates types of income and different donors:

Grant
  Government
  Corporate
Donation
  Regular
  Matching
Membership Dues
  Individual
  Corporate
  Contributing
  Platinum Circle

Product Items

Products you sell to customers fall into three categories: ones you keep in inventory, ones you special order, and ones you assemble. QuickBooks can handle inventory as long as your company passes the tests on page 114. Likewise, products you purchase specifically for customers or jobs are no problem. And as explained on page 130, QuickBooks can handle lightly assembled products like gift baskets or gizmos made from widgets—but you'll need QuickBooks Premier edition to do more than that.

Choose one of these three QuickBooks item types for the products you sell:

- **Inventory Part.** Use this type for products you purchase and keep in stock for resale. Retailers and wholesalers are the obvious examples of inventory-based businesses, but other types of companies like building contractors may track inventory, too. With inventory parts, you can track how many you have, how much they're worth, and when you should reorder. The box on page 128 explains how to keep track of the financial details for inventory.

NOTE You can create Inventory Part items only if you turn on QuickBooks' inventory feature as described on page 615.

- **Non-inventory Part.** If you purchase products specifically for a job or customer and don't track how many products you have on hand, use Non-inventory Part items. Unlike an Inventory Part item, this type has at most two account fields: one for income you receive when you sell the part, and another for the expense of purchasing the part in the first place.

- **Inventory Assembly.** This item type (available only in QuickBooks Premier and Enterprise editions) is perfect when you sell products built from your inventory items. For example, say you stock wine bottles and related products like corkscrews and glasses, and you assemble them into gift baskets. With an Inventory Assembly item, you can track the number of gift baskets you have on hand, as well as the individual inventory items. You can also assign a different price for the gift basket than the total of the individual products, as described in the box on page 130. (The box on page 135 describes another way to track products you build from other items.)

ACCOUNTING CONCEPTS

Following the Inventory Money Trail

Inventory Part items are the most complicated type of item because, in accounting, the cost of inventory moves from place to place as you purchase, store, and finally sell your products. Table 5-1 and the following steps show the path that the inventory money trail takes:

1. You spend money to purchase faux pony chairs to sell in your store. Your checking or credit card account shows the money you pay going out the door.

2. Because you spent money to purchase inventory, which has value, it represents an asset of your company. Hence, the value of the purchased inventory appears in an inventory asset account in your chart of accounts.

3. When you sell some chairs, QuickBooks posts the sale to an income account (such as Product Income) and the money your customer owes you shows up in Accounts Receivable.

4. The chairs leave inventory, so QuickBooks deducts the value of the chairs you sold from the inventory asset account. The value of the sold chairs has to go somewhere, so QuickBooks posts it to a *cost of goods sold account*.

In the financial reports you create, the gross profit of your company represents your income minus the cost of goods sold (in this example, $1,000 income minus $500 cost of goods sold for $500 gross profit). As soon as you turn on QuickBooks' inventory-tracking preference (page 615), the program adds cost of goods sold and inventory asset accounts to your chart of accounts.

TABLE 5-1 *Following inventory money through accounts*

TRANSACTION	ACCOUNT	DEBIT	CREDIT
Buy inventory	Checking Account		$500
Buy inventory	Inventory Asset	$500	
Sell inventory	Product Income		$1,000
Sell inventory	Accounts Receivable	$1,000	
Sell inventory	Inventory Asset		$500
Sell inventory	Cost of Goods Sold	$500	

Inventory Part Fields

As described in the box on page 128, money moves between accounts as you buy and sell inventory. Here's how you can use the fields for an Inventory Part item (shown in Figure 5-8) to define your company's inventory money trail and, at the same time, keep track of how much inventory you have:

- **Manufacturer's Part Number.** If you want your purchase orders to include the manufacturer's part number or unique identifier for the product, enter it here.

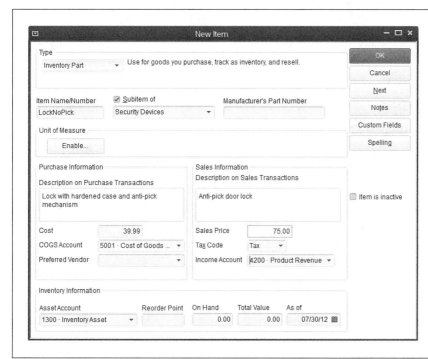

FIGURE 5-8

When you create a new Inventory Part item, QuickBooks includes fields for purchasing and selling that item. The fields in the Purchase Information section show up on purchase orders. The Sales Information section sets the values you see on sales forms, such as invoices and sales receipts. The program simplifies recording your initial inventory by letting you type in the quantity you already have on hand and its value.

NOTE If you use QuickBooks Premier or Enterprise, you'll also see a "Unit of Measure" section, which lets you specify the units the inventory part comes in (bottles, cases, tons, cubic feet, or whatever). When you define units for an inventory part, they appear on invoices, sales forms, and reports. To turn this feature on, in the New Item (or Edit Item) dialog box, click the Enable button and then choose whether you want to assign one or several units of measure to each item. Once this feature is turned on, the New Item and Edit Item dialog boxes display the U/M box in the "Unit of Measure" section. Choose the unit you want to apply from the drop-down list.

- **Description on Purchase Transactions.** Whatever you type here appears on the purchase orders you issue to buy inventory items. Describe the product in terms that the vendor or manufacturer understands; you can use a different and more customer-friendly description for the invoices that customers see.

- **Cost.** Enter what you pay for one unit of the product. QuickBooks assumes you sell products in the same units that you buy them. So, for example, if you purchase four cases of merlot but sell wine by the bottle, enter the price you pay *per bottle* in this field.

- **COGS Account.** Choose the account to which you want to post the cost *when you sell the product.* (COGS stands for "cost of goods sold," which is an account for tracking the underlying costs of the things you sell in order to calculate your gross profit, which you'll learn about on page 469.)

NOTE If you don't have a cost of goods sold account in your chart of accounts, QuickBooks creates one for you as soon as you type the name of your first Inventory Part item in the New Item window.

POWER USERS' CLINIC

Assembling Products

In the Premier and Enterprise editions of QuickBooks, you can create an Inventory Assembly item that gathers Inventory Part items into a new item that you sell as a whole. As shown in Figure 5-9, the New Item window for an assembled item is similar to the one for an inventory part.

The main difference is that you select other inventory items or Inventory Assembly items as the building blocks of your new item. In the "Bill of Materials" section, you specify the components and the quantity of each, and QuickBooks then calculates the total cost of the *bill of materials*—that is, the list of all the materials that make up the assembled product. You set the price you charge for the entire ball of wax in the Sales Price field, regardless of the cost of the individual pieces.

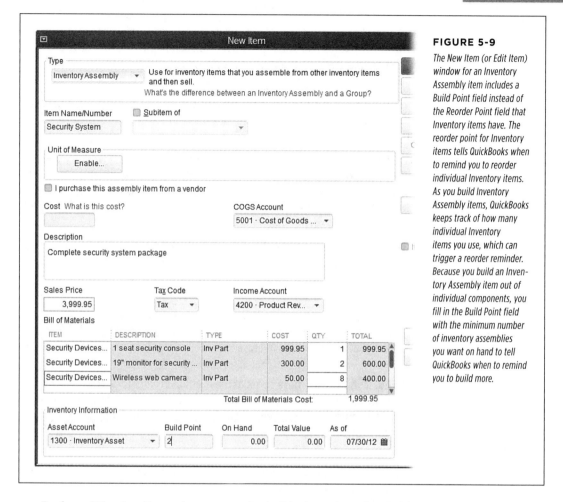

FIGURE 5-9

The New Item (or Edit Item) window for an Inventory Assembly item includes a Build Point field instead of the Reorder Point field that Inventory items have. The reorder point for Inventory items tells QuickBooks when to remind you to reorder individual Inventory items. As you build Inventory Assembly items, QuickBooks keeps track of how many individual Inventory items you use, which can trigger a reorder reminder. Because you build an Inventory Assembly item out of individual components, you fill in the Build Point field with the minimum number of inventory assemblies you want on hand to tell QuickBooks when to remind you to build more.

- **Preferred Vendor.** If you choose a vendor in this drop-down list, QuickBooks selects that vendor when you add this Inventory Part item to a purchase order.

- **Description on Sales Transactions.** QuickBooks automatically copies what you typed in the Description on Purchase Transactions field into this box, so it appears on sales forms like invoices, credit memos, and sales receipts. If your customers wouldn't recognize that description, type a more customer-friendly one here.

- **Sales Price.** Type in how much you charge for the product, and make sure that the Cost field uses the same units. For example, if you sell a bottle of merlot for $15, type *15* in this field and type the price you pay *per bottle* in the Cost field.

- **Tax Code.** When you add an item to an invoice, QuickBooks checks this field to see whether the item is taxable. (QuickBooks comes with two tax codes: *Non* for nontaxable items and *Tax* for taxable items.) Most products are taxable, although groceries are a common exception.

- **Income Account.** This drop-down list includes all the accounts in your chart of accounts. Choose the *income* account for the money you receive when you sell one of these products.

- **Asset Account.** Choose the asset account for the value of the inventory you buy. Suppose you buy 100 bottles of merlot, which are each worth the $8 a bottle you paid; QuickBooks posts $800 into your inventory asset account. When you sell a bottle, QuickBooks deducts $8 from the inventory asset account and adds that $8 to the COGS account.

- **Reorder Point.** Type the quantity on hand that would prompt you to order more. When your inventory hits that number, QuickBooks adds a reminder to reorder this product to the Reminders List (page 621).

> **TIP** If you can receive products quickly, use a lower reorder point to reduce the money tied up in inventory and prevent write-offs due to obsolete inventory. If products take a while to arrive, set the reorder point higher. Start with your best guess and then edit this field as business conditions change.

- **On Hand.** If you already have some of the product in inventory, type the quantity in this field. From then on, if you use QuickBooks' inventory feature (Chapter 19) to record inventory you receive, you can rely on it to accurately post inventory values in your accounts.

- **Total Value.** If you filled in the On Hand field, fill in *this* field with the total value of the quantity on hand. QuickBooks increases the value of your inventory asset account accordingly.

- **As of.** The program uses this date for the transaction it creates in the inventory asset account.

> **NOTE** You can enter values for the last three fields listed above only when you create a new item, not when you edit an existing one. From then on, QuickBooks calculates how many you have on hand based on the numbers you've sold and received.

Turning Parts into Products

Inventory Assembly items don't work the way many manufacturers treat assembled items. Manufacturers and distributors often build batches of assembled items, pool the manufacturing costs for the batch, and then assign a value to the resulting batch of products that goes into inventory. To use this approach in QuickBooks, you track the parts you use to build products (Non-inventory Parts) as *assets* instead of Inventory Assembly items. Here's how it works:

1. As you buy ingredients for a batch, assign the costs (via bills and so on) to an asset account specifically for inventory you build (such inventory is often referred to as WIP for "work in progress").

2. When the batch is complete, make an inventory adjustment to add the items you made to inventory. Choose Vendors→Inventory Activities→Adjust Quantity/Value on Hand.

3. In the "Adjust Quantity/Value on Hand" window, in the Adjustment Type drop-down list, choose "Quantity and Total Value."

4. In the Adjustment Account drop-down list, choose the asset account for your WIP.

5. In the New Quantity column, type the number of items you built from your pool of parts. In the New Value column, type the value of the parts you used.

6. Click Save & Close to save the adjustment, which places the value of the new inventory in your inventory asset account. Because the inventory value matches what you paid for parts, the value adjustment also reduces the WIP asset account's balance to zero, in effect moving the value of your parts from the WIP asset account to your inventory asset account.

You have to know how many units you got out of the parts pool, so this approach works only if you build products in batches. If you constantly manufacture products, you need a program other than QuickBooks to track your inventory. To find one, go to *http://marketplace.intuit.com*. On the menu bar, click Find Software→Find Solutions by Industry. Then, on the By Industry tab, click Manufacturing. Finally, in that same tab under the Manufacturing heading, click Inventory Management.

Non-Inventory Part Fields

You'll need Non-inventory Part items if you use purchase orders to buy supplies or other products that you don't track as inventory. For example, suppose you're a general contractor and you buy materials for a job. When you use Non-inventory Part items, QuickBooks posts the cost of those products to an expense account and the income from selling them to an income account. You don't have to bother with an inventory asset account because you transfer ownership of these products to the customer almost immediately. (See page 298 to learn how to charge your customer for these reimbursable expenses.)

The good news is that Non-inventory Part items use all the same fields as Service items (page 123), although there are a few subtle differences you need to know. Take the following disparities into account when you create Non-inventory Part items:

- **This item is used in assemblies or is purchased for a specific customer:job.** This checkbox goes by a different name than the one in Service items, but its effect is the same. Turn it on when you want to use different values on purchase and sales transactions for items you resell. If the Non-inventory Part item is for office supplies you want to place on a purchase order, then leave this checkbox off because you won't have sales values.

  When this checkbox is on, QuickBooks displays Purchase Information and Sales Information sections, like the ones you saw in Figure 5-7 (page 126). For Non-inventory Part items, choose income and expense accounts you set up specifically for products. Read on to find out what happens when you turn this checkbox off.

- **Account.** If you don't resell this product, leave the "This item is used in assemblies or is purchased for a specific customer:job" checkbox turned off, and you'll see only one Account field. QuickBooks considers the account in this field the expense account for the purchase.

- **Tax Code.** This works exactly the same way as it does for a Service item. Choose Non if the products are nontaxable (like groceries), and Tax if they're taxable. (This field appears only if you've turned on QuickBooks' sales tax feature, as described on page 628.)

> **TIP** Many companies don't bother with purchase orders—forms that record what you order from a vendor—when buying office supplies. But if you want to track whether you receive the supplies you bought, you can create purchase orders for them (page 230). Then use Non-inventory Part items for supplies you add to purchase orders but don't track as inventory. (Remember, purchase orders are non-posting transactions, so they don't affect the balances in your accounts.)

■ Other Types of Items

If a line on a sales form isn't a service *or* a product, read this section to figure out the type of item you need.

Other Charge

The Other Charge item is aptly named because you use it for any charge that isn't quite a service or a product, like shipping charges, finance charges, or bounced check charges. Other Charge items can be percentages or fixed amounts. For example, you might set up shipping charges that are the actual cost of shipping, or calculate shipping as a percentage of the product cost.

If a customer holds back a percentage of your charges until you complete the job satisfactorily, create an Other Charge item for the *retainer* (the portion of your fee that the customer doesn't pay initially). Then, when you create the invoice, enter a negative percentage so QuickBooks deducts the retainer from the invoice total. When your customer approves the job, create another invoice, this time using another Other Charge item, called Retention, to charge the customer for the amount she withheld.

> **TIP** Progress invoices (page 315) are another way to invoice customers for a portion of a job. They're ideal if you invoice the customer based on the percentage of the job you've completed or on the parts of the job that are complete.

Other Charge items can be linked to expenses—or not. Here are your options:

- **A charge linked to expenses.** For Other Charge items, the checkbox for hiding or showing purchase fields is labeled "This item is used in assemblies or is a reimbursable charge." Turn on this checkbox when you want to set the Cost field to what you pay and the Sales Price field to what you charge your customers. You'll see the same sets of fields for purchases and sales as you do for Service and Non-inventory Part items.

- **A charge without associated expenses.** You can create charges that don't link directly to expenses by leaving the "This is used in assemblies or is a reimbursable charge" checkbox turned off. You can then create a percentage, which is useful for calculating shipping based on the value of the products being shipped. With the checkbox off, instead of the Cost and Sales Price fields, you see the "Amount or %" field. If you want to create a charge for a specific amount (like the value for a country club's one-time initiation fee), type a whole or decimal number in this field, as shown in Figure 5-10. To create a percentage-based charge, type a number followed by "%", such as *10%,* in this field instead.

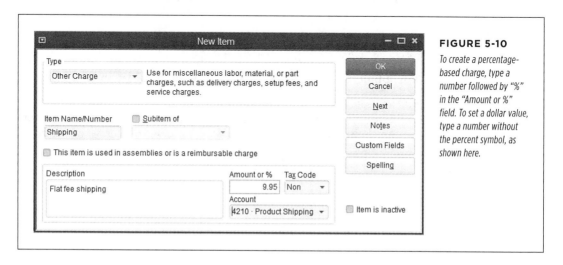

FIGURE 5-10

To create a percentage-based charge, type a number followed by "%" in the "Amount or %" field. To set a dollar value, type a number without the percent symbol, as shown here.

NOTE When you add a percentage-based Other Charge item to an invoice, such as shipping, QuickBooks applies the percentage to the previous line in the invoice. If you want to apply the Other Charge percentage to *several* items, add a Subtotal item (explained next) to the invoice before the Other Charge item.

Subtotal

You'll need a Subtotal item if you apply sales tax to all the products you include on a sales form, discount only some of the items on a form, or calculate shipping based on the value of the order. You need to create only *one* Subtotal item in QuickBooks, because a Subtotal item does just one thing: totals all the amounts for the preceding lines up to the last subtotal or the beginning of the invoice. That means you can add more than one subtotal to an invoice. For example, you can use one Subtotal item to add up the services you sell before applying a preferred-customer discount and a second Subtotal item for product sales when you have to calculate shipping. Because you can't change a Subtotal item's behavior, Subtotal items have just two fields: Item Name/Number and Description. You can type any name and description you wish in these fields, but in practically every case, Subtotal says it all.

Group

Group items are great timesavers, and they're indispensable if you tend to forget things. As the name implies, a Group item represents several related items you often buy or sell together. Create a Group item that contains items that always appear together, such as each service you provide for a landscaping job. That way, when you add the Landscaping Group item to an invoice, QuickBooks automatically adds the Service items for the various phases, such as Excavation, Grading, Planting, and Cleanup.

You can also use a Group item to show or hide the underlying items, which is useful mainly when you create fixed-price invoices (page 288) and you don't want the customer to know how much profit you're making. Here's how you set up a Group item to do these things:

- **Group Name/Number.** Type a name for the group that gives a sense of the individual items within it, such as Security Package.

- **Description.** Type the description that you want to appear on sales forms.

- **Print items in group.** To show all the underlying items on your invoice, turn on this checkbox. Figure 5-11 (top) shows an invoice that prints all the items in a group, and what an invoice looks like when you leave this checkbox turned off (bottom).

FIGURE 5-11

Top: If you turn on the "Print items in group" checkbox when you create a Group item (Security Package, in this example) and then add it to an invoice, QuickBooks adds all the individual items it contains.

Bottom: If you leave the "Print items in group" checkbox turned off when you create the Group item, you'll see the individual items in the Create Invoices window, but the invoice you print to send to the customer will list only the Group item itself, along with the total price for all the items in the group.

Quantity	Description	Rate	Amount
		P.O. No.	Terms	Project
4	Review system security and physical building security	200.00	800.00
8	Install custom-designed security system	150.00	1,200.00
1	1 seat security console	2,000.00	2,000.00T
4	Wireless web camera	95.95	383.80T
5	Wireless web camera	95.95	479.75T
	Full package for security including audit, install, basic equipment		4,863.55

Quantity	Description	Rate	Amount
		P.O. No.	Terms	Project
	Full package for security including audit, install, basic equipment		4,863.55

- **Item.** To add an item to a group, click a blank cell in the Item column, shown in Figure 5-12, and then choose the item you want. You can also create a new item by choosing <Add New> from the drop-down list.

- **Qty.** Group items can include different quantities of items, just like a box of notecards usually includes a few more envelopes than cards. For each item in the group, type how many you typically sell as part of that group. If the quantity of each item varies, type *0* in the Qty cells. You can then specify the quantities on your invoices after you add the Group item.

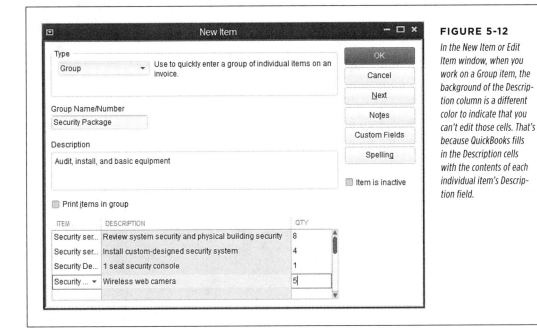

FIGURE 5-12

In the New Item or Edit Item window, when you work on a Group item, the background of the Description column is a different color to indicate that you can't edit those cells. That's because QuickBooks fills in the Description cells with the contents of each individual item's Description field.

Discount

As you know, a discount is an amount you deduct from the standard price you charge, such as a volume discount, customer-loyalty discount, or sale discount. QuickBooks' Discount item calculates deductions like these. By using both Subtotal and Discount items, you can apply discounts to some or all of the charges on a sales form.

Discount items deduct either a dollar amount or a percentage for discounts you apply at the time of sale, such as volume discounts, damaged-goods discounts, or customer-appreciation discounts.

> **NOTE** Early payment discounts don't appear on sales forms because you won't know that a customer pays early until long after that form is complete. You apply early payment discounts in the Receive Payments window, described on page 378.

The fields for a Discount item are similar to those of an Other Charge item with a few small differences:

- **Amount or %.** To deduct a dollar amount, type a positive number (whole or decimal) in this field. To deduct a percentage, type a whole or decimal number followed by "%," like *5.5%*.

- **Account.** Choose the account to which you want to post the discounts you apply. You can post discounts to either income or expense accounts. When you post discounts to an income account, they appear as negative income, so your gross profit reflects what you actually earned after deducting them. Posting discounts to expense accounts, on the other hand, makes your income look better than it actually is. But the discounts increase the amounts in your expense accounts, so your net profit is the same no matter which approach you use.

- **Tax Code.** Most of the time, you choose a taxable code in this field (which only appears if you have the program's sales-tax features turned on) so that QuickBooks applies the discount before it calculates sales tax. For instance, if customers buy products on sale, they pay sales tax on the *sale* price, not the original price. If you choose a nontaxable code in this field, QuickBooks applies the discount after it calculates sales tax. You'll rarely want to do this, though, because it means you'll collect less sales tax from customers than you have to send to the tax agencies.

Payment

When customers send you payments, you can record them in QuickBooks by using the Receive Payments feature (page 371). But if you're in the middle of creating invoices when the checks arrive, you can avoid that task by recording those payments right in your invoices by adding a Payment item. As Figure 5-13 explains, Payment items do more than reduce the amount owed on the invoice.

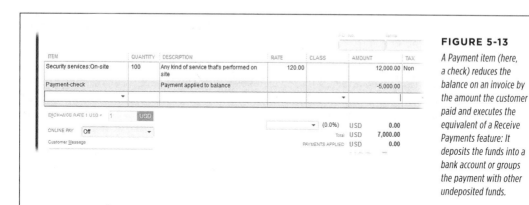

FIGURE 5-13

A Payment item (here, a check) reduces the balance on an invoice by the amount the customer paid and executes the equivalent of a Receive Payments feature: It deposits the funds into a bank account or groups the payment with other undeposited funds.

In addition to the Type, Item Name/Number, and Descriptions fields, Payment items boast fields unlike those for other items. These unique fields tell QuickBooks the method of payment that a customer uses and whether you deposit the funds in a specific bank account or group them with other undeposited funds. For example, you group payments with other undeposited funds if you save up the checks customers send so you can make one trip to deposit them all in your bank. For credit card payments, banks sometimes transfer them into an account individually and sometimes make a single deposit each day with all the charges for that day. Here are the details:

- **Payment Method.** Choose a method such as cash, check, or brand of credit card. That way, when you open the Make Deposits window (page 396) to make a deposit and the "Payments to Deposit" window opens, you can filter pending deposits by payment method.

- **Group with other undeposited funds.** Choose this option if you want to add the payment to other payments you received. That way, when you add this Payment item to a sales form, QuickBooks adds the payment to the list of undeposited funds. To actually complete the deposit of all your payments, choose Banking→Make Deposits (page 397).

- **Deposit To.** If payments flow into an account without any action on your part, such as credit card or electronic payments, choose this option and then choose the appropriate bank account in the drop-down list.

Setting Up Sales Tax

If you don't have to collect and remit sales tax, skip this section and give thanks. Sales taxes aren't much more fun in QuickBooks than they are in real life. QuickBooks has two features for dealing with sales tax: *codes* and *items*:

- **Sales Tax Codes** specify whether an item you sell is taxable—that is, whether QuickBooks calculates sales tax for the item when you add it to a sales form.

- **Sales Tax items**, on the other hand, provide the nitty-gritty detail: They let you calculate and organize sales taxes charged by state and local authorities for the items on your invoices and other sales forms.

This section describes both features and how to use them. If you sell products in a place burdened with multiple sales taxes (state, city, and local, say), you can use a Sales Tax Group item to calculate the total sales tax you have to charge. That way, your sales form shows only the total, but QuickBooks keeps track of what you owe to each agency.

> **NOTE** Before you can dive into the details of setting up sales tax, you need to turn on QuickBooks' sales tax feature. Page 628 explains how.

For most product sales in most areas, you have to keep track of the sales taxes you collect and then send them to the appropriate tax agencies. Labor usually isn't taxable, whereas products usually are. (Groceries are a notable nontaxable exception.) To simplify applying sales tax to the right items or subtotals on your invoices, create separate items for the things you sell that are taxable and the things that are nontaxable. After you assign sales tax codes to the items you create, QuickBooks takes care of calculating the sales tax that's due.

Sales Tax Codes

Sales tax codes are QuickBooks' way of letting you specify whether to apply sales tax. Out of the box, the program's Sales Tax Code List comes with two self-explanatory options: Tax and Non. If you'd like to further refine taxable status (to specify *why* a sale isn't taxable, for example), you can add more choices, as explained on page 142. You can apply tax codes to customers or to individual sales items.

■ ASSIGNING TAX CODES TO CUSTOMERS

Nonprofit organizations and government agencies are usually tax-exempt, meaning they don't have to pay sales taxes. To tell QuickBooks whether a customer pays sales tax, open the Edit Customer window, click the Sales Tax Settings tab, and then fill in the fields as described on page 72. Here's how QuickBooks interprets a customer's tax-exempt status:

- **Nontaxable customer.** When you assign Non or another nontaxable sales tax code to customers (page 72), QuickBooks doesn't calculate sales tax on *any* items you sell to them.

- **Taxable customer.** When you assign Tax or any taxable sales tax code to a customer, the program calculates sales tax only on the taxable items on their invoices and other sales forms.

■ ASSIGNING TAX CODES TO ITEMS

Some items aren't taxable regardless of whether a customer pays sales tax. For example, most services and non-luxury goods like food don't get taxed in most states. If you look carefully at the invoice in Figure 10-7 on page 285, you'll notice Non or Tax to the right of some of the amounts. QuickBooks applies the sales tax only to taxable items to calculate the sales taxes on the invoice.

Items include a Tax Code field so you can designate them as taxable or nontaxable. To assign a tax code to an item, in the Create Item or Edit Item window (page 132), choose a code in the Tax Code drop-down list.

> **NOTE** Taxable and nontaxable items can live together peacefully assigned to the same income account. QuickBooks figures out what to do with sales taxes based on tax codes, tax items, and whether a customer has to pay sales tax.

■ CREATING ADDITIONAL SALES TAX CODES

Tax codes let you mark customers and items as either taxable or nontaxable. The two built-in options, Non and Tax, pretty much cover all possibilities, but you may want to create additional sales tax codes to classify nontaxable customers by their *reason* for exemption (nonprofit, government, wholesaler, out-of-state, and so on). If that's the case, here's how to create additional sales tax codes in QuickBooks:

1. **Choose Lists→Sales Tax Code List.**

   QuickBooks opens the Sales Tax Code List window.

2. **To create a new code, press Ctrl+N or, at the bottom of the window, click Sales Tax Code→New.**

   The New Sales Tax Code window opens.

3. **In the Sales Tax Code box, type a one- to three-character code.**

   For example, type *Gov* for government agencies, *Whl* for wholesalers who resell your products, *Oos* for out-of-state customers, and so on.

4. **In the Description box, add some details about the code.**

   For example, type a description that explains the purpose of the code, like *Government* for Gov.

5. **Choose the Taxable or Non-Taxable option.**

   Sales tax codes are limited to taxable or nontaxable status.

6. **Click Next if you want to add another code.**

   The code you created appears in the Sales Tax Code List window.

7. **When you've added all the codes you want, click OK to close the New Sales Tax Code window.**

As you can see, QuickBooks' sales tax codes don't let you specify a sales tax percentage or note which tax office to send the collected sales taxes to. That's where Sales Tax *items* (described next) come into play.

Sales Tax Items

QuickBooks' built-in sales tax codes are fine for designating taxable status, but you also have to tell QuickBooks the rate and which tax authority levies the tax. If you sell products in more than one state, Sales Tax items are the way to deal with varying tax regulations. (Like the IRS, each tax agency wants to receive the taxes it's due.) To track what you owe, create a Sales Tax item for *each* agency. Also, if you sell products through direct mail, you'll need a Sales Tax item for each state you ship to that charges sales tax.

For example, suppose *both* local and state taxes apply to products you sell in your store. For customers to whom you ship goods in *other* states, sales taxes for those other states apply. You can create separate Sales Tax items for your local tax and the state sales taxes for each state in which you do business. Or, if one tax authority collects several sales taxes, QuickBooks has a Sales Tax Group feature (page 144) to help you collect them all in one shot.

Unlike sales tax codes, which can apply to both customers and products, Sales Tax items apply only to customers, which makes sense, since sales tax rates usually depend on the customer's location. If the customer is in the boonies, you might assign the state Sales Tax item because the customer pays only that one tax. Alternatively, a customer smack in the middle of downtown might have to pay state tax, city tax, and a special district tax. Once you assign Sales Tax items to customers (page 72), QuickBooks automatically fills in the Sales Tax item on your invoices and other sales forms to show the customer the sales taxes they pay.

To create a Sales Tax item, open the Item List (click Items & Services on the Quick-Books Home page) and then press Ctrl+N to open the New Item window (page 124). From the Type drop-down list, choose Sales Tax Item. Then fill in the fields (shown in Figure 5-14) as follows:

- **Sales Tax Name.** Type in a name for the tax. You can use the same identifiers that the tax authority does, or a more meaningful name like Denver City Tax. You can fit up to 31 characters in this field—more than enough to use the four- or five-digit codes that many states use for sales taxes.

- **Description.** If you want QuickBooks to display a description of the tax on your invoices or sales forms, type it here.

- **Tax Rate (%).** Type the percentage rate for the tax here. QuickBooks automatically adds the percent sign, so simply type the decimal number—for example, *4.3* for a 4.3 percent tax rate.

- **Tax Agency.** In this drop-down list, choose the tax authority that collects the sales tax. If you haven't created the vendor for the tax authority yet, choose <Add New> and create a vendor record (page 91).

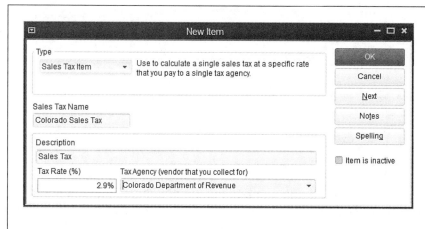

FIGURE 5-14

The "Tax Rate (%)" field sets the percentage of the tax. The Tax Agency drop-down list shows the vendors you've set up, so you can choose the agency to which you remit the taxes. If a tax authority collects the sales taxes for several government entities, a Sales Tax Group is the way to go (see the box on page 144).

Sales Tax Groups

A Sales Tax Group item calculates the total tax for multiple Sales Tax items—perfect when you sell goods in an area rife with state, city, and local sales taxes. The customer sees only the total tax, but QuickBooks tracks how much you owe to each agency. This item works the same way as the Group item (page 136), except that you add Sales Tax items to it instead of Service, Inventory, and Other Charge items.

As shown in Figure 5-15, a Sales Tax Group item applies several Sales Tax items at once. QuickBooks totals the individual tax rates into a total rate for the group, which is what the customer sees on the invoice. For example, businesses in Denver charge a combined sales tax of 7.62 percent, which is made up of a Denver sales tax, the Colorado sales tax, an RTD tax, and special district taxes.

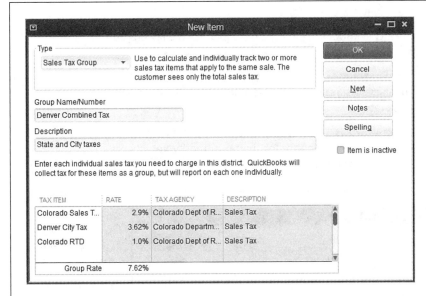

FIGURE 5-15

Before you can create a sales tax group, you first need to create each of the Sales Tax items that you plan to include in it. After you type the name or number of the sales tax group and a description, click the Tax Item cell and then click the drop-down list to choose one of the individual Sales Tax items to include in the group. QuickBooks fills in the rate, tax agency, and description from the Sales Tax item.

Modifying Items

You can change information about an item even if you've already used the item in transactions. The changes you make don't affect *existing* transactions, but when you create *new* transactions using that item, QuickBooks uses the updated information to fill in fields.

In the Item List window (List→Item List), double-click the item you want to edit. QuickBooks opens the Edit Item window. Simply make the changes you want and then click OK. If you want to modify several items at once, use the Add/Edit Multiple List Entries feature (page 94) instead.

NOTE If you change an account associated with an item (like the income account to which sales post), the Account Change dialog box appears when you save the edited item. This dialog box tells you that all future transactions for that item will use the new account. If you also want to change the account on all *existing* transactions using the item, consult with your accountant to make sure that change is OK before you click Yes. Click No to keep the old account on existing transactions that use the item.

Be particularly attentive if you decide to change an item's Type field. You can change only Non-inventory Part or Other Charge items to other item types, and they can be changed into only certain item types: Service, Inventory Part, Inventory Assembly (available only in QuickBooks Premier and Enterprise), Non-inventory Part, or Other Charge. If you conclude from this that you can't change a Non-inventory Part item *back* once you change it to an Inventory part, you're absolutely correct. To prevent type-change disasters, back up your QuickBooks file (see page 179) before switching item types.

TIP Parts that you keep in inventory have value that shows up as an asset of your company, but Non-inventory Parts show up simply as expenses. If you change a Non-inventory Part item to an Inventory Part item, be sure to choose a date in the "As of" field that's *after* the date of the last transaction that uses the item in its non-inventory guise.

◼ Hiding and Deleting Items

Deleting items and hiding them are two totally different actions, although the visible result is the same: QuickBooks doesn't display the items in the Item List window or in item drop-down lists. The only time you'll delete an item is when you create it by mistake and want to eliminate it permanently from the Item List. You can delete an item only if you've never used it in a transaction.

Hiding items doesn't have the same restrictions as deleting them, and offers a couple of advantages to boot. First, when you hide items, they don't appear in the Item List, which prevents you from selecting them accidentally. And unlike deleting, hiding is reversible: You can switch items back to active status if you start selling them again. Suppose you hid the item for bell-bottom hip-huggers in 1974. Decades later, now that '70s retro has become cool again, you can reactivate that item and use it on sales forms. (Of course, you'll probably want to edit the cost and sales price to reflect today's economy.)

Hiding Items

As mentioned above, if you've sold an item in the past, then the only way to remove it from the Item List is to hide it. Hiding items means that your Item List shows only the items you currently use, so you'll scroll less to find the items you want and you're less likely to pick the wrong item by mistake. If you start selling a hidden item again, you can reactivate it so that it appears on the Item List once more.

Here's a guide to hiding and reactivating items:

- **Hide an item.** In the Item List, right-click the item and choose Make Item Inactive from the shortcut menu. The item disappears from the list.

- **View all items, active or inactive.** At the bottom of the Item List window, turn on the "Include inactive" checkbox. QuickBooks displays a column with an X as its heading and shows an X in that column for every inactive item in the list. (The "Include inactive" checkbox is grayed out when all your items are active.)

- **Reactivate a hidden item.** First, turn on the "Include inactive" checkbox to display all items. Then, click the X next to the name of the item you want to reactivate. When you click the X next to a *parent* item, QuickBooks opens the Activate Group dialog box. If you want to reactivate all the subitems as well as the parent, click Yes; to reactivate only the parent item, click No.

If you find that you're constantly hiding items you no longer sell, your Item List might be too specific for your constantly changing product list. For example, if you create 100 items for the clothes that are fashionable for teenagers in May, those items will be obsolete by June. So consider creating more generic items, such as pants, shorts, T-shirts, and bathing suits. You can then reuse these items season after season, year after year, without worrying about running out of room in the Item List, which is limited to 14,500 entries.

> **TIP** To see how many items you have, press F2 to open the Product Information window. In the List Information section on the right side of the window, look for the Total Items figure (you may have to scroll down in the List Information box to see it).

Deleting Items

If you erroneously create an item and catch your mistake immediately, deleting the offender is no sweat. Open the List Item window (Lists→Item List) and then use one of these methods:

- Select the item and then press Ctrl+D.

- Right-click the item and then choose Delete Item on the shortcut menu.

- Select the item, and then head to the main QuickBooks menu bar and choose Edit→Delete Item.

- At the bottom of the Item List window, click Item→Delete Item.

If you try to delete an item that's used in even *one* transaction, QuickBooks warns you that you can't delete it. Say you created an item by mistake and then compounded the problem by inadvertently adding the item to an invoice. When you realize your error and try to delete the item, QuickBooks refuses to oblige. Fortunately, it's pretty easy to run a report to find the transactions that contain the item and then replace it with another item:

1. **Open the Item List window (Lists→Item List), and then right-click the item and choose "QuickReport: <item name>" on the shortcut menu.**

   QuickBooks opens the Item QuickReport report window. Depending on how your report preferences are set, the Modify Report dialog box might open as well.

2. **If the Modify Report dialog box appears, on the Display tab, choose All at the top of the Dates drop-down list and then click OK.**

   If the Modify Report dialog box *doesn't* appear, in the Item QuickReport window, choose All in the Dates drop-down list.

3. **To edit a transaction to remove an item, in the report window, double-click the transaction.**

   Based on the type of transaction you double-click, QuickBooks opens the corresponding dialog box or window. For example, if you double-click an invoice, QuickBooks opens the Create Invoices window and displays the invoice you chose. In the Create Invoices window's Item column, click the cell containing the item you want to delete, click the downward-pointing arrow in that cell, and then choose the replacement item from the Item drop-down list.

4. **To save the transaction with the revised item, click Save & Close.**

   You'll know that you've successfully eliminated the item from all sales transactions when the Item QuickReport window shows no transactions.

TIP To be sure that you've removed all links to the item, in the button bar at the top of the report window, click Refresh to update the report based on the current data in your QuickBooks file.

---

5. **To close the report window, click the X button at its upper right.**

   QuickBooks takes you back to the Item List window.

6. **Finally, back in the Item List window, select the item you want to delete and then press Ctrl+D. In the Delete Item message box, click OK to confirm that you want to get rid of the item.**

   The item disappears from your Item List for good, and you're ready to get back to work.

Setting Up Other QuickBooks Lists

Open any QuickBooks window, dialog box, or form, and you're bound to bump into at least one list. These drop-down lists make it easy to fill in transactions and forms. Creating an invoice? If you pick the customer and job from the Customer:Job List, QuickBooks fills in the customer's address, payment terms, and other fields for you. Selecting payment terms from the Terms List tells the program how to calculate an invoice's due date. If you choose an entry in the Price Level List, QuickBooks calculates the discount you extend to your customers for the goods they buy. Even the products and services you sell to customers come from the Item List, which you learned about in Chapter 5.

In this chapter, you'll discover what many of these lists can do for you and whether you should bother setting them up for your business. Because some lists have their own unique fields (such as the Price Level Type for a Price Level entry), you'll also learn what the various fields do and how to fill them in. If you already know which lists and list entries you want, you can skip to "Creating and Editing List Entries" on page 164 to master the techniques that work for most lists in QuickBooks, such as adding and tweaking entries, hiding entries, and so on. Once you learn how to work with one QuickBooks list, the doors to almost every other list open, too.

NOTE A few lists—such as the Customer, Vendor, and Employee lists—behave a little differently from the ones described in this chapter. Here are the other chapters that provide instructions for working with other QuickBooks lists:

- The **chart of accounts**, which is a list of your bookkeeping accounts, is covered in Chapter 3.

- The **Customer:Job List**, which includes entries for both customers and their jobs, is the topic of Chapter 4.

- The **Vendor List** is also described in Chapter 4.

- The **Item List** helps you fill in invoices and other sales forms with services and products you sell; it's covered in Chapter 5.

- Although the **Sales Tax Code List** appears on the Lists menu, sales tax codes are inextricably linked to how you handle sales tax. The details of setting up this list are described in Chapter 5 on page 141.

- Chapter 12 shows you how to have QuickBooks memorize transactions and store them in the **Memorized Transaction List** so you can reuse them.

- If you turn on QuickBooks' payroll feature (page 619), the Lists menu includes the **Payroll Item List**, which covers the deposits and deductions on your payroll. Payroll items are quite specialized, and you use them only if you use one of QuickBooks' payroll services.

Categorizing with Classes

Classes are the only solution if you want to classify income and expenses by categories that span multiple accounts in your chart of accounts or multiple customers, jobs, and vendors. Classes help you track financial results by categories such as business unit, location, partner, or consultant.

Suppose you have business units that sell to the same customers and rack up the same types of expenses. By creating classes that represent business units in Quick-Books' Class List, you can track the profitability of each unit. Classes also come in handy for tracking the allocation of functional expenses that nonprofit organizations have to show on financial statements.

TIP Before you decide to use classes, use QuickBooks without them for a few weeks or months. If it turns out that you can generate all the reports you need *without* classes, then don't burden yourself with another field to fill in. But if you work without classes and then decide to use them after all, you can go back and edit past transactions to assign classes to them, or just start using classes at the beginning of a new fiscal period. For more help deciding whether to use classes, see the box on page 151.

If you choose to work with classes, be sure to follow these guidelines to get the most out of them:

- **Pick one use for classes**. QuickBooks has only one list of classes, so every class should represent the same type of classification. Moreover, you can assign just one class to a transaction, so classes add only one additional way to categorize transactions. For example, once you assign a class for a business unit to a transaction, there's no way to assign another class—to identify the office branch, say—to the same transaction.

- **Use classes consistently**. Make sure to use classes on *every* transaction that relates to your classification method. For example, if you classify income and expenses by partner, assign a class to every invoice and expense that is related to a partner's work; otherwise, your class-based reports won't be accurate. However, if expenses are overhead and don't relate to the work partners do, you can leave a transaction's class field blank.

- **Create a catchall class**. Set up a class like Other so that you can still classify transactions even if they don't fit into any of the specific classes you've defined.

UP TO SPEED

Do You Need Classes?

Not every company needs classes, so don't feel that you *have* to use them. You can call on several other QuickBooks features to help you track your business. Each tracking feature has its advantages, so how do you decide which one(s) to use to evaluate your performance? Here's a brief description of each feature and the best time to use it:

- **Accounts**. You can use accounts to segregate income and expenses in several ways. For instance, keep income from your physical store separate from your website sales by creating two separate income accounts. Accounts are the fastest way to see performance because QuickBooks' built-in Profit & Loss reports (page 468) automatically display results by account.

- **Customer, job, and vendor types**. To analyze income by wholesale, retail, online, and other types of customers, use customer types to classify your customers. That way, you can filter the reports you generate to show results for a specific kind of customer. However, types are more limited in scope than accounts—for example, customer

types apply only to customers (page 158). Likewise, job types and vendor types (page 159) help you categorize only by job and vendor, respectively.

- **Classes**. Classes cut across accounts, customers, jobs, *and* vendors because you assign a class to an individual transaction, such as a check, bill, or invoice. So classes are perfect for categories that span accounts, customers, vendors, and types. Suppose the partners in your company help customers implement technology and tighten their security. You've decided to use separate income accounts to track technology sales and security sales, and you use customer types to track work for the government versus the private sector. You also want to track income and expenses by partner, but each partner works on all types of service for all types of customers. Happily, you can create classes to track partners' sales and expenses, regardless of which service they deliver or the type of customer. A Profit & Loss report by class (page 474) will then tell you how each partner is performing.

Turning on Class Tracking

You have to turn on QuickBooks' class-tracking feature before you can start assigning classes. To see whether classes are turned on, in the main QuickBooks menu bar, click Lists. If you don't see a Class List item in the menu, the class-tracking feature is turned off. Here's how to turn it on:

1. **Choose Edit→Preferences→Accounting, and then click the Company Preferences tab.**

    To turn class tracking on, you need to be a QuickBooks administrator, because classes affect everyone in your organization who uses the program. (If you aren't a QuickBooks administrator, you'll have to persuade someone who is to turn on classes.)

2. **Turn on the "Use class tracking for transactions" checkbox.**

When you do, QuickBooks automatically turns on the "Prompt to assign classes" checkbox. With this checkbox turned on, if you try to save a transaction without an entry in the Class field, QuickBooks gives you a chance to add the class (or save the transaction without one). Turn this checkbox off if you don't want to be reminded to assign classes.

3. **Click OK to close the Preferences window.**

The Class List entry now appears on the Lists menu.

Setting Up Classes

Once QuickBooks' class-tracking feature is turned on, here's how you create classes:

1. **In the main QuickBooks menu bar, choose Lists→Class List.**

The Class List window opens.

2. **In the Class List window, press Ctrl+N or click Class→New.**

The New Class window opens.

3. **In the Class Name box, type a name for the class.**

If you want to create a class that's the subclass of a parent (to set up subclasses for each region within a business unit, say), turn on the "Subclass of" checkbox. Then, in the drop-down list, choose the parent class you want.

4. **Click Next to create another class, or click OK to close the New Class window.**

If you realize you need another class while you're working on a transaction, you can create an entry by choosing <Add New> in the Class drop-down list, shown in Figure 6-1.

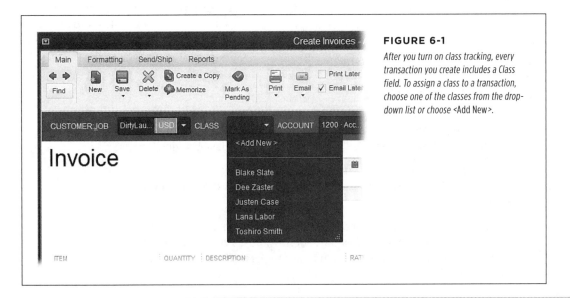

FIGURE 6-1

After you turn on class tracking, every transaction you create includes a Class field. To assign a class to a transaction, choose one of the classes from the drop-down list or choose <Add New>.

▧ Price Levels

Whether you give your favorite customers price breaks or increase other customers' charges because they keep asking for "just one more thing," you can apply discounts and markups when you create invoices. But remembering who gets discounts and how big is tough when you have a lot of customers, and it's bad form to mark up a favorite customer's prices by mistake.

Say hello to QuickBooks' Price Level List. When you define price levels and assign them to customers, QuickBooks takes care of adjusting the prices on every invoice you create. You can also apply a price level to specific lines on invoices to mark up or discount individual items. For example, suppose you create a price level that represents a 15 percent discount. If you apply that price level to a customer, the sales forms you create for that customer automatically discount prices by 15 percent. And if you apply that price level to a product on a customer's invoice, the product's price gets reduced by 15 percent.

Creating a Price Level

To create a price level, do the following:

1. **Make sure the Price Level preference is turned on (you have to be a Quick-Books administrator to turn it on).**

   If QuickBooks' Price Level preference is turned off, you won't see the Price Level List item in the Lists menu. Choose Edit→Preferences→Sales & Customers, and then click the Company Preferences tab. Turn on the "Use price levels" checkbox, and then click OK.

2. **Choose Lists→Price Level List.**

   The Price Level List window opens.

3. **In the Price Level List window, press Ctrl+N or click Price Level→New.**

   The New Price Level window, shown in Figure 6-2, opens.

4. **In the Price Level Name box, type a name for the level.**

   If you have a fixed set of discounts, you might name the various levels by the percentage, like Discount 10 and Discount 20, for example. An alternative is to name them by their purpose, like Customer Loyalty or User Group Discount. That way, it's easy to change the discount amount without changing the price level's name.

5. **In the "This price level will" box, choose "increase" or "decrease" based on whether you want the price level to mark up or discount items, and then enter the percentage in the "item prices by" box.**

   In QuickBooks Pro, the Price Level Type box is automatically set to "Fixed %" because you can create price levels that increase or decrease prices only by a fixed percentage. See the box on page 155 to learn about the Per Item price level available in QuickBooks Premier and Enterprise.

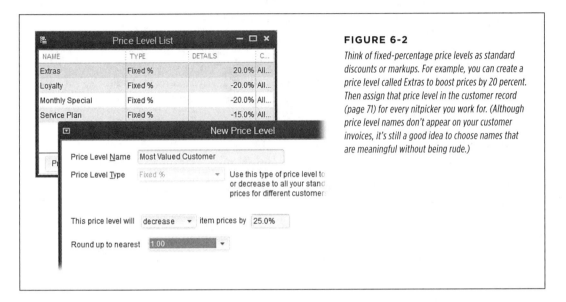

FIGURE 6-2

Think of fixed-percentage price levels as standard discounts or markups. For example, you can create a price level called Extras to boost prices by 20 percent. Then assign that price level in the customer record (page 71) for every nitpicker you work for. (Although price level names don't appear on your customer invoices, it's still a good idea to choose names that are meaningful without being rude.)

6. **For percentage price levels, in the "Round up to nearest" drop-down list, choose the type of rounding you want to apply.**

   The "Round up to nearest" feature is handy if the percentages you apply result in fractions of pennies or amounts too small to bother with. This setting lets you round discounts to pennies, nickels, dimes, quarters, half-dollars, and even whole dollars (if you *really* hate making change). The box on page 156 explains other, fancier rounding you can apply.

7. **Click OK to close the New Price Level window.**

   To create another price level, repeat steps 3–7.

Per-Item Price Levels

In QuickBooks Premier and Enterprise, you can create price levels that apply to individual items in your Item List. To do that, in the New Price Level window's Price Level Type drop-down list, choose Per Item. The window then displays a table containing all your items. In the Custom Price column, type the price for an item at that price level. For example, suppose you sell calendars to retail stores for $5 each. The Standard Price column would show 5.00 for the calendar item. If you're creating a price level for nonprofit organizations, you could type *3.50* in the item's Custom Price cell so that a nonprofit would pay only $3.50 for a calendar.

If you want to apply percentages to several items in the table displayed in the New Price Level window, there's a shortcut for calculating custom prices:

1. Turn on the checkboxes for the items that use the same percentage increase or decrease.

2. In the "Adjust price of marked items to be" box, type the percentage. In the drop-down list next to it, choose "lower" or "higher." And in the "than its" drop-down list, choose an entry to tell QuickBooks to calculate the price level based on the standard price, the cost, or the current custom price.

3. Click the Adjust button. QuickBooks fills in the Custom Price cells for the marked items with the new custom prices.

4. To apply different percentages to another set of items, clear any checkmarks and then select the next set of items and repeat the steps to define the percentage adjustment.

If you work with more than one currency and turn on the multiple currency preference, you can create price levels for individual items to set their prices in different currencies. Here's how: In the New Price Level window, choose the currency in the Currency drop-down list. Then, in the Custom Price cell, type the price for the item in the foreign currency. After that, when you add the item to an invoice, simply choose the currency price level in the Rate drop-down list, and QuickBooks recalculates the price.

NOTE You can't create price levels on the fly while you're creating an invoice. The easiest solution to a missing price level is to adjust the price on the invoice manually. Then, after the invoice is done, add the price level to your Price Level List.

Applying Price Levels

You can apply price levels in two ways:

- **Applying a price level to a customer record** (page 71) tells QuickBooks to automatically adjust all the prices on every new invoice for that customer by that price level percentage (page 284).

- **Applying a price level to line items in an invoice** adjusts the prices of those items whether or not a customer has a standard price level. To do so, in the Create Invoices window, click an item's Rate cell, click the down arrow that appears, and then choose the price level you want from the drop-down list.

Rounding Price Level Values

When you use percentages to calculate markups and discounts, the resulting values may not be what you want. The basic choices in the New Price Level window's "Round up to nearest" drop-down list take care of the most common rounding—to the nearest penny, dime, quarter, dollar, and so on. Other entries on the list let you give QuickBooks more complex rounding instructions, which can come in handy.

The seven entries that include the word "minus" help you position prices at magic marketing prices like $29.99 or $1.95. For example, the ".10 minus .01" entry ensures that the price always ends in 9. With this rounding choice, if the discounted price comes out to $8.74, QuickBooks rounds up to the nearest 10 cents ($8.80) and then subtracts 1 cent, so the rounded value is $8.79.

If you like to undercut your competitors with unusual price points, in the "Round up to nearest" drop-down menu, choose "user defined." QuickBooks then displays several boxes and options for defining your own rounding:

- **The "nearest" drop-down menu**. In the unlabeled drop-down menu below "user defined," you can choose "to nearest," "up to nearest," or "down to nearest." "To nearest" rounds in whichever direction is closest (for example, rounding from 1.73 to 1.70 or from 1.77 to 1.80).

- **The first $ box**. Type the value you want to round to, like .01, .25, or 1.00.

- **Plus or Minus and the second $ box**. Select the Plus or Minus option depending on whether you want to add or subtract money after you've rounded the value. In the $ box, type the amount you want to add or subtract from the rounded value. (If you don't want to use this feature, just leave the second $ box set to 0.)

Customer and Vendor Profile Lists

Filling in fields goes much faster when you can choose info from drop-down lists instead of typing values. The lists that appear on the Customer & Vendor Profile Lists submenu (choose Lists→Customer & Vendor Profile Lists to see it) pop up regularly, whether you're creating an invoice, paying a bill, or generating a report. For example, when you create an invoice, QuickBooks fills in the Payment Terms field with the terms you assigned to the customer's record (page 70), but you can choose different terms from the drop-down list to urge your customer to pay more quickly.

For many of these lists, creating list entries involves nothing more than typing the entry's name and specifying whether that entry is a subentry of another. This section describes how to add entries to each list and how to put these lists to work for you.

Sales Rep List

The Sales Rep List is perfect when you want to assign people as points of contact for your customers. The people you add to this list can be sales reps you pay on commission or employees who are dedicated contacts for customers. For example, if you assign people as sales reps to your customers (page 73) and add the appropriate rep to your sales transactions, you can then generate reports by sales rep (page 559). But first you have to add the names of your sales reps and contacts to the Sales Rep List.

NOTE The Intuit Commissions Center is an add-on service for QuickBooks that calculates commissions for sales reps. When you use this feature, you can flag items that don't pay commissions and assign commissions as percentages or dollar amounts. To learn more, go to *http://workplace.intuit.com/appcenter*, click All Apps, and then, below the Sales Management heading, click Intuit Commissions Manager. Alternatively, to find a third-party program for sales commissions, go to *http://marketplace.intuit.com*. In the Search Apps Now box, type *sales commission* and then press Enter.

To add a name to the Sales Rep List:

1. **Choose Lists→Customer & Vendor Profile Lists→Sales Rep List; in the Sales Rep List window that opens, press Ctrl+N or click Sales Rep→New.**

   The New Sales Rep List dialog box opens.

2. **In the Sales Rep Name drop-down list, choose a name; in the Sales Rep Initials box, type the person's initials.**

   The Sales Rep Name list displays names from the Employee List (page 202), the Vendor List (page 91), and the Other Names List (page 158). If the name you want doesn't exist, choose <Add New> at the top of the list. (In the Select Name Type dialog box that appears, select Vendor, Employee, or Other, and then click OK. Then, in the New Name window, fill in the Name box and any other fields you want.)

   QuickBooks automatically fills in the Sales Rep Type field with Employee, Vendor, or Other Name, depending on which list the name came from or, if you just added the name, the type you assigned when you added that person. (The box on page 158 gives hints about when to use the Other Names List.)

3. **Click Next to add another sales rep, or click OK to close the New Sales Rep window.**

   If you select a name and realize that it's misspelled, you can edit the name from the New Sales Rep window. Click Edit Name, and QuickBooks opens the Edit Employee, Edit Vendor, or Edit Name dialog box so you can change the name.

When to Use the Other Names List

If you have more than a few names on your Other Names List, you're probably not getting the most out of QuickBooks. In fact, unless you're a sole proprietor or several partners share ownership of your company, you can run QuickBooks without *any* names on the Other Names List.

The entries in the Other Names List show up in the drop-down menus for a few types of transactions, such as checks and credit card charges (page 259). But they don't appear when you create invoices, purchase orders, sales receipts, or any other type of transaction.

So what are Other Names good for? People who aren't customers, vendors, or employees—for example, *your* name as sole proprietor or the names of company partners. That way, when you write partners' distribution checks to pay partners, you can choose their names from the Other Names List.

To create an entry on the Other Names List:

1. Choose Lists→Other Names List.

2. When the Other Names List window opens, press Ctrl+N.

3. Fill in the fields in the New Name window, which are similar to the ones in the New Customer dialog box (page 66).

The Other Names List can also serve as a holding tank. If you aren't sure which list to put someone on, you can add that person to the Other Names List temporarily. Then, when you figure out which list she should go on, you can move her. Because QuickBooks needs to close all open windows to move people between lists, it's best to save this task for a lull in your workday. When you're ready, open the Other Names List window and click Activities→Change Other Name Types. In the Change Name Types dialog box that appears, find the person's name and then click the cell in the appropriate column (Customer, Vendor, or Employee) to assign that type. Click OK to complete the makeover.

Merging entries in the Other Names List is similar to merging customers (page 86). For example, if you realize that you created two entries for the same person in the Other Names List, you can merge one into the other. The alternative is to change one of the two entries to inactive, as described on page 88, and then use the other entry for all future transactions.

Customer Type List

Customer types help you analyze your income and expenses by customer category (page 79). For example, a healthcare provider might create Government and Private customer types to see how much a change in government reimbursement might hurt revenue.

You first create customer types in the Customer Type List and then assign one of those types in each customer's record. Creating all your customer types up front is fast—as long as you already know what entries you want to create:

1. **Choose Lists→Customer & Vendor Profile Lists→Customer Type List; when the Customer Type List dialog box opens, press Ctrl+N.**

   The New Customer Type window (Figure 6-3) opens.

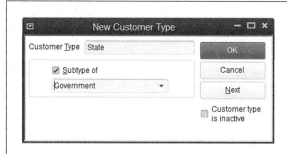

FIGURE 6-3

The only thing you have to fill in here is the Customer Type field. If this type represents a portion of a larger customer category, turn on the "Subtype of" checkbox and choose the parent type. For example, if you have a Government customer type, you might create subtypes like Federal, State, County, and so on.

2. **Enter a name in the Customer Type field.**

   If the new type is a subtype of another, turn on the "Subtype of" checkbox and then choose the parent type from the drop-down list.

3. **Click OK if you're done, or click Next to create another type.**

You can also create entries as you work: If you're creating or modifying a customer in the New Customer or Edit Customer dialog box, click the Additional Info tab. In the Customer Type drop-down list, choose <Add New>, which opens the New Customer Type window. Then you can create a new customer type, as shown in Figure 6-3.

Vendor Type List

Vendor types work similarly to customer types—you can filter reports or subtotal expenses by different types of vendors. For example, if you create a Communications vendor type, you could generate a report showing the expenses you've paid to your telephone, Internet, and satellite communication providers.

You create Vendor Type entries the way you create Customer Type entries: Choose Lists→Customer & Vendor Profile Lists→Vendor Type List, and then press Ctrl+N to open the New Vendor Type window.

> **TIP** To create a new vendor type while you're creating a vendor, in the New Vendor dialog box, click the Additional Info tab; in the Vendor Type drop-down list, choose <Add New> to open the New Vendor Type window.

Job Type List

Job types also follow the customer-type lead. You can use job types to classify the projects you perform for customers, as described on page 82. For instance, you can filter a Profit & Loss report to show how profitable your spec house projects are compared with your remodeling contracts. You create Job Type entries the way you create Customer Type entries (page 158). Open the Job Type List window by choosing Lists→Customer & Vendor Profile Lists→Job Type List.

Terms List

The Terms List includes both the payment terms you require of your customers and the payment terms your vendors ask of you. If you assign terms in a customer's record, then QuickBooks automatically fills in the Terms box on the invoices you create for that customer. Likewise, filling in terms in a vendor record means that QuickBooks fills in the Terms box on bills you enter.

To add a new term, open the Terms List window (Lists→Customer & Vendor Profile Lists→Terms List), and then press Ctrl+N. The fields that you fill in to create terms (Figure 6-4) are different from those in other Customer & Vendor Profile lists. The following sections explain the New Terms window's Standard and Date Driven options.

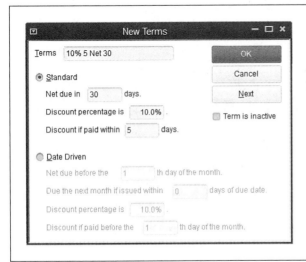

FIGURE 6-4

Because payment terms apply to both vendors and customers, consider using generic names that say something about the terms themselves. For example, the "10% 5 Net 30" entry shown here is an enticement for early payments because it means that the amount is due 30 days from the invoice date, but you can deduct 10 percent from your bill if you pay within 5 days.

■ SETTING UP TERMS USING ELAPSED TIME

The New Terms window's Standard option is ideal when the due date is a specific number of days after the invoice date (or the date you receive a bill from a vendor). If you send invoices whenever you complete a sale, choose the Standard option so that payment is due within a number of days of the invoice date. Here's what the Standard option fields do:

- **Net due in _ days**. Type the maximum number of days after the bill or invoice date that you or a customer can pay. For example, if you type *30*, customers have up to 30 days to pay an invoice or you have up to 30 days to pay a bill. If you charge penalties for late payments, QuickBooks can figure out when customer payments are late so you can assess finance charges (page 388).

- **Discount percentage is**. If you or your vendor offers a discount for early payments, type the discount percentage in this box.

- **Discount if paid within _ days**. Type the number of days after the invoice date within which you or a customer has to pay to receive the early payment discount.

NOTE When terms reduce a customer's bill for early payments, QuickBooks deducts these discounts in the Receive Payments window (page 378), where the program can determine whether the customer paid early. If a vendor offers discounts for early payments, you can take advantage of those in the Pay Bills window (page 245).

■ SETTING UP DATE DRIVEN TERMS

The Date Driven option sets up terms for payments that are due on a specific date, regardless of the date on the invoice. This option is handy if you or your vendors send invoices on a schedule—say, on the last day of the month. For example, home mortgages often assess a late fee if payments arrive after the 15th of the month.

Here's what the New Terms window's Date Driven options do:

- **Net due before the _th day of the month**. Type the day that the payment is due. For example, if a payment is due before the 15th of the month, no matter what date appears on your statement, type *15* in this box.

- **Due the next month if issued within _ days of due date**. Your customers might get annoyed if you require payment by the 15th of the month and send out your invoices on the 14th. They would have no way of paying on time, unless they camped out in your billing department.

  You can type a number of days in this box to automatically push the due date to the following month when you issue invoices too close to the due date. Suppose payments are due on the 15th of each month and you type *5* in this box. In that case, for invoices you create between August 10 and August 15, QuickBooks automatically changes the due date to September 15.

- **Discount percentage is**. If you or your vendors extend a discount for early payments, type the discount percentage in this box.

- **Discount if paid before the _th day of the month**. Type the day of the month before which you or a customer has to pay to receive the early payment discount.

Customer Message List

When you create an invoice, you can add a short message to it, such as "If you like the service we deliver, tell your friends. If you don't like our service, tell us." To save time and prevent embarrassing typos, add your stock messages to the Customer Message List (Lists→Customer & Vendor Profile Lists→Customer Message List).

The New Customer Message dialog box (which you open by pressing Ctrl+N while the Customer Message List window is open) has only one field—Message—which can hold up to 101 characters (including spaces).

TIP Don't use the Customer Message List for notes that change with every invoice (like one that specifies the date range that an invoice covers) because you'll fill the list with unique messages and won't be able to add any more. If you want to include unique information, do so in the cover letter (or email) that accompanies your invoice.

Payment Method List

Categorizing payments by the method the customer uses can be handy. For instance, when you select Banking→Make Deposits (page 396), you can choose to process all the payments you've received via a specific payment method—deposit all the checks and cash you received into your checking account, say, but deposit the payments you receive via credit cards to a dedicated merchant account.

You categorize payments by using the entries on the Payment Method List. QuickBooks starts the list for you with entries for cash, check, and credit cards (such as American Express and Visa). To add another payment method—for payments through PayPal, for example—choose Lists→Customer & Vendor Profile Lists→Payment Method List, and then press Ctrl+N. In the New Payment Method dialog box, type a name for the method, and then choose a type. For instance, if you use two Visa credit cards, you can create two entries with the Visa payment type. Other payment types include Debit Card, Gift Card, and E-Check.

Ship Via List

When your invoices include the shipping method that you use, your customers know whether to watch for the mailman or the UPS truck. QuickBooks creates several shipping methods for you: DHL, Federal Express, UPS, and US Mail. If you use another shipping method, like a bike messenger in New York City or your own delivery truck, simply create additional entries in the Ship Via List window (Lists→Customer & Vendor Profile Lists→Ship Via List) by pressing Ctrl+N. In the Shipping Method field (the only field in the New Ship Method dialog box), type a name for the method and then click OK.

> **TIP** If you use one shipping method most of the time, you can have QuickBooks fill in the Shipping Method field on invoices with that entry automatically. See page 627 to learn about the Usual Shipping Method preference and the Usual Free on Board location.

Vehicle List

If you want to track mileage (page 210) on the vehicles you use for your business, create entries for your cars and trucks in the Vehicle List (Lists→Customer & Vendor Profile Lists→Vehicle List). Press Ctrl+N and then use the Vehicle box to name the vehicle: *Ford Prefect 1982 Red*, for example. The Description field holds up to 256 characters, so you can use it to store the VIN, license plate, and even the insurance policy number.

> **TIP** If you want to charge your customers for mileage, see page 214.

Fixed Asset Items

Assets that you can't convert to cash quickly—such as backhoes, buildings, and supercomputers—are called *fixed assets*. If you track information about your fixed assets in another program or have only a few fixed assets, there's no reason to bother with the Fixed Asset Item List. As you can see in Figure 6-5, QuickBooks can track info such as when you bought the item and how much you paid. But in QuickBooks Pro, *you* have to calculate depreciation (see the box on page 463) for each asset at the end of the year and create journal entries to adjust the values in your asset accounts.

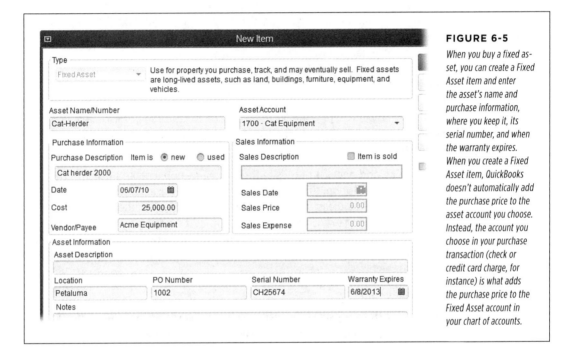

FIGURE 6-5

When you buy a fixed asset, you can create a Fixed Asset item and enter the asset's name and purchase information, where you keep it, its serial number, and when the warranty expires. When you create a Fixed Asset item, QuickBooks doesn't automatically add the purchase price to the asset account you choose. Instead, the account you choose in your purchase transaction (check or credit card charge, for instance) is what adds the purchase price to the Fixed Asset account in your chart of accounts.

NOTE QuickBooks Premier Accountant edition and QuickBooks Enterprise edition include the Fixed Asset Manager, which figures out the depreciation on your assets and posts depreciation to an account in your QuickBooks company file. If you have an accountant prepare your depreciation schedule, go with the number your accountant gives you. The depreciation that QuickBooks calculates may be close to, but different from, the number your accountant calculates.

When you sell an asset, open the Edit Item dialog box (choose Lists→Fixed Asset Item List, and then press Ctrl+E) and turn on the "Item is sold" checkbox. When you do that, the sales fields come to life so you can specify when you sold the asset, how much you got for it, and any costs associated with the sale.

If you decide to track the details about your fixed assets outside QuickBooks, you still need to include the *value* of those assets in your financial reports. Simply create Fixed Asset accounts (page 52) to hold the value of your assets. Then each year, add a general journal entry to record the amount of depreciation for your fixed assets.

Creating and Editing List Entries

Every list in QuickBooks responds to the same set of commands. As your business changes, you can add new entries, edit existing ones, hide entries that you no longer use, and (in some lists) merge two entries into one. If you make a mistake creating an entry, you can delete it. You can also print your QuickBooks lists to produce a price list of the products you sell, for example. Using the following techniques, you'll be able to do what you want with any list or entry you might need.

Creating Entries

If you're setting up QuickBooks, creating all the entries for a list at the same time is fast and efficient. Open the New dialog box for the type of list entry you want (New Customer Type, for example), and you'll soon get into a rhythm creating one entry after another.

You can also add new list entries in the middle of bookkeeping tasks without too much of an interruption. (If you launch a new line of business selling moose repellent, for example, you can add a Burly Men customer type in the middle of creating an invoice.) But don't rely on this approach to add every entry to every list—you'll spend so much time jumping from dialog box to dialog box that you'll never get to your bookkeeping.

Each list has its own collection of fields, but the overall process for creating entries in lists is the same:

1. **To open the window for the list you want to work on, on the main QuickBooks menu bar, click Lists and then select the list you want on the submenu.**

   For example, to open the Class List window, choose Lists→Class List.

   Several lists are tucked away one level deeper on the Lists menu. For lists that include characteristics of your customers or vendors, such as Vendor Type or Terms, choose Lists→Customer & Vendor Profile Lists, and then choose the list you want, as shown in Figure 6-6.

2. **To create a new entry, press Ctrl+N or, right-click the list window and choose New on the shortcut menu that appears. Or, at the bottom of the window, click the button with the list's name on it, and then choose New.**

   For instance, to create an entry in the Class List, make sure that the Class List window is active and then press Ctrl+N. Or, at the bottom of the Class List window, click Class→New. Either way, QuickBooks opens the New Class window.

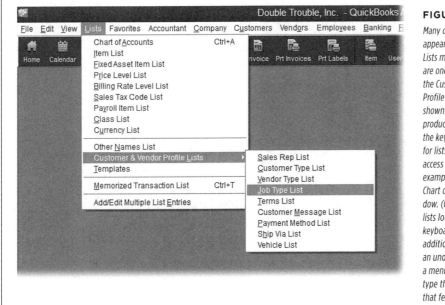

FIGURE 6-6

Many of QuickBooks' lists appear directly on the Lists menu, but some are one level lower on the Customer & Vendor Profile Lists submenu, shown here. To boost your productivity, take note of the keyboard shortcuts for lists you're likely to access most often. For example, Ctrl+A opens the Chart of Accounts window. (Online Appendix C lists lots of other handy keyboard shortcuts.) In addition, when you see an underlined letter in a menu entry, you can type that letter to launch that feature. For example, when the Lists menu is open, press "c" to open the Class List window.

3. **After you've completed one entry, simply click Next to save the current entry and begin another. To save the entry you just created and close the dialog box, click OK.**

To toss an entry that you botched, click Cancel to throw it away and close the dialog box.

NOTE Unlike all the other New dialog boxes for lists, the New Price Level window doesn't include a Next button.

Editing Entries

To modify a list entry, open the window for that list. (You can customize the columns that appear in list windows so it's easier to see values associated with list entries; the box on page 166 tells you how.) Then select the entry you want to edit and press Ctrl+E (or double-click the entry). When the Edit dialog box opens, make the changes you want, and then click OK.

Customizing Columns in List Windows

Some list entries don't come with many fields, such as the items in the Ship Via List, so all you need to see in that list window is the names of the shipping methods you've created. But other lists, such as Terms, store a plethora of information, including discounts and days of the month associated with the terms. You can customize the columns that appear in list windows so you can see list entries' values without editing the entries. Here's how:

1. At the bottom of the list window, click the button with the list's name on it, and then choose Customize Columns.

2. In the "Customize Columns - <list name>" dialog box that appears, in the Available Columns list, select a field you want to display, and then click Add. The column moves to the Chosen Columns list.

3. Repeat step 2 to add more columns.

4. To remove a column from the window, in the Chosen Columns list, select the field, and then click Remove.

5. To move a field to another position, select it in the Chosen Columns list, and then click Move Up or Move Down until it's in the position you want.

6. When you're done customizing, click OK. The fields appear in the window, as shown in Figure 6-7 (background).

FIGURE 6-7

You can add, remove, or reorder the fields in the Customize Columns dialog box. The fields are listed from top to bottom in the Chosen Columns list, but they appear from left to right in the list window.

Hiding and Deleting List Entries

Deleting entries is only for discarding entries that you create by mistake. If you've already used list entries in transactions, hide the entries you don't use anymore so your historical records are complete. For example, you wouldn't delete the "Net 30" payment term just because you're lucky enough to have only Net 15 clients right now; you may still extend Net 30 terms to some clients in the future.

Hiding Entries

Hiding list entries that you no longer use does two things:

- **Keeps your records intact**. Your previous transactions still use the entries you've hidden, so your historical records don't change.

- **Declutters your lists**. When you create new transactions, the hidden entries don't appear in drop-down lists, so you can't choose them by mistake.

The methods for hiding and reactivating list entries are exactly the same regardless of which list you're working on:

- **To hide an entry**: In the list's window, right-click the entry and choose "Make <list name> Inactive" from the shortcut menu, where <list name> is the list you're editing. The entry disappears from the list.

- **To view all the entries in a list**: At the bottom of the list window, turn on the "Include inactive" checkbox so you can see both active and hidden entries. QuickBooks adds a column with an X as its heading and displays an X in that column for every inactive entry in the list.

- **To reactivate an entry**: First, view all the entries, and then click the X next to the entry that you want to reactivate. If the entry has subentries, in the Activate Group dialog box that appears, click Yes to reactivate the entry *and* all its subentries.

Deleting Entries

You can delete a list entry only if nothing in your QuickBooks company file references it in any way. To delete a list entry, open the appropriate list window and select the entry you want to delete, and then press Ctrl+D or choose Edit→"Delete <list name>." If you haven't used the entry in any records or transactions, QuickBooks asks you to confirm that you want to delete the entry; click Yes.

Finding List Entries in Transactions

If QuickBooks won't let you delete a list entry because a transaction is still using it, don't worry—it's easy to find transactions that use a specific list entry. Here's how:

1. **Open the list that contains the entry you want to find and, in the list window, right-click the entry and choose Find on the shortcut menu.**

   The Find dialog box opens already set up to search for transactions that use the list entry you selected.

2. **Click Find.**

   The table at the bottom of the Find dialog box displays all the transactions that use that entry.

3. **To modify the list entry a transaction uses, select the transaction in the table, and then click Go To.**

   QuickBooks opens the window or dialog box that corresponds to the type of transaction. If you're trying to eliminate references to a list entry so you can delete it, choose a different list entry and then save the transaction.

■ Sorting Lists

QuickBooks sorts lists alphabetically by name, which is usually what you want. The only reason to sort a list another way is if you're having trouble finding the entry you want to edit. For example, if you want to find equipment you bought within the last few years, you could sort the Fixed Asset List by purchase date to find the machines that you're still depreciating. Figure 6-8 shows you how to change the sort order.

NOTE Sorting in a list window doesn't change the order in which entries appear in drop-down lists, unless you manually sort a list by dragging the diamond icons to the left of list items' names.

FIGURE 6-8

To sort a list by a column, click the column's heading, such as Purchase Date. The first time you click the heading, Quick-Books sorts the list in ascending order. To toggle between ascending and descending order, click the heading again. The small black triangle in the heading (circled) points up when the list is in ascending order, as shown here, and down when it's in descending order.

NOTE If you use a different column to sort a list, QuickBooks displays a gray diamond to the left of the column heading that it used to sort the list initially. For example, the Fixed Asset Item List shows items in alphabetical order by Name. If you sort the list by Purchase Date instead, a gray diamond appears to the left of the Name heading, as shown in Figure 6-8. To return the list to the order that QuickBooks originally used, click the diamond.

◼ Printing Lists

After you spend all that time building lists in QuickBooks, you'll be happy to know that it's much easier to get information about those lists *out* of the program than it was to put it in. For instance, suppose you want to print a price list of all your fixed asset items. QuickBooks makes short work of printing lists or turning them into files that you can use in other programs.

Blasting Out a Quick List

Here's the fastest way to produce a list, albeit one that doesn't give you any control over the report's appearance:

1. **At the bottom of a list window, click the button labeled with the list's name—like Price Level, for example—and then, in the drop-down menu, choose Print List (or press Ctrl+P).**

   QuickBooks might display a message box telling you to try list reports if you want to customize or format your reports. That method is covered in the next section. For now, in the message box, click OK. The Print Lists dialog box opens.

NOTE To print Customer, Vendor, or Employee lists, in the Customer Center, Vendor Center, or Employee Center toolbar, click Print and then choose Customer & Job List, Vendor List, or Employee List.

---

2. **To print the list, select the Printer option and then choose a printer in the drop-down list. If you want to output the list to a file, choose the File option instead and then select the file format you want.**

   If you go with the Printer option, you can specify print settings, as you can in many other programs. Choose landscape or portrait orientation, the pages to print, and the number of copies.

   If you choose File, you can create ASCII text files, comma-delimited files, or tab-delimited files (page 649).

3. **Click Print.**

   QuickBooks prints the report or creates the type of file you selected.

Customizing a Printed List

If the Print List feature described in the previous section scatters fields over the page or produces a comma-delimited file that doesn't play well with your email program, you'll be happy to know that QuickBooks might offer a report closer to what you have in mind. For example, an Other Names Phone List is only two clicks away.

To access the reports that come with QuickBooks, in the program's main menu bar, go to Reports→List and then choose the report you want. If these reports fall short, you can modify them to change the fields and records they include, or format them in a variety of ways.

Chapter 21 explains how to customize reports, but if you click Customize Report in a report window's toolbar, you can make changes to the list report before you print it or create a file containing the list's info. In the Modify Report window that appears, you can:

- **Choose fields**. On the Display tab, the Columns box includes every field for that type of list entry. When you click a field's name, QuickBooks puts a checkmark next to it and adds that field to the report.

- **Sort records**. On the Display tab, choose the field you want to sort by from the "Sort by" drop-down menu and whether you want the report sorted in ascending or descending order.

- **Filter the report**. You can use the settings on the Filters tab to limit the records in a report. For example, you can produce an employee report for active employees (which refers to their employment status, not the level of effort they devote to their jobs). You can also filter by employee name or by values in other fields.

- **Set up the report's header and footer**. On the Header/Footer tab, you can choose the information that you want to show in the report's title and in the footer at the bottom of each page. The title identifies the data in the report, and the footer can include the date the report was prepared so you know whether it's current.

- **Format text and numbers**. On the Fonts & Numbers tab, you can choose the font that QuickBooks uses for different parts of the report. For instance, labels should be larger than the lines in the report. You can also choose how to display negative numbers: The In Bright Red checkbox controls whether red ink truly applies to your financial reports. If you like, turn on the Divide By 1,000 checkbox to make QuickBooks remove three zeroes from the end of each number before displaying it in the report so it's easier to differentiate thousands from millions.

Managing QuickBooks Files

W hen company ledgers were made of paper, you had to be careful not to tear the pages or spill coffee on them. Today's electronic books require their own sort of care and feeding. Protecting your QuickBooks files is essential, not only because they tell the financial story of your company, but also because computers are notorious for chewing up data in all sorts of ways.

QuickBooks files have a few advantages over their paper-based relatives. Most importantly, you can make copies of them for safekeeping. (QuickBooks can also create a *special* copy of your company file so you and your accountant can both work on it at the end of the year; see page 490 for details.) If several people work on your QuickBooks file simultaneously, you'll learn when and how to switch from multi-user mode to single-user mode so you can perform the housekeeping tasks that require dedicated access. This chapter focuses on the most important things you can do with your QuickBooks files: back them up and copy them. It also explains why and how to verify, condense, and delete your files, which you'll do less often—if ever.

■ Switching Between Multi- and Single-User Mode

In QuickBooks, some maintenance tasks require that only one person have access to the company file. So if you told QuickBooks to set up your company file in multi-user mode when you created it, you have to switch to *single-user mode* for the following tasks:

- Merge or delete accounts and items.
- Set up some aspects of your company file, such as finance charges.

- Condense or export data from a company file.

- Save an accountant's copy of your company file (although you can open or convert an existing one while in multi-user mode.)

TIP You can verify data while in multi-user mode, although the verification isn't as rigorous as the one performed while in single-user mode. Single-user mode can also speed up time-consuming tasks like running humongous reports.

To see which mode your company file is currently in, display QuickBooks' File menu. If you see "Switch to Multi-user Mode" on the menu, it's in single-user mode. If you see "Switch to Single-user Mode" instead, it's in multi-user mode.

The good news is that you don't have to remember which tasks demand single-user mode; QuickBooks reminds you to switch modes if you try to perform a single-user-mode task when the company file is chugging away in multi-user mode. Because everyone else has to close the company file before you can switch it to single-user mode, you may find it easiest to wait until no one else is working on the company file (early in the morning or after business hours, say).

Here's how you switch from multi-user mode to single-user mode:

1. **If your single-user task can't wait until off hours, ask everyone else to close the company file you want to work on.**

   They can choose File→Close Company/Logoff or simply exit QuickBooks to close the company file.

2. **When everyone else has closed the company file, open it in QuickBooks by choosing File→Open Previous Company, and then selecting the company file in the submenu.**

   If the company file doesn't appear on the Open Previous File submenu, choose File→"Open or Restore Company" instead. In the "Open or Restore Company" dialog box, select the "Open a company file" option, and then click Next. In the "Open a Company" dialog box that appears, navigate to the folder where you store the file, and then double-click its filename.

3. **Choose File→"Switch to Single-user Mode." In the message box that appears telling you the file is in single-user mode, click OK.**

   QuickBooks closes all open windows before it switches to single-user mode. After you click OK, it reopens the windows, and you're ready to work solo on the company file.

4. **After you finish your single-user task, switch back to multi-user mode by choosing File→"Switch to Multi-user Mode." When the message box appears telling you the file is in multi-user mode, click OK.**

   You'll see all the windows in QuickBooks close. After you click OK, they re-appear, and the company file is back in multi-user mode.

Don't forget to tell your colleagues that they can log back into the company file.

Backing Up Files

If you already have a backup procedure for *all* your computer files, QuickBooks' Backup feature might seem about as useful as your appendix. Your company-wide backups regularly squirrel your data files away in a safe place, ready to rescue you should disaster strike. Still, QuickBooks Backup complements even the most robust backup plan. And if you run a mom-and-pop business, online backups let you back up all your data without hiring an IT staff. Here are some ways you can put the program's Backup feature to work:

- **Back up one QuickBooks company file**. Before you experiment with a new QuickBooks feature, you don't want to back up *all* your data—just the company file. That way, if the experiment goes terribly wrong, you can restore the backup and try a different approach. You can also call on QuickBooks Backup when you've worked hard on your company file (pasting hundreds of inventory items into the file from Excel [page 654], say) and the thought of losing that work makes you queasy. In both these situations, running a QuickBooks *manual backup* (page 179) creates a backup file immediately.

- **Schedule backups of your QuickBooks data**. If you have trouble remembering to back up your work, QuickBooks' scheduled and automatic backups can help. You can set the program up to automatically back up a company file after you've opened it a certain number of times. That way, if you mangle your data or it gets corrupted in some way, you can use one of these backups to recover. The program can also create company-file backups automatically according to the schedule you specify—Tuesdays through Saturdays at 2:00 a.m., for example.

- **Back up your data online**. Online backups are a handy alternative to setting up your own backup plan—scheduling regular backups, rotating backup media, storing backups offsite, and so on. You can select which data you want to back up and when. That way, when QuickBooks creates the backups, your backup files are encrypted and stored at secure data centers managed by IT professionals. If you don't have IT staff to back up your data and keep it secure, this method may be worth every penny. See the box on page 180 to learn more.

> **NOTE** QuickBooks backup files aren't merely copies of your company files—they're compressed files that take up less space (about 20 to 25 percent less, depending on what you store in your company file).

Whether you want to set up options for your backups, schedule backups, or run a backup immediately, open the Create Backup dialog box by choosing File→Backup Company→Create Local Backup.

NOTE What and how often you back up are up to you (or your company's system administrators). It depends on what information you can't afford to lose and how much data you're willing to recreate in case of a disaster. Most companies back up their data every night and also create additional backup copies daily or weekly to store off site.

If you rely on your company-wide backups, consider testing their reliability at least once a year. Tell the IT folks that you've deleted your QuickBooks company file and see if they can provide you with a recent backup. (Then, bring them donuts the next day as a thank you.)

Choosing Standard Backup Settings

For each company file that you back up, you can choose when, where, and how many backups QuickBooks creates. These standard settings are great timesavers and make for consistent backups. For example, you can tell QuickBooks to ask you about backing up your data after you've closed the company file a specific number of times, or have it automatically append the date and time that you run the backup to the name of the backup file. You simply choose these settings once for each company file, and QuickBooks then uses them for every backup of that file—until you change the settings, of course.

Here's how to choose your backup settings:

1. **Choose File→Backup Company→Create Local Backup.**

    The Create Backup dialog box opens with the "Local backup" option selected.

2. **Click Options.**

    The Backup Options dialog box (Figure 7-1) lays out your choices for backing up the current company file.

3. **In the "Tell us where to save your backup copies (required)" box, click Browse. In the "Browse for Folder" dialog box, choose where you want to save the backup file, and then click OK to return to the Backup Options dialog box.**

    To protect your data from both human error and hardware failure, back up your file to a different hard drive than the one where you company file is stored, or to removable media like a CD, DVD, or USB thumb drive. That way, your backup file will be safe if the hard drive where you keep your company file crashes. For that reason, if you choose a backup location that's on the same drive as where you store your company file, when you click OK in the Backup Options dialog box (step 8 below), QuickBooks displays a dialog box with two buttons: Change Location and "Use this location." As long as you run company-wide backups that store your data on another disk or removable media, backing up your company file to a hard drive is fine for protection during the day; in that case, click "Use this location." To save the backup in a different spot, click Change Location, which returns you to the Backup Options dialog box so you can click Browse again.

FIGURE 7-1

The top section of this dialog box includes settings that apply only to local backups, like the location and the number of backup copies you want to save. The settings in the "Online and local backup" section, on the other hand, apply whether you create a backup on your computer or use one of Intuit's online backup services (page 180). For example, you can specify how thoroughly you want the program to verify that your data isn't corrupted.

NOTE The "Browse for Folder" dialog box doesn't let you create a new folder. So if you want to save your backups in a folder that doesn't exist yet, click Cancel and create the new folder in Windows Explorer. Then, in the Backup Options dialog box, click Browse.

4. **So that you never overwrite a backup file, make sure the "Add the date and time of the backup to the file name (recommended)" checkbox is turned on.**

   With this setting turned on, when QuickBooks creates the backup file, it tacks a timestamp onto the end of the filename prefix so that the name looks something like *Double Trouble, Inc (Backup Jul 19,2012 08 46 PM).qbb*. That way, unless you make multiple backups within a minute of each other, you can be sure that your filenames are unique.

5. **To cap the number of backup copies you save, keep the "Limit the number of backup copies in this folder to" checkbox turned on and choose a number.**

   With this setting on, QuickBooks takes care of deleting older backup files. QuickBooks automatically sets the limit to three, which is fine if you use a full-fledged backup program to back up all your data including your company files. If you back up your files to an insatiable hard disk, you can change this setting to save up to 99 backups before QuickBooks starts deleting older ones.

NOTE When you create a backup that hits the limit you set for manual backup copies in the folder, QuickBooks displays the Delete Extra Backups? dialog box, which asks you if you want to keep or delete the oldest manual backup file. Click "Yes, Delete" to delete the oldest file, or "No, Don't Delete" if you decide to keep the file after all.

6. **To have QuickBooks nudge you to back up your file every so often, in the "Online and local backup" section, make sure the "Remind me to back up when I close my company file every _ times" checkbox is on.**

   That way, when you've closed the company file that number of times (it's set to four unless you change it), QuickBooks displays the Automatic Backup message box. To create a backup of your company file, click Yes, which takes you to the Create Backup dialog box so you can run a manual backup. If you decide to bypass this automatic backup, click No in the message box instead.

NOTE The "Remind me to back up when I close my company file every _ times" checkbox in the Backup Options dialog box sounds a lot like the "Save backup copy automatically when I close my company file every _ times" checkbox for scheduled backups (page 181), but they do different things. The checkbox in the Backup Options dialog box tells QuickBooks to *ask* you if you want to back up your file after you've closed it that many times, whereas the "Save backup copy automatically when I close my company file every _ times" checkbox for scheduled backups tells QuickBooks to create a backup file automatically—*without asking*—after you close the company file that many times.

7. **Select a verification option.**

   If your company file is in single-user mode, QuickBooks automatically selects "Complete verification." For a file in multi-user mode, the program automatically selects "Quicker verification," because complete verification isn't available for multi-user files. Quicker verification, as its name suggests, is speedier than "Complete verification" but risks letting some corrupted data slip through. If you want to make sure that the data you save isn't corrupt, first switch your company file to single-user mode and then, in the Backup Options dialog box, select the "Complete verification (recommended)" option. At the other extreme, for high speed—and higher risk—select "No verification."

8. **When all the settings look good, click OK to close the Backup Options dialog box.**

   If you see a dialog box that includes a Change Location button, see step 3 for help deciding which option to choose.

9. **Back in the Create Backup dialog box, click Finish to run a backup with the settings you chose.**

   Click Cancel to close the dialog box without running a backup.

Backing Up Manually

If you just spent several hours recording tricky transactions in QuickBooks, you definitely want to save that work. To run a backup right away, here's what you do:

1. **If you want to back up your file to removable media like a CD, or DVD, put the disc in the drive.**

   You don't *have* to put the media in until just before you click Save, but you may as well do it now so you don't forget.

2. **Choose File→Backup Company→Create Local Backup.**

   The Create Backup dialog box opens.

3. **To save the file to your computer, choose "Local backup" (if it isn't already selected), and then click Next.**

   The Create Backup dialog box includes options for backing up your file locally—on your computer—or online. To create an online backup, select (you guessed it) the "Online backup" option. QuickBooks' online backup service isn't free, but it has its advantages, as the box on page 180 explains.

4. **For a local backup, on the "When do you want to save your backup copy?" screen, choose "Save it now" (if it isn't already selected), and then click Next.**

   The Save Backup Copy dialog box opens to the folder you specified in Quick-Books' backup options (page 176), as Figure 7-2 shows. If you want to save the file somewhere else, browse to the folder.

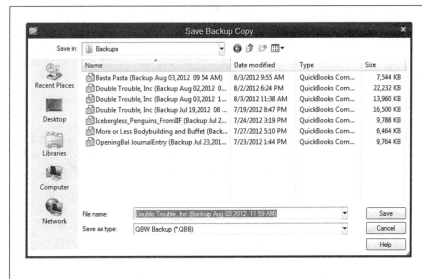

FIGURE 7-2

QuickBooks automatically fills in the "File name" box with the same filename prefix as your company file and adds a timestamp to show when you made the backup—unless you told it not to (see step 4 on page 177). For example, if you're backing up your Double Trouble.qbw file, the backup file prefix is something like "Double Trouble (Backup Aug 03,2012 11 38 AM)." In the "Save as type" box, the program automatically selects "QBW Backup (*.QBB)," which is what you want.

5. **Click Save.**

The Working message box shows QuickBooks' progress as it verifies the data and creates the backup. When the backup is complete, another message box tells you the backup was successful. Click OK to close the box.

Backing Up Online

Online backup services cost money, but as long as your Internet connection is relatively fast, an online backup service is usually a worthwhile investment. You can use it to back up *all* your data—databases, documents, and email—so your backups reside in a data center managed by IT experts who live, eat, and breathe effective backup procedures.

Intuit Data Protect (*http://marketplace.intuit.com/AppID-3356-Overview.aspx*) can back up your entire computer and automatically runs backups in the background every day so they don't interrupt your work—even if you have your QuickBooks company file open. Intuit recommends that you run Intuit Data Protect on only one PC. The service costs $4.95 a month to back up one QuickBooks company file or $9.95 a month to back up your entire PC.

You can check out the service with a 30-day free trial. Intuit's backup services aren't the only game in town. If the benefits of backing up online sound good, look at other services before you make your decision. Dropbox (*www.dropbox.com*) is a backup

and synchronization service, perfect for financial professionals on the go. When you store files in a special folder on your computer, Dropbox copies them to your online account. If you hit the road with your laptop, Dropbox synchronizes the files onto your laptop when you go online. You get 2 GB of storage for free; 100 GB, 200 GB, or 500 GB of data costs $9.99, $19.99, or $49.99 a month, respectively. SugarSync (*www.sugarsync.com*) is a similar backup and synchronization service, which offers 5 GB of storage free, 30 GB for $4.99 per month, and up to 500 GB for $39.99 per month.

Another option with a different approach is CrashPlan (*www.crashplan.com*), which lets you back up files to the destination of your choice: another hard disk on your computer, from your laptop to your desktop computer, a computer in another location, even from a Mac to a PC. CrashPlan compresses your files, so backups take no time at all. You can download CrashPlan software at no charge, or purchase its online backup service. See *www.crashplan.com* for pricing details.

Automated Backups

QuickBooks can back up your data without your help in two different ways:

- **Automatic backup**. This kind of backup runs after you close a company file a specific number of times, which is great for protecting the work you do in a few back-to-back QuickBooks sessions. You simply close the company file at the end of a session and, if this session hits the magic number, QuickBooks asks if you want to create a backup.

- **Scheduled backups**. You can also schedule backups to run at a specific date and time (typically when you aren't around). A scheduled backup for a single company file is ideal when your QuickBooks data is the *only* data on your computer or you want to back up your books more often than your other data. Otherwise, you're better off using your operating system's backup feature (or an online backup service—see the box on page 180) to schedule a backup that captures *all* your data.

This section explains the differences between these options and how you set up each one.

■ SETTING UP AUTOMATIC BACKUPS

Automatic backups require a bit of setup. You tell QuickBooks where you want to store the backup files and the number of sessions between backups, and from then on, they spawn themselves quietly in the background. Here's what you do:

1. **Choose File→Backup Company→Create Local Backup. In the Create Backup dialog box, select the "Local backup" option, and then click Next.**

   The "When do you want to save your backup copy?" screen appears.

2. **To tell QuickBooks when to create automatic backups, select the "Only schedule future backups" option, and then click Next.**

   QuickBooks displays the settings you can use to define both automatic and scheduled backups (Figure 7-3).

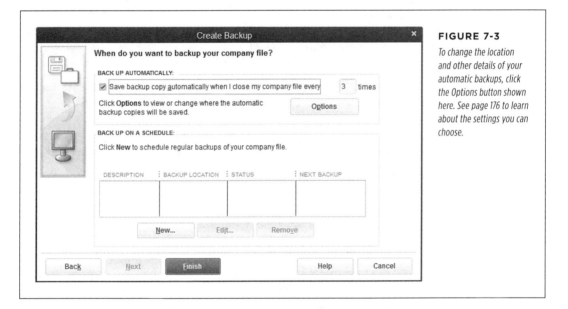

FIGURE 7-3

To change the location and other details of your automatic backups, click the Options button shown here. See page 176 to learn about the settings you can choose.

3. **Turn on the "Save backup copy automatically when I close my company file every _ times" checkbox. In the text box, type the number of sessions you want in between automatic backups.**

   For example, if you type *5*, QuickBooks creates an automatic backup when you close the company file the fifth time since the last backup.

4. **Click Finish.**

QuickBooks starts counting. After you've completed the number of sessions you specified for the company file, the QuickBooks Automatic Backup message box appears, telling you that it's creating the backup as promised.

The file-naming convention that QuickBooks uses for automatic backup files is:

ABU_0_<company name> <date stamp> <time stamp>

For example, the first automatic backup file might be *ABU_0_Double Trouble, Inc Mar 13,2013 05 17 PM* (ABU stands for "automatic backup"). When QuickBooks creates the next automatic backup, it renames the file that begins with ABU_0 to start with ABU_1 (*ABU_1_Double Trouble, Inc Mar 13,2013 05 17 PM*, for example), renames the ABU_1 file to start with ABU_2, and so on. With this system, you always know that the automatic backup file that starts with ABU_0 is the most recent.

■ SCHEDULING BACKUPS FOR A SINGLE COMPANY FILE

Although most companies back up all their computers on a regular schedule, you can set up a scheduled backup for your QuickBooks company file for an extra layer of safety. If you back up your data every other day, for example, you may want to back up your company file every night, and a QuickBooks scheduled backup is the ideal way to do that. Here's how you schedule backups:

1. **Choose File→Backup Company→Create Local Backup. In the Create Backup dialog box, select the "Local backup" option, and then click Next.**

The "When do you want to save your backup copy?" screen appears.

2. **Select the "Only schedule future backups" option, and then click Next.**

If you want to make a backup right away as well as set up the schedule, select the "Save it now and schedule future backups" option instead. Either way, the screen that appears includes a table showing scheduled backups you've already set up (if any), plus each backup's description, location, status, and next occurrence.

3. **To set up a schedule, below the table, click New.**

QuickBooks opens the Schedule Backup dialog box (Figure 7-4), which includes all the options you need to set up a regularly scheduled backup.

4. **In the Description box, type a meaningful name for the backup, like** *Daily* **or** *Monthly Offsite*.

When you finish defining the schedule, this description will appear in the table in the Create Backup dialog box. Consider including the backup's frequency and location (such as the network drive or offsite location) in the name.

5. **Click Browse to specify the backup location.**

QuickBooks opens the "Browse for Folder" dialog box. To choose a folder, hard drive, or other location on your computer, expand the Computer or My Computer entry (depending on your operating system), and then choose the location you want. To store the backup on another computer on your network, expand the Network or My Network Places entry instead, and then choose a location. Click OK when you're done.

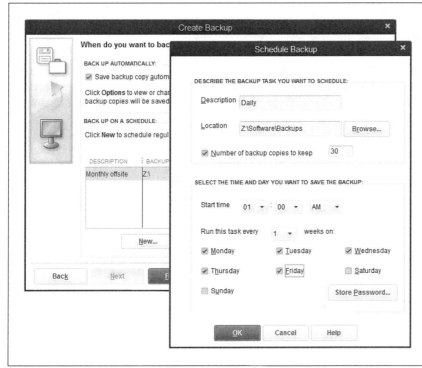

WARNING If you've scheduled backups, don't turn off your computer when you go home, or the backups won't work. And if you back up to a hard drive on another computer, leave that computer running, too.

6. **If you back up your company file to a hard drive and don't want to overwrite the previous backup each time the scheduled backup runs, turn on the "Number of backup copies to keep" checkbox and, in the box to the right of the label, type the number of previous backups you want to keep.**

When you turn on this checkbox, QuickBooks uses the filename *SBU_0_<company name> <date stamp> <time stamp>*. For example, your scheduled backup file might be *SBU_0_Double Trouble, Inc Sep 24,2013 01 00 AM* (SBU stands for "scheduled backup"). Each time QuickBooks creates a new scheduled backup file, it renames the previous backups to the next number in the list, and then replaces the SBU_0 file with the new backup. For example, if you keep four backups, the SBU_2 backup becomes the SBU_3 file; the SBU_1 file becomes the SBU_2 file; the SBU_0 backup file becomes the SBU_1 file; and the new backup becomes the new SBU_0 file. The most recent backup always starts with "SBU_0."

7. **In the "Start time" boxes, choose when you want the backup to run.**

   These boxes work on a 12-hour clock, so specify the hour, the minute, and AM or PM.

TIP It's easy to confuse midnight and noon on a 12-hour clock (midnight is 12:00 a.m., noon is 12:00 p.m.). Avoid this gotcha by running your scheduled backups at 11:00 p.m., 1:00 a.m., or later.

---

8. **To set the backup's frequency, in the "Run this task every _ weeks on" box, select the number of weeks you want between backups, and then turn on the checkboxes for each day of the week on which you want the backup to happen.**

   For example, for daily backups, in the "Run this task every _ weeks on" box, choose *1*, and then turn on the checkbox for each weekday.

9. **Click Store Password, and then type your Windows user name and password.**

   QuickBooks needs this info so it can log into the computer to run the backup.

10. **When you're done, click OK.**

    QuickBooks adds this backup to your list of scheduled backups.

■ Restoring Backups

Having backup files can reduce your adrenaline level in a number of situations:

- You merge two customers by mistake or commit some other major faux pas that you want to undo.

- Your company file won't open, which can happen if it's been damaged by a power outage or a power surge.

- You recently assigned a password to your administrator login and can't remember what it is.

- Your hard disk crashes and takes all your data with it.

WARNING Hard disk crashes used to be dramatic events accompanied by impressive grinding noises. With today's smaller, faster hard disks, crashes can be deceptively quiet. So if you hear any odd sounds emanating from your computer—little chirps or squeaks, for instance—stop what you're doing immediately and take it to a computer repair shop to see if they can fix it or recover your data. If you shut down your computer and it won't reboot because of a disk crash, a data-recovery company can sometimes salvage some of your data, but the price is usually in the thousands of dollars. And if smoke wafts from your computer, don't bother with shutting down—just pull the plug and get that puppy to a repair shop.

NOTE QuickBooks 2011 and later versions can restore backup files to a format you can use in QuickBooks 2010 or earlier—if, for example, a client is still using QuickBooks 2009 and asks you for a copy of her company file. The box on page 187 tells you why and how to restore a backup for an earlier QuickBooks version.

Here's how to restore a QuickBooks backup when you need to recover from a mistake or damaged data:

1. **If you backed up your data to removable media, put the disc containing the backup in the appropriate drive.**

   If you backed up your data to another hard drive on your computer or on a network, make sure you have access to that drive.

2. **Choose File→Backup Company→Restore Previous Local Backup, and then choose the backup you want to restore on the submenu that appears.**

   If the backup you want isn't listed in the submenu, choose File→"Open or Restore Company." In the "Open or Restore Company" dialog box, shown in Figure 7-5, select the "Restore a backup copy" option, and then click Next. Select "Local backup," and then click Next. In the Open Backup Copy dialog box, navigate to your backup file and double-click its name.

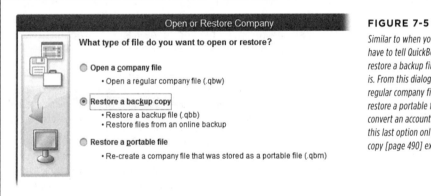

FIGURE 7-5

Similar to when you create backups, you have to tell QuickBooks that you want to restore a backup file and where that file is. From this dialog box, you can open a regular company file, restore a backup, restore a portable file (page 189), or convert an accountant's copy (you'll see this last option only if an accountant's copy [page 490] exists).

3. **In the "Open or Restore Company" dialog box, the "Where do you want to restore the file?" screen makes it clear that you need to choose the restore location carefully. Click Next and, in the "Save Company File as" dialog box, choose the folder where you want to restore the file.**

   If you restore the backup to your regular company-file folder, you run the risk of overwriting your existing company file. If that's what you want, fine. If it's not, that file may be gone for good. To be safe, restore the backup to your desktop. Then, once you know that the restored company file is the one you want, you can move it to the folder where you store your regular company files.

4. In the "File name" box, type a new name for the file you're about to restore.

QuickBooks fills in the "File name" box with the company file's name (minus the timestamp). The safest approach is to modify the name to include a unique identifier, so you don't overwrite your existing company file.

> **TIP** If you give a restored file a different name as a precaution—"Double Trouble Copy," for example—you can trick QuickBooks into renaming the file after you're sure it's the one you want. To do that, create a manual backup of the file (page 179). Then, immediately restore it with the company filename you want ("Double Trouble," in this example).

5. Click Save.

If you're restoring a backup of a company file that already exists and didn't use a unique filename in step 4, QuickBooks warns you that you're about to overwrite an existing file. If the original file is corrupt or won't open for some reason, click Yes because that's exactly what you want to do. In the Delete Entire File dialog box that appears, you also have to type *Yes* to confirm that you want to delete the file. (It's better to take these precautions than to overwrite the wrong file and have to dig out yet another backup.)

If the restored file has a password, you have to log in, just as you do in a regular company file. When you see a message that says your data has been restored successfully, click OK to open the company file and reenter any transactions that the backup doesn't include.

> **NOTE** If restoring a backup copy from removable media (CD, DVD, or USB thumb drive) doesn't work, try copying the contents of the backup media to your hard drive and restoring the backup file from there. If the restore *still* doesn't work, your backup file is probably damaged, so try restoring the next-most-recent backup.

If none of your backups work, Intuit offers data-recovery services to extract data from your backup files. The service isn't free, but it might be cheaper than rebuilding your entire company file. To arrange for this service, choose Help→Support. On the QuickBooks Support web page, click "Contact support" and then call the telephone number listed there. If the support person can't resolve the problem with your file, he or she will transfer you to the Intuit Data Recovery Services team.

■ Sending Company Files to Others

QuickBooks company files can grow quite large as you add year after year of financial transactions. Fortunately, QuickBooks can create *portable* company files, a slim format that flies through the email ether and slips effortlessly into removable media like USB thumb drives and CDs. You can email a portable company file to your accountant or transfer the file to a colleague before you head out on vacation.

TIP If you intend to work on the company file at the same time as your accountant and want to merge her changes into your copy, create an accountant's copy (page 490) instead of a portable copy. But, before you transmit the file electronically, be sure you've added a password to it so nobody else can intercept it and access your financial data.

For example, a company file that's more than 10 MB in size turns into a portable company file of less than 1 MB. Portable company files have a .qbm file extension, but QuickBooks converts them to regular company files with a .qbw file extension when you open them.

NOTE If the person you send the file to is going to make any changes and send the file back, he needs a username and password to login.

DON'T PANIC

Restoring to an Earlier QuickBooks Version

QuickBooks 2010 and more recent versions use a new and improved method to compress backup files that doesn't work with earlier versions of the program. But, when it converts a company file to work with a new version of the program, QuickBooks backs up your file so you can restore it in case you run into trouble. So if you switch back to an earlier version of the program, you can't restore a QuickBooks 2010 or later backup file *directly* in that earlier version. Here's what to do instead:

1. In QuickBooks 2010 or later, choose File→Utilities→Restore Backup For Earlier QuickBooks Version.

2. In the "Select the backup file you want to restore" section of the Restore Your Company File dialog box, click the ellipsis button (...). The Open Backup Copy dialog box appears, displaying the contents of the folder where you last saved backup files.

3. Select the QuickBooks backup file you want to restore, and then click Open.

4. In the "Where do you want to save the restored file?" section of the Restore Your Company File dialog box, click the ellipsis button (...). The "Save Company File as" dialog box appears showing the contents of the backup folder.

5. Navigate to the folder where you want to save the restored file; for example, you might choose the folder you use to store your company files (page 703).

6. In the "File name" box, type a unique name for the restored file, such as *CompanyFileRestored_01052013*, and then click Save.

7. Back in the Restore Your Company File dialog box, click OK. A message box appears telling you that the file has been restored and where it is. Click OK to close the message box.

Now you can open the restored file as a regular company file in the earlier version of QuickBooks.

Creating a Portable Company File

Creating a portable company file is just a wee bit more complicated than saving a file. (You need to be in single-user mode to create a portable company file, so if you're in multi-user mode, switch to single-user mode as explained on page 173 before getting started.)

Here are the steps:

1. **Choose File→Create Copy.**

   This feature lets you create a backup file, a portable company file, *or* an accountant's copy.

2. **In the "Save Copy or Backup" dialog box, select the "Portable company file" option, and then click Next.**

   QuickBooks opens the Save Portable Company File dialog box (Figure 7-6). It automatically fills in the "File name" box with the name of your company file, followed by "(Portable)," and sets the "Save as type" box to "QuickBooks Portable Company Files (*.QBM)."

FIGURE 7-6

Unlike the Save Backup Copy dialog box (page 179), the Save Portable Company File dialog box opens to your computer's desktop the first time around. If you want to save the file to a folder, choose the folder. From then on, QuickBooks opens this dialog box to the last folder you selected.

3. **Choose the folder where you want to restore the file.**

   The Save Portable Company File dialog box opens to your computer's desktop the first time you open it. After that, it opens to the last location where you saved a backup file or copy.

4. **If you want to use a different filename, change the name in the "File name" box. Then click Save.**

   The "Close and reopen" dialog box tells you that you need to close and reopen your company file to create a portable file.

5. **Click OK to create the file.**

   A message box appears when QuickBooks finishes creating the portable company file. Click OK to reopen your company file. (You can tell that the company file is open when you see its name in the main QuickBooks window's title bar.

However, you might have to reopen windows such as the Home page or the Chart of Accounts window.)

Feel free to view the portable company file in Windows Explorer and admire its sleek size.

Opening a Portable Company File

Opening a portable company file is almost identical to restoring a backup file, except for a few different setting labels. When you open a portable company file, QuickBooks essentially converts it into a full-size, bona fide company file. Here's what you do:

1. **Choose File→"Open or Restore Company."**

   If the No Company Open window is visible, you can click "Open or restore an existing company." Either method opens the "Open or Restore Company" dialog box.

2. **In the "Open or Restore Company" dialog box, select the "Restore a portable file" option, and then click Next.**

   QuickBooks opens the Open Portable Company File dialog box to the last folder you selected for portable company files. QuickBooks sets the "Files of type" box to "QuickBooks Portable Company Files (*.QBM)" so the dialog box's list shows only portable company files.

3. **Double-click the portable file you want to restore.**

   Alternatively, click its filename and then click Open.

4. **Back in the "Open or Restore Company" dialog box, the "Where do you want to restore the file?" screen makes it clear that you should choose the location carefully. Click Next.**

   If you restore the portable file to your regular company-file folder, you'll overwrite your existing company file. If that's what you want, fine. Otherwise, be sure to choose another folder or change the filename in the next step.

5. **In the "Save Company File as" dialog box, choose the folder to which you want to restore the file. In the "File name" box, type a new name.**

   The dialog box opens to the folder you last chose for portable files. If you want to replace your company file, choose the folder that holds your everyday company file.

   The safest approach is to modify the filename to include a unique identifier, such as "_restoredportable", so you can easily identify the file you restored. You can then rename the file later (page 186 describes a quick way to do so).

6. **Click Save.**

   If you're restoring a portable file for a company file that already exists, Quick-Books warns you that you're about to overwrite an existing file. If that's what you want, click Yes, and then type *Yes* to confirm that you want to delete the existing file.

The Working message box shows its progress (restoring a portable file can take several minutes). When the file is ready, the QuickBooks Login dialog box appears or, if you don't use a password, the file opens.

Verifying Your QuickBooks Data

QuickBooks files hiccup now and then. Perhaps you worked through a spectacular thunderstorm and a power spike zapped a bit of your company file, for example. Fortunately, QuickBooks has a feature that can scan your company files and tell you whether they've suffered any damage: the Verify Data utility.

It's a good idea to run this utility every so often, just to make sure your company file is OK. How often you should run it depends on how hard you work your company file, but monthly verifications are in order for most companies. The utility is indispensable, though, if you notice any of the following symptoms:

- **The company file won't open.** Sometimes, memorized transactions become corrupt, which prevents you from opening the company file.

- **Error messages**. If you see errors in message boxes when you run QuickBooks, you almost certainly have a damaged company file.

- **Discrepancies on reports**. Your balance sheet doesn't show all your accounts, or transactions show negative values instead of positive ones.

> **TIP** If the totals in your reports don't seem right, first check that the report dates are correct and that you're using the right cash or accrual accounting setting (see page 625).

- **Missing transactions and names**. Transactions or names that you're sure you entered don't appear in reports or lists.

- **You can't save transactions**. QuickBooks doesn't save a transaction or shuts down when you try to save a transaction.

- **QuickBooks misbehaves**. It's a good idea to verify your company file if QuickBooks shuts down on its own, your computer crashes, a "Company file in use, please wait" message appears, or you see other strange behavior from QuickBooks or your computer.

Running the Verify Data Utility

Whether you're just giving your company file a checkup or you see signs of problems, the Verify Data utility is easy to use:

1. **Close QuickBooks and then restart it.**

   This makes QuickBooks create a new *QBWIN.log* file, which will contain only the results of the data verification you run in step 3.

NOTE   You can verify data in multi-user mode, although no other users will be able to use QuickBooks while it's verifying the company file. In addition, the program can perform a more thorough verification when the file is in single-user mode. So you're best off switching to single-user mode (page 173) before running this utility.

2. **Choose File→Utilities→Verify Data to start the utility. (If any windows are open, click OK to give QuickBooks permission to close them.)**

    You can close all QuickBooks windows before you run the utility by choosing Window→Close All.

3. **If you see the message "Your data has lost integrity," then your company file has some problems. Continue to the next section to learn how to rebuild your data.**

    If QuickBooks displays a message saying that it detected no problems with your data, congratulations—your file is healthy!

Reviewing Problems

If your company file has "lost integrity," the Verify Data utility writes down any errors it finds in a file named *QBWIN.log*. Before you run the Rebuild Data utility (which can help fix the problems QuickBooks found), it's a good idea to take a look at this log file and review your company file's problems. However, you'll need a map to find the log file. Here's how:

1. **Open Windows Explorer and locate the folder where QuickBooks stores *QBWIN.log*.**

    In Windows 7, it's *C:\Users\<your user name>\AppData\Local\Intuit\Quick-Books\log\23.0*.

    In Windows XP, it's *C:\Documents and Settings\<your user name>\Local Settings\Application Data\Intuit\QuickBooks\log\23.0*.

NOTE   Windows initially hides application-data folders like the log folder you're looking for here. If you don't see the folder, in Windows Explorer's menu bar, choose Organize→"Folder and search options" (in Windows 7) or Tools→Folder Options (in Windows XP). Then click the View tab. In the "Advanced settings" list, under "Hidden files and folders," select "Show hidden files, folders, and drives."

2. **Open the log file by double-clicking its name.**

    The file opens in Notepad, and you can use Notepad's features to move around the file. (If the file doesn't open, launch Notepad, choose File→Open, and then double-click the *QBWIN.log* filename.)

    When you verify data, QuickBooks automatically renames the previous *QBWIN.log* file to *QBWIN.log.old1* so that the *QBWIN.log* file contains information for only the most recent verification. QuickBooks also renames other old files, changing *QBWIN.log.old1* to *QBWIN.log.old2*, and so on.

Running the Rebuild Data Utility

If your file is damaged, QuickBooks' Rebuild Data utility tries to fix it. Intuit recommends that you run the Rebuild Data utility *only* if an Intuit technical support person tells you to. *Always* make a backup of your company file before trying to rebuild it, and take extra care to prevent overwriting your previous backups—those files might be your only salvation if the rebuild doesn't work.

To run the Rebuild Data utility, choose File→Utilities→Rebuild Data. When the utility is done working, close your company file and reopen it; this refreshes the lists in the company file so you can see if the problems are gone. Then run the Verify Data utility once more to see if any damage remains. If this second Verify Data run still shows errors, then restore a recent backup of your company file (page 184).

Condensing Data

As you add transactions and build lists in QuickBooks, your company file gets larger. Although larger company files aren't too big of a hassle, you might be alarmed when your company file reaches hundreds of megabytes. Backups will take longer and use up more storage space. Meet the Condense Data utility, which creates an archive file and deletes obsolete list items and transactions prior to the date you choose.

WARNING The Condense Data utility removes the audit trail information for transactions that it deletes. So if you're watching transaction activity, print an Audit Trail report and back up your company file *before* condensing.

When QuickBooks condenses data, it replaces the detailed transactions prior to the date you specify with general journal entries that summarize the deleted transactions by month. As a result, some of your financial details are no longer available for running reports, filing taxes, and other accounting activities. Still, there are a couple of compelling reasons to condense your data:

- **You no longer refer to old transactions**. If you're a QuickBooks veteran, you probably *don't* need the finer details from eight or more years ago. And if you ever do need details from the past, you can open an archive file to run reports.

- **You have obsolete list items**. Cleaning up a company file can remove list items that you don't use, like customers you no longer sell to. This option comes in handy if you're nearing the program's limit on the number of names you can store (page 68).

NOTE If Condense Data isn't the housekeeper you hoped for, you have a couple of options. One is to start a fresh company file. That way, you can export all the lists from your existing company file (page 649) and import them (page 657) into the new one so you start with lists but no transactions. Set your accounts' opening balances (page 58) to the values for the start date of the new file. Or, you can hand your company file over to a company that provides file cleanup and repair services, such as "QB or not QB" (*www.qbornotqb.com*).

An archive file created by the Condense Data utility is a regular company file that contains all your transactions, but it's *read-only*, meaning you can't add data to it or edit it, so you can't inadvertently enter new transactions. If QuickBooks runs into trouble condensing your file, it automatically pulls transaction details from the archive file. An archive copy *isn't* a backup file, which means you can't restore it to replace a corrupt company file. So even if you create an archive copy, you still need to back up your data.

If you decide to condense your company file, here's what you can expect to find afterward, depending on the settings you choose:

- **General journal entries that summarize deleted transactions**. QuickBooks replaces all the deleted transactions that happened during each month with one general journal entry. For example, instead of 20 separate invoices for the month of June, you'll see one journal entry transaction with the total income for June for each income account.

NOTE   If you see other transactions for the same month, it means that QuickBooks wasn't able to delete those transactions for some reason. For instance, if you tell it not to, QuickBooks won't delete unpaid invoices or other transactions with an open balance, nor will it delete any transactions in the queue to be printed (page 345) or ones that you haven't reconciled (page 426).

- **Inventory adjustments that reflect the average cost of items**. If you tell it to, QuickBooks removes inventory transactions that are complete, such as invoices that have been paid in full. Because inventory transactions use the average cost of inventory items, QuickBooks adds an inventory adjustment to set the average cost of the items as of the condense date. When the program finds an inventory transaction that it can't condense (perhaps because the payment is outstanding), it keeps all the inventory transactions from that date forward.

- **Reports might not include the details you want**. You can still generate summary reports because QuickBooks can incorporate the info in the monthly general journal entries. Likewise, sales tax reports still include data about your sales tax liabilities. But detailed reports won't include transaction details before the cutoff date you chose for condensing the file (see page 194). And cash accounting reports (page 625) might not be accurate because they need the dates for detailed transactions. Talk with your accountant to see how your cash basis reports might be affected.

- **You still have payroll info for the current year**. QuickBooks keeps payroll transactions for the current year and the previous year regardless of the cutoff date you chose for condensing the file.

- **QuickBooks deletes estimates for closed jobs**. If a job has any status other than Closed, QuickBooks keeps the estimates for that job. Or, you can tell QuickBooks to remove *all* estimates, sales orders, purchase orders, and pending invoices.

- **QuickBooks retains unbilled expenses, items, time, and mileage**. The program keeps any unbilled charges, unless you tell it to delete those transactions.

Running the Condense Data Utility

If you're ready to condense your company file, first consider *when* to do it. The cleaning process can take several hours for a large company file, and a slow computer or a small amount of memory exacerbates the problem. You might want to condense your file over the weekend so the utility has plenty of time to run before folks come in Monday morning.

Here's how to condense a company file:

1. **If you've created budgets in QuickBooks, export them (page 526) before you condense your data.**

   After you condense your data, you can import them back into your company file (page 529).

2. **Choose File→Utilities→Condense Data.**

   The Condense Data dialog box opens.

3. **Select the "Transactions before a specific date" option.**

   This option deletes old transactions and things like unused accounts and items.

   The "All transactions" option removes transactions but keeps your preferences, lists, and service subscriptions—such as payroll—intact. You won't use this option often, but it comes in handy if, for example, you want to offer your clients a template company file that contains typical list entries but no transactions.

4. **In the "Remove transactions before" box, type or select the ending date for the period you want to condense, and then click Next.**

   If you use an Intuit payroll service (page 409), you can't clean up data for the current year. QuickBooks also won't let you clean up transactions that are newer than the closing date on your company file (page 600). Choosing a date at least two years in the past ensures that you can compare detailed transactions for the current year and the previous year. For example, if it's March 1, 2013, consider using January 1, 2011, or earlier as your cutoff date.

NOTE If there are no transactions to condense before the date you picked, you'll see the message "There are no transactions to remove on or before the date you entered. Please verify the Condense process date." Either pick a date closer to today's date or click Cancel, because there aren't any transactions to condense.

5. **If you see the How Should Transactions Be Summarized screen (you may not), select your preferred method.**

   Your options are to have QuickBooks create one summary journal entry for all the transactions it condensed, create a summary journal entry for each month prior to the date you selected, or not create a summary at all. QuickBooks automatically selects the first option, and you're best off sticking with that so you have a record of your previous transactions without dozens of summary journal entries cluttering your company file.

6. **If you see the How Should Inventory Be Condensed? screen, keep the "Summarize inventory transactions (recommended)" option selected and click Next.**

   This removes inventory transactions that QuickBooks can condense and replaces them with inventory adjustments (page 513).

7. **On the Do You Want To Remove The Following Transactions? screen, turn *off* the appropriate checkboxes if you want to *keep* transactions that the clean-up process would condense, and then click Next.**

   Figure 7-7 shows your choices. QuickBooks turns on all the checkboxes initially. Before you click Next, carefully review your company file to make sure that the settings you choose here won't delete transactions you want to keep.

FIGURE 7-7

These checkboxes let you remove transactions that the Condense Data utility would normally leave alone—like transactions marked "To be printed" that you don't need to print. If you have very old, unreconciled transactions, invoices, or estimates marked "To be sent," or transactions with unreimbursed costs, leave the appropriate checkboxes turned on to remove them during the condensing.

Within the figure:

Condense Data   ✕

Do You Want To Remove The Following Transactions?

QuickBooks recommends that you remove the following transactions:

☑ Uncleared (unreconciled) bank and credit card transactions
☑ Transactions marked 'To be printed'
☑ Invoices and Estimates marked 'To be sent'
☑ ALL Estimates, Sales Orders, Purchase Orders, and Pending Invoices
☑ ALL Time and Mileage activities
☑ Transactions containing unbilled expenses and items

[Select None]

Archive

[Back] [Next] [Begin Condense]   [Help] [Cancel]

8. **On the Do You Want To Remove Unused List Entries? screen, turn off the appropriate checkboxes if you want QuickBooks to keep specific list items. Then click Next.**

   Accounts, customers, vendors, other names, and invoice items might become orphans when you delete old transactions they're linked to. You can neaten your file by removing these list items, which now have no links to the transactions that still remain. QuickBooks initially turns on all the checkboxes on this screen. But keep in mind that you might still work with one of these vendors or customers later. If that's the case, turn off checkboxes to tell the program to keep unused list entries.

9. **On the Begin Condense screen, click Begin Condense.**

   If you're not sure of the options you chose, or if you have any doubts about condensing your file, click Back to return to a previous screen, or click Cancel to exit without condensing.

When you click Begin Condense, QuickBooks first creates an archive copy file (a QuickBooks company file, not a backup file) in the same folder as your original company file. The filename for the archive copy has the format *<company name> mm-dd-yyyy Copy.qbw*, where "mm-dd-yyyy" represents the month, day, and year that you created the file.

As QuickBooks proceeds with the condensing process, it scans your data *three* times. You might see message boxes wink on and off in rapid succession; then again, you might not see anything happen for a while if your file is large. But if your hard disk is working, the condensing process is still in progress. When it's finished, QuickBooks displays a message telling you so and shows you where it stored the archive copy of your company file.

> **TIP** After your file is condensed, run a balance sheet report (page 474) and compare your account balances in the condensed file to those in the uncondensed file.

Cleaning Up after Deleting Files

QuickBooks doesn't include a feature for deleting company files, which is no biggie. If you want to get rid of a practice file you no longer use, you can easily delete it right in Windows. But you'll still have to do some housekeeping to remove all references to that file from QuickBooks. For example, a deleted company file will still appear in QuickBooks' list of previously opened files (page 19), but the program won't be able to find the file if you choose it in the list.

Here's how to delete a company file and eliminate stale entries in the QuickBooks list of previously opened files:

1. **In Windows Explorer, navigate to the folder where your QuickBooks company files are stored, and find the company file you want to delete.**

   What to look for when searching for your company file depends on how you've set up your folder view. If your folder shows the full names of files, look for a file with a .qbw file extension, such as *Double Trouble, Inc.qbw*. If the folder includes a Name column and a Type column, the type you want is QuickBooks Company File.

   Files with .qbx extensions represent accountant's copies (page 490). Files with .qbb file extensions are backup copies of company files. Portable files come with .qbm file extensions. If you delete the company file, go ahead and delete the backups, accountant's copies, and portable files as well if you no longer need them.

2. **Right-click the file and on the shortcut menu, choose Delete.**

   Windows displays the File Delete message box. Click Yes to move the file to the Recycle Bin. If you have second thoughts, click No to keep the file.

3. **In QuickBooks, choose File→Open Previous Company→"Set number of previous companies."**

   If this menu item is grayed out, it means you don't have a company file open. In that case, in the File→Open Previous Company submenu, choose a file *other* than the file you just deleted. Alternatively, if the No Company Open window is visible, open the company file that you typically work with by double-clicking it. Either way, you should now be able to select the "Set number of previous companies" menu item.

4. **In the "How many companies do you want to list (1 to 20)?" box, type *1* and then click OK.**

   If you choose File→Open Previous Company again, you'll notice that only one company appears—the company file you opened last. The No Company Open window also shows only the company file you opened last.

5. **To reset the number of previously opened companies, with a company file open, choose File→Open Previous Company→"Set number of previous companies."**

   In the "How many companies do you want to list (1 to 20)?" box, type the number of companies you'd like to see in the list, and then click OK.

As you open different company files, QuickBooks adds them to the list in the No Company Open window and the Open Previous Company menu.

Tracking Time and Mileage

Whom customers pay for your services, they're really buying your knowledge of how to get the job done the best and fastest possible way. That's why an inexperienced carpenter charges $15 an hour, whereas a master who hammers faster and straighter than a nail gun charges $80 an hour. When it comes right down to it, time is money, so you want to keep track of both with equal accuracy. Product-based companies track time, too. For example, companies that want to increase productivity often start by tracking the time that employees work and what they work on.

There are hordes of off-the-shelf and homegrown time-tracking programs out there, but if your time-tracking needs are fairly simple, you can record time directly in QuickBooks or use its companion Timer program, which you can provide to each person whose work hours you want to track. The advantage of tracking time in QuickBooks is that the hours you record are ready to attach to an invoice (see page 297) or use in payroll (see page 411). In this chapter, you'll learn how to record time in QuickBooks itself. Appendix D (online at *www.missingmanuals.com/cds*) explains the ins and outs of the standalone Timer program.

> **NOTE** Intuit's two online time-tracking services, Time Tracker and Time and Billing Manager, have been discontinued. If your time-tracking needs outpace the time tracking features of QuickBooks itself, Intuit's marketplace (*http://marketplace.intuit.com*) lists almost 50 time-tracking solutions that integrate with QuickBooks. Click Search By Business Need and then click Time Tracking. You can then turn on the checkboxes that appear to specify features you're looking for, such as online access or the ability to track time against projects. To search further afield, type keywords like "QuickBooks time tracking" into your favorite Internet search engine.

Mileage is another commodity that many businesses track—or should. Whether your business hinges on driving or merely requires the occasional jaunt, the IRS lets you deduct vehicle mileage, as long as you can document the miles you deduct. And you might charge customers for the miles driven in conjunction with the work you do for them. As you'll learn in this chapter, QuickBooks can help you track the mileage of company vehicles, which you can use for tax deductions or to charge customers.

Setting Up Time Tracking

For many businesses, *approximations* of time worked are fine. For example, employees who work on only one or two tasks each day can review the past week and log their hours in a weekly timesheet. But for people with deliciously high hourly rates, you want to capture every minute spent on an activity.

QuickBooks can help you track time whether you take a conscientious approach or a more cavalier one. You can choose from two different ways of recording time with QuickBooks:

- **Enter time data in QuickBooks**. You can enter time for individual activities or fill in a weekly timesheet. In the Time/Enter Single Activity dialog box, you can type in the number of hours for a single activity. The dialog box also includes a stopwatch, so you can have it track the time you're working on a task.

- **Use the QuickBooks Timer stopwatch**. This program, which comes on the QuickBooks CD, lets you time activities as you work so you can track your time to the second—as long as you remember to start and stop the Timer at the right moments. (If you forget to turn the Timer on or off, you can edit time entries to correct them.) The best thing about Timer is that you can use it to record time even when QuickBooks isn't running. Moreover, you can give a copy of Timer to all your employees and subcontractors so they can send you time data to import into QuickBooks.

NOTE If you download QuickBooks and want the Timer program, you'll have to order a CD from Intuit.

No matter which technique you use to capture time, the setup is the same: You tell QuickBooks that you want to track time and then set up the people who have to track their time (employees and outside contractors alike). You use the customers and items you've set up in QuickBooks to identify the billable time you work. If you want to track nonbillable time, you need a few more entries in QuickBooks, which you'll learn about in the following sections.

Turning on Time Tracking

If you told QuickBooks that you want to track time when you created your company file (page 14), the time-tracking preferences and features should be ready to go. To see whether time tracking is turned on, choose Edit→Preferences→Time & Expenses, and then click the Company Preferences tab (only a QuickBooks administrator can turn time tracking on or off). If the Yes option below "Do you track time?" (shown in Figure 8-1) isn't selected, click it. (If your company file is in multi-user mode, QuickBooks tells you that you have to switch to single-user mode [page 173] first.)

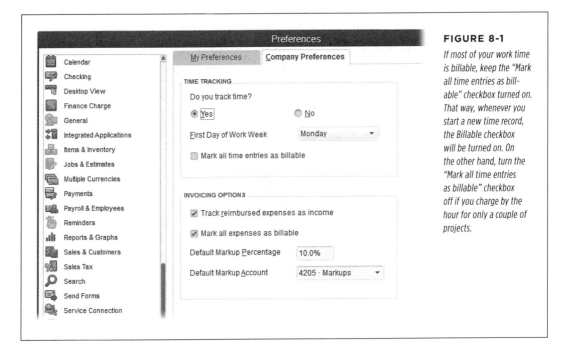

FIGURE 8-1

If most of your work time is billable, keep the "Mark all time entries as bill-able" checkbox turned on. That way, whenever you start a new time record, the Billable checkbox will be turned on. On the other hand, turn the "Mark all time entries as billable" checkbox off if you charge by the hour for only a couple of projects.

QuickBooks automatically sets the First Day of Work Week box to Monday to match the Monday-through-Friday workweek of so many businesses. For round-the-clock services, self-employed people, and workaholics, choose whichever day of the week feels most like the beginning of the week. For example, many companies on a seven-day workweek start the week on Sunday. If you use QuickBooks to generate hours for payroll, you should set the program's workweek to end on the same day as your pay periods. For instance, if you pay employees on Fridays, in the First Day of Work Week drop-down list, choose Saturday so that QuickBooks' workweek ends on Friday, just like your payroll.

> **TIP** To learn about time-related invoicing options, see page 297.

Setting Up the People Who Track Time

You can't enter or import people's time into QuickBooks unless their names appear in one of your name lists (the Employee List, Vendor List, or Other Names List). If someone whose time you want to track isn't on one of those lists yet, here's how you decide which list to use:

- **Employee List**. Use this list for your employees whether you pay them by using QuickBooks' payroll features or in some other way.

- **Vendor List**. Add subcontractors and outside consultants (people or companies that send you bills for time) to this list, whether or not their time is billable to customers. (Their time is undoubtedly billable to *you*.)

- **Other Names List**. By process of elimination, anyone who isn't a vendor or an employee belongs on this list, such as owners who take a draw or partners who take distributions instead of a paycheck (page 404).

People who enter time in QuickBooks (with a weekly timesheet or in the Time/Enter Single Activity dialog box, not with the standalone Timer program) need the program's permission to do so. When you set up QuickBooks users (page 688), you can set their permissions so they can enter time.

Setting Up Items and Customers for Time Tracking

The good news is that you don't have to do any additional item and customer setup to be able to bill time to your customers. The Service items (page 123) and customer records (page 66) you create for invoicing also work for tracking billable time. When you enter time, you choose the Service item you're working on. Then QuickBooks totals your hours and figures out how much to charge the customer based on the number of hours you worked and how much you charge per hour for that service.

The only reason you'd need additional items is if you track *all* the hours that people work, both billable and nonbillable. For example, if you're trying to reduce overhead costs, you might add items to track the time spent on administrative work or providing customer service, as shown in Figure 8-2. (Page 121 explains how to add items.) The level of detail for nonbillable activities is up to you.

Here's how you fill in item fields when you create items to track time that you *don't* bill to a customer:

- **Type**. Use the Service item type (page 123) because that's the only one QuickBooks' time tracking recognizes.

- **Rate**. In the New Item or Edit Item dialog box, the Rate box is where you enter how much you charge for the service. Because no money changes hands for nonbillable time, leave this box set to 0.

- **Account**. You can't create an item without assigning it to an account. Go ahead and create an expense account (page 51) and call it something like Nonbillable Work or Overhead Time. If you number accounts, assign a number that places the account near the end of your Expense type accounts (like 8230).

- **This service is used in assemblies or is performed by a subcontractor or partner**. If a subcontractor performs nonbillable work for you, turn on this checkbox. That way, you can assign the subcontractor's costs to an expense account and use time tracking to make sure the subcontractor's bills are correct. For nonbillable items performed by owners and partners, leave this checkbox turned off.

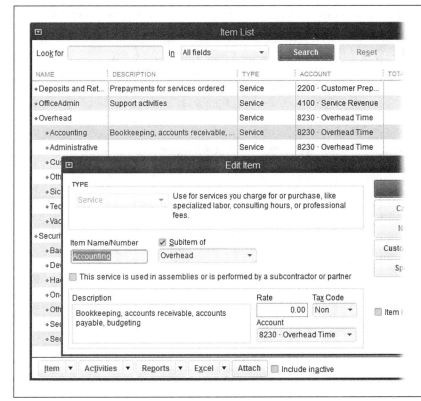

FIGURE 8-2

If you want to capture non-billable activities in one big pot, create a single Service item called Overhead. For greater detail about nonbill-able time, you can create a top-level Overhead item, and then create subitems for each type of nonbillable work you want to track. Be sure to create one catchall item, such as Other, to capture the time that doesn't fit in any other nonbillable category.

Entering Time in QuickBooks

QuickBooks lets you enter and view time for a single activity or for whole weeks. If you record time after the fact, a weekly timesheet is the fastest way to enter time (and you can enter weekly timesheets for more than one person at once). If you already have one timesheet filled out, you can copy it to speed up your data entry, as the box on page 207 explains. To time work as you perform it, the Time/Enter Single Activity dialog box (explained starting on page 207) is the way to go.

Filling out Weekly Timesheets

QuickBooks' weekly timesheet is the fastest way to enter time for several activities or work that spans several days. Here's what you do:

1. **In the Home page's Employees panel, click Enter Time and then, on the drop-down menu, choose Use Weekly Timesheet.**

   QuickBooks opens the Weekly Timesheet window.

NOTE   Although you can track time for people other than employees, you can also access time tracking by choosing Employees→Enter Time→Use Weekly Timesheet.

2. **In the Name drop-down list, choose the person who performed the work.**

   Because time tracking is rarely limited to only the people with permission to run QuickBooks, you can enter time for yourself or anyone else. After you choose a name, the program displays a timesheet for the current week and shows any time already entered for that week, as shown in Figure 8-3. (See the box on page 205 to learn how to create a batch of timesheets in one fell swoop.)

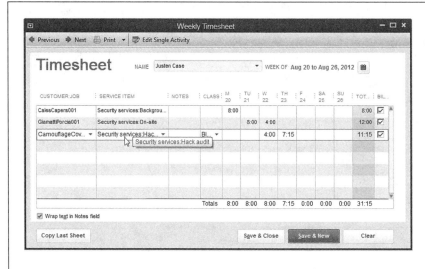

FIGURE 8-3

The weekly timesheet doesn't provide much room to display customer names, job names, or more than a few letters of the Service item for the task performed. To see the full contents of a cell in a pop-up tooltip like the one shown here, position your cursor over the cell. You can also drag a corner of the window to resize it or click the Maximize button near the top right of the window to enlarge it.

3. **To enter time for a different week, in the window's toolbar, click Previous or Next until the week you want appears.**

   To choose a week that's quite a ways in the past, click the calendar icon to the right of the week's date range. In the Set Date dialog box that appears, click the arrows to the left or right of the month heading to move to a past or future month. Click any date during the week to choose that workweek. For example, choosing 16 in the May 2013 calendar switches the timesheet to the week beginning May 13, 2013.

TIP   If an earlier timesheet has entries with customers and items that apply to the current timesheet, you can copy the earlier timesheet as described in the box on page 207.

4. **In the first blank Customer:Job cell (the first column of the timesheet table), choose the customer or job associated with the work that was performed, if applicable.**

If the work is billable, choose the customer or job that pays for it. If the time isn't billable, you can leave this cell blank or choose the customer you created to track nonbillable time. Depending on whether you prefer to keep your hands on the keyboard or the mouse, you can then move to the Service Item cell by clicking it or by pressing Tab.

GEM IN THE ROUGH

Time by the Batch

The Weekly Timesheet window lets you create timesheets for several people at the same time. The only limitation is that the entries in the weekly timesheet have to be identical for all the people you select—that is, the same customer and job, Service item, notes, class, and hours each day. And if the people are paid through payroll, the payroll item has to be the same, too.

Here's how to create a batch timesheet:

1. In the Home page's Employees panel, click Enter Time and then, on the drop-down menu, choose Use Weekly Timesheet.

2. In the Weekly Timesheet window's Name drop-down list, choose "Multiple names (Payroll)" if the people are paid through your payroll service or "Multiple names (Non-

Payroll)" if they're paid another way, such as vendors, contractors, or owners who take an owners' draw.

3. In the "Select Employee, Vendor or Other Name" dialog box, keep the Manual option selected and then click the name of each person you want to add to the batch timesheet to add a checkmark to the left of their names.

4. Click OK.

5. Fill out the weekly timesheet as you would for a single person and then click Save & Close.

QuickBooks creates a timesheet for each person you selected with the information you entered in the timesheet. For example, if you recorded 40 hours of work in the timesheet, each person has a timesheet showing 40 hours.

---

5. **In the Service Item cell, choose the item that represents the work the person performed.**

If you use a QuickBooks' payroll service and pay employees by the hours they work, the Payroll Item column appears to the right of the Service Item column, so you can also fill in the payroll-related item that applies to the time worked. For example, for billable work, choose a payroll item such as Salary or Employee Income. If the hours are for vacation or sick time, choose the payroll item you've created for that kind of time.

6. **In the Notes cell, type any additional information about the work.**

If your customers require details about the work performed, store that info in the Notes cell, which then appears on the invoices you create (see page 301).

TIP To see the entire contents of Notes cells, make sure the "Wrap text in Notes field" checkbox at the bottom of the Weekly Timesheet window is turned on. That way, each row in the Timesheet table takes up more space, but you won't have to position your cursor over every Notes cell to see what it contains.

---

7. **If you use classes to track income (page 150), in the Class column, choose one for the work.**

This column appears only if you've turned QuickBooks' class preference on. If you track income by partner, for example, choose the class for the partner who handles that customer. If you use classes to track office branches, choose the class for the branch where the person works.

8. **To enter time for a day during the week, click the cell for that day or press Tab until you reach the right cell.**

You can enter time in several ways. If you know the number of hours, type them as a decimal or as hours and minutes. For example, for seven and a half hours, type either *7.5* or *7:30*. QuickBooks displays the hours in the timesheet based on the time format preference you set (page 613). If you know the starting and ending time, QuickBooks can calculate the hours for you. For example, if you type *9-5* in a cell, the program transforms it into eight hours when you move to a different cell (by pressing Tab or clicking another cell).

As you enter time for each day of the week, the Total *column* on the right side of the table shows the total hours for each activity. The numbers in the Totals *row* below the table show the total hours for each day and for the entire week.

NOTE Each row in a weekly timesheet represents one service item, one customer or job, and one note. So if you perform the same type of work for two different customers, you have to enter that time in two separate rows. You also have to create another row if you want to record a different note for the same customer and the same service item. You might do this if, for example, you did web-development work for a customer, but want to differentiate the work you did on its online store web page and its marketing web pages.

---

9. **If the time is for overhead or you aren't billing the customer for the work and the checkmark in the "Billable?" column is turned on, click it to turn it off. Conversely, if the checkmark is turned off and the time is billable, click the checkbox to turn it on.**

If you've turned on the "Mark all time entries as billable" preference (page 633), QuickBooks puts a checkmark in the "Billable?" column automatically. If this preference is turned off, the "Billable?" checkbox is blank unless you click it.

TIP Adding billable time to customer invoices is easy; it's described in detail on page 297.

---

10. **To save the timesheet, click Save & Close or Save & New.**

If you're entering time for a number of people, click Save & New to save the current timesheet and open a new blank one. Clicking Save & Close saves the timesheet and closes the Weekly Timesheet window.

UP TO SPEED

Copying Timesheets

People often work on the same tasks from week to week. QuickBooks can reduce tedium and mistakes—and save you time—by copying entries from a person's previous timesheet. Here's how:

1. In the Weekly Timesheet window's Name field, choose the person's name.

2. Display the weekly timesheet you want to copy information *into* by clicking Previous or Next, or clicking the calendar icon.

3. At the bottom of the dialog box, click the Copy Last Sheet button. If the timesheet that's currently displayed is empty, QuickBooks fills in all the rows with the entries from the person's last timesheet, including the customer, service item, class, notes, and hours. If the timesheet already has values, QuickBooks asks whether you want to replace the entries. Click Yes to replace the entries with the ones from the last timesheet you opened. Click No to append the entries from the last timesheet as additional rows in this week's timesheet. To keep the currently displayed timesheet just the way it is, click Cancel.

Entering Time for One Activity

Entering time in a weekly timesheet is quick, but the width of the columns makes it hard to see which customer and service item you're tracking. If you prefer readability to speed, the Time/Enter Single Activity window is a better choice. This window also includes a stopwatch you can use to time your work.

TIP One drawback to the Time/Enter Single Activity window is that you have to fill in every field for every activity. If you grow tired of this form of time entry, then in the window's toolbar, click Timesheet to switch to the Weekly Timesheet window. The weekly timesheet that appears is for the person you selected in the Time/Enter Single Activity window and the week that includes the selected day.

Here's how to enter time for one activity at a time:

1. **In the Home page's Employees panel, click Enter Time and then, on the drop-down menu, choose Time/Enter Single Activity.**

   The Time/Enter Single Activity window opens to today's date.

2. **If you want to record time for a different day, then in the Date field, click the calendar icon and choose the date when the work took place.**

   When you first open the Time/Enter Single Activity window, QuickBooks selects all the text in the Date box. You can replace that date by simply typing a new one, like *3/07/13*.

3. **In the Name drop-down list—which includes vendors, employees, and names from the Other Names List—select the person who performed the work.**

   Employees and other names are near the end of the list.

NOTE   In the Time/Enter Single Activity window, when you select an employee who's paid based on her time (page 411), you'll see the Payroll Item field. Select the payroll item to which the time applies so that the time data generates the values on the person's paycheck. However, if you choose the name of a person who isn't paid based on her time, the Payroll Item field disappears.

4. **In the Customer:Job drop-down list, choose a customer or job.**

   If someone performs work for a real customer or job, choose that customer or job whether or not you bill the time. To track overhead time, choose the customer you created for nonbillable work (page 202).

5. **If the time is billable and the "Billable?" checkbox in the upper-right corner of the window is turned off, click it to turn it on. For nonbillable time, make sure the Billable checkbox is turned off.**

   If you've turned on the "Mark all time entries as billable" preference (page 633), QuickBooks puts a checkmark in the "Billable?" checkbox automatically. If that preference is turned off, the "Billable?" checkbox is blank unless you click it.

6. **In the Service Item drop-down list, choose the item that represents the work performed.**

   Choose the appropriate item, whether it's one you use to invoice customers or a nonbillable item you created to track overhead activities. When you're done, press Tab to move to the Duration box.

7. **In the Duration box, enter the hours worked.**

   If you press Tab to move to the Duration box, QuickBooks automatically selects the contents of the box, so you can simply type the hours worked. If you *click* the Duration box instead, drag to select its contents.

   Enter hours as a decimal or as hours and minutes, such as *5.5* or *5:30*. Or, if you know the starting and ending time, type the range to have QuickBooks calculate the hours. For example, if you type *11-5,* the program fills converts it to *6:00* when you Tab or click away from the Duration box.

   If you work in QuickBooks most of the time, you can also use the Time/Enter Single Activity window to time your work, as shown in Figure 8-4.

NOTE   If you click Previous at the top of the Time/Enter Single Activity window to display another single activity for today and then click Start, the stopwatch feature starts adding additional time to what you've already recorded.

8. **If you track classes, in the Class field, choose the appropriate one. (This field appears only if classes are turned on.) To add notes about the activity, type text in the Notes box.**

   These notes appear in the Notes column of the Weekly Timesheet window and, for billable work, appear on invoices you generate from time worked.

9. **To save the transaction, click Save & New or Save & Close.**

   When you click Save & New, the saved activity represents time for only one day. To record time for another day's work even if it's for the same worker, customer, and Service item, you have to create a new activity.

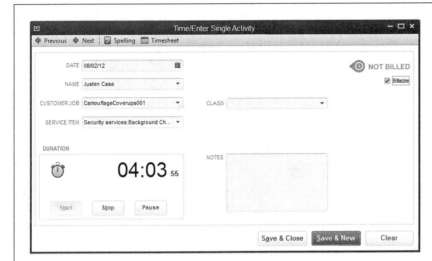

FIGURE 8-4

To time your current activity, the Date field has to be set to today, since, unless you have special time-travel powers, you can't run a stopwatch for work performed on a different day. To start the stopwatch, click the Start button, which is grayed out here. You'll see the seconds that are passing to the right of the Duration box (where it says "55" here) to show that it's timing your work. To pause the stopwatch, click Pause; click Start to start timing again. When you finish the task, click Stop. As long as the stopwatch isn't timing, you can edit the time by typing the time you want.

Running Time Reports

Customers don't like being charged for too many hours, and workers are quick to complain if they're paid for too few. Before you use time records either for billing customers or feeding your payroll records, it's a good idea to generate reports to make sure your time data is correct. (Page 411 explains how to set up employees in QuickBooks so their reported time links to your QuickBooks payroll.)

To generate a time report in QuickBooks, choose Reports→"Jobs, Time & Mileage," and then select the report you want. Here are the ones you can choose from and what they're useful for:

- **Time by Job Summary**. If you bill by the job, this handy report shows hours by customer or job, summarized by Service items, which helps you review the total hours worked on a job during a period. Because of its high-level view, this report is perfect for spotting time charged to inappropriate Service items or hours that exceed job limits. Overly high or low hours—or Service items that don't belong on a job—are red flags for data entry errors. If hours seem too high or low, you can drill down with the Time by Job Detail report to investigate.

- **Time by Job Detail**. Use this report to verify that hours were correctly set as billable or nonbillable. It's grouped first by customer/job and then by Service item, but each time entry shows the date the hours were worked, who performed the work, and whether the work is billable (the billing status is Unbilled for billable hours not yet invoiced, Billed for invoiced billable hours, or Not Billable).

- **Time by Name**. This report shows the hours people have worked on each customer or job, as shown in Figure 8-5. QuickBooks sets the date range to This Fiscal Year-to-date, but if you want to check timesheets for accuracy, you can change it to Last Week, This Week, or whatever time period you want. If a person reports too many or too few hours for a period, use the Weekly Timesheet window (page 203) to look for signs of inaccurate or missing time reports.

- **Time by Item**. This report groups hours by Service item and then by customer or job. You can use this report to analyze how your billable and nonbillable time is spent, either to cut unproductive activities or to determine staffing needs.

Tracking Mileage

If you charge customers for mileage, keeping track of the billable miles you drive helps you get all the reimbursements you're due. But *all* business-related mileage is tax-deductible, so tracking nonbillable business mileage is important, too. Customers and the IRS alike want records of the miles you drive, and QuickBooks can help you produce that documentation.

> **NOTE** QuickBooks' mileage-tracking feature is intended for tracking the miles you drive using company vehicles (and, if you run your own company, the business miles you drive using your own car), not other vehicle expenses, such as fuel or tolls. Likewise, you don't use QuickBooks to record miles driven by employees, vendors, or subcontractors, which instead go straight to an expense account. For example, if a vendor bills you for mileage, when you enter the bill in QuickBooks (page 219), you assign that charge to an expense account, such as Travel-Mileage. When you write a check to reimburse an employee for mileage driven, you assign that reimbursement to the expense account for mileage.

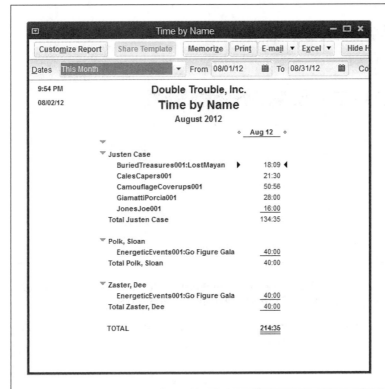

FIGURE 8-5

The Time by Name report summarizes the hours someone works for each customer or job. To see the dates and times of the work, put your cursor over an hourly total. When the magnifying glass icon appears (not shown here), double-click the time to open a "Time by Name Detail" report.

Adding a Vehicle

To track mileage for a company vehicle, you first have to add the vehicle to Quick-Books' Vehicle List. Here's how:

1. **Open the Vehicle List window by choosing Lists→Customer & Vendor Profile Lists→Vehicle List.**

2. **To add a new vehicle, press Ctrl+N or click Vehicle→New.**

   The New Vehicle window (Figure 8-6) opens.

3. **In the Vehicle field, type a name for the vehicle.**

   To easily identify your company cars and trucks, include the type of vehicle and a way to differentiate it from others. For instance, if your company's cars are all white Jeeps, use the license plate number as the name rather than the make and color.

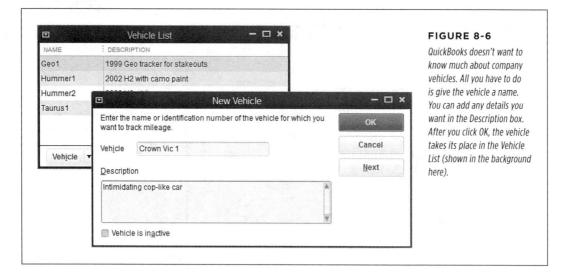

FIGURE 8-6

QuickBooks doesn't want to know much about company vehicles. All you have to do is give the vehicle a name. You can add any details you want in the Description box. After you click OK, the vehicle takes its place in the Vehicle List (shown in the background here).

4. **In the Description box, type additional info such as the year, make, model, license plate number, or Vehicle Identification Number (VIN).**

   To change this information later, in the Vehicle List window, double-click the vehicle's name, and then, in the Edit Vehicle dialog box, edit the name or description.

5. **Click OK.**

That's it. The name and description appear in the Vehicle List window.

Setting the Mileage Rate

For tax purposes, you can deduct mileage expenses based on a standard rate or by tracking the actual costs of operating and maintaining your vehicles. Using a standard mileage rate is convenient—simply multiply the miles you drove by the rate to calculate your vehicle deduction. The box on page 214 explains how you charge customers for mileage if your mileage charge differs from the IRS standard rate. (You don't *have* to set a mileage rate to record the miles you drive, but you'll need a rate in place before you run your tax reports.)

> **TIP** If you own an expensive car with expensive maintenance needs, actual costs might provide a larger deduction. (You can deduct either the standard-rate amount *or* your actual costs, but not both.) But to deduct what you spend on gas, tires, repairs, insurance, and so on, you have to keep track of these expenses. As usual, the tax rules for deducting operating and maintenance costs are, well, taxing. So before you choose this approach, ask your accountant or the IRS if you can deduct actual costs and whether it's the best approach.

QuickBooks stores multiple mileage rates along with their effective dates, because standard mileage rates usually change at the beginning of each calendar year. Here's how to set a mileage rate:

1. **Choose Company→Enter Vehicle Mileage.**

   The Enter Vehicle Mileage window opens.

2. **In the window's toolbar, click Mileage Rates.**

   QuickBooks opens the Mileage Rates window shown in Figure 8-7.

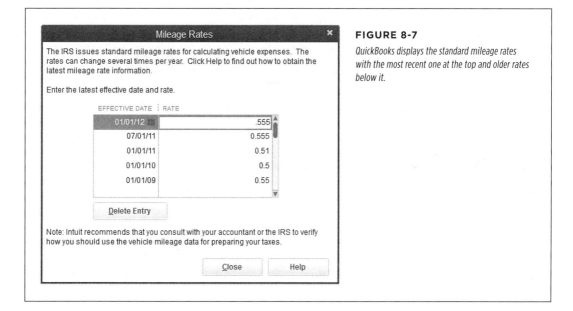

FIGURE 8-7

QuickBooks displays the standard mileage rates with the most recent one at the top and older rates below it.

3. **To add a new rate, click the first blank Effective Date cell at the bottom of the list, and then choose the date that the new mileage rate becomes effective, such as 1/1/2013.**

   You can either type the date or click the calendar icon.

4. **In the Rate cell, type the rate in dollars, such as .555 for 55.5 cents.**

   The mileage rate is 55.5 cents per mile beginning January 1, 2012, as documented on the IRS website, *www.irs.gov*. If you're reading this in 2013, be sure to check that site to see if this rate has changed.

5. **Click Close when you're done.**

Mileage Rates and Invoice Items

What if the IRS's rate is different from the rate I charge customers for mileage?

The rates you enter in the Mileage Rates window (page 213) are the standard rates set by the IRS for tax purposes. The IRS doesn't care one whit what you charge your customers for miles, so you can charge them whatever you want.

For the reimbursable miles that you drive, you need to create a Service or Other Charge item in your Item List. (In the Enter Vehicle Mileage window, the Item drop-down list includes only these two types of items.) When you create the item, you can assign it the rate that you charge customers per mile or leave the rate at zero if you charge variable mileage rates.

For an Other Charge item, the "Amount or %" box is the place to enter the mileage rate, as shown in Figure 8-8. (For a Service type item, use the Rate box instead.) In the Account box, choose the income or expense account you use for reimbursable mileage, whether it's specific to mileage or an overall reimbursable cost account.

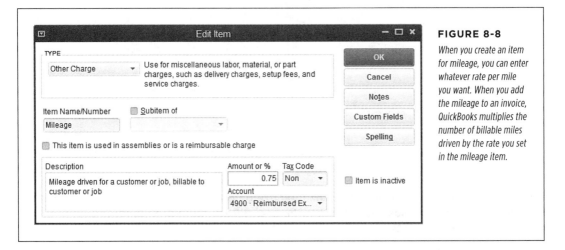

FIGURE 8-8

When you create an item for mileage, you can enter whatever rate per mile you want. When you add the mileage to an invoice, QuickBooks multiplies the number of billable miles driven by the rate you set in the mileage item.

Recording Mileage Driven

Once you've added a vehicle to the Vehicle List, you're ready to record mileage. Here's how you fill in the Enter Vehicle Mileage window to record billable and non-billable miles you've driven:

1. **Open the Enter Vehicle Mileage window (Company→Enter Vehicle Mileage) and, in the Vehicle box, choose the vehicle that you drove.**

   If you forgot to add the vehicle to the list, you can create it now by choosing <Add New> from the drop-down menu.

2. **In the Trip Start Date and Trip End Date boxes, choose when you started and completed the trip, respectively.**

If you're recording mileage for one day of onsite work, choose the same day in both boxes. On the other hand, if you used a company car to drive to another city for several days, the Trip Start Date is the day you headed out of town and the Trip End Date is the day you returned.

3. **In the Odometer Start box and Odometer End boxes, type what the vehicle's mileage was before you began driving and what it was when you returned, respectively, as shown in Figure 8-9. Or just type how far you drove into the Total Miles box.**

If you fill in the Odometer boxes, QuickBooks automatically calculates the miles you drove and plops that number in the Total Miles box.

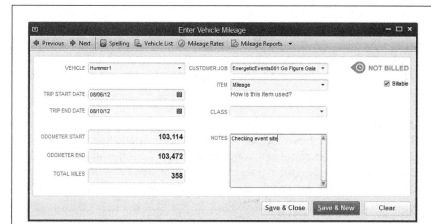

FIGURE 8-9

If you usually forget to check the starting mileage, you can ignore the Odometer Start and Odometer End boxes entirely. Instead, in the Total Miles box, type the mileage you drove, such as 358 for a 358-mile trip for your customer. You can type the mileage with or without commas (1,500 or 1500).

NOTE The drawback to filling in the Enter Vehicle Mileage dialog box's Total Miles field is that your mileage record doesn't include the odometer readings that the IRS wants to see. But if every mile you drive is for business, you can prove your deduction by showing the IRS an odometer reading at the beginning of the year and one at the end of the year.

4. **If your mileage is billable to a customer or job, turn on the Billable checkbox. Then, in the Customer:Job box, choose the customer or job to which you want to assign the mileage, and in the Item drop-down list, choose the item you created for mileage (page 214).**

If the mileage *isn't* billable to a customer, keep the Billable checkbox turned off and leave the Customer and Item boxes blank.

5. **If you track classes, then in the Class box, choose the appropriate one.**

   For example, if you use classes to track branch performance, choose the class for the branch. However, if you track partner income with classes and the mileage is nonbillable, you don't need to assign a class.

6. **To further document the reason for the mileage, type details in the Notes box. Then, to save the mileage and close the dialog box, click Save & Close.**

   If you want to enter additional mileage for other customers and jobs, click Save & New instead.

■ Generating Mileage Reports

Mileage records come in handy when you prepare your taxes or if your customers question their mileage charges. These reports are simple, mainly because you don't track that much mileage information in QuickBooks. You can generate mileage reports by choosing Reports→"Jobs, Time & Mileage" and then selecting a report. Or, if you have the Enter Vehicle Mileage window open, in the window's toolbar, click the down arrow to the right of the Mileage Reports button and select a report.

Here are the reports you can choose and what they're useful for:

- **Mileage by Vehicle Summary**. For your tax documentation, this report shows the total miles you drove each vehicle and the corresponding mileage expense (which QuickBooks calculates using the standard mileage rate in effect at the time). The date range is set initially to This Tax Year. If you wait until after January 1 to gather your tax documentation, then in the Dates box, choose Last Tax Year.

- **Mileage by Vehicle Detail**. This report shows each trip that contributed to a vehicle's mileage. For each one, the report includes the trip's end date, miles driven, mileage rate, and mileage expense. If you have questions about your deductions, double-click an entry to open the Enter Vehicle Mileage window for that transaction.

- **Mileage by Job Summary**. If you charge customers for mileage, run this report both for total miles driven and the billable mileage by customer and job. Quick-Books uses the rate you set in the Service or Other Charge item to calculate the billable amount.

- **Mileage by Job Detail**. If a customer has a question about mileage you charged, this report is the quickest way to find the charges in question. The report groups mileage by customer or job but lists each trip in its own line. The report shows each trip's start date, end date, miles driven, billing status, mileage rate, and billable amount, so you can answer almost any mileage-related question a customer might have.

Paying for Expenses

Although most small business owners sift through the daily mail looking for envelopes containing checks, they usually find more containing *bills*. One frustrating aspect of running a business is that you often have to pay for the items you sell before you can invoice your customers for the goods.

If you want your financial records to be right, you have to tell QuickBooks about the expenses you've incurred. And, if you want your vendors to leave you alone, you have to pay the bills they send. Paying for expenses can take several forms, but QuickBooks is up to the challenge.

This chapter explains your choices for paying bills (now or later) and describes how to enter bills and record your bill payments. If you pay right away, you'll learn how to write checks, use a debit or credit card, and pay with cash in QuickBooks, among other options. If you enter bills in QuickBooks for payment later, you'll learn how to handle the recurring ones, such as rent, as well as reimbursable expenses and inventory.

QuickBooks is happy to help you through every step of the process: entering bills you receive if you want to pay later, setting up bill payments, and even printing checks you can mail to vendors. But for modest enterprises with few expenses, writing checks by hand and entering them in the program works just as well.

When to Pay Expenses

When it comes to handling expenses, you can pay now or pay later; QuickBooks has features for both options. (You can choose to *not* pay bills, but QuickBooks can't help you with collection agencies or represent your company in bankruptcy court.)

If bills arrive about as often as meteor showers, go ahead and pay each one immediately so you're sure they're paid on time. In QuickBooks, paying immediately means writing a check, entering a debit card or ATM transaction, entering a credit card charge, making an online payment, or using money from petty cash—all of which are described in this chapter. When you pay immediately, you don't have to enter a bill in QuickBooks; you can simply record the expense payment transaction.

But when bills arrive as steadily as latte orders at the local coffee shop, you'll probably want to set aside time to pay them all at once when it won't interfere with delivering services or selling products. What's more, most companies don't pay bills until just before they're due—unless there's a good reason (like an early payment discount). Setting up vendor bills for later payment is known as *using accounts payable* because you store the unpaid expenses in an Accounts Payable account.

In QuickBooks, entering bills for later payment delivers all the advantages of convenience and good cash management. You can tell the program when you want to pay bills—for instance, to take advantage of an early payment discount or the grace period that a vendor allows. Then you can go about your business without distraction, knowing that QuickBooks will let you know when bills are on deck for payment.

TIP For the eternally forgetful, QuickBooks can add bills to your Reminders List (page 621). Choose Edit→Preferences→Reminders, and then click the Company Preferences tab. Set the Bills to Pay option to Show Summary or Show List, and then enter the number of days of lead time you want before bills are due.

Once you decide whether you're going to pay bills now or later, use that method consistently. Otherwise, you could pay for something twice by entering a bill in QuickBooks and then, a few days later, writing a paper check for the same expense. To prevent duplicate payments, always enter bills you receive in the mail (or email) as bills in QuickBooks and pay them by using the Pay Bills feature (page 244). The Enter Bills window includes a list of recent transactions, shown in Figure 9-1, which you can use to look for payments you've already made.

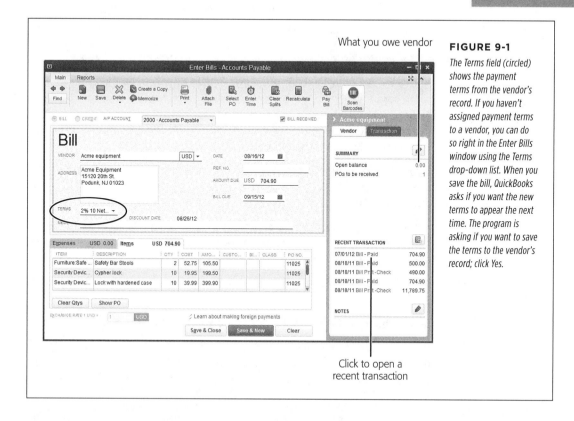

What you owe vendor

FIGURE 9-1

The Terms field (circled)
shows the payment
terms from the vendor's
record. If you haven't
assigned payment terms
to a vendor, you can do
so right in the Enter Bills
window using the Terms
drop-down list. When you
save the bill, QuickBooks
asks if you want the new
terms to appear the next
time. The program is
asking if you want to save
the terms to the vendor's
record; click Yes.

Click to open a
recent transaction

NOTE If you pay for something when you're out of the office by charging expenses to your credit card or writing checks by hand, you simply enter those transactions in QuickBooks without entering a corresponding bill. (See page 262 for info on recording credit card charges and page 257 for info on writing checks.)

■ Entering Bills

At first glance, entering bills in QuickBooks and then paying them later might *seem* like more work than just writing checks. But as you'll learn in this chapter, there are several advantages to entering bills in QuickBooks, and the program makes it incredibly easy to pay them.

To get started, open the Enter Bills window using any of the following methods:

- On the Home page, click Enter Bills in the Vendors panel.

- Choose Vendors→Enter Bills.

- In the Vendor Center's icon bar, click New Transactions→Enter Bills.

The fields in the Enter Bills window are similar to the ones on invoices you create. In fact, if your vendors use QuickBooks, the bills you receive are just another company's QuickBooks invoices (see Chapter 10) or statements (see Chapter 11).

Here's how to enter a bill in QuickBooks' Enter Bills window:

1. **In the Vendor drop-down list, choose the vendor who billed you.**

    Above the Bill area, QuickBooks automatically chooses the Bill option so you can record a vendor bill. (You'll learn about recording a credit from a vendor on page 243.) The program also turns on the Bill Received checkbox. Turn *off* this checkbox *only if* you receive a shipment of inventory without a bill; you'll learn how to deal with such shipments page 236.

    If you set up any pre-fill accounts in the vendor's record (page 93), QuickBooks automatically adds them to the table on the Expenses tab near the bottom of the Enter Bills window.

2. **If you have open purchase orders with the vendor you selected and the bill corresponds to one or more of those POs, then in the message box that appears, click Yes.**

    Page 233 explains how to record bills that correspond to purchase orders you've created.

3. **In the Date box, type or select the date you received the bill.**

    If you set up payment terms in the vendor's record (page 92), QuickBooks figures out when the bill is due and fills in the Bill Due field, as shown in Figure 9-1. For example, if the bill date is 8/16/2013 and the vendor's payment terms are Net 30, the bill is due 30 days after the bill date—9/15/2013.

    If QuickBooks fills in a date that doesn't match the due date on the bill you received, then in the Bill Due field, enter the date printed on the vendor's bill—it's the one to go by.

TIP The right side of the Enter Bills window summarizes the vendor's info and your recent transactions with that vendor. For example, the Summary section shows your balance and open purchase orders with that vendor. If you see any info you want to change, like the terms or address, click the Edit button (its icon looks like a pencil) to open the vendor's record in the Edit Vendor dialog box. The Recent Transactions section lists bills, bill payments, credits, and other transactions, which is a great way to catch that you have a credit available or already paid the bill you're about to enter. To open one of these recent transactions in its corresponding window, click a link, like the "Bill - Paid" link shown in Figure 9-1.

---

4. **In the Ref. No. box, type the vendor's invoice number, the statement date, or another identifying feature of the bill you're paying.**

The Ref. No. box accepts any alphanumeric character, not just numbers, so you can type in things like "1242," "Invoice 1242," and "Statement 1/6/2013."

If you want to include additional notes about the bill, type them in the Memo box.

5. **In the Amount Due box, type the total from the bill.**

The only time you'd type a different amount is when you take a discount that the vendor forgot to apply or deduct a portion of the bill because the goods were defective.

In the lower half of the Enter Bills window, QuickBooks initially displays the Expenses tab, which is where you enter information about expenses such as utility bills, office supply bills, and attorney's fees. If you assign only one pre-fill account (page 93) to this vendor, QuickBooks automatically fills in the first cell in the table's Amount column with the Amount Due value.

NOTE The box on page 224 tells you what to do when you receive a bill from a vendor who uses a different currency.

6. **In the first cell of the Expenses tab's Account column, choose the expense account from your chart of accounts that corresponds to the first expense on the bill.**

When you click a cell in the Account column, a down arrow appears. Clicking the arrow displays a drop-down list of every account in your chart of accounts, but QuickBooks automatically displays the expense account section of the list. To choose a different expense account—the account for your legal fees, say—scroll in the drop-down list and select the account you want.

7. **If the bill covers several types of expenses (such as airfare and your travel agent's fees), in the first Amount cell, type the amount that belongs to the expense account in the first row.**

If you assign more than one pre-fill account to a vendor, QuickBooks subtracts the amount you typed in the first row from the total amount due and puts the remaining amount in the second row. Bottom line: You have to type the amounts in each row's Amount cell.

TIP You can increase or decrease the width of drop-down lists (to see the full names of the accounts in your chart of accounts, for example). When the drop-down list is open, position your cursor over the list's lower-right corner. When the cursor changes to a two-headed arrow, drag to adjust the list's width and height. In addition, you can change the width of the columns on the Expenses and Items tabs: Position your cursor over the vertical line between two column headings and drag to the left or right to shrink or widen the column on the left.

8. **If an expense relates to a job, in the Customer:Job column, choose the customer or job.**

   If you fill in the Customer:Job cell, QuickBooks puts a checkmark in the "Bill-able?" column. If you don't want to charge the customer for the expense, turn off the checkmark.

TIP If you're recording reimbursable expenses, which will eventually appear on a customer's invoice (page 298), be sure to type a meaningful description in each Memo cell. QuickBooks uses the text in this cell as the description of the expense on your invoice. If there's no Memo text, your invoice includes charges without descriptions, which are bound to generate a call from the customer.

9. **If you're tracking classes, choose the appropriate class for the expense.**

   The Class column appears only if you use QuickBooks classes (page 150).

10. **If the bill you're entering includes different types of expenses, repeat steps 6–9 to add a row for each type of expense, as shown in Figure 9-2.**

    As soon as you finish one row in the table, QuickBooks fills in the Amount cell in the next row with the amount that's still unallocated. For the first through the next-to-last line, you have to edit the amount that the program fills in to match your expense. The amount QuickBooks enters in the last line should be correct if you haven't made any typos.

    If the multiple accounts and amounts are hopelessly mangled, at the top of the Enter Bills window, click Clear Splits to clear the table so you can start over.

11. **Click Save & Close to save the bill and close the window.**

    Or, if you have other bills to enter, click Save & New to save that bill and display a new blank one.

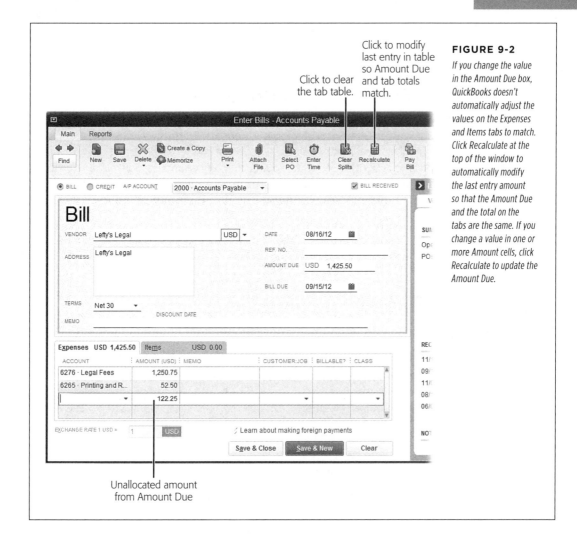

Click to clear
the tab table.

Click to modify
last entry in table
so Amount Due
and tab totals
match.

FIGURE 9-2

*If you change the value
in the Amount Due box,
QuickBooks doesn't
automatically adjust the
values on the Expenses
and Items tabs to match.
Click Recalculate at the
top of the window to
automatically modify
the last entry amount
so that the Amount Due
and the total on the
tabs are the same. If you
change a value in one or
more Amount cells, click
Recalculate to update the
Amount Due.*

Unallocated amount
from Amount Due

TIP You can't change a vendor's currency after you've recorded your first transaction for that vendor. To switch to a different currency, you have to create a new vendor record that uses the new currency. The alternative is to calculate the bill's values in your home currency based on the going exchange rate and then enter the bill in QuickBooks with those converted values.

■ Automating Recurring Bills

Many of your bills are due at the same time every month, and some are even the same *amount* every month. For example, your electric bill is due the 19th of the month, but the amount varies each time, whereas your rent check is due the first of every month and it's always $1,000. Each time you reorder office supplies or inventory, the items you buy are often the same, but the quantities and cost totals are different. These sorts of bills are perfect candidates for QuickBooks' memorized transaction feature.

QuickBooks can memorize bills and reuse them. You can even create a group of bills so that you can process all the bills due on the same day of the month. Even when some fields change, recalling a transaction with *most* of the fields filled in saves you time.

FREQUENTLY ASKED QUESTION

Bills and Foreign Currencies

How do I enter a bill that has values in a foreign currency?

You have to turn on multiple currencies (page 610) before you can enter bills with values in foreign currencies. Once you do that, the Enter Bills window displays the currency in several places. The currency you apply to a vendor appears in the window's title bar and to the right of the vendor's name, as shown in Figure 9-3. The Amount Due box shows the foreign currency to the left of the amount, with the corresponding value in your home currency below the line. And the Expenses and Items tabs both show the foreign currency to indicate that the values you enter are in that currency. (See page 482 to learn how to enter or download currencies into the Currency List.)

Here's how to fill out a bill a vendor submitted in a foreign currency:

1. In the Enter Bills window's A/P Account box, choose the Accounts Payable account that corresponds to the foreign currency.

2. In the Amount Due box, type the bill's value in the foreign currency.

3. On the Expenses and Items tabs, type the amounts in the foreign currency.

4. Below the Expenses and Items tabs, in the "Exchange Rate 1 <currency> =" box, type the exchange rate from the foreign currency to your home currency (Chinese Yuan Renminbi to U.S. dollars in Figure 9-3).

5. Click Recalculate at the top of the window to calculate the bill's total in your home currency.

Currency

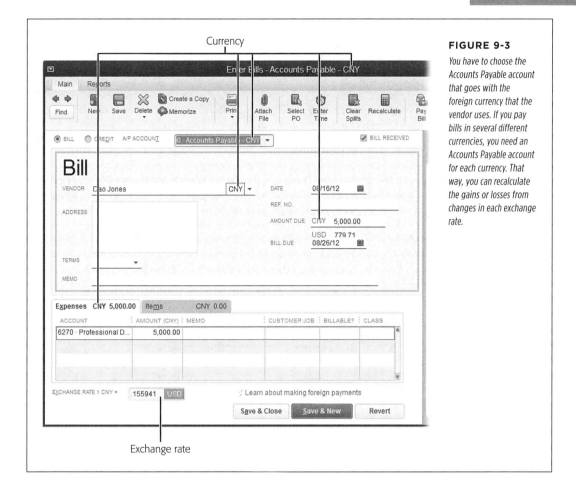

FIGURE 9-3

You have to choose the Accounts Payable account that goes with the foreign currency that the vendor uses. If you pay bills in several different currencies, you need an Accounts Payable account for each currency. That way, you can recalculate the gains or losses from changes in each exchange rate.

Exchange rate

TIP If you get the same bill only once in a blue moon, memorizing it might be overkill. Instead, you can create a duplicate whenever you need it. In the Vendor Center, on the Transactions tab, click Bills, and then double-click the bill you want to reuse to open it in the Enter Bills window. Then right-click in the Enter Bills window and choose Duplicate Bill from the shortcut menu, or click "Create a Copy" at the top of the window. Make any changes you want, like the date and amount, and then click Save & Close.

Memorizing a Bill

Here's how to make QuickBooks memorize a bill:

1. **On the Home page, click Enter Bills or choose Vendors→Enter Bills.**

   QuickBooks opens the Enter Bills window.

2. **Fill in all the fields that will be the same on each bill, as shown in the background in Figure 9-4.**

   If a field changes for each bill, such as an Account, simply leave it blank (or, if it's an amount field, set it to 0.00). Later, when you use this memorized bill to enter a bill, simply fill in the empty fields with the values on the bill that the vendor sent.

3. **When the bill is set up the way you want, press Ctrl+M to open the Memorize Transaction dialog box (shown in the foreground in Figure 9-4). In the Name box, type a name for the memorized bill.**

   QuickBooks automatically fills in the Name box with the vendor's name, but it's a good idea to enter something more meaningful. For example, naming a memorized bill Rent Broomfield Office is more helpful than using the landlord's name.

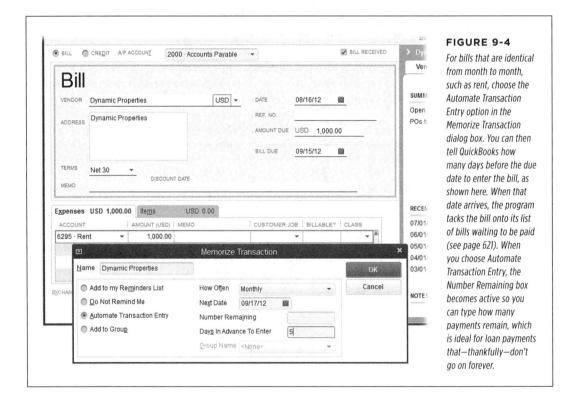

FIGURE 9-4

For bills that are identical from month to month, such as rent, choose the Automate Transaction Entry option in the Memorize Transaction dialog box. You can then tell QuickBooks how many days before the due date to enter the bill, as shown here. When that date arrives, the program tacks the bill onto its list of bills waiting to be paid (see page 621). When you choose Automate Transaction Entry, the Number Remaining box becomes active so you can type how many payments remain, which is ideal for loan payments that—thankfully—don't go on forever.

NOTE If you've already memorized a bill for this vendor, the Replace Memorized Transaction message box appears instead. To replace the existing memorized bill, click Replace. To add a new memorized bill for the vendor, click Add; when you do, QuickBooks then opens the Memorize Transaction dialog box so you can specify a new name and options for the memorized transaction. If you change your mind about memorizing the bill, click Cancel.

4. **If you want QuickBooks to remind you when it's time to pay the bill, choose the "Add to my Reminders List" option and then tell the program when to remind you.**

   If bills don't arrive on a regular schedule (like ones for snowplowing), choose the Do Not Remind Me option. Then, when you receive a bill, you can call up the memorized transaction as described in the next section.

   For bills that you receive regularly, in the How Often box, choose the frequency, such as Monthly or "Every four weeks," and in the Next Date field, choose the next due date. For example, if the monthly bill you're memorizing is set for 8/16/2013, choose 9/16/2013.

5. **To memorize the bill, click OK.**

   QuickBooks adds the bill to the Memorized Transaction List, closes the Memorize Transaction dialog box, and returns to the Enter Bills window.

   If you want to add the bill to the queue of bills to be paid, click Save & Close. If you created the bill *only* to memorize it, click the window's Close button (the X in its top-right corner), and then click No when QuickBooks asks if you want to save the transaction.

Using a Memorized Bill

How you generate a bill from a memorized transaction in QuickBooks depends on whether you've opted for a reminder, no reminder, or total automation:

- **Add to my Reminders List**. When you tell QuickBooks to remind you and the scheduled date arrives, the program adds the bill to the Reminders List (page 621). If the Reminders List displays only the "Bills to Pay" heading, double-click it to display the bills that are due to be paid. Then, below the "Bills to Pay" heading, double-click a bill to open the Enter Bills window. The bill that you see contains only the memorized information. Make any changes you want, fill in the empty fields, and then click Save & Close.

TIP For reminders that are hard to miss, tell QuickBooks to display the Reminders List each time you open the company file. That way, as soon as you log into the file, you'll see the tasks awaiting you. To set this up, choose Edit→Preferences→Reminders and, on the My Preferences tab, turn on the "Show Reminders List when opening a Company file" checkbox.

- **Do Not Remind Me**. When you memorize a bill that you use only occasionally or that occurs on an irregular schedule, choosing Do Not Remind Me stores the bill in the Memorized Transaction List in case you need it. When you want to use that memorized bill, click it in the Memorized Transaction List (choose Lists→Memorized Transaction List or press Ctrl+T), and then click Enter Transaction.

- **Automate Transaction Entry**. If you create a memorized bill with the Automate Transaction Entry option, that's exactly what the program does: When the next scheduled date for the bill arrives, QuickBooks creates a new bill and adds it to the list of bills waiting to be paid.

Creating Memorized Groups of Bills

The first day of the month is the nemesis of bill payers everywhere because so many bills are due then. QuickBooks can't ease the pain of watching your money go out the door, but it can at least ease the burden of entering all those bills in your company file. Memorized bills are a start, but why enter individual memorized bills when you can enter several at once? You can set up memorized transaction *groups* that act like their individual memorized counterparts—to remind you about all the bills due on a specific day or enter all the recurring transactions automatically.

You might wonder how to add a memorized transaction to a group when you open the Memorize Transaction dialog box (page 226) for the very first time; the Add to Group option and the Group Name box are visible, but grayed out. To add a memorized transaction to a group, you have to first create a *memorized group*. Here's how you do that:

1. **Press Ctrl+T to open the Memorized Transaction List. At the bottom of the window, click Memorized Transaction→New Group.**

   QuickBooks opens the New Memorized Transaction Group dialog box—identical to the Memorize Transaction dialog box except that it doesn't include the Add to Group option or Group Name box.

2. **Name the group something meaningful like Monthly Bills, and fill in the other fields as you would for a memorized transaction (page 227).**

   Tell QuickBooks how and when you want to be reminded about the bills in this group.

3. **Click OK to save the group.**

   Now that the group exists, you can add individual transactions to it.

4. **To add an existing memorized transaction to the group, in the Memorized Transaction List window, select the transaction you want to add, and then press Ctrl+E to edit it.**

   The Schedule Memorized Transaction dialog box opens.

5. **Select the Add to Group option. In the Group Name box, choose the group you just created, and then click OK.**

When you add a memorized transaction to a group, QuickBooks tucks the transaction underneath the group in the Memorized Transaction List, as shown in Figure 9-5.

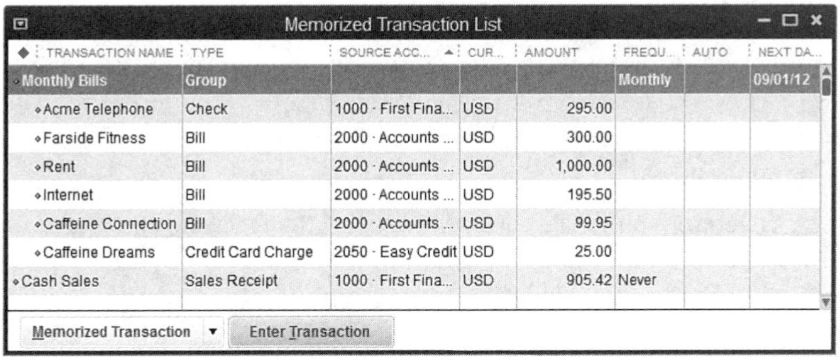

FIGURE 9-5

Individual memorized transactions take on the schedule and reminder settings of the memorized group you put it in. So if you edit a memorized transaction that belongs to a group, the How Often, Next Date, Number Remaining, and Days In Advance To Enter boxes are grayed out.

TIP Create separate memorized groups for bills with consistent amounts and for ones whose amounts vary. That way, you can set up the unvarying memorized group with the Automate Transaction Entry option so QuickBooks simply adds all the bills in that group to your list of bills to be paid without any intervention from you. Then you can set the second memorized group to use the "Add to my Reminders List" option so you can go through each bill and fill in the amount before you record it.

Purchasing Inventory

Purchasing and paying for inventory items is *mostly* the same as paying for other expenses. But as you learned in Chapter 5, inventory always seems more complicated than the other things you sell.

Part of the problem with inventory is that you have to keep track of how much you have. As inventory wends its way from your warehouse to your customers, it also hops among accounts in your chart of accounts (see page 128): An income account tracks the money you make from selling inventory; a cost of goods sold account tracks the cost of the inventory you've sold; and an asset account tracks the value of the inventory you still own.

Purchasing inventory involves three actions in QuickBooks:

- Adding the inventory you purchase to an inventory asset account
- Entering the bill you receive for the inventory you bought
- Paying the bill for the inventory

What's tricky is that you don't know whether the bill or the inventory will arrive first. In many cases, the bill arrives with or after the shipment. But Samurai Sam requires a deposit before he starts crafting your swords. In that case, you can record the deposit payment you make and then apply that payment when the final bill arrives. In the following sections, you'll learn how to use QuickBooks' features to handle any order of bill and inventory arrival.

Turning on QuickBooks Inventory

If you want to track inventory in QuickBooks, your first task is turning on the preference for inventory and purchase orders (page 615) if you didn't do that when you created your company file (page 14). Although the program turns on purchase-order features as part of tracking inventory, you can skip purchase orders if you don't use them in your business.

As soon as you turn on the inventory preference, the following changes occur in QuickBooks:

- Icons for purchase orders and inventory appear on the Home page.

- Inventory-related features like Create Purchase Orders and Receive Items appear on the Vendors menu.

- A non-posting account called Purchase Orders appears in the chart of accounts.

Creating Purchase Orders

Before you get around to receiving inventory and paying the corresponding bills, it's a good idea to make sure that the inventory you ordered actually arrives. If you ordered corsages for Mother's Day but the box that shows up contains corsets, the mistake is obvious. Remembering what you ordered is tougher when products and quantities vary. Most businesses address this problem by creating *purchase orders* for the inventory they buy. That way, when an order arrives, they can compare the shipment to the purchase order to confirm that the items and quantities are correct. Because purchase orders are typically the first step in purchasing, the QuickBooks Home page places the Purchase Orders icon in the pole position in the Vendors panel.

> **NOTE** You can create all the purchase orders you want without altering the balances in your income, expense, and asset accounts; and the purchase orders won't appear in your Profit & Loss or Balance Sheet reports, either. That's because purchase orders are known as *non-posting* transactions: No money changes hands (or accounts), so there's nothing to post in your chart of accounts. In QuickBooks, the first posting for purchased inventory happens when you receive either the inventory or the bill.

The Create Purchase Orders dialog box is like a mirror image of the Create Invoices dialog box that you'll meet in Chapter 10. You choose a vendor instead of a customer, and the Ship To address is your company's address, as shown in Figure 9-6.

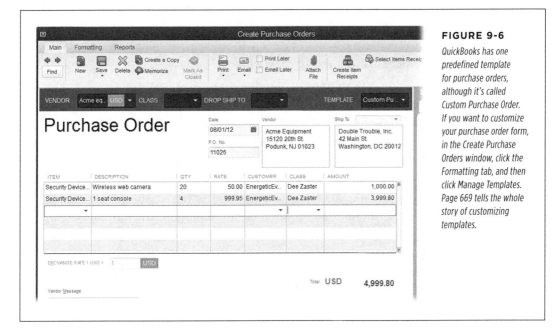

FIGURE 9-6

QuickBooks has one predefined template for purchase orders, although it's called Custom Purchase Order. If you want to customize your purchase order form, in the Create Purchase Orders window, click the Formatting tab, and then click Manage Templates. Page 669 tells the whole story of customizing templates.

Here's how to create a purchase order:

1. **On the Home page, click the Purchase Orders icon or choose Vendors→Create Purchase Orders.**

   In the Create Purchase Orders window, QuickBooks fills in the current date, and there's no reason to change that because purchase orders are a paper trail of what you order.

2. **In the Vendor box, choose the vendor you're ordering inventory from.**

   QuickBooks fills in the Vendor box in the header area with the vendor's name and address (from the vendor record you created on page 91) as shown in Figure 9-6.

NOTE If you use multiple currencies, the vendor's currency appears to the right of the vendor's name. The "Exchange Rate 1 <unit> =" box becomes active below the Item table if the vendor is set up to use a currency different from your home currency.

---

3. **If you use classes to categorize income and expenses (page 150), choose a class for the purchase order.**

   If you use classes and skip the Class box, when you try to save the purchase order, QuickBooks might remind you that you didn't assign a class. If that happens, click Cancel to return to the purchase order so you can choose a class, or click Save Anyway to save the purchase order without a class.

4. **If you're ordering inventory that you want shipped directly to one of your customers, in the Drop Ship To drop-down list, choose that customer (or job).**

QuickBooks changes the address in the Ship To box from your company's address to the customer's or job's address.

5. **If you're creating your first purchase order, in the P.O. No. box, type the number that you want to start with.**

From then on, QuickBooks increments the number in the P.O. No. box by one. If you order your products over the phone or through an online system and the vendor asks for your purchase order number, give him this number.

6. **In the drop-down list for the first Item cell in the table, choose the item that corresponds to the first product you're purchasing.**

The Item drop-down list shows all the entries in your Item List, even though companies usually create purchase orders only for inventory items. (As you type the first few letters of an item's name, QuickBooks displays matching entries. You can keep typing or click the item you want as soon as it appears.)

When you choose an item, QuickBooks fills in other cells in the row with information from that item's record (see Chapter 5). The Description cell gets filled with the item record's description, which you can keep or edit. The Rate cell grabs the value from the Cost field of the item's record (that's the price you pay for the item).

7. **In the cell in the Qty column, type the quantity you want to purchase.**

QuickBooks fills in the Amount cell with the total purchase price for the item: the quantity multiplied by the rate.

8. **If you're purchasing inventory specifically for a customer or job, choose the customer or job in the drop-down list in the Customer column.**

The Create Purchase Orders dialog box doesn't include a column for designating purchases as billable. Don't worry: You'll tell QuickBooks that an item is billable when you create a bill or receive the item into inventory.

9. **Repeat steps 6–8 for each product you're purchasing.**

You can add and delete lines in a purchase order: To add a line, right-click a line and then choose Insert Line from the shortcut menu; to delete one, choose Delete Line from the shortcut menu instead.

10. **At the bottom of the Create Purchase Orders dialog box, in the Memo box, type a summary of what you're ordering to help you identify the purchase order.**

The contents of the Memo field show up when it's time to apply a purchase order to a bill (as you'll learn shortly), so you can identify the right purchase order.

11. **If you have additional purchase orders to create, click Save & New to save the current purchase order and start another.**

To save the one you just created and close the Create Purchase Orders window, click Save & Close. Click Clear to throw out your choices or changes on the purchase order.

Recording a Vendor Deposit

Suppose a vendor requires a deposit before you receive a service or product. You can record the payment so it shows up as a credit to that vendor. Then, when the bill arrives, you can apply that credit to the bill. Here's what you do:

1. **Write a check (page 257) or enter a credit card charge (page 262) to pay the deposit.**

   If you have an open purchase order for inventory items, QuickBooks displays a message box about it; click No because it's too early to use the purchase order.

2. **In the Write Checks or Enter Credit Card Charges window, click the Expenses tab. In the first Account cell, choose the Accounts Payable account.**

   Choosing the Accounts Payable account creates a credit for you with that vendor.

3. **In the first Amount cell, enter the amount of the deposit.**

   When you click away from the Amount cell, the check amount at the top of the window changes to the deposit amount you entered.

4. **Save the transaction.**

   You don't have to do anything else until the final bill arrives.

5. **When you receive the bill, enter it in QuickBooks as you would any other bill.**

   Fill in the Account fields with the expense accounts for the services or products you received (page 221).

6. **Apply the vendor credit to the bill as described on page 243.**

   The credit reduces the balance due.

7. **Save the bill.**

   You're done!

TIP You can also use this technique to edit a check or credit card charge so you can apply it to a bill that you forgot you'd already entered. Simply edit the check or credit card charge and change the account to Accounts Payable. Then, use the credit to pay the bill.

Receiving Inventory and Bills Simultaneously

For many orders, you'll find the bill tucked into one of the boxes of your shipment like a bonus gift. Although a bill isn't the most welcome of gifts, receiving a bill and inventory simultaneously *is* a bonus because you can record the inventory and accompanying bill at the same time in QuickBooks. Here's how:

1. **On the Home page, click Receive Inventory and then choose Receive Inventory with Bill, or choose Vendors→Receive Items and Enter Bill.**

   Either way, QuickBooks opens the Enter Bills window that you first met on page 219 and automatically turns on the Bill Received checkbox just as it does when you create a regular bill.

2. **In the Vendor drop-down list, choose the vendor who sent the bill.**

   QuickBooks looks for any open purchase orders for that vendor.

3. **If there are any open purchase orders for that vendor and you want to apply the shipment you received to one of them, in the Open POs Exist message box, click Yes. (If the items you received don't go with any open purchase orders, click No and skip to step 5.) If you don't see this message box, skip to step 5.**

   When you click Yes, QuickBooks opens the Open Purchase Orders dialog box (shown in the foreground of Figure 9-7). This dialog box lists purchase order dates, numbers, and memos.

   If the vendor's bill includes the purchase order number, picking the correct one is easy. Or, if you filled in the Memo field when you created the purchase order, that note may help you identify the right one. But if you don't know which one to pick, click Cancel to close the Open Purchase Orders dialog box. Then, to view a report of open purchase orders, choose Reports→Purchases→Open Purchase Orders. Double-click a purchase order to view its details, and then head back to the Open Purchase Orders dialog box once you know which one to select.

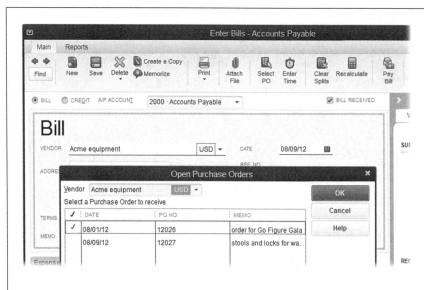

FIGURE 9-7

In the Enter Bills window, when you choose the vendor who shipped the items you've received (from the Vendor drop-down list), QuickBooks checks for any open purchase orders for that vendor. If it finds any, it displays the Open POs Exist message box (not shown here). If you click Yes in that box, the open Purchase Orders dialog box appears so you can select a PO, which then applies the items you've received from that purchase order to the bill.

TIP   Another way to display the Open Purchase Orders dialog box is to click Select PO at the top of the Enter Bills window.

4. **To select the existing purchase order that goes with the shipment you received, in the "Select a Purchase Order to receive" table, click the checkmark column (the first column) for the purchase order you want, and then click OK.**

QuickBooks displays a checkmark in the purchase order's checkmark cell. When you click OK, the program closes the Open Purchase Orders dialog box and fills in the bill fields with purchase order info, like the amount and the items ordered, as shown in Figure 9-8. When you work from a purchase order, QuickBooks displays the order's number in the PO No. column in the Items tab, which appears only if you choose a purchase order. To open the selected purchase order in the Create Purchase Orders dialog box, click Show PO below the Item table.

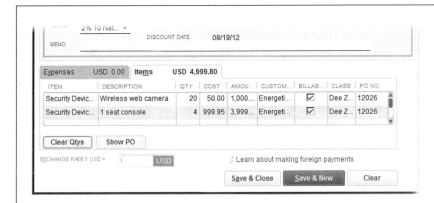

FIGURE 9-8

When you choose an open purchase order, QuickBooks uses the information from it to fill in fields in the Enter Bills window, such as the Amount Due field in the header (not shown) and the Items tab with most of the information about the items you ordered.

TIP   It's always a good idea to compare the quantities you received in the shipment to the quantities on your purchase order. If you received fewer items than you ordered, in the Qty cell for the item, enter the number you actually received and adjust the amount due to match what you received.

5. **In the Enter Bills window's Date box, enter the date you received the bill.**

If you've already defined the payment terms in the vendor's record (page 92), QuickBooks fills in the Terms box and automatically fills in the Bill Due box. If the bill you received shows different terms or a different due date, update the values in the Bill Due and Terms boxes to match the vendor's bill. (When you save the bill, QuickBooks offers to save the new terms in the vendor's record.)

6. **If you didn't create a purchase order for the shipment you received, fill in the fields as you would for a regular bill.**

In the Amount Due field, type the amount due from the vendor's bill. You'll also have to fill in the Items table manually: For each item you received, in a blank line in the table, specify the item, quantity, customer or job, and class (if you use classes). QuickBooks fills in the Description and Cost cells by using the values in the item's record (see Chapter 5) and then calculates the Amount by multiplying the quantity by the item's cost.

7. **Click Save & New or Save & Close.**

When you save a combination inventory/bill transaction, QuickBooks goes to work behind the scenes. For the inventory you received, the program debits your inventory account the amount you paid for the items and updates the quantity on hand for the item (page 505). It also increases the balance in your Accounts Payable account by the amount of the bill.

TIP If you want to see how many of a particular product you have on hand, on the Home page, click Items & Services. In the Item List window, look at the Total Quantity On Hand column for the item you're interested in.

Receiving Inventory before the Bill

When you receive inventory, you want to record it in QuickBooks so you know that it's available to sell. If you receive inventory without a bill, the best solution is to *pretend* that you received the bill. By creating the bill in QuickBooks, your Accounts Payable stays in sync with what you've purchased. Then you can edit the QuickBooks bill later to match the real one you receive.

Another approach is to record the received inventory in QuickBooks without a bill. (You can do this because the program has separate features for receiving inventory and entering bills when they arrive.) The box on page 237 explains how QuickBooks posts amounts to accounts when you receive inventory without a bill. The fields that you specify and the options at your disposal are the same as when you receive inventory *with* a bill (as described in the previous section); they just appear in different windows.

Posting Inventory Received

When you receive inventory before the bill arrives, your accountant might squawk about how QuickBooks posts inventory to your accounts. In standard accounting practice, only bills show up as credits to the Accounts Payable account. But QuickBooks credits the Accounts Payable account when you receive inventory items without a bill.

When you receive items without a bill, QuickBooks adds an entry for the items you received to the Accounts Payable register. (To view the register, press Ctrl+A to open the Chart of Accounts window, and then double-click the Accounts Payable account.) The program fills in the Type cell with ITEM RCPT to indicate that the entry isn't a bill. Later, when you enter the bill, QuickBooks overwrites the same transaction, replacing the ITEM RCPT type with BILL.

The result in your company file is correct after you both receive inventory and enter bills. However, your accountant might complain about the incomplete audit trail because the transaction changes without some kind of record. If you want to track inventory, bills, and price differences between your purchase orders and the final bills, you can do so outside of QuickBooks. Then when you possess both the inventory and the corresponding bill, you can record the transaction in QuickBooks.

To receive inventory in your company file before the bill arrives:

1. **On the Home page, click the Receive Inventory icon and then choose "Receive Inventory without Bill," or choose Vendors→Receive Items.**

   QuickBooks opens the Create Item Receipts window, which is a close relative of the Enter Bills window. In fact, other than the title of the dialog box, only three things are different, all of which are shown in Figure 9-9.

TIP If you open the Create Item Receipts window and then realize that you *do* have the bill, there's no need to close the window and choose a different feature. Simply turn on the Bill Received checkbox in the top right of the window. When you do, the window changes to the Enter Bills window so you can receive the items and create the bill at the same time (page 233).

Similar to what happens when you receive inventory and a bill at the same time (page 233), the Create Item Receipts window reminds you about open purchase orders that you can select to fill in the items received automatically. The rest of the fields behave like the ones in the Enter Bills window, explained on page 219.

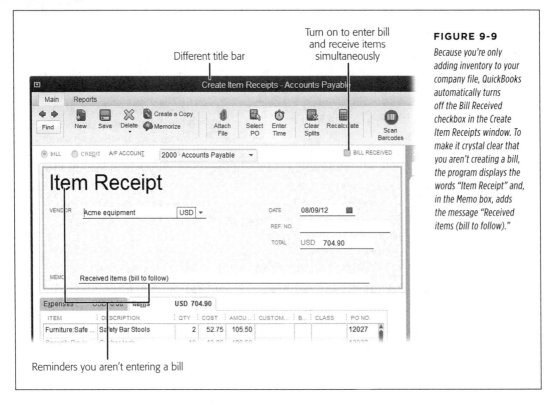

Turn on to enter bill
and receive items
simultaneously

Different title bar

FIGURE 9-9

Because you're only adding inventory to your company file, QuickBooks automatically turns off the Bill Received checkbox in the Create Item Receipts window. To make it crystal clear that you aren't creating a bill, the program displays the words "Item Receipt" and, in the Memo box, adds the message "Received items (bill to follow)."

Reminders you aren't entering a bill

2. **When you've added all the items you received and updated any quantities that differ from those on your purchase order, click Save & Close.**

   QuickBooks records the inventory in your company file, as described in the box on page 237.

   Then, when the bill for the items you received finally arrives, here's what you do:

1. **Choose Vendors→"Enter Bill for Received Items," or on the Home page, click the Enter Bills Against Inventory icon.**

   The box on page 239 tells you how to recover if you choose Vendors→Enter Bills by mistake.

2. **In the Select Item Receipt dialog box, choose the vendor that sent the shipment; then select the shipment that corresponds to the bill you just received and click OK.**

   QuickBooks opens the Enter Bills window and fills in the fields with info from your Receive Items transaction.

TIP The Select Item Receipt dialog box's Ref. No. and Memo columns identify the shipments you've received. If those columns are blank, the Date column won't be enough to let you select the right item receipt, so click Cancel and then choose Vendors→Receive Items. At the top of the Create Item Receipts window, click the left arrow (Previous) or right arrow (Next) to display the item receipt you want, and then fill in its Ref. No. field with the purchase order number for the shipment or the carrier's tracking number. After you save the item receipt with an identifying reference number, choose Vendors→"Enter Bill for Received Items" once more.

3. **If the prices and quantities on the vendor's bill are different from those QuickBooks used, on the Items tab near the bottom of the window, update the prices and quantities.**

   When prices and quantities differ, don't take the vendor's bill as the final word—check your record to see where the discrepancy arose.

4. **If the bill includes sales tax and shipping that you didn't include on your purchase order, click the Expenses tab, and then fill in additional lines for those charges.**

   If you changed anything on the Items or Expenses tab, at the top of the Create Item Receipts window, click Recalculate to update the Amount Due field with the new total.

5. **Click Save & Close.**

   You'll see a message box asking if you want to save the changes you made—even if you didn't make any. QuickBooks asks this question because *it* has changed the item receipt transaction to a bill in your Accounts Payable account, as the box on page 237 explains. Click Yes to save the changes.

TROUBLESHOOTING MOMENT

Double (Posting) Trouble

When you want to enter a bill for items you received earlier, be extra careful to choose Vendors→"Enter Bills for Received Items" (or click Enter Bills Against Inventory on the Home page). If you choose Vendors→Enter Bills instead, you'll end up with *two* postings for the same items in your Accounts Payable account. The first posting appears when you receive the items in QuickBooks (the one identified with the type ITEM RCPT); the second posting is for the bill.

If you accidentally create one of these double entries, here's how to correct the problem:

1. In the Chart of Accounts window, double-click the Accounts Payable account.

2. In the Accounts Payable register, select the bill and then choose Edit→Delete Bill, or right-click the bill and then choose Delete Bill on the shortcut menu.

3. Recreate the bill using the "Enter Bills for Received Items" feature.

Handling Reimbursable Expenses

Reimbursable expenses are costs you incur that a customer subsequently pays. Products you purchase specifically for a customer or a subcontractor you hire to work on a customer's job are costs you pass on to customers. For example, travel costs are a common type of reimbursable expense, and you've probably seen telephone and photocopy charges on your attorney's statements.

There are two ways to track reimbursable expenses, and QuickBooks can handle them both:

- **As income**. With this method, QuickBooks posts the expenses on a bill you pay to the expense account you specify. When you invoice your customer, Quick-Books posts the reimbursement as income in a separate income account. Your income is higher this way, but it's offset by higher expenses. This approach is popular because it lets you compare income from reimbursable expenses to the reimbursable expenses themselves to make sure they match. The box on page 242 describes the income accounts you need for tracking reimbursable expenses this way.

- **As expenses**. Tracking reimbursements as expenses doesn't change the way QuickBooks handles bills—expenses still post to the expense accounts you specify. But, when your customer pays you for the reimbursable expenses, QuickBooks posts those reimbursements right back to the expense account, so the expense account balance looks as if you never incurred the expense in the first place.

> **NOTE** If you track reimbursable expenses as expenses, you don't have to do any special setup in QuickBooks. When you pay a bill, the expenses simply post to the expense account. When you invoice a customer, you add the reimbursable expenses to the invoice. QuickBooks then posts the reimbursements back to the same expense account.

Setting Up Reimbursements as Income

If you want to track reimbursable expenses as income, choose Edit→Preferences→Time & Expenses. Then, on the Company Preferences tab, turn on the "Track reimbursed expenses as income" checkbox. With this preference turned on, whenever you create or edit an *expense* account (in the Add New Account or Edit Account windows), QuickBooks adds a "Track reimbursed expenses in Income Acct." checkbox and drop-down list to the bottom of the window, as shown in Figure 9-10.

Here's what happens as you progress from paying bills to invoicing customers:

1. **When you assign an expense on a bill as reimbursable to a customer, Quick-Books posts the money to the expense account you specified.**

2. **When you create an invoice for that customer, the program reminds you that you have reimbursable expenses.**

3. **When you add the reimbursable expenses to the customer's invoice, they post to the income account you specified for that type of expense. (See the box on page 242 to learn more about creating income accounts for reimbursable expenses.)**

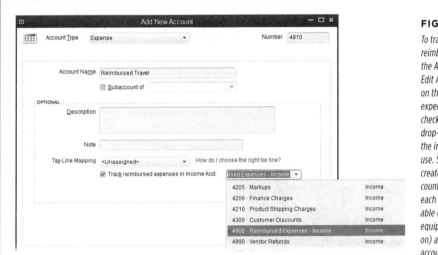

FIGURE 9-10

To track an expense as reimbursable income, in the Add New Account or Edit Account window, turn on the "Track reimbursed expenses in Income Acct." checkbox and then, in the drop-down list, choose the income account to use. Since you've already created your expense accounts, you'll have to edit each one that's reimbursable (travel, telephone, equipment rental, and so on) and add the income account as shown here.

Recording Reimbursable Expenses

As you enter bills (page 219) or make immediate payments with checks or credit cards, you add designated expenses as reimbursable, as shown in Figure 9-11. When you choose a customer or job in the Customer:Job column, QuickBooks automatically adds a checkmark to the "Billable?" cell. Be sure to type a note in the Memo cell to identify the expense, because QuickBooks uses the text in that cell as the description of the reimbursable expense on your invoice.

FIGURE 9-11

The tables in the Enter Bills, Write Checks, and Enter Credit Card Charges windows all include columns to designate reimbursable expenses and the customers or jobs to which they apply. (You can click Splits in an account register to access these columns.)

WORKAROUND WORKSHOP

Accounts for Reimbursable Expenses

QuickBooks won't let you assign the same income account to more than one reimbursable expense account, so you have to create a separate income account (see Chapter 3) for each type of reimbursable expense.

To keep your chart of accounts neat, create a top-level income account called something like Reimbursed Expenses. Then create an income subaccount for each type of reimbursable expense. When you're done, your income accounts will look something like this:

- 4100 Service Revenue
- 4200 Product Revenue
- 4900 Reimbursed Expenses - Income

Subaccounts for account 4900:

- 4910 Reimbursed Telephone
- 4920 Reimbursed Postage
- 4930 Reimbursed Photocopies
- 4940 Reimbursed Travel

An alternative approach is to create Other Charge items for each type of reimbursable expense. By doing so, you can assign those items to a single income account. However, you can still see the details of each reimbursable category by running a Sales By Item report (page 481).

TIP Sometimes you want to track expenses associated with a customer or job, but you don't want the customer to reimburse you, like when you have a fixed-price contract. In that situation, click the "Billable?" cell for that expense to remove the checkmark.

◼ Recording Vendor Refunds and Credits

Say you ordered 30 dozen lightweight polypropylene T-shirts for your summer Death Valley marathon, but your vendor mistakenly silk-screened the logo on long-sleeved cotton T-shirts heavy enough to survive a nuclear blast. If you raise a ruckus, the vendor may issue you a refund check or a credit. Either way, it's easy to record the money you get back in QuickBooks.

Here's how to deposit a vendor's refund check or credit card refund:

1. **On the Home page, click Record Deposits or choose Banking→Make Deposits.**

2. **If the "Payments to Deposit" window appears, turn on the checkmark cell for each payment you want to deposit along with the refund check.**

   The "Payments to Deposit" window opens if you have other deposits to make.

3. **Click OK to open the Make Deposits window. In the Make Deposits window's Deposit To drop-down list, choose a bank account.**

   If you selected other deposits in the "Payments to Deposit" window in the previous step, they appear in the table.

4. **In the first blank Received From cell, choose the vendor who issued the refund check.**

   You can choose a customer, employee, or other name if the check isn't from a vendor.

5. **In the From Account cell, choose the account associated with the refund.**

   For a refund for shirts you purchased, you might choose a cost of goods sold account that you use for products you buy specifically for a customer. If the refund is for office supplies, choose the expense account for office supplies.

6. **Fill in the other fields and then click Save & Close.**

   Fill in the Memo cell with a note about the refund, the check number, and payment method to record a refund check or a credit card refund, and the amount of the refund.

If the vendor insists on issuing a credit instead of a refund check, here's how to record that credit in QuickBooks:

1. **On the Home page, click Enter Bills or choose Vendors→Enter Bills.**

   QuickBooks opens the Enter Bills window as if you're going to enter a bill.

2. **Just below the window's Main tab, choose the Credit option.**

   QuickBooks changes the giant heading in the window to Credit and the Amount Due label to Credit Amount. The other fields stay the same.

3. **On the Expenses and Items tabs, fill in the cells with the items for which you received credit.**

Enter positive numbers just as you did when you entered the original bill. QuickBooks takes care of posting the credit amounts to your accounts. Your inventory account decreases due to the inventory items you return, and your expense accounts' balances decrease due to expense credits. The total credit amount also reduces the balance in your Accounts Payable account.

4. **Click Save & Close.**

That's it! (See page 246 to learn how to *apply* a credit.)

■ Paying Your Bills

Entering bills in QuickBooks isn't the same as *paying* bills. The bills you enter are a record of what you owe and when, but they do nothing to send money to your vendors. Pay Bills is the feature that actually pushes your money out the door. With this feature, you can select the bills you want to pay, how much to pay on each one, as well as the payment method, account, and date. If you have credits or early payment discounts, you can include those, too.

TIP If you want to evaluate all your unpaid bills before you pay them, the Unpaid Bills Detail report displays the bills due up to the current date, grouped by vendor. To run it, choose Reports→Vendors & Payables→Unpaid Bills Detail.

Selecting Bills to Pay

You begin the payment process by choosing the bills you want to pay. When you choose Vendors→Pay Bills (or click the Pay Bills icon on the Home page), QuickBooks opens the Pay Bills window and displays the bills due within the next two weeks. As Figure 9-12 shows, you can change which bills are displayed, view bill details, or apply credits and discounts.

NOTE If you don't use multiple currencies, the Pay Bills window doesn't include the A/P Account or Exchange Rate fields.

You can select bills to pay in the Pay Bills window by clicking their checkboxes in the first column of the window's table. Clicking the Select All Bills button below the table makes QuickBooks select *all* the bills displayed in the window's table. (The button's label changes to Clear Selections when at least one bill is selected.) Either way, QuickBooks fills in the Amt. To Pay cells for the selected cells with the total due on each bill.

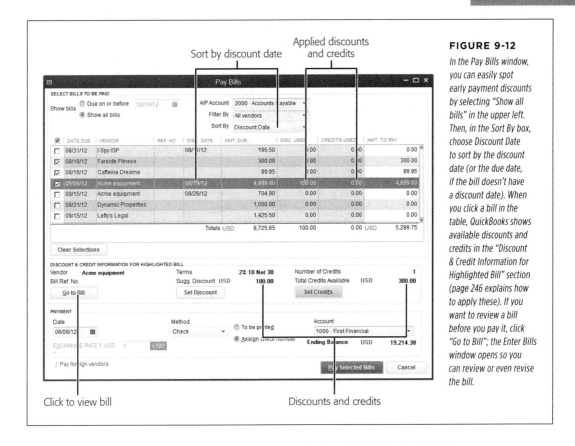

Sort by discount date

Applied discounts and credits

Click to view bill

Discounts and credits

FIGURE 9-12

In the Pay Bills window, you can easily spot early payment discounts by selecting "Show all bills" in the upper left. Then, in the Sort By box, choose Discount Date to sort by the discount date (or the due date, if the bill doesn't have a discount date). When you click a bill in the table, QuickBooks shows available discounts and credits in the "Discount & Credit Information for Highlighted Bill" section (page 246 explains how to apply these). If you want to review a bill before you pay it, click "Go to Bill"; the Enter Bills window opens so you can review or even revise the bill.

NOTE When you select more than one bill from the same vendor, QuickBooks automatically combines those bills onto one check when you pay them.

To use two different payment methods (check and credit card, for example), make two passes through the Pay Bills window. On the first pass, choose all the bills that you pay by check and then, in the Payment section's Method box, choose Check. On the second pass, in the Method box, choose Credit Card.

NOTE A standard accounting rule that accountants live by is to never pay one current liability (Accounts Payable in this example) with another current liability (a credit card, for example). However, small businesses do this all the time, regardless of what their accountants recommend.

Similarly, to pay bills submitted in different currencies, you have to make a separate pass through the Pay Bills window for each currency. QuickBooks creates an Accounts Payable account for each currency you assign to vendors. To pay bills from vendors using a specific currency, choose the corresponding Accounts Payable account in the A/P Account drop-down list. The Pay Bills window then displays the bill amounts in the foreign currency, and the amount you have to pay in your home currency.

Modifying Payment Amounts

Whether you select individual bills or all the bills in the list, the program automatically fills in the selected bills' Amt. To Pay cells with the total amounts that are due. Paying bills in full means you don't have to worry about the next due date or paying late fees, but making partial payments can stretch limited resources to appease more of your unpaid vendors, as the box below explains. To pay only part of a bill, in a bill's Amt. To Pay cell, type how much you want to pay.

> **TIP** If you keep your cash in an interest-bearing account until you need it, you'll want to know how much money you need to transfer to your checking account to pay the bills. In the Pay Bills window, the number at the bottom of the Amt. Due column is the total of all the bills displayed, and the number at the bottom of the Amt. To Pay column is the total of all the bills you've selected. If you select all the bills in the list, the two totals are initially the same. But if you change a value in an Amt. To Pay cell, click another cell to update the Amt. To Pay total.

When Cash Is Tight

If your cash accounts are dwindling, you may face some tough decisions about whom to pay and when. To help keep your business afloat until the hard times pass, here are a few strategies to consider:

- Pay government obligations (taxes and payroll withholdings) first. In the Pay Bills window's Sort By box, choose Vendor to make it easy to spot all your government bills.

- Pay the vendors whose products or services are essential to your business.

- Make partial payments to all your vendors rather than full payments to some and no payments to others.

- If you want to pay small bills in full, in the Sort By box, choose Amount Due to sort your outstanding bills by dollar value.

Applying Discounts and Credits to Payments

Most companies like to use their discounts and credits as soon as possible. By far the easiest way to deal with discounts and credits you receive from vendors is to let QuickBooks handle them automatically. Here's how to delegate applying early payment discounts and available credits to QuickBooks:

1. **Choose Edit→Preferences→Bills, and then click the Company Preferences tab.**

   The settings you choose here apply to every person who logs into your company file. Because the settings are on the Company Preferences tab, you have to be a QuickBooks administrator to change them.

2. **To make QuickBooks apply available credits automatically, turn on the
"Automatically use credits" checkbox.**

   With this setting turned on, QuickBooks automatically deducts vendor credits
   from the corresponding vendor's bills. If you'd rather choose when to apply
   credits, leave this checkbox turned off.

3. **Turn on the "Automatically use discounts" checkbox and, in the Default
   Discount Account box, choose the account you use to track vendor discounts.**

   If you haven't set up an account for vendor discounts, in the Default Discount
   Account drop-down list, choose <Add New>, and then create a new account
   (page 51) called something like Vendor Discounts.

NOTE   Whether you create an income account or an expense account for vendor discounts is neither an
accounting rule nor a QuickBooks requirement, but a matter of how you view vendor discounts. If you think of
them as expenses you've saved by paying early, create an expense account. If you view them as money you've
made, create an income account instead. Either way, vendor discounts are different from discounts you extend
to your customers. So, in the Default Discount Account box, choose an account specifically for *vendor* discounts,
not your customer discount account.

As you'd expect, turning on these checkboxes tells QuickBooks to apply early payment discounts and available credits to bills without further instructions from you.
The program uses your payment terms to figure out the discount you've earned, and
it adds all available credits to their corresponding bills. Whether these checkboxes
are on or off, you can still control the discounts and credits QuickBooks applies to
your bills, as you'll learn on the following pages. For example, you might want to
delay a large credit until the following year to increase your expenses in the current
year—which decreases this year's taxable income.

■ APPLYING DISCOUNTS MANUALLY

If you want to apply discounts by hand or change a discount that QuickBooks added,
here's what to do:

1. **On the Home page, click the Pay Bills icon or choose Vendors→Pay Bills.**

2. **In the Pay Bills window's table, turn on the checkbox next to the bill whose
   discount you want to edit.**

   In the "Discount & Credit Information for Highlighted Bill" section, QuickBooks
   shows the discount and credits that are available for the selected bill. More
   importantly, the program activates the Set Discount and Set Credits buttons
   so you can click them to apply discounts and credits. (If the bill's checkbox is
   turned off, QuickBooks shows the suggested discount and available credits, but
   the Set Discount and Set Credits buttons are dimmed.)

TIP   When you're applying discounts manually, look for dates in the Disc. Date column that are in the *future*.
Those bills qualify for early payment discounts.

---

3. **To apply or modify a discount to the selected bill, click Set Discount.**

QuickBooks opens the "Discount and Credits" dialog box (Figure 9-13). If you've turned on multiple currencies, the currency you set for the vendor appears to the left of the Suggested Discount label and in the "Amount of Discount" box.

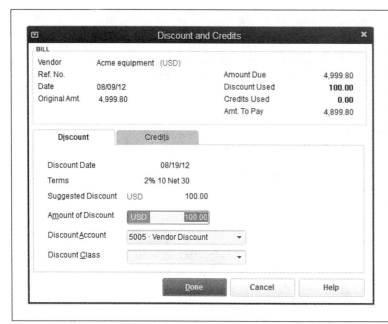

FIGURE 9-13

In the "Discount and Credits" dialog box, QuickBooks automatically selects the Discount tab and displays your payment terms, the discount date, and the amount of discount you deserve. If the suggested discount is worth an early separation from your money, click Done to deduct the discount from your bill. Otherwise, click Cancel. If you also want to work on credits (page 249), when you're done modifying the discount, click the Credits tab.

4. **In the "Amount of Discount" box, QuickBooks fills in the suggested discount. If you want to apply a different discount, type the new value.**

Many companies try to save money by taking early payment discounts when they haven't actually paid early. Some companies apply discounts regardless of what their payment terms are, and most vendors honor these undeserved discounts in the name of goodwill.

5. **In the Discount Account drop-down list, choose the account you use to track vendor discounts.**

If you use an income account, discounts appear as positive numbers and increase the balance of the income account. If you use an expense account, discounts appear as negative numbers because they reduce how much you spend on expenses.

TIP If you want to track discounts on inventory separately from other discounts you receive, create a cost of goods sold account specifically for inventory discounts. For example, if QuickBooks created account 5000 for Cost of Goods Sold, you can create two subaccounts: 5005 for Cost of Inventory Sold and 5010 for Inventory Discounts. In your financial reports, the two subaccounts show your original cost and the discounts you receive. Account 5000 adds the two subaccounts together to show your net cost of goods sold.

6. **If you track classes, choose the class for the discount.**

   Typically, you'll choose the same class for the discount that you used for the original expense.

7. **Click Done.**

   QuickBooks closes the "Discount and Credits" dialog box. Back in the Pay Bills window, the program adds the discount you entered in the bill's Disc. Used cell and recalculates the value in the Amt. To Pay cell by subtracting the discount from the amount due.

■ **APPLYING CREDITS MANUALLY**

When you select a bill in the Pay Bills window, the "Discount & Credit Information for Highlighted Bill" section shows the credits that are available for that bill. If the "Discount and Credits" dialog box is already open because you've applied a discount, just click the Credits tab and then perform step 4 of the list below. Otherwise, here's how to apply available credits to a bill or remove credits that QuickBooks applied for you:

1. **On the Home page, click the Pay Bills icon or choose Vendors→Pay Bills.**

2. **Select a bill by turning on its checkbox in the Pay Bills window's table.**

   In the "Discount & Credit Information for Highlighted Bill" section, QuickBooks shows the credits available for the vendor, if any. The program also activates the Set Credits button.

3. **To apply a credit to the selected bill, click Set Credits.**

   QuickBooks opens the "Discount and Credits" dialog box, and displays the Credits tab, shown in Figure 9-14. Credits that are already applied to the bill are checked.

4. **Turn on the checkmark cell for each credit you want to apply. If you want to use a credit later, turn off its checkmark cell. Then click Done.**

   QuickBooks closes the dialog box and applies the credits.

Setting the Payment Method and Account

After you've selected the bills to pay and applied any discounts and credits, you still have to tell QuickBooks how and when you want to pay those bills. These payment settings at the very bottom of the Pay Bills window are the last ones you have to adjust before paying your vendors:

- **Date**. QuickBooks fills in the current date automatically. To predate or postdate your payments, choose a different date. (Page 603 explains how to get Quick-Books to date checks using the day you print them.)

- **Method**. In this drop-down list, choose how you want to pay the bills: Check, Credit Card, or (if you subscribe to QuickBooks' online bill-payment service) Online Bank Pmt. If you pick Check, you have one other choice to make here:

- If you print your checks from QuickBooks, choose the **To be printed** option, and the program automatically adds the bills you selected to its queue of checks to be printed. (You'll learn about printing these checks on page 255.)

- If you write checks by hand, choose the **Assign check number** option. That way, you can assign check numbers when you click the Pay Selected Bills button (explained in a moment).

- **Account**. If you specified a default account for the Pay Bills window to use (page 602), QuickBooks automatically selects that account here. To use a different one, in this drop-down list, choose the one you use to pay bills, such as a checking or credit card account.

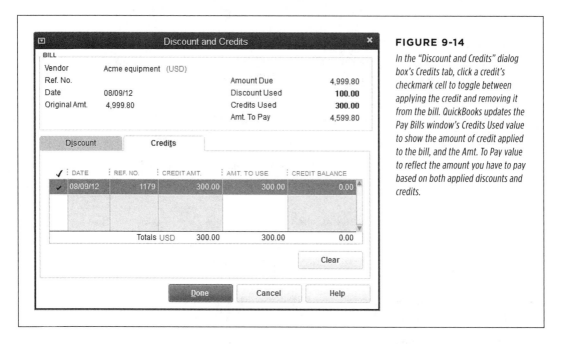

FIGURE 9-14

In the "Discount and Credits" dialog box's Credits tab, click a credit's checkmark cell to toggle between applying the credit and removing it from the bill. QuickBooks updates the Pay Bills window's Credits Used value to show the amount of credit applied to the bill, and the Amt. To Pay value to reflect the amount you have to pay based on both applied discounts and credits.

Paying Selected Bills

When you're done setting up bills to pay, it's time to pay them. Here are the steps:

1. **Click the Pay Bills window's Pay Selected Bills button.**

   If you write paper checks for your bills and chose the "Assign check number" option, the program opens the Assign Check Numbers dialog box. If you use any other payment method, jump to step 3.

2. **In the Assign Check Numbers dialog box, if you want to start with the next unused check number, choose the "Let QuickBooks assign check numbers" option, and then click OK.**

If you instead want to specify the check numbers for each check you write, choose the "Let me assign the check numbers below" option. Fill in the check numbers in the Check No. cells, and then click OK.

3. **In the Payment Summary dialog box, click the button for the action you want to take next.**

The Payment Summary dialog box shows the payments you've made and adds those payments to the appropriate checking or credit card account register. All you have to do is click the appropriate button:

- **If you write paper checks**, click Done. Then write the checks and mail them, as described in the next section.

- **If you print checks via QuickBooks**, click Print Checks and see page 255 for details. Or, if you aren't ready to print checks just yet, click Done.

- **To create another batch of bill payments** (for example, to pay bills by using another method), click Pay More Bills.

NOTE If you open the Enter Bills window, you'll see a PAID stamp on bills you've paid.

▨ Producing Checks

When you choose Check in the Pay Bills window's Method field, your checking account register shows check transactions, but you still have to generate checks to send to your vendors. For companies that produce lots of checks, printing them in QuickBooks can prevent carpal tunnel syndrome. But for a sole proprietorship that generates only a few checks each month, writing them by hand is easy enough. As this section explains, QuickBooks accepts either approach with equal aplomb.

Writing Checks by Hand

Handwriting checks doesn't require any work in QuickBooks, but you still have to keep your company file in sync with your paper checks. Whether you're writing checks for bills you've paid in QuickBooks or scratching out a spur-of-the-moment check to the fortune-teller for this week's corporate horoscope, you want to make sure that the check numbers in your bank account register match your paper checks.

If you already recorded your check transactions in QuickBooks by paying bills (page 244) or recording a check transaction for an immediate payment (page 257), synchronizing check numbers is as easy as writing the paper checks in the same order as you entered them in QuickBooks. Simply open the checking account register window and use the check transactions to guide your paper check writing, as shown in Figure 9-15.

Bill paid by check

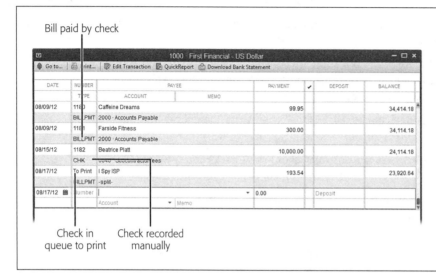

FIGURE 9-15

*To open the checking ac-
count register, first press
Ctrl+A to open the Chart
of Accounts window.
Then, double-click the
checking account's
row (or right-click the
checking account's row,
and then choose Use
Register). In a register
window, the code CHK
in the Type cell indicates
a check transaction. The
code BILLPMT along with
a check number indicates
a bill paid by check.*

Check in   Check recorded
queue to print   manually

NOTE If the next check number in QuickBooks isn't the one on your next paper check, figure out why they don't match. The answer might be as simple as a voided check that you forgot to enter in QuickBooks or a check you wrote earlier that was out of sequence. But if someone is walking off with blank checks, you need to take action.

Until you find the reason for the mismatched check number, editing the check numbers that QuickBooks assigns in the checking account register is the easiest way to get checks into the mail. In the register window, simply double-click an incorrect check number and then type the number that's on your paper check.

Setting Up QuickBooks to Print Checks

If you have scads of checks to generate, printing on preprinted computer checks is well worth the small amount of setup you have to do. And if you dedicate a printer to check printing and keep it stocked with checks, setup is truly a one-time event.

TIP Lock up your preprinted checks and any printer stocked with them. Otherwise, you might discover checks missing, which can lead to money disappearing from your bank account.

The first step is telling QuickBooks which printer to print to and the type of checks you use. The program remembers these settings, so you need to go through this process just once. After you've specified your check-printing settings, QuickBooks fills them in automatically in the Print dialog box. (You can always change those options before you print.)

Here's how you set QuickBooks up to print checks:

1. **Open the "Printer setup" dialog box by choosing File→Printer Setup.**

   The dialog box's Form Name drop-down list includes all the forms you can print in QuickBooks, so you can choose different print settings for each one.

2. **In the Form Name drop-down list, select Check/PayCheck.**

   The Check Style section appears in the bottom of the dialog box; step 4 describes what to choose there.

3. **In the "Printer name" drop-down list, choose the printer you want to use.**

   If you choose a printer brand that QuickBooks recognizes (there are only a few it doesn't), the program automatically fills in the "Printer type" box. If you use a very old or very odd printer, you'll have to manually choose the type of printer. "Page-oriented (Single sheets)" refers to printers that feed one sheet at a time. Choose Continuous (Perforated Edge) if the printer feeds a roll of paper.

NOTE   If you print to checks on continuous-feed paper, properly aligning the paper in the printer is critical. You can save time and a lot of wasted checks by aligning the paper *before* you print batches of checks, as described on page 342.

---

4. **In the Check Style section, choose the option that represents the type of check you purchased. (The box on page 254 explains where you can buy checks.)**

   The "Printer setup" dialog box displays examples of each check style it can deal with, making it easy to choose the right one, as shown in Figure 9-16. Voucher checks print one to a page, so they're by far the easiest to use. However, if you use standard or wallet checks to save paper, see the box on page 256 to learn how to tell QuickBooks how you want to print partial pages of checks.

5. **If the company you buy checks from wants too much money to print your company info and logo on the checks, turn on the "Print company name and address" and "Use logo" checkboxes.**

   Turning on the "Print company name and address" checkbox tells QuickBooks to print the company name and address you filled in when you created your company file (page 8). If you turn on the "Use logo" checkbox, the program opens the Logo dialog box. Click File and then, in the Open Logo File dialog box, select the file containing your logo and click Open. (QuickBooks can handle BMP, GIF, JPEG, PNG, and TIFF formats.) Back in the Logo dialog box, click OK.

   If your company info and logo are preprinted on your checks, leave these checkboxes turned off.

6. **If you have an image of your signature saved on your computer, you can print it on your checks by turning on the Print Signature Image checkbox.**

QuickBooks opens the Signature dialog box. Click File and then, in the Open Logo File dialog box, locate and double-click the file containing your signature. (One way to create a graphic file of your signature is by signing a piece of paper and scanning it to your computer.)

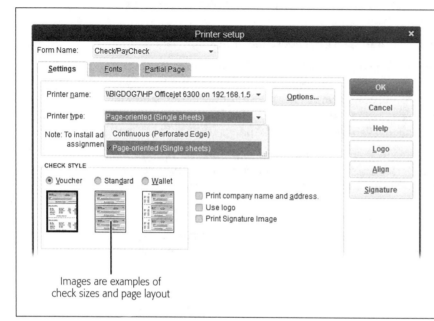

Images are examples of check sizes and page layout

FIGURE 9-16

The Voucher option represents one-page forms that include both a check and a detachable stub for payroll or check info. The Standard option sets QuickBooks up to print to checks that fit in a #10 business envelope; these checks typically come three to a page. Wallet checks are narrower than standard business checks, and have a perforation on the left for tearing the check off, leaving a stub containing check information that you can file.

FREQUENTLY ASKED QUESTION

Buying Preprinted Checks

Do I have to order checks from Intuit?

The short answer is no, but there are compelling reasons to go with Intuit's checks. The company sells competitively priced preprinted checks that work with QuickBooks. The program keeps track of the checks you've used and tells you when to order more. It then automatically sends the correct bank account number with your order.

To order Intuit checks, at the top of the Write Checks window, click Order Checks (if you don't see this button, click the arrow at the right end of the button bar to display it). If you haven't ordered from Intuit before, select the "Ordering from Intuit for the first time?" option. QuickBooks turns on the checkbox

to use your company and bank account information to fill out your order form. Click Order Now to open the Checks web page and set up your order.

You can also purchase checks from your bank or a business-form company (such as Clarke American or Deluxe) just as easily. The checks have to be preprinted with your bank account number, bank routing number, and the check number, because QuickBooks prints only the payment information, such as date, payee, and amount. So if you order checks from a company other than Intuit, be sure to tell them that you use QuickBooks, since the checks need to have fields positioned to match where QuickBooks prints data.

NOTE If you want to change the fonts on the checks you print, click the "Printer setup" dialog box's Fonts tab. There, you can change the font for the entire check form by clicking Font, or designate a special font for the company name and address by clicking Address Font.

7. **Click OK to save your check-printing settings.**

The next section tells you how to actually print checks.

Printing Checks

In the Pay Bills window's Method section, if you choose the "To be printed" option, QuickBooks adds the checks you've selected for payment to a print queue when you click the Pay Selected Bills button. You can also tell QuickBooks to add a check to a print queue by turning on the Print Later checkbox at the top of the Write Checks window. After you confirm that your preprinted checks are in the printer and that the checks are aligned properly, you can print queued-up checks by following these steps:

1. **If the Payment Summary dialog box is open, click Print Checks. Otherwise, choose File→Print Forms→Checks.**

   QuickBooks opens the "Select Checks to Print" dialog box and selects all the unprinted checks, as shown in Figure 9-17.

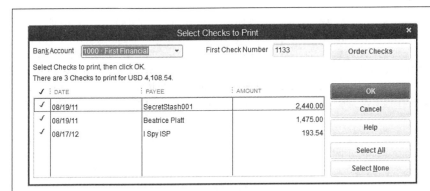

FIGURE 9-17

The first time you print checks, QuickBooks sets the First Check Number box to 1. If necessary, change this number to match the one on the first check loaded in your printer.

2. **If you don't want to print a particular check that's listed, turn off its check-box. When only the checks you want to print are selected, click OK.**

   QuickBooks opens the Print Checks dialog box, which looks much like the "Printer setup" dialog box for checks (Figure 9-16).

3. **If the first page of checks in your printer is a partial page, in the "Number of checks on first page" box, type how many checks there are.**

   You won't see this box if you're printing to voucher checks, because they print one to a page. But for standard or wallet checks, this box lets you use leftover checks from previous print runs when you have a page-oriented printer. Type the number of leftover checks on the partial page, and then insert that page into your printer's envelope feeder. After QuickBooks prints checks to that page, it will begin feeding full sheets of checks from the paper tray.

4. **Click Print.**

Because of the problems that can happen during printing (paper jams, low toner, or an unfortunate margarita spill), QuickBooks opens the "Print Checks – Confirmation" dialog box after it prints checks.

5. **If there was a problem, in the "Print Checks – Confirmation" dialog box, click the Reprint cell for each check that didn't print correctly.**

If the whole batch is a loss, click Select All.

6. **Click OK to reprint the checks.**

In addition to printing the checks, QuickBooks also removes the words To Print from those checks in your checking account register, replacing them with the check numbers it used.

GEM IN THE ROUGH

Using Leftover Checks

If you use voucher checks, you don't have to worry about leftovers, because each check prints on its own page. However, when you print standard or wallet checks to single sheets of paper, you might print only one or two of the checks on the last sheet, leaving a leftover or two. Happily, QuickBooks includes a setting that lets you print on those orphaned checks. Here are the steps:

1. Choose File→Printer Setup, and then choose Check/PayCheck in the Form Name drop-down list.

2. Click the Partial Page tab.

3. Choose the option (Side, Center, or Portrait) that corresponds to how your printer feeds envelopes, and then click OK to save the setting.

The Side and Portrait options are the most common methods. If you select Side, you insert the partial page of checks into the envelope feeder sideways, with the top of the first check aligned with the left side of the envelope feed. With the Por-

trait option, you feed the top of the first check straight into the envelope feeder. (Whether you insert pages face up or down depends on the type of printer you have. Print a sample page of checks to determine which direction you have to feed pages. Then tape a note to the printer with instructions like "print side down, top edge in first" so you don't misprint any pages in the future.)

Before you start printing, feed the pages with orphaned checks into your printer's envelope feeder. That way, QuickBooks prints to those orphaned checks before printing to the full pages of checks in the paper tray.

If you have an old dot-matrix printer taking up space in a junk closet, consider putting it to work printing checks. Its continuous-feed mechanism means you can stop printing anywhere and resume right where you left off, so you won't need the Partial Page feature. An added bonus is that you don't have to worry about accidentally printing reports on preprinted checks or printing checks to blank paper.

Writing Checks Without Entering Bills

You might enter bills in QuickBooks for the majority of your vendor transactions so you can take advantage of early payment discounts or pay bills just before they're due. But you're still likely to handwrite a quick check from time to time to pay for an expense immediately. For example, when the person who plows your parking lot knocks on the door and asks for payment, he won't want to wait while you step through the bill-entering and bill-paying process in QuickBooks—he just wants his $100. And if you write only a couple of checks a month, there's nothing wrong with writing checks to pay vendors without entering a bill in QuickBooks.

When you're new to QuickBooks and want some guidance, use the Write Checks window to make sure you enter all the required info. Once you're more experienced, you can record checks directly in QuickBooks' checking account register. This section describes how to do both.

NOTE Entering checks in the register is best reserved for paper checks that you write, but you can print checks you enter in the register: First, record the check. Then right-click it and choose Edit Check to open the Write Checks window and, in the window's menu bar, click Print. Alternatively, in the register, type *To Print* in the transaction's Number cell and then click Record; QuickBooks adds the check to the queue of checks waiting to be printed. (Page 255 explains how to print these queued-up checks.)

Using the Write Checks Window

The Write Checks window is like a trimmed-down version of the Enter Bills window. Because you're paying immediately, there's no need for fields such as Bill Due or Terms. For a payment without a bill, you have to provide information about the expenses or items you're paying for, which is why the Write Checks window includes the Expenses and Items tabs. QuickBooks fills in a few fields for you, and the rest are like the ones you've met already in the Enter Bills window (page 220).

NOTE Don't use the Write Checks (or Enter Bills) window to write checks for sales tax, payroll, payroll taxes, or liabilities. Instead, see page 266 to learn how to pay sales tax, and Chapter 14 for info about payroll transactions.

To write a check in the Write Checks window, follow these steps:

1. **Open the Write Checks window by pressing Ctrl+W, choosing Banking→Write Checks, or clicking the Write Checks icon on the Home page.**

   As you can see in Figure 9-18, QuickBooks tries to flatten the learning curve by making the upper part of the window look like a paper check. If you use multiple currencies, QuickBooks lists the currency for your checking account in the Bank Account box, the currency for the vendor on the right side of the "Pay to the Order of" box, and the currency for the check to the left of the check amount.

   If you set up bank account preferences (page 602), such as which bank account to use when you open the Write Checks window, QuickBooks automatically chooses that account for you.

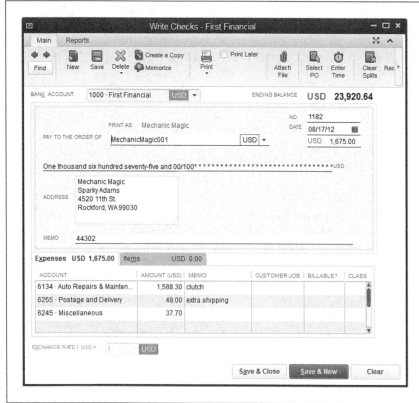

FIGURE 9-18

Choosing a name in the "Pay to the Order of" field fills in the Address box, which is perfect for printing checks for mailing in window envelopes. Even though the company name appears in the "Pay to the Order of" field, the Address box also displays the company name to show you what it prints on checks. If you include account numbers in your vendor records, QuickBooks adds the account number to the Memo field.

2. **If you want to print the check, at the top of the window, make sure the Print Later checkbox is turned on and then skip to step 4. If you're writing checks by hand, turn off the Print Later checkbox and then continue with step 3.**

   When this checkbox is on, the words "To Print" appear to the right of the No. label, and QuickBooks adds the checks you create to a print queue. When you print those checks (page 255), QuickBooks replaces "To Print" with check numbers.

3. **If the "Print Later" checkbox is turned off, make sure the number in the No. box is correct.**

   When you turned off the Print Later checkbox, QuickBooks automatically filled in the No. box with the next check number for the selected bank account. If the number it filled in doesn't match the check you're writing by hand, type in the number from your paper check. If you type a check number that's already been used, QuickBooks warns you about the duplicate number when you try to save the check. In the warning message box, click Cancel, and then, in the Write Checks window, edit the value in the No. field.

TIP If you suspect that there's more than one check number awry, open the checking account register to review multiple checks at once. To renumber a check in the register window, double-click a transaction's Number cell, type the new number, and then press Enter to save the change. As long as you keep editing check numbers until all the duplicates are gone, it's perfectly acceptable to save a duplicate check number.

4. **In the "Pay to the Order of" drop-down list, choose who you want to pay.**

   The drop-down list includes customers, vendors, employees, and names from the Other Names List. If you filled in the "Print on Check as" box with a vendor name when you set up the vendor, you'll see "Print As: <name>" above the "Pay to the Order of" line.

5. **Add entries to the Expenses and Items tabs for the things the check is paying for, just like you do when you enter a bill (page 221).**

   QuickBooks calculates the check amount as you add entries on these tabs. If you fill in the check amount and *then* start adding expenses and items, you'll know that the check total and the posted amounts match when no unallocated dollars remain. If you mangle the entries on either tab, you can start over by clicking the Clear Splits button at the top of the window.

6. **Click Save & Close to record the check.**

   To write another check, click Save & New. To throw away any values in the window and start over, click Clear.

Adding Checks to an Account Register

In QuickBooks, entering checks in a bank account register is fast, easy, and—for keyboard aficionados—addictive. By combining typing and keyboard shortcuts, such as tabbing from cell to cell, you can make short work of entering checks. Here's how to create checks in a register window:

1. **Press Ctrl+A to open the Chart of Accounts window, and then double-click your bank account.**

   You can also open the register by clicking Check Register in the Home page's Banking section; then, in the Use Register dialog box, select the checking account and click OK. Either way, QuickBooks opens the account register window and positions the cursor in the Date cell of the first blank transaction.

2. **To adjust the check's date by a few days, press the plus key (+) or minus key (–) until the date is what you want.**

   See Appendix C (online at *www.missingmanuals.com/cds*) for more date-related keyboard shortcuts.

3. **Press Tab to move to the Number cell.**

   QuickBooks automatically fills in the next check number for that bank account. If the number doesn't match the paper check you want to write, press + or – until the number is correct or simply type the new number. (The box on page 261 explains how to fill in the Number cell if you make a payment with a debit card, ATM card, electronic transaction, or other method.)

4. **Press Tab to move to the Payee cell, and then start typing the name of the payee.**

   QuickBooks scans the lists of names in your company file and selects the first one that matches all the letters you've typed so far. As soon as it selects the one you want, press Tab to move to the Payment cell.

5. **In the Payment cell, type the amount of the check.**

   If you previously recorded a check for that vendor, QuickBooks fills in this cell with the amount from the previous check. To use a different amount, simply type the new value.

6. **Press Tab to jump past the Deposit cell to the Account cell.**

   If the payee is a vendor with pre-fill accounts assigned (page 93), QuickBooks adds "-split-" to the Account cell. In that case, click Splits to open the Splits panel (see Figure 9-19) so you can enter amounts for more than one account. For each allocation, specify the account, amount, memo, customer, and class (if you track classes), and then click Close. If you modify the value in the Payment cell or any values in the Amount cells, click Recalc to change the check payment amount to the total of the splits.

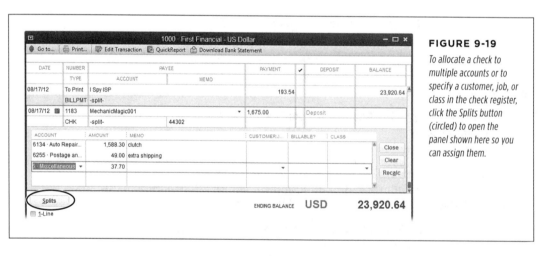

FIGURE 9-19

To allocate a check to multiple accounts or to specify a customer, job, or class in the check register, click the Splits button (circled) to open the panel shown here so you can assign them.

7. **If the check applies to only one expense account, in the Account drop-down list, choose the appropriate account.**

   You can also choose an account by typing the account's number or the first few letters of its name. As you type, QuickBooks selects the first account that matches what you've typed. When the account is correct, press Tab to move to the Memo cell.

If your check covers more than one type of expense, you can click Splits and allocate the payment among several accounts, as shown in Figure 9-19.

8. **To add a description of the check, in the Memo cell, type your notes. When you've filled in all the fields you need, click Record to save the check.**

Lather, rinse, repeat.

UP TO SPEED

Paying with a Debit Card

Paying with a debit card is like writing a check, because the transaction removes money from your bank account. For that reason, you use the Write Checks window to record debit card transactions. In fact, you can also use the Write Checks window to record ATM withdrawals, electronic funds transfers, and payments you make through PayPal. The only difference between these transactions and regular checks is what you enter in the window's No. field.

Instead of putting the check number in this field, you can use a code to identify the type of payment. For example, enter *ATM* for an ATM transaction, *DB* for a debit card, *EFT* for electronic

transactions like an online bill payment you make with your bank's bill-payment service, or *PP* for PayPal. If you have several ATM or debit cards for your bank account, you may want to include the last four digits of the card number after the code so you can tell your transactions from your partner's transactions.

Debit card transactions are different from credit card charges, which is why you don't use the Enter Credit Card Charges window to record them. Debit card charges reduce the balance in your bank account, which is a current asset account (page 52), whereas credit card charges increase the balance in your credit card account, which is a current liability account (page 52).

■ Paying with Cash

If you carry company cash around in your wallet (called *petty cash*, and described in detail on page 447) or if you receive a cash advance toward travel expenses, you eventually have to record the details of your cash transactions in QuickBooks. For example, on a business trip, you might pay cash for meals, parking, tips, and tolls. When you return with your receipts, your bookkeeper can enter a transaction documenting those expenses in the petty cash account.

Entering cash transactions in the petty cash account register is even easier than entering checks in the checking account register. (To open it, in the Chart of Accounts window, double-click the account you created for petty cash.) For cash transactions, the key fields are the amount and the account. You can skip the Payee field altogether to keep your Vendor List concise. If you want a record of where you spent the cash, type the business name in the Memo cell. QuickBooks automatically assigns a check number to such cash transactions, which you might as well keep. Or, if you hand out petty cash receipts that have receipt numbers, you can type that value in the Number cell instead.

Paying with Credit Cards

When you make credit card purchases, the easiest way to record those charges in your company file is by signing up for online banking (page 571) and downloading the transactions (page 579). But you can also enter credit charges manually.

> **TIP** Whether you download charges or not, entering charges manually is a great way to catch erroneous or fraudulent charges that appear on your statement. For example, after entering your charges manually, you can download the charges from your credit card company. If you see additional charges that don't match the ones you entered, either you forgot a charge or there's an error in your account.

Recording credit card charges is almost the same as writing checks except that, instead of the Write Checks window, you work in the Enter Credit Card Charges window, shown in Figure 9-20. Behind the scenes, QuickBooks adds the credit card charge to your credit card account, which is a current liability account. That means the balance in the account increases because you owe more money. (When you write a check out of your checking account, the account's balance decreases because you have less money in that *asset* account.)

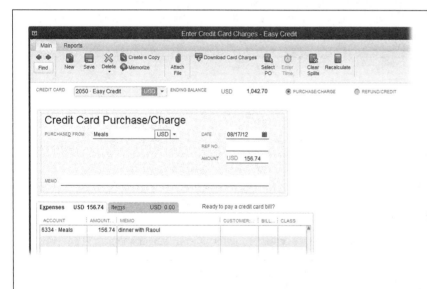

FIGURE 9-20

Unless you want your Vendor List awash with every pizza parlor, gas station, and parking lot you patronize, consider creating generic vendors such as Restaurant, Gas, and Parking. If you want to track the specific vendors, type their names in the Memo field. You can leave the Ref. No. field blank or enter your receipt number there. Allocating a charge to multiple accounts or to a customer works the same as for bills (page 221).

To open the Enter Credit Card Charges window, choose Banking→Enter Credit Card Charges. You can also enter charges directly in the credit card account register, just as you do with checks.

> **NOTE** To enter a refund for a credit card charge, near the top of the Enter Credit Card Charges window, choose the Refund/Credit option and fill in the rest of the fields based on the refund you received.

▓ Running Expense-Related Reports

Vendors & Payables reports tell you how much you owe each vendor and when the bills are due. The reports in the Purchases category, on the other hand, focus on how much you've bought from each vendor you work with. This section tells you how to put the reports in these two categories to work.

A/P Aging and Vendor Balance Reports

If your company is flush with cash and you pay bills as soon as they appear in the Pay Bills window, your A/P Aging reports and Vendor Balance reports will contain mostly zeroes. If you want an overview of how much you owe each vendor and how much is overdue, use one of the following reports listed under Reports→Vendors & Payables:

- **A/P Aging Summary**. This report shows all the vendors you owe money to and how old your balances are for each one. Double-click a value to see a report of the transactions that produced the amount owed.

- **A/P Aging Detail**. Run this report to see each unpaid bill sorted by its billing date and grouped into bills that are current, those that are 1 to 30 days overdue, 31 to 60 days overdue, 61 to 90 days overdue, and more than 90 days late.

- **Vendor Balance Detail**. This report shows your bills and payments grouped by vendor.

> **TIP** You can also see the details of a vendor's balance in the Vendor Center: Select the vendor and then, on the right side of the window, click the Open Balance link.

- **Unpaid Bills Detail**. If you want to evaluate all your unpaid bills before you pay them, this report displays the bills due up to the current date, grouped by vendor. To include bills due in the future, in the Dates box, choose All. If you want to inspect a bill more closely, double-click anywhere in its row, and the Enter Bills window opens with the bill's details.

Purchases Reports

These reports, not surprisingly, are listed under Reports→Purchases. When you run the Purchases by Vendor Summary report and see high dollar values, you might want to negotiate volume discounts or faster delivery times. This summary report can also show when you rely too heavily on one vendor—a big risk should that vendor go out of business.

The Purchases by Item Summary report shows how many inventory items you've purchased and the total you paid. The Purchases by Item Detail report shows each purchase transaction with the quantity, cost, and vendor.

If your supplies are dwindling, the Open Purchase Orders report shows when more items are due. The report displays only the PO's date, vendor, number, and delivery date. Double-click a purchase order to open the Create Purchase Orders window, which shows the products on the order.

Paying Sales Tax

Sales tax can be complicated, particularly in states where the number of tax authorities has exploded. You might have to pay sales taxes to several agencies, each with its own rules about when and how much. QuickBooks' sales tax features can't eliminate this drudgery, but they can help you pay the right tax authorities the right amounts at the right time—and that's something to be thankful for.

After governmental paperwork, the chief aggravation of sales tax is that setting it up spans several areas of QuickBooks. If you're new at collecting sales tax for your products, make sure you've completed the tasks in the following list so you're collecting and tracking sales taxes properly. Only then can you pay the sales taxes you owe.

Here's the sales tax setup you have to do:

- **Sales tax preferences**. If you're liable for sales tax, be sure to turn on Quick-Books' sales tax feature, as described in the next section.

- **Customer records**. When you create a customer in the Customer:Job List, you can assign tax codes and tax items to that customer (page 72). If you do, QuickBooks automatically calculates and applies the correct Sales Tax items to taxable sales on the customer's invoices.

- **Items**. When you create items in the Item List, you can specify whether they're taxable or not (page 132). That way, when you add these items to invoices or other sales forms, QuickBooks automatically applies the correct tax status. (See pages 142–144 to learn how to set up Sales Tax items and sales tax groups. When you add these to invoices, QuickBooks calculates the sales taxes you need to remit.)

- **Invoices and other sales forms**. QuickBooks calculates sales tax on invoices and other sales forms based on whether items are taxable and whether customers are tax exempt.

NOTE The Manage Sales Tax window contains commands for all your sales-tax tasks. To open it, in the Home page's Vendors panel, click the Manage Sales Tax icon.

Sales Tax Payment Preferences

To turn on QuickBooks' sales tax features, choose Edit→Preferences→Sales Tax. Then, on the Company Preferences tab, in the "Do you charge sales tax?" section, choose Yes. In the Preferences dialog box's "Your most common sales tax item" drop-down list, choose the sales tax item or sales tax group for your state. After you set these preferences, QuickBooks automatically creates a liability account in your chart of accounts called Sales Tax Payable the first time you add sales tax to an invoice.

The preference settings you choose for paying sales taxes aren't up to you. Tax agencies decide when your sales taxes are due, usually based on how much sales tax you collect. When you receive a notice about your required payment interval from the state or other tax authority, be sure to update your QuickBooks preferences to match. QuickBooks provides two sets of payment options to satisfy the tax agencies you're beholden to:

- **When do you owe sales tax?** If your tax agency deems sales taxes due when you add them to customer invoices (known as *accrual basis payment*), choose the "As of invoice date (Accrual Basis)" option. If your tax agency says sales taxes are due when your customers pay them (known as *cash basis payment*), choose the "Upon receipt of payment (Cash Basis)" option. When you generate sales tax reports (explained in the next section), QuickBooks uses the setting you choose to calculate the sales taxes you have to remit.

- **When do you pay sales tax?** Tax agencies determine how frequently you have to remit sales taxes based on how much sales tax you collect. If your sales taxes are only a few dollars, you might pay only once a year. But if you collect thousands of dollars of sales tax, you can be sure that the tax agency wants its money more quickly, such as quarterly or monthly. When your tax agency informs you of your remittance frequency, choose Monthly, Quarterly, or Annually, as appropriate.

Producing Reports of the Sales Tax You Owe

Tax agencies are renowned for their forms. You have to fill out forms to tell the agencies how much sales tax you've collected and how much you're required to remit to them. Fortunately, QuickBooks can take *some* of the sting out of tax paperwork with reports that collate the sales tax info you need. Here are the reports you can generate (they're listed under Reports→Vendors & Payables, or you can run them from the Manage Sales Tax window):

- **Sales Tax Liability**. This report summarizes the sales taxes you've collected for each tax agency. As shown in Figure 9-21, QuickBooks automatically sets the report's dates to match the payment interval preference you chose.

- **Sales Tax Revenue Summary**. This report shows the dollar value of taxable and non-taxable sales.

Remitting Sales Taxes

You don't have to enter a bill to pay sales taxes. QuickBooks not only keeps records of the sales taxes you owe, but it also provides a dialog box especially for sales tax payments. Here's how you keep the tax agencies off your back:

1. **Choose Vendors→Sales Tax→Pay Sales Tax, or in the Manage Sales Tax window, click Pay Sales Tax.**

   Either way, QuickBooks opens the Pay Sales Tax dialog box and fills in the amounts you owe for the last collection period (as defined in your Sales Tax preferences [page 265]), as shown in Figure 9-22.

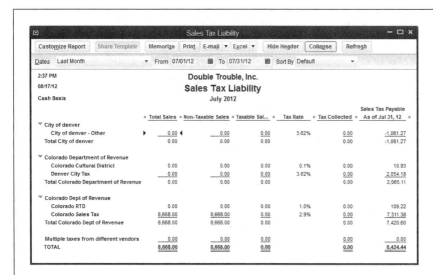

FIGURE 9-21

If you remit sales taxes to several tax agencies, each with its own payment interval, you can rerun this report with a different interval to calculate the sales tax you owe to other agencies. In the Dates drop-down list, choose another interval, such as Last Calendar Quarter.

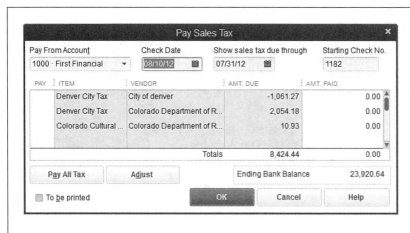

FIGURE 9-22

If you remit sales taxes to only one tax agency or all your sales tax payments are on the same schedule, you can click Pay All Tax to select every payment in the table. But chances are that you make payments to different agencies on different schedules—in which case, select all the agencies on the same schedule, and then repeat these steps for agencies that are on a different timetable.

2. **If you use more than one checking account, in the Pay From Account drop-down list, choose the account you want to use.**

   QuickBooks automatically selects an account here if you set the "Open the Pay Sales Tax form with _ account" preference (page 603).

> **NOTE** Make sure the date in the "Show sales tax due through" box is the last day of the current sales-tax reporting period. For example, if you pay sales taxes quarterly, choose a date like 6/30/2013.

3. **In the Pay column, click cells to select the payments you want to make.**

   QuickBooks adds a checkmark to indicate that a payment is selected and puts the amount of the remittance in the Amt. Paid cell.

> **NOTE** In some states, you may need to adjust the payments you make to a tax agency; for example, to apply a discount for timely payment. In cases like that, click the Adjust button to open the Sales Tax Adjustment dialog box. You can increase or decrease the tax by a dollar value, and you have to specify the account to which you want to post the adjustment (the Sales Tax Payable account, say). If the Entry No. box seems vaguely familiar, that's because this dialog box actually creates a journal entry (page 451) for the adjustment.

4. **If you want to print the sales tax remittance checks from QuickBooks, turn on the "To be printed" checkbox, and then click OK.**

   With this checkbox turned on, you'll see the remittance checks the next time you choose File→Print Forms→Checks. If the "To be printed" checkbox is turned off, whip out your checkbook and write those remittance checks.

Invoicing

Telling your customers how much they owe you and how soon they need to pay is an important step in accounting. After all, if money isn't flowing into your organization from outside sources, eventually you'll close up shop and close your QuickBooks company file for the last time.

Although businesses use several different sales forms to bill customers, the *invoice* is the most popular, and, unsurprisingly, customer billing is often called *invoicing*. This chapter begins by explaining the differences between invoices, statements, and sales receipts—each of which is a way of billing customers in QuickBooks—and when each is most appropriate.

After that, you'll learn how to fill in invoice forms in QuickBooks, whether you're invoicing for services, products, or both. If you send invoices for the same items to many of your customers (and don't use the program's multiple currencies feature), QuickBooks' batch invoice feature can help: You select the customers, add the items you want on the invoices, and QuickBooks creates all the invoices for you. If you track billable hours with QuickBooks, you can also have the program add your billable-hour charges to invoices. And if you designate expenses as billable to customers, QuickBooks can chuck them into the invoices you create, too.

Finally, you'll find out how to handle a few special billing situations, like creating invoices when products you sell are on backorder. You'll also learn how to create estimates for jobs and then use them to generate invoices as you perform the work. And, since you occasionally have to give money back to customers (like when they return the lime-green polyester leisure suits that suddenly went out of style), you'll learn how to assign a credit to a customer's account, which you can then deduct from an existing invoice, refund by cutting a refund check, or apply to the customer's next invoice.

NOTE Chapter 11 continues the invoicing lesson that starts with this chapter by teaching you how to produce statements that show your customers' account status. It also explains how to create sales receipts when customers pay you right away. Chapter 12 explains how to get any kind of sales form into your customers' hands, along with a few other timesaving techniques, like finding transactions and memorizing them for reuse.

Choosing the Right Type of Form

In QuickBooks, you can choose from three different sales forms to document what you sell, and each form has strengths and limitations. Invoices can handle any billing task you can think of, so they're the best choice if you have any doubts about which one to use. Table 10-1 summarizes what each sales form can do. The sections that follow explain the forms' capabilities in detail and give guidance on when to choose each one.

TABLE 10-1 *What each QuickBooks sales form can do*

ACTION	SALES RECEIPT	STATEMENT	INVOICE
Track customer payments and balances		X	X
Accept payments in advance	X	X	X
Accumulate some charges before sending sales form	X	X	X
Collect payment in full at time of sale	X	X	X
Create summary sales transaction	X	X	X
Apply sales tax	X		X
Apply percentage discounts	X		X
Use group items to add charges to form	X		X
Add long descriptions for items	X		X
Subtotal items	X		X
Include customer message	X		X
Include custom fields on form	X		X

NOTE   QuickBooks Premier and Enterprise editions include one more type of sales form: the sales order. In those editions, when you create a sales order for the products that a customer wants to buy, you can create an invoice for the items that are in stock and keep track of out-of-stock items that you'll need to send to your customer when a new shipment arrives (page 307).

Sales Receipts

The sales receipt is the simplest sales form that QuickBooks offers, and it's also the shortest path between making a sale and having money in the bank (at least in QuickBooks). But this form is suitable *only* if your customers pay the full amount at the time of the sale—for example, in a retail store, restaurant, or beauty salon. However, you can accumulate charges for time and billable expenses as described on page 208 and page 222, and then add them to a sales receipt. But for products you sell, sales receipts handle only payment in full.

When you create and save a sales receipt in QuickBooks, the program immediately posts the money you receive to the Undeposited Funds account or to the bank account you choose. As you'll learn in this chapter and the next, invoices and statements take several steps to move from billing to bank deposits.

Sales receipts can handle sales tax, discounts, and subtotals—or any other item in your Item List. But when you operate a cash business, creating a sales receipt in QuickBooks for each newspaper and pack of gum your newsstand sells is *not* good use of your time. Instead, consider creating a sales receipt that summarizes a day's or week's sales, using a customer named Cash Sales that you create specifically for that purpose (see the box on page 68).

Statements

Suppose you're a lawyer and you spend 15 minutes here and 15 minutes there working on a client's legal problem over the course of a month. Each time you do so, that's another charge to the client's account. In QuickBooks, each of those charges is called a *statement charge*, and you can enter them individually (page 328). (If you track time in QuickBooks, you can add your time to an invoice just as easily, as described on page 297.)

Businesses often turn to statements when they charge the same amount each month, such as a fixed monthly fee for Internet service or full-time work as a contract programmer. Although statements work for these fixed fees, you can also use memorized invoices (page 352) and QuickBooks' batch invoice feature (page 294) to do the same thing just as easily.

Where statements really shine is summarizing a customer's account. Behind the scenes, a statement adds up all the transactions that affect the customer's open balance over a period of time, which includes statement charges, payments, and invoices. The statement shows the customer's previous balance, any payments that the customer has made, any invoices that they haven't paid, and any new charges on the account. From all that information, QuickBooks calculates the total and displays it on the statement, so you know how much money is outstanding and whether or not it's overdue.

- Tracking sales tax

- Using Group items to add several items

- Accepting multi-paragraph descriptions of services or products

- Subtotaling items

- Applying percentage discounts to items sold

- Including a message to the customer

- Including custom fields

- Summarizing the services and products sold (on statements, each service or product you sell appears
as a separate statement charge)

Invoices

If statements or sales receipts don't work for your situation, don't be afraid to use
invoices. They accept any item you've created in your Item List (see Chapter 5) *and*
they track what customers owe you.

Besides the features in Table 10-1, an invoice is the only type of QuickBooks sales
form you can generate from an estimate (page 314). If you're a general contractor
and prepare a detailed estimate of the services and products for a job, you'll save
a huge chunk of time by turning that estimate into an invoice for billing. And if you
have to refund some of your customer's money, you can also turn an invoice into a
credit memo (page 320).

■ Sales Forms and Accounts

An invoice or other sales form is the first step in the flow of money through your
company, so now is a good time to look at how QuickBooks posts income and expenses from your invoices to the accounts in your chart of accounts. Suppose your
invoice has the entries shown in Figure 10-1. Table 10-2 shows how the amounts on
that invoice post to accounts in your chart of accounts.

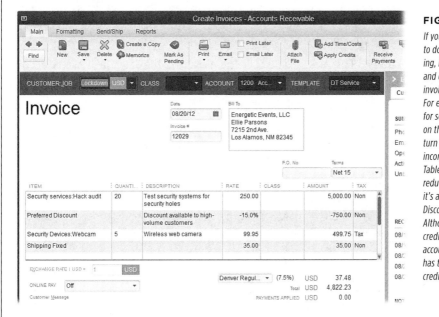

FIGURE 10-1

If you're still getting used to double-entry account-ing, balancing the debit and credit amounts for an invoice is a brainteaser. For example, the items for services and products on the invoice shown here turn up as credits in your income accounts, as in Table 10-2. The discount reduces your income, so it's a debit to the Sales Discounts income account. Although the debits and credits appear in different accounts, the total debit has to equal the total credit.

TABLE 10-2 *Debits and credits have to balance*

ACCOUNT	DEBIT	CREDIT
Accounts Receivable	4822.23	
Services Revenue		5000.00
Product Revenue		499.75
Sales Discounts	750.00	
Sales Tax Payable		37.48
Shipping income		35.00
Cost of Goods Sold	249.78	
Inventory		249.78
Total	5822.01	5822.01

NOTE   The lines on the invoice in Figure 10-1 don't show *all* the movements between accounts listed in Table 10-2. The money transferring to cost of goods sold and inventory happens behind the scenes.

Here's why the amounts post the way they do:

- You sold $5,000 of services and $499.75 of products, which is income. The income values appear as credits to your Services Income and Product Revenue accounts to increase your income because you sold something. In this example, the discount is in an income account, so the discount is in the Debit column to *reduce* your income.

- The $37.48 of sales tax you collect is a credit to the Sales Tax Payable account.

- The shipping charge ($35.00) is a credit in your shipping income account to show what you charged for shipping.

- All those credits need to balance against a debit. Because your customer owes you money, the amount owed ($4822.23) belongs in the Accounts Receivable account, indicated by the debit.

- You also sold some products from inventory. You credit the Inventory account with the cost of the products, $249.78, which decreases the Inventory account's balance. You offset that credit with a debit for the same amount to the Cost of Goods Sold account, which is an income statement account.

■ Creating Invoices

Depending on which edition of QuickBooks you use, you have up to three options for creating invoices:

- **Create Invoices** can handle everything you throw at it: services, products, billable time, and billable expenses. It's available in QuickBooks Pro and higher.

- **Create Batch Invoices** (page 294) lets you select all the customers to which you want to send the same invoice (that is, the same items and the same amounts.) If you send the same invoice to the same customers all the time, you can set up a billing group for those customers and, from then on, simply choose the group. After you create the invoice, you can print or email it to the customers in the list. This feature is available in QuickBooks Pro and higher, as long as you don't use multiple currencies.

- **Invoice for Time & Expenses**, available only in QuickBooks Premier and Enterprise editions, can do everything that the Create Invoices feature can do, but it's a real time-saver when you invoice for billable time and expenses. As you'll learn on page 299, you specify a date range and QuickBooks shows you all the customers who have billable time and expenses during that period. When you choose a customer or job and tell the program to create an invoice, it opens the Create Invoices window, fills in the usual fields, *and* fills the invoice table with the customer's billable time and expenses. Once you're in the Create Invoices window, you can add any other items you want, like products you sold or discounts you're offering. And in QuickBooks 2012 and 2013, this feature also lets you create batch invoices for time and expenses (page 294).

Invoices tell your customers everything they need to know about what they purchased and the payment they're about to make. If you created customers and jobs with settings such as payment terms, tax item, and sales rep (page 70), as soon as you choose a customer and job in the Create Invoices window's Customer:Job field, QuickBooks fills in many of the fields for you.

Some invoice fields are more influential than others, but they all come in handy at some point. To understand the purpose of the fields on an invoice more easily, you can break the form up into three basic parts (see Figure 10-2). Because the invoices you create for product sales include a few more fields than the ones for services only, the following sections use a product invoice to explain how to fill in each field you might run into on the invoices you create. These sections also tell you what to do if the information that QuickBooks fills in for you is incorrect.

NOTE   If you charge customers based on the progress you've made on a project, invoices are a *little* more complicated, but you'll learn how to handle this situation on page 315.

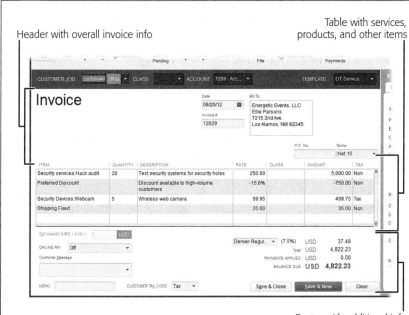

Header with overall invoice info

Table with services, products, and other items

Footer with additional info

FIGURE 10-2

The top of the invoice has overall sale information, such as the customer and job, the invoice date, who to bill and ship to, and the payment terms. The table in the middle has info about the products and services sold, and other items, such as subtotals and discounts. Below the table, QuickBooks fills in the tax field (the unlabeled drop-down list below the line-item table) and the Customer Tax Code field with values from the customer's record, but you can change any values that the program fills in. You can also add a message to the customer, choose your send method, or type a memo to store in your QuickBooks file.

Creating an Invoice

In the sections that follow, you'll find details about filling in all the fields on an invoice. For now, here's the basic procedure for creating and saving one or more invoices by using the Create Invoices feature:

1. **In the Customers panel on the Home page, click the Create Invoices icon; press Ctrl+I; or—in the Customer Center toolbar—choose New Transactions→Invoices.**

   If you use QuickBooks Pro or the preference for invoicing time and expenses isn't turned on, clicking Create Invoices opens the Create Invoices window immediately.

   If you use QuickBooks Premier or Enterprise and you've turned on the preference to invoice for time and expenses (page 633), the Home page displays the Invoices icon instead of the Create Invoices icon. Clicking Invoices displays a shortcut menu with two entries: "Invoice for Time & Expenses" and Create Invoices. Choose Create Invoices to create a regular invoice. See page 299 to learn how to use the shortcut menu's other entry to invoice for billable time and expenses.

2. **In the Create Invoices window's Customer:Job box, choose the customer or job associated with the invoice.**

   When you choose a customer or job, QuickBooks fills in many of the invoice fields with values from the customer's record (see page 66), the job's record if you selected a job (page 76), and the preferences you set for them (page 626). For example, QuickBooks pulls the data for the Bill To address, Terms, and Rep fields from the customer's or job's record. And your Sales & Customers preferences provide the values for the Via and F.O.B. fields. (FOB stands for "free on board," which is the physical point where the customer becomes responsible for damage to or loss of the shipment.)

> **NOTE** Depending on the QuickBooks edition you use and transactions you've entered, a few other windows may open when you choose a customer or job. If the customer or job you selected has an available estimate, the Available Estimates dialog box opens so you can fill in the invoice simply by selecting an estimate and clicking OK. If you use QuickBooks Premier and there's an outstanding sales order (page 307), the Available Sales Order window appears so you can select the one you want to invoice.
>
> In QuickBooks Premier, if the preference for invoicing time and expenses is turned on and the customer or job has associated time or expenses, the Billable Time/Costs dialog box opens with the "Select the outstanding billable time and costs to add to this invoice" option selected. If you don't want to add the time and expenses to this invoice, select the option whose label begins with "Exclude," and then click OK. To learn more about invoicing for time and expenses, see page 297.

3. **For each product or service sold, in the line-item table, enter the info for the item, including its quantity and price (or rate).**

   If you want, you can also fill in the boxes below the line-item table, such as Customer Message and Memo. If you've signed up for online payments, you can choose whether to include an online payment link on the invoice you send. And you'll rarely need to change the sales tax rate associated with the customer, but you can if necessary.

4. **Maintain your professional image by checking for spelling errors before you send the invoice.**

   To run QuickBooks' spell-checker, in the Create Invoices window, click the Formatting tab, and then click Spelling. (If you checked spelling when you created your customers and invoice items, then the main source of spelling errors will be edits you've made to item descriptions.) If the spell-checker doesn't work the way you want, then change your Spelling preferences (page 631).

5. **To save the invoice you just created and close the -Create Invoices window, click Save & Close.**

   If you're unhappy with the choices you made in the current invoice, click Clear to start over with a fresh, blank invoice. If you have additional invoices to create, click Save & New to save the current invoice and begin another.

NOTE If you create or modify an invoice and then click the Print icon, QuickBooks saves the invoice before printing it, which helps prevent financial hanky-panky.

Filling in Invoice Header Fields

If you fill in all the fields in your customer and job records (see Chapter 4), QuickBooks takes care of filling in most of the invoice header section. Here's what the header fields do and where QuickBooks gets the values it fills in automatically.

■ CHOOSING THE CUSTOMER OR JOB

The selection you make in the Customer:Job field (shown in Figure 10-3) is your most important choice for any invoice. In addition to billing the correct customer for your work, QuickBooks uses the settings from the customer's or job's record to fill in many of the invoice's fields.

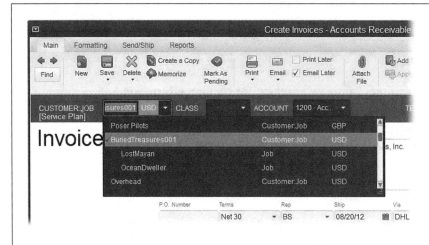

FIGURE 10-3

If you work on different jobs for a customer, click the name of the job, which is indented underneath the customer's name. If your work for a customer doesn't relate to jobs, just click the customer's name. The column to the right of the customer and job names provides another way to differentiate customers and jobs: It displays "Customer:Job" for a customer entry, and "Job" for a job entry.

NOTE If you've turned on the preference for multiple currencies, the last column in the Customer:Job drop-down list shows the customer's currency.

The panel on the right side of the Create Invoices window (Figure 10-4) shows a summary of the customer's account and its recent transactions. The Customer tab displays the customer's open balance and the credit limit you've set for that customer so you can see whether the new invoice exceeds that limit. You can also review recent transactions to check whether payments have come in before you send an invoice for finance charges. Notes that you've entered for the customer appear at the bottom of the panel. Click the arrow at the panel's top left to expand or collapse it.

NOTE The right-hand panel's Transaction tab shows information about the transaction that's currently displayed in the Create Invoices window. The Summary section shows who created and edited the transaction and when. If there are related transactions, such as a payment or credit memo, they appear in the Related Transactions section.

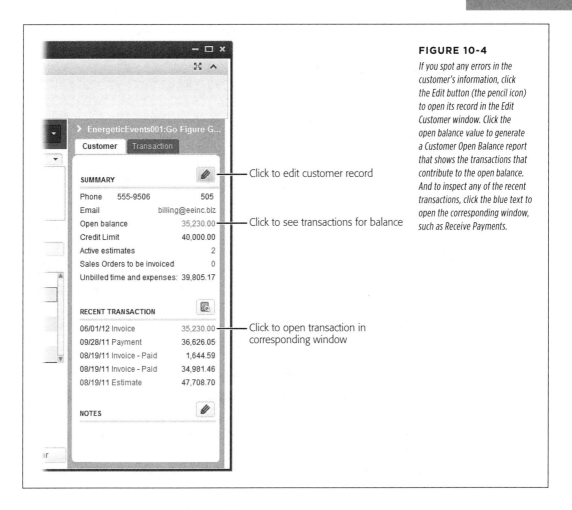

FIGURE 10-4

If you spot any errors in the customer's information, click the Edit button (the pencil icon) to open its record in the Edit Customer window. Click the open balance value to generate a Customer Open Balance report that shows the transactions that contribute to the open balance. And to inspect any of the recent transactions, click the blue text to open the corresponding window, such as Receive Payments.

Click to edit customer record

Click to see transactions for balance

Click to open transaction in corresponding window

■ CHOOSING AN INVOICE TEMPLATE

The template you choose in the Template drop-down list (near the top right of the Create Invoices window) determines which fields appear on your invoices and how they're laid out. For example, you might use two templates: one for printing on your company letterhead and one for invoices you send electronically. Choosing a template *before* doing anything else is the best way to prevent printing the wrong invoice on expensive stationery.

QuickBooks remembers the template you chose when you created your last invoice. So if you use only one invoice template, choose it on your first invoice and the program chooses it for you from then on. But if you switch between invoices, be sure to select the correct template for the invoice you're creating.

NOTE Templates aren't linked to customers. If you pick a template when you create an invoice for one customer, QuickBooks chooses that same template for your next invoice, regardless of which customer it's for.

You can switch templates anytime. When you choose a template, the Create Invoices window displays the appropriate fields and layout. If you've already filled in an invoice, changing the template doesn't throw out the data; QuickBooks simply displays the data in the new template. However, QuickBooks won't display settings like your company logo, fonts, and other formatting until you print or preview the invoice (page 345).

Many small companies are perfectly happy with the invoice templates that QuickBooks provides. When you create your first invoice, you might not even think about the layout of the fields. But if you run across a billing task that the current template can't handle, don't panic: You can choose from several built-in templates. And if you want your invoices to reflect your company's style and image, you can create your own custom templates (see page 669).

The options you see in the Template drop-down list depend on the QuickBooks edition you use. Before you accept the template that QuickBooks chooses, in the Template drop-down list, quickly select and review the templates to see whether you like any of them better. Here are a few of the more popular built-in templates:

- **Intuit Product Invoice**. If you sell products with or without services, this template is set up to show information like the quantity, item code, price for each item, total charge for each item, sales tax, and shipping info—including the ship date, shipping method, and FOB.

- **Intuit Service Invoice**. This template doesn't bother with shipping fields because services are performed, not shipped. The template includes fields for the item, description, quantity, rate, amount, tax, and purchase order number.

- **Intuit Professional Invoice**. The only difference between this template and the Intuit Service Invoice is that this one doesn't include a P.O. Number field, and the quantity (Qty) column follows the Description column.

- **Progress Invoice**. If you bill customers based on the progress you've made on their jobs, use this template, which has columns for your estimates, prior charges, and new totals. It appears in the Template drop-down list only if you turn on the preference for progress invoicing (see page 617).

NOTE The Intuit Packing Slip template also appears in the Template drop-down list even though it isn't an invoice template. It's listed because, when you ship products to customers, you can print an invoice *and* packing slip from the Create Invoices window (see page 348).

- **Fixed Fee Invoice**. This template drops the quantity and rate fields, since the invoice shows only the total charge. It includes fields for the date, item, description, tax, and purchase order number.

- **Time & Expense Invoice**. If you bill customers by the hour, this template is the one to use. It includes a column for hours and hourly rate, and it calculates the resulting total. (The Attorney's Invoice template is identical to this one except in name.)

■ THE OTHER HEADER FIELDS

As Figure 10-5 shows, QuickBooks can fill in most of the remaining header fields for you. Although the following fields don't appear on every invoice template, here's how to fill in any empty fields or change the ones that QuickBooks didn't complete the way you want:

- **Class**. If you turned on the class-tracking feature (page 150) to categorize your income and expenses in different ways, choose a class for the invoice. If you skip this box and have the class reminder preference set, QuickBooks tells you that the box is empty when you try to save the invoice. Although you *can* save the invoice without a class if classes don't apply to the transaction, it's important to assign classes to every class-related transaction if you want your class-based reports to be accurate. For example, if you use classes to track income by partner and save an invoice without a class, the partner who delivered the services on the invoice might complain about the size of her paycheck.

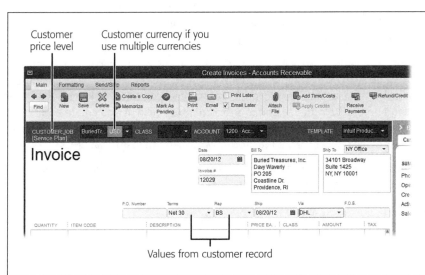

Customer price level

Customer currency if you use multiple currencies

Values from customer record

FIGURE 10-5

After you choose a customer, if you've assigned a price level to that customer's record (page 71), the unlabeled price level appears in brackets below the Customer:Job label. You can change the customer's price level by editing the customer's record (page 78), or you can choose existing price levels to change the price you charge as you add items to your invoice (see the box on page 284).

NOTE If you work with multiple currencies and the customer is set up to use a currency other than your home one, then at the top of the Create Invoices window, the Account box appears and shows the Accounts Receivable (AR) account for the invoice's income. To store income in other currencies, QuickBooks creates additional Accounts Receivable accounts (page 52), such as Account Receivable-EUR.

- **Date**. Out of the box, QuickBooks fills in the current date, which is fine if you create invoices when you make a sale. But service businesses often send invoices on a schedule—the last day of the month is a popular choice. If you want to get a head start on your invoices, you can change your QuickBooks preferences so the program uses the same date for every subsequent invoice (until you change the date), making your end-of-month invoicing a tiny bit easier. Page 612 tells you how.

- **Invoice #**. When you create your first invoice, type the number that you want to start with. For example, if you'd rather not reveal that this is your first invoice, type a number such as 245. Then, each time you create a new invoice, Quick-Books increases the number in this field by one: 246, 247, and so on.

TIP Press the plus (+) or minus (–) key to increase or decrease the invoice number by one, respectively. When you save the current invoice, QuickBooks considers its invoice number the starting point for subsequent numbers.

If your last invoice was a mistake, the best thing to do is to void it (page 325). If you delete it instead, you'll end up with a gap in your invoice numbers. For example, when you delete invoice number 203, QuickBooks has already set the next invoice number to 204. So, if you notice the gap, in the Invoice # box, type the number you want to use to get QuickBooks back on track and void incorrect invoices from now on.

- **Bill To**. This field is essential if you mail invoices. When the customer record includes a billing address (page 69), QuickBooks puts that address in this field. If you email invoices, a billing address isn't necessary—the customer name in this field simply identifies the customer on the emailed form.

- **Ship To**. If you sell services, you don't need an address to ship to. But if you sell products, you need a shipping address to send the products to your customer. When you use a template like Intuit Product Invoice, QuickBooks puts the shipping address from the customer's record in this field. If you create additional shipping addresses (for instance, for different office locations), click the down arrow to the right of the Ship To drop-down list and choose the address you want.

- **P.O. Number**. If your customer issued a purchase order for the goods and services on your invoice, type that purchase order number here.

- **Terms**. Typically, you set up payment terms when you create customers, and you then use those terms for every invoice. When the customer's record includes payment terms (page 70), QuickBooks uses them to fill in this field. However, if you decide to change the terms—perhaps due to the customer's failing financial strength—choose a different term here, such as "Due on receipt."

NOTE If QuickBooks fills in fields with incorrect values, make the corrections on the invoice. When you save the invoice, QuickBooks asks if you'd like the new values to appear the next time, as shown in Figure 10-6.

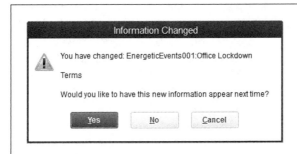

FIGURE 10-6

If you click Yes here, QuickBooks changes the corresponding fields in the customer and job records. If you click No, it changes the values only on this particular invoice.

- **Rep**. If you assigned a sales rep in the customer's record (page 73), QuickBooks fills in this field for you. If the sales rep changes from invoice to invoice (for instance, when the rep is the person who takes a phone order) and you left the Rep field blank in the customer's record, choose the right person here, or leave the field blank if the transaction doesn't have a sales rep.

- **Ship**. QuickBooks fills in the current date here. If you plan to ship on a different date (when the products arrive from your warehouse, for example), type or choose the correct date.

- **Via**. If you specify a value in the Usual Shipping Method preference (page 627), QuickBooks enters that value here. To choose a different shipping method for this invoice—for instance, when your customer needs the order right away—click this field and select the one you want. (Some templates use the label Ship Via for this field.)

- **F.O.B.** This stands for "free on board" and signifies the physical point at which the customer becomes responsible for the shipment. That means that if the shipment becomes lost or damaged beyond the FOB point, it's the customer's problem. If you set the Usual FOB preference (page 627), QuickBooks enters that location here. To choose a different FOB for this order, type the location you want.

FREQUENTLY ASKED QUESTION

Adjusting Price Levels

One of my Service items costs $150 per hour. But when I created a customer invoice for that item, the Price Each came up as $120. What's going on?

Before you rush to correct that Service item's price, look near the top of the Create Invoices window, immediately below the Customer:Job label. If you see text in square brackets, such as "[Loyalty]," you'll know that you set up your customer with a price level (page 71). Instead of a mistake, this price adjustment on your invoice is actually a clever and convenient feature.

Price levels are percentages (either increases or decreases) that you can apply to the prices you charge. For example, you can set up price levels to give discounts to your high-volume customers or mark up prices for customers known for their frequent use of your customer-service line. To use price levels, you first have to turn on the Price Level preference (page 628).

If you assign a price level to a customer, QuickBooks automatically applies that price-level percentage to every item you add to invoices for that customer. The only indication that QuickBooks has applied the price level is the price level's name below the Customer:Job label (and the item's altered cost).

You can also apply price levels to individual items on an invoice. For example, suppose you offer a 20 percent discount on a different item each month. When an item is the monthly special, you can apply the Monthly Special price level to just that item, as shown in Figure 10-7.

When you use price levels, your customers don't see that the price increases or decreases, which means they could take your discounts for granted. If you want to emphasize the discounts you apply, use a Discount item instead to visibly reduce prices on your invoices (see page 289).

Entering Invoice Line Items

If you dutifully studied Chapter 5, you know about the different types of items you can add to an invoice. This section describes how to fill in a line in the Create Invoices window's line-item table to charge your customers for the things they buy. (The box on page 287 explains a shortcut for speeding up this process.)

The order in which you add items to an invoice is important. For example, when you add a Subtotal item, QuickBooks subtotals all the preceding items up to the previous Subtotal item (if there is one). QuickBooks does nothing to check that you add items in the correct order—you can add a Subtotal item as the first line item, even though that does nothing for your invoice. See page 289 for the full scoop on adding Subtotal, Discount, and Sales Tax items in the right order.

NOTE If multiple currencies are turned on and you have customers set up to use foreign currencies, QuickBooks automatically applies the exchange rate you entered for that currency to item prices and service rates. (See the box on page 482 to learn how to download exchange rates and obtain exchange rates for certain dates.) To use a specific exchange rate in an invoice, fill in the "Exchange Rate 1 <currency> =" box with the exchange rate *before* you add items to the invoice. (If you forgot to change the exchange rate before adding items, delete the lines in the invoice, set the exchange rate, and then add the items again.)

Customer price
level applies

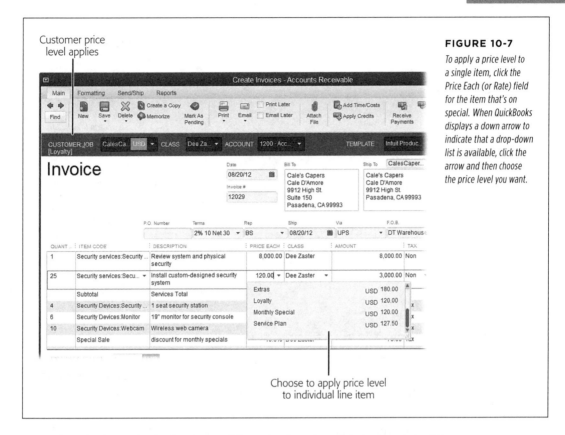

FIGURE 10-7

*To apply a price level to
a single item, click the
Price Each (or Rate) field
for the item that's on
special. When QuickBooks
displays a down arrow to
indicate that a drop-down
list is available, click the
arrow and then choose
the price level you want.*

Choose to apply price level
to individual line item

The order of columns in the line-item table varies from template to template. This section lists the columns in the order they appear on the Intuit Product Invoice template (shown in Figure 10-8):

- **Quantity**. For products, type the quantity. For services you sell by the hour (or other unit of time), type the number of time units. (See page 302 to learn how to select hours from a timesheet.) If you sell services at a flat rate, you can leave this cell blank and simply fill in the Amount cell.

> **NOTE** If you type a quantity for a product that exceeds how many you have on hand, QuickBooks Pro simply warns you that you don't have enough. QuickBooks Premier displays the warning *and* tells you how many you have on hand, how many are on sales orders (page 307), and the total available.

Quantity doesn't apply if the item is a discount, subtotal, or sales tax. So if you choose one of these items after entering a quantity, QuickBooks removes the value in the Quantity cell.

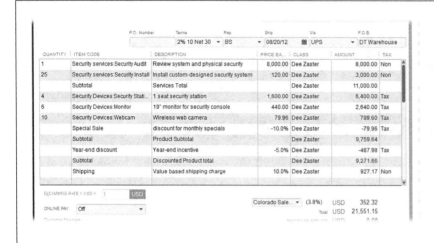

FIGURE 10-8

When you use the Intuit Product Invoice, the Quantity column comes first. After you choose an item, make sure to check the value in the Amount cell. If the number looks too large or small, the quantity you entered might not match the units for the item. For example, if you charge for developing training materials by the hour but charge for teaching a training class by the day, the quantity for developing training materials has to be in hours and the quantity for teaching in days.

- **Item Code**. Click this cell and then choose an item from the drop-down list (see Chapter 5 for details on items). Depending on the info you entered when you created this item (page 124), QuickBooks may fill in the Description and Price Each (or Rate) cells for you.

- **Description**. If you set up inventory items with standard descriptions, Quick-Books automatically puts them in this cell. But you can edit a description to, for example, add details—like changing the generic description "Security service" to the more specific "Nightly rounds every two hours."

- **Price Each (or Rate)**. Depending on the type of item you're adding to the invoice, QuickBooks goes to the item's record (see Chapter 5) and grabs the value in the Sales Price field or Rate field and puts it here. For example, an inventory part's price always comes from the Sales Price field, whereas Service items use the Rate field (unless a partner or subcontractor performs the work, in which case they use the Sales Price field).

- **Class**. If you turn on the Class feature (page 150), you can fill in this cell with the class for this item.

- **Amount**. QuickBooks calculates the total in this cell by multiplying the quantity by the value in the Price Each (or Rate) field. But nothing stops you from simply typing a value in this field, which is exactly what you want for a fixed-fee contract.

- **Tax**. QuickBooks fills in this cell with the taxable status you specified in the item's record, and fills in the Tax box *below* the table with the sales tax item you set in the customer's record. (The tax rate for the sales tax item you select appears to the right of the box.) With the taxable status of your customers (page 72) and the items you sell (page 132) in place, QuickBooks can automatically handle sales tax on your invoices. For example, when an item is taxable *and* the customer is liable for paying sales tax, the program calculates the total sales tax that appears below the table (see Figure 10-8) by adding up all the taxable items on your invoice and multiplying that number by the tax rate set in the Tax box below the table.

> **TIP** If you notice that an item's taxable status isn't correct, don't change the value in the Tax cell. You're better off correcting the customer's or item's tax status so QuickBooks can calculate tax correctly in the future.

POWER USERS' CLINIC

Adding Group Items to Invoices

If the same items frequently appear together on your invoices, you can add all those items in one step by creating a Group item (page 136).

For example, customers who buy your deluxe vinyl sofa covers also tend to purchase the dirt-magnet front hall runner and the faux-marble garage floor liner. So you could create a Group item, perhaps called the Neat Freak Package, that includes the items for the sofa cover, runner, and liner, with the quantity you typically sell of each item. Any type of item is fair game

for a Group item, so you can include service items, discounts, subtotals, and other charges.

To add a Group item to an invoice, in the Create Invoices window's item drop-down list (labeled Item or Item Code depending on the invoice template you're using), simply choose the Group item you created. QuickBooks fills in the first line by putting the name of the Group item in the item cell. Then, the program adds additional lines (including quantity, description, and price) for the individual items in the group, such as the sofa cover, runner, and liner.

■ INSERTING AND DELETING LINE ITEMS

Sometimes, you forget to add line items you need. For example, say you've added several services and inventory items to your invoice, and then realize that you need Subtotal items following the last service and last inventory items so you can apply a shipping charge only to the inventory items. Here's how to insert and delete lines in the line-item table:

- **Insert a line**. Right-click the line above which you want to add a line, and then choose Insert Line from the shortcut menu, as shown in Figure 10-9. If you prefer keyboard shortcuts, press Ctrl+Insert instead.

- **Delete a line**. Right-click the line you want to get rid of and choose Delete Line from the shortcut menu, or press Ctrl+Delete.

QuickBooks adjusts the invoice's lines accordingly.

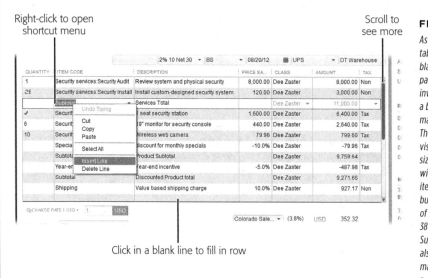

Right-click to open
shortcut menu

Scroll to
see more

FIGURE 10-9

*As you add items to the
table, QuickBooks adds
blank lines (and new
pages, if needed) to your
invoice. Tab into or click
a blank line to add as
many lines as you need.
The number of items
visible depends on the
size of the Create Invoices
window. To view more
items, click the Supermax
button at the top right
of the window (see page
38 for the full scoop on
Supermax mode). You can
also resize the window by
maximizing it or dragging
a corner of it, or move the
scroll bar up or down.*

Click in a blank line to fill in row

GEM IN THE ROUGH

Invoicing Fixed-Price Contracts

Fixed-price contracts are risky because you have to swallow any cost overruns beyond the fixed price you charge. But if you've sharpened your skills on similar projects in the past and can estimate your costs with reasonable accuracy, fixed-price contracts can provide opportunities for better-than-average profit.

Once you and your customer agree on the fixed price, that amount is all that matters to the customer. Even if *you* track the costs of performing a job, your customer never sees those numbers. In QuickBooks, you can invoice fixed-price contracts in two different ways:

- **Group item**. If you use the same sets of services and products for multiple jobs, create a Group item that includes each service and product you deliver and set

up the Group item to hide the details of the underlying services and products (page 136). After you add the Group item to your invoice, change the price of the Group item to your fixed price.

- **Service item**. If every fixed-price job is different, create a Service item (page 123) called something like "Fixed Fee" and leave its Rate field set to 0.00. When you add the item to an invoice, fill in its Rate field with the full amount of the fixed-price contract. Then, when you reach a milestone that warrants a payment, create a progress invoice: In the Quantity column, type the decimal that equates to the percentage completed (*.25* for 25 percent, for example), and QuickBooks calculates the payment by multiplying the quantity by the fixed-price amount.

Applying Subtotals, Discounts, and Percentage Charges

Services, Inventory Parts, and Non-inventory Parts (see Chapter 5) are standalone items; when you add them to an invoice's line-item table, they don't affect their neighbors in any way. However, when you offer percentage discounts on what you sell or include Other Charge items that calculate shipping as a percentage of price, the order in which you add items becomes crucial. And if you want to apply a percentage calculation like a discount or a shipping fee to several items, you'll need one or more Subtotal items to make the calculations work.

You first learned about Subtotal, Discount, and Other Charge items in Chapter 5. Figure 10-10 shows how to combine them to calculate percentage discounts and add markups to the items on your invoices.

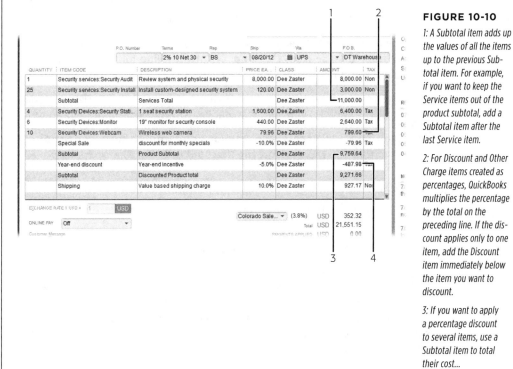

FIGURE 10-10

1: A Subtotal item adds up the values of all the items up to the previous Subtotal item. For example, if you want to keep the Service items out of the product subtotal, add a Subtotal item after the last Service item.

2: For Discount and Other Charge items created as percentages, QuickBooks multiplies the percentage by the total on the preceding line. If the discount applies only to one item, add the Discount item immediately below the item you want to discount.

3: If you want to apply a percentage discount to several items, use a Subtotal item to total their cost...

4: ...and then add a percentage Discount or Other Charge item on the line following that subtotal.

Here are the steps for arranging Subtotal, Discount, and Other Charge items to calculate percentages on invoice items:

1. **If you want to discount several items on an invoice, enter all those items one after the other.**

   Even though the Balance Due field below the line-item table shows the total of all items, to apply a discount to all of them, you'll need to add a Subtotal item to the line-item table.

2. **Add a Subtotal item after the last item you want to discount, like the Product Subtotal item in Figure 10-10.**

   The Subtotal item adds up all the preceding line items up to the previous Subtotal. For example, in Figure 10-10, the Services Total item (labeled "1") is a subtotal of all the Service items on the invoice. The Product Subtotal item (labeled "3") adds up all items between the Services Subtotal and the Product Subtotal items.

3. **To apply a percentage discount or charge to the subtotal, add a Discount or Other Charge item (labeled "4") to the line immediately below the Subtotal item.**

   If you've already added other items to the invoice, right-click the line immediately below the Subtotal item and then choose Insert Line from the shortcut menu.

4. **If you have additional items that you don't want to include in the discount or charge, add those below the Discount or Other Charge item.**

> **NOTE** These steps also work for Other Charge items that you set up as percentages, such as shipping, as shown at the bottom of Figure 10-10.

Adding a Message to the Customer

You can include a message to your customers on your invoices—for instance, thanking them for their business or asking for feedback. In the Customer Message drop-down list, choose the message you want to include. The messages in the drop-down list are the ones you've added to the Customer Message List (page 161). If the message you want to use isn't listed, then click <Add New> to open the New Customer Message dialog box.

Adding an Online Payment Link

The Online Pay box, which sits below the Create Invoices window's line-item table, is your key to quick and easy payments from customers. Choose one of the online payment entries in the drop-down list and your customer will receive an online payment link to pay you electronically from their back account or credit card via Intuit's Online PaymentNetwork. When your customers use the links to pay you, the money gets deposited into your bank account and you can download the payment transactions into QuickBooks (page 371). (There are no setup, cancellation, or monthly fees for this service. You pay a flat 50 cents for each bank payment you receive; fees for credit card payments vary.) This section describes how you turn on and use this feature.

> **NOTE** If you don't want to use Intuit's Online PaymentNetwork, you can turn off all online payment links in one fell swoop. Choose Edit→Preferences→Payments, and then on the Company Preferences tab, click Turn Off Online Payments. When you do so, QuickBooks turns off all online payments links on all invoices for all customers, even if links were previously turned on.

■ SIGN UP FOR INTUIT PAYMENTNETWORK

Before customers can pay you through an online payment link, you have to create a PaymentNetwork account. (If your customers try to use the online payment links before you create your account, they'll see a message that you haven't signed up yet.) To sign up, choose Customers→Intuit PaymentNetwork→About PaymentNetwork. The "Get paid Online on QuickBooks invoices" screen appears in a browser window. (After this screen appears, the "Quick intro: Online invoice payments" screen pops up in front of it. There, you can watch a video or click Continue to get back to the "Get paid Online..." screen.) You have to provide the email address and password you want to use for the account (or you can sign up using your Intuit account if you have one), as well as information about the bank account you want deposits sent to. When you finish filling in the fields, click Complete Set Up.

> **NOTE** QuickBooks automatically puts the email address associated with your company file in the QuickBooks Email Address field. If this field is blank or contains an incorrect email address, be sure to type in the correct one. PaymentNetwork communicates with you through this email address and, more importantly, uses it to direct customer payments to your bank account.

■ SET ONLINE PAYMENT LINK PREFERENCES

QuickBooks gives you several ways to control when online payment links appear:

- **All invoices for all customers.** To include online payment links on every invoice you create, you turn on the Invoice Payments preference. Choose Edit→Preferences→Payments, and then click the Company Preferences tab. Turn on the "Include online payment link on invoices" checkbox. In the drop-down list, choose the payment methods you want to accept: "bank account" or "bank account and credit card." To include links on printed invoices, too, turn on the "Also include on printed invoices" checkbox.

- **All invoices for a customer.** You can specify whether to include online payments links on all the invoices for a particular customer by editing the customer's record. Page 72 tells you how. The Add Online Payment Link To Invoices setting is on the Payment Settings tab of the Create Customer or Edit Customer window. You can also change a customer's setting from an invoice. To do so, on the Main tab of the Create Invoices window, click the Online Pay button and then choose Settings.

NOTE If you choose a setting for a specific customer, it overrides the setting you chose for all invoices in the Preferences dialog box. For example, if you tell QuickBooks to include online payment links on all invoices and then edit a customer's record to not show such links, online payment links will show up on all future invoices *except* ones for that customer.

- **Individual invoice.** When the invoice is visible in the Create Invoices window, choose the setting you want for that invoice in the Online Pay box below the line-item table.

Choosing How to Send the Invoice

On the Create Invoices window's Main tab, you'll find two checkboxes that simplify sending invoices to customers: Print Later and Email Later. But these checkboxes don't tell the whole story—you actually have *five* options for sending invoices:

- **Print now**. If you create only the occasional invoice and send it as soon as it's complete, turn off both checkboxes. Then, on the Create Invoices window's Main tab, click Print and follow the instructions on page 345.

- **Print later**. If you want to add the invoice to a queue to print later, turn on the Print Later checkbox. That way, you can print all the invoices in the queue, as described on page 346.

- **Email now**. In the Create Invoices window's Main tab, click the Email button (it looks like an envelope) and follow the instructions for emailing invoices on page 350.

Shipping Products

If you sell products, making regular runs to the FedEx or UPS office gets old quickly. But sitting quietly within QuickBooks is a free service that could change the way you ship packages.

The Shipping Manager feature is built into QuickBooks, so you can sign up for shipping services and start sending out packages right away. You can print FedEx, UPS, and U.S. Postal Service shipping labels; schedule pickups; and even track package progress right in QuickBooks. Shipping Manager fills in shipping labels with customer addresses from your QuickBooks invoices, sales receipts, or customer records. All you pay are the FedEx, UPS, or postal service charges on your shipment.

Here's where you can find Shipping Manager:

- If you're creating an invoice for products you plan to ship, in the Create Invoices window, click the Send/Ship tab, and then click the button for the shipping company you want to use. In the drop-down menu that appears, choose what you want to do, such as ship a package, schedule a pickup, or track a package that's already on its way.

- The Sales Receipt window also includes a Send/Ship tab, which works in the same way as the one in the Create Invoices window.

- Choose File→Shipping, and then choose Ship FedEx Package, Ship UPS Package, or Ship USPS Package.

The first time you choose a shipping action, such as Ship FedEx Package, a setup wizard steps you through creating an account for that shipping company.

- **Email later**. If you want to add the invoice to a queue to email later, turn on the Email Later checkbox. You can then send all the invoices in the queue, as described on page 352.

> **TIP** See page 629 if you want to set a preference that automatically turns on the Email Later checkbox if the customer's Preferred Delivery Method is email. And page 349 explains how QuickBooks works with email programs.

- **Print *and* email later**. Turn on both checkboxes if you want to email invoices to get the ball rolling and then follow up with paper copies.

If you're sending an invoice for products you've sold, you also have to ship those products to your customer. See the box on page 292 to learn a convenient and money-saving way to ship products.

Adding a Memo to Yourself

The Create Invoices window includes a Memo box, which works just like Memo boxes throughout QuickBooks. You can use it to remind yourself about something special on the invoice or to summarize the transaction. For example, if the invoice is the first one for a new customer, you can note that in the Memo box. The memo won't print on the invoices you send to your customers. However, it *does* appear on your sales reports and customer statements, so be careful what you put in the Memo box.

ALTERNATE REALITIES

Invoicing for Nonprofits

If you sell products and services, then you create invoices when someone buys something. For nonprofits, however, invoices can record the pledges, donations, grants, or other contributions you've been promised.

Invoicing for nonprofits differs from the profit world's approach. First of all, many nonprofits don't send invoices to donors. Nonprofits might send reminders to donors who haven't sent in the pledged donations, but they don't add finance charges to late payments.

Moreover, because some donors ask for specific types of reports, nonprofits often use several Accounts Receivable accounts to track money coming from grants, dues, pledges, and other sources. When you use multiple Accounts Receivable accounts, the Create Invoices window includes an Account field so you can choose the Accounts Receivable account (just like when you work with multiple currencies, as described in the Note on page 282). For example, when you create an invoice for pledges, you'd choose the Pledges Receivable account.

To compensate for this additional field, QuickBooks provides a handy feature when you use multiple Accounts Receivable accounts: The program remembers the last invoice number used for each income account in your QuickBooks Chart of Accounts, so you can create unique invoice numbering schemes for each one. For example, if you create an invoice for the Pledges Receivable account and set the Invoice # field to "PL-100," QuickBooks automatically assigns invoice number "PL-101" to the next invoice you create for that account.

Creating Batch Invoices

If you send invoices with the same items and the same quantities to many of your customers, QuickBooks offers a great invoicing timesaver. Instead of creating individual invoices for each customer, you can set up a single *batch invoice* and send it to as many customers as you want. And you can speed things up even more by creating a billing group that includes all the customers that receive the invoice, so you don't have to re-select them the next time you send a batch invoice.

NOTE You can't use the batch invoice feature if you have multiple currencies turned on (page 617). When that preference is turned on, the Create Batch Invoices entry doesn't appear on the Customers menu.

Batch invoices use the payment terms, sales tax rates, and send methods you specify for each customer, so be sure to fill in these fields in customers' records before you create your first batch invoice. These fields are on the Payment Settings, Sales Tax Settings, and Additional Info tabs (page 70, page 72, and page 73, respectively) of the Create Customer and Edit Customer windows. You can use the Add/Edit Multiple List Entries window (page 94) to find and fill in any missing values.

Here's how to create a batch invoice for several customers:

1. **Choose Customers→Create Batch Invoices.**

   The Batch Invoice window opens (Figure 10-11).

   NOTE If this is your first time using Create Batch Invoices, the "Is your customer info set up correctly?" message box appears, reminding you that you need to fill in terms, sales tax, and send method settings for your batch invoice customers. Click OK to close it and open the Batch Invoice window. If you need to fill in more information for your customers, close the Batch Invoice window and choose Lists→Add/Edit Multiple List Entries to open the Add/Edit Multiple List Entries window to complete your customers' records.

2. **In the Batch Invoice window, either select individual customers in the Search Results list and then click Add to add them to the Customers In This Group box on the right side of the window, or choose an existing group from the Billing Group drop-down list.**

   If you select individual customers, you can select adjacent names by clicking the first customer's name and then Shift-click the last customer's name. You can also Ctrl-click each customer name you want to select.

If you choose a billing group, the name of the group appears above the Customers In This Group box and the individual names appear in the box, as shown in Figure 10-11. (The box on page 297 explains how to create billing groups.)

NOTE If you add individual customers and a billing group to the "Customers in this Group" list, when you click away from the list, a Batch Invoice message box asks if you want to save the changes to the billing group. Click Yes to add the individual customers to this billing group and use the full list for the batch invoice. Click No to use the list of customers for the batch invoice while leaving the saved billing group as it is. Or click Cancel to return to the Batch Invoice window to make additional changes.

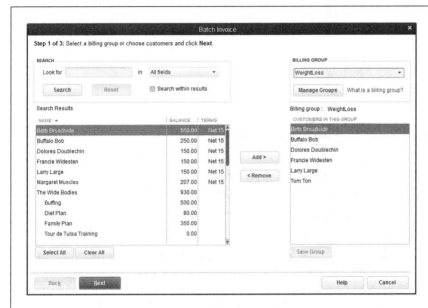

FIGURE 10-11

You can rename or delete the billing groups you create by clicking Manage Groups. To select a different billing group, choose it from the Billing Group drop-down list. If you modify the customers in the list, click Save Group to update the billing group with the current set of customer names.

3. **After you add the appropriate customers to the Customer In This Group list, click Next.**

   In the "Step 2 of 3" screen that appears, QuickBooks automatically puts today's date in the Date box and displays a table for the next step in the process: adding items to the invoice.

4. **To use a different date, choose it in the Date box.**

   You can also choose a different invoice template from the Template drop-down list.

5. **In the line-item table (Figure 10-12), fill in the items you want to add to the invoice just as you do in a regular invoice (page 284).**

   You can add any item from your Item List to a batch invoice.

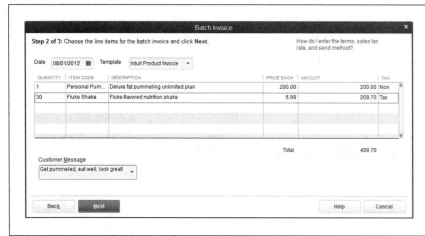

FIGURE 10-12

Fill in the items for the batch invoice as you do the line items in the Create Invoices window. (The fields you see in the table depend on the invoice template you're using.)

6. **After you fill in the items for the invoice, click Next.**

   The "Step 3 of 3" screen displays a summary of the customers who will receive the invoice, including their terms, send methods, tax codes, and other information. If you notice any errors or omissions, click Back to correct them.

7. **When everything looks good, click Create Invoices.**

   QuickBooks creates the invoices for the selected customers. The Batch Invoice Summary dialog box appears and shows how many invoices are set up to print and how many to email, based on the customers' preferred delivery methods. (The dialog box mentions the customer's Preferred Send Method, but the field in the customer record is actually named Preferred Delivery Method.) If the Preferred Delivery Method for any of the customers is set to None, the dialog box's "unmarked" entry shows how many invoices aren't marked to be mailed or emailed; you can send them later by choosing File→Send Forms or File→Print Forms.

   > **TIP** You can view or change each customer's delivery method selection in the Customer Center. Simply right-click the customer's name and choose Edit. Then click the Payment Settings tab to see your selections.

8. **Click Print to print the invoices marked to print; click Email to send the invoices marked to be emailed.**

   If you want to print or email the invoices later, click Close. Then you can print or email them by choosing File→Print Forms→Invoices or File→Send Forms.

Creating a Billing Group

Billing groups make it easy to select all the customers who receive the same batch invoice. Once you set up a billing group, you can select it in the Batch Invoice window and QuickBooks automatically adds all the customers in it to the Customers In This Group list in one fell swoop.

Here's how to create a billing group:

1. In the Batch Invoice window (Customers→Create Batch Invoices), before you select customer names, in the Billing Group drop-down list, choose <Add New>.

2. In the Group Name dialog box, type a name of the group,

like *WeightLoss* for all the customers on your monthly diet plan, for example. Then click Save.

3. In the Batch Invoice window's Search Results list, Ctrl-click all the customers you want to add to the group, and then click Add to copy the names to the Customers In This Group list.

4. Click the Save Group button below the Customer In This Group list.

QuickBooks saves your new billing group so you can use it again simply by selecting it in the Batch Invoice window.

Invoicing for Billable Time and Costs

When you work on a time-and-materials contract, you charge the customer for labor costs plus job expenses. Cost-plus contracts are similar except that you charge a fee on top of the job costs. Contracts like these are both low-risk and low-reward—in effect, you're earning an hourly wage for the time you work. For these types of contracts, it's critical that you capture all the expenses associated with the job or you'll lose some of the profit that the contract offers.

QuickBooks helps you get those billable items into your invoices. You have to tell the program about every hour worked and every expense you incur for a customer or job. But once you do that, it's easy to build an invoice that captures these billable items. You can add billable time and costs to an invoice when it's open in the Create Invoices window. And, when you open the Create Invoices window in QuickBooks Pro or Premier and choose a customer or job, the program reminds you about outstanding billable time and costs. QuickBooks Premier also has a separate feature specifically for creating invoices for billable time and costs. The following sections tell you how to perform all these tasks.

Setting Up Invoicing for Time and Costs

In some industries, like consulting and law, invoicing for time and expenses is the norm. But before you can pop your billable time and expenses into QuickBooks invoices, you first need to record them as billable items and assign them to the correct customer or job. Here are the billable items you can add to invoices and the chapters that tell you how to track them:

- **Billable time**. Chapter 8 (page 203) describes how to track billable time and assign hours to a customer or job.

- **Mileage**. Chapter 8 (page 210) describes how to track mileage and assign billable mileage to a customer or job.

- **Purchases and expenses related to a customer or job**. Reimbursable expenses include products you purchase specifically for a job, services performed by a subcontractor, and other expenses such as shipping and postage. Chapter 9 describes how to make items and expenses reimbursable to a customer or job (page 222) as you enter bills, checks, or credit card charges in QuickBooks.

Adding Billable Time and Costs to Invoices

If you use QuickBooks Pro or Premier, you can add billable time and costs directly in the Create Invoices window. Here's how:

1. **Press Ctrl+I or choose Customers→Create Invoices to open the Create Invoices window.**

2. **In the Customer:Job drop-down list, choose the customer or job you want to invoice.**

   If the customer or job has outstanding billable time or expenses, the Billable Time/Costs dialog box opens and automatically selects the "Select the outstanding billable time and costs to add to this invoice?" option, as shown in Figure 10-13 (foreground).

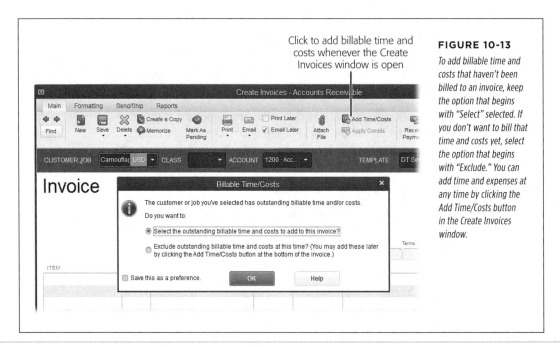

Click to add billable time and costs whenever the Create Invoices window is open

FIGURE 10-13

To add billable time and costs that haven't been billed to an invoice, keep the option that begins with "Select" selected. If you don't want to bill that time and costs yet, select the option that begins with "Exclude." You can add time and expenses at any time by clicking the Add Time/Costs button in the Create Invoices window.

3. **In the Billable Time/Costs dialog box, click OK.**

   The Choose Billable Time and Costs dialog box opens.

NOTE   You can open the Choose Billable Time and Costs dialog box any time the Create Invoices window is
open by clicking the Add Time/Costs button on the window's Main tab.

---

4. **To select the time and costs you want to add to the invoice, follow the in-structions that begin with step 1 on page 302.**

Using "Invoice for Time & Expenses"

If you have QuickBooks Premier or Enterprise, you can set the program up to include a special feature for adding billable items to invoices. The "Invoice for Time & Expenses" feature shows you every customer with billable time and expenses waiting to be invoiced and how much there is of each type, so it's easy to see all your outstanding billable hours and reimbursable expenses.

To set the preference for this feature, choose Edit→Preferences→Time & Expenses. On the Company Preferences tab, turn on the "Create invoices from a list of time and expenses" checkbox. (Leave this checkbox turned off if invoicing for time and expenses is the exception rather than the rule. If you leave it off, you can still add time and other costs to an invoice in the Create Invoices window, as described in the previous section.)

■ INVOICING ONE CUSTOMER OR JOB FOR TIME AND EXPENSES

If you want to create an invoice for billable time and expenses for one customer or job, here's how to put this feature to use:

1. **Choose Customers→Invoice for Time & Expenses or, on the Home page, click the Invoices icon, and then choose Invoice for Time & Expenses on the drop-down menu.**

   QuickBooks opens the Invoice for Time & Expenses window, which lists the customers and jobs that have billable time and expenses associated with them. The table shows the amount of billable time, expenses, and mileage for each customer and job. The Items column shows the reimbursable amount for products that you purchased specifically for the customer or job.

2. **In the Date Range From and To boxes, type the starting and ending dates for the time and expenses you want to invoice.**

   For example, if you want to invoice for billable time and expenses for the previous month, type the first and last days of the month, like *8/1/2012* and *8/31/2012*. To invoice for all outstanding time and expenses up to a certain date, leave the Date Range From box blank.

3. **To select a customer or job, click anywhere in its row.**

   QuickBooks highlights the customer or job you clicked.

4. **To choose specific billable time and costs to add to the invoice, turn on the "Let me select specific billable costs for this Customer:Job" checkbox at the bottom of the window.**

   This checkbox is active only when one customer or job is selected. If you select more than one customer or job (see page 301 to learn how to create a batch of time and expenses invoices), the checkbox is grayed out.

5. **Click Create Invoice.**

   If you turned on the "Let me select specific billable costs for this Customer:Job" checkbox, QuickBooks opens the Choose Billable Time and Costs dialog box shown in Figure 10-14, which includes tabs for time, expenses, mileage, and items (products). (This dialog box is the same one you see if you click Add Time/Costs in the Create Invoices window.) Proceed to the section "Selecting Billable Time and Costs" on page 302 to learn how to add specific billable time and costs to an invoice.

   If you left the "Let me select specific billable costs for this Customer:Job" checkbox turned off, the Create Invoices window opens with your invoice already filled out. All you have to do is save the invoice by clicking Save & Close.

FIGURE 10-14

On the Choose Billable Time and Costs dialog box's Time tab (background), click the Options button to tell QuickBooks how to handle different activities. In the Options for Transferring Billable Time dialog box (foreground), the program automatically selects the option that displays the total hours for each service item. However, you can choose the other option to tell QuickBooks to add a separate line for each activity, to show the hours worked each day, for instance. If each activity is on its own line, you can transfer activity descriptions, notes, or both to the invoice.

■ CREATING A BATCH OF TIME AND EXPENSES INVOICES

If your company is set to use a single currency and you have QuickBooks Premier or Enterprise, you can create time and expenses invoices for more than one customer or job. Here are the steps:

1. **Choose Customers→Invoice for Time & Expenses or, on the Home page, click the Invoices icon, and then choose Invoice for Time & Expenses on the drop-down menu.**

   The Invoice for Time & Expenses window shows all the customers with out-standing billable time and expenses and includes a checkmark column on the left side of the table.

2. **In the Date Range From and To boxes, select the date range you want.**

3. **To select several customers or jobs, click the checkmark cells for the ones you want.**

   When a customer or job is selected, a checkmark appears in the checkmark column, as shown in Figure 10-15.

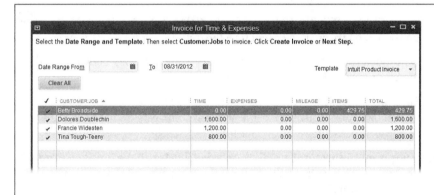

FIGURE 10-15

You can select more than one customer, as long as you use QuickBooks Premier or Enterprise and don't use multiple currencies. If your company file is set to a single currency, the Invoice for Time & Expenses window includes a checkmark column. You can click individual checkmark cells or drag over the cells to toggle them on or off.

4. **Click Next Step.**

   The Batch Invoice for Time & Expenses dialog box opens with the customers and jobs you selected.

5. **To specify the options for the invoices, click Edit Options below the table. Choose the settings you want and then click OK.**

   The Options for Transferring Billable Time dialog box (Figure 10-14) has options for showing each item on a separate line in the invoice or showing the total hours for each service item. If each activity is on its own line, you can transfer descriptions, notes, or both to the invoice. You can also specify a markup percentage and account for expenses.

6. **To look at the details for a customer or job, click Review Billables.**

   In the Review Billable Time and Costs dialog box, click the down arrow to the right of the Time and Costs For box and choose a customer or job. Click OK when you're done.

7. **Click Create Invoices.**

   QuickBooks creates the invoices for the selected customers. The Time & Expenses Summary dialog box appears and shows how many invoices are set up to print and how many to email, based on your customers' preferred delivery methods (page 71). Click Print to print the invoices marked to print; click Email to send the invoices marked to be emailed. To print or email the invoices later, click Close. Then, you can print or email them by choosing File→Print Forms→Invoices or File→Send Forms.

Selecting Billable Time and Costs

Regardless of how you open the Choose Billable Time and Costs dialog box (Figure 10-14), the steps for selecting the billable time and costs to add to an invoice are the same. Here's what you do:

1. **In the Choose Billable Time and Costs dialog box, to select all the entries on the Time tab, click the Select All button.**

   QuickBooks adds a checkmark in the first column for every activity. To add or remove a row, click its checkmark cell to toggle it on or off.

   Each tab in the dialog box shows the total value of the entries you've selected on that tab. The "Total billable time and costs" value below the table is the total of all the selected items on all four tabs.

2. **If you want the invoice to include only one line for all the time and expenses you've selected, turn on the "Print selected time and costs as one invoice item" checkbox below the table.**

   After you create the invoice in step 6, in the Create Invoices window, you'll see separate entries for billable items so you can verify that the invoice is correct. However, with this checkbox turned on, the printed invoice will include only one line, labeled "Total Reimbursable Expenses."

If you've created the invoice with one line for time and costs, it takes several steps to recreate it showing individual costs. To change an invoice back to a line-by-line listing, in the Create Invoices window, delete the Total Reimbursable Expenses line item. Then click Add Time/Costs in the window's Main tab to open the Choose Billable Time and Costs dialog box and reselect all the entries you want. Finally, turn off the "Print selected time and costs as one invoice item" checkbox and then click OK.

3. **Click the Expenses tab, and then click the checkmark cell for each expense (like meals, airfare, and other costs) you want to add to the invoice.**

   If you mark up expenses, such as phone calls and postage, the Expenses tab lets you track your markups. In the "Markup Amount or %" box, type the markup's dollar value or percentage. Then choose the income account for the markup. (The box on page 304 tells you how to apply different markups to different expenses.)

   To have QuickBooks calculate the sales tax, turn on the "Selected expenses are taxable" checkbox. (If the customer is tax exempt, QuickBooks doesn't add sales tax even if you turn on this checkbox.)

NOTE On the Expenses tab, the Memo column displays what you typed in the Memo field of the original vendor bill, check, or credit card charge. QuickBooks uses the entries in this column as the description on the invoice. (You can't edit the Memo text in this dialog box. So, if you didn't enter a Memo in the original expense transaction, you'll have to type the description for each expense once it's added to the invoice.)

4. **Click the Mileage tab and select the mileage you want to add to the invoice.**

   Like you did on the Time tab (Figure 10-14), click Options to tell QuickBooks whether to show one line for mileage or a separate line for each trip.

5. **On the Items tab, select any products that you bought specifically for this customer or job.**

   Click an item's checkmark cell to add it to the invoice.

6. **When you've selected all the billable items you want to add from every tab, click OK.**

   QuickBooks adds all the items you selected to the invoice, as shown in Figure 10-16. If it looks good, click Save & Close. If not, edit the invoice to include what you want or click Clear to start from scratch.

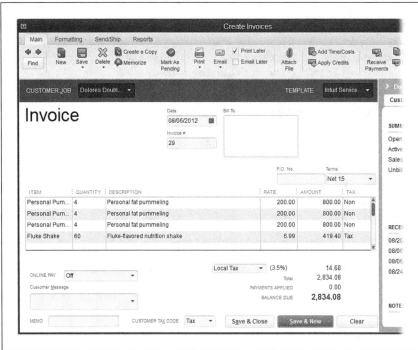

FIGURE 10-16

If you didn't type memos in the original expense transactions, you have to type the descriptions for billable expenses directly into the Description fields here. Because the invoice is open in the Create Invoices window, you can add additional line items to the invoice before you save it.

Adding Different Markups to Billable Expenses

The Choose Billable Time and Costs dialog box's Expenses tab has only one "Markup Amount or %" box, which might seem like a problem if you add different markups to some of your billable expenses. But there's nothing stopping you from adding these expenses to your invoice in more than one batch with a different markup amount or percentage for each batch. Here's how:

1. In the Choose Billable Time and Costs dialog box, click the Expenses tab.

2. In the "Markup Amount or %" box, type the markup for the first batch of expenses.

3. Turn on the checkmark cell for each expense that you want to apply that markup to.

4. Click OK to add the selected expenses to the invoice.

5. In the Create Invoices window's Main tab, click Add Time/Costs.

6. In the Choose Billable Time and Costs dialog box, click the Expenses tab.

7. Change the value in the "Markup Amount or %" box to the next markup and then turn on the checkmark cell for the expenses at this markup. Click OK to close the dialog box.

8. Repeat steps 5–7 for each additional markup.

This technique works just as well when some of the expenses are taxable while others aren't. Simply choose the taxable items, turn on the "Selected expenses are taxable" checkbox, and then add the taxable expenses to the invoice. Next, reopen the Choose Billable Time and Costs dialog box, choose the nontaxable items, turn off the "Selected expenses are taxable" checkbox, and then add the nontaxable expenses to the invoice.

Checking for Unbilled Costs

Most Customers & Receivables reports focus on charges you've already invoiced. If you invoice customers for reimbursable expenses, forgetting to invoice for reimbursable costs takes a bite out of your profits. So be sure to regularly run the Unbilled Costs by Job report (Reports→Customers & Receivables→Unbilled Costs by Job) to look for expenses that you've forgotten to invoice. This report shows costs that you designated as billable to a customer or job that haven't yet been added to an invoice.

Invoicing for Backordered Products

Placing a product order to fulfill your customers' orders is known as a *backorder*. If backorders are a regular part of your business day, you should consider finding suppliers who deliver more quickly, and maybe upgrading to QuickBooks Premier or Enterprise, which has a built-in sales order form for tracking backordered items. If you have QuickBooks Pro, you can handle backorders using pending invoices.

When you tell customers that a product is out of stock, they might ask you to handle the backorders in different ways. Here are the most common requests for backorders:

- **Remove the backordered items from the order**. Customers in a hurry may ask you to fill the order with only the products you have in stock. If they can't find the backordered products anywhere else, they can call in a new order.

- **Ship all items at once**. If convenience is more important than speed, you can hold the customer's order until the backordered products arrive and then ship the whole order at once.

- **Ship backordered items when they arrive**. Many customers request that you process their orders for the products you *do* have in stock, and then send the backordered products when you receive them.

If your customer wants you to remove backordered items from an order, you can ship the rest of the order and invoice the customer immediately. But when customers ask you to hold all or part of their orders until backordered products arrive, they usually expect you to invoice them for backordered products only when you ship them. So you don't want the income appearing in your account balances until the order ships. This section describes two ways to handle this situation.

TIP   If you need help remembering how customers want you to handle their backorders, store backorder preferences in a custom field in customer records (page 73). An alternative approach is to add a note in the Customer Center (select the customer and then click the Notes tab). When you choose a customer in the Create Invoices window, the Notes section on the right side displays notes you've added to the customer's record.

Using Pending Invoices for Backorders

If you don't have QuickBooks Premier or Enterprise, a pending invoice is the way to track backorders. In QuickBooks, setting an invoice's status to Pending places it in a holding pattern with no income or expenses posting to your accounts. Such invoices are easy to spot in the Create Invoices window—they sport a Pending stamp.

To set an invoice to pending status, follow these steps:

1. **Press Ctrl+I to open the Create Invoices window.**

   Fill in the invoice fields as usual (page 276).

2. **On the Create Invoices window's Main tab, click Mark As Pending (or right-click the Create Invoices window and then choose Mark Invoice As Pending from the shortcut menu).**

   QuickBooks adds a "Pending/non-posting" stamp to the invoice, as shown in the background of Figure 10-17.

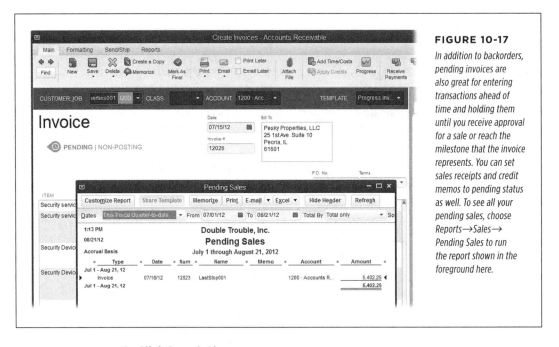

FIGURE 10-17

In addition to backorders, pending invoices are also great for entering transactions ahead of time and holding them until you receive approval for a sale or reach the milestone that the invoice represents. You can set sales receipts and credit memos to pending status as well. To see all your pending sales, choose Reports→Sales→ Pending Sales to run the report shown in the foreground here.

3. **Click Save & Close.**

   The invoice is ready for action, but none of its values post to any accounts.

4. **When the backordered products arrive, open the invoice in the Create Invoices window (choose Reports→Sales→Pending Sales and then double-click the invoice to open it). In the window's Main tab, choose Mark As Final, and then click Save & Close.**

   QuickBooks posts the invoice's values to the appropriate income and expense accounts.

Using Sales Orders for Backorders

QuickBooks Premier and Enterprise have a sales order form that's perfect for backorders. The Create Sales Orders window looks like the Create Invoices window, except that the item table includes an Ordered column, which holds the number of items the customer ordered but that you haven't yet invoiced. In effect, it's a record of how much stock you need to have on hand to fill the order.

TIP To see all your sales orders at once, choose Reports→Sales and then select either Open Sales Order by Customer or Open Sales Orders by Item.

If you try to add more items to an invoice than you have in stock, you'll see an error message warning of the shortfall. QuickBooks Pro simply warns you that you don't have enough. But in QuickBooks Premier and Enterprise, this message tells you how many you have on hand, how many are on other sales orders, and the remaining quantity available. (For example, if you have 10 items on hand and sales orders for 6 of them, the quantity available is 4.) When you see this message, click OK to close the message box and then click Clear to cancel the invoice. Then create a sales order instead.

If you already know that your inventory is woefully low or nonexistent (and you use QuickBooks Premier or Enterprise), simply create a sales order for the customer's order. Then, if a review of your inventory shows that some items are in stock, you can create a partial invoice for the items you have and use the sales order to track the backordered items. Since QuickBooks keeps a running balance of backordered items based on your sales orders, you can easily create a purchase order to restock the products you need. (See Chapter 19 to learn more about managing inventory.)

Here's how to create a sales order for backordered items:

1. **Make sure the preference for using sales orders is turned on.**

   Choose Edit→Preferences→Sales & Customers, and then click the Company Preferences tab. In the Sales Orders section, make sure that the Enable Sales Orders checkbox is on.

2. **On the Home page, click Sales Orders or choose Customers→Create Sales Orders.**

   The Create Sales Orders window opens.

3. **Fill in the sales order's fields as you would the fields in an invoice (page 276).**

   The only difference is that the column where you record the quantity of items you're ordering is labeled "Ordered" instead of "Quantity."

4. **On the Create Sales Orders window's Main tab, click Create Invoice.**

   The aptly named Create Invoice Based On Sales Order(s) dialog box opens (Figure 10-18).

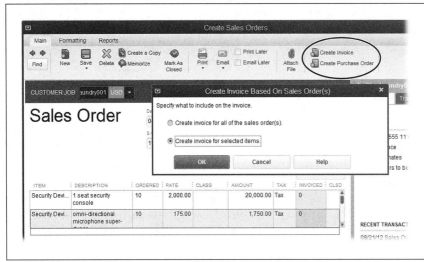

FIGURE 10-18

The Create Sales Order window's Main tab has two buttons for creating transactions associated with the sales order (circled). Click Create Invoice to create a customer invoice for the items you have on hand to ship. Click Create Purchase Order to order items that customers have purchased but that you don't have on hand to ship.

5. **To create a partial invoice for the items you have in stock, select the "Create invoice for selected items" option and then click OK.**

   The "Specify Invoice Quantities for Items on Sales Order(s)" dialog box (Figure 10-19) appears. Turn on the "Show quantity available instead of quantity on hand" checkbox to see how many items are *really* available to ship and invoice. (Quantity available is the quantity that's physically on hand minus the quantity that's already committed on other sales orders or already used in Inventory Assembly items.)

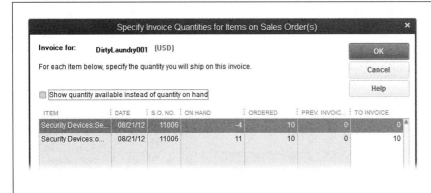

FIGURE 10-19

This dialog box lists each item on the sales order and shows how many items you have in stock. QuickBooks automatically fills in the To Invoice column with the number of items on hand because you usually invoice for only the products you can ship, but you can edit the quantity if you want to invoice the customer for the full order.

6. **Click OK to create the invoice for the in-stock items.**

   QuickBooks opens the Create Invoices window and fills in the invoice. You might see a message telling you that the invoice has at least one zero amount item (the one that's backordered) with instructions for preventing QuickBooks from printing those items on the invoice. Click OK to close the message box. Click Save & Close.

7. **Open the Create Sales Orders window again (see step 2) and, on the Main tab, click the left arrow (Previous) until you see the sales order on which you based the invoice.**

   It's a good idea to place an order for the backordered items while it's still fresh in your mind. The quantity of backordered items appears in the window's Ordered column.

8. **On the window's Main tab, click Create Purchase Order, circled in Figure 10-18.**

   The "Create Purchase Order Based on the Sales Transaction" dialog box appears.

9. **Select the "Create purchase order for selected items" option, and then click OK.**

   The "Specify Purchase Order Quantities for Items on the Sales Transaction" dialog box opens. If you specified a preferred vendor in the item's record (page 131), QuickBooks automatically fills in Preferred Vendor cell. It also fills in the Qty cells with how many items you have to order to fulfill the backorder.

10. **Click the checkmark cell for each item you want to order.**

    Select only the items you want to purchase from one vendor. If you purchase the items from multiple vendors, you'll have to create separate purchase orders for each vendor.

11. **If you want to order some spare inventory, edit the values in the Qty cells, and then click OK.**

    The Create Purchase Orders window appears, filled in with the items you're ordering. Although QuickBooks automatically puts the preferred vendor's name in the Vendor box, you can choose a different one from the drop-down list.

12. **When the purchase order is filled out the way you want, click Save & Close and then send it to the vendor.**

    After you receive the items you ordered to replenish your inventory, return to step 4 to create a final invoice from the sales order.

Estimating Jobs

Many customers ask for an estimate before hiring you. If you're good with numbers, you might tot up the costs in your head and scribble the estimate on a napkin. But creating estimates in QuickBooks not only generates a more professional-looking estimate, it also feeds numbers into your customers' invoices as you perform work for them. When you create an estimate in QuickBooks, you add the items you'll sell or deliver and set the markup on those items.

NOTE The estimate feature needs to be turned on before you can create estimates in QuickBooks. Choose Edit→Preferences→Jobs & Estimates, and then click the Company Preferences tab. In the "Do You Create Estimates?" section, make sure that Yes is selected, and then click OK.

QuickBooks estimates make short work of pricing time and materials for small jobs. But QuickBooks estimating isn't for every business. Particularly in construction, where a major project might require hundreds or even thousands of items, you definitely don't want to enter all the data you'd need to build the Item List for your project. That's why most construction firms turn to third-party estimating programs, which come with databases of the services and products you need. Many of these estimating programs integrate with QuickBooks, which means you can import an estimate you created in another program and use it to produce your invoices (see Chapter 24).

NOTE The totals on estimates don't post to accounts in your chart of accounts. After all, an estimate doesn't mean that your customer has committed to going ahead with the job. The estimates show the *potential* value of a job without showing up in your financial reports. When the preference for estimates is turned on (page 617), QuickBooks creates a *non-posting* account called Estimates, where it stores estimate values. (If you use account numbers [page 598], its number is 4.)

Creating an Estimate

If you've mastered QuickBooks' invoices, you'll feel right at home with the fields that appear in a QuickBooks estimate. Figure 10-20 shows the Create Estimates window.

Here's how to create an estimate and handle the small differences between invoices and estimates:

1. **On the Home page, click the Estimates icon or choose Customers→Create Estimates.**

   QuickBooks opens the Create Estimates window. (The program may choose a different estimate template depending on which edition of QuickBooks you use.) If you've created your own estimate template (page 669), choose it from the Template drop-down list (QuickBooks automatically uses your custom template from then on).

2. **As you would for an invoice, build your estimate by adding items to the line-item table (page 284).**

In a blank line in the table, in the Item drop-down list, choose the item that you want to add to the estimate. When you fill in the quantity, QuickBooks uses the cost and sales price from the item's record to fill in the Cost, Amount, Markup, and Total cells.

The markup percentage is based on how much you pay for the item and the sales price you charge. If you want to apply a different markup percentage, click the item's Markup cell and either type the percentage you want to use or choose a price level (page 153) from the drop-down list. (The markup you add is visible only while you work on the estimate. When you print it or email it to your customer, only the Cost and Total columns appear in the form.)

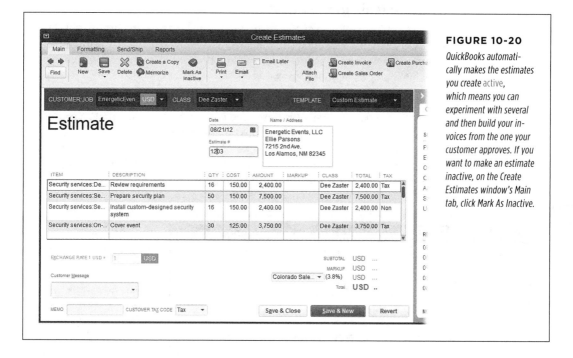

FIGURE 10-20

QuickBooks automatically makes the estimates you create active, *which means you can experiment with several and then build your invoices from the one your customer approves. If you want to make an estimate inactive, on the Create Estimates window's Main tab, click Mark As Inactive.*

NOTE   The calculated value in an item's Total cell isn't set in stone. If you change the Total value, QuickBooks recalculates the markup percentage for you. Likewise, if you change the percentage in the Markup cell, QuickBooks recalculates the value in the Total cell.

3. **To email the estimate to your customer, in the window's Main tab, turn on the Email Later checkbox.**

   QuickBooks queues up the estimate to be emailed later (page 349). For reasons unknown, you can't queue up an estimate to *print* later. If you want to print an estimate, in the Create Estimates window's Main tab, click Print and then choose Estimate on the drop-down menu. Alternatively, you can choose Print→Save as PDF, and then print the PDF later.

4. **When the estimate is complete, click Save & Close to save it and close the Create Estimates window.**

   After you've created an estimate and printed it or emailed it to your customer, you don't do much with it until the customer gives you the nod for the job.

Creating Multiple Estimates

Whether you're creating a second estimate because the customer thought the first price was too high or creating separate estimates for each phase of a multiyear job, it's easy to build and manage several estimates for the same job. You've got the following methods at your disposal:

- **Creating an estimate.** You can create additional estimates for a job simply by creating a new estimate (as described in the previous section). When you create additional estimates, QuickBooks makes them active so they appear in the Available Estimates dialog box (page 276) when you choose the corresponding customer in the Create Invoices window. Active estimates also appear in the Estimates by Job report, shown in Figure 10-21.

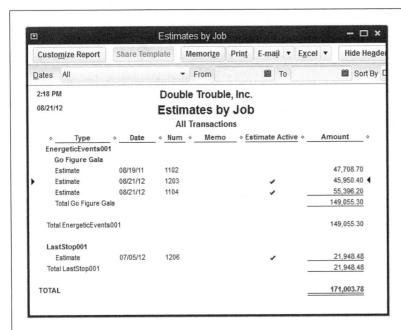

FIGURE 10-21

If you have too many estimates to find the right one by clicking Previous and Next in the Create Estimates window, try looking at the Estimates by Job report (Reports→Jobs, Time & Mileage→Estimates by Job). This report includes an Estimate Active column, which contains a checkmark if the estimate is active. Double-click anywhere in a line to open that estimate in the Create Estimates window.

- **Duplicating an estimate.** If you want to play what-if games with an existing estimate, duplicate it and then make your adjustments. In the Create Estimates window, display the estimate you want to copy and then, on the Main tab, click "Create a Copy," or right-click the estimate and choose Duplicate Estimate from the shortcut menu. Either way, QuickBooks pulls everything from the existing estimate onto a new one, and assigns it the next estimate number in sequence. After you make the changes you want, click Save & Close or Save & New. (The box on page 314 tells you how to create boilerplate estimates, which is faster if you intend to duplicate an estimate frequently.)

- **Finding an estimate.** When you know the estimate you want exists, you can search for it based on the customer or job, when you created it, its number, or the amount. On the Create Estimates window's Main tab, click Find or right-click in the window and then choose Find Estimates from the shortcut menu. In the Find Estimates dialog box that appears, fill in what you know about the estimate and then click Find. If you click Advanced, QuickBooks opens the full-blown Find window, so you can set up more specific criteria (page 361).

- **Making an estimate inactive.** When you create several estimates for the same work, eventually you and your customer will pick one to run with. Once you've picked an estimate, make the others inactive. To do that, display the estimate in the Create Estimates window and then, on the Main tab, click Mark As Inactive. Click Save & New to save the estimate while keeping the Create Estimates window open. If you want to make another estimate inactive, on the Main tab, click the left arrow (Previous) or the right arrow (Next) until the estimate appears, and then repeat these steps.

  QuickBooks won't display inactive estimates in the Available Estimates dialog box (page 276), but you still have a record of your other attempts, which you can see by clicking the right arrow (Next) or the left arrow (Previous) in the Create Estimates window's Main tab or by running the Estimates by Job report.

- **Deleting an estimate.** Deleting an estimate isn't the no-no that deleting an invoice is. (Your only risk is that you'll realize you wanted to keep the estimate as soon as you delete it.) In the Create Estimates window, display the estimate and then, on the Main tab, click Delete or right-click the estimate in the Create Estimates window and then choose Delete Estimate from the shortcut menu. In the Delete Transaction dialog box, click OK to get rid of the estimate.

NOTE To protect profit margins from being nibbled away by small changes, many businesses keep track of every change that a customer requests (called *change orders*). The Contractor and Accountant editions of QuickBooks let you track change orders on estimates.

Building Boilerplate Estimates

Suppose you've put a lot of thought into the typical tasks you perform and materials you need for different types of jobs. You can capture this information in QuickBooks estimates to quickly produce an estimate that takes into account your performance on similar jobs in the past. Your new customer will be impressed by your speedy response, and you'll be confident that you haven't forgotten anything.

To create a boilerplate estimate, build an estimate with all the information you reuse and then have QuickBooks memorize it. Here's how:

1. In the Create Estimates window, fill in all the fields and line items you want in the boilerplate. If you want to capture the items you use but not the quantities, in the line-item table, leave the quantity (Qty) cells blank.

2. To memorize the estimate, press Ctrl+M or right-click the estimate and then choose Memorize Estimate from the shortcut menu. You can also click Memorize on the Create Estimates window's Main tab.

3. QuickBooks tells you that it will remove the Customer: Job so you can use the memorized estimate for any customer. Click OK to dismiss the message.

4. In the Memorize Transaction dialog box, type a name for the estimate, for example, Fire Mitigation for a boilerplate estimate for fire mitigation.

5. Because you'll recall this estimate only when you get a similar job, choose the Do Not Remind Me option.

6. Click OK to add the estimate to your Memorized Transaction List.

7. When you bid on a similar job, press Ctrl+T to open the Memorized Transaction List window.

8. Double-click the memorized estimate to open the Create Estimates window with the memorized estimate's information displayed. QuickBooks fills in the current date and the next estimate number in the sequence.

9. In the Customer:Job box, choose the new customer. Make any other changes you want.

10. Click Save & Close.

Creating an Invoice from an Estimate

Whether you create one estimate for a job or several, you can generate invoices from your estimates. In fact, if you open the Create Invoices window and then choose a customer or job for which estimates exist, QuickBooks displays the Available Estimates dialog box, which lists all the active estimates for that customer or job.

NOTE This section explains how to turn an *entire* estimate into an invoice. See page 315 to learn how to use estimates to generate progress invoices when you reach milestones on large projects.

To use an estimate to create an invoice, do the following:

1. **Press Ctrl+I to open the Create Invoices window and then, in the Customer:Job drop-down list, choose the customer or job you want to invoice.**

   If one or more estimates exist for that customer or job, the Available Estimates dialog box opens, showing the active estimates for that customer or job, as shown in Figure 10-22. (You don't have to use your estimate to create an invoice if, say, you want to invoice for your actual time and materials. In that situation, click Cancel. The Available Estimates dialog box closes, and the Create Invoices window is ready for you to fill in the line-item table.)

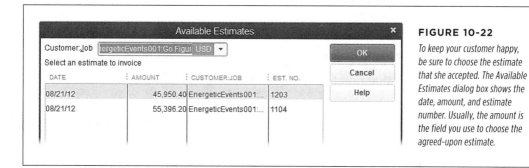

FIGURE 10-22

To keep your customer happy, be sure to choose the estimate that she accepted. The Available Estimates dialog box shows the date, amount, and estimate number. Usually, the amount is the field you use to choose the agreed-upon estimate.

2. **In the Available Estimates dialog box, click anywhere in the row for the estimate you want, and then click OK.**

   QuickBooks enters the information from the estimate in the Create Invoices window.

3. **Make any changes you want and then click Save & Close.**

   You're done!

Comparing Estimates to Actuals

Customers who write you blank checks for jobs are rare, so most jobs require estimates of what the work will cost. When you finish a job that you estimated, take some time to run the Job Estimates vs. Actuals Summary report (it's on the Reports→Jobs, Time & Mileage submenu) to see how you did compared to your estimate. Do this a few times and the accuracy of your estimates should improve dramatically.

If you invoice jobs based on the progress you've made (as described in the next section), run the Job Progress Invoices vs. Estimates report instead (it's on the Reports→Jobs, Time & Mileage submenu if you have the progress invoicing preference [page 617] turned on). It compares your estimate to actual performance through your most recent progress invoice.

■ Creating Progress Invoices

When you work on jobs and projects that take more than a few days, you probably don't want to wait until a job is completely finished to charge for some of your work. *Progress invoices* include charges based on your estimate *and* the progress you've made on the job. These invoices are common for jobs that are broken into phases or when payments are made when you reach milestones. Since most large jobs start with an estimate, you won't have to start from scratch when it's time to invoice your customer—QuickBooks can convert your estimates into progress invoices with only a few additional pieces of information.

NOTE To produce progress invoices, the preferences for creating estimates and progress invoicing (page 617) must both be turned on.

Progress Invoicing Options

Progress invoices are still invoices; they just happen to link to estimates you've created for a job. In the Create Invoices window, when you choose a customer or job, QuickBooks checks to see if an estimate exists. If there's at least one estimate for that customer or job, QuickBooks opens the Available Estimates dialog box so you can choose an estimate to invoice against.

To get started creating a progress invoice, select an estimate in the Available Estimates dialog box and then click OK; QuickBooks opens the Create Progress Invoice Based On Estimate dialog box (Figure 10-23). When you create your *first* progress invoice for a job, this dialog box lets you choose to invoice the entire estimate or only a portion. Here are your options and when you might use them:

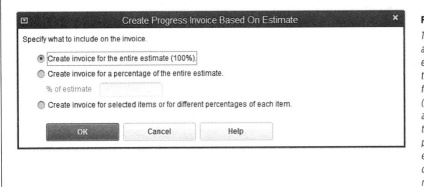

FIGURE 10-23

The first time you create a progress invoice for an estimated job is the only time the "Create invoice for the entire estimate (100%)" option is available. After that, you have to invoice based on a percentage of the entire estimate, by picking individual items, or for the remaining amounts on the estimate (this option isn't shown here).

- **Create invoice for the entire estimate (100%)**. This option is perfect if you prepared an estimate to get approval before starting a job, and you completed the job in a short period of time. QuickBooks takes care of the grunt work of transferring all the services, products, and other items from the estimate to the invoice.

NOTE You can edit the invoice amounts that come from an estimate, which is handy if your actual costs were higher than your estimates, for instance. However, the contract you signed determines whether your customer will actually *pay* the revised amounts!

- **Create an invoice for the remaining amounts of the estimate**. For every progress invoice *after* the first one for a job, you'll see this option instead of "Create invoice for the entire estimate (100%)." Use this option when you're ready to create your last invoice for the job. Its sole purpose is to save you the hassle of calculating the percentages that haven't yet been billed.

- **Create invoice for a percentage of the entire estimate**. Choose this option if you negotiated a contract that pays a percentage when you reach a milestone, such as 15 percent when the house's foundation is complete. (Of course, you and the customer have to agree that a milestone is complete; QuickBooks can't help you with that.) This option is also handy if your contract specifies a number of installment payments. In the "% of estimate" box, type the percentage you've completed.

   Don't use this option if you include inventory on the estimate, because the invoice you create might contain fractional quantities of inventory items. For example, if you estimate 10 inventory items and then create a progress invoice for 33 percent of the job, the invoice will include 3.33 inventory items. You can avoid this by invoicing using the selected items option, described next.

TIP Suppose your contract includes a clause that covers cost overruns, and the job ended up costing 20 percent more than the estimate. You might wonder how you can charge for that extra 20 percent. The hidden solution is that the "% of estimate" box doesn't limit the percentage to 100 percent. So in this example, you'd type *120* percent for the last invoice to reflect the costs that exceeded the estimate.

- **Create invoice for selected items or for different percentages of each item**. This option is the most flexible and a must if you bill customers only for the work that's actually complete. For example, if you're building an office complex, one building might be complete while another is still in the framing phase. When you select this option, you can choose the services and products to include on the invoice and specify different percentages for each one. When you click OK, the "Specify Invoice Amounts for Items on Estimate" dialog box appears, initially showing your estimated amounts and any previously invoiced amounts. The next section tells you how to fill in this dialog box.

Fine-Tuning a Progress Invoice

When you click OK in the Create Progress Invoice Based On Estimate dialog box (or the "Specify Invoice Amounts for Items on Estimate" dialog box if you choose items to invoice), QuickBooks automatically fills in the estimate items, percentages, and amounts, as shown in Figure 10-24. You don't have to stick with the numbers that QuickBooks comes up with—you can reconfigure the charges on the invoice any way you want. However, it's always a good idea to review the customer's contract and get approval before you make any increases or additions not covered by the contract.

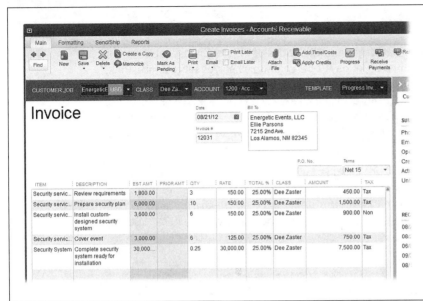

FIGURE 10-24

When you provide materials for a job, they're either onsite or not. Assigning 50 percent to materials only makes sense if half the boxes made it. If you created an invoice for 25 percent of the job, you can change the invoice to cover 100 percent for materials by editing the values in the "Total %" column. Changing a "Total %" cell also solves the problem of one task that's far behind—or far ahead.

You can modify line items directly in a QuickBooks invoice, but that approach doesn't create a history of your changes. If you want to keep a record of the changes you make between the estimate and the progress invoice, follow these steps instead:

1. **Open the progress invoice in the Create Invoices window (press Ctrl+I and then click the window's left arrow [Previous] button until the progress invoice you want appears).**

   You can also open an invoice from the Customer Center: On the center's Customers & Jobs tab, select the customer you want. Then, on the Transactions tab at the Customer Center's lower right, in the Show drop-down list, click Invoices. Finally, double-click the invoice you want to open.

2. **On the Create Invoices window's Main tab, click Progress.**

   QuickBooks opens the "Specify Invoice Amounts for Items on Estimate" dialog box.

3. **Before you begin changing values, make sure that the correct columns are visible. Turn on the "Show Quantity and Rate" checkbox or the Show Percentage checkbox.**

   QuickBooks remembers the checkboxes you turn on and turns the same ones on the next time you open this dialog box.

4. **To change a value on the progress invoice, click the cell that you want to change, as shown in Figure 10-25.**

Changing a rate is a rare occurrence. However, it might happen if, say, you have a contract that bumps your consulting rate by 10 percent for the next calendar year. If the job runs into the next calendar year, you can increase the rate for the hours worked in January.

When you change a value, QuickBooks recalculates the other columns. For example, if you type a percentage in a "Curr %" (current percentage) cell, Quick-Books calculates the amount to invoice by multiplying your estimated amount by the current percentage. The "Tot %" column shows the total percentage, including previously invoiced amounts and the current amount.

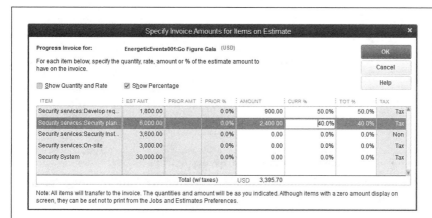

FIGURE 10-25

You can change only the cells in columns with a white background. (The columns with a gray background simply show the values from the estimate and previous progress invoices.)

5. **To apply the changes, click OK.**

The "Specify Invoice Amounts for Items on Estimate" dialog box closes, taking you back to the modified progress invoice.

6. **Save the progress invoice by clicking Save & New or Save & Close.**

■ Handling Refunds and Credits

If a customer returns a product or finds an overcharge on her last invoice, you have two choices: Issue a credit against her balance, or issue a refund by writing her a check. In the bookkeeping world, the documents that explain the details of a credit are called *credit memos*. On the other hand, when a customer doesn't want to wait to get the money she's due or she isn't planning to purchase anything else from you, a refund check is the logical solution. In either case, refunds and credits both begin with a credit memo, like the one shown in Figure 10-26.

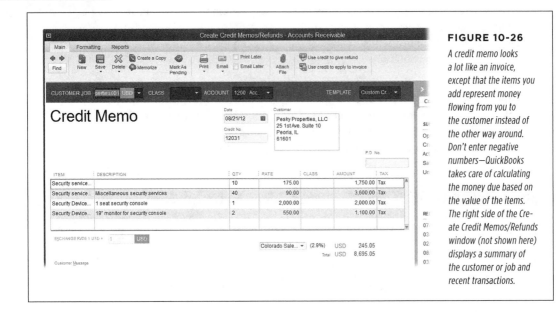

FIGURE 10-26

A credit memo looks a lot like an invoice, except that the items you add represent money flowing from you to the customer instead of the other way around. Don't enter negative numbers—QuickBooks takes care of calculating the money due based on the value of the items. The right side of the Create Credit Memos/Refunds window (not shown here) displays a summary of the customer or job and recent transactions.

Creating a Credit Memo from an Invoice

Here's how to transform an invoice into a credit memo to refund a customer's money:

1. **Open the invoice in the Create Invoices window.**

   The easiest way to find and open the invoice is by clicking Find on the Create Invoices window's Main tab. In the Find box, type the customer's name or the invoice number, and then click Find. When you see the invoice in the Find box, click the invoice and then click Go To.

2. **On the right end of the Create Invoices window's Main tab, click the Refund/Credit button.**

   QuickBooks opens the Create Credit Memos/Refunds window (Figure 10-26) and copies the information from the invoice into the credit memo.

3. **If you want to change anything in the credit memo, edit it.**

   For example, if you want to refund only a portion of the invoice, you can delete lines from the credit memo. Simply right-click a line in the line-item table and choose Delete Line on the shortcut menu.

4. **If you want to print or email the credit memo, turn on the Print Later or Email Later checkbox.**

5. **Click Save & Close when you're done.**

The Available Credit dialog box appears with three options for handling the credit, as shown in Figure 10-27.

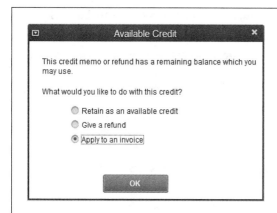

FIGURE 10-27

When you save a credit memo with available credit, QuickBooks displays this dialog box. To keep the credit around and apply it later (page 322)—to the next invoice you create for the customer, for example—choose "Retain as an available credit." If you choose "Give a refund," QuickBooks opens the Issue a Refund window so you can write the refund check. Don't choose "Apply to an invoice" unless you have an open invoice for the customer to apply the refund to.

Creating Credit Memos

You can also create a credit memo from scratch. Here's how:

1. **On the Home page, click Refunds & Credits or choose Customers→Create Credit Memos/Refunds.**

   QuickBooks opens the Create Credit Memos/Refunds window. (If you stay on top of your invoice numbers, you'll notice that the program automatically uses the next invoice number as the credit memo's number.)

2. **As you would for an invoice, choose a Customer:Job.**

   Choose a class if you use classes, and, if necessary, choose the credit memo template you want to use.

3. **In the line-item table, add a line for each item you want to credit.**

   Be sure to include *all* the charges you want to refund, including shipping and taxes.

> **TIP** If you want to include a message to the customer, in the Customer Message box, choose it from the list.

4. **If you want to print or email the credit memo, turn on the Print Later or Email Later checkbox.**

5. **Click Save & Close when you're done.**

When you save a credit memo with an available credit balance, the Available Credit dialog box appears with three options for handling the credit, as shown in Figure 10-27.

Creating Refund Checks

If your customer is dreadfully disgruntled, you'll probably want to write a refund check. If you didn't do that when the Available Credit dialog box appeared (see the previous section), here's how to do it now:

1. **Open the Customer Center and, on the Customers & Jobs tab, select the customer.**

2. **On the Transactions tab in the window's lower right, in the Show drop-down list, choose Credit Memos.**

   The list of open credit memos for that customer appears.

3. **Double-click the credit memo that you want to refund as a check.**

   The Create Credit Memos/Refunds window opens to that credit memo.

4. **In the window's Main tab, click the "Use credit to give refund" button.**

   QuickBooks opens the Issue a Refund window and fills in all the information you need to create the refund.

5. **In the Issue a Refund window, make sure the settings are correct.**

   In the window's "Issue this refund via" box, QuickBooks chooses Check, and selects the checking account you set in your checking preferences (page 602). If the red-faced customer is staring at you from across the counter, choose Cash instead, and then click OK.

   If the Issue a Refund window's "To be printed" checkbox is turned on (which it is automatically), QuickBooks adds the check to the queue of checks waiting to be printed. Click OK to close the Issue a Refund window, and then click Save & Close in the Create Credit Memos/Refunds window.) Then, to print the refund check right away, find the check in your checking account register and open it in the Write Checks window (right-click the check transaction and then choose Edit Check from the shortcut menu). Then, in the Write Checks window's Main tab, click Print.

> **NOTE** If you've signed up for the QuickBooks Merchant Service (see the box on page 350) and accept credit card payments, you can also refund money via credit card. Or you can choose other methods, such as E-Check and EFT, depending on the payment services you've signed up for.

Applying Credits to Existing Invoices

If a customer has an unpaid invoice or statement, you can apply a credit to it and reduce the amount that the customer owes. Applying a credit to an invoice is *almost* like receiving a payment, so when you choose a customer or job in the Receive Payments window, QuickBooks tells you if the customer has available credits and discounts. Here's how to apply that credit to an invoice:

1. **On the Home page, click Receive Payments.**

   QuickBooks opens the Receive Payments window.

2. **In the Received From drop-down list, choose the customer whose credit you want to apply.**

   Below the invoice table, QuickBooks displays a message that the customer has available credit and shows the amount of the credit below the Available Credits label.

3. **To select the invoice or statement to which you want to apply the credit, click anywhere in the line for the invoice or statement *except* the checkmark column (Figure 10-28).**

   Clicking an invoice's checkmark column tells QuickBooks that you received a *real* payment from that customer.

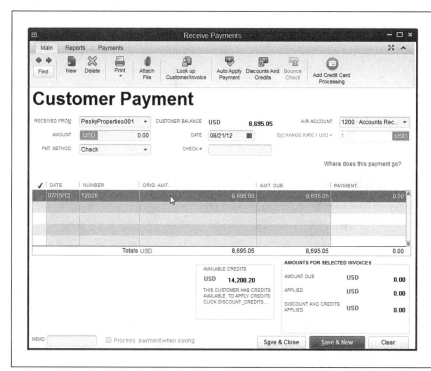

FIGURE 10-28

If you chose a customer in the Received From drop-down list rather than a job, the Available Credits value represents the total credits available for all jobs for that customer. To select an invoice for a credit, click anywhere in the invoice's row—except the checkmark cell, which selects the invoice for payment.

4. **On the Receive Payments window's Main tab, click the Discounts and Credits button.**

   QuickBooks opens the Discount and Credits dialog box shown in Figure 10-29.

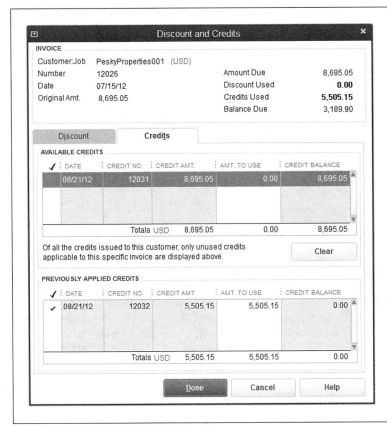

FIGURE 10-29

When you turn on credit checkmarks, the Credits Used value near the top of the dialog box shows the total amount of credit you applied, and the Balance Due number shows how much is still due on the invoice. If the original invoice balance is less than the available credit, QuickBooks applies only enough of the credit to set the invoice's balance to zero. You can apply the remaining credit to another invoice by repeating the steps in this section.

5. **To apply one of the customer's credits, click the checkmark cell for that credit to turn it on.**

    If the customer has only one credit, QuickBooks turns on its checkmark cell automatically. If you don't see the credit you expect, it might apply to a different job or to the customer only. In that case, click Cancel and start again with step 2.

6. **In the Discount and Credits dialog box, click Done.**

    After all this, the Receive Payments window doesn't look very different, but there's one important change: The Credits column for the open invoice displays the value of the credit. (The amount due won't change until you receive the actual payment.)

7. **Click Save & Close to apply the credit to the invoice.**

Now, if you open the invoice in the Create Invoices window, you'll see the credit amount in the Payments Applied field and the Balance Due reduced by the amount of the credit.

Applying Credits to New Invoices

If you create a new invoice for a customer who has a credit due, on the Main tab of the Create Invoices window, you'll see the Apply Credits button come to life. Here's how to apply a credit to reduce the balance of the invoice:

1. **With the new invoice visible in the Create Invoices window (press Ctrl+I to open it), on the Main tab, click Apply Credits.**

   QuickBooks opens the Apply Credits dialog box, which looks like the Discount and Credits dialog box except that it has only a Credits tab.

2. **Turn on the checkmarks for each credit you want to apply to the invoice, and then click Done.**

   In the Create Invoices window, you'll see the credit amount in the Payments Applied field and the Balance Due reduced by the amount of the credit.

Editing Invoices

While you're in the process of creating an invoice or a sales receipt, you can jump to any field and change its value, delete lines, or insert new ones. Even after you've saved an invoice, editing it is easy. Any time an invoice is visible in the Create Invoices window, you can click any field and make whatever change you want. If you've already printed the invoice, turn on the Print Later checkbox so you don't forget to reprint the form with the changes you made.

TIP If you've received a payment against an invoice, editing that invoice is *not* the way to go, because the edits can disrupt the connections between payment, invoice, and accounts to the point that you'll never straighten it out. If you undercharged the customer, simply create a new invoice with the missing charges on it. If you charged the customer for something she didn't buy, issue a credit memo or refund (see page 321).

Voiding and Deleting Invoices

Sometimes, you want to eliminate an invoice—for instance, when you create one by mistake and want to remove its values from your accounts. QuickBooks provides two options, but for your sanity's sake, you should *always* void invoices that you don't want rather than deleting them.

When you void an invoice, QuickBooks resets its dollar values to zero so that your account balances show no sign of the transaction. It also marks the transaction as void so you know what happened to it when you stumble upon it in the future.

If you delete an invoice, QuickBooks *truly* deletes the transaction, removing its dollar values from your accounts and deleting any signs of it. All that remains is a hole in your invoice-numbering sequence and an entry in the audit trail that says you deleted the transaction (page 694). If your accountant or the IRS looks at your books a few years down the road, your chances of remembering what happened to the transaction are slim. If an invoice has a payment attached to it, deleting it is even more problematic: You have to delete the bank deposit first, followed by the customer's payment, and finally the invoice.

To void an invoice:

1. **Open the Create Invoices window, and then, on the Main tab, click Find.**

2. **In the Find Invoices dialog box, fill in the invoice number, customer name, or date, and then click Find. In the Find dialog box that appears, double-click the invoice you want to void.**

   The invoice appears in the Create Invoices window.

3. **On the Create Invoices window's Main tab, choose Delete→Void Invoice, or right-click in the window and then choose Void Invoice from the shortcut menu.**

   All the values in the form change to zero, and QuickBooks adds "VOID" to the Memo field. To remind yourself why you voided that transaction, type the reason after "VOID."

4. **Click Save & Close.**

NOTE If you open the Accounts Receivable register's window, you might get nervous when you see the word Paid in the Amt Paid column of a voided transaction. Don't get excited: Notice that the amount paid is zero, and that the word "Void" is in the Description field. The word Paid in the Amt Paid column is just QuickBooks' way of telling you the invoice is no longer open.

Producing Statements

S tatements are the perfect solution for businesses that charge individuals for time and other services in bits and pieces, such as law offices, wireless telephone service providers, or astrology advisors. Statements can summarize the charges racked up during the statement period (usually a month). But they're also great for showing payments and outstanding balances, the way your cable bill shows the charges for your monthly service, the Pay-Per-View movies you ordered, your last payment, and your current balance. So even if you invoice your customers, you can send statements to show them their previous balances, payments received, new charges, and overdue invoices. (To learn about what statements *don't* do, see page 272.)

However, business-to-business invoicing is another story. Most accounting departments process only vendor invoices and credit memos for payments, so statements end up in the wastebasket. So if you do business only with other businesses, you're better off turning off QuickBooks' statements feature (the Note on page 328 explains where to find the preference to do that).

In this chapter, you'll find out how to produce statements, whether you accumulate charges over time or simply summarize your customers' account status.

Generating Statements

Think of a statement as a report of all the charges and payments during the statement period that you then send to your customer. The dates you choose for the statement determine its previous balance and the charges and customer payments it includes. Businesses typically send statements out once a month, but you can generate them for any time period you want.

> **NOTE** To work with statements and statement charges, make sure the statements preference is turned on. Choose Edit→Preferences→Desktop View and then click the Company Preferences tab. Check that the "Statements and Statement Charges" checkbox is turned on, and then click OK.

In QuickBooks, creating statements is a simple process:

1. **If you want to charge your customers directly on statements, in the Accounts Receivable account register, enter** *statement charges* **(explained in a moment) for the services or other items you delivered to your customers.**

   If you use statements simply to show invoices, payments, and the resulting balance, you can skip this step.

2. **Generate statements for your customers.**

The following pages explain how to complete both these steps.

Creating Statement Charges

Statement charges are charges for services and items you deliver to your customers that you add directly to the Accounts Receivable account. They look like the line items you see on invoices, except for a few small but important omissions. When you select an item for a statement charge, you won't see any Sales Tax, percentage discount, Subtotal, or Group items in your Item List because QuickBooks doesn't let you use those features in statements. When you generate statements (as explained in the next section), QuickBooks automatically grabs any payments that have been made, so you don't see Payment items in the Item drop-down list, either.

Here are the types of items in your Item List that you can use to create statement charges:

- Service items

- Inventory Part items

- Inventory Assembly items (if you use QuickBooks Premier or Enterprise)

- Non-inventory Part items

- Other Charge items

TIP Statement charges don't handle sales tax. For that reason, you should use an invoice to bill for taxable items so QuickBooks can calculate the sales tax for you. That way, when you generate statements, QuickBooks scoops up that invoice and pops it into the appropriate statement.

Unlike invoice line items, you create statement charges directly in the Accounts Receivable register for the customer or job that has racked up the charges, as shown in Figure 11-1. A statement charge has fields much like those for a line item in an invoice, although they're scrunched into two lines in the Accounts Receivable register. If you track your time and billable expenses in QuickBooks, you can use the Time/Costs feature to add billable time and expenses to the customer's Accounts Receivable register without going through the steps to create statement charges. This section explains how to add statement charges directly to the Accounts Receivable register and how to use the Time/Costs feature.

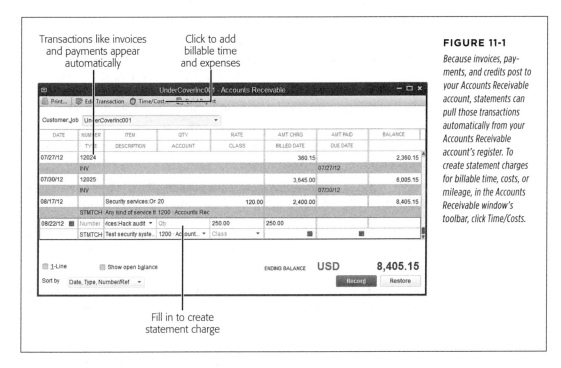

FIGURE 11-1

Because invoices, payments, and credits post to your Accounts Receivable account, statements can pull those transactions automatically from your Accounts Receivable account's register. To create statement charges for billable time, costs, or mileage, in the Accounts Receivable window's toolbar, click Time/Costs.

You enter statement charges in a customer's Accounts Receivable register, which is where QuickBooks stores the customer's invoices, credits, and payments, so the total in the register represents the customer's balance. Here's how to create a statement charge:

1. **Choose Customers→Enter Statement Charges or, in the Customers panel of the Home page, click the Statement Charges icon.**

   The Accounts Receivable window opens.

2. **In the Customer:Job drop-down list, choose the customer to whom you want to assign the statement charge.**

The Accounts Receivable window filters the transactions to show only accounts receivable for the customer or job you choose.

> **NOTE** If you set up the customer or job to use a foreign currency, you can't record statement charges for that customer or job directly in the Accounts Receivable register. To record a statement charge, using a foreign currency, choose Company→Make General Journal Entry and then record the charge as a journal entry. (You can also open the Make General Journal Entries window by clicking Edit Transaction in the Accounts Receivable window's toolbar.)

3. **If you track billable time, costs, or mileage, create statement charges for those items by clicking Time/Costs in the Accounts Receivable window's toolbar.**

The Choose Billable Time and Costs window that opens is the same one you see when you add billable time and costs to an invoice (page 302). Select the time and expenses you want to add, and then click OK. QuickBooks adds the selected items to the Accounts Receivable register and sets their Type to STMTCHG to indicate that the charges will appear on a statement instead of an invoice.

4. **To add a statement charge to the Accounts Receivable register, choose the item you want to charge for from the Item drop-down list in a blank line of the register.**

Figure 11-2 shows the fields for a blank transaction. When you choose an item, QuickBooks fills in the Rate and Description fields with the rate and description from the item's record (page 124), and sets the Type to STMTCHG to denote a charge that appears on a statement rather than an invoice. The program also copies the value in the Rate field to the Amt Chrg field (the total amount for the charge).

5. **Press Tab to move to the Qty field, and then type a quantity for the item. (If you don't use a quantity and rate, type the amount charged in the Amt Chrg field instead.)**

If you enter a quantity (based on the units for the item as described on page 616), when you move to another field (by pressing Tab or clicking the field), QuickBooks updates the total amount in the Amt Chrg field by multiplying the rate by the quantity.

6. **If you want to change the rate, press Tab to move to the Rate field, and then type the value you want.**

When you edit the value in the Rate field, QuickBooks recalculates the amount in the Amt Chrg field.

7. **If you want to revise the charge's description (which will appear on the statement you create), edit the Description field.**

QuickBooks automatically fills in this field with the first paragraph of the Description field (labeled "Description on Sales Transaction" if the service is performed by a subcontractor or partner) from the item's record, but you can see only a smidgeon of it. To see the whole thing, put your cursor over the Description field, and QuickBooks displays the full contents of the field in a pop-up tooltip just below the field.

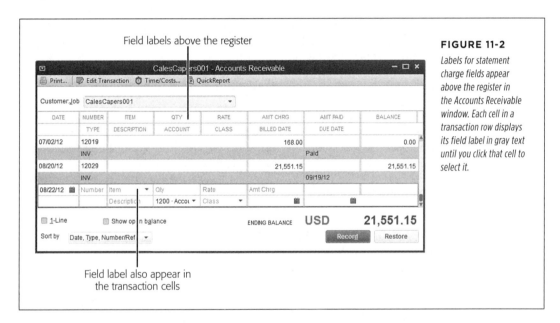

Field labels above the register

Field label also appear in
the transaction cells

FIGURE 11-2

Labels for statement charge fields appear above the register in the Accounts Receivable window. Each cell in a transaction row displays its field label in gray text until you click that cell to select it.

8. **If you use classes (page 150), in the Class field, choose the one you want.**

You can skip the Class field if it doesn't apply to the statement charge. If you set the preference to make QuickBooks prompt you about classes (page 598), when you try to save the statement charge, QuickBooks asks if you want to save it without a class. Click Save Anyway to omit the class, or click Cancel to return to the transaction so you can add a class.

9. **To control which statement the charge appears on, in the Billed Date field, choose a date for the charge.**

QuickBooks uses the value in the Date field to determine which statement includes the charge. When you add a statement charge that you want to save for a future statement, be sure to choose a billed date within the correct time period. For example, if a membership fee comes due in April, choose a billed date that falls in April. That way, the statement charge won't show up until you generate the customer's April statement. On the other hand, if you forgot a charge from the previous month, set its billed date to a day in the current month so the charge appears on this month's statement.

10. **If you plan to assess finance charges for late payments, in the Due Date field, choose the day when payment is due.**

QuickBooks uses this date along with your preferences for finance charges (page 608) to calculate any late charges due. (The due date is based on the terms you apply to the customer [page 70].) But late-charge calculations don't happen until you generate statements.

11. **To save the statement charge, click the Record button.**

TIP If you charge the same amount every month, memorize the first statement charge: With the statement charge filled in and selected in the register, press Ctrl+M or right-click the statement charge and then choose Memorize Stmt Charge on the shortcut menu. In the Memorize Transaction dialog box, set its recurrence schedule to the same day each month and choose the option to record the transaction automatically (page 352) and then click OK. QuickBooks then takes care of entering your statement charges for you, so all you have to do is generate customer statements once a month.

Generating Customer Statements

QuickBooks is smart, but it can't read your mind. The statements it generates include only the statement charges and other transactions you've entered. So before you produce monthly statements, double-check that you've entered all payments, credits, and refunds that your customers are due, and all new statement charges for the period.

As Figure 11-3 shows, everything about the statements you generate appears in the Create Statements window, including the date range for the statements, the customers you want to send statements to, the template you're using, printing options, and finance charges. To begin creating statements, in the Customers panel of the Home page, click the Statements icon (or choose Customers→Create Statements). The sections that follow explain your options and the best way to apply them.

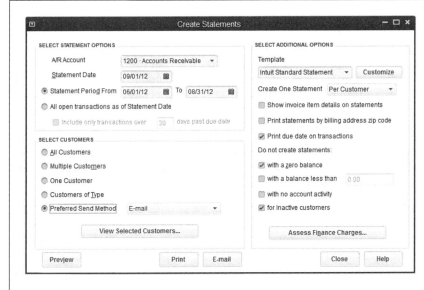

FIGURE 11-3

The options in the Select Customers section let you create statements for a subset of your customers, which comes in handy if you send statements to some customers by email and to some by U.S. mail, for example. In that case, you'd create two sets: one for email and the other for paper. You might also create a statement for a single customer if you made a mistake and want a corrected version. Or you can generate statements only for customers with balances.

■ CHOOSING THE DATE RANGE

Statements typically cover a set period of time, like a month. But the statement's date doesn't have to be during that period. For example, you might wait until the day after the period ends to generate the statement so you're sure to capture every transaction. In the Create Statements window's Select Statement Options section, you can adjust the following settings:

- **Statement Date**. In this field, type the date that you want to appear on the statement. In Figure 11-3, for example, the statement date is the day after the last day of the statement period.

- **Statement Period From _ To _**. Select this option to create statements for a period of time. For example, if you produce monthly statements, in the From box, choose the first day of the month, and in the To box, choose the last day of the month. Or you can choose dates to generate statements for a quarter.

- **All open transactions as of Statement Date**. Choosing this option adds every unpaid statement charge to the statement, regardless of when the charges happened. This option is particularly helpful when you want to generate a list of all overdue charges so you can send a reminder to woefully tardy customers. To filter the list of open transactions to only those overdue by a certain number of days, turn on the "Include only transactions over _ days past due date" checkbox, and type the number of days late.

NOTE If you've turned on the multiple currency preference (page 617), the Create Statement window displays the A/R Account box at the top left. Use that drop-down menu to choose the correct Accounts Receivable account for the currency that applies to the statements you want to create. Repeat the statement-generation steps for each currency you use.

■ SELECTING CUSTOMERS

QuickBooks initially selects the All Customers option because most companies send statements to every customer. But you can choose another option to limit the list of recipients. (The next time you open the Create Statements window, QuickBooks remembers the option you chose and selects it automatically.) Here are your other customer options and the reasons you might choose each one:

- **Multiple Customers**. To specify the exact set of customers to whom you want to send statements, choose this option. For example, you can select customers who received statements with errors on them.

  After you choose this option, click the Choose button that appears to its right. In the Print Statements dialog box that opens, QuickBooks automatically selects the Manual option, so you can choose each customer or job that you want to send a statement to (click individual customers or jobs or drag over adjacent customers to select them and display checkmarks next to their names). The Automatic option isn't really automatic—you have to type a customer's name *exactly* as it appears in the Customer Name field in the customer's record to select that single customer. So it's much easier to select the Manual option and then scroll to the name you want.

- **One Customer**. To create a corrected statement for a single customer, choose this option. In the drop-down list that appears, click the down arrow, and then choose the customer or job.

- **Customers of Type**. If you categorize customers by type and process their statements differently, choose this option. For example, you might spread your billing work out by sending statements to your corporate customers at the end of the month and to individuals on the 15th. In the drop-down list that appears, choose a customer type.

- **Preferred Send Method**. If you print some statements and email others, you'll have to create statements in two batches. Choose this option and, in the drop-down list that appears, pick one of the send methods. For example, choose E-mail here and then click the E-mail button at the bottom of the window to send statements to the customers who prefer to receive bills that way. (Page 349 explains how to email documents.)

TIP If you loathe stuffing envelopes and licking stamps, offer your customers a discount for receiving their statements (or invoices and credit memos) via email. They're likely to say yes, and you can then shoot statements out from QuickBooks in the blink of an eye.

- **View Selected Customers**. Before you generate statements by clicking Print or E-mail, click this button to make sure you've chosen the correct customers.

■ SETTING ADDITIONAL OPTIONS

In the Create Statement window's Template box, QuickBooks automatically selects Intuit Standard Statement, but you can choose your own customized template instead. You can also control what QuickBooks adds to statements and which statements it should skip:

- **Create One Statement**. In this drop-down list, choosing Per Customer can save some trees because it makes QuickBooks generate one statement for each customer, no matter how many jobs you do for them (on the statements, charges are grouped by job). If each job has its own mailing address, you can create separate statements for each job by choosing Per Job here instead.

- **Show invoice item details on statements**. Turning this checkbox on is usually unnecessary because your customers already have copies of the invoices you've sent, and these extra details merely clutter your statements.

- **Print statements by billing address zip code**. Turn on this checkbox if you have a bulk-mail permit, which requires that you mail by Zip code.

- **Print due date on transactions**. QuickBooks turns on this checkbox automatically because you'll typically want to show the due date for each entry on your statements.

- **Do not create statements**. Printing statements that you don't need is a waste of time and paper. QuickBooks includes several settings that you can choose to skip certain statements. For example, you can turn on the "with a zero balance" checkbox to skip statements for customers who don't owe you anything. Leave this checkbox off if you want to send a statement to show that the customer's last payment arrived and that their balance due is zero.

  You might also decide to skip customers unless their balance exceeds your typical cost of processing a statement. With the cost of a first-class stamp and letterhead, envelope, and a label, you might skip statements unless the balance is at least $5 or so. Turn on the "with a balance less than" checkbox and, in the box to its right, type a dollar value.

  You can also skip customers with no activity during the statement period—no charges, no payments, no transactions whatsoever—by turning on the "with no account activity" checkbox. QuickBooks automatically turns on the "for inactive customers" checkbox because there's no reason to send statements to customers who aren't actively doing business with you.

- **Assess Finance Charges**. Not surprisingly, you have to turn on QuickBooks' finance charge feature before you can assess finance charges (see page 388). Once you've done that, you can click Assess Finance Charges to add finance charges to your statements. In the Assess Finance Charges dialog box, you have the opportunity to turn off the checkmarks for individual customers. For example, if a squirrel ate your customer's last statement, you can turn off the checkmark in that customer's entry to tell QuickBooks not to penalize her with a finance charge. (You can also assess finance charges before you start the statement process by clicking the Finance Charges icon on the Home page.)

Previewing Statements

Before you print statements on expensive letterhead or send statements to your customers, it's a good idea to preview them to make sure you've chosen the right customers and that the statements are correct. Here's how to preview statements before you print or email them:

1. **In the Create Statements window, click Preview.**

   QuickBooks opens the Print Preview window (Figure 11-4), which works like its counterparts in other programs.

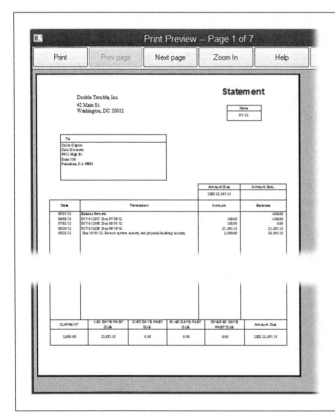

FIGURE 11-4

If you generate statements for a given time period, the first line in the body of a statement is "Balance forward," which is the amount due prior to this statement's opening date. The value in the Amount Due field is the total amount the customer owes you, which is the sum of the Balance forward plus all the transactions for that customer or job that happened during the statement's date range, including payments. At the bottom of the statement, the Amount Due figure is carved up into how much is current and how much is past due.

2. **In the Print Preview window, click "Prev page" or "Next page" to view your statements.**

If you left your reading glasses at home, click Zoom In to get a closer look. (The button's label switches to read "Zoom Out" so you can return to a bird's-eye view.)

3. **To return to the Create Statements window and print or email your statements, click Close.**

The Print Preview window includes a Print button, but it's not the best way to print statements. Clicking it begins printing your statements immediately so you have no chance to set your printer options, like which printer to use or the number of copies. To adjust those settings as described on page 335, click Close, and then click Print in the Create Statements window instead.

Generating Statements

When you're absolutely sure the statements are correct, in the Create Statements window, click Print or E-mail to generate your statements. This section describes how to do both.

■ EMAILING STATEMENTS

To email statements directly from QuickBooks, in the Create Statements window, click E-mail. If you use Microsoft Outlook, QuickBooks creates email messages in Outlook and automatically fills in the customers' email addresses. The messages contain the standard message you've set up for statements (page 630).

If you set up QuickBooks to use a web-based email service instead (page 630), the Select Forms To Send dialog box opens, showing the statements you're about to email. There, you can select additional statements, turn off statements you don't want to send, and click a statement to preview its content. Click Send Now to dispatch them to your customers.

■ PRINTING STATEMENTS

To print statements:

1. **In the Create Statements window, click Print.**

QuickBooks opens the Print Statement(s) dialog box.

2. **Choose the printer you want to use.**

For example, if you have a printer loaded with preprinted forms, select it in the "Printer name" drop-down list. (See page 340 to learn how to designate a printer so QuickBooks uses it every time you print statements.)

3. **Select one of the "Print on" options.**

   If you select "Intuit Preprinted forms," QuickBooks doesn't print the name of the form or the lines around fields, because they're already on the preprinted page. The "Blank paper" option tells the program to print the statement exactly the way you see it in the Print Preview window. The Letterhead option shrinks the form to leave a 2-inch band at the top of the page for your company logo.

   > **TIP** If your letterhead is laid out in an unusual way (your logo down the left side of the page, for instance), create a custom statement template (page 669) that leaves room for your letterhead elements, and then choose the "Blank paper" option.

4. **In the "Number of copies" box, type the number of copies of each statement you want to print.**

   For example, if you want one copy for the customer and one for your files, type 2.

5. **Click Print.**

Transaction Timesavers

QuickBooks can zip you through the two basic ways of distributing invoices and other sales forms: on paper and electronically. But within those two distribution camps, you can choose to send forms as soon as you complete them or place them in a queue to send in batches. For sporadic sales forms, it's easier to print or email them as you go. But when you generate dozens or even hundreds of sales orders, invoices, or statements, printing and emailing batches is a much better use of your time.

If you have workhorse transactions that you enter again and again, QuickBooks can memorize them and then fill in most, if not all, of the fields in future transactions for you. For transactions that happen on a regular schedule—like monthly customer invoices or vendor bills—the program can remind you when it's time to record the transaction, or even add the transaction without any help from you. You can also memorize transactions that you use occasionally, such as estimates, and call on them only when you need them.

QuickBooks' search features can also save you time, which you can appreciate if you've ever hunted frantically for a transaction. Whether you want to correct a billing problem on a customer's invoice, check whether you paid a vendor's bill, or look for the item you want to add to an estimate, QuickBooks gives you several ways to search: You can look for different types of transactions within various date ranges in the Customer, Vendor, and Employee Centers—and the Inventory Center if you use QuickBooks Premier or Enterprise. The Item List window sports a few search boxes for finding the items you want. Form windows, such as Create Invoices, have a Find button on their Main tabs so you can quickly find transactions of the corresponding type. You can use the Search feature to search throughout your company file or QuickBooks. And, the full-blown Find feature is perfect for surgical searches. This chapter explains all your options.

Printing Sales Forms

Before you start printing, you have some setup to do. But once QuickBooks' print settings are in place and there's paper in your printer, you can print forms with just a click or two. If you want to apply special settings to certain types of forms, for each one, QuickBooks needs to know the printer you want to use, the paper you print to (like preprinted forms or letterhead), and a few other details. The program remembers these settings, so you have to go through this process only once. From then on, QuickBooks fills in the Print dialog box's settings automatically when you choose a type of form to print, although you can change the settings before you print.

With these prep tasks behind you, you're ready to print. You can either print a form right away or add it to a queue to print in batches. This section explains how to accomplish all these printing tasks.

TIP   If you want to make sure you don't forget to send sales forms, you can create reminders (page 621) for invoices, credit memos, sales receipts, and—if you use QuickBooks Premier or Enterprise—sales orders that are queued up to print.

Setting Print Options

Before you print *any* documents in QuickBooks (not only invoices and other sales forms, but also timesheets, pay stubs, reports, and so on), take a few minutes to set up the printer(s) you use. The program lets you assign a different printer for each type of document. Why would you want to do that? Because it can save you a lot of time, wasted paper, and frustration, especially if you print invoices on multipart forms, paychecks on preprinted check forms, statements on letterhead, and reports on plain paper. Keep each printer stocked with the right type of paper, and you can print your documents with barely a glance at the print options.

Although you can assign a different printer to each type of QuickBooks form, you probably have only one or two printers stocked with special paper. So you can bypass printer setup for the forms you print using basic settings, such as printing to your workhorse printer on blank paper, using portrait orientation.

If you set up print settings in QuickBooks before you print, the program will fill in those settings for you automatically when you choose a type of form. (Print dialog boxes still appear, so you can change any print options before committing your documents to paper.)

TIP Many of the options in the "Printer setup" dialog box are the same as options you can set within your operating system, as Figure 12-1 shows. However, QuickBooks keeps the options you choose in its "Printer setup" dialog box separate from your operating system settings. So, for example, if you use Windows' printer options to set your most popular printer to use portrait orientation, you can set that same printer to use landscape orientation in QuickBooks.

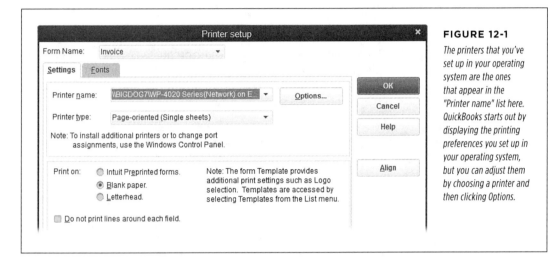

FIGURE 12-1

The printers that you've set up in your operating system are the ones that appear in the "Printer name" list here. QuickBooks starts out by displaying the printing preferences you set up in your operating system, but you can adjust them by choosing a printer and then clicking Options.

To assign and set up printers for forms in QuickBooks, choose File→Printer Setup. Then adjust the following settings:

- **Form Name.** In QuickBooks, each form has its own print settings, so you're free to print invoices on letterhead, timesheets in landscape orientation, and checks to a printer filled with preprinted checks. In this drop-down list, choose the form you want to set up for printing.

- **Printer name.** Choose a printer here to anoint it as the standard for the form you selected. When you're printing that type of form, QuickBooks automatically selects this printer, but you can choose a different printer—for instance, when you switch between printing paper documents and creating Adobe PDF files that you can email.

- **Options.** If you want to adjust the properties for the printer you chose, click this button. In the dialog box that appears, depending on the type of printer, you can change the document's orientation, page order, pages per sheet, print quality, paper tray, color, and so on.

NOTE The rest of the settings in this list appear for most of the forms in the Form Name drop-down list, but not when you select Report or Graph. See page 548 to learn about print settings for reports.

- **Printer type**. When you choose a printer name, QuickBooks fills in this box with its best guess of the type (it usually guesses right). If it guesses wrong, simply choose the correct type in this drop-down list. If the printer feeds individual pages through, such as letterhead or blank paper, choose "Page-oriented (Single sheets)." If it feeds continuous sheets of paper with perforations on the edges, such as the green-striped paper so popular in the past, choose "Continuous (Perforated Edge)."

- **Print on**. QuickBooks gives you three options here:

  - **Intuit Preprinted forms**. If you purchase preprinted forms, which typically include your company's information, field labels, and lines that separate fields, choose this option. When you print your documents, QuickBooks sends only the form data to fill in the form.

TIP If you use preprinted forms, a small misalignment can make your documents look sloppy and unprofessional. See page 342 to learn how to align documents to the paper in your printer.

  - **Blank paper**. This option tells QuickBooks to print everything on your document template: company info, logo, labels, and data. This is the easiest way to print because you don't have to worry about aligning the paper and the form. If you set up a template with your company logo and attractive fonts (page 672), you can produce a professional-looking form on blank paper.

  - **Letterhead**. When you print to letterhead that already includes your company's address and other information, you don't need to print that info on your documents. Choose this option to tell QuickBooks to skip printing your company information.

TIP The Letterhead option tells QuickBooks to start printing the form 2 inches from the top of the paper. If your letterhead has your logo and company information somewhere other than the top of the page, don't use this option. Instead, create a custom template for your form (page 669) to leave room for the logo. Then, when you print, select the "Blank paper" option.

- **Do not print lines around each field**. Turning on this checkbox is a matter of personal preference. Lines around each field make it clear which information belongs to which label, but you might consider those lines unnecessary. If your template separates fields to your satisfaction, turn off this checkbox to print only the labels and data, not borders around each field. (Because preprinted forms include borders, QuickBooks automatically turns on this checkbox if you choose the "Intuit preprinted forms" option.)

Aligning Forms and Paper

If you've ever gotten lost at an office-supply store, you understand why printing includes so many options. You can print on different types of paper using different types of printers, and making the two line up properly can be a delicate process.

And besides invoices and other sales forms, you might also print ancillary documents like mailing labels and packing slips.

To save some trees and your sanity, make sure the paper in your printer is aligned properly *before* you print, especially if you use fancy letterhead or preprinted forms. When you use preprinted forms or continuous-feed paper with perforations for page breaks, the alignment of the paper is crucial: If it's not lined up properly, your data won't appear next to the correct labels or an invoice might print over a page break. It's a good idea to print a sample to check the alignment of your forms and paper every time you print, but it's particularly important if you're printing a big batch of forms. If the sample's alignment is off, here's how to save time, paper, and your mental health:

1. **Choose File→Printer Setup.**

   The "Printer setup" dialog box opens.

   > **NOTE** You can also align forms in the "Printer <form>" dialog box just before you print a batch of forms: Choose File→Print Forms, and then choose the type of form you want to align. In the "Select <form> to Print" dialog box, select the ones you want to print and then click OK to open the "Print <form>" dialog box, such as Print Invoices if you're printing invoices. In that dialog box, click Align.

2. **From the Form Name drop-down list, choose the type of form you want to align, and then click Align.**

   If you have more than one template to choose from, QuickBooks opens the Align Printer dialog box. Choose the template you want to use to align your paper, and then click OK. If you have only one template, the program goes straight to the Fine Alignment or "Use 'Coarse' for Big Vertical Adjustments" dialog box, depending on whether the "Printer type" setting in the "Printer setup" dialog box is Continuous (Perforated Edge) or Page-oriented (Single sheets). If you use a page-oriented printer, the Fine Alignment dialog box appears and you can skip to step 4. If you use a continuous feed printer, you'll perform both steps 3 and 4.

3. **If the Printer type is Continuous (Perforated Edge), the "Use 'Coarse' for Big Vertical Adjustments" dialog box opens. If the alignment is way off, position the paper so the print head is just below a page break, click Coarse, and then click OK to print a sample form.**

   Don't adjust the paper in your printer (QuickBooks warns you several times not to). The form that prints includes text indicating a pointer line. When the Coarse Alignment dialog box appears, in the Pointer Line Position box, type the number of the line preprinted in the paper's margin. QuickBooks uses that number to align the form and the paper. Click OK to print another sample. When the alignment is correct, click Close. You can then perform a fine alignment, if necessary, by clicking Fine.

4. **In the Fine Alignment dialog box's Vertical and Horizontal boxes (Figure 12-2), type numbers to represent the hundredths of an inch to move the form to line it up with the paper.**

After you tweak the alignment, click Print Sample to check the printed form's appearance. When the form is aligned, click OK—and keep your mitts off the paper in the printer.

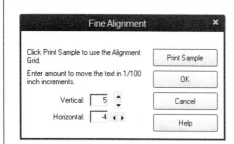

FIGURE 12-2

A positive number in the Vertical box moves the form toward the top of the page. A positive number in the Horizontal box moves the form to the right on the page. Negative vertical and horizontal numbers move the form down and to the left, respectively.

GEM IN THE ROUGH

Managing Documents

QuickBooks offers a document-management feature that lets you attach files to records in your company file, like an electronic copy of a job contract to a customer record or a photo to an item's record, for example. Introduced in QuickBooks 2012, Attached Documents is an integrated—and free—feature. It lets you attach documents that you scan in with a scanner or drag over from Outlook or folders on your computer. In the Customer Center, Vendor Center, Employee Center, or Inventory Center, select the name or item you want to attach the document to and then click the Attach button at the top right of the window (it has a paperclip icon on it). In a transaction window like Create Invoices, display the transaction you want to attach something to and then click the Attach File button in the window's Main tab. In the Attachments window that appears, click an icon at the top of the window to choose the file you want to attach, or simply drag the file onto the window.

If you plan to keep all your bookkeeping-related files attached to records in QuickBooks, Attached Documents is handy. However, if you want to attach files that you use in other ways, such as correspondence, there are some caveats to be aware of.

When you create an attachment in QuickBooks, you aren't attaching the original document. (Some programs, like Word and Excel, let you insert hyperlinks to files so the hyperlink can open the original file regardless of where it's located, but QuickBooks doesn't work that way.) Instead, QuickBooks creates a copy of the file and attaches the copy. So if you edit your original document, you won't see those changes in the attached document. QuickBooks puts the copies it creates in a set of subfolders within the folder that holds your company file. Say your company file is stored in *My Documents\Data_Files*. If you attach a document to an invoice, QuickBooks stores a copy of the file in the folder *My Documents\Data_Files\Attach\<company file name> \Txn\<ID>*, where "ID" represents the transaction. If you attach a document to a customer's record, the copy ends up in *My Documents\Data_Files\Attach\<company file name> \List\ Name\<ID>*, where "ID" is a code that represents the customer.

Fortunately, you don't have to navigate to those folders to find your file attachments. You can manage your attached files in the Doc Center. Choose Company→Documents→Doc Center to open it.

Choosing a Print Method

At the top of each QuickBooks form's window are the same basic printing options, as shown in the Create Invoices window in Figure 12-3. Here's a guide to your choices for printing documents:

- **Print one form**. If you want to print the current form, at the top of the form window, click Print and then choose the type of form from the drop-down menu (in Figure 12-3, that's Invoice). From that menu, you can also choose other printing-related features. For instance, you can preview the form you're about to print, print all the forms in your queue as a batch, or print special forms such as packing slips or envelopes.

- **Printing in batches**. If the Print Later checkbox at the top of the form window is turned on (which it is by default), QuickBooks adds the current form to a queue of forms that you can print as a batch. To print the batch of forms, at the top of the form window, click Print and then choose Batch from the drop-down menu.

FIGURE 12-3

From a form's window, you can print one document at a time or queue them up to print in batches. To process batches of different types of documents, you can also choose File→Print Forms from the main QuickBooks menu bar and then choose the type of form you want to print.

NOTE For invoices and sales receipts, printing a shipping label for the current form is easy: At the top of the Create Invoices or Enter Sales Receipt window, click Print and then choose Shipping Label. If you choose Envelope from drop-down menu instead, you have to specify the size and whether you want to include the return address (you don't if your envelopes already have your return address on them). You can even print a delivery barcode for addresses in the United States.

Printing One Form

When you display a form in its corresponding window, you can preview and print it right away. For example, at the top of the Create Invoices window, to print the displayed invoice, click Print and then choose the form type (Invoice, in this example). QuickBooks displays the Print One Invoice dialog box, where you can choose the printer and paper. To preview the form before you print it, click Print and then choose Preview.

NOTE To prevent embezzling, QuickBooks automatically saves forms when you print them. That way, if you change a form after you print it, the audit trail shows a record of the change.

Printing in Batches

If the Print Later checkbox is turned on before you save a form, QuickBooks adds that form to a print queue. After you've checked that your printer contains the correct paper and that the paper is aligned properly, you can print all the forms in the queue in just a few steps:

1. **Choose File→Print Forms and then choose the type of form you want to print. (Or, in the form's window—like Create Invoices, for example—click Print, and then choose Batch.)**

   QuickBooks opens the "Select <form> to Print" dialog box with all your unprinted forms selected, as shown in Figure 12-4. You can turn checkmarks on or off one at a time or by dragging down the checkmark column. You can also select or deselect all the invoices by clicking Select All or Select None.

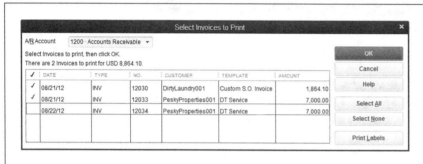

FIGURE 12-4

To remove any of the forms from the batch, click their checkmarks to turn them off. If you want to print labels, click the Print Labels button. (As explained in the next section, you have to print labels before forms.) Then, after the labels have printed, click OK to print the forms.

2. **Click OK to print the selected forms. In the "Print <form>" dialog box, click Print.**

   Because problems can occur during printing (paper jams, low toner, or smears), the program opens the "Print <form> - Confirmation" dialog box after it prints the forms.

3. **If the forms printed correctly, click OK to close the dialog box.**

   If a problem occurred, in the "Print <form> - Confirmation" dialog box, click the Reprint cell for each form that didn't print correctly and then click OK to reprint them. If the whole batch is a loss, click Select All.

Printing Mailing and Shipping Labels

QuickBooks can print mailing labels to go with some of the forms you print, such as invoices. But after you print customer forms, the program removes the forms in the "Select <form> to Print" dialog box, so you have to print the labels *before* you print the forms. Here's how:

1. **Choose File→Print Forms, and then choose the type of forms for which you want labels.**

   QuickBooks opens the "Select <form> to Print" dialog box with all your un-printed forms selected.

2. **In the "Select <form> to Print" dialog box, click Print Labels.**

   QuickBooks opens the "Select Labels to Print" dialog box and automatically chooses the Name option, which prints labels for the customers or vendors associated with each form that's waiting to print.

TIP If you've created forms for a specific customer type or vendor type, in the "Select Labels to Print" dialog box, choose the Customer Type or Vendor Type option and then, in the drop-down list, select the type you want to print labels for. These options are better suited for printing labels *not* associated with your queued forms—for example, when you want to send a letter to your retail customers informing them of product rebates. Or you might use them if you process forms for retail and wholesale customers at different times of the month. Alternatively, if you want to print labels for a mailing without an associated form (like an open-house announcement) choose File→Print Forms→Labels.

---

3. **To filter the printed labels by location, turn on the "with Zip Codes that start with" checkbox, and then type the beginning of the Zip code you want, as shown in Figure 12-5.**

   For example, if you're offering a seminar for people in the Denver area, you'd type *801* in the box.

4. **In the "Sort labels by" box, choose Name or Zip Code.**

   If you use bulk mail, choose Zip Code so you can bundle your mail by Zip code as your bulk-mail permit requires.

5. **If you want to print shipping labels rather than labels that use billing addresses, turn on the "Print Ship To addresses where available" checkbox.**

   The "Print labels for inactive names" checkbox can come in handy from time to time—for instance, if you need to send a letter to past and present customers to tell them about a product recall.

   When you want to send communications to different addresses for each job, even if the jobs are for the same customer, turn on the "Print labels for jobs" checkbox.

FIGURE 12-5

If you want to print labels for a mailing that has nothing to do with money (like an announcement about your new office location), choose File→Print Forms→Labels. The "Select Labels to Print" dialog box opens, so you can jump right to selecting the recipients.

6. **After making sure that you've selected the labels you want, click OK.**

   QuickBooks opens the Print Labels dialog box.

7. **If you've already chosen the printer and settings for labels in Printer Setup, click Print and you're done.**

   If you want to print to different labels, in the Label Format drop-down list, choose the type of label you're using. (You can find the vendor and label number—like Avery #5262—on the box of labels.) The drop-down list includes popular Avery formats along with several other options.

   After you print your labels, QuickBooks closes the Print Labels dialog box. If you clicked Print Labels in the "Select <form> to Print" dialog box, that dialog box reappears so you can click OK to proceed to printing your queued forms.

Printing Packing Slips

When you ship products to a customer, it's common to include a packing slip that tells them what should be in the shipment. In QuickBooks, you have to print each packing slip individually from the Create Invoices window. The packing-slip template that Intuit provides is basically an invoice without prices.

Here are the steps for printing the packing slip for an invoice:

1. **Open the Create Invoices window by pressing Ctrl+I.**

   Display the invoice for which you want to print a packing slip by clicking the left arrow (Previous) at the top of the Create Invoices window.

2. **Click Print, and then choose Packing Slip.**

   QuickBooks changes the form template to the packing slip template and opens the Print Packing Slip dialog box, where you can set print options, if necessary.

3. **Once the settings look good, click Print.**

   QuickBooks closes the Print Packing Slip dialog box and prints the packing slip.

4. **Back in the Create Invoices window, click Save & Close.**

   QuickBooks changes the Template box from the packing slip template back to the invoice template.

TIP If you want QuickBooks to always use a particular packing slip template, change the packing-slip template preference as described on page 627.

■ Emailing Sales Forms

If you've lost interest in paper-shuffling, sending invoices and other forms electronically is much more satisfying. But to make your electronic sending as efficient as possible, be sure that all your customer records include email addresses. Otherwise, you'll waste time typing email addresses one after another, and the chance of a typo increases with each address you type.

If you use a popular email program, such as Outlook, QuickBooks automatically uses your email program to send forms. When you email a form in QuickBooks as described in this section, the program opens new messages in your email program, which you can edit as you would any email. When you send the emails, they show up in your Sent Items folder or Sent box. You can also tell QuickBooks to use a web-based email service, like Gmail or Hotmail. This section explains all your emailing options.

Choosing a Send Method

QuickBooks gives you three ways to send sales forms: Similar to printing, you can email the current form or add it to a queue to send in batches; or you can use QuickBooks Billing Solution (a subscription service described in the box on page 350).

Here are the ways you can send emails without paying for a subscription:

- **Send one form**. If you want to email the current form, at the top of the form window, click the Email button, and then choose the form name, such as Invoice, as shown in Figure 12-6.

- **Sending in batches**. When you turn on the Email Later checkbox at the top of a form window, QuickBooks adds the current form to the queue of forms that you'll email all at once. You can send them by clicking the window's Email button and then choosing Batch.

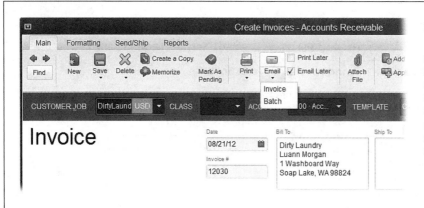

FIGURE 12-6

When you click the Email button, you can choose the form's name (Invoice, in this example) to email the form that's open in the window, or choose Batch to email all the forms in your to-be-emailed queue.

ALTERNATE REALITY

QuickBooks Billing Solution

Intuit offers the QuickBooks Billing Solution, a subscription service that helps you invoice customers and get paid faster. This service costs money ($14.95 a month plus 79 cents per invoice), but it prints, folds, and mails your invoices to customers. So if you're short of both time and office staff, it could be worth the price. Invoices go to a centralized mail center that prints customized black-and-white, invoices using your logo and invoice template, stuffs envelopes, and mails invoices with remittance tear-offs and return envelopes.

If you add the Merchant Services feature (another subscription service), then your customers can pay via credit card. By subscribing to the Billing Solution *and* Merchant Services, your customers can pay any invoice online using a credit card—no matter how you sent it. This approach also means you can download payments into QuickBooks, reducing the number of transactions you have to enter. And Merchant Services gets your payments into your bank account faster. Intuit's merchant services come in several forms. Go to *www.payments.intuit. com* to learn more.

Emailing One Form

Here's how to email a form when you're looking at it in its corresponding window (these steps use the Create Invoices window as an example, but they work equally well for other sales forms):

1. **In the Create Invoices window, click the Email button, and then choose Invoice (or the corresponding form name).**

   What happens when you choose Email→Invoice depends on the email program you use. For many popular email programs, the program opens and creates a new message with the fields from QuickBooks filled in.

If you use web-based email (see page 629 to learn how to set it up), the "Send <form>" dialog box opens with the email fields filled in. If you use online payment links, the link for payment appears in the E-mail Text box, as shown in Figure 12-7.

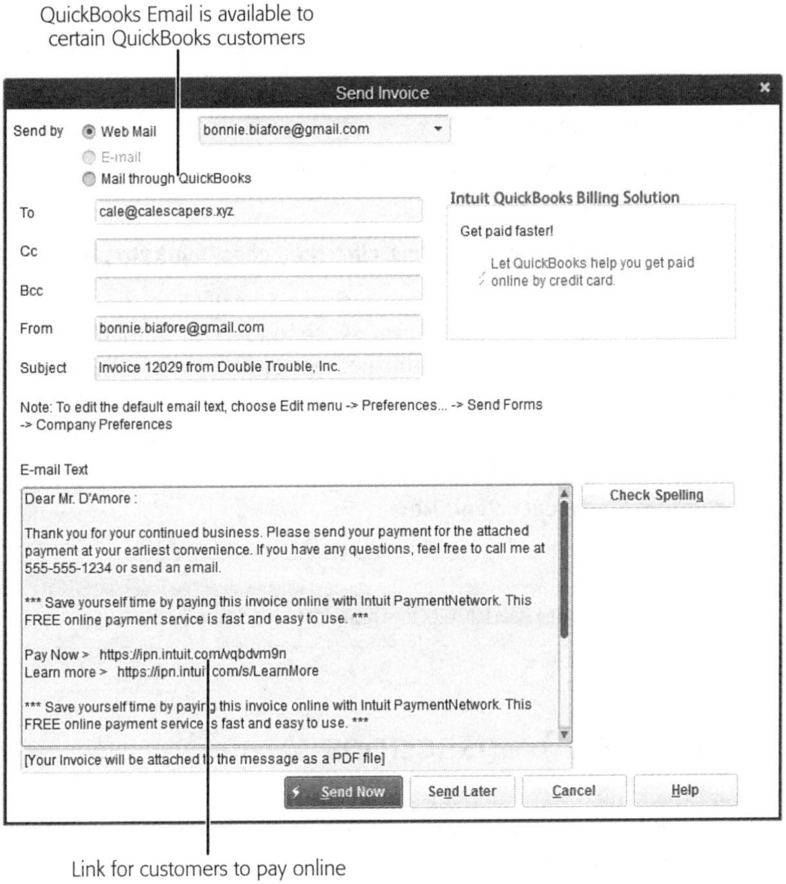

QuickBooks Email is available to certain QuickBooks customers

FIGURE 12-7

You send a QuickBooks-generated message just as you would an email you created in your email program. In Outlook, for example, simply click Send. When you email an invoice, QuickBooks attaches it to the email message as an Adobe PDF file. Customers who don't have Acrobat Reader installed on their computers can click the Acrobat Reader link in the body of the email message to download it for free. Otherwise, the customer can just double-click the PDF file link to open the attachment.

Link for customers to pay online

NOTE If you're looking for an alternative to Outlook, QuickBooks Email is a subscription service that's available if you subscribe to one or more of Intuit's other subscription services, such as QuickBooks Payroll, Intuit Merchant Services, or QuickBooks Billing Solution.

2. **Modify the message in any way you want.**

   You can change the email addresses, subject, and email text that QuickBooks automatically adds.

3. **If you use web-based email, click the "Send <form>" dialog box's Send Now or Send Later button. If you use a desktop email program, click its Send button.**

Emailing in Batches

When you turn on the Email Later checkbox for forms you create, QuickBooks adds them to an email queue. You can then send all the forms you've queued up in just a couple of steps:

1. **Choose File→Send Forms.**

   QuickBooks opens the Select Forms to Send dialog box, which lists and selects all your unsent forms.

2. **If you want to skip some of the forms, click their checkmarks to turn them off.**

   Click Select None to deselect all the forms, or Select All to choose them all. You can also drag over several checkmarks to toggle their settings. When you select a form to send, a preview of the message appears below the table. If you want to change the message, click the Edit E-mail button. In the "Send <form>" dialog box that appears, edit the message and then click OK to return to the Select Forms to Send dialog box.

3. **When you're ready, click Send Now.**

> **NOTE** You can also email batches of forms from the window where you create those forms. For example, in the Create Invoices window, on the Main tab, click the Email button and choose Batch.

◼ Memorized Transactions

If you enter the same transactions over and over, having QuickBooks memorize them for reuse saves time. The program can then fill in most, if not all, the fields for you. Once it memorizes a transaction, all you have to do is choose the transaction you want to reuse and make sure that the values in the new transaction are correct before you save it.

QuickBooks can also remind you to enter a transaction, such as a recurring client invoice for retainers, or even add the transaction without any help from you. For example, if your company's Internet service costs $259 each month and you pay it with an automatic credit card payment, you can tell QuickBooks to memorize that charge and automatically enter it each month.

> **NOTE** Memorizing bills you pay regularly is described in detail on page 226. And the box on page 314 explains how to memorize a boilerplate estimate to use on similar jobs in the future. Although you can memorize bills, you can't memorize a bill *payment*. The same goes for deposits and invoice payments, because you have to choose the bills or invoices that the payments apply to.

The Memorized Transactions List is an anomaly on the Lists menu because you don't create memorized transactions the way you do entries on other lists. Instead, you tell QuickBooks to memorize *existing* transactions. Here's how:

1. **Open the window for the type of transaction you want to memorize (for example, the Create Invoices window for an invoice).**

   You can memorize any kind of transaction, including checks, credit card charges, bills, invoices, journal entries, and so on.

2. **Fill in any fields that remain the same each time you use that transaction. If a value changes, leave its field blank.**

   For example, add the invoice items and their rates. If your hours change from invoice to invoice, leave the Quantity field blank. Or, for a check, enter the payee and the account to post the expense to. If the amount is the same each time, fill in the amount; if the amount changes, leave the amount field blank. Later, when you use the memorized transaction, QuickBooks fills in all the fields except the ones you left blank, which you fill in with the correct values.

3. **In the transaction window (Create Invoices, for example), press Ctrl+M to open the Memorize Transaction dialog box, shown in Figure 12-8.**

   QuickBooks automatically fills in the Name box with the transaction's Payee name or the name in a form.

TIP Memorize sales forms with the Print Later or Email Later checkbox turned on so that the form is added to your print or email queue.

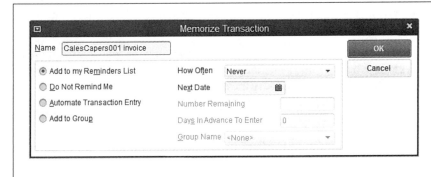

FIGURE 12-8

You can also open this dialog box by right-clicking in a transaction window, such as the Create Invoices window, and then choosing Memorize Invoice (or Memorize Check, Memorize Credit Card Charge, or whatever). Or you can click Memorize at the top of the window.

4. **In the Memorize Transaction dialog box's Name field, type a name that you'll recognize when you see it in the Memorized Transaction List.**

   You can use names like Monthly Telephone Bill or Health Insurance Premium for bills you pay, a customer name combined with a sales form's name, or the type of retainer, such as Full-time Programming Contract.

5. **Tell QuickBooks whether you want it to remind you when to enter transactions.**

   Choosing the "Add to my Reminders List" option is great for recurring transactions: QuickBooks adds the memorized transaction to the Reminders List and prompts you when it's time to enter the next occurrence (though you can choose to skip the transaction). If you select this option, specify how often you want to be reminded and pick the next reminder date. For example, if you pay your phone bill on the 10th of each month, in the How Often box, choose Monthly and in the Next Date box, pick the 10th of the next month.

   If you don't use a transaction on a regular schedule, choose the Do Not Remind Me option and QuickBooks won't add the memorized transaction to the Reminder List. When you want to use the transaction again, press Ctrl+T to open the Memorized Transaction List window, select the transaction, and then click Enter Transaction.

   If you want QuickBooks to enter the transaction on its next scheduled date without any action on your part, choose the Automate Transaction Entry option. When you select this option, be sure to specify, in the Number Remaining box, how many times QuickBooks should enter the transaction. Otherwise, your company might continue to make an installment payment long after the last payment was due. You can also specify how many days in advance you want QuickBooks to enter the transaction. Providing a few days of lead time helps you avoid late payments and insufficient funds charges from your bank.

   You can also set up groups of memorized transactions (page 228) and enter them all at once. To add a memorized transaction to a memorized group, select the Add to Group option to use the reminder setting you chose for the group. (If the Add to Group option and the Group Name box are grayed out, you don't have any memorized groups.)

6. **To memorize the transaction, click OK.**

   If you created an invoice or other form simply to set up a memorized transaction, click Clear in the form window, and then click the window's Close button (the X in its upper right) to close it without saving the form.

TIP See page 621 to learn how to get QuickBooks to display reminders whenever you open your company file so you actually *see* them. That way, when you open the company file, the program displays a Start Up box that asks if you want to enter memorized transactions. Click Now to add them.

Using a Memorized Transaction

If you memorize a transaction that you use from time to time, you need a way to create a new transaction based on it. (You'll also use this technique if you set up a memorized transaction on a schedule but want to create one right away.) Here's how to use a memorized transaction:

1. **Choose Lists→Memorized Transaction List or press Ctrl+T.**

   The Memorized Transaction List window opens.

2. **Select the transaction you want, and then click the Enter Transaction button.**

   The corresponding transaction window opens, such as Create Invoices, Write Checks, or Enter Credit Card Charges.

3. **Make any changes you want, and then click Save & Close.**

   That's all there is to it!

Editing a Memorized Transaction

If you want to change a memorized transaction's recurrence schedule or reminder settings, select the memorized transaction in the Memorized Transaction List window (press Ctrl+T to open it), and then press Ctrl+E to edit it. The Schedule Memorized Transaction dialog box appears with settings for reminders and the recurrence schedule (page 354).

If you want to edit the info *within* a memorized transaction, such as the items and services sold, you technically have to edit the existing transaction and rememorize it. Choose Lists→Memorized Transaction List to open the Memorized Transaction List window. Next, select the transaction and then click the Enter Transaction button. In the corresponding form window, do your editing, and then press Ctrl+M to rememorize it with the changes you've made. When you click Replace in the dialog box that appears, the edited transaction takes the place of the previous one in the Memorized Transaction List. (If you want to save both the old and new versions, click Add instead.)

■ Finding Transactions

When you want to answer a customer's question about what she owes, it's easier if you have the invoice in front of you. The Create Invoices window shows only one invoice at a time, but there are several ways to find one specific invoice out of the hundreds you've sent. Whether you want to find overdue invoices, purchase orders, or paychecks, the Customer, Vendor, and Employee Centers (and the Inventory Center if you use QuickBooks Premier or Enterprise) make it easy to find transactions for a particular customer, vendor, or employee. And the Item List window has a few tools for finding the items you want.

QuickBooks also offers two additional features for searching. The Search feature scours every inch of QuickBooks and your company file. The Find feature, on the other hand, is best suited for more precise searches—to find a specific invoice number, transactions related to a specific customer, invoices overdue more than a certain number of days, and so on. (QuickBooks' form windows all include a Find button at their top-left corners.) This section explains how to use all these features.

Searching with QuickBooks Centers

The Customer Center is a quick way to answer basic questions about your customers, like "What sales orders are still open?" or "Has the customer paid all the invoices I've sent?" Likewise, you can track down bills, bill payments, and other vendor transactions in the Vendor Center. The Employee Center performs similar tasks for transactions like paychecks and non-payroll transactions. And if you use QuickBooks Premier or Enterprise, you can find out what's going on with your inventory in the Inventory Center.

Here are ways you can use QuickBooks centers to find transactions, using the Customer Center as an example (to open it, on the Home page or icon bar, click the Customers button):

- **Display transactions for any customer or job**. On the Transactions tab on the left side of the center, click the type of transaction you want to search for. When you do, the right side of the center lists all the transactions of that type. You can filter the transactions to see all of them, only open transactions, or ones within a certain date range.

- **Filter the list of customers**. To narrow the customer list to those that fit the criteria you want, on the Customers & Jobs tab, click the first unlabeled box (it's usually set to Active Customers). In the drop-down list, choose one of the entries, like Customers with Open Balances, Customers with Overdue Invoices, or Customers with Almost Due Invoices.

- **Find a customer**. If you have trouble finding a customer on the Customers & Jobs tab, in the tab's second unlabeled box, type part of the customer's name and then click the "Find in common fields" button, which has a magnifying glass on it.

- **Review a customer's account**. In the upper-right part of the Customer Center are several links you can click to see various things about a customer's account:

  - **QuickReport** shows all transactions for the customer within the date range you specify.

  - **Open Balance** generates a report of all the accounts-receivable transactions that contributed to the customer's current open balance, like invoices and payments.

  - **Show Estimates** generates a report of any estimates you've created for that customer or job.

  - **Customer Snapshot** opens the Company Snapshot window to the Customer tab, where you can see statistics like the average days the customer takes to pay, total sales this year, and total sales for the same period last year.

- **Display the transactions for a customer**. When you select a customer on the Customers & Jobs tab, the transactions for that customer appear in the Transactions tab in the lower-right part of the Customer Center. To see a specific type of transaction, in the Show drop-down list above the transaction table, choose the transaction type like Invoices or Refunds, as shown in Figure 12-9. QuickBooks initially displays all the transactions of that type, but you can filter them as explained next.

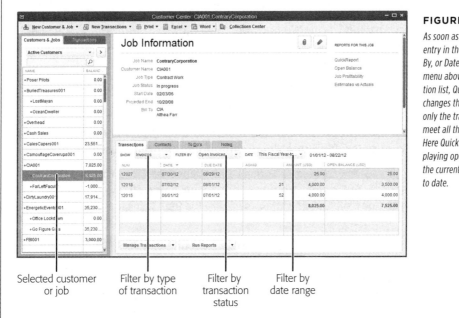

Selected customer   Filter by type   Filter by   Filter by
or job   of transaction   transaction date range
                                     status

FIGURE 12-9

As soon as you choose an entry in the Show, Filter By, or Date drop-down menu above the transaction list, QuickBooks changes the list to show only the transactions that meet all three criteria. Here QuickBooks is displaying open invoices for the current fiscal year to date.

- **Filter transactions by status**. In the Transaction tab's Filter By drop-down menu, choose a category like Open Invoices or Overdue Invoices. The choices in this drop-down menu vary depending on the transaction type. For example, if you search for refunds, the choices are All Refunds, Cash/Check Refunds, and Credit Card Refunds.

- **Filter transaction by date range**. In the Transaction tab's Date drop-down menu, choose a period. Your choices here are the same as the ones you can choose for reports (page 553).

- **Open a transaction**. Double-click a transaction in the Transaction tab's table to open the corresponding window to that transaction.

Finding Items

The Item List window has its own abbreviated search feature: You type what you're looking for, such as an item name or keyword, and the field you want to search, and then QuickBooks filters the list for matching results. Here's how to search for an item:

1. **To open the Item List window, choose Lists→Item List or, on the Home page, click Items & Services.**

2. **In the "Look for" box, type the text or value you want to find.**

   If you type more than one word, QuickBooks looks for items that contain the whole phrase you typed. For example, enter *fiber optic* to find all your fiber-optic electronic devices.

3. **In the "in" drop-down list, choose the field you want to search.**

   QuickBooks automatically selects "All fields" here. To narrow your search, choose Item Name/Number, Description (Sales), Purchase Description, Man. Part Number, or another field. You can also choose "Custom fields" to search fields you've created (page 73).

4. **Click Search (you may need to resize the window to see this button).**

   The Item List window displays only the items that match your search criteria.

5. **To narrow your search, type a new word or phrase in the "Look for" box, turn on the "Search within results" checkbox, and then click Search.**

   Turning on the "Search within results" checkbox tells QuickBooks to search for the new search term only in the items currently displayed in the list. (If you don't see the checkbox, maximize the Item List window or drag one of its corners to enlarge it.)

   To reset the window's list to display all your items, click Reset.

Using QuickBooks Search

The QuickBooks Search feature can look through your company file or QuickBooks help files, although it automatically searches only your company file. If you want to find something in your company file, simply type in a few key words or values, and it combs through your entire company file for them. For example, type *webcam* and it looks for that value in your transactions, Customer List, Vendor List, other name records, items, descriptions, notes, and memos. But if you're trying to find information about a QuickBooks feature, type the feature's name in the Search box, choose Help in the box's drop-down list, and Search tells you which menu it's on.

TIP The Search feature is quick and easy if you want to search by date range or fairly simple filters, such as a specific amount. But if you have really specific search criteria, like invoices that are more than 30 days overdue and more than $10,000, the Find feature (explained on page 360) is a better tool.

Here's how to use Search:

1. **Type the value you want to look for in the Search box (which is at the top of the left icon bar or the right end of the top icon bar), and then click the Search button (which looks like a magnifying glass) or press Enter.**

The Search window (shown in Figure 12-10) opens. (If you've hidden the icon bar, you can also open this window by choosing Edit→Search.)

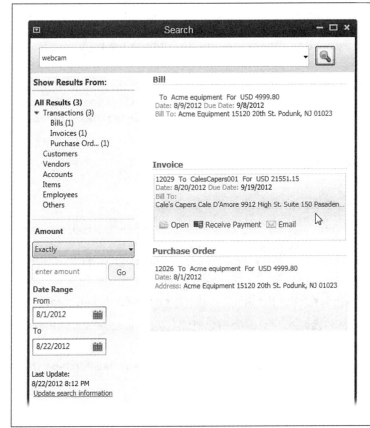

FIGURE 12-10

Below the Search box at the top of this window, you see a summary of the results, such as where the results were found. If you get too many results, you can filter the list by clicking the type of result you want in the Show Results From section, like Transactions. The results list on the right then displays only that type of result, as shown here.

2. **To filter the results, click the type of result you want below the Show Results From heading.**

To see all transactions that matched your criteria, click Transactions. To search for a specific type, click the type, such as Invoices or Bills. You can also choose a date range to specify a period to search. If you're looking for an amount, choose an option to look for an amount equal to, less than, or greater than the amount.

3. **Put your cursor over a search result.**

Icons appear below the search result that represent the actions that you can perform, like Open for an invoice (see Figure 12-10) or Edit for an item in the Item List. Click the icon for the action you want.

Using the Find Feature

The Find feature is ideal for finding transactions that match several criteria. For example, it lets you search for the exact invoice number that a customer is asking about, all invoices that include a product you've recalled, or all the invoices for work performed by one partner (using classes). In fact, the Find feature can mine every transaction field except Description (to search descriptions, use the Search feature instead [page 358]).

The Find window has a Simple tab for straightforward searches and an Advanced tab where you can build searches as detailed as you want. QuickBooks remembers which one you used for your last search and displays that tab the next time you open the window.

■ FINDING MADE SIMPLE

To use the simple version of the Find feature:

1. **Choose Edit→Find or press Ctrl+F.**

   If you have a form window (like Create Invoices) open, the dialog box that opens is a smaller version of the Find window's Simple tab. Click Advanced in this simplified dialog box to open the full-blown Find window. If you *don't* have any form windows open, the full Find window opens automatically.

2. **In the Find window, click the Simple tab if it's not already selected.**

   The Transaction Type box at the top of the tab is set to Invoice, and all the other fields are blank.

3. **In the Transaction Type drop-down list, choose a type like Purchase Order or Bill.**

   The search fields are almost identical no matter which transaction type you choose, with a few exceptions, as explained in Figure 12-11. From, To, and Amount fields appear for every type.

4. **Fill in the values you want to search for and then click the Find button.**

   You can fill in as many or as few fields as you want. When you click Find, the matching transactions appear in the table at the bottom of the window. Double-click a transaction to open it in its corresponding window, like Create Invoices for an invoice.

5. **To clear all the fields and start a new search, click Reset.**

   Click Close when you're done.

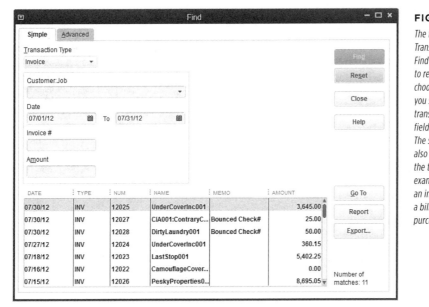

FIGURE 12-11

The first field after Transaction Type in the Find window changes to reflect the type you choose. For example, if you select Bill for the transaction type, the field changes to Vendor. The second-to-last field also varies depending on the transaction type; for example, it's Invoice # for an invoice, Ref. No. for a bill, and P.O. No. for a purchase order.

ADVANCED FIND METHODS

The Find window's Advanced tab lets you search any transaction field. You can build up a set of filters to locate exactly the tra nsaction you want. Here's how:

1. **Choose Edit→Find (or press Ctrl+F), and then click the Advanced tab.** (If a simplified Find dialog box opens, click its Advanced button.)

   The Advanced tab starts with an almost clean slate every time you open the Find window—the filter list always starts with Posting Status set to Either.

2. **In the Filter list (Figure 12-12), choose the first field you want to search.**

   Frequently used search fields—like Account, Amount, Date, Item, and Transaction Type—appear near the top of the Filter list, followed by other, less common fields. If you've turned on multiple currencies, you'll see Currency and Foreign Amount, too.

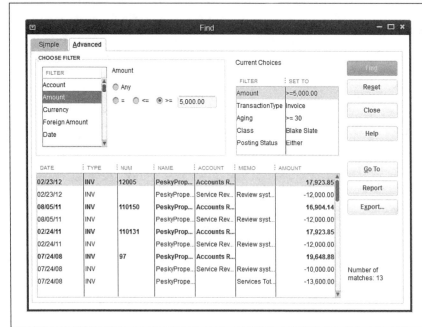

FIGURE 12-12

In the Filter list, the most common search fields are listed first, followed by less common transaction fields, which are listed alphabetically starting with Aging. If you find other fields at the bottom of the Filter list that aren't in alphabetical order, they're custom fields you've defined (page 73).

3. **Select settings to the right of the Filter list to specify how you want to search the selected field.**

   The settings change depending on the field you select. For example, if you choose TransactionType in the Filter list, you see only a single drop-down list of QuickBooks transaction types. Choosing Date in the Filter list displays a drop-down list of time periods, along with From and To boxes to specify dates. And selecting Aging in the Filters list gives you options to help find late invoices (=, <=, and >=); for instance, you can find invoices that are more than 30 days late by choosing the >= option and typing *30* in the box.

4. **To add another filter to your search, repeat steps 2 and 3.**

   You can add as many filters as you want. The Current Choices table lists the fields you're searching and what you're searching for in each one.

5. **Click Find.**

   The table at the bottom of the window lists all the matching transactions (or line items within a transaction).

6. **If you get too many or too few results, repeat steps 2 and 3 to add or change filters, and then click Find again.**

   To edit a filter, select the field in the Filter list and change its settings. To remove a filter from the Current Choices list, select the filter, and then press Backspace or Delete. To clear all the filters, click the Reset button.

7. **Click Close when you're done.**

■ USING SEARCH RESULTS

After you find what you're looking for, you can inspect your results more closely using the following buttons in the Find window:

- **Go To**. Select one of the results and then click this button to see the transaction in the corresponding transaction window (like Create Invoices for an invoice) or account register.

- **Report**. This button opens the Find Report window, which includes all the transactions in your search results.

- **Export**. To export your results, click this button. (See page 649 for more on exporting.)

Managing Accounts Receivable

In between performing work, invoicing customers, and collecting payments, you have to keep track of who owes you how much (known as *accounts receivable*) and when the money is due. Sure, you can tack on finance charges to light a fire under your customers' accounting departments, but such charges are rarely enough to make up for the time and effort you spend collecting overdue payments. Far more preferable are customers who pay on time without reminders, gentle or otherwise.

Because companies need money to keep things running, you'll have to spend *some* time keeping track of your accounts receivable and the payments that come in. In this chapter, you'll learn the ins and outs of tracking what customers owe, receiving payments from them, and dinging them if they don't pay on time. QuickBooks Collections Center helps you find customers with overdue or almost-due invoices, so you won't forget to collect what they owe. It gathers all the info you need to collect what customers owe, and makes it easy to send out reminders.

On the other hand, sales receipts are the simplest and most immediate sales forms in QuickBooks. When your customers pay in full at the time of the sale—at your used-CD store, for example—you can create a sales receipt so the customer has a record of the purchase and payment. At the same time, QuickBooks posts the money from the sale into your bank account (in QuickBooks, anyway) or the Undeposited Funds account. (Sales receipts work only when customers pay in full, because that type of sales form can't handle previous customer payments and balances.) In this chapter, you'll learn how to create sales receipts for one sale at a time and to summarize a day's worth of merchandising.

Receivables Aging

You don't have to do anything special to *create* accounts receivable—they're the by-product of billing and invoicing your customers. But receivables that are growing long in the tooth are the first signs of potential collection problems. With the Company Snapshot, Customer Center, and built-in QuickBooks reports, you have three ways to check the state of your accounts receivable in record time.

The Company Snapshot can show the balance each customer owes, as you can see in Figure 13-1. To view it, choose Company→Company Snapshot or click Snapshots in the icon bar. In the Company Snapshot window, click the Company tab if it's not already selected. (When you want to see more detail about receivables, turn to QuickBooks' built-in aging reports instead; they're described in the next section.)

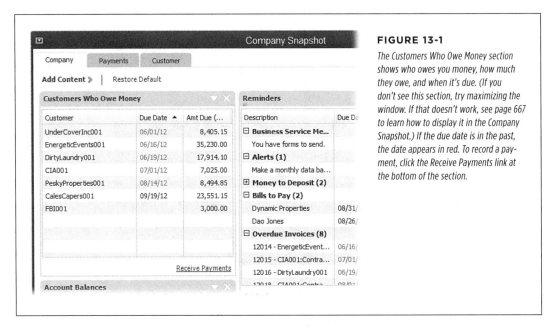

FIGURE 13-1

The Customers Who Owe Money section shows who owes you money, how much they owe, and when it's due. (If you don't see this section, try maximizing the window. If that doesn't work, see page 667 to learn how to display it in the Company Snapshot.) If the due date is in the past, the date appears in red. To record a payment, click the Receive Payments link at the bottom of the section.

When you open the Customer Center (choose Customers→Customer Center or, on the Home page, click Customers), QuickBooks automatically displays the Customers & Jobs tab, which lists your customers and jobs and the balance owed by each one. If you select a customer or job in the list, you can see the invoices or other sales transactions that generated the open balance on the right side of the window, as shown in Figure 13-2.

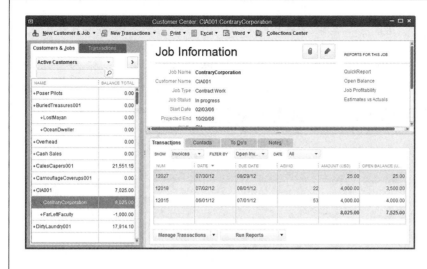

FIGURE 13-2

To see all the transactions that make up a customer's balance, select the customer in the Customers & Jobs tab. On the Transactions tab in the lower right part of the window, in the Show drop-down list, choose All Sales Transactions. If you want to focus on overdue invoices, in the tab's Show drop-down list, choose Invoices; and in the tab's Filter By drop-down list, choose Overdue Invoices, as shown here. A value in an invoice's Aging cell indicates the number of days the invoice is past its due date.

NOTE In Figure 13-2 the customer's balance on the Customers & Jobs tab doesn't equal the open balance in the Show table. That's a clue that the customer has transactions other than invoices that affect the balance, such as a credit that hasn't been applied yet or a statement charge.

Accounts Receivable Aging Reports

Aging reports tell you how many days have passed since you sent each open invoice, and viewing them is the first step in keeping your accounts receivable from growing overly ripe. It's a fact of business life that the longer a customer hasn't paid, the more likely it is that you'll never see that money. Taking action before an account lags too far behind limits bad debts and protects your profits.

QuickBooks includes two built-in aging reports: A/R Aging Summary and the A/R Aging Detail. These reports show how much your customers owe for the current billing period (invoices that are less than 30 days old), as well as unpaid invoices from previous periods (invoices that are between 1 and 30 days late, 31 to 60 days late, 61 to 90 days late, and more than 90 days late). The Accounts Receivable Graph can also show you some useful info. Here's a bit more about each one:

- **A/R Aging Summary**. For a quick look at how much money your customers owe you and how old your receivables are, choose Reports→Customers & Receivables→A/R Aging Summary. To see the transactions that make up a customer's total, put your cursor over a summary value. When the cursor change to a magnifying glass, as shown in Figure 13-3, double-click the transaction.

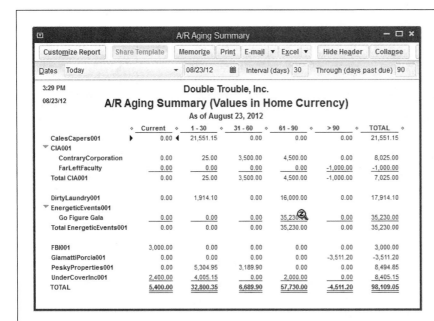

FIGURE 13-3

In the A/R Aging Summary report, QuickBooks lists customers and jobs, and shows the money they owe in each aging period. Ideally, you should see more zero balances as you look at older periods. When you're on a mission to collect overdue accounts, start with the oldest aging period on the right side of the report.

NOTE If you work with more than one currency, the A/R Aging reports and the Accounts Receivable Graph use your home currency for all values. You can modify the A/R Aging Summary report to see transactions in the currencies in which they were recorded: In the report's window, click Customize Report. On the Display tab of the dialog box that appears, below the "Display amounts in" label, select the "The transaction currency" option, and then click OK.

- **A/R Aging Detail**. To see accounts receivable transactions for all your customers categorized by age, choose Reports→Customers & Receivables→A/R Aging Detail.

- **Accounts Receivable Graph**. This graph doesn't show as much detail as either of the A/R Aging reports, but its visual nature makes aging problems stand out. To display this graph, choose Reports→Customers & Receivables→Accounts Receivable Graph. Ideally, you want to see the bars in the graph get smaller or disappear completely as the number of days overdue increases. To see more details for a particular period, double-click a bar in the graph to open a QuickZoom Graph.

To see more detail about a customer, double-click the customer's name in the legend, or double-click the slice in the pie chart that corresponds to the customer.

POWER USERS' CLINIC

Watching Receivables Trends

In the investment world, financial analysts study trends in accounts receivable. For example, if accounts receivable are increasing faster than sales, it means that customers aren't paying for everything they bought, either because they're on thin ice financially or they don't like the products or services they've received.

One way to measure how good a job your company does collecting receivables is with *days sales outstanding*, which is the number of days' worth of sales it takes to match your accounts receivable. If accounts receivable grow faster than sales (meaning customers aren't paying), you'll see this value get larger. Here's the formula for days sales outstanding:

Days sales outstanding =

Accounts receivable / (Sales/365)

Days sales outstanding below 60 (collecting accounts receivable with two months' worth of sales) is good. But if your company is in the retail business, you should aspire to the performance of high-volume giants such as WalMart and Home Depot, who collect their receivables in less than a week.

Customer and Job Reports

Aging reports aren't the only goodies you can generate in QuickBooks. To see all the reports associated with customers and what they owe, choose Reports→Customers & Receivables. Here's an overview of when it makes sense to use these reports:

- **Customer Balance Summary**. This report shows the balances for each job and then the total balance for the customer. You can find this same total balance information on the Customer Center's Customers & Jobs tab, but unlike the Customers & Jobs tab, you can easily print this report.

- **Customer Balance Detail**. This report shows every transaction that makes up customers' balances, so it could get pretty long. It lists every transaction (such as invoices, payments, statement charges, and credit memos) for *every* customer and job, whether the customer is late or not. To inspect transaction details, double-click anywhere in the transaction's row to see it in its corresponding window (Create Invoices for an invoice, for example). If you'd rather see the transactions for just one customer, open the Customer Center, select the customer, and then, on the right side of the window, click the Open Balance link.

- **Open Invoices**. This report includes unpaid invoices and statement charges, as well as payments and unapplied credits, so you can see if a payment or unapplied credit closes out a customer's balance. This report is sorted and subtotaled for each customer and job, so you can find an unpaid invoice quickly. When you find the invoice you want, double-click anywhere in its row to open it.

- **Collections Report**. When you're on a mission to collect the money that's owed to you, this report provides all the info you need. It shows the past-due invoices and statement charges by customer and job with the due date and number of days that the transaction is past due. To make it easy to contact customers, the report includes each one's contact name and phone number. Give this report to your most persistent employees and get ready to receive payments. If a customer has questions about a transaction, double-click the transaction's row to view it in detail.

TIP When customers have pushed their credit limits—and your patience—too far, you can easily create collection letters by merging information for overdue customers with mail-merge collection letters in Word (see page 638 for details).

- **Average Days to Pay Summary/Average Days to Pay**. These reports show how long customers take to pay your invoices. The summary report lists each customer and the average days it took them to pay based on all transactions. If you notice customers going far beyond your limits, you might consider increasing your finance charges or looking for new customers.

- **Unbilled Costs by Job**. Another way you might leave money on the table is by forgetting to add reimbursable expenses to invoices. Run this report to see if there are expenses you haven't billed, the type of expense, and when you incurred the cost, among other info. If you spot older expenses that you haven't yet billed, add them to the next invoice (page 302).

- **Collections Center**. This feature isn't a report, but it offers another way to contact customers about the money they owe. In the Customer Center's toolbar, click Collections Center. The Overdue tab that appears shows customers with overdue invoices, the number of days overdue, and the customers' phone numbers. To send out email reminders, click "Select and Send Email" near the top-right of the window. QuickBooks creates emails for each customer with an overdue balance; simply click Send to get the reminders on their way.

NOTE After you clean up all your overdue invoices, click the Collection Center's Almost Due tab to see invoices that are due in the near future.

■ Receiving Payments for Invoiced Income

To record a payment, most of the time, you'll click Receive Payments on the Home page, but you can also choose Customers→Receive Payments. Either way, Quick-Books opens the Receive Payments window, which handles full and partial payments, early payment discounts, credits, and downloaded online payments.

The Receive Payments window works for most payments, but you record some types of payments in other places. Here are the windows that can record payments and when to use them:

- **Receive Payments**. When customers send you money, on the Home page, click Receive Payments (or choose Customers→Receive Payments) to record the payment as explained below. This window is for full or partial payments that you receive *after* you've made a sale. It lets you apply early payment discounts, credits for returns, and downloaded online payments. (See page 398 to find out how to record the deposits for any type of payments.)

- **Create Invoices**. As explained in the box on page 381, this window is where you record a partial payment that you receive *before* you prepare an invoice. These payments appear on the next invoice you create and reduce its balance. If you happen to receive a payment while you're preparing the customer's next invoice, you can add the payment to the invoice right then.

- **Enter Sales Receipts**. When your customers pay in full at the time of sale (with cash, check, or credit card), record payments in this window (page 391).

> **NOTE** If you add online payment links (page 290) to the invoices you send out, the payments that customers make using these links show up as electronic funds transfers into your bank account, either from the customer's bank or from your merchant services account if they pay with a credit card.

For full or partial payments with or without discounts or credits, follow these steps to record payments you receive from customers:

1. **On the Home page, click Receive Payments.**

   QuickBooks opens the Receive Payments window.

2. **In the Received From box, choose the customer or the job for which you received a payment, as shown in Figure 13-4.**

   If the customer sent a payment that covers more than one job, in the Received From box, choose the customer's name rather than a job. QuickBooks then adds the Job column to the Receive Payments table and fills in the rows with all the outstanding invoices for all the customer's jobs. When an invoice applies to a specific job, the job's name appears in the table. If the cell in the Job column is blank, the invoice applies directly to the customer, not to a job.

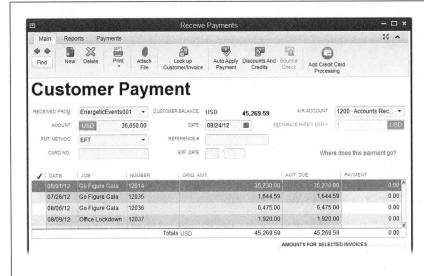

FIGURE 13-4

When you choose a customer or job in the Received From box, the Customer Balance to its right shows the corresponding balance, and QuickBooks fills in the table with every unpaid invoice for that customer or job. If you choose a customer (as shown here), the table adds the Job column and fills in the rows with the customer's outstanding invoices. The cell in the Job column lists the job's name when an invoice applies to a specific job and is blank when the invoice applies to the customer, not to a job.

TIP If you choose a job and don't see the invoice you expect, in the Received From box, choose the customer to see all invoices for that customer *and* its jobs.

3. **In the Amount box, type the amount of the payment (if the customer uses a foreign currency, type the amount received in the foreign currency).**

   If you select a customer who is set up to use a foreign currency, the A/R Account box automatically selects the Accounts Receivable account for that currency. For euros, for example, you'll see "Accounts Receivable - EUR."

4. **If you turned off the "Automatically apply payments" preference (page 618), in the unpaid invoice table, turn on the checkmark cells (in the first column) for the invoices to which you want to apply the payment, as shown in Figure 13-5.**

   If the "Automatically apply payments" preference is turned on, here's what happens after you enter the payment amount and either press Tab or click another box: QuickBooks automatically selects an invoice for you. But if a payment doesn't match any of the customer's invoice amounts, QuickBooks applies the payment to the oldest invoices first. If you don't notice that QuickBooks selected the wrong invoices, you could end up paying your accountant to straighten out the mess. If the program doesn't select the correct invoices, turn off the checkmark cells that QuickBooks selected and turn on the checkmark cells for the invoices you want.

TIP On the other hand, turning on the "Automatically calculate payments" preference (page 618) is handy. In the Receive Payments window, as you choose invoices, QuickBooks calculates what the payment should be and applies that amount. If the customer underpaid, QuickBooks asks you if you want to keep the underpayment or write off the amount that the customer didn't pay.

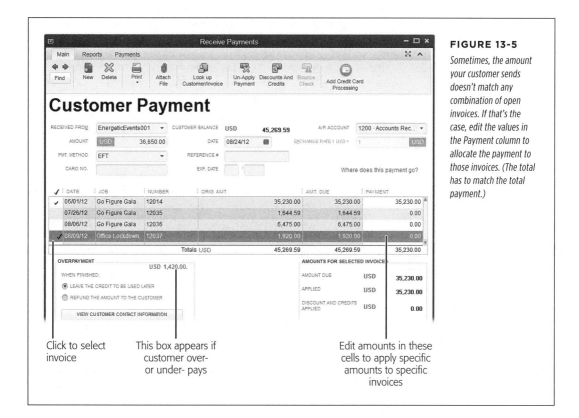

FIGURE 13-5

Sometimes, the amount your customer sends doesn't match any combination of open invoices. If that's the case, edit the values in the Payment column to allocate the payment to those invoices. (The total has to match the total payment.)

Click to select invoice

This box appears if customer over- or under- pays

Edit amounts in these cells to apply specific amounts to specific invoices

TIP When you select a customer who is set up to use a foreign currency, the "Exchange Rate 1 <currency> =" box comes to life below the Date box, filled in with the current exchange rate set in QuickBooks. If you want to use a different rate, type it in the "Exchange Rate 1 <currency> =" box. If the exchange rate you use when you receive the payment is different from the rate you used on the invoice, QuickBooks automatically calculates the gain or loss (page 482) for the transaction.

5. In the Pmt. Method box, choose the method the customer used to make the payment.

If you choose Cash, QuickBooks displays the Reference # box where you can type a receipt number or other identifier. When you choose Check, Quick-Books displays the Check # box instead, so you can type the number from the customer's check. For any type of credit card or EFT, in the Card No. box and Exp. Date boxes, type the card's number and the month and year that it expires. The Reference # box that appears is perfect for storing the credit card transaction number.

NOTE If you already subscribe to QuickBooks Merchant Services (see the box on page 350) and you want to process the payment on the customer's credit card, turn on the "Process payment when saving" checkbox at the bottom of the window. (When you choose a credit card in the Pmt. Method box, this checkbox's label changes to something like "Process Visa payment when saving.") You can then download transactions for the payments you received online or via credit card by clicking Get Online Pmts at the top of the Receive Payments window.

6. If the Deposit To box is visible, choose the account for the deposit, such as your checking account, money market account, or Undeposited Funds account.

Out of the box, the Use Undeposited Funds preference (page 618) is turned on, which tells QuickBooks to deposit payments into your Undeposited Funds account automatically. When this setting is on, you won't see the Deposit To box. The program holds the payment in that account until you tell it to deposit those payments into a specific bank account. If you're the impatient type or if your checking account balance is desperately low, you can deposit a payment directly to the bank account—as long as you follow that QuickBooks transaction with a real-world bank deposit.

TIP To make reconciling your bank statement a bit easier (page 426), choose the Deposit To account based on the way your bank statement shows the deposits you make—for example, if your bank statement shows only a deposit total, regardless of how many checks were in the deposit, put payments in the Undeposited Funds account. But if your bank shows every check you deposit, choose your QuickBooks bank account so that each payment appears separately. (Page 618 explains how to set your QuickBooks preferences so that the program always chooses Undeposited Funds for payments.)

7. If your customer reduced the payment by the amount of their available credit, at the top of the Receive Payments window, click the Discounts and Credits button; in the Discount and Credits dialog box (Figure 13-6), apply the credit to the payment.

If the customer paid too much or too little, you'll see an overpayment or under-payment message like the one shown in Figure 13-5. Before you edit values in the Payment column, see if the Available Credits value equals the Underpayment value. If it does, your customer reduced the payment by their available credit. See page 375 for more details about applying credits.

8. **If you want to print a payment receipt, at the top of the Receive Payments window, click Print→Payment.**

   QuickBooks opens the Print Lists dialog box. If necessary, change the print settings, and then click Print.

9. **Click Save & Close to assign the payment to the selected invoices and close the window.**

   If you want to apply another payment, click Save & New.

TIP Say you realize thatyou've applied a payment to the wrong invoice. The easiest way to change a recent payment is to choose Customers→Receive Payments, and then click the left arrow (Previous) at the top of the Receive Payments window until the payment in question appears. In the invoice table, turn off the checkmark cell for the currently selected invoice, turn on the checkmark cell for the correct invoice, and then click Save & Close.

◼ Applying Credits to Invoices

When something goes awry with the services or products you sell, customers won't be bashful about asking for a refund or credit. And customers who buy from you regularly might *prefer* a credit against their next order rather than a refund, so that checks aren't flying back and forth in the mail (page 321 tells you how to create a credit). In a business sense, a credit is a lot like a customer payment that you can apply to invoices. In QuickBooks, the steps for applying credits are different from those for applying actual customer payments, although you do both in the Receive Payments window.

TIP For small credits, it's easier to wait until the customer sends a payment to apply the credit. When the customer sends a payment and you choose that customer in the Receive Payments window, QuickBooks reminds you about the available credits. Then you can apply the payment and the credit in the same transaction.

If a customer's credit is sizable and the customer has unpaid invoices, you can apply the credit to those invoices even if the customer hasn't sent an actual payment.

When you're ready to apply a credit to an invoice, here's what to do:

1. **On the Home page, click Receive Payments (or choose Customers→Receive Payments).**

   QuickBooks opens the Receive Payments window.

2. **In the Received From drop-down list, choose the customer or job you want.**

   If you choose a customer or job with an available credit, the Available Credits label appears below the window's table and shows the amount of credit that's available. If you choose a customer, the Available Credits value represents all the credits available for all jobs for that customer.

3. **If your customer gave you instructions about which invoice should get the credit, click anywhere in the line for that invoice or statement** *except* **the checkmark column.**

If you click a cell in the checkmark column, QuickBooks selects that invoice to receive a *real* payment.

4. **To apply the credit to the invoice or statement you selected, at the top of the Receive Payments window, click the Discounts and Credits button.**

QuickBooks opens the Discount and Credits dialog box, shown in Figure 13-6.

FIGURE 13-6

When you click a credit's checkmark cell, the Credits Used value changes to show the total credit that has been applied to the invoice. The Balance Due value shows how much is still due on the invoice. If you applied other credits to the invoice in the past, they appear in the Previously Applied Credits table at the bottom of the dialog box.

5. **To apply a credit, click its checkmark cell to turn it on.**

If the customer asked you not to apply a credit, turn off that credit's checkmark cell. If the credit doesn't appear in the Discount and Credits dialog box, it probably relates to a different job or to the customer only. If you want to apply a credit to a different job or to the customer's account, see the box on page 381.

6. Click Done.

When QuickBooks closes the Discount and Credits dialog box and returns to the Receive Payments window, you'll see the applied credit, as shown in Figure 13-7.

Applied credit

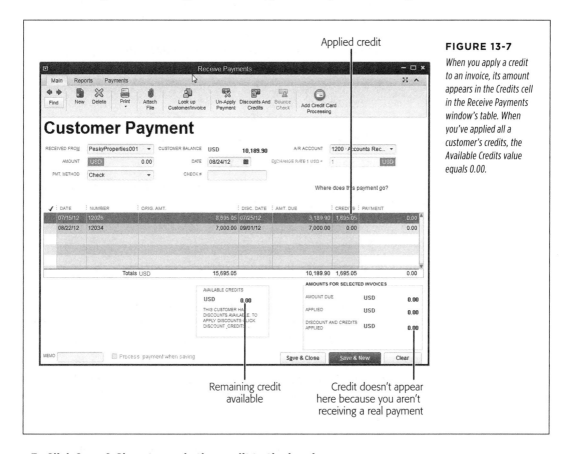

FIGURE 13-7

When you apply a credit to an invoice, its amount appears in the Credits cell in the Receive Payments window's table. When you've applied all a customer's credits, the Available Credits value equals 0.00.

Remaining credit
available

Credit doesn't appear
here because you aren't
receiving a real payment

7. Click Save & Close to apply the credit to the invoice.

If the customer's available credit is greater than the total for an invoice, you can still apply the credit to that invoice. QuickBooks reduces the invoice's balance to zero but keeps the remainder of the credit available so you can apply it to another invoice. Simply repeat these steps to apply the leftover credit to another invoice.

■ Discounting for Early Payment

Customers aren't eligible for early payment discounts until they actually *pay early*, so it makes sense that you apply such discounts in the Receive Payments window. The process for applying an early payment discount is almost identical to applying a credit. In fact, if an invoice qualifies for both a credit and an early payment discount, you can apply them both in the Discount and Credits dialog box.

NOTE If the discount is for something other than an early payment, such as a product that's on sale, add a Discount item to the invoice instead (page 289).

Here's how to apply an early payment discount to a customer:

1. **On the Home page, click Receive Payments.**

2. **In the Receive Payments window's Received From drop-down list, choose the customer or job for the payment you received.**

   In the table of open invoices, QuickBooks shows all the invoices or statements that aren't paid.

3. **In the Amount cell, type the amount of the payment.**

   When you click away from the field, QuickBooks applies the payment to open invoices. If QuickBooks doesn't apply the payment to the correct invoices, you can choose the ones you want (page 372). If the customer already deducted the early payment discount, the Receive Payments window shows an underpayment (Figure 13-8, background).

4. **To apply the early payment discount, at the top of the Receive Payments window, click the Discounts and Credits button.**

   QuickBooks opens the Discount and Credits dialog box. If the Credits tab is visible, click the Discount tab to display the Discount fields shown in Figure 13-8. If the date of the payment is earlier than the Discount Date that's listed, QuickBooks uses the early payment percentage from the customer's payment terms to calculate the Suggested Discount. For example, if the customer gets a 2 percent discount for paying early, the suggested discount is 2 percent of the invoice total.

NOTE Customers often deduct their early payment discounts despite sending their payments after the early payment cutoff date. The typical reaction of most business owners is a resigned sigh. Although QuickBooks shows the suggested discount as zero when a customer doesn't actually pay early, you can show your customer goodwill and accept its payment. In the Amount of Discount box, simply type the discount that the customer took.

5. **In the Discount Account box, choose the income account you've set up to track customer discounts.**

   You might think it makes sense to post customer discounts to one of your income accounts for products or services you sell. But customer discounts tend to fall off your radar when they're buried in your regular income. The best course of action is to keep track of the discounts you give by creating an income account specifically for them, called something imaginative like Customer Discounts.

   If you spot an *expense* account called Discounts, don't use that as your customer discount account, either. An expense account for discounts is meant to track the discounts *you* receive from your vendors.

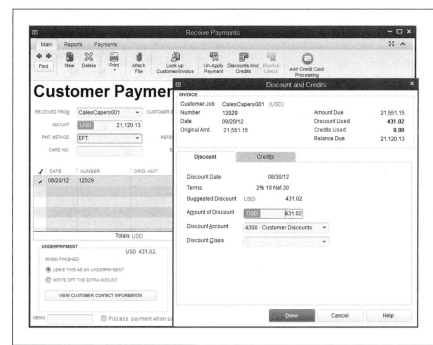

FIGURE 13-8

In the Amount of Discount box, QuickBooks automatically fills in the suggested discount. But you can type a different amount—if the customer paid only part of the invoice early, for instance. The Invoice section at the top of the dialog box shows the amount due on the invoice and the balance due after applying the early payment discount you chose. If the customer has already paid the invoice in full, the early payment discount becomes a credit for the next invoice.

6. **If you use classes, in the Discount Class box, choose the appropriate one.**

This class is typically the same one you used for the invoice.

7. **Click Done.**

When QuickBooks closes the Discount and Credits dialog box and returns to the Receive Payments window, you'll see the discount in two or three places, as shown in Figure 13-9. The early payment discount appears both in the invoice table's Discount column and below the table next to the Discount and Credits Applied label. If the customer paid the invoice in full, the early payment discount also becomes an overpayment (not shown in Figure 13-9).

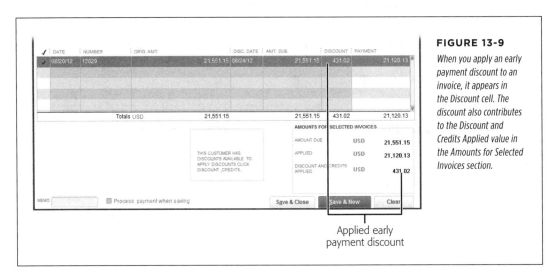

FIGURE 13-9

When you apply an early payment discount to an invoice, it appears in the Discount cell. The discount also contributes to the Discount and Credits Applied value in the Amounts for Selected Invoices section.

Applied early
payment discount

TIP If a customer overpays, at the bottom left of the Receive Payments window, QuickBooks displays two options: Create a credit for future use, or refund the amount to the customer. Unless your customer wants a refund, keep "Leave the credit to be used later" selected.

8. **Click Save & Close when you're done.**

You've just recorded the payment with the discount applied.

Different Ways to Apply Payments

Most of the time, customers send payments that bear a clear relationship to their unpaid invoices. For those payments, QuickBooks' preference that automatically selects invoices (page 618) is a fabulous timesaver: You type the payment amount in the Receive Payments window's Amount box, and the program selects the most likely invoice for payment. When a payment matches an invoice amount exactly, this feature works perfectly almost every time.

But every once in a while you'll receive a payment that doesn't match up, and you have to tell QuickBooks how to apply the payment. For example, if the payment and the customer's available credit (taken together) match an open invoice, you can use the method explained on page 372 to apply them to the invoice. (If you have no idea what the customer had in mind, don't guess—contact the customer and ask how to apply the payment.)

Regardless of the situation, in the Receive Payments window, you can adjust the values in the Payment column to match your customer's wishes. Here's how to handle some common scenarios:

- **Customer includes the invoice number on the payment.** If QuickBooks selects an invoice other than the one the customer specifies, click the selected invoice's checkmark cell to turn it off. Then turn on the checkmark for the desired invoice to make QuickBooks apply the payment to it and type the amount of the payment in the Payment cell.

- **Payment is less than any outstanding invoices.** In this case, QuickBooks applies the payment to the oldest invoice. Click Save & Close to apply the payment as is. Your customers will thank you for helping them avoid (or reduce) your finance charges.

- **Payment is greater than the total of the customer's invoices.** If the payment is larger than all the customer's unpaid invoices, apply the payment to all its open invoices and adjust the Payment cells accordingly. Then create a credit or write a refund check for the amount of the overpayment (page 319).

Deposits, Down Payments, and Retainers

Deposits, down payments, and retainers are all *prepayments*: money that customers give you that you haven't actually earned. For example, a customer might give you a down payment to reserve a spot in your busy schedule. Until you perform services or deliver products to earn that money, the down payment is more like a loan from the customer than income.

Receiving money for something you didn't do feels good, but don't make the mistake of considering that money yours. Prepayments belong to your customers until you earn them, and they require a bit more care than payments you receive for completed work and delivered products. This section explains how to manage all the intricacies of customer prepayments.

Applying a Credit for One Job to a Different Job

If you work on several jobs for the same customer, your customer might ask you to apply a credit from one job to another. For example, perhaps the job with the credit is already complete and the customer wants to use that credit for another job that's still in progress.

QuickBooks doesn't have a ready-made feature to transfer credits between jobs. If you want to transfer the credit *and* satisfy your accountant, a couple of journal entries do the trick, but first you have to create an account to hold these credit transfers. In your chart of accounts, create an account (page 51) using the Other Expense type and call it something like Credit Memo Transfers, Credit Memo Swap Account, or Clearing Account.

Because you're moving money in and out of Accounts Receivable and QuickBooks allows only one Accounts Receivable account per journal entry, you need *two* journal entries to complete the credit transfer: one that moves the credit from the first job into the clearing account, and a second that completes the transfer from the clearing account to the new job. Figure 13-10 shows what the two journal entries look like.

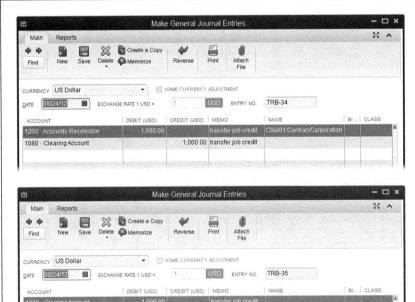

FIGURE 13-10

Top: The first journal entry transfers the amount of the credit memo from the first job into the clearing account; you have to choose the customer and job in the Name cell. (Adding a memo can help you follow the money later.)

Bottom: The second journal entry transfers the amount of the credit memo from the clearing account to the second job.

Setting Up QuickBooks for Prepayments

If you accept prepayments of any kind, you'll need an account in your chart of accounts to keep that money separate from your income. You'll also need an item that you can add to your invoices to deduct prepayments from what your customers owe:

- **Prepayment account**. If your customer gives you money and you never do anything to earn it, the customer is almost certain to ask for it back. Because unearned money from a customer is like a loan, create an Other Current Liability account in your chart of accounts (see page 52) to hold prepayments. Call it something like Customer Prepayments.

- **Prepayment item**. Create a prepayment item in your Item List, as shown in Figure 13-11.

FIGURE 13-11

Whether you accept deposits or retainers for services or product deposits, create a Service item for these prepayments. When you create this item, assign it to the prepayment account (a current liability account) you created.

Recording Prepayments

When a customer hands you a check for a deposit or down payment, the first thing you should do is wait until she's out of earshot to yell, "Yippee!" The second thing is to record the prepayment in QuickBooks. You haven't done any work yet, so there's no invoice to apply the payment to. A sales receipt not only records a prepayment in QuickBooks, but when you print it, it also acts as a receipt for your customer. Here's how to create one:

1. **Make sure the Sales Receipts preference is turned on.**

   If you don't see a Create Sales Receipts icon on the QuickBooks Home page, choose Edit→Preferences→Desktop View, and then click the Company Preferences tab. Turn on the Sales Receipts checkbox, and then click OK.

2. **On the Home page, click the Create Sales Receipts icon (or choose Customers→Create Sales Receipts).**

   QuickBooks opens the Enter Sales Receipts window to a blank receipt.

3. **In the Customer:Job box, choose the customer or job from which you received a deposit or down payment.**

   QuickBooks fills in some of the fields, such as the customer's address in the Sold To box, with information from the customer's record.

4. **Fill in the other header boxes as you would for a regular sales receipt or an invoice (page 281).**

   If you use classes, in the Class box, choose a class to track the prepayment. If you have a customized template just for prepayments (page 669), in the Template drop-down list, select that template. In the Date box, choose the date that you received the prepayment. In the Payment Method box, pick the method the customer used to pay you. If the customer paid by check, in the Check No. box, type the check number for reference.

5. **In the table, click the first Item cell and use its drop-down list to choose the prepayment item you want to use (for example, a Service item called something like "Deposits and Retainers," as described on page 383).**

   This step is the key to recording a prepayment to the correct account. Because your prepayment items are tied to an Other Current Liability account, QuickBooks doesn't post the payment as income, but rather as money owed to your customer.

6. **In the Amount cell, type the amount of the deposit or down payment.**

   You don't need to bother with entering values in the Qty or Rate cells—the sales receipt simply records the total that the customer gave you. You'll add the details for services and products later when you create invoices.

7. **Complete the sales receipt as you would any other payment form.**

   For example, add a message to the customer, if you like. At the top of the Enter Sales Receipt window, click Email or Print to provide the customer with a receipt. In the Deposit To box at the bottom left of the window, choose Undeposited Funds if you plan to hold the payment and deposit it with others. (You won't see this box if you turned on the preference to use the Undeposited Funds account [page 168].) If you're going to race to the bank as soon as your computer shuts down, choose your bank account instead.

8. **Click Save & Close.**

   QuickBooks posts the payment to your prepayment account and closes the Enter Sales Receipts window.

Applying a Deposit, Down Payment, or Retainer to an Invoice

When you finally start to deliver stuff to customers who've paid up front, you invoice them as usual. But the invoice you create has one additional line item that deducts the customer's prepayment from the invoice balance.

Create the invoice as you normally would with items for the services, products, charges, and discounts (Chapter 10). After you've added all those items, add the item for the prepayment and fill in the Amount cell with a *negative* number to deduct the prepayment from the invoice amount, as shown in Figure 13-12 (top).

NOTE If the charges on the invoice are less than the amount of the customer's deposit, deduct only as much of the deposit as you need; you can use the rest of it on the next invoice.

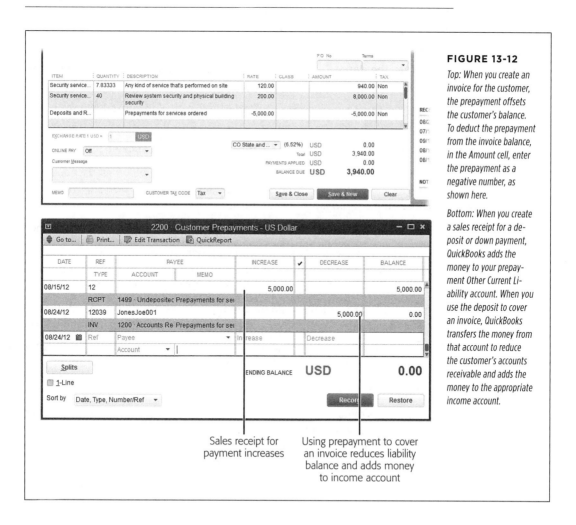

FIGURE 13-12

Top: When you create an invoice for the customer, the prepayment offsets the customer's balance. To deduct the prepayment from the invoice balance, in the Amount cell, enter the prepayment as a negative number, as shown here.

Bottom: When you create a sales receipt for a deposit or down payment, QuickBooks adds the money to your prepayment Other Current Liability account. When you use the deposit to cover an invoice, QuickBooks transfers the money from that account to reduce the customer's accounts receivable and adds the money to the appropriate income account.

Sales receipt for payment increases

Using prepayment to cover an invoice reduces liability balance and adds money to income account

Refunding Prepayments

Deposits and down payments don't guarantee that your customers will follow through with their projects or orders. For example, a customer might make a deposit on decor for his bachelor pad. But when he meets his future wife at the monster truck rally, his plan for the bachelor pad is crushed as flat as the cars under the trucks' wheels. Of course, your customer wants his money back, which means you share some of his disappointment.

Your first step is to determine how much money the customer gets back. For example, if a customer cancels an order before you've purchased the products, you might refund the entire deposit. However, if the leopard-print wallpaper has already arrived, you might keep part of the deposit as a restocking fee.

After you decide how much of the deposit you're going to keep, you have to do two things: move the portion of the deposit that you're keeping from the prepayment account to an income account, and then refund the rest of the deposit. Here's how to do both:

1. **To turn the deposit you're keeping into income, create an invoice for the customer or job.**

    Open the Create Invoices window (Ctrl+I), and in the Customer:Job box, choose the customer.

2. **In the first Item cell, choose an item related to the canceled job or order.**

    For example, if you're keeping a deposit for products you ordered, choose the item for those products. If the deposit was for services you planned to perform, choose the appropriate Service item instead.

3. **In the item's Amount cell, type the amount of the deposit that you're keeping.**

    Because items are connected to income accounts (see Chapter 5), this first line in the invoice is where you assign the amount of the deposit that you're keeping to the correct income account for the products or services you sold.

4. **In the table's second line, add the prepayment item and fill in the amount of the deposit you're keeping as a negative amount, as shown in Figure 13-13.**

    This item removes the amount of the deposit you're keeping from your liability account so you no longer owe the customer that money.

5. **Click Save & Close.**

    QuickBooks removes the deposit you're keeping from the prepayment liability account and posts that money to one of your income accounts. If you're keeping the whole deposit, you're done. But if you aren't keeping the entire amount, you have to refund the rest to the customer, so continue on to the next step.

FIGURE 13-13

In the first row's Amount cell, enter the amount of the deposit you're keeping as a positive number. Then, in the Amount cell for the prepayment (the second row), type a negative number, which makes the invoice's balance zero. The prepayment item also deducts the deposit from the prepayment liability account, so you no longer "owe" your customer that money.

6. **To refund the rest of the deposit, create a credit memo for the remainder (page 319).**

   In the Create Credit Memos/Refunds window's table, add the prepayment item you used in the invoice. In the Amount cell, type the amount that you're refunding.

7. **Click Save & Close.**

   QuickBooks removes the remaining deposit amount from your prepayment liability account. Because the credit memo has a credit balance, QuickBooks opens the Available Credit dialog box.

8. **In the Available Credit dialog box, choose the "Give a refund" option and then click OK.**

   QuickBooks opens the Issue a Refund dialog box and fills in the customer or job, the account from which the refund is issued, and the refund amount. If you want to refund the deposit from a different account, choose a different refund payment method or account.

9. **Click OK to create the refund.**

   All that's left for you to do is mail the refund check.

Applying Finance Charges

If you've tried everything but some customers still won't pay, you can resort to finance charges. These charges usually don't cover the cost of keeping after the slackers, but QuickBooks at least minimizes the time you spend on this vexing task.

NOTE Typically, only small businesses actually pay finance charges. Corporations usually ignore them, so you may decide to skip finance charges for your corporate clients. You'll just have to reverse the charges later on.

Customers tend to get cranky if you spring finance charges on them without warning, so spend some time up front determining your payment policies: what interest rate you'll charge, what constitutes "late," and so on. Include these terms in the contracts your customers sign and on the sales forms you send. Then, after you configure QuickBooks with your finance-charge settings, a few clicks is all it'll take to add those penalties to customer accounts.

Finance Charge Preferences

Before you apply finance charges, you need to tell QuickBooks how steep your finance charges are, when they kick in, and a few other details. The Preferences dialog box's Finance Charge section (Edit→Preferences→Finance Charge) is where all these settings reside. Because your finance-charge policies should apply to *all* your customers, these settings are on the Company Preferences tab, which means only a QuickBooks administrator can change them. To learn how to set these preferences, see page 608.

Assessing Finance Charges on Overdue Balances

QuickBooks creates finance-charge invoices for customers tardy enough to warrant late fees, but you don't have to print or send these invoices. Instead, you can assess finance charges just before you print customer statements (page 388) to have QuickBooks include the finance-charge invoices on statements, along with any outstanding invoices and unpaid charges for the customer.

TIP Make sure you apply payments and credits to invoices *before* you assess finance charges. Otherwise, you'll spend most of your time reversing finance charges and working to get back into your customers' good graces.

Here's how to assess finance charges for slow-paying customers:

1. **On the Home page, click the Finance Charges icon or choose Customers→ Assess Finance Charges.**

   The Finance Charges icon appears only if you've turned on the preference for finance charges and selected an account to track finance charges (page 608). The Assess Finance Charges window (Figure 13-14) opens.

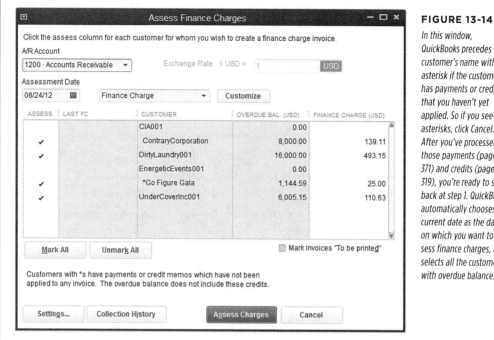

FIGURE 13-14

In this window, QuickBooks precedes a customer's name with an asterisk if the customer has payments or credits that you haven't yet applied. So if you see any asterisks, click Cancel. After you've processed those payments (page 371) and credits (page 319), you're ready to start back at step 1. QuickBooks automatically chooses the current date as the date on which you want to assess finance charges, and selects all the customers with overdue balances.

2. **If you begin the process of preparing statements a few days before the end of the month, in the Assessment Date box, change the date to the last day of the month.**

   The last day of the month is a popular cutoff date for customer statements. When you change the date in the Assessment Date box and move to another field, QuickBooks recalculates the finance charges to reflect the charges through that new date.

3. **If you don't want to assess finance charges on one of the customers in the list, in the Assess column, click that customer's Assess cell to turn off the checkmark.**

   QuickBooks automatically selects all customers with overdue balances, but you can let some of them slide without penalty. Since there's no way to flag a customer as exempt from finance charges, you have to do this manually. If you reserve finance charges for your most intractable customers, click Unmark All to turn off all the finance charges. Then, in the Assess column, click only the cells for the customers you want to penalize.

To view a customer's invoices, payments, and credits, click the row for that customer and then click Collection History. QuickBooks displays a Collections Report with every transaction for that customer.

4. **If you want to change the finance charge amount, in the Finance Charge column, click the cell you want to edit and then type the new amount.**

   The only time you might want to do this is when you've created a credit memo (page 319) for a customer but you don't want to apply it to an invoice. As long as the credit memo is out there, it's simpler to forgo the finance charges until you've applied the credit.

5. **If you want to print and send the finance-charge invoices, turn on the "Mark Invoices 'To be printed'" checkbox.**

   If you plan to send customer statements, turn off this checkbox. Sending customers statements to remind them of overdue balances is one thing, but sending a statement *and* a finance-charge invoice borders on nagging.

6. **To finalize the finance-charge invoices for the selected customers, click the Assess Charges button.**

   QuickBooks adds the finance-charge invoices to the queue of invoices to be printed. When you print all the queued invoices (page 346), the program prints the finance-charge invoices as well.

■ Cash Sales

Receiving payment when you deliver the service or products is known as a *cash sale*, even though your customer might pay you with cash, check, or credit card. For example, if you run a thriving massage therapy business, your customers probably pay for their stress relief before they leave your office—and no matter how they pay, QuickBooks considers the transaction a cash sale.

If your customers want records of their payments, you give them sales receipts. In QuickBooks, a sales receipt can do double-duty: It records the cash sale in the program, *and* you can print it as a paper receipt for your customer.

NOTE Although a cash sale is a simultaneous exchange of money for goods (or services), you don't actually have to create a QuickBooks sales receipt at the time of the sale.

Here are the two most common ways of handling cash sales:

- **Recording individual sales**. If you want to keep track of which customers purchase which products, create a separate sales receipt for each cash sale. Individual sales receipts track both customers' purchases and the state of your inventory.

NOTE If you keep QuickBooks open on the computer in your store, you can print individual sales receipts for your customers. But keeping QuickBooks running on the store computer could be risky if the wrong people started snooping around in your records. And, unless you're completely proficient with the program's sales receipts, you might find paper sales receipts faster when your store is swamped. Then, when there's a lull in your store's traffic, you can enter individual receipts into your QuickBooks company file.

- **Recording batch sales**. If your shop gets lots of one-time customers, you don't care about tracking who purchases your products, but you still need to know how much inventory you have and how much money you've made. In this situation, you don't have to create a separate sales receipt for each sale. Instead, create one for each business day, which shows how much money you brought in for the day and what you sold.

Creating Sales Receipts

Creating sales receipts in QuickBooks is like creating invoices, except for a few small differences. Here's what you do:

1. **On the Home page, click Create Sales Receipts (or choose Customers→Enter Sales Receipts).**

   The Create Sales Receipt icon appears only if you've turned on the sales receipt preference (page 608). The Enter Sales Receipt window opens.

2. **If the customer paid with a check, fill in the Check No. box with the customer's check number.**

   For cash or credit cards, leave this box blank.

3. **In the Payment Method drop-down list, choose the method of payment, such as Cash, Check, or Visa.**

4. **Fill in the item table with the items your customer purchased.**

5. **In the Deposit To box—which appears only if you've turned off the preference to use the Undeposited Funds account (page 618)—choose an account to tell QuickBooks where to plop the money (page 374) you made from the sale.**

6. **If you want to print the sales receipt for your customer after you've filled in all the Enter Sales Receipt window's fields, at the top of the window, click Print→Sales Receipt to have QuickBooks open the Print One Sales Receipt dialog box.**

   To learn more about your printing options, see page 340.

WARNING Keeping track of customers who make one-time cash sales can clog your Customer:Job List with unnecessary information. To keep your customer list lean, create a customer called Cash Sales (page 66).

Editing Sales Receipts

If you're in the process of creating a sales receipt, you can jump to any field and change its value. You can also insert or delete lines in the sales receipt's line-item table as your customer tosses another book on the pile or puts one back on the shelf.

Although you can edit sales receipts after you've saved them, you won't do so very often. After all, the sale is complete, and your customer has left with her copy. However, you may want to edit the sales receipt after the sale to add more detailed descriptions to items, for example. To do so, in the Enter Sales Receipts window, click the left arrow (Previous) or right arrow (Next) until you see the receipt you want (or click Find, which is described on page 360), and then make your changes.

Voiding and Deleting Sales Receipts

If you created a sales receipt by mistake and want to remove its values from your accounts, you might think about simply deleting the receipt. However, you should *always* void sales receipts that you don't want rather than deleting them.

If you delete a sales receipt, it's gone for good: QuickBooks removes the dollar values and any sign of the transaction from your accounts. You'll see a hole in your numbering sequence of sales receipts and an entry in the audit trail that says you deleted the transaction (page 694). Voiding a sales receipt, on the other hand, resets the dollar values for the transaction to zero so that your account balances show no sign of the transaction, and marks the transaction as void, so you have a record of it.

To void a sales receipt, do the following:

1. **On the Home page, click Create Sales Receipts (or choose Customer→Enter Sales Receipts).**

   The Enter Sales Receipts window opens.

2. **Click the left or right arrow until you see the receipt in question, and then right-click the Sales Receipt window, and then choose Void Sales Receipt on the shortcut menu, as shown in Figure 13-15.**

   All the values in the form change to zero, and QuickBooks adds the word "VOID" to the Memo field. To remind yourself why you voided that transaction, type a reason after the colon.

3. **Click Save & Close.**

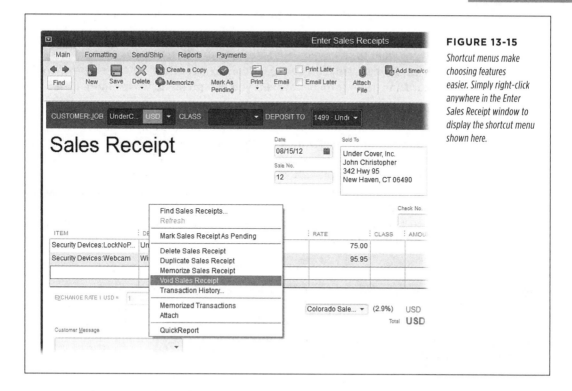

FIGURE 13-15

Shortcut menus make choosing features easier. Simply right-click anywhere in the Enter Sales Receipt window to display the shortcut menu shown here.

Memorizing a Batch Sales Transaction

If you want to reduce your paperwork by recording one batch sales receipt for each business day's sales, why not go one step further and *memorize* a batch sales receipt that you can reuse every day? Here's how:

1. **On the Home page, click Create Sales Receipts or choose Customers→Enter Sales Receipts.**

   QuickBooks opens the Enter Sales Receipts window.

2. **In the Customer:Job box, choose the generic customer you created for cash sales.**

   If you haven't set up a cash sale customer, in the Customer:Job box, choose <Add New>. In the New Customer dialog box's Customer Name box, type a name like *Cash Sales*. Then click OK to save the customer and use it for the sales receipt.

3. **If you typically sell the same types of items every day, in the table's Item cells, choose those items.**

Leave the Qty cells blank because those values are almost guaranteed to change every day.

4. **If you want to split your daily sales among different types of payments (like Visa, MasterCard, and so on), add a Payment item for each type of credit card and other form of payment you accept, as shown in Figure 13-16.**

Because sales receipts are meant to handle cash, the total at the bottom of the form represents the bank deposit you make at the end of the day. But it can be helpful to know exactly which forms of payments customers used that day. To set up the memorized sales receipt so you can record that info, in the Item table, choose a Payment item, like Payment-Visa. (When you create a Payment item [page 139], choose the "Group with other undeposited funds" option so you can control when you deposit the money.) Leave the Amount cell blank; you'll fill in the actual amounts when you use the memorized sales receipt to record the sales for a particular day.

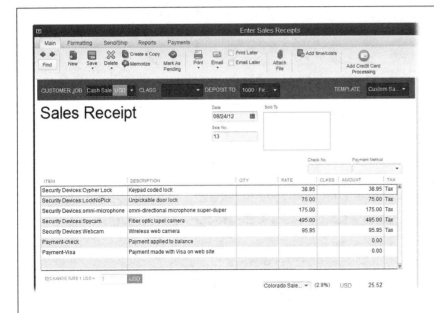

FIGURE 13-16

Add a Payment item for every form of payment you accept (American Express, Discover, debit cards, checks, and so on). Then, when you use the memorized transaction to record batch sales receipts each day, type a negative number for the amount charged to each type of payment. If the Total value doesn't match the amount of your cash deposit, add an item for excess or short cash to make your bank deposit balance. (The next section explains how to use excess and short cash items.)

TIP By splitting a sales receipt among different types of payments, you can make a single deposit (page 396) to each merchant card account at the end of the day. To do so, choose Banking→Make Deposits. In the Payments to Deposit dialog box, choose the payment type in the "View payment method type" drop-down list. Select the deposits for that card, and then click OK to deposit them to the bank or merchant card company. Repeat this process for each type of payment you accept. (This technique works as long as your merchant card company deducts its fees as a single amount, instead of as a fee on every charge transaction.)

5. **When the sales receipt is set up the way you want, press Ctrl+M to open the Memorize Transaction dialog box.**

   In the Name box, type a name for the reusable sales receipt, such as *Day's Cash Sales*.

6. **If you want to use this memorized sales receipt only on the days you have cash sales, choose the Do Not Remind Me option.**

   If you receive cash sales every day, choose the Remind Me option and then, in the How Often box, choose Daily.

7. **To memorize the sales receipt, click OK.**

   QuickBooks closes the Memorize Transaction dialog box and adds the batch sales receipt to the Memorized Transaction List.

Now that you've memorized the batch sales receipt, you can create a new sales receipt for a given day by pressing Ctrl+T to open the Memorized Transaction List window. In the window, click the memorized transaction for your batch sales receipt and then click Enter Transaction. QuickBooks opens the Enter Sales Receipts window with a sales receipt based on the one you memorized. You can then edit the items in the window's table, their quantities, and the prices to reflect your day's sales. When the sales receipt is complete, click Save & Close.

Reconciling Excess and Short Cash

When you take in paper money and make change, you're bound to make small mistakes. Unless you're lucky enough to have one of those automatic change machines, the money in the cash register at the end of the day rarely matches the sales you recorded. Over time, the amounts you're short or over tend to balance out, but that's no help when you have to record sales in QuickBooks that don't match your bank deposits.

The solution to this reality of cash sales is one final sales receipt at the end of the day that reconciles your cash register's total with your bank deposit slip. But before you can create this reconciliation receipt, you need to create an account and a couple of items:

- **Over/Under account**. To keep track of your running total for excess and short cash, create an Income account named something like Over/Under. If you use account numbers, give the account a number so that it appears near the end of your Income accounts. For example, if Uncategorized Income is account number 4999, make the Over/Under account 4998.

- **Over item**. Create an Other Charge item to track the excess cash you collect, and assign it to the Over/Under account. Make sure that you set up this item as nontaxable.

- **Under item**. Create a second Other Charge item to track the amounts that you're short and assign it to the Over/Under account. This item should also be nontaxable.

At the end of each day, compare the income you recorded (run a Profit & Loss report and set the Date box to Today) to the amount of money in your cash register. Then create a sales receipt to make up the difference. Here's how:

- **If you have less cash than you should**, create a sales receipt and, in the first Item cell, add the Under item. In the Amount cell, type the amount that you're short as a *negative* number. When you save this receipt, QuickBooks adjusts your income record to match the money in the cash register.

- **If you have too much cash**, create a sales receipt and, in the first Item cell, add the Over item. In the Amount cell, type the excess amount as a positive number. This receipt increases your recorded income to match the money you have on hand.

NOTE If you notice that your cash count at the end of the day is always short, a fluke of probability could be at work. But the more likely answer is that someone is helping herself to the cash in your till.

Making Deposits

Whether customers mail you checks or hand over wads of cash, taking those deposits to the bank isn't enough—you also have to record them in QuickBooks. In the Receive Payments window, if you designate a bank account as the Deposit To account (page 374), there's nothing more to do after you save the payment—QuickBooks records the payment as a deposit to that account. However, if you initially store payments in the Undeposited Funds account, you have to work your way through two dialog boxes to first record payments you receive, and then to record the deposits you make in your bank account. (The box on page 401 explains how QuickBooks moves money between accounts as you record these transactions.) This section explains this two-step process. (The box on page 399 explains how to record deposits made with different payment types.)

Choosing Payments to Deposit

If you store payments in the Undeposited Funds account, you end up with a collection of payments ready for deposit that coincide with the paper checks or cash you have to take to the bank. When you have payments queued up for deposit and choose Banking→Make Deposits (or, in the Home page's Banking panel, click Record Deposits), QuickBooks opens the Payments to Deposit dialog box, where you can choose the payments you want to deposit in several ways, as shown in Figure 13-17.

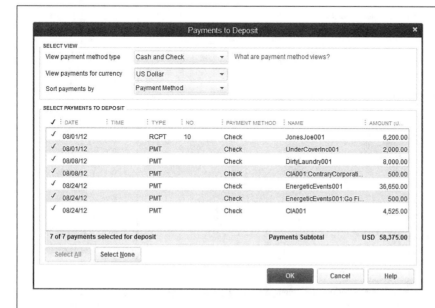

FIGURE 13-17

You can filter payments by payment method. In the "View payment method type" box, choose a method to display only those types of payments. If you want to record deposits for payments made in a foreign currency, in the "View Payments for currency" drop-down list (which you'll only see if you have multiple currencies turned on), choose the currency. You enter your bank's exchange rate for the deposit in the Make Deposits window (as explained below).

NOTE If you have other checks to deposit, such as an insurance claim check or a vendor's refund, you'll have a chance to add those to your deposit in the Make Deposits window as explained below.

To choose specific payments to deposit, in the checkmark column, click each one you want to deposit. To select every payment listed, click Select All. When you've selected the payments you want, click OK. QuickBooks closes the Payments to Deposit dialog box and opens the Make Deposits window, described next.

Recording Deposits

The Make Deposits window is like an electronic deposit slip, as you can see in Figure 13-18. The payments you chose to deposit are already filled in. If you have other checks to deposit besides customer payments, they won't show up automatically in this window, but you can add them to the table.

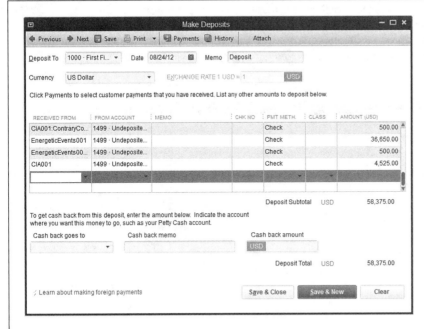

FIGURE 13-18

In the Make Deposits window, you can specify the account into which you're depositing funds, the date, and each payment in the deposit. If you're in the habit of withdrawing some petty cash from your deposits, you can record that as well. To avoid bouncing checks, in the Date box, be sure to choose the date that you actually make the deposit.

NOTE If you're depositing a payment made in a foreign currency, in the "Exchange Rate 1 <currency> =" box, type the exchange rate that your bank used for the transaction (to find it, look at your bank statement or review the transaction on your bank's website). The table of deposits shows the deposit amount in the foreign currency, and the bottom of the window shows the deposit total in both the foreign currency and your home currency.

After you make your foreign-currency deposits, you can see how much you gained or lost due to changes in the exchange rate by choosing Reports→Company & Financial→Realized Gains & Losses. This report shows the payment amounts in your home currency, the exchange rate, and the resulting gain or loss.

Here's how to add these additional deposits:

1. **Click the first blank Received From cell and choose the vendor or name of the source of your deposit. Then, in the From Account cell, choose the account to which you're posting the money.**

   For example, if you're depositing a refund check for some office supplies, choose the expense account for office supplies.

2. If you like, fill in the rest of the cells.

This step is optional. For refunds or checks from other sources, memos can help you remember why people sent you money. In case a question arises, typing the check number gives your customer or vendor a reference point.

TIP If you want to withdraw some money from your deposit for petty cash, in the "Cash back goes to" box, choose your petty cash account. Then, in the "Cash back amount" box, type the amount you're deducting from the deposit.

Keep in mind that you can't just withdraw money for your personal use. By accounting for the cash in a petty cash account, you can record your cash expenditures in QuickBooks. If you own a sole proprietorship, you can also withdraw cash for yourself by choosing your owners' draw account in the "Cash back goes to" box.

---

3. When you've filled in all the fields you want, click Save & Close.

QuickBooks posts the deposits to your accounts.

UP TO SPEED

Putting Payment Deposit Types to Work

Choosing different types of payments before you get to the Make Deposits window takes extra work, but it's a good idea for several reasons. Here are a few reasons you might make multiple passes through the deposit process:

- **Different deposit types**. Many banks group different types of deposits, such as checks versus electronic transfers. To group your payments in QuickBooks the way your bank groups them on your monthly statements, in the Payments to Deposit window's "View payment method type" box, choose a payment method, and then click Select All to process those payments as a group.

- **Different deposit accounts**. If you deposit some payments in your checking account and others in a savings account, in the Payments to Deposit window, select all the payments you want to deposit in the checking account and then, in the Make Deposits window, select that account in the Deposit To box. Then run through the deposit process a second time to deposit other checks to your savings account.

- **Reconciling cash deposits**. As you learned on page 395, the cash-counting process is prone to error, so you're probably used to your bank coming up with a different cash deposit total than you did. Although QuickBooks groups cash and checks as one payment type, process your cash and check payments as two separate deposits. That way, if the bank changes the deposit amount, it's easy to edit your cash deposit.

Depositing Money from Merchant Card Accounts

When you accept payment via credit card, the merchant bank you work with collects your customers' credit card payments and deposits them in your bank account as a lump sum. However, you record your deposits in QuickBooks the way they appear on your bank statement, which might or might not show lump sums. For example, your merchant bank might show payments and merchant bank fees separately, whereas the amount deposited in your checking account is the net after the fees are deducted.

Here's how to record deposits of merchant credit card payments and fees into your bank account to match the way they appear on your bank statement:

1. **On the Home page, click Record Deposits or choose Banking→Make Deposits.**

   In the Payments to Deposit dialog box's "View payment method type" drop-down list, choose the merchant card whose payments you want to deposit.

2. **Select the credit card payments you want to deposit and then click OK.**

   QuickBooks opens the Make Deposits window, which lists the credit card payments in the deposit table. If the Deposit Subtotal amount doesn't match the deposit that appears on your bank statement, the merchant bank probably deducted its fees; you'll record those fees in the next step.

   TIP To make merchant card deposits easier to track, ask your merchant card company to charge one lump sum for fees instead of charging for each transaction; it will almost certainly say yes.

3. **In the Make Deposits window's table, in the first blank row's Account cell, choose the account to which you post merchant card fees (such as Bank Service Charges). Then, in the Amount cell, type the merchant card fees as a negative number.**

   The Deposit Subtotal should equal the deposit that appears on your bank statement.

4. **Click Save & Close when you're done.**

   NOTE How soon you can enter your merchant card deposits in QuickBooks depends on how wired your company is. For example, QuickBooks' online banking service (Chapter 22) downloads your merchant card deposits into your company file automatically. If you have online account access to your merchant card account, make the deposit in QuickBooks when you log into your merchant card account online and see the deposit in your transaction listing. If you don't use any online services, enter the deposit in QuickBooks when the merchant card statement arrives in the mail.

Following the Money Trail

If you use QuickBooks' windows to create transactions, the program posts debits and credits to accounts without any action on your part. But in case you're interested in how money weaves its way from account to account, here's what happens from the time you create an invoice to the time you deposit the customer's payment into your bank account.

- **Create Invoices**. When you create an invoice, QuickBooks credits your income accounts because you've earned income, and debits the Accounts Receivable account because your customers owe you money.

- **Receive Payments**. When you receive payments into the Undeposited Funds account, QuickBooks credits the Accounts Receivable account because the customer's balance is now paid off. The program also debits the Undeposited Funds account because the money is now in that account waiting to be deposited.

- **Make Deposits**. When you deposit the payments queued in the Undeposited Funds account, QuickBooks credits the Undeposited Funds account to remove the money from it and debits your bank account to increase its balance by the amount of the deposit.

Doing Payroll

U nless you run an all-volunteer operation, sooner or later, your employees are going to want to get paid. When that time comes, you face the daunting task of dealing with *payroll*, which is the name for all the financial records you have to keep for employees' salaries, wages, bonuses, and deductions. This chapter explains how to pay yourself without payroll, how to record do-it-yourself payroll transactions, and how to record the payroll transactions processed by a payroll-service company.

If you run a one-person shop, like a sole proprietorship, partnership, or a small Subchapter S corporation, you can withdraw money from the company as compensation without fussing over payroll. But to take advantage of retirement savings options like a Simplified Employee Pension (SEP), you have to deal with special rules regarding eligible compensation. For sole proprietors and partners, all you have to do to determine your eligibility for a SEP is calculate your compensation, which is based on company net profits. However, a Subchapter S corporation has to pay you an actual salary for you to be eligible for a SEP plan.

If you're one of the poor souls who has to deal with payroll, you can process payroll on your own by adding transactions to QuickBooks for your payroll checks and the payroll tax payments you make to federal and state government agencies. (The box on page 404 explains what you're in for if you decide to do payroll on your own.)

But you can also outsource the headaches of payroll to a payroll-service company (as many businesses do). For small companies, outside services are a pretty good deal, since they take care of all the grunt work for the equivalent of the cost of a few hours of your time. If you go that route, then you simply use values from the payroll-service company's reports to fill out a couple of transactions for each payroll in QuickBooks—to allocate salaries and wages, payroll taxes, and any other payroll expenses to the accounts in your chart of accounts. Not surprisingly, Intuit offers payroll services of its own. Its options range from a bare-bones service that provides only updated tax tables to a full-service payroll; page 409 has the details.

Preventing Payroll Migraines

Payroll regulations are painfully complex and vary depending on the size of your payroll and the tax agencies to which you remit payroll taxes. If you've just started a new business and are new to payroll, it's almost impossible to handle payroll on your own. Even if you get it right, you'll spend hours working on it—time you could spend more productively doing other things, like lining up more business or enjoying hard-earned leisure time.

The easiest way to handle payroll is to hire a payroll service (page 408) to handle the headaches for you. For a few hundred dollars a year, the service will help you set up the accounts you need with tax agencies and then crunch all the numbers, fill out all the right forms, and submit them when they're due.

If you opt for this route, don't wait until December to hire a payroll service. Instead, give the company a call no later than July. Ask your representative to set you up with a small monthly salary of, say, $1,000. Then, in November, you and your accountant will decide how much you want your annual salary to be ($30,000, for example). After that, you can call your payroll representative in early December and ask her to set up an *annual shareholder's distribution reclassification* (defined on page 405) for you. For example, if you've already received $7,000 in salary, this distribution would be $23,000 to make up your $30,000 salary. She'll say, "Sure thing!" and you're done. (See page 408 to learn how to record the transactions that your payroll service creates.)

If you aren't convinced of a payroll service's value, consider what you have to do to process payroll yourself:

- Apply for an account with the Electronic Federal Tax Payment System so you can remit payroll taxes to the federal government.

- Apply for the appropriate payroll tax-related accounts with your state. (Depending on the state, you might need accounts with more than one agency or department, such as a revenue agency or a department of unemployment.)

- Determine which tax forms you have to fill out and when you need to submit them. Federal forms include the IRS's Form 941 Employer's Quarterly Federal Tax Return, Form 940 Employer's Annual Federal Tax Return, W-2, and W-3 (Transmittal of Wage and Tax Statements). You might have to submit two or three state forms as well, such as an Annual Transmittal of State W-2s and unemployment insurance reports.

- Remember to order all the forms you have to submit or learn how to submit them electronically.

- Figure out how to remit your payroll taxes to each agency.

- Learn how to calculate what you owe to each agency.

- Once you've identified all your responsibilities, perform them every month, every quarter, and at the end of every year, so you aren't dinged with penalties for late payments.

If that list didn't dissuade you from wanting to process payroll yourself, you're a brave soul...and a glutton for punishment.

Paying Yourself

If you own a sole proprietorship, partnership, or Subchapter S corporation (named after Subchapter S of the U.S. tax code), you can take money out of the company for your personal use. These withdrawals go by different names depending on the type of company. For a sole proprietor, the money you withdraw is called *owners' draw*, or simply *draw*. Partners withdraw money and call it *partner's draw*. And if you're a shareholder in a Subchapter S corporation, the money you withdraw is called *shareholder's distributions*.

If you don't pay yourself a salary, you pay taxes when the company's profits flow through to your personal tax return. However, if you're a Subchapter S shareholder, you can pay yourself using a *combination* of salary and shareholder's distribution. That way, you can contribute to a pension plan, like a SEP, based on your corporate salary. This section explains how to pay yourself no matter which type of business structure you've established.

Taking a Draw

As your company makes money, you can withdraw funds. The easiest way to do this in QuickBooks is to write a check (page 257) made out to yourself, as shown in Figure 14-1. If you're a sole proprietor and own your own company, choosing the Owners' Contribution/Draw account for the check tells QuickBooks to post the check to show that you've withdrawn equity from your company. You use the same process if you're a partner except that you choose the Partners' Contribution/Draw account instead. The Shareholders' Distribution account shown in Figure 14-1 represents the draw account for shareholders in a Subchapter S corporation.

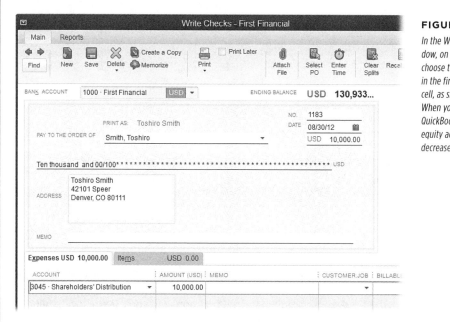

FIGURE 14-1

In the Write Checks window, on the Expenses tab, choose the draw account in the first blank Account cell, as shown here. When you save the check, QuickBooks debits that equity account, which decreases its balance.

NOTE   If you're a sole proprietor, you typically make an initial investment of capital into your business. You record this investment into the Owners' Contribution/Draw equity account (page 463 explains how). If your company runs low on cash later on, you can contribute more money and record this addition in the same account.

Reclassifying Shareholder's Distribution to Salary

If you withdraw money from your Subchapter S corporation for personal use, you may want to turn some of that shareholder's distribution into salary so, for example, you can contribute to a retirement account. To prepare your own payroll in this situation, you have to calculate the applicable payroll withholdings (like federal and state taxes, Social Security, and Medicare) and company payroll taxes, as you can see in Figure 14-2. (Alternatively, you can ask your accountant or bookkeeper to calculate them for you.) You also have to record your payroll check (if you issue one) and checks that you send to federal and state tax agencies for withholdings and payroll taxes. (And don't forget about preparing and filing federal and state payroll tax returns, including forms W-2 and W-3.)

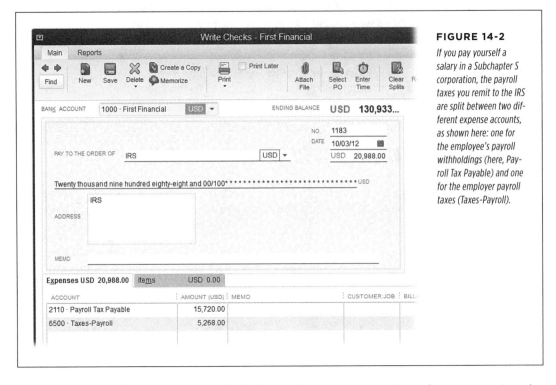

FIGURE 14-2

If you pay yourself a salary in a Subchapter S corporation, the payroll taxes you remit to the IRS are split between two different expense accounts, as shown here: one for the employee's payroll withholdings (here, Payroll Tax Payable) and one for the employer payroll taxes (Taxes-Payroll).

If you take a shareholder's distribution, you can use a journal entry to recategorize some of those dollars as salary. For example, you could assign the money to a salary expense account called Officers Salaries, as shown in Figure 14-3. (You'll learn about the Payroll Tax Payable credit in the next section, and you'll learn how to handle the employer portion of payroll tax on page 407.)

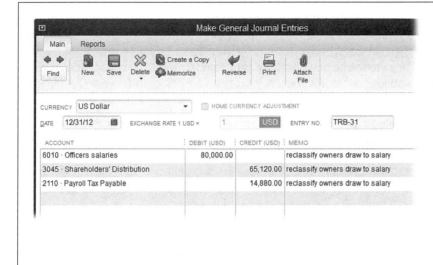

FIGURE 14-3

To recategorize a distribution as salary, you credit the Shareholder's Distribution account and debit the salary expense account. The credit to the Shareholder's Distribution account increases the balance in the equity account (which decreased when you took the distribution), whereas the debit to the salary expense account shows your salary as an expense. The Payroll Tax Payable amount represents your employee portion of payroll tax withholdings.

■ RECLASSIFYING PAYROLL WITHHOLDINGS

After you reclassify your shareholder's distribution as salary, you still have to account for your payroll withholdings, such as the federal and state income taxes you pay, and other payroll taxes. When you remit payroll taxes to tax agencies like the IRS, you have to allocate them to the correct payroll accounts in your company file.

The journal entry in Figure 14-3 set your salary to $80,000. However, companies and employees split the bill for Social Security taxes and Medicare taxes. Because employees don't know anything about remitting payroll tax withholdings, they let their employers include those withholdings in the employer's payroll tax payments. The credit to the Payroll Tax Payable account in Figure 14-3 allocates part of your salary to your employee payroll tax withholdings so they appear in the Payroll Tax Payable current liability account.

When you remit payroll taxes, the amount you pay includes *both* the employer payroll taxes and employees' payroll tax withholdings. That's why the IRS check in Figure 14-2 is split between two accounts. The line assigned to the Taxes-Payroll account represents the employer portion of federal payroll taxes (which includes the employer's portion of Social Security and Medicare taxes, and the employer's federal unemployment tax). The line for Payroll Tax Payable, on the other hand, represents the employees' payroll tax withholdings (estimated federal income tax and the employees' portion of Social Security and Medicare taxes).

Recording Transactions from a Payroll Service

Lots of companies use outside payroll services (ADP and Paychex are two popular ones) to avoid the brain strain of figuring out tax deductions and complying with payroll regulations. When you use one of these services, you send them your payroll data. They then write and distribute your company's payroll checks and send you reports about the transactions they processed. They even take care of remitting payroll taxes and other withholdings to the appropriate agencies.

None of these payroll transactions appear in your QuickBooks company file until you add them. Fortunately, you don't have to enter every last detail. You can simply create a journal entry debiting the payroll expense accounts and crediting your bank account (page 454). Or you can create a vendor for payroll and record a split transaction that distributes the money from your checking account into the appropriate expense accounts, as shown in Figure 14-4; here's how:

1. **Create a vendor for your payroll transactions.**

   On the QuickBooks Home page, click the Vendors button. In the Vendor Center's toolbar, click New Vendor→New Vendor. You don't have to fill in all the fields in the New Vendor window; simply type something like *Payroll Service* in the Vendor Name box and then click OK.

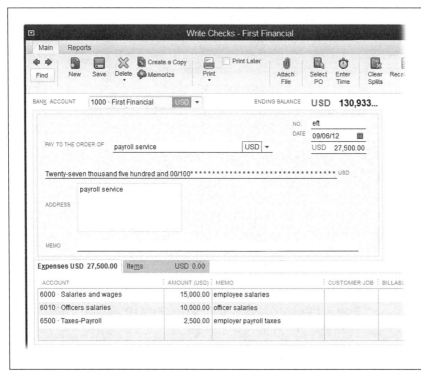

FIGURE 14-4

In most cases, your payroll falls into three categories: Salaries and wages represent the gross pay that employees receive on their paychecks. Officers' salaries represent gross salaries for corporate officers. And payroll taxes are the employer payroll taxes that the company pays, such as Social Security and Medicare taxes.

NOTE The example in Figure 14-4 applies when your employees are paid using direct deposit, where the money is deposited into their bank accounts electronically. If you don't use direct deposit, you also have to record the actual paychecks in QuickBooks in order to reconcile your bank account.

2. **Press Ctrl+W or choose Banking→Write Checks.**

   In the Bank Account drop-down list, choose the account you use for your payroll.

3. **In the No. field, type *EFT* for electronic funds transfer.**

   Most payroll services transfer the funds from your bank account electronically.

4. **In the Pay To The Order Of field, type the name of the payroll vendor you just set up.**

5. **If necessary, on the Expenses tab, fill in the Account and Amount fields for each payroll expense.**

   If the accounts are already in place, but the values differ, simply edit the numbers in the Amount fields.

NOTE To record the payroll service's fee, you can record a separate transaction in the payroll bank account, using the payroll service as the vendor. Assign the transaction to an expense account named something like Payroll Service.

6. **When the transaction is correct, click Save & Close.**

TIP If you turned on the preference to recall the last transaction (page 612), QuickBooks automatically fills in the amounts and accounts the next time you record a transaction for the payroll service.

Using an Intuit Payroll Service

Intuit offers three payroll services that let you process payroll in QuickBooks, and three others that process payroll even if you *don't* use QuickBooks. These services help you calculate deductions, enter the results into your company file, print paychecks, remit payroll taxes, and generate the appropriate payroll tax reports. Depending on the Intuit payroll service you choose, you have to perform some or all aspects of gathering payroll info and processing payroll.

NOTE Although Intuit offers do-it-yourself payroll services, you typically need an accountant to help you set up payroll correctly. Then you'll still have to carve time out of your workday each time you run payroll. Intuit and third-party payroll services that do payroll work for you are a great way to place the burden of payroll tasks on someone else's shoulders—and they don't cost that much when you consider the value of your time. For all those reasons, this book doesn't include the instructions for using QuickBooks' built-in payroll feature.

If you're interested in Intuit's payroll services, you can choose among a low-cost basic service, a moderately priced and moderately featured service, and a more costly but comprehensive service. The payroll options fall into do-it-yourself or delegate-to-Intuit categories. Those in the know swear by the Assisted Payroll service, but here's a quick overview of all your choices:

- **Basic Payroll** is the first do-it-yourself option. You have to set everything up at the start. Then, for each payroll, you enter hours or payroll amounts, and QuickBooks uses the data in tax tables (which you download so they're always up-to-date) to calculate deductions and payroll taxes for you. The program then spits out reports with the info you need to fill out the federal and state tax forms you have to file. You still have to print the paychecks from QuickBooks (or use direct deposit for an additional fee), fill out the payroll tax forms, and then send the forms in with your payments. Basic Payroll costs $149 a year for up to three employees, or $249 a year for four or more employees.

- **Enhanced Payroll** is a do-it-yourself payroll service. You set everything up at the start. Then, for each payroll, you enter hours or payroll amounts, and the service calculates deductions and payroll taxes for you. Enhanced Payroll handles preparing both federal and state payroll forms, and reminds you when it's time to submit forms and pay taxes. You print the forms, add your John Hancock, and then mail them in. If the tax agencies you work with support e-file or e-pay services, Enhanced Payroll can also file your tax forms and pay payroll taxes. This service can handle workers' compensation, too. It costs $236 for the first year ($295 per year after that) for up to three employees, or $316 the first year ($395 a year after that) for four or more employees.

- **Intuit Online Payroll** offers two do-it-yourself payroll service options: Online Payroll Basic and Online Payroll Plus. With both services, you don't need Quick-Books, although QuickBooks and the payroll services are integrated so you can easily get your payroll transactions into your company file. Online Payroll Basic is similar to QuickBooks Basic Payroll except that it also provides W-2 forms at the end of a year. Online Payroll Plus offers the same features as QuickBooks Enhanced Payroll but you don't need QuickBooks to use it.

- **Assisted Payroll** handles making federal and state payroll tax deposits, filing required tax reports during the year, and preparing W-2 and W-3 forms at the end of the year. In addition, Intuit guarantees that your payroll and payroll tax deposits and filings will be accurate and on time. Of course, you have to send Intuit the correct data on time in the first place. But if Assisted Payroll then makes a mistake or misses a deadline, Intuit pays the resulting payroll tax penalties. The price of the service varies depending on your payroll schedule and number of employees; it starts at $79 per month but you'll pay more depending on how many employees you have, the number of states you work with, the W-2s you require, and whether you use direct deposit.

- **Full Service Payroll** takes Assisted Payroll one step further—this service per-forms payroll setup for you. It starts at $99 per month with add-on fees similar to Assisted Payroll.

NOTE With all these Intuit payroll services, direct-depositing employee paychecks costs extra.

Building Paychecks from Time Worked

If you pay your employees by the hour, time tracking can automate your payroll process a bit. To use QuickBooks' time-tracking feature, the people you pay via QuickBooks payroll have to be on your Employee List. When you link employees to their QuickBooks timesheets, the program takes care of calculating how much they've earned. Here's how to link employees and timesheets to take advantage of this feature:

1. Open the Employees Center by choosing Employees→ Employee Center.

2. On the Employees tab, double-click an employee whom you pay by the hour.

3. In the Edit Employee window, click the Payroll Info tab.

4. Turn on the "Use time data to create paychecks" checkbox (the time-tracking preference has to be turned on [page 200] for you to see it), and then click OK to save the record.

Employees can still track time without this checkbox turned on, which is ideal if you *don't* need a connection between the hours worked and the employee's paycheck. For example, turn the checkbox *off* if you bill customers for employee time but pay those employees a straight salary.

Bank Accounts and Petty Cash

You've opened your mail, plucked out the customer payments, and deposited them in your bank account (Chapter 13). In addition to that, your bills are paid (Chapter 9). Now you can sit back and relax knowing that *most* of the transactions in your bank and credit card accounts are accounted for. What's left?

Some stray transactions might pop up—an insurance claim check to deposit, restocking your petty cash drawer, or handling the aftermath and fees from your bank for a customer's bounced check, to name a few. Plus, running a business typically means that money moves between accounts—from interest-bearing accounts to checking accounts or from merchant credit card accounts to savings. For any financial transaction you perform, QuickBooks has a way to enter it, whether you prefer the guidance of transaction windows or the speed of an account-register window.

Reconciling your accounts to your bank statements is another key process you don't want to skip. You and your bank can both make mistakes, and reconciling your accounts is the way to catch these discrepancies. Once the bane of bookkeepers everywhere, reconciling is practically automatic now that you can download transactions electronically and let QuickBooks handle the math.

In this chapter, the section on reconciling (page 426) is the only must-read. And if you want to learn the fastest way to enter any type of bank account transaction, don't skip the first section (page 414). You can read about transferring funds, loans, bounced checks, and other financial arcana covered in this chapter as the need arises.

◼ Entering Transactions in an Account Register

QuickBooks includes windows and dialog boxes for making deposits, writing checks, and transferring funds, but you can also record these transactions right in a bank account's register window. Working in a register window has two advantages over other windows and dialog boxes:

- **Speed**. Entering a transaction in a register window is fast, particularly when keyboard shortcuts (like pressing Tab to move between fields) are second nature.

- **Visibility**. Transaction windows, such as Write Checks, keep you focused on the transaction at hand; but they take up lots of screen real estate, so it's tough to see more than one of these windows at a time. But in a register window, you can look at previous transactions for reference.

Opening a Register Window

You have to open a register window before you can enter transactions in it. Luckily, opening these windows couldn't be easier. Here's how to open *any* kind of account's register window:

1. **If the Chart of Accounts window isn't open, press Ctrl+A (or, on the Home page, click Chart of Accounts) to open it.**

   The window pops open, listing all the accounts in your chart of accounts.

TIP If you use the top icon bar, you can open a bank account or credit card register by double-clicking the account you want to see in the Account Balances section on the right side of the Home page. If you use the left icon bar, click View Balances in its middle section and then, in the View Balances section at the top of the icon bar, double-click the account you want.

---

2. **In the Chart of Accounts window, double-click the account whose register window you want to open (Figure 15-1).**

   This method can open register windows for more than just bank accounts. See the box on page 418 to learn about different ways to handle credit card accounts.

NOTE Income and expense accounts don't have registers in QuickBooks. When you double-click an income or expense account in the Chart of Accounts window, QuickBooks generates a QuickReport of the transactions for that account. In the report window, you can take a closer look at a transaction by double-clicking it.

FIGURE 15-1

You can open a register window by double-clicking any type of account that can have a balance, including checking, savings, money market, and petty cash accounts. In fact, double-clicking opens the register for any account on your balance sheet (Accounts Receivable, Accounts Payable, Credit Card, Asset, Liability, and Equity accounts).

Creating a Transaction in an Account Register

The steps for creating a check in your checking account register (page 259) work for deposits and transfers, too, with only a few minor adjustments. Here's how to fill in the cells in the register window to create any kind of bank transaction:

- **Date**. When you first open a bank account's register window, QuickBooks automatically selects the date in the Date field of the first blank transaction. Out of the box, QuickBooks puts the current date in the Date cell, but you can set a preference to have the program fill in the last date you used (page 612). Tweaking the date by a few days is as easy as pressing + or – until the date is the one you want. (To become a master of date-related keyboard shortcuts, read the box on page 416.)

- **Number**. When you jump to the Number cell (by pressing Tab), QuickBooks automatically fills in the next check number for that bank account. If the number doesn't match the paper check you want to write, press + or – until the number is correct.

NOTE For some types of accounts, like credit cards and assets, the register window has a Ref field instead of a Number field. You can fill in a reference number for the transaction or leave it blank.

Keyboard Shortcuts for Dates

Pressing + or – to increment dates is a great timesaver, but you might also want to add some of the following keyboard shortcuts to your date-selection arsenal. When the cursor is in the Date field, these can help you jump directly to favorite dates:

- **Press T (for Today)** to change the date to today.

- **Press M (for Month)** to select the first day of the current month. Pressing M additional times jumps to the first day of previous months.

- **Press H (for montH)** to select the last day of the current month. Pressing H additional times jumps to the last day of future months.

- **Press W (for Week)** to choose the first day of the current week. Pressing W additional times jumps to the first day of previous weeks.

- **Press K (for weeK)** to choose the last day of the current week. Pressing K additional times jumps to the last day of future weeks.

- **Press Y (for Year)** to choose the first day of the current year. Pressing Y additional times jumps to the first day of previous years.

- **Press R (for yeaR)** to choose the last day of the current year. Pressing R additional times jumps to the last day of future years.

You can press these letters multiple times to pick dates further in the past or the future and combine them with pressing + and – to reach any date you want. But face it: After half a dozen keystrokes, it might be easier to type a numeric date, such as *3/14/13*, or to click the Calendar icon and choose the date.

To make an online payment (see Chapter 22), in the Number cell, type *S*, which QuickBooks promptly changes to *Send* (if you've set up an online payment service, that is.) To enter a deposit, you can bypass the Number and Payment cells regardless of what values they have, as shown in Figure 15-2.

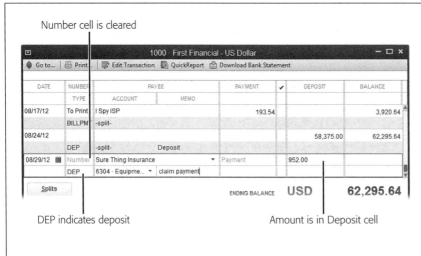

Number cell is cleared

DEP indicates deposit

Amount is in Deposit cell

FIGURE 15-2

You aren't alone if you frequently type a deposit amount in the Payment cell by mistake. To record a deposit correctly, be sure to enter its value in the Deposit cell. When you move to another cell, QuickBooks springs into action, automatically clearing the check number out of the Number cell and the value out of the Payment cell. It also replaces the code CHK in the Type cell with DEP for deposit.

NOTE QuickBooks keeps track of handwritten and printed check numbers separately. When you use the register window to create a check, QuickBooks fills in the Number cell by incrementing the last *handwritten* check number. When you choose File→Print Forms→Checks, the program fills in the First Check Number box by incrementing the last *printed* check number.

- **Payee**. QuickBooks doesn't require a value in this cell. In fact, if it's a payee you only occasionally work with, it's better to not type the vendor's or other name in the Payee cell for deposits, transfers, or petty cash transactions so your Vendors list doesn't fill up with names you rarely use. Instead, type a generic name like *Deposit* or *Petty Cash* and then fill in the Memo cell with a description of the transaction, like *Insurance Claim*.

  As you start typing the payee's name, QuickBooks scans the names in the various lists in your company file (Vendors, Customers, Other Names, and so on) and selects the first one it finds that matches the letters you've typed so far. As soon as QuickBooks selects the one you want, press Tab to move to the Payment cell.

- **Payment** or **Charge**. For checks you write, fees that the bank deducts from your account, and petty cash withdrawals, type the amount in the Payment cell. In a credit card register, this field is named Charge for the credit card charges you make.

- **Deposit** or **Payment**. For deposits you make to checking or petty cash, or interest you've earned, type the amount in the Deposit cell. In a credit card register, this field is called Payment, because you make payments *to* a credit card account (the opposite of making payments *from* a checking account).

NOTE In QuickBooks transactions, money either goes out or comes in—there's no in-between. So when you enter a value in the Payment cell, QuickBooks clears the Deposit cell's value, and vice versa.

- **Account**. This cell can play many roles. For instance, when you're creating a check, choose the account for the expense it represents. If you're making a deposit, choose the income or expense account to which you want to post the deposit. (Depositing an insurance claim check that pays for equipment repair reduces the balance of the expense account for equipment maintenance and repair.) If you're transferring money to or from another bank account, choose that account instead.

- **Memo**. Filling in this cell can jog your memory no matter what type of transaction you create. Enter the bank branch for a deposit (in case your deposit ends up in someone else's account), the name of the restaurant for a credit card charge, or the items you purchased with petty cash. The contents of the Memo cell appear in the reports you create.

TIP Remember your accountant's insistence on an audit trail? If you create a transaction by mistake, don't delete it. Although QuickBooks' audit trail keeps track of deleted transactions, the omission can be confusing to others—or to you after some time has passed.

Instead of deleting transactions, void them. That way, the payment or deposit amount changes to zero, but the voided transaction still appears in your company file, so you know that it happened. Because the amount is zero, the transaction doesn't affect any account balances or financial reports. Before you void a transaction, type a note in its Memo cell that explains why you're voiding it. Then, in a register window, right-click a transaction and choose the appropriate Void feature (Void Check, Void Deposit, and so on) on the shortcut menu.

FREQUENTLY ASKED QUESTION

Managing Credit Card Accounts

Are credit cards accounts or vendors?

In QuickBooks, the credit cards you use can be set up as accounts *or* vendors, depending on how you prefer to record your credit card transactions. Here's the deal:

- **Credit card account**. If you prefer to keep your expenditures up-to-date in your company file, create an account for your credit card and enter the charges as they happen (which takes no time at all if you download credit card transactions; page 576 explains how). Then, reconcile the credit card account as you would a checking account (page 426), which is easy in QuickBooks. To prevent credit card charge payee names from filling your Vendor List with entries you don't need, store names in the Memo cell or create more general vendors like Gas, Restaurant, and Office Supplies.

- **Credit card vendor**. If you set up a credit card as a vendor, you don't have an account to reconcile when you receive your credit card statement. In addition, the name of every emporium and establishment you bless with credit card purchases won't fill up your Vendor List. The drawback to this approach is that you still have to allocate the money you spent to the appropriate accounts, and you can't download that split transaction from your credit card company. With statement in hand, open the Write Checks window (page 257) and write a check for the total amount on your credit card statement. Then, on the window's Expenses and Items tabs, add entries to allocate charges to the appropriate expense accounts. (You can also use QuickBooks' Enter Credit Card Charges feature [page 262] to enter a single transaction allocating the total to each of the charges you made. The advantage to this approach is that recording a transaction this way does double duty by reconciling your charges to the statement, which will make your accountant happy.)

Handling Bounced Checks

Bouncing one of your own checks is annoying and embarrassing. It can be expensive, too, since banks charge for each check you bounce (and, often, they craftily pay your larger checks before the smaller ones to rack up as many bounced-check charges as possible). Besides depositing more money to cover the shortfall and paying those bank fees, you have to tell people to redeposit the checks that bounced or write new ones.

When someone pays *your* company with a rubber check, it's just as annoying. In addition to the charges your bank might charge for redepositing a bounced check, you have to do a few things to straighten out your records in QuickBooks when a customer's check bounces:

- Record a transaction that removes the amount of the bounced check from your checking account, because the money never made it there.

- Record any charges that your bank levies on your account for your customer's bounced check.

- Invoice the customer to recover the original payment, your bounced-check charges, and any additional charges you add for your trouble.

The following sections explain the details.

Setting Up QuickBooks to Handle Bounced Checks

Before you can re-invoice your customers, you first need to create items for bounced checks and their associated charges.

▩ BOUNCED CHECK REIMBURSEMENT ITEM

When a check you deposit bounces, you'll see two transactions on your next bank statement: the original deposit and a second transaction that removes the amount when the check bounces. You have to create the same transactions in your company file so you don't overestimate your bank balance and write bad checks of your own. Because the customer hasn't really paid you, the amount of the check should go back into your Accounts Receivable account.

To create an item that removes the amount of the bounced check from your bank account, create an Other Charge item. Here's how:

1. **Choose Lists→Item List to open the Item List window, and then press Ctrl+N.**

    The New Item window opens.

2. **In the Type drop-down list, choose Other Charge.**

    The Other Charge item type is perfect for miscellaneous charges that don't fit any other category.

3. **In the Item Name/Number box, type a name for the item, like *BadCheck*. In the Account drop-down list, choose your bank account, and then click OK.**

    The new item appears in the Item List.

▩ SERVICE CHARGES FOR BOUNCED CHECKS

Companies typically request reimbursement for bounced-check charges, and many companies tack on *additional* service charges for the inconvenience of processing a bounced check. Depending on how you account for these charges, you'll use one or two Other Charge type items:

- **Bounced-check charge reimbursement.** To request reimbursement from a customer for your bank's bounced-check charges, you need an Other Charge item that you can add to an invoice, called something like BadCheck Charge.

(Be sure to choose a nontaxable code for the item so that QuickBooks doesn't calculate sales tax on it.)

QuickBooks doesn't care whether you post this item to an income account or an expense account, but an income account is easier if you plan to charge customers an extra service charge for bounced checks, as you'll learn shortly. You can post reimbursed bounced-check charges to the same income account you use for other types of service charges. Although the customer's reimbursement appears as income, the bank charge you paid is an expense. The effect on your net profit (income minus expenses) is zero.

- **Bounced-check service charge.** If you post your bank's bounced-check charges to an income account (such as a Service Charge account), you can use the same item for any *extra* service charge you apply for the hassle of handling bounced checks.

NOTE Alternatively, you can post bounced-check reimbursements directly to the same expense account you use for bank service charges. Then when you pay your bank's bounced-check charge, it shows up as an expense in the bank service charge account. When the customer pays you back, QuickBooks credits the bank service charge account to reduce your service charge expenses. The effect on net profit is still zero.

When you use this approach, you need an additional item if you ding your customer with a bounced-check service charge. Create an Other Charge type item for the additional service charge, and for the item's Account, choose your service charge income account. Like the bounced-check charge reimbursement item, make this charge nontaxable.

Recording Bank Charges

The easiest place to record a bounced-check charge is in the bank account's register window. This technique works for any charge your bank drops on your account, and for service charges and interest your credit card company levies:

1. **Press Ctrl+A to open the Chart of Accounts window and then, in the window, double-click your bank account to open its register window.**

2. **In the Date cell for the first blank transaction, choose the date when the bank assessed the charge.**

   QuickBooks automatically fills in the Number cell with the next check number. Be sure to delete that number before saving the transaction to keep your QuickBooks check numbers synchronized with your paper checks.

3. **In the Payee cell, type a generic payee name like *Bank Charge*.**

   Alternatively, you can type the name of your bank or credit card company.

4. **Type the details of the charge in the Memo cell, as shown in Figure 15-3.**

   For a bounced check charge, include the name of the customer, a note that their check bounced, and the number of the check that bounced.

FIGURE 15-3

In the Memo cell, type a description of the bank charge, such as "bounced check charge," "minimum balance charge," the bounced check's number, and so on.

5. **In the Payment cell, type the amount of the charge. In the Account cell, choose the account you use to track bank charges or bounced-check charges.**

   For a bounced-check charge, choose the income or expense account you use for that purpose (page 419). For other bank service charges, choose the corresponding expense account. You have to include a bounced-check charge item on a new invoice in order to recoup this cost, as described in the next section.

TIP The Customer:Job cell provides a shortcut to invoicing a customer for bounced-check charges: While the transaction is still selected in the register window, click Splits to open the Splits table. The Account, Amount, and Memo fields are already filled in with the values you've provided so far. To make the bank charge billable to the customer who bounced the check, in the Customer:Job cell, choose the customer, and in the "Billable?" cell, turn on the checkbox. Then you can add this billable charge along with any others to the customer's next invoice (as described in step 5 on page 422).

---

6. **Click Record.**

   QuickBooks saves the bank charge in your account.

Re-invoicing for Bounced Checks

With the bounced-check items described on page 419, you can update all the necessary account balances just by re-invoicing the customer for the bounced check. Here's the short-and-sweet approach:

1. **On the Home page, click the Create Invoices icon (or Invoices→Create Invoices if you've set up time-tracking in QuickBooks).** Or simply press Ctrl+I.

   The Create Invoices window opens.

2. **In the Customer:Job box, choose the customer who wrote the bad check.**

   You don't have to bother filling in fields like P.O. No. and Ship.

3. **In the item table, add an item for the bounced check (like the BadCheck item in Figure 15-4).**

FIGURE 15-4

To re-invoice the customer for the amount of the check that bounced, in the first Item cell, choose the item for a bounced check (BadCheck, in this example). In the Amount cell, type the amount of the bounced check. In the second item cell, choose the item you created for bounced-check charges. This item's amount represents the bank's charge for a bounced check and any additional service fee you charge.

4. **In the Amount cell for the bounced-check item, type the amount of the returned check.**

   Include the full amount of the bounced check.

5. **Add a second item to recoup the bounced-check fees that your bank charged you and any additional service charges you want to include. In the Amount cell for the bad-check-charge item, type the amount you're charging.**

   If you really want to deter customers from writing bad checks, in addition to making them pay your bank fees, you can add on a fee for your trouble. In Figure 15-4, the BadCheck Charge item covers the bank's $25 charge plus an additional $25 fee your company collects.

   If you recorded the bounced-check charge in your bank account as a billable cost to your customer (page 421), the Billable Time/Costs dialog box opens. Keep the "Select the outstanding billable time and costs to add to this invoice" option selected and click OK. In the Choose Billable Time and Costs dialog box, click the Expenses tab and select the bank charge, and then click OK to add that charge to the invoice.

6. **When you save the invoice, QuickBooks updates your bank account and Accounts Receivable account balances, as shown in Figure 15-5.**

   When you first invoice a customer, the invoice amount gets added on to your Accounts Receivable balance. The customer's original payment reduced the Accounts Receivable balance, but the bounced check means you have to remove the original payment amount from your records. By re-invoicing the customer, you reestablish the balance as outstanding and add the invoice amount back into Accounts Receivable.

Bad check amount deducted
from bank balance

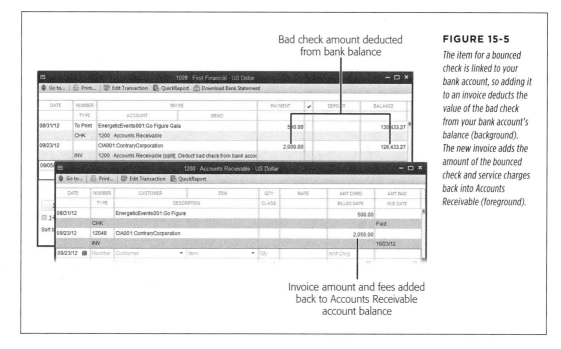

FIGURE 15-5

The item for a bounced check is linked to your bank account, so adding it to an invoice deducts the value of the bad check from your bank account's balance (background). The new invoice adds the amount of the bounced check and service charges back into Accounts Receivable (foreground).

Invoice amount and fees added
back to Accounts Receivable
account balance

7. **When the customer sends you a check for this new invoice, click the Receive Payments icon on the Home page to apply that check as a payment for the invoice.**

   QuickBooks reduces the Accounts Receivable balance by the amount of the payment. (If your customer and the money they owe you are gone for good, see the box on page 424 to learn what to do next.)

Writing Off Bad Debt

If you try contacting a customer about a payment only to find that the phone is disconnected, the forwarding address has expired, and an eviction notice is stapled to the office door, you probably aren't going to get your money. In accounting, admitting that the money is gone for good is called *writing off bad debt*.

The invoice you create for a customer represents income *only if* the customer pays it. So, to write off bad debt, you have to remove the income for the unpaid invoice from your financial records. You do that by offsetting the income with an equal amount of expense—you guessed it: the bad debt.

Suppose you invoiced a customer for $5,000, which means that $5,000 is sitting in your Accounts Receivable account as an asset, but you now realize that you'll never see the money. Here's how to remove that money from the Accounts Receivable account by means of a bad-debt expense:

1. If you don't have an account for bad debt, create an Other Expense type account (page 52) and name it Bad Debt.

2. Create an Other Charge item (page 134) and name it Bad Debt. Point it to the Bad Debt account you created, and be sure to make it nontaxable.

3. On the Home page, click the Refunds & Credits icon.

4. In the Create Credit Memos/Refunds window's Customer:Job box, choose the customer.

5. In the first item cell, choose the Bad Debt item. When the warning about the item being associated with an expense account appears, simply click OK.

6. In the Amount cell, type the amount that you're writing off as bad debt.

7. Click Save & New to save the credit memo. Then, at the top of the window, click the left arrow to display the credit memo you just saved.

8. The Available Credit dialog box opens and asks you what you want to do with the credit. Select the "Apply to an invoice" option and then click OK.

9. In the Apply Credit to Invoices dialog box, turn on the checkmark for the invoice(s) that the customer isn't going to pay.

10. Click Done.

11. Back in the Create Credit Memos/Refunds window, click Save & Close.

When you apply the write-off as a credit against an invoice, QuickBooks removes the money from the Accounts Receivable account, so the program no longer thinks your customer owes the money. And it adds the credit amount to the appropriate income account and to the Bad Debt expense account, so your net profit shows no sign of the income. In addition, if you run a Job Profitability Detail report for that customer, the bad debt appears as a negative number in the Actual Revenue column—that is, a cost that reduces the profitability of the job.

Transferring Funds

With the advent of electronic banking services, transferring funds between accounts has become a staple of account maintenance. Companies stash cash in savings and money market accounts to earn interest and then transfer money into checking right before they pay bills.

Fund transfers have nothing to do with income or expenses—they merely move money from one balance-sheet account to another. For example, if you keep money in savings until you pay bills, the money moves from your savings account (an asset account in your chart of accounts) to your checking account (another asset account). Your income, expenses, and, for that matter, your total assets, remain the same before and after the transfer.

Transferring funds in QuickBooks is easy, whether you use the Transfer Funds dialog box or enter the transaction directly in an account register window. The steps for creating a transaction in an account register appear on page 414. If you create a transfer in a bank account register (a savings account, for example), in the Account field, choose the bank account to which you're transferring funds (checking, say). Here's how to use the Transfer Funds Between Accounts window:

1. **Choose Banking→Transfer Funds.**

   QuickBooks opens the Transfer Funds Between Accounts window (Figure 15-6).

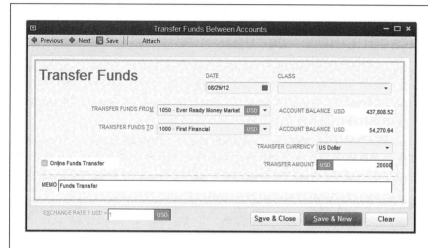

FIGURE 15-6

This window has one advantage over entering transfers in a bank account register: You can't create a payment or deposit by mistake. That's because you can't save a transfer in the window until you specify both the account that contains the money and the account into which you want to transfer the funds. In addition, the Transfer Funds From and Transfer Funds To drop-down menus show only balance-sheet accounts (bank, credit card, asset, liability, and equity accounts).

2. **After you choose the accounts for the transfer, in the Date box, select the date of the transfer and, in the Transfer Amount field, type the amount you're transferring.**

   To record the reason for the transfer, in the Memo box, replace "Funds Transfer" (which QuickBooks adds automatically) with your reason.

   If you track classes, the window includes a Class box, too. Depending on the preferences you've set, the program might warn you if you leave this box blank. However, transfers usually don't require a class assignment, so you can dismiss the warning.

NOTE If the two accounts you select are both set up for online banking at the same financial institution, the Online Funds Transfer checkbox appears in the transfer Funds Between Accounts window. Turn this checkbox on if you want to send the transfer instruction to your bank through QuickBooks.

3. **Click Save & Close. (If you've got more transfers to make, click Save & New instead.)**

   You still have to transfer the funds between your real-world bank accounts, of course. If you turned on the Online Funds Transfer checkbox to send the transfer instructions, you have to open the Online Banking Center (Banking→Online Banking→Online Banking Center) and then click Send/Receive.

   In the account register window for either account in the transfer, QuickBooks identifies the transaction by putting TRANSFR in the Type cell.

◼ Reconciling Accounts

Reconciling a bank statement with a paper check register is tedious and error-prone. Besides checking off items on two different paper documents, the check register and the bank statement never seem to agree—likely due to arithmetic mistakes you've made.

With QuickBooks, you can leave your pencils unsharpened and stow your calculator in a drawer. When all goes well, you can reconcile your account in QuickBooks with just a few mouse clicks. Discrepancies crop up less often because the program does the math without making mistakes. But problems occasionally happen—transactions might be missing or numbers don't match. Fortunately, when your bank statement and QuickBooks account don't agree, the program helps you find the problems.

Preparing for the First Reconciliation

If you didn't set the beginning balance for the QuickBooks account to the beginning balance on a bank statement, you might wonder how you can reconcile the bank account the first time around. The best way to resolve this issue is to enter the transactions that happened between that statement's beginning date and the day you started using QuickBooks. Or you can create a journal entry (page 454) to record the beginning balance. (You'll select these items as part of your first reconciliation, as described on page 427.)

NOTE Alternatively, QuickBooks can align your statement and account the first time you reconcile, as described in the box on page 431. The program generates a transaction that adjusts your account's opening balance to match the balance on your bank statement. Account opening balances post to your Opening Bal Equity account, so these adjustments affect your balance sheet. If you use this method, let your accountant know that you changed the opening balance so she can address that change while closing your books at the end of the year.

Preparing for Every Reconciliation

QuickBooks lets you create and edit transactions in the middle of a reconciliation, but reconciling your account flows more smoothly when your transactions are up-to-date. So take a moment *before* you reconcile to make sure that you've entered all the transactions in your account:

- **Bills**. If you paid bills by writing paper checks and forgot to record them in QuickBooks, then on the program's Home page, click the Pay Bills icon and enter those payments (page 244).

- **Checks**. If you find that checks are not in your checkbook but you don't see check transactions in QuickBooks, chances are that you wrote a paper check and didn't record it in your company file. Create any missing check transactions in the account register (page 414) or choose Banking→Write Checks.

- **Transfers**. Create missing transfers in the account register (page 414) or choose Banking→Transfer Funds.

- **Deposits**. If you forgot to record deposits of customer payments in QuickBooks, on the program's Home page, click the Record Deposits icon to add them to your bank account (page 397). If a deposit appears on your bank statement but doesn't show up in the Payments to Deposit dialog box, you might have forgotten to receive the payment in QuickBooks. For deposits unrelated to customer payments, create the deposit directly in the account's register (page 414).

> **TIP** The easiest way to spot payments you haven't deposited in QuickBooks is to open the register window for the Undeposited Funds account (double-click it in the Chart of Accounts window). If the balance is greater than zero, you haven't deposited all the payments you received.

- **Online transactions**. If you use Online Payment or Online Account Access, download online transactions (page 571).

> **TIP** If you let several months go by without reconciling your account, don't try to reconcile multiple months at once to catch up—doing so makes discrepancies harder to spot, and locating the source of problems will tax your already-overworked brain. Instead, put your bank statements in chronological order and then walk through the reconciliation process for each statement.

Starting a Reconciliation

Reconciling an account is a two-part process, and QuickBooks has separate dialog boxes for each phase. The first phase includes choosing the account you want to reconcile, entering the ending balance from your bank statement, and entering service charges and interest earned during the statement period. Here's how to kick off a reconciliation:

1. **On the Home page, click the Reconcile icon or choose Banking→Reconcile (or Banking→Reconcile Credit Card if you have a credit card account selected in the Chart of Accounts window). In the Begin Reconciliation dialog box's Account drop-down list, choose the account you want to reconcile.**

   The Begin Reconciliation dialog box displays information about the previous reconciliation for this account, as shown in Figure 15-7. The date of the previous reconciliation appears to the right of the Account box. (No date appears if you're reconciling this account for the first time.) QuickBooks fills in the Statement Date box with a date one month after the previous reconciliation date. If that date doesn't match your bank statement's ending date, replace it with the date from your statement.

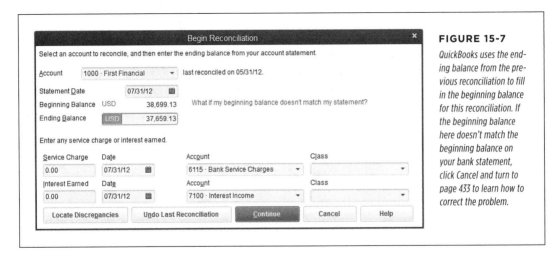

FIGURE 15-7

QuickBooks uses the ending balance from the previous reconciliation to fill in the beginning balance for this reconciliation. If the beginning balance here doesn't match the beginning balance on your bank statement, click Cancel and turn to page 433 to learn how to correct the problem.

TIP If the bank account's register window is already open, it's easier to start reconciling by right-clicking the register window and choosing Reconcile on the shortcut menu that appears (or by choosing Banking→Reconcile or Banking→Reconcile Credit Card on the QuickBooks main menu bar). With this approach, the Begin Reconciliation dialog box opens and automatically selects the active bank account.

2. **In the Ending Balance box, type the ending balance from your bank statement.**

   If you turned on multiple currencies, the account's currency appears to the right of the Beginning Balance and Ending Balance labels. For a foreign-currency account, enter the ending balance in the foreign currency, which is the ending balance that appears on your bank statement.

3. **If your bank levies a service charge on your account, in the Service Charge box, type the charge amount. (If you download transactions from your bank, leave this box blank.)**

   In the Date box to the right of the Service Charge box, choose the date that the charge was assessed if it differs from the statement ending date. In the Account box, choose the account to which you want to post the charge (usually Bank Service Charges or something similar). QuickBooks creates a transaction for you.

   TIP If you use online banking, chances are you've already downloaded your service charge and interest transactions. In that case, don't enter them in the Begin Reconciliation dialog box or you'll end up with duplicate transactions.

4. **If you're reconciling an account that pays interest, in the Interest Earned box, type the interest you earned from the bank statement.**

   As you did for the service charge, specify the date and the account that you use to track interest.

   NOTE If you track service fees and interest earned by class, in the Class boxes, choose the appropriate one. For example, classes might apply if you use them to track performance by region. However, if you use classes to track sales by partner, you don't have to specify a class for interest earned.

5. **Click Continue to start reconciling individual transactions.**

   QuickBooks opens the Reconcile window, where you reconcile the individual transactions, as described in the next section.

Reconciling Transactions

The Reconcile window groups checks and payments on the left side and deposits and other credits on the right side. (For a credit card account, charges and cash advances appear on the left side of the window—since they reduce your balance—and payments and credits appear on the right side.) Marking transactions as cleared is a matter of turning on their checkmarks, as you can see in Figure 15-8. For each transaction that appears on your bank statement, turn on the checkmark for the matching QuickBooks transaction. (If you turn on a checkmark by mistake, just click it again to turn it off.)

NOTE QuickBooks initially sorts transactions by date with the earliest transaction listed first. If you want to sort them by another field, click the column heading for that field. For example, click "Chk #" if you're trying to find the check that's preventing you from reconciling successfully. An up arrow next to the heading indicates that the column is sorted in ascending order (smallest to largest values). Click the column heading again to reverse the order (largest to smallest).

Click to toggle
checkmark on and off

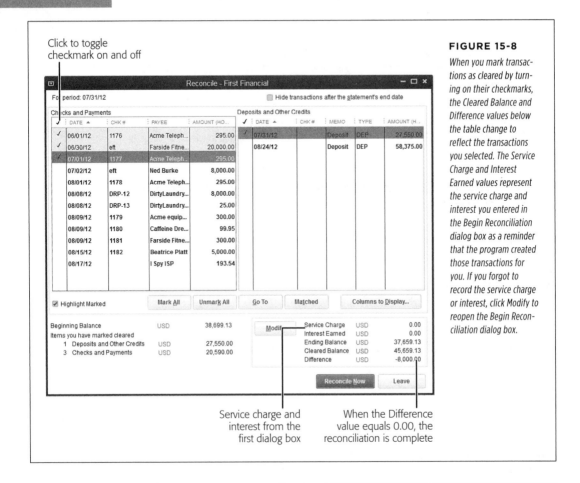

Service charge and interest from the first dialog box

When the Difference value equals 0.00, the reconciliation is complete

TIP Initially, the Reconcile window lists *all* uncleared transactions in the account regardless of when they happened. If transactions after the statement ending date are mixed in, you could select unnecessary transactions by mistake. To filter the list to likely candidates for clearing, turn on the "Hide transactions after the statement's end date" checkbox at the top right of the window. If you don't see transactions that appear on your bank statement, turn this checkbox off; you might have created a transaction with the wrong date.

QuickBooks includes several shortcuts for marking a transaction as cleared:

- **Mark All**. If you usually end up clearing most of the transactions in the list, click Mark All below the table to select all the transactions. Then, turn off the checkmarks for the ones that don't appear on your bank statement. If you were distracted and selected several transactions by mistake, click Unmark All to start over.

- **Selecting contiguous transactions**. Dragging down the checkmark column selects every transaction you pass. (This approach isn't that helpful if you compare one transaction at a time or if your transactions don't appear in the same order as those on your bank statement.)

- **Online account access**. If you've set up online banking in QuickBooks, click Matched to automatically clear the transactions that you've already matched from your QuickStatement (see Chapter 22). Enter the ending date from the printed statement, and then click OK.

When the Difference value changes to 0.00, your reconciliation is a success. To officially complete the process, click Reconcile Now. The Select Reconciliation Report dialog box opens. If you don't want to print a reconciliation report, simply click Close.

> **NOTE** When you reconcile a credit card account and click Reconcile Now, QuickBooks opens the Make Payments window. There, you can choose to write a check or enter a bill to make a payment toward your credit card balance.

WORKAROUND WORKSHOP

Adjusting an Account that Won't Reconcile

When the Difference value in the Reconcile dialog box obstinately refuses to change to 0.00, reconciling without finding the problem *is* an option. For example, if you're one penny off and you can't solve the problem with a quick review, that 1 cent isn't worth any more of your time. As you complete the reconciliation, QuickBooks can add an adjustment transaction to make up the difference.

In the Reconcile window, if you click Reconcile Now without zeroing the Difference value, QuickBooks opens the Reconcile Adjustment dialog box. The program tells you what you already know: That there's an unresolved difference between

the Ending Balance from your bank statement and the Cleared Balance in QuickBooks. If you want to try to fix the problem, click Return to Reconcile. Or click Leave Reconcile if you want to research the problem. (When you restart the reconciliation, all the work you've done so far will still be there.)

To create an adjustment transaction, click Enter Adjustment, and QuickBooks creates a general journal entry to zero out the balance. If you stumble across the source of the discrepancy later, you can either void the adjustment journal entry or create a reversing entry (page 459).

Reconciliation Reports

After you click Reconcile Now in the Reconcile window, you might notice a short delay while QuickBooks generates your reconciliation reports. These reports may come in handy as a benchmark when you try to locate discrepancies in a future reconciliation.

When the Select Reconciliation Report dialog box opens, you can display or print reconciliation reports. Choose the Summary option for a report that provides the totals for the checks and payments you made, and for the deposits and credits you received. To save the reports for future reference, click Print. Click Close to close the dialog box without printing or viewing the reports. You can look at them later by choosing Reports→Banking→Previous Reconciliation. (If you use QuickBooks

Premier or Enterprise, in the Select Previous Reconciliation Report dialog box, the Statement Ending Date box lists the dates of the previous reconciliations for the account. Click the statement ending date you want and then click Display to run the report.) Figure 15-9 shows what a detailed reconciliation report looks like.

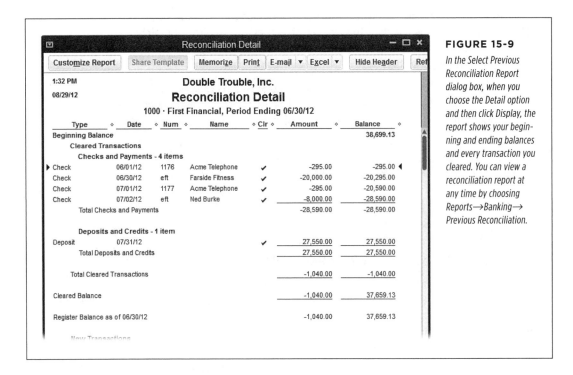

FIGURE 15-9

In the Select Previous Reconciliation Report dialog box, when you choose the Detail option and then click Display, the report shows your beginning and ending balances and every transaction you cleared. You can view a reconciliation report at any time by choosing Reports→Banking→ Previous Reconciliation.

Modifying Transactions During Reconciliation

QuickBooks immediately updates the Reconcile window with changes you make in the account register window, so it's easy to complete a reconciliation. Missing transactions? Incorrect amounts? Other discrepancies? No problem. You can jump to the register window and make your changes. Then, when you click back to the Reconcile window, the changes are there.

> **TIP** If you have opened both the register window and the reconciliation window (page 414), click the one you want to work on. If the Open Windows list appears in the navigation bar on the left side of the QuickBooks window (choose View→Open Window List if you use the top icon bar), you can click names there to change the active window or dialog box. If you use the left icon bar, click Open Windows in the bar's middle section to see the same type of list at the top of the bar; simply click the name of the window you want to work with.

Here's how to make changes while reconciling:

- **Adding transactions**. If a transaction appears on your bank statement but isn't in QuickBooks, switch to the account's register window and add the transaction (page 414).

- **Deleting transactions**. If you find duplicate transactions, in the account's register window, right-click the transaction and choose the corresponding Delete entry on the shortcut menu (or select the transaction and press Ctrl+D). When you confirm your decision and QuickBooks deletes the transaction, the transaction also disappears from the Reconcile window.

- **Editing transactions**. If you notice an error in a transaction, in the Reconcile window, double-click the transaction to open its corresponding window (Write Checks for checks, Make Deposits for deposits, and so on). Correct the mistake and then save the transaction by clicking Record or Save, depending on the window.

Stopping and Restarting a Reconciliation

If your head hurts and you need a break, don't worry about losing the reconciliation work you've already done. Here's how to stop and restart a reconciliation:

1. **In the Reconcile window, click Leave.**

   Although QuickBooks closes the window, it remembers what you've done. In the account's register window, you'll see asterisks in the checkmark column for transactions that you've marked as cleared, which indicates that your clearing of that transaction is pending.

2. **When you're reenergized, open the account's register window, right-click it, and then choose Reconcile on the shortcut menu.**

   The Begin Reconciliation dialog box opens with the ending balance, service charge, and interest amounts already filled in.

3. **Click Continue.**

   The transactions you marked are, happily, still marked. Pick up where you left off by marking the rest of the transactions that cleared on your bank statement.

Correcting Discrepancies

If you modify a transaction that you've already reconciled, QuickBooks displays a dialog box warning you that you changed a reconciled transaction and that your change will affect your reconciliation balance. After all, if you cleared a transaction because it appeared on your bank statement, the transaction is complete, and changing it in QuickBooks doesn't change it in your bank account. While you technically *can* change or delete cleared transactions in QuickBooks, doing so is usually a bad idea. (The one situation that usually calls for editing reconciled transactions is when you're trying to correct a reconciliation problem. The box on page 435 provides one example of this type of change.)

Changing previously cleared transactions is the quickest way to cause mayhem when reconciling accounts. For example, in the account register window, clicking a checkmark cell resets the status of that transaction from reconciled (indicated by a checkmark) to cleared (indicated by an asterisk), which then removes that transaction's amount from the Begin Reconciliation dialog box's Beginning Balance when you try to reconcile the account. And *that* means that the Beginning Balance won't match the beginning balance on your bank statement, which is one reason you might be reading this section. The box on page 435 explains how to perform a mini-reconciliation if the Beginning Balance is off because you deleted a reconciled transaction on purpose, and the following sections explain how to hunt down transactions that are causing discrepancies.

■ THE DISCREPANCY REPORT

If your statement and QuickBooks records don't agree and you don't know why, the Discrepancy Report can help you find the transactions that are the culprits. This report shows you changes that were made to cleared transactions, so you can restore them to their original state.

To run the Discrepancy Report, in the Begin Reconciliation window, click Locate Discrepancies, and then, in the Locate Discrepancies window, click Discrepancy Report. (You can also choose Reports→Banking→Reconciliation Discrepancy.) To edit a transaction listed in the report, double-click the transaction to open its corresponding window or dialog box.

Seeing transactions on the Discrepancy Report is a big step toward correcting reconciliation problems. Here's how to interpret the crucial columns in the report:

- **Entered/Last Modified**. This is the date that the transaction was created or modified, which doesn't help you restore the transaction but might help you figure out who's changing reconciled transactions.

- **Reconciled Amount**. This column shows the value the transaction had when you cleared it during reconciliation. If the transaction's amount has been changed, use this value to restore the transaction to its original value. For example, –99.95 in this column represents a check or charge for $99.95.

- **Type of Change**. This indicates what aspect of the transaction was changed. For example, "Amount" means that the transaction's amount changed, "Uncleared" indicates that someone removed the reconciled checkmark in the account register, and "Deleted" means that the transaction was deleted. (The only way to restore a deleted transaction is to recreate it from scratch.)

- **Effect of Change**. This value indicates how the change affected the beginning balance for your reconciliation. For example, a $99.95 check that was reset added $99.95 to your bank account. When the Beginning Balance is off and the amount in this column matches that discrepancy, you can be sure that restoring these transactions to their original states will fix your problem.

Using a Mini-Reconciliation

Suppose you recorded a transaction by using the wrong form, such as writing a check to remit your sales tax instead of using the Pay Sales Tax dialog box. Then, to make matters worse, you reconcile that incorrect transaction as part of your bank account reconciliation. If you delete the check so you can pay the sales tax using the correct QuickBooks feature, your beginning reconciliation balance won't agree with the one on your bank statement. Fortunately, you can perform a surgical reconciliation to accept your corrected transaction. Here are the steps:

1. In the bank account register window, delete the transaction that you recorded using the wrong method by right-clicking the transaction and choosing "Delete <transaction>" from the shortcut menu. (In this example, the transaction is a check to pay sales tax, so you would choose Delete Check, but it could be a check for payroll or another type of transaction). By deleting this transaction, the beginning balance for your reconciliation will be reduced by the amount of the check. Although the best approach to removing a transaction is to void it, in this case, you delete the transaction, because you'll recreate it in the next step.

2. Recreate the transaction using the correct method (in this case, by choosing Vendors→Sales Tax→Pay Sales Tax).

3. Choose Banking→Reconcile and then, in the Account drop-down list, choose the bank account you want to mini-reconcile (if it isn't already selected).

4. In the Begin Reconciliation dialog box, change the date in Statement Date box to the date on the bank statement that contains the transaction you deleted and recreated. For example, if you made your sales tax payment gaff on September 15, fill in the statement date for your September bank statement.

5. In the Ending Balance box, fill in the ending balance from the bank statement (the September statement, in this example).

6. Click Continue.

7. In the Reconcile window, find the recreated transaction in the Checks and Payments list and click its checkmark cell to turn on its checkmark. By doing so, the Difference value will change to 0.00.

8. Click Reconcile Now to complete the mini-reconciliation.

The next time you reconcile the account, the beginning balance will match the beginning balance on your bank statement.

■ OTHER WAYS TO FIND DISCREPANCIES

Sometimes, your QuickBooks records don't match your bank's records because of subtle errors in transactions or because you've missed something in the current reconciliation. Try the following techniques to help spot problems:

- **Search for a transaction equal to the amount of the discrepancy**. Press Ctrl+F to open the Find window. On the Advanced tab, in the Choose Filter list, select Amount. Next, choose the = option and type the amount in the text box, and then click Find to run the search.

  You can also use the Search feature to find a transaction for that amount: Press F3 to open the Search window. In the Amount box, type the amount of the discrepancy and then click Go.

NOTE   Using Find or Search in this way works only if the discrepancy is caused by *one* transaction that you cleared or uncleared by mistake. If more than one transaction is to blame, the amount you're trying to find is the total of all the erroneously cleared transactions, so these methods won't find a matching value.

- **Look for transactions cleared or uncleared by mistake**. Sometimes, the easiest way to find a discrepancy is to start the reconciliation over. In the Reconcile window, click Unmark All to remove the checkmarks from all the transactions. Then begin checking them off as you compare them to your bank statement. Make sure that every transaction on the statement is cleared in the Reconcile window, and that no *additional* transactions are cleared in that window.

- **Look for duplicate transactions**. If you create transactions in QuickBooks *and* download transactions from your bank's website, it's easy to end up with duplicates. And when you clear both of the duplicates, the mistake is hard to spot. If that's the case, you have to scroll through the register window looking for multiple transactions with the same date, payee, and amount.

TIP   Count the number of transactions on your bank statement, and then compare that to the number of cleared transactions displayed on the left side of the Reconcile window (Figure 15-8). Of course, this count won't help if you enter transactions in QuickBooks differently than they appear on your bank statement. For example, if you deposit every payment individually but your bank shows one deposit for every business day, your transaction counts won't match.

- **Look for a deposit entered as a payment or vice versa**. To find an error like this, look for transactions whose amounts are half the discrepancy. For example, if a $500 check becomes a $500 deposit by mistake, your reconciliation will be off by $1,000—$500 because a check is missing and another $500 because you have an extra deposit.

- **Look at each cleared transaction for transposed numbers or other differences between your statement and QuickBooks**. It's easy to type *$95.40* when you meant *$59.40*.

NOTE   If these techniques don't uncover the problem, your bank might have made a mistake. See page 437 to learn what to do in that case.

Undoing the Last Reconciliation

If you're having problems with this month's reconciliation but suspect that the guilty party is hiding in *last* month's reconciliation, you can undo the last reconciliation and start over. When you undo a reconciliation, QuickBooks returns the transactions in it to an uncleared state.

In the Begin Reconciliation dialog box (choose Banking→Reconcile), click Undo Last Reconciliation to open the Undo Previous Reconciliation dialog box. (Although the button's label and the dialog box's title don't match, they both represent the same process.) In the dialog box, click Continue. When the Undo Previous Reconciliation message box appears telling you that the previous reconciliation has been success-fully undone, click OK.

QuickBooks unclears all the transactions back to the beginning of the previous reconciliation and returns you to the Begin Reconciliation dialog box. Change the values in the dialog box, and then click Continue to try another reconciliation.

> **NOTE** Although QuickBooks removes the cleared status from all the transactions, including service charges and interest, it doesn't remove the service charge and interest transactions that it added. So when you restart the reconciliation, don't re-enter the service charges or interest in the Begin Reconciliation dialog box.

When Your Bank Makes a Mistake

Banks do make mistakes: Digits get transposed, or amounts are flat wrong. When this happens, you can't ignore the difference. In QuickBooks, add an adjustment transac-tion (page 431) to make up the difference, and be sure to tell your bank about the mistake. (It's always a good idea to be polite in case the error turns out to be yours.)

When you receive your *next* statement, check that the bank made an adjustment to correct its mistake. You can then delete your adjustment transaction or add a revers-ing journal entry to remove your adjustment and reconcile as you normally would.

> **TIP** For a reminder to check your next statement, create a To Do Note (choose Company→To Do List, and then click Add To Do).

▨ Managing Loans

Unless your business generates cash at an astonishing rate, you'll probably have to borrow money to purchase big-ticket items that you can't afford to do without, such as a deluxe cat-herding machine.

In real life, the asset you purchase and the loan you assume are intimately linked—you can't get the equipment without borrowing the money. But in QuickBooks, loans and the assets they help purchase aren't connected in any way. You create an asset account to track the purchase price of an asset that you buy. If you take out a loan to pay for that asset, you create a liability account to track the balance of what you owe on the loan. With each payment you make on the loan, you pay off a little bit of the loan's principal as well as a chunk of interest.

> **NOTE** On your company's balance sheet, the value of your assets appears in the Assets section, and the balance owed on loans shows up in the Liabilities section. The difference between the asset value and the loan balance is your *equity* in the asset. For example, suppose your cat-herding machine is in primo condition and is worth $70,000 on the open market. If you owe $50,000 on the loan, then your company has $20,000 in equity for that machine.

Most loans *amortize* your payoff, which means that each payment represents a different amount of interest and principal. At the beginning of a loan, amortized payments are mostly interest and very little principal, which means the lender gets more of its money up front, but it's also great for your company's tax deductions. By the end, the payments are almost entirely principal. Making loan payments in which the values change each month would be a nightmare if not for Loan Manager, a separate program that comes with QuickBooks that can gather information from your company file. Loan Manager calculates your loan's amortization schedule, posts the principal and interest for each payment to the appropriate accounts, and handles escrow payments and fees associated with your loans. This section explains how to use Loan Manager.

NOTE Loan Manager doesn't handle loans in which the payment covers only the accrued interest (called *interest-only loans*). For loans like these, you have to set up payments yourself (page 444) and allocate the payment to principal and interest using the values on your monthly loan statement.

Setting Up a Loan

Regardless of whether you use Loan Manager, you have to create accounts to keep track of your loan. You probably already know that you need a liability account for the amount of money you owe. But you also need accounts for the interest you pay on the loan and escrow payments (such as insurance or property tax) that you make:

- **Liability account.** Create a liability account (page 51) to track the money you've borrowed. For mortgages and other loans whose terms are longer than a year, use the Long Term Liability type. For short-term loans (ones with terms of one year or less), use the Other Current Liability type.

  When you create the liability account, forgo the opening balance. The best way to record money you borrow is with a journal entry (see Chapter 16), which credits the liability account for the loan and debits either the bank account where you deposited the money or the fixed asset account for the asset you purchased.

TIP If you've just started using QuickBooks and have a loan that you've partially paid off, fill in the journal entry with what you owed on the loan statement that's dated just before your QuickBooks company file's start date. Then, enter any loan payments you've made since that statement's ending date to get the account to the current balance.

- **Loan interest account.** The interest that you pay on loans is an expense, so create an Expense account (or an Other Expense account if that's the type of account your company uses for interest paid) called something like Interest Paid. (Loan Manager shows Other Expense accounts in its account drop-down lists, although the accounts are listed in alphabetical order, not by type.)

- **Escrow account.** If you make escrow payments for things like property taxes and insurance, create an account to track the escrow you've paid. Because escrow represents money you've paid in advance, use a Current Asset account type.

- **Fees and finance charge expense account.** Chances are you'll pay some sort of fee or finance charge at some point before you pay off the loan. If you don't have an account for finance charges you pay, set up an Expense account for them.

There's one last QuickBooks setup task to complete *before* you start Loan Manager: You have to create the lender in your Vendor List (page 91). The box below tells you what to do if you forgot to perform any of these steps before starting Loan Manager.

WORKAROUND WORKSHOP

Where Are My Accounts and Vendors?

Loan Manager looks like an item in QuickBooks' Banking menu, but it's actually a separate small program. When you start Loan Manager, it gleans information from your company file, such as the liability account you created for the loan and the vendor entry you set up for your lender.

If you forgot to create accounts or your lender in QuickBooks before launching Loan Manager, you'll probably jump to your

Chart of Accounts window or Vendor List and create them. Unfortunately, you *still* won't see those new elements in Loan Manager's drop-down lists. To get them to appear, you have to close Loan Manager (losing all the data you've already entered) and create those entries in QuickBooks. Then, after you've created the vendor and all the accounts you need, choose Banking→Loan Manager to restart Loan Manager, which now includes your lender and loan accounts in its drop-down lists.

Adding a Loan to Loan Manager

Loan Manager makes it so easy to track and make payments on amortized loans that it's well worth the steps required to set it up. Before you begin, gather your loan documents like chicks to a mother hen, because Loan Manager wants to know every detail of your loan, as you'll soon see.

■ BASIC SETUP

With your account and vendor entries complete (see page 438 and the box above), follow these steps to tell Loan Manager about your loan:

1. **Choose Banking→Loan Manager.**

   QuickBooks opens the Loan Manager window.

2. **In the Loan Manager window, click the Add a Loan button.**

   QuickBooks opens the Add Loan dialog box, which has several screens for all the details of your loan. After you fill in each screen, click Next to move to the next one.

3. **In the Account Name drop-down list, choose the liability account you created for the loan.**

   QuickBooks lists only Current Liability and Long Term Liability accounts. After you choose the correct account, Loan Manager displays the current balance for that account.

NOTE If Loan Manager shows the loan's balance as zero, you aren't off the hook for paying back the loan. Loan Manager grabs this balance from the QuickBooks liability account you created for the loan. The loan balance in Loan Manager is zero if you forgot to create a journal entry to set the liability account's opening balance. To correct this, click the Add Loan dialog box's Cancel button, and then close Loan Manager. In QuickBooks, create a journal entry to set the liability account's opening balance, and then restart Loan Manager and set up the loan.

4. **In the Lender drop-down list, choose the vendor you created for the company you're borrowing money from.**

   If you haven't set up the lender as a vendor in QuickBooks, you have to close Loan Manager. After you create the vendor in QuickBooks, choose Banking→Loan Manager to restart Loan Manager, which now shows the lender in the Lender drop-down list.

5. **In the Origination Date box, choose the origination date on your loan documents.**

   Loan Manager uses this date to calculate the number of payments remaining, the interest you owe, and when you'll pay off the loan.

6. **In the Original Amount box, type the total amount you borrowed when you first took out the loan.**

   The Original Amount box is aptly named because it's *always* the amount that you originally borrowed. For new loans, the current balance on the loan and the Original Amount are the same. If you've paid off a portion of a loan, your current balance (shown below the Account Name box in Figure 15-10) is lower than the Original Amount. If the current balance is zero, you forgot to record the money you borrowed in the liability account (page 438).

7. **In the Term boxes, specify the full length of the loan (such as 360 months for a 30-year loan) and then click Next to advance to the screen where you enter payment information (explained next).**

■ PAYMENT INFORMATION

When you specify a few details about your loan payments, Loan Manager can calculate a payment schedule for you. To make sure you don't forget a loan payment (and incur outrageous late charges), you can tell Loan Manager to create a QuickBooks reminder for your payments. Here's how:

1. **In the Due Date of Next Payment box, choose the next payment date.**

   For a new loan, choose the date of the first payment you'll make. For an existing loan, choose the date of the next payment, which usually appears on your last loan statement.

2. **In the Payment Amount box, type the total amount of your next payment including principal and interest.**

If you don't know what your payment amount is, you can find it on your loan documents. Loan Manager automatically puts 1 in the Next Payment Number box. For loans that you've made payments on already, replace this with the number of the next payment (this, too, should be on your last loan statement).

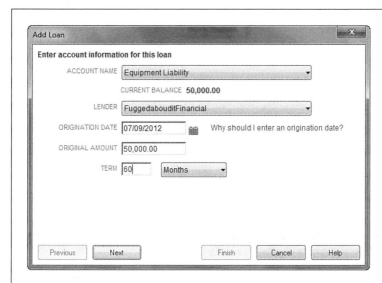

FIGURE 15-10

Loan Manager automatically selects Months in the Term drop-down list. Specifying the number of months for a 30-year loan is a great refresher for your multiplication tables, but you don't want to confuse Loan Manager by making an arithmetic error. If your loan's term is measured in something other than months, in the Term drop-down list, choose the appropriate period (such as Years). Then you can fill in the Term box with the number of periods shown on your loan documents.

3. **In the Payment Period drop-down list, choose the frequency of your payments.**

Loans typically require monthly payments, even when their terms are in years. Regardless of which period you specified in the first Add Loan screen's Term drop-down list, in the Payment Period drop-down list, choose how often you make loan payments.

4. **If your loan includes an escrow payment, choose the Yes option.**

Specify the amount of escrow you pay each time and the account to which you want to post the escrow, as shown in Figure 15-11.

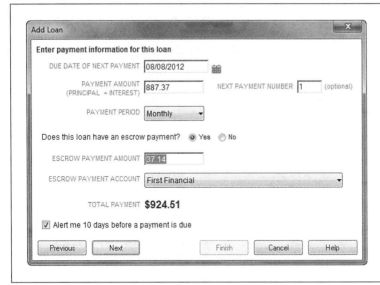

FIGURE 15-11

Most mortgages include an escrow payment for property taxes and property insurance. Escrow accounts are asset accounts because you're setting aside some money to pay expenses later. When you add an escrow payment, Loan Manager updates the Total Payment value to include principal, interest, and escrow.

5. **If you want a reminder before a loan payment is due, leave the "Alert me 10 days before a payment is due" checkbox turned on.**

   Loan Manager then tells QuickBooks how often and when payments are due, so QuickBooks can create a loan-payment reminder in its Reminders List (page 227). You can't set the number of days before a payment is due for the reminder, but 10 days is usually enough to get your payment in on time.

6. **Click Next to advance to the screen for entering interest rate information (explained next).**

■ INTEREST RATE INFORMATION

For Loan Manager to calculate your amortization schedule (the amount of principal and interest paid with each payment) you have to specify the interest rate. Here's how:

1. **In the Interest Rate box, type the loan's interest rate.**

   Use the rate that appears on your loan documents. For example, although you probably make monthly payments, the documents usually show the interest rate as an annual rate.

2. **In the Compounding Period box, choose either Monthly or Exact Days, depending on how the lender calculates compounding interest.**

   If the lender calculates the interest on your loan once a month, choose Monthly.

   If the lender calculates interest using the annual interest rate divided over a fixed number of days in a year, choose Exact Days instead. When you do, Loan

Manager activates the Compute Period box. In the past, many lenders simplified calculations by assuming that a year had 12 months of 30 days each; if your lender uses this method, choose 365/360 as the Compute Period. Today, lenders often use the number of days in a year; in that case, choose the 365/365 Compute Period option instead.

3. **In the Payment Account drop-down list, choose the account from which you make loan payments, whether you write checks or pay electronically.**

   Loan Manager includes all your bank accounts in this list.

4. **In the Interest Expense Account drop-down list, choose the account you use to track interest you pay. In the Fees/Charges Expense Accounts drop-down list, choose the account you use for fees and late charges you pay.**

   Expense accounts and Other Expense accounts are comingled in these drop-down lists, because they appear in alphabetical order, not sorted by account type.

5. **Click Finish.**

   Loan Manager calculates the payment schedule for the loan and adds it to its list of loans, shown in Figure 15-12.

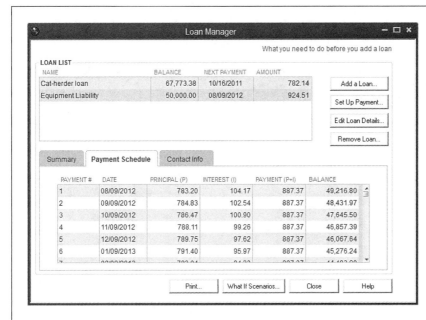

FIGURE 15-12

When you select a loan in the Loan List table, the tabs at the bottom of the Loan Manager window display information about that loan. Most of the information on the Summary tab is stuff you entered, although Loan Manager does calculate the maturity date (the date when you'll pay off the loan). The Payment Schedule tab (shown here) lists every payment and the amount of principal and interest each one represents. The info on the Contact Info tab comes directly from the lender's vendor record in QuickBooks.

Modifying Loan Terms

Some loan characteristics change from time to time. For example, if you have an adjustable-rate mortgage, the interest rate changes every so often. And your escrow payment changes based on your property taxes and insurance premiums. To make changes like these, in the Loan Manager window (choose Banking→Loan Manager), select the loan, and then click Edit Loan Details.

Loan Manager takes you through the same series of screens you saw when you first added the loan (page 439). If you change the interest rate, the program recalculates your payment schedule. For a change in escrow, the program updates your payment to include the new escrow amount.

Setting Up Payments

You can set up a loan payment check or bill in Loan Manager, which hands off the payment info to QuickBooks so the program can record it in your company file. Although Loan Manager can handle this task one payment at a time, it can't create recurring payments to send the payment that's due each month. When you see the QuickBooks reminder for your loan payment, you have to run Loan Manager to generate the payment, like so:

1. **In the Loan Manager window (Banking→Loan Manager), select the loan you want to pay and then click Set Up Payment.**

   Loan Manager opens the Set Up Payment dialog box and fills in the information for the next payment, as you can see in Figure 15-13.

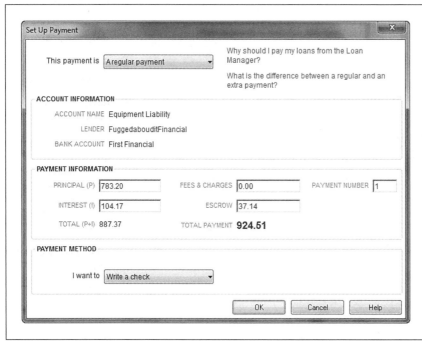

FIGURE 15-13

When you click Set Up Payment, Loan Manager fills in the Payment Information section of this dialog box with the principal and interest amounts from the loan payment schedule for the next payment that's due. It also fills in the Payment Number box with the number of the next payment due.

NOTE If you want to make an extra payment, in the "This payment is" drop-down list, choose "An extra payment." Because extra payments aren't part of the loan's payment schedule, Loan Manager changes the values in the Principal (P), Interest (I), Fees & Charges, and Escrow boxes to zero. If you want to prepay principal on your loan, type the amount that you want to prepay in the Principal (P) box. Or, if you want to pay an annual fee, fill in the Fees & Charges box.

2. **In the "I want to" drop-down list at the bottom of the window, choose "Write a check" or "Enter a bill," and then click OK.**

   Loan Manager opens the QuickBooks Write Checks or Enter Bills window, respectively, and fills in the boxes with the payment information. You can change the payment date or other values if you want.

3. **In the Write Checks or Enter Bills window, click Save & Close.**

   The window closes and you're back in the Loan Manager window, where the value in the loan's Balance cell has been reduced by the amount of principal that the payment paid off.

If you want to print the payment schedule for your loan, in the Loan Manager window, click Print. Or, if you pay off a loan and want to remove it from Loan Manager, select the loan, and then click Remove Loan. (Removing a loan from Loan Manager doesn't delete any loan transactions or loan accounts in QuickBooks.)

NOTE If your loan payments include escrow, each payment deposits the escrow amount into your QuickBooks escrow asset account. When your loan statement shows that the lender paid expenses from escrow—like insurance or property taxes—you can record the corresponding payment in QuickBooks: Open the escrow account's register window (page 414) and, in the first blank transaction, choose the date and the payee, such as the insurance company or the tax agency. In the Decrease field, type the payment amount (because the payment reduces the balance in the escrow account), and then click Record.

What-If Scenarios

Because economic conditions and interest rates change, loans aren't necessarily stable. For example, if you have an adjustable-rate loan, you might want to know what your new payment amount is. Or you might want to find out whether it makes sense to refinance an existing loan when interest rates drop. Loan Manager's What If Scenarios button is your dry-erase board for trying out loan changes before you make up your mind. When you click this button, Loan Manager opens the What If Scenarios dialog box, where you can pick from different loan scenarios depending on whether you've already created a loan:

- **How much will I pay with a new loan?** You don't have to go through the third degree to see what a loan will cost. Choose this scenario to quickly enter the key information for a loan and evaluate the payment, total payments, total interest, and final balloon payment.

- **Evaluate two new loans**. Type in the details of two loans to see which one is better.

- **What if I change my payment amount?** This scenario is listed only if you've already created a loan in QuickBooks. Paying extra principal can shorten the length of your loan and reduce the total interest you pay. Choose this scenario and then, in the Payment Amount box, type the new amount you plan to pay each month. When you click Calculate, Loan Manager calculates your new maturity date, how much you'll pay overall, and how much you'll pay in interest.

NOTE The changes you make in the What If Scenarios dialog box don't change your existing loans. And if you switch to a different scenario or close the dialog box, Loan Manager doesn't save the information you've entered. So if you want a record of different scenarios, click Print.

- **What if I change my interest rate?** If you have an adjustable-rate loan set up in QuickBooks, choose this scenario to preview the changes in payment, interest, and balloon payment for a different rate (higher or lower).

- **What if I refinance my loan?** This scenario is listed only if you've already created a loan in QuickBooks. When interest rates drop, companies and individuals alike consider refinancing their debt to save money on interest. With this scenario, type in a new term, payment, interest rate, and payment date to see whether it's worth refinancing, as shown in Figure 15-14.

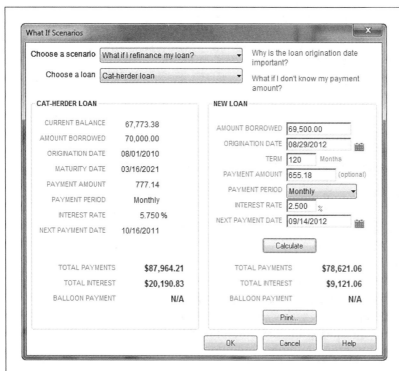

FIGURE 15-14

Loan Manager's refinance calculator doesn't provide everything you need to decide whether to refinance. Many loans come with closing costs that you should take into account. In this example, the new loan costs $78,621.06 over the life of the loan, and the current loan costs $87,964.21. But if the new loan had closing costs of $3,000, that would eat into the savings from switching loans.

■ Tracking Petty Cash

Dashing out to buy an extension cord so you can present a pitch to a potential client? Chances are you'll get money from the petty cash drawer at your office. *Petty cash* is the familiar term for money spent on small purchases, typically less than $20.

Many companies keep a cash drawer at the office and dole out dollars for small, company-related purchases that employees make. But for the small business owner with a bank card, getting petty cash is as easy as withdrawing money from an ATM. Either way, petty cash is still company money, and that means you have to keep track of it and how it's spent. The following sections explain how.

Recording ATM Withdrawals and Deposits to Petty Cash

In QuickBooks, adding money to your petty cash account mirrors the real-world transaction: You either write a check made out to Cash (or the trustworthy employee who's cashing the check), or you withdraw money from an ATM. To write a check to withdraw cash for your petty cash account, simply open the Write Checks window (choose Banking→Write Checks or, on the Home page, click the Write Checks icon). If you withdraw cash from an ATM, open the Transfer Funds window (choose Banking→Transfer Funds) instead.

If creating transactions in the account register window is OK with you, here are the steps for replenishing your petty cash with a check:

1. **In the Chart of Accounts window (press Ctrl+A to open it), double-click your checking account to open its register window.**

   QuickBooks selects the date in the first blank transaction. Depending on the date preference you choose (page 612), the program fills in either the current date or the last date you entered in a transaction. If you added money to petty cash on a different day, choose the correct date.

2. **If you're withdrawing money from an ATM, clear the value in the Number cell.**

   If you're writing a check to get petty cash and QuickBooks fills in the Number cell with the correct check number, continue to the Payee cell. Otherwise, type the correct check number in the cell.

3. **Whether you're writing a check or using an ATM, in the Payee cell, type a name such as *Cash* or *Petty Cash*.**

   If you made a check out to one of your employees, in the Payee cell drop-down list, choose that person's name.

4. **In the Payment cell, type the amount that you're moving from the checking account to petty cash.**

   If you track classes in QuickBooks, this is one time to *ignore* the Class cell. You assign classes only when you record purchases made with petty cash (as explained in the next section).

5. **In the Account cell, choose your petty cash account.**

If you don't already have a petty cash account in your chart of accounts, be sure to choose the Bank type when you create the account here by choosing <Add New>. That way, your petty cash account appears at the top of your balance sheet with your other savings and checking accounts.

6. **Click Record to save the transaction.**

That's it!

> **TIP** If you make a withdrawal from an ATM to get petty cash, use the Transfer Money feature (page 424) to record the transaction. In the Transfer Funds From box, choose your bank account; in the Transfer Funds To box, choose your petty cash account.

Recording Purchases Made with Petty Cash

As long as company cash sits in a petty cash drawer or your wallet, the petty cash account in QuickBooks keeps track of it. But when you spend some of the petty cash in your wallet or an employee brings in a sales receipt for purchases, you have to record what was bought.

The petty cash account's register is as good a place as any to record these purchases. In the Chart of Accounts window, double-click the petty cash account to open its register window. Then, in a blank transaction, follow these guidelines to record your petty cash expenditures:

- **Number cell**. Although petty cash expenditures don't use check numbers, QuickBooks automatically puts the next check number in this cell anyway. The easiest thing to do is ignore the number and move on to the Payee or Payment cell.

- **Payee cell**. You don't have to enter anything here, and for many petty cash transactions, entering a Payee would just clog your lists of names, so leave this cell blank.

- **Memo cell**. Type the vendor's name or details of the purchase here.

- **Payment cell**. Enter the amount that was spent.

- **Account cell**. Choose an account to track the expense.

> **TIP** To distribute the petty cash spent to several accounts, click Splits. In the table that appears, specify the account, amount, customer or job, class, and a memo for each split (page 260).

Petty Cash Advances

Good management practices warn against dishing out petty cash without a receipt. But suppose an employee asks for cash in advance to purchase a new lava lamp for the conference room? There's no receipt, but you really want the lava lamp to impress the CEO of a tie-dye company.

The solution in the real world is to write a paper IOU and place it in the petty cash drawer until the employee coughs up a receipt. In QuickBooks, record the advance as if the purchase were already complete. For the lava lamp, create the transaction using entries like these:

- In the Amount cell, type the amount of money you advanced to the employee.

- In the Account cell, choose the account that corresponds with the expense, such as Office Supplies.

- In the Memo cell, type a note about the employee who received the advance, the IOU in the petty cash drawer, and what the advance is for.

When the employee comes back with a receipt, you can update the transaction's Memo cell to show that the IOU has been repaid. If the employee brings change back, create a deposit to put that money back in the petty cash account.

Making Journal Entries

M ost of the time, you don't need to know double-entry accounting (page xxii) to use QuickBooks. When you write checks, receive payments, and perform many other tasks in QuickBooks, the program unobtrusively handles the double-entry accounting for you. But every once in a while, QuickBooks transactions can't help, and your only choice is moving money around directly between accounts.

In the accounting world, these direct manipulations are known as *journal entries*. For example, if you posted income to your only income account but have since decided that you need several income accounts to track the money you make, journal entries are the way to reclassify money in that original income account to the new ones.

The steps for creating a journal entry are deceptively easy; it's assigning money to accounts in the correct way that's maddeningly difficult for weekend accountants. And unfortunately, QuickBooks doesn't have any magic looking glass that makes those assignments crystal clear. This chapter gets you started by showing you how to create journal entries and providing examples of journal entries you're likely to need. However, you'll want to talk to your bookkeeper or accountant about the journal entries you need and the accounts to use in them.

NOTE In the accounting world, you'll hear the term "journal entry" and see it abbreviated JE. Although QuickBooks uses the term "general journal entry" and the corresponding abbreviation GJE, both terms and abbreviations refer to the same account register changes.

Balancing Debit and Credit Amounts

In double-entry accounting, both sides of any transaction have to balance, as the transaction in Figure 16-1 shows. When you move money between accounts, you increase the balance in one account and decrease the balance in the other—just as shaking some money out of your piggy bank decreases your savings balance and increases the money in your pocket. These changes in value are called *debits* and *credits*. If you commit anything about accounting to memory, it should be the definitions of debit and credit, because they're the key to successful journal entries, accurate financial reports, and understanding what your accountant is talking about.

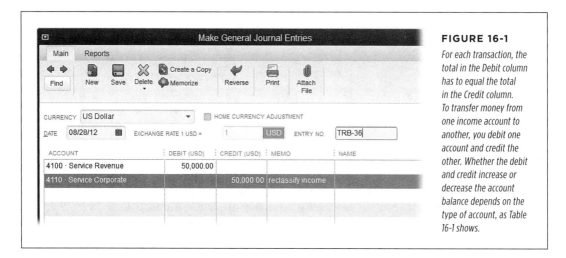

FIGURE 16-1

For each transaction, the total in the Debit column has to equal the total in the Credit column. To transfer money from one income account to another, you debit one account and credit the other. Whether the debit and credit increase or decrease the account balance depends on the type of account, as Table 16-1 shows.

Table 16-1 shows what debits and credits do for different types of accounts and can take some of the pain out of creating journal entries. For example, buying a machine is a debit to the equipment asset account because it increases the value of the equipment (assets) you own. A loan payment is a debit to your loan account because it decreases your loan balance (a liability). And (here's a real mind-bender) a credit card charge is a credit to your credit card liability account because purchases on credit increase the amount you owe.

TABLE 16-1 *How debits and credits change the values in accounts*

ACCOUNT TYPE	DEBIT	CREDIT
Asset	Increases balance	Decreases balance
Liability	Decreases balance	Increases balance
Equity	Decreases balance	Increases balance
Income	Decreases balance	Increases balance
Expense	Increases balance	Decreases balance

NOTE   One reason that debits and credits are confusing is that the words have the *exact opposite* meanings when your bank uses them. In your personal banking, a debit to your bank account decreases the balance and a credit to that account increases the balance.

As you'll see in examples in this chapter, you can have more than one debit or credit entry in one journal entry. For example, when you depreciate equipment, you can include one debit for depreciation expense and a separate credit for the depreciation on each piece of equipment.

Some Reasons to Use Journal Entries

Here are a few of the more common reasons that businesses use journal entries:

- **Setting up opening balances in accounts**. You can fill in the opening balanced for most of your balance sheet accounts with a single journal entry based on your trial balance from your previous accounting system. The box on page 457 explains how.

- **Reassigning accounts**. As you work with QuickBooks, you might find that the accounts you originally created don't track your business the way you want. For example, suppose you started with one income account for everything you sell—services and products alike. But now you want two income accounts: one for income from services and another for income from product sales. To move income from your original account to the correct new account, you debit the income from the original account and credit it to the new account, as described on page 459.

- **Correcting account assignments**. If you assigned an expense to the wrong expense account, you or your accountant can create a journal entry to reassign the expense to the correct account. If you've developed a reputation for misassigning income and expenses, your accountant might ask you to assign any transactions you're unsure about to an uncategorized income or expense account. That way, when she gets your company file at the end of the year, she can create journal entries to assign those transactions correctly. You can verify that the assignments and account balances are correct by running a trial balance report (page 484).

- **Reassigning jobs**. If a customer hires you for several jobs, that customer might ask you to apply a payment, credit, or expense from one job to another. For example, if expenses come after one job is complete, your customer might want to apply them to the job still in progress. QuickBooks doesn't have a feature to transfer money between jobs, but a general journal entry does the trick, as page 460 explains.

- **Reassigning classes**. If you use QuickBooks' class feature, journal entries can transfer income or expenses from one class to another. For example, nonprofits often use classes to assign income to programs. If you need to reassign money to a different program, create a journal entry that has debit and credit entries for the same income account, but changes the class (see page 457).

- **Depreciating assets**. Each year that you own a depreciable asset, you decrease its value in the appropriate asset account in your chart of accounts. Because no real cash changes hands, you use a journal entry to handle depreciation of assets. As you'll learn on page 461, a journal entry for depreciation debits the depreciation expense account (increases its value) and credits the asset account (decreases its value).

- **Recording transactions for a payroll service**. If you use a third-party payroll service like Paychex or ADP, the payroll company sends you reports. To get the numbers from those reports into your company file where you need them, you can use journal entries. For example, you can reclassify some of your owners' draw as salary and make other payroll-related transformations, as page 459 explains in detail.

- **Recording year-end transactions**. The end of the year is a popular time for journal entries, whether your accountant is fixing your more creative transactions or you're creating journal entries for non-cash transactions before you prepare your taxes. For example, if you run a small business out of your home, you might want to show a portion of your utility bills as expenses for your home office. When you create a journal entry for this transaction, you debit the office utilities account and credit an equity account for your owner's contributions to the company.

Creating General Journal Entries

In essence, every transaction you create in QuickBooks is a journal entry: When you write checks, the program balances the debits and credits behind the scenes. To *explicitly* create general journal entries in QuickBooks, open the Make General Journal Entries window by choosing Company→Make General Journal Entries. Or, if the Chart of Accounts window is open, right-click anywhere in the window and then choose Make General Journal Entries on the shortcut menu, or click Activities→Make General Journal Entries.

Here are the basic steps for creating a general journal entry in QuickBooks:

1. **In the Make General Journal Entries window, choose the date on which you want the general journal entry to happen.**

   If you're creating a general journal entry to reassign income or an expense to the correct account, you should use today's date. However, when you or your accountant make end-of-year journal entries—to add the current year's depreciation, say—it's common to use the last day of the fiscal year instead.

NOTE If you turn on the multiple currency preference (page 617), the Make General Journal Entries window includes boxes for the currency and the exchange rate. If you select an account that uses a foreign currency in a journal entry line, QuickBooks fills in the exchange rate and asks you to confirm that the rate is correct. If it isn't, open the Currency List (choose Lists→Currency List) and update the exchange rate for that currency.

2. **Although QuickBooks automatically assigns numbers to general journal entries, you can specify a different number by typing it in the Entry No. box.**

   When you type an entry number, QuickBooks fills in the entry number for your *next* entry by incrementing the one you typed. For example, suppose your accountant adds several journal entries at the end of the year and uses the entry numbers ACCT-1, ACCT-2, ACCT-3, and so on. When you begin using the file again, you can type a number to restart your sequence, such as DRP-8. When you create your next journal entry, QuickBooks automatically fills in the Entry No. box with DRP-9.

   Since you can type both letters and numbers in this field, you can also use it to store words that indicate the type of journal entry you're creating. For example, you can label the journal entries that record payroll transactions for your outside payroll service with PAY.

TIP If you don't want QuickBooks to number general journal entries automatically, you can turn off the automatic numbering setting in the Accounting preferences (page 599).

3. **Fill in the first line of your general journal entry, which can be either a debit or a credit. (The next section has details about filling in each field in a general journal entry line.)**

   When you click the Account cell in the next line, QuickBooks automatically enters the offsetting balance, as shown in Figure 16-2.

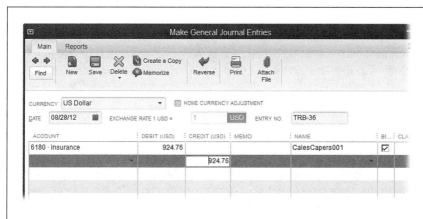

FIGURE 16-2

The total in the Debit column must match the total in the Credit column. If the first line you enter is a debit, QuickBooks helpfully enters the same amount in the Credit column in the second line, as shown here. If your first line is a credit, QuickBooks fills in the second line with the same amount in the Debit column.

4. **Fill in the second line of the general journal entry.**

If the offsetting value that QuickBooks adds to the second line is what you want, all you have to do is choose the account for that line, and then click Save & Close.

If the second line doesn't balance the Debit and Credit columns, continue adding additional lines until you've added debit and credit amounts that balance.

5. **When the debit and credit columns are the same, click Save & Close to save the general journal entry and close the Make General Journal Entries window.**

If you want to create another general journal entry, click Save & New instead.

Filling in General Journal Entry Fields

Each line of a general journal entry includes a number of fields, although for most journal entries, the key fields are Account, Debit or Credit, and Memo. But every field comes in handy at some point, so they're all worth knowing about. Here's what each field does and when you might fill them in:

- **Account**. Choose the account that you want to debit or credit. Every line of every general journal entry has to have an account assigned.

- **Debit**. To debit the account on the line, type the amount of the debit in this field.

- **Credit**. To credit the account on the line, type the amount of the credit in this field.

- **Memo**. Entering a memo is a huge help when you go back to review your journal entries. For example, if you're reclassifying an uncategorized expense, type something like "Reclassify expense to correct account." For depreciation, you can include the dates covered by the journal entry.

NOTE In QuickBooks Premier and Enterprise editions, the "Autofill memo in general journal entry" preference on the My Preferences tab, (Edit→Preferences→Accounting) tells the program to fill each subsequent Memo field with the text from the first one.

- **Name**. If you're debiting or crediting an AR or AP account, you have to choose a name, as explained in the box on page 457. However, you might also fill in this field if you're creating a journal entry for billable expenses and want to assign the expenses to a customer.

- **Billable?** This field lets you designate part of your journal entry as billable expenses. When you choose a name in the Name field, QuickBooks automatically adds a checkmark in this field, as shown in Figure 16-2, which reassigns some of your existing expenses to be billable to the customer. If you don't want to make the value billable to the customer (for example, to assign expenses to a customer's job to reflect its true profitability), then turn off the checkmark in this field.

- **Class**. General journal entries are transactions just like checks and invoices, which means that, if you use classes, you should choose a class for each line to keep your class reports accurate. If you create a general journal entry to reassign income or expenses to a different class, select the same account on each line, but different classes.

TIP You can use the Search and Find features to track down a journal entry. To use Search, choose Edit→Search. In the Search window, click Transactions and then click Journals. To use Find, choose Edit→Find (or press Ctrl+F) to open the Find window. Click the Advanced tab and then, in the window's Filter list, choose Transaction Type. In the Transaction Type drop-down list, choose Journal. Then click Find to display the journal entries you've created.

WORKAROUND WORKSHOP

Creating Opening Balances with Journal Entries

QuickBooks has rules about Accounts Payable (AP) and Accounts Receivable (AR) accounts in general journal entries. Each general journal entry can have only one AP or AR account, and that account can appear on only one line of the journal entry. And if you do add an AP account, you also need to choose a vendor in the Name field. (For AR accounts, you have to choose a *customer's* name in the Name field.)

These rules are a problem only when you want to use general journal entries to set the opening balances for customers or vendors. The hardship, therefore, is minute, because the preferred approach for building opening balances for vendors and customers is to enter bills and customer invoices. These transactions provide the details you need to resolve disputes, determine account status, and track income and expenses.

You can get around QuickBooks' AP and AR limitations by setting up the opening balances in all your accounts with a journal entry based on your trial balance (page 484) from your previous accounting system. Simply create the journal entry without the amounts for accounts payable and accounts receivable, as shown in Figure 16-3.

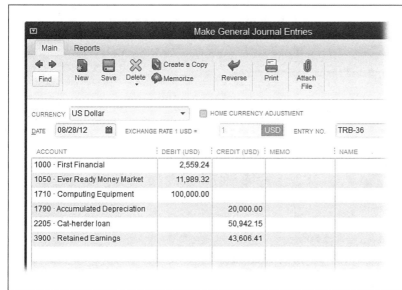

FIGURE 16-3

When you use journal entries to create opening balances, you have to adjust the values in your equity account (like retained earnings) to reflect the omission of AP and AR. Then you can create your open customer invoices and unpaid vendor bills to build the values for accounts receivable and accounts payable. When your AP and AR account balances match the values on the trial balance, the equity account will also match its trial balance value.

Checking General Journal Entries

If you stare off into space and start mumbling "Debit entries increase asset accounts" every time you create a general journal entry, it's wise to check that the journal entry did what you wanted. Those savvy in the ways of accounting can visualize debits and offsetting credits in their heads, but for novices, thinking about the changes you expect in your Profit & Loss report or balance sheet is easier.

For example, if you plan to create a journal entry to reassign expenses in the Uncategorized Expenses account to their proper expense-account homes, you'd expect to see the value in the Uncategorized Expenses account drop to zero and the values in the correct expense accounts increase. Figure 16-4 shows how to use a Profit & Loss report (see page 468) to check your general journal entries.

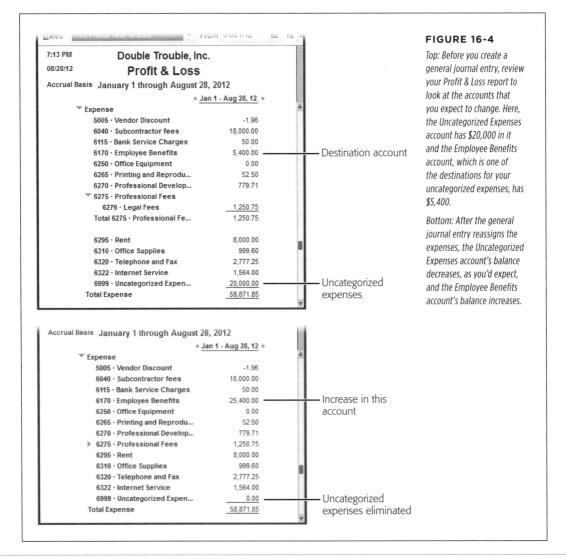

FIGURE 16-4

Top: Before you create a general journal entry, review your Profit & Loss report to look at the accounts that you expect to change. Here, the Uncategorized Expenses account has $20,000 in it and the Employee Benefits account, which is one of the destinations for your uncategorized expenses, has $5,400.

Bottom: After the general journal entry reassigns the expenses, the Uncategorized Expenses account's balance decreases, as you'd expect, and the Employee Benefits account's balance increases.

NOTE Some general journal entries affect both Balance Sheet and Profit & Loss reports. For example, as you'll see on page 461, a depreciation journal entry uses an asset account, which appears only in the Balance Sheet, and an expense account, which appears only in the Profit & Loss report. In situations like this, you have to review both reports to verify your numbers.

Reclassifications and Corrections

As you work with your QuickBooks file, you might realize that you want to use different accounts. For example, as you expand the services you provide, you might switch from one top-level income account to several specific income accounts. Expense accounts are also prone to change—when the Home Office account splits into separate accounts for utilities, insurance, and repairs, for example. Any type of account is a candidate for restructuring, as one building grows into a stable of commercial properties, say, or you move from a single mortgage to a bevy of mortgages, notes, and loans.

Reclassifying Accounts

Whether you want to shift funds between accounts because you decide to categorize your finances differently or you simply made a mistake, you're moving money between accounts of the same type. The benefit to this type of general journal entry is that you only have to think hard about *one* side of the transaction—as long as you pick the debit or credit correctly, QuickBooks handles the other side for you.

Debits and credits work differently for income and expense accounts, and Figure 16-5 shows you how to set them up for different types of adjustments.

Accountants sometimes create what are known as *reversing journal entries*, which are general journal entries that move money in one direction on one date and then move the money back to where it came from on another date. Reversing journal entries are common at the end of the year, when you need your books configured one way to prepare your taxes and another way for your day-to-day bookkeeping.

TIP It's easy enough to create two general journal entries, each using the same accounts, but with opposite assignments for debits and credits. But in QuickBooks Premier edition, the Make General Journal Entries window includes a Reverse feature in the toolbar, which automatically creates a reversing journal entry for you.

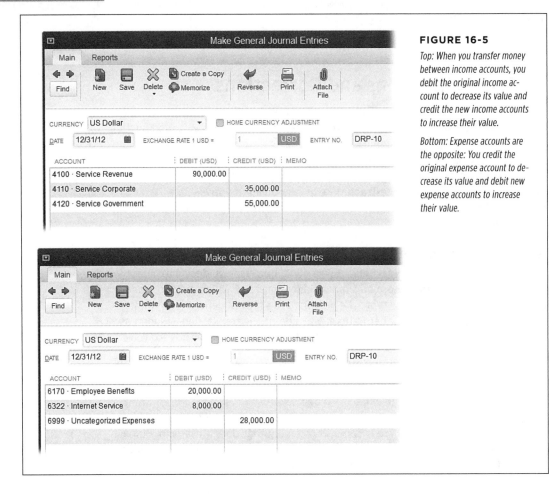

FIGURE 16-5

Top: When you transfer money between income accounts, you debit the original income account to decrease its value and credit the new income accounts to increase their value.

Bottom: Expense accounts are the opposite: You credit the original expense account to decrease its value and debit new expense accounts to increase their value.

Reassigning Jobs

If you need to transfer money between different jobs for the same customer, general journal entries are the answer. For example, your customer might ask you to apply a credit from one job to another because the job with the credit is already complete.

When you move money between jobs, you're transferring that money in and out of Accounts Receivable. Because QuickBooks allows only one AR account per journal entry, you need *two* journal entries to transfer the credit completely. (Figure 13-10 on page 382 shows what these journal entries look like.) You also need a special account to hold the credit transfers; an Other Expense account called something like Clearing Account will do. After you have the holding account in place, here's how the two journal entries work:

- **Transfer the credit from the first job to the holding account**. In the first journal entry, debit accounts receivable for the amount of the credit. (Be sure to choose the customer and job in the Name field.) This half of the journal entry removes the credit from the job's balance. In the second line of the journal entry, choose the holding account. The amount is already in the Credit cell, which is where you want it for moving the amount into the holding account.

- **Transfer the money from the holding account to the second job**. In this journal entry, debit the holding account for the money you're moving. Then the AR account receives the amount in its Credit cell. In the Name cell in the AR account line, choose the customer and the second job. This journal entry transfers the money from the holding account to the second job's balance.

Recording Depreciation with Journal Entries

When you own an asset, such as the Deluxe Cat-o-matic Cat Herder, the machine loses value as it ages and clogs with fur balls. *Depreciation* is an accounting concept, intimately tied to IRS rules, that reduces the value of the machine and lets your financial reports show a more accurate picture of how the money you spend on assets links to the income your company earns. (See the box on page 463 for an example of how depreciation works.)

Typically, you'll calculate depreciation in a spreadsheet so you can also see the asset's current depreciated value and how much more it will depreciate. But depreciation doesn't deal with hard cash, which is why you need to create a general journal entry to enter it. Unlike some other general journal entries, which can use a wide range of accounts, depreciation journal entries are easy to create because the accounts you can choose are limited. Here's how it works:

- The **debit account** is an expense account, usually called Depreciation Expense. (If you don't have a Depreciation Expense account, see page 51 to learn how to create one.)

- The **credit account** is a fixed asset account called something like Less Accumulated Depreciation. Figure 16-6 (top) shows how to set up your fixed asset accounts for things like machinery, vehicles, and furniture. You create a parent fixed asset account called Depreciable Assets and then create separate fixed asset subaccounts within Depreciable Assets so you can see the total value of all your fixed assets on your balance sheet. The Accumulated Depreciation account appears after the depreciable asset accounts at the same level as the parent Depreciable Assets, so you can see how much depreciation you're deducting, as shown in Figure 16-6 (bottom).

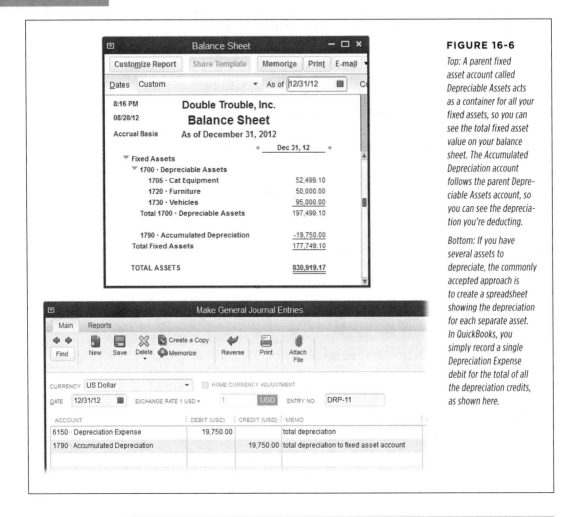

FIGURE 16-6

Top: A parent fixed asset account called Depreciable Assets acts as a container for all your fixed assets, so you can see the total fixed asset value on your balance sheet. The Accumulated Depreciation account follows the parent Depreciable Assets account, so you can see the depreciation you're deducting.

Bottom: If you have several assets to depreciate, the commonly accepted approach is to create a spreadsheet showing the depreciation for each separate asset. In QuickBooks, you simply record a single Depreciation Expense debit for the total of all the depreciation credits, as shown here.

TIP If you depreciate the same amount each year, memorize the first depreciation transaction you create (page 352). The following year, when it's time to enter depreciation, press Ctrl+T to open the Memorized Transaction List window. Select the depreciation transaction, and then click Enter Transaction.

Another way to copy a journal entry is to open the Make General Journal Entries window and then click Previous until you see the journal entry you want. Then right-click the window and choose Duplicate Journal Entry from the shortcut menu. Make the changes you want and then click Save & Close.

For a depreciation general journal entry, you want to reduce the value of the fixed asset account and add value to the Depreciation Expense account. If you remember that debit entries increase the value of expense accounts, you can figure out that the debit goes with the expense account and the credit goes to the fixed asset account. Figure 16-6 shows how depreciation debits and credits work.

UP TO SPEED

How Depreciation Works

When your company depreciates assets, you add dollars here, subtract dollars there, and none of the dollars are real. It sounds like funny money, but depreciation is an accounting concept that presents a more realistic picture of financial performance. To see how it works, here's an example of what happens when a company depreciates a large purchase.

Suppose your company buys a Deep Thought supercomputer for $500,000. You spent $500,000, and you now own an asset worth $500,000. Your company's balance sheet moves that money from your bank account to a fixed asset account, so your total assets remain the same.

The problem arises when you sell the computer, perhaps 10 years later when it would make a fabulous boat anchor. If you don't depreciate the computer, the moment you sell it, its value plummets from $500,000 to your selling price—$1,000, say. The decrease in value shows up as an expense, putting a huge dent in your profits for the 10th year. Shareholders don't like it when profits change dramatically from year to year—up or down. With depreciation, though, you can spread the cost of a big purchase over several years, which does a better job of matching expenses to the revenue generated by the asset. As a result, shareholders can see how well you use assets to generate income.

Depreciation calculations come in several flavors: straight-line, sum of the years' digits, and double declining balance.

Straight-line depreciation is the easiest and most common. To calculate annual straight-line depreciation over the life of the asset, subtract the *salvage* value (how much the asset will be worth when you sell it) from the purchase price, and then divide by the number of years of useful life, like so:

- Purchase price: $500,000
- Expected salvage value after 10 years: $1,000
- Useful life: the 10 years you expect to run the computer
- Annual depreciation: $499,000 divided by 10, which equals $49,900

Every year, you use the computer to make money for your business, and you show $49,900 as an equipment expense associated with that income. On your books, the value of the Deep Thought computer drops by another $49,900 each year, until the balance reaches the $1,000 salvage value at the end of the last year. This decrease in value each year keeps your balance sheet (page 474) more accurate and avoids the sudden drop in asset value in year 10.

The other, more complex methods depreciate your assets faster in the first few years (called *accelerated depreciation*), making for big tax write-offs in a hurry. Page 461 explains how to record journal entries for depreciation, but your best bet is to ask your accountant how to post depreciation in your QuickBooks accounts.

■ Recording Owners' Contributions

Most attorneys suggest that you contribute some cash to get your company off the ground. However, you might make a non-cash contribution to the company, like your home computer, printer, and other office equipment. Then, as you run your business from your home, you may want to allocate a portion of your mortgage interest, utility bills, homeowners' insurance premiums, home repairs, and other house-related expenses to your company. In both these situations, journal entries are the way to get money into the accounts in your chart of accounts.

TIP If you contribute cash to jump-start your company's checking account balance, simply record a deposit to your checking account (page 396) and assign that deposit to your owners' equity account.

Recording Initial Noncash Contributions

When you contribute equipment to your company, you've already paid for the equipment, so you want the value of your equipment to show up in your company file. You can't use the Write Checks window to make that transfer, but a journal entry can record that contribution:

- Credit the owners' equity account (or common stock account if your company is a corporation) with the value of the equipment you're contributing to the company.

- Debit the equipment asset account so its balance shows the value of the equipment that now belongs to the company.

Recording Home-Office Expenses

If you use a home office for your work, the money you spent on home-office expenses is already out the door, but those expenditures are equivalent to personal funds you contribute to your business. If your company is a corporation, you credit your equity account with the amount of these home-office expenses. Here's how you show this contribution in QuickBooks:

- Credit the total expenses for your home office to an equity account for your shareholders' distribution or owner's contributions to the company.

- Debit the expense accounts for each type of home-office expense, as shown in Figure 16-7.

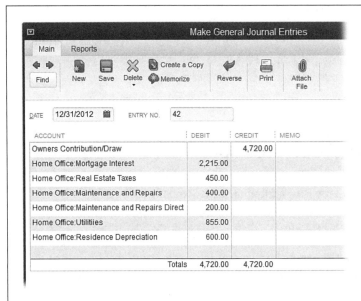

FIGURE 16-7

After you credit the owner's contribution account and debit the home-office expense accounts, your home-office expenses show up in a Profit & Loss report (page 468) and your owner's contribution appears on the Balance Sheet (page 474).

TIP Another way to handle a home office is to charge your company rent for your office space. That way you, as the homeowner, have rental property, so you can depreciate the portion of your home rented to your company. (However, this depreciation complicates things down the road when you sell your home.) If your company is a corporation, it gets to take a tax deduction for rent on its corporate tax return.

If your business is a sole proprietorship, you handle home-office expenses differently: You write business checks to pay all your home expenses. When you do that, your Profit & Loss report will show your total home expenses as business expenses. But only a percentage of those expenses are business related, so you need a way to subtract the expenses that correspond to your personal use of your home. The solution? At the end of the year, create a journal entry to reallocate the personal percentage of home expenses to your owners' draw equity account, so that only the business portion of your home expenses show up on the Profit & Loss report. Then you'll have a section in your Profit & Loss report similar to Table 16-2.

NOTE The "Maintenance and Repairs Direct" line represents expenses *directly* related to the home office, so the full amount goes toward the home-office expenses. Similarly, the Residence Depreciation line is the amount of depreciation for the portion of the home used as a home office.

TABLE 16-2 *Business expenses for a sole proprietorship*

ACCOUNT	EXPENSE AMOUNT
Business Use of Residence	This is a summary account for the accounts starting with Mortgage Interest to Other Utilities.
Mortgage Interest	$9,000.00
Real Estate Taxes	$2,250.00
Real Estate Insurance	$750.00
Maintenance and Repairs	$2,400.00
Maintenance and Repairs Direct	$200
Other Utilities	$3,200.00
Less 80.0% Personal Use	$14,080
Residence Depreciation	$1,000
Total Business Use of Residence	$4,720

Generating Financial Statements

When you keep your company's books day after day, all those invoices, checks, and other transactions blur together. But hidden within that maelstrom of figures is important information for you, your accountant, your investors, and the IRS. When consolidated and presented the right way, your books can tell you a lot about what your company does right, does wrong, could do better, and has to pay in taxes.

Over the years, the Financial Accounting Standards Board (FASB) has nurtured a standard of accounting known as GAAP (generally accepted accounting principles). GAAP includes a trio of financial statements that together paint a portrait of company performance: the income statement (also known as the Profit & Loss report), the balance sheet, and the statement of cash flows.

Generating financial statements in QuickBooks is easy. But unless you understand what these statements tell you and you can spot suspect numbers, you may simply end up generating fodder for your paper shredder. If you're new to business, get started by reading the first part of this chapter, which is about what the income statement, balance sheet, and statement of cash flows show. If you're already an expert in all that, jump to the section on generating these reports in QuickBooks (page 471).

> **NOTE** When you close out a year on your company's books, these three special financial reports are a must. You'll learn how financial statements fit into your year-end procedures in Chapter 18. If you're a business maven and need a bunch of additional reports to manage your business, Chapter 21 has instructions for finding the reports you need and customizing them to your demanding specifications.

The Profit & Loss Report

The Profit & Loss report is more like a video than a snapshot. It covers a period of time (usually a month, a quarter, or a full year) and shows whether your company is making money—or hemorrhaging it.

The money you make selling services or products (called *revenue* or *income*) sits at the top of the Profit & Loss report. Beneath it, your expenses gradually whittle away at that income until you're left with a profit or loss at the bottom. The Profit & Loss report (Reports→Company & Financial→Profit & Loss Standard) and the following list explain the progression from sales to the net income your company earned after paying the bills:

- **Income.** The first category in a Profit & Loss report is income, which is simply the revenue your company generates by selling products and services. Regardless of how you earn revenue (selling services, products, or even charging fees), the report shows all the income accounts in your chart of accounts and how much you brought into each, as shown in Figure 17-1.

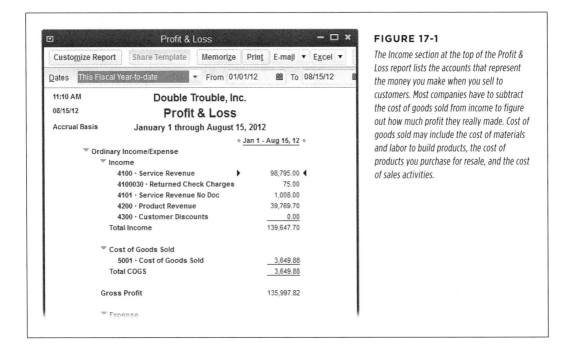

FIGURE 17-1

The Income section at the top of the Profit & Loss report lists the accounts that represent the money you make when you sell to customers. Most companies have to subtract the cost of goods sold from income to figure out how much profit they really made. Cost of goods sold may include the cost of materials and labor to build products, the cost of products you purchase for resale, and the cost of sales activities.

TIP The Profit & Loss report lists accounts in the order they appear in your company file's chart of accounts. If you want to report your income and expenses in a specific order, you can rearrange the accounts in the Chart of Accounts window (press Ctrl+A to open it). To do that, put your cursor over the diamond to the left of an account's name. When the cursor changes to a four-headed arrow, drag the account to where you want it.

- **Cost of Goods Sold**. Unless you gather rocks from your yard and then sell them as alien amulets, the products you sell carry some initial cost. For example, with products you purchase for resale, the cost of those goods includes the original price you paid for them, the shipping costs you incurred to get them, and so on. In the Profit & Loss report, the Cost of Goods Sold section adds up the underlying costs associated with your product sales.

NOTE If you don't sell inventory items, you might not have a Cost of Goods Sold section in your report. QuickBooks creates a Cost of Goods Sold account when you create your first inventory item. However, if you want to track other costs associated with selling goods—such as how much you paid for the labor required to build the products you sell, the cost of shipping, the cost of sales, and so on—you can create as many additional Cost of Goods Sold accounts as you want (page 51).

- **Gross Profit**. Gross profit is the profit you make after subtracting the cost of goods sold from your total income. For example, if you paid $60,000 to purchase equipment and then sold that equipment for $100,000, your gross profit is $40,000. The box on page 470 explains how to see whether your gross profit is in line with your industry.

- **Expense**. The next and longest section is for expenses—all the things you spend money on running your business, which are sometimes called *overhead*. For example, office rent, telephone service, and bank fees all fall into the overhead expense bucket. The name of the game is to keep these expenses as low as possible without hindering your ability to make money.

- **Net Ordinary Income**. QuickBooks uses the term "net ordinary income" to describe the money that's left over after you pay the bills. (You've probably also run across this measure referred to as *net profit* or *net earnings*.) Figure 17-2 shows the expenses and net ordinary income portions of a Profit & Loss report.

- **Other Income/Expense**. Income and expenses that don't relate to your primary business fall into this category. The most common entrants are the interest income you earn from your savings at the bank, the interest you pay on loans, and bad debt. In this category, income and expense are bundled together and offset each other. The result is called net other income. For example, if you have only a smidgeon of cash in savings but a honking big mortgage, your net other income will be a negative number.

- **Net Income**. At long last, you reach the end of the report. Net income is the money that's left after subtracting all the costs and expenses you incur. If this number is positive, congratulations—your company made money! If it's negative, your expenses were more than your income, and something's gotta give.

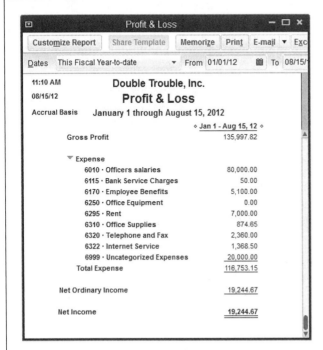

FIGURE 17-2

If your company makes more money than it spends, your net income (also called net profit) is a positive number, as shown here. Profit Profit & Loss reports don't label your result a loss when your company spends more than it makes. Instead, a loss shows up as a negative net income number, whether it's net ordinary, other, or overall net income.

Profit Percentage

There's no question that sales are important. But the *percentage gross profit* you achieve is the real test of whether you're keeping up with your competitors. Compare the ratio of gross profit to sales to see if your company is in line with your industry. For example, in construction, gross profit between 40 and 60 percent is typical. (The business reference section of your local library is a great place to find industry statistics, and many libraries offer online access to their reference materials.)

QuickBooks is happy to calculate percentage gross profit for you. Here's what you do:

1. In the Profit & Loss report window's menu bar, click Customize Report.

2. In the Modify Report: Profit & Loss dialog box, click the Display tab (if it isn't already selected).

3. Turn on the "% of Income" checkbox at the bottom right of the dialog box, and then click OK.

QuickBooks adds another column to the report showing the percentage of income that each row in the report represents, as you can see in Figure 17-3. The Gross Profit value in the "% of Income" column is your gross profit.

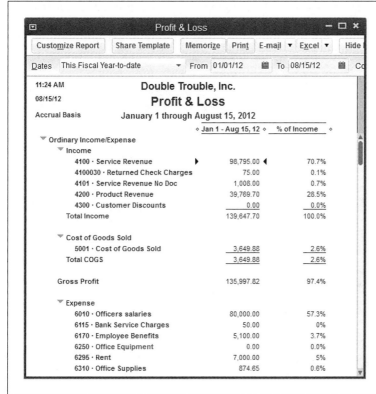

FIGURE 17-3

You can use the percentages in the "% of Income" column to analyze company performance in various ways. For example, when you're trying to find places to cut costs, look for expense accounts that take up a large percentage of your income. Or compare the percentage of net profit to the average for your industry.

Generating a Profit & Loss Report

If you choose Reports→Company & Financial, QuickBooks gives you several built-in Profit & Loss reports to choose from. Choose Profit & Loss Standard to see a month-to-date report, which, if you've built your mom-and-pop shop into a merchandising monster, might be just the one you want.

> **NOTE**   Before you generate your first financial statements, be sure that QuickBooks reports your numbers by using your company's accounting basis. The Summary Reports Basis preference (page 625) sets your reports to either accrual or cash accounting. If you choose the Cash option, your Profit & Loss reports show income only after you receive customer payments, and show expenses only after you pay bills. With the Accrual option, income appears in Profit & Loss reports as soon as you record an invoice or other type of sale, and expenses show up as soon as you enter bills.

But for many small companies, month-to-date numbers can be rather sparse. You can change the month-to-date Profit & Loss report that QuickBooks produces into a quarter-to-date or year-to-date report instead, as described in Figure 17-4. (Page 563 tells you how to save a Profit & Loss report after you tweak it to look the way you want.)

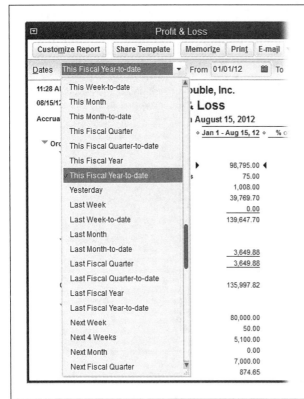

FIGURE 17-4

The Dates drop-down list includes dozens of commonly used date ranges for the current and previous fiscal year. If you choose "This Fiscal Year-to-date," for example, the dates in the From and To boxes change to the first day of your fiscal year and today's date, respectively. To select specific dates, in the From and To boxes, type or choose the dates you want.

Other Profit & Loss Reports

If the Profit & Loss Standard report described in the previous section isn't what you want, take a few minutes to see if any of the other built-in reports fit the bill. Here's a guide to the other Profit & Loss reports on the Reports→Company & Financial menu and when you might use them:

- **Profit & Loss Detail**. Only the tiniest of companies—or the most persnickety of bookkeepers—uses this report regularly. It's a year-to-date report that includes a separate line for every service and product you sold, every other charge that produced revenue, and every item on every bill you paid. It comes in handy when, for example, you restore a backup copy of your company file and want to look at your previous company file to identify the transactions you have to recreate in the restored backup.

TIP If you spot a questionable number in a Profit & Loss report, double-click the number for a closer inspection. When you put your cursor over a number, it changes to an icon that looks like a Z (for zoom) inside a magnifying glass; that's your clue that double-clicking the number will drill down into the details. For example, if you double-click a number in a Profit & Loss Standard report, QuickBooks displays a Transaction Detail By Account report that lists each transaction that contributed to the total. In a Profit & Loss Detail report, double-clicking a transaction opens the Create Invoices window (or corresponding window) so you can view that transaction.

- **Profit & Loss YTD Comparison**. This report puts the profit and loss results for two periods side by side: the current month to date and the year to date. However, most businesses compare a period to its predecessor from the previous year to see business trends more clearly, as the next report does.

- **Profit & Loss Prev Year Comparison**. If you own a gift shop or other seasonal business, you know that sales are highest during your peak season around the holidays. If you compare the last quarter of one year to the first quarter of the next, the Profit & Loss report would look pretty grim: Sales would be down and possibly exacerbated by returns from holiday purchases. To see whether your business is growing, compare your previous year to the current year with this report (shown in Figure 17-5).

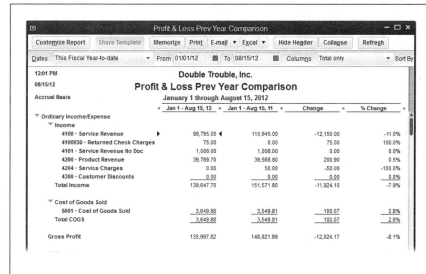

FIGURE 17-5

This report sets the Dates box to "This Fiscal Year-to-date" and shows your results for the current year in the first column and those from the previous year in the second column. If you want to see where growth is strong or stagnant, include columns that show the change in dollars or percentages (page 555). Right after your fiscal year ends, you can change the Dates box to Last Fiscal Year to compare the year you just finished to the one before it.

- **Profit & Loss by Job**. If you suspect that some of your customers and jobs are less profitable than others—and you want to learn from your mistakes—run this report. It displays each of your customers and jobs in its own column so you can compare how much profit you made for each. The box page 474 tells you how to compare apples to apples in this report.

- **Profit & Loss by Class**. If you use classes to track performance for different business units or locations, use this report to produce a Profit & Loss report for each class. It includes a column for each class. If you'd rather generate a Profit & Loss report that displays only one class, modify this report to filter for that class. The last column in this report is Unclassified, which shows all the transactions that don't have a class assignment.

- **Profit & Loss Unclassified**. Before you pretty up and print your class-based Profit & Loss reports, run this one to see the numbers for transactions without class assignments. Depending on how you use classes, unclassified transactions might be perfectly acceptable. For example, if you track income by partner, overhead expenses aren't related to individual partners. In that situation, most income accounts should have values, but some expense accounts could have zero balances.

UP TO SPEED

Comparing Profitability

Because jobs vary in size, it's hard to compare profitability by looking at the raw numbers. For example, one job may produce $50,000 in total income with $10,000 in net income. Another job also produces $50,000 in total income, but only $5,000 in net income. To see how profitable customers and jobs truly are, percentages are the answer. For example, suppose each job's total income represents 10 percent of your total income for the year. The job with $10,000 in net income may represent 15 percent of your net income, while the other job, at $5,000 net income, is only 7.5 percent.

To add columns that show the percentage that a job contributes to your overall income and profit, do the following:

1. In the Profit & Loss by Job report window's menu bar, click Customize Report.

2. In the Modify Report: Profit & Loss dialog box, click the Display tab (if it isn't already selected).

3. Turn on the "% of Income" checkbox and then click OK.

QuickBooks adds another column for each job showing the percentage of income that each number in the job column represents. The Net Income value at the bottom of the "% of Income" column shows the net profit margin for a job. That's the number you want to focus on. When a job's net income percentage is higher than the total income percentage, that customer is more profitable than average.

The Balance Sheet

If a Profit & Loss report is like a video, a balance sheet is more like a portrait. This report (Reports→Company & Financial→Balance Sheet Standard) shows how much your company owns (assets), how much it owes (liabilities), and the resulting equity in the company at a given point in time. While a Profit & Loss report tells you whether you're making money, the balance sheet helps you analyze your company's financial strength.

Understanding the Balance Sheet

One thing you can count on with a balance sheet is that there's a steady relationship among the total assets, total liabilities, and equity, as you can see in Figure 17-6. The Balance Sheet report earns its name from math, not magic; here's the formula that puts the "balance" into balance sheets:

```
Assets - Liabilities = Equity
```

As you buy more or borrow more, the value of your equity changes to make up the difference between the value of your assets and liabilities. Another way to look at this equation is that your asset value equals the sum of your liabilities and equity.

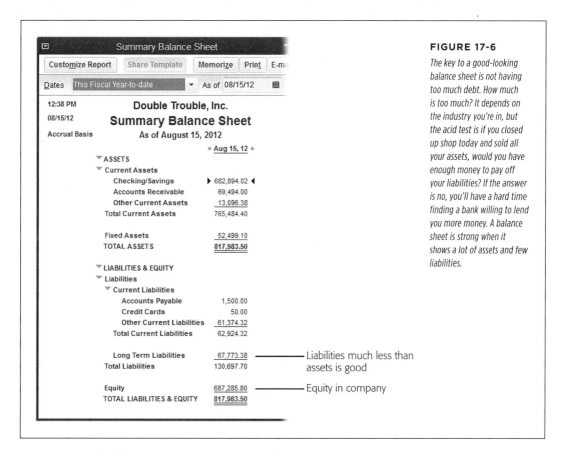

FIGURE 17-6

The key to a good-looking balance sheet is not having too much debt. How much is too much? It depends on the industry you're in, but the acid test is if you closed up shop today and sold all your assets, would you have enough money to pay off your liabilities? If the answer is no, you'll have a hard time finding a bank willing to lend you more money. A balance sheet is strong when it shows a lot of assets and few liabilities.

Here's what to look for in each section of a balance sheet:

- **Assets**. Assets are things of value that a company owns, such as equipment, land, product inventory, accounts receivable, cash, and even brand names. On a balance sheet, you want to see significantly more money in the Assets section than in the Liabilities section.

NOTE Even with assets, you can have too much of a good thing. Assets aren't corporate collectors' items—companies should use assets to make money. A measure called *return on assets* (the ratio of net income to total assets) shows whether a company is using assets effectively to produce income. Return on assets varies from industry to industry, but, typically, less than 5 percent is poor.

- **Liabilities**. Liabilities include accounts payable (bills you haven't yet paid), un-paid expenses, loans, mortgages, and even future expenses such as pensions. Debt on its own isn't bad; it's *too much* debt that can drag a company down, particularly when business is slow, since debt payments are due every month whether your business produced revenue or not.

- **Equity**. Equity on a balance sheet is the corporate counterpart of the equity you have in your house. When you buy a house, your initial equity is the down payment you make. But both the decreasing balance on your mortgage and any increase in the value of your house contribute to an increase in your equity. Equity in a company is the dollar value that remains after you subtract liabilities from assets.

Generating a Balance Sheet Report

A balance sheet is a snapshot of accounts on a given date. The various built-in Balance Sheet reports that QuickBooks offers differ in whether they show only account balances or all the transactions that make up those balances. Choose Reports→Company & Financial, and you can pick from any of the following reports:

- **Balance Sheet Standard**. This report includes every asset, liability, and equity account in your chart of accounts except for ones with zero balances, as shown in Figure 17-6. QuickBooks automatically sets the Dates box to "This Fiscal Year-to-date" so the report shows your balance sheet for the current date. If you want to see the balance sheet for the end of a quarter or end of the year, in the Dates box, choose This Fiscal Quarter, This Fiscal Year, or Last Fiscal Year.

- **Balance Sheet Detail**. This report shows the transactions over a period in each of your asset, liability, and equity accounts. If a number on your Balance Sheet Standard report looks odd, use this report to verify your transactions. Double-click a transaction's value to open the corresponding window, such as Enter Bills.

- **Balance Sheet Summary**. If you want to see the key numbers in your balance sheet without scanning past the individual accounts in each section, this report shows subtotals for each category of a balance sheet.

- **Balance Sheet Prev Year Comparison**. If you want to compare your financial strength from year to year, this report has four columns at your service: one each for the current and previous years, one for the dollar change, and the fourth for the percentage change.

NOTE When you review your Balance Sheet Prev Year Comparison report, you typically want to see decreasing liabilities. If liabilities have *increased*, then assets should have increased as well, because you don't want to see more debt without more assets to show for the trouble. Equity is the value of your—and your shareholders'—ownership in the company, so it should increase each year. (If you use QuickBooks to keep the books for your one-person consulting company, the equity may not increase each year if, for example, you don't have many company assets and you withdraw most of the profit you make as your salary.)

- **Balance Sheet by Class**. This report lists your asset, liability, and equity accounts, and includes a column for each class. However, to obtain accurate results from this report, you have to enter transactions in a specific way (for example, using only one class in each transaction, and recording transactions using QuickBooks features like Create Invoices and Receive Payments). To learn more about this report, search QuickBooks Help for "balance sheet by class report."

The Statement of Cash Flows

Thanks to noncash accounting anomalies like accrual reporting and depreciation, Profit & Loss reports don't tell you how much cash you have on hand. Looking at your cash flow helps you figure out whether your company generates enough cash to keep the doors open. Your balance sheet might look great—$10 million in assets and only $500,000 in liabilities, say—but if a $50,000 payment is due and you have only $3,000 in the bank, you have cash flow problems.

Understanding the Statement of Cash Flows

The concept of cash flow is easy to understand. In the words of every film-noir detective, follow the money. Cash flow is nothing more than the real money that flows in and out of your company—not the noncash transactions, such as depreciation, that you see on a Profit & Loss report. Figure 17-7 shows sources of cash in a sample Statement of Cash Flows.

WARNING When you sell an asset (which is an investing activity), it shows up as a gain or loss on the Profit & Loss report, which *temporarily* increases or reduces your net income. Beware: The effect of investing activities on the Profit & Loss report can hide problems brewing in your operations, which is why you should examine the Statement of Cash Flows report. If your income derives mainly from investing and financing activities instead of operating activities, you've got a problem.

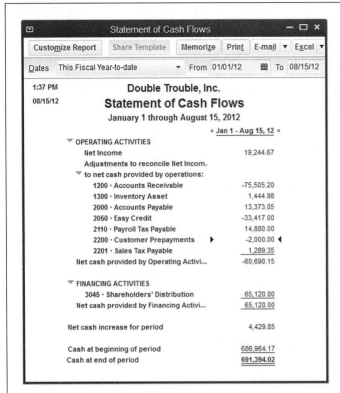

FIGURE 17-7

A Statement of Cash Flows report organizes transactions into various activity categories. Cash from operating activities is the most desirable; when a company's ongoing operations generate cash, the business can sustain itself without cash coming from other sources. Buying and selling buildings or making money in the stock market by using company money are investing activities. Borrowing money or selling stock in your company brings in cash from outside sources, called financing activities. (New companies often have no other source of cash.)

Generating a Statement of Cash Flows

To create a Statement of Cash Flows, QuickBooks automatically assigns the accounts that appear in your company's balance sheet to one of the three cash flow categories—operating, investing, or financing—and the program almost always gets those assignments right. For example, Accounts Receivable and Inventory appear as operating accounts, fixed asset accounts show up as investing, and accounts for loans fall under financing. Unless you're a financial expert or your accountant gives you explicit instructions about a change, you're better off leaving QuickBooks' account classifications alone. If you need to reassign accounts for your Statement of Cash Flows report, this section tells you how.

Generating a Statement of Cash Flows is easy because you have only one report to choose from. Simply choose Reports→Company & Financial→Statement of Cash Flows, and QuickBooks creates a report like the one shown in Figure 17-7, displaying your cash flow for your fiscal year to date. To view the Statement of Cash Flows report for a quarter or a year, in the Dates box, choose This Fiscal Quarter or This Fiscal Year.

NOTE The Operating Activities section of the report includes the label "Adjustments to reconcile Net Income to net cash provided by operations." If you're wondering what that means in non-accounting language, QuickBooks calculates the net income at the top of the Statement of Cash Flows report on an accrual basis (meaning income appears as of the invoice date, not the day the customer pays). But the Statement of Cash Flows is by nature a cash-based report, so the program has to add and subtract transactions to get net income on a cash basis.

The account assignments for the Statement of Cash Flows report are controlled by a collection of preferences you can find in the Preferences dialog box. Here's how to view the account assignments or change them:

1. **In the Statement of Cash Flows report window's toolbar, click the Classify Cash button.**

   The Preferences dialog box opens to the Reports & Graphs section and selects the Company Preferences tab (as long as you have QuickBooks administrator privileges, that is). You can also open this dialog box by choosing Edit→Preferences→Reports & Graphs.

2. **Click the Classify Cash button.**

   QuickBooks opens the Classify Cash dialog box. As Figure 17-8 explains, this is where you change your account categories.

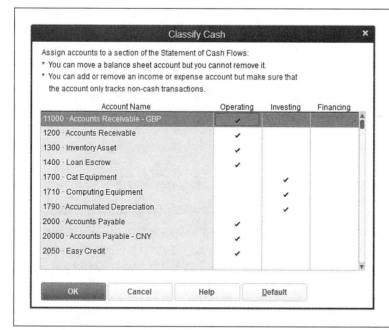

FIGURE 17-8

To change the category to which an account belongs, click the cell in the column for the new category. If you made changes and fear you've mangled the settings beyond repair, click Default to reset the categories to the ones QuickBooks used initially.

3. **When the assignments are the way you want, click OK to close the dialog box.**

   That's it—you've reassigned the accounts.

Expert Cash Flow Analysis

Thanks to today's accounting rules, cash isn't always connected to revenues and expenses. And a dollar in sales isn't necessarily a dollar of cash. Here's what financial analysts look for when they evaluate a company's health based on its statement of cash flows:

- Net income on the Profit & Loss report that's close to the cash from operating activities means net income is mostly from business operations and the company can support itself.

- Cash from operations that's growing at the same rate or faster than the growth of net income indicates that the company is maintaining—or even improving—its ability to sustain business.

- Cash that's increasing means the company won't have to resort to financing to keep the business going.

- Negative cash flow is often the sign of a rapidly growing company—without financing, the company grows only as fast as it can generate cash from operations. If a company isn't growing quickly and *still* can't generate cash, something's wrong.

- If an increase in cash comes primarily from selling assets, the company's future looks grim. Selling assets to raise cash sometimes means the company can't borrow any more because banks don't like what they see. Because assets often produce sales, selling assets means less cash generated in the future—and you can see where that leads.

Other Helpful Financial Reports

Although financial statements are the ones that people like shareholders and the IRS want to see, other financial reports help you, the business owner, keep tabs on how your enterprise is doing. Here are a few QuickBooks reports that can help you evaluate your business's performance:

NOTE Reports that apply to specific bookkeeping and accounting tasks are explained in the chapters about those tasks, such as accounts receivable reports in Chapter 13.

- **Reviewing income and sales.** If you're introducing enhanced services to keep your best customers—or you're looking for the customers you *want* your competition to steal—use the Income by Customer Summary report (Reports→Company & Financial→Income by Customer Summary). It shows total income for each of your customers; that is, the total dollar amount from all of a customer's invoices and statement charges. Customers with low income totals might be good targets for more energetic sales pitches. If you find that most of your income comes from only a few customers, you may want to protect your income stream by lining up more customers. (One thing this report *doesn't* show is how profitable your sales to customers are; the box on page 474 explains how to see that.)

TIP   If you want to produce a report showing performance over several years to evaluate trends, you can set a report's date range to include the years you want to compare. Then modify the report as explained on page 555 to include columns for each year.

- **Reviewing expenses.** On the expense side, the Expenses by Vendor Summary report (Reports→Company & Financial→Expenses by Vendor Summary) shows how much you spend with each vendor. If you spend tons with certain vendors, maybe it's time to negotiate volume discounts, find additional vendors as backups, or set up electronic ordering to speed up deliveries.

- **Comparing income and expenses.** The Income & Expense Graph (Reports→Company & Financial→Income & Expense Graph) includes a bar graph that shows income and expenses by month and a pie chart that breaks down either income or expenses (click Income or Expense at the bottom of the report's to choose which pie chart is displayed). To specify how income or expense is broken down, click By Account, By Customer, or By Class in the window's icon bar. You can't change the time periods for each set of bars on the graph.

- **What you've sold.** Most companies analyze their sales to find ways to improve. Maybe you want to beef up sales to customers who haven't bought from you in a while, turn good customers into great ones, or check how well your stuff is selling. The Sales by Customer Summary report (Reports→Sales→Sales by Customer Summary) is a terse listing of customers and how much you've sold to each one during the timeframe you specify; it initially shows "This Month-to-date" figures.

  The Sales Graph (Reports→Sales→Sales Graph), on the other hand, presents sales data in a cheery rainbow of colors, and you can quickly switch the graph to show the breakdown of sales by customer, item, and sales rep. The bar graph shows sales by month for the year to date. If you want to change the duration covered by the graph, click Dates and specify the date range you want. The pie chart shows sales slices based on the category you choose. In the window's toolbar, click By Item, By Customer, or By Rep to switch between seeing pie slices for items, customers, or sales reps.

  The Sales by Item Summary report (Reports→Sales→Sales by Item Summary) shows how much you sell of each item in your Item List, starting with inventory items, then non-inventory parts, and finally service items. This report includes a column for average cost of goods sold (COGS) and gross margin, which apply only to inventory items you sell.

- **Forecasting cash flow.** You may be wondering whether you have any invoices due that will cover a big credit card bill that's coming up or whether income over the next few weeks is enough to meet payroll. At times like that, use the Cash Flow Forecast report (Reports→Company & Financial→Cash Flow Forecast) to see how much cash you should have over the next four weeks, as shown in Figure 17-9. The Beginning Balance line shows the current balance for your Accounts Receivable, Accounts Payable, and bank accounts. The Proj Balance column shows how much money you should have in your bank accounts at the end of each week (or longer if you choose a different period in the Periods drop-down list). If a number in the column starts flirting with zero, you're about to run out of cash. You'll have to speed up some customer payments, transfer cash from another account, or look into a short-term loan.

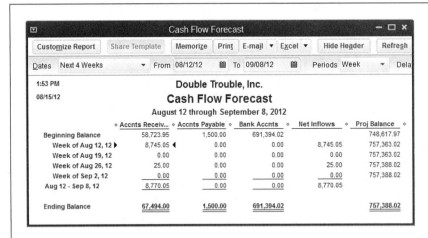

FIGURE 17-9

To view more than four weeks, type the date range you want in the From and To boxes or, in the Dates drop-down list, choose Next Fiscal Quarter or Next Fiscal Year. To change the length of each period in the report, in the Periods drop-down list, choose from Week, Two Weeks, Month, and so on.

Realized Gains and Losses

If you work with more than one currency, changes in exchange rates can lead to gains or losses on your transactions. Say you send a customer an invoice for €1,000 when the euro-to-dollar exchange rate is 1.459 (that is, 1 euro equals 1.459 dollars). The invoice total in your home currency (dollars, in this example) is $1,459. However, by the time you deposit the customer's payment, the euro-to-dollar exchange rate is 1.325, which means each euro is worth fewer dollars. At that exchange rate, your bank records a deposit of $1,325 in your account, and you've lost $134 on the transaction.

To see how much you've gained or lost on foreign currency transactions, choose Reports→Company & Financial→Realized Gains & Losses. To see *potential* gains or losses based on the latest exchange rate, choose Reports→Company & Financial→Unrealized Gains & Losses. In the Enter Exchange Rates dialog box, type the exchange rates you want to apply. When you click Continue, the Unrealized Gains & Losses report shows gains and losses for the balances in your AR and AP accounts.

To report your financial results accurately, you have to adjust the value of accounts set up in foreign currencies (page 482) based on the exchange rate as of the end date for the report. You can download the most recent exchange rates by choosing Company→Manage Currency→Download Latest Exchange Rates. Or, to find exchange rates for a given date, point your web browser to *www.xe.com/ict*. Then, in QuickBooks, you can choose Lists→Currency List and edit the currencies to enter the exchange rates you found online.

To adjust account values, choose Company→Manage Currency→Home Currency Adjustment. In the Home Currency Adjustment window, select the date for the adjustment, and then pick the currency and the exchange rate you want to use. Click Calculate Adjustment, and customers and vendors who use that currency appear in the window's table. Select the ones you want to adjust, and then click Save & Close.

Performing End-of-Year Tasks

As if your typical workday isn't hectic enough, the end of the year brings an assortment of additional bookkeeping and accounting tasks. As long as you've kept on top of your bookkeeping during the year, you can delegate most of these year-end tasks to QuickBooks with a few mouse clicks. (If you shrugged off your data entry during the year, even the mighty QuickBooks can't help.) This chapter describes the tasks you have to perform at the end of each fiscal year (or other fiscal period, for that matter) and how to delegate them to QuickBooks. (The box on page 484 describes a QuickBooks feature that helps you remember these various tasks.)

■ Checking for Problems

If you work with an accountant, you may never run a report from the Reports→ Accountant & Taxes submenu unless your accountant asks you to. But if you prepare your own tax returns, running the following reports at the end of each year will help sniff out any problems:

- Run the **Audit Trail** report, especially if several people work on your company file, to watch for suspicious transactions, like deleted invoices or modifications to transactions after they've been reconciled. People make mistakes, and this report is also good for spotting inadvertent changes to transactions. Quick-Books initially includes only transactions entered or modified today, but you can choose a different date range to review changes since your last review (in the Audit Trail report's window, choose a date range in the Date Entered/Last Modified drop-down list, or type dates in the From and To boxes).

- The **Voided/Deleted Transactions Summary** and **Voided/Deleted Transactions Details** reports focus on transactions that—you guessed it—have been voided or deleted.

NOTE The QuickBooks Accountant edition (page xxi) has a host of features that help accountants and bookkeepers spiff up your books at the end of the year. For example, the Client Data Review tool lists review and cleanup tasks to perform. If your accountant finds any issues, she can add notes about what she plans to do. If you didn't classify transactions correctly, your accountant can use the Reclassify Transactions features to correct classifications in a jiffy.

GEM IN THE ROUGH

QuickBooks' Year-End Guide

QuickBooks Help contains a guide to typical year-end tasks, which is especially handy if you aren't familiar with what you have to do to wrap up a year for your business. When you choose Help→Year-End Guide, the program opens a special browser window displaying the Year-End Guide (Figure 18-1). It includes a list of activities related to general tax preparation and end-of-year dealings with subcontractors or employees. You may find some end-of-year tasks you didn't know you had!

The first time you view the guide, turn on the checkmarks for each issue that pertains to your organization. Since the guide is an HTML document, it works just like a web page. If you need help with the steps for an activity, click its link to open the corresponding QuickBooks Help topic. Click Save Checkmarks to make QuickBooks remember your choices—a handy reminder of your to-do list for the next fiscal year.

Viewing Your Trial Balance

The *Trial Balance* report is named after the report's original purpose: totaling the balances of every account in the debit and credit columns to see whether the pluses and minuses balanced. If they didn't, the bookkeeper had to track down the mistakes and try again.

QuickBooks doesn't make arithmetic mistakes, so you don't need a trial balance to make sure that debits and credits match. Nonetheless, the Trial Balance report is still handy. Accountants like to examine it for errant account assignments before diving into tax preparation or giving financial advice—and for good reason: The Trial Balance report is the only place in QuickBooks where you can see all your accounts *and* their balances in the same place, as shown in Figure 18-2.

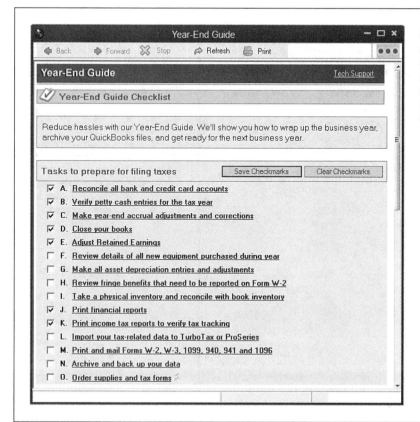

FIGURE 18-1

Click Save Checkmarks to store your choices. That way, when you open the Year-End Guide again next fiscal year, the checkmarks will be there to remind you of your to-do list.

To display this report, choose Reports→Accountant & Taxes→Trial Balance. Quick-Books then generates a Trial Balance report for the previous month. If you want to see the trial balance for your entire fiscal year, choose This Fiscal Year in the Dates box. The accounts appear in the same order that they're listed in the Chart of Accounts window (page 47).

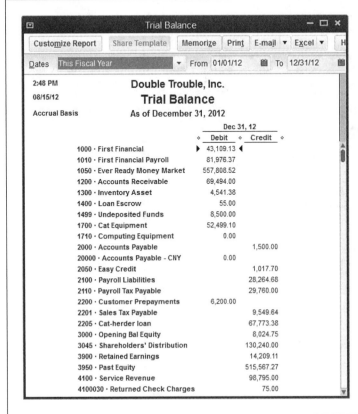

FIGURE 18-2

If the account balances in your Trial Balance report look a little off, check the heading at the report's top left. If you see the words "Accrual Basis" in the heading but you use cash accounting for your business (see page 625 to learn how to set this preference), you've found the culprit. The same goes if the heading says "Cash Basis" but you use accrual accounting. To set things right, click Customize Report in the report window's menu bar. In the Modify Report dialog box that appears, on the Display tab, choose the Accrual or Cash option, and then click OK.

Generating Year-End Financial Reports

At the end of every year, tax preparation stimulates a frenzy of financial reporting as companies submit fiscal-year Profit & Loss reports and balance sheets as part of their tax returns. But tax forms aren't the only reason to run year-end reports before you hand over your company file to your accountant or prepare final reports for your tax return.

Run year-end reports for these reasons, too:

- If you work with more than one currency, adjust account balances to reflect the currencies' current values based on exchange rates (page 482 explains how).

- Inspect year-end reports for funny numbers. They might mean that you posted a transaction to the wrong account or created a journal entry incorrectly.

- Analyze your annual results to spot problems with your operations or to look for ways to improve.

After you complete your initial review of the year-end reports and make any corrections to transactions, generate a revised set of year-end reports. (Chapter 17 has the full scoop on generating financial statements.) Then your accountant (if you work with one) is next in line to see your company file (page 490).

FREQUENTLY ASKED QUESTION

Net Income and Retained Earnings

I just changed the date on my Balance Sheet report from December 31 of last year to January 1 of this year, and the Net Income and Retained Earnings numbers are different. What's the deal?

At the end of a fiscal year, account balances go through some changes to get your books ready for another year of commerce. For example, at the end of one fiscal year, your income and expense accounts show how much you earned and spent during that year. But come January 1 (or whatever day your fiscal year starts), all those accounts have to be zero so you can start your new fiscal year fresh. QuickBooks makes this happen by adjusting your net income behind the scenes.

Say your net income on the Profit & Loss report is $18,276.97 on December 31, 2012. That number appears at the bottom of the Balance Sheet report as the value of the Net Income account (in the Equity section). At the beginning of the new

fiscal year, QuickBooks automatically moves the previous year's net income into the Retained Earnings equity account, which resets the Net Income account to zero.

Some companies like to keep equity for the current year separate from the equity for all previous years. To do that, you need one additional equity account and one simple journal entry. Create an equity account (page 52) called something like Past Equity with an account number greater than the one you use for Retained Earnings. (For example, if Retained Earnings is 3900, set Past Equity to 3950.) Then, when you close your books at the end of the year, create a journal entry to move the current value ($14,209.11 in this example) from the Retained Earnings account to the Past Equity account. That way, when QuickBooks moves the current year's net income into the Retained Earnings equity account, you can see both current and past equity values, as shown in Figure 18-3.

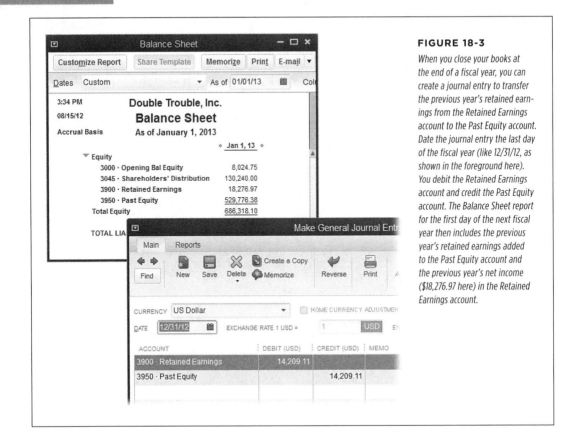

FIGURE 18-3

When you close your books at the end of a fiscal year, you can create a journal entry to transfer the previous year's retained earnings from the Retained Earnings account to the Past Equity account. Date the journal entry the last day of the fiscal year (like 12/31/12, as shown in the foreground here). You debit the Retained Earnings account and credit the Past Equity account. The Balance Sheet report for the first day of the next fiscal year then includes the previous year's retained earnings added to the Past Equity account and the previous year's net income ($18,276.97 here) in the Retained Earnings account.

Generating Tax Reports

Whether your accountant has the honor of preparing your taxes or you keep that excitement for yourself, you can save accountant's fees and your own sanity by making sure your company file is ready for tax season. The key to a smooth transition from QuickBooks to tax preparation is linking each account in your chart of accounts to the correct tax line and tax form.

Reviewing the Income Tax Preparation report (Reports→Accountant & Taxes→Income Tax Preparation) can not only save you money on accountant's fees, but it can also prevent IRS penalties (as well as keep more of your hair attached to your scalp). As shown in Figure 18-4, this report lists the accounts in your chart of accounts and shows the tax lines to which you assigned them. If an account isn't linked to the correct tax line—or worse, not assigned to *any* tax line—the Income Tax Summary report, which lists each line on your tax return with the amount you have to report, won't display the correct values. See page 56 to learn more about choosing tax lines for accounts.

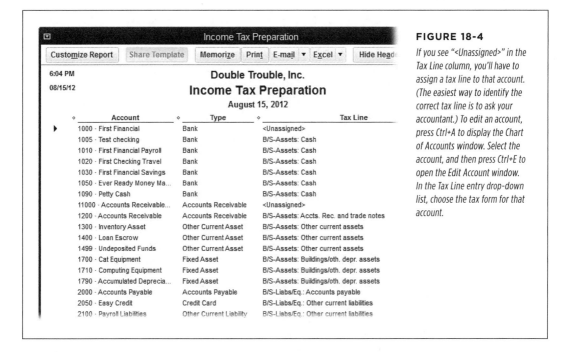

FIGURE 18-4

If you see "<Unassigned>" in the Tax Line column, you'll have to assign a tax line to that account. (The easiest way to identify the correct tax line is to ask your accountant.) To edit an account, press Ctrl+A to display the Chart of Accounts window. Select the account, and then press Ctrl+E to open the Edit Account window. In the Tax Line entry drop-down list, choose the tax form for that account.

When all the accounts in your chart of accounts are assigned to tax lines, you can generate a report with all the values you need for your company's tax return. Choose Reports→Accountant & Taxes→Income Tax Summary. Because you usually run this report after the fiscal year ends and all the numbers are in, QuickBooks automatically fills in the Dates box with Last Tax Year.

NOTE As one last reminder of unassigned accounts, the last two lines of the Income Tax Summary report are "Tax Line Unassigned (balance sheet)" and "Tax Line Unassigned (income/expense)." To see the transactions that make up one of these unassigned values, double-click the number in the corresponding line.

Year-End Journal Entries

Journal entries run rampant at the end of the year. If your accountant makes journal entries for you or gives you instructions, you might be perfectly happy not knowing what these journal entries do. But if you go it alone, you need to know which journal entries to make.

For example, if you purchase fixed assets, you need to create a general journal entry to handle depreciation. You might also create journal entries to record home-office expenses as owners' contributions to your company.

If you aren't an accounting expert, don't waste precious time trying to figure out your journal entry needs; the cost of an accountant's services is piddling in comparison. Once you know what journal entries you need, Chapter 16 explains how to create them.

Sharing a Company File with Your Accountant

If you work with an accountant who uses QuickBooks, there are times when a tug-of-war over your company file is inevitable. You want to perform your day-to-day bookkeeping, but your accountant wants to review your books, correct mistakes you've made, enter journal entries to prepare your books for end-of-quarter or end-of-year reports, and so on. QuickBooks has two ways for you and your accountant to share:

- With an **accountant's review copy**, the two of you can stop squabbling because you each get your own copy of the company file. That way you can work on everyday bookkeeping tasks while your accountant tackles cleaning up earlier periods.

- The **external accountant user** is a super-powered user who can look at anything in your company file—except sensitive customer information like credit card numbers. You set up an external accountant user in your company file for your accountant so he can log into your file, review every nook and cranny of your company's data (with QuickBooks' Client Data Review tool designed specially for accountants), make changes, and keep track of which changes are his and which are yours.

This section explains both these approaches.

Creating an Accountant's Review Copy

The secret to an accountant's review copy is a cutoff date that QuickBooks calls the *dividing date*. Transactions before this date are fair game for your accountant, who can work in the comfort of his own office. Transactions after that date are under your command in your original company file. When your accountant sends a file with changes back to you, the program makes short work of merging his changes into your company file. The box below describes other ways you can collaborate with your accountant.

Ways to Work with an Accountant

For most companies, QuickBooks is no substitute for an accountant. As financial professionals, accountants have the inside track on how best to handle your business finances. In addition to (or instead of) giving your accountant a review copy of your company file, here are other ways you can integrate your accountant's advice into your company file:

- **A backup or portable copy**. You can give your accountant *exclusive* access to your company file by sending her a backup or portable copy (page 187) of the file. When she finishes evaluating your books and making the changes she wants, you can either begin using the copy she sends back to you or make adjustments in your company file based on her recommendations. For example, your accountant can send you a document listing the journal entries you have to create to adjust your accounts along with copies of what your income statement and balance sheet should look like. After you create those journal entries, your company file contains all of your transactions and the adjustments she requested. You can confirm that

you entered the journal entries correctly by making sure your financial reports match the ones she produced.

- **Working onsite**. An accountant can work on the company file right in your office with a login password from you (the external accountant user feature gives your accountant special tools for working with your data). However, accountants are prone to doing things that require the company file to be in single-user mode, which might disrupt your day-to-day bookkeeping process.

- **The paper method**. If your accountant prefers to work with her own accounting system, you'll have to print the lists and reports that she requires. Then, when she gives you a list of changes and journal entries, you'll have to make those changes in your company file.

In addition to these options, QuickBooks Premier and Enterprise editions include a remote-access service, which lets your accountant access your QuickBooks company file over the Internet. Or you can use a remote-access service like those offered at *www.mypc.com* or *www.logmein.com*.

You have to be in single-user mode to create an accountant's copy. To switch to single-user mode, first make sure that everyone else is logged out of the company file, and then choose File→"Switch to Single-user Mode." After that, creating an accountant's review copy is a lot like creating other kinds of copies of your company file:

TIP If you have a few dozen windows open and laid out just the way you want, there's no need to gnash your teeth as QuickBooks closes all your windows to create the accountant's copy. Before you create the accountant's copy, save the current window arrangement so the program can reopen all those windows for you: Simply choose Edit→Preferences→Desktop View and, on the My Preferences tab, choose the "Save current desktop" option.

1. **Choose File→Accountant's Copy→Save File. In the Save As Accountant's Copy dialog box, which automatically selects the Accountant's Copy option, click Next.**

   If your accountant needs unrestricted access to the file, select the "Portable or Backup File" option instead and see page 187 to learn how to create those types of files.

2. **On the "Set the dividing date" screen shown in Figure 18-5, choose the date when control over transactions changes hands. Click Next and then, in the message box about closing windows, click OK.**

Use the Dividing Date drop-down list to choose the date you want as the dividing line between your work and your accountant's work. The upper part of the screen explains what each of you can do before and after the dividing date.

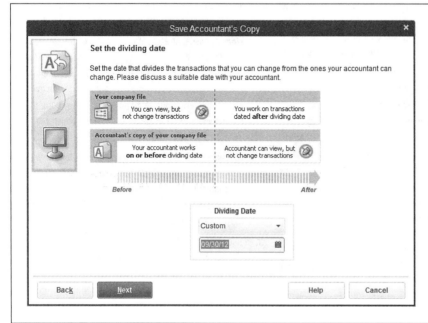

FIGURE 18-5

The dividing date you use is often the end of a fiscal period. The Dividing Date drop-down list gives you only a few choices, one of which is Custom. If you want to specify a date, choose Custom and then type or choose the date in the box that appears. Your other dividing date choices are End of Last Month, 2 Weeks Ago, and 4 Weeks Ago.

3. **Choose the folder or drive where you want to save the copy.**

QuickBooks sets the "Save as type" box to "QuickBooks Accountant's Copy Transfer Files (*.QBX)," and automatically names the file by using the company file's name followed by "Acct Transfer" and the date and time you created the file. (The extension .qbx stands for QuickBooks Accountant Transfer File.) As usual, you're free to edit the filename. Accountant's review copies use the Quick-Books portable file format, so they're usually small enough to email or save to a USB thumb drive. For example, a 10-megabyte company file may shrink to an accountant's review copy that's less than 1 MB.

4. **To create the accountant's review copy, click Save.**

Once you create an accountant's copy, QuickBooks reminds you that it exists: In the QuickBooks program window's title bar, you'll see the words "Accountant's Changes Pending" immediately after the company name.

5. **Send the file to your accountant.**

Email the file to your accountant, or copy it to a CD or a USB thumb drive and send it to him.

> **NOTE** If you use a password on your company file (an excellent idea, no matter how tiny your company is), don't forget to tell your accountant the password for the account you've set up for him.

FREQUENTLY ASKED QUESTION

Bookkeeping During Accountant's Review

Are there any limitations I should know about before I create an accountant's review copy?

QuickBooks locks parts of your company file when an accountant's review copy exists, so both you and your accountant have to live with a few minor restrictions. Fortunately, most of the taboo tasks can wait during the few weeks that your accountant has a copy of your file.

While you're sharing the company file, you can work on transactions after the dividing date, so your bookkeeping duties are unaffected. You can also add entries to lists or edit the information in list entries, but you *can't* merge or delete list entries until you import your accountant's changes. Similarly, you can add accounts, but you can't edit, merge, or deactivate accounts. Adding subaccounts is a no-no, too.

With a few restrictions, your accountant can work on transactions dated on or before the dividing date, whether she's

adding, editing, voiding, or deleting transactions. For example, payroll, non-posting transactions (like estimates), transfers, sales tax payments, and inventory assemblies are completely off limits. Because the limitations vary depending on what your accountant is trying to do, QuickBooks highlights fields in an accountant's copy to show the changes she can make that go back to you. (Fields that aren't sent back to you aren't highlighted.)

Your accountant can reconcile periods that end before the dividing date or change the cleared status of these earlier transactions. She can also add accounts to the chart of accounts and add items to some lists. For example, she can add customers, vendors, items, classes, fixed assets, sales tax codes, employees, and other names. Whether she can edit, inactivate, merge, and delete list items depend on the list. However, even if editing the list is off limits, your accountant can still *view* lists.

Sending a Copy Directly to Your Accountant

Intuit is happy to act as a go-between for accountant's review copies. You can tell QuickBooks to create an accountant's review copy *and* send it to your accountant; the copy goes up on a secure Intuit server, and your accountant gets an email that the file is waiting there. This method may be faster than creating and shipping the accountant's copy yourself. Here's how to start the ball rolling:

1. **Choose File→Accountant's Copy→Send to Accountant.**

   The Send Accountant's Copy dialog box opens and tells you about Intuit's Accountant's Copy File Transfer service. Click Next.

2. **On the "Set the dividing date" screen, choose the date that marks when you or your accountant is in charge, and then click Next.**

   The Dividing Date drop-down list has the same options described in Figure 18-5.

3. **Fill out the "Information for sending the file (1 of 2)" screen.**

   In the first and second box, type your accountant's email address. Make sure this address is correct—you don't want to accidentally send your financial information to the wrong person! Type your name and email address in the other boxes, so your accountant knows who the copy came from, and then click Next.

4. **On the "Information for sending the file (2 of 2)" screen, type a password to protect your file.**

   Type the password in the "Reenter password" box to prevent typos from sneaking in. The password has to be strong: at least seven characters, at least one number, and at least one uppercase letter. In the Note box, type any instructions for your accountant. *Don't* include the password in the Note box; instead, tell your accountant what the password is over the phone or in a separate email.

5. **Click Send.**

   QuickBooks closes all its windows and tells you that it's creating and sending an accountant's copy. You'll see a confirmation dialog box in QuickBooks (click OK to close it) and a confirmation email in your inbox when the copy has settled successfully onto Intuit's server.

   Your accountant receives an email that the file is waiting with a link to the download page. (The link is good for 14 days; then Intuit deletes your file from its server.) All you have to do is wait for your accountant to send you a file with changes and then import those changes as described in the next section.

Merging Accountant Changes into Your Company File

The company file your accountant sends back to you will have the file extension .qby instead of .qbx to indicate that it's an accountant's review copy import file. (Y follows X in the alphabet. Get it?) If you've imported data (like customer records) into QuickBooks before (page 654), the following steps should be familiar:

1. **If your company file isn't open, open it and back it up (page 175) before you import your accountant's changes.**

2. **Choose File→Accountant's Copy→Import Accountant's Changes from File. In the Import Changes From Accountant's Copy dialog box, navigate to the disk or folder that contains the accountant's file and then double-click the filename.**

   QuickBooks displays the changes your accountant made, as shown in Figure 18-6. Click the Expand All button to see the entire list. Review the changes to see if any of them conflict with work that you've done while your accountant worked on the copy. Each change comes with an explanation of how to deal with these conflicts.

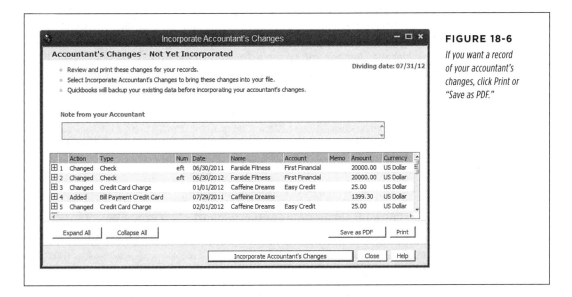

FIGURE 18-6

If you want a record of your accountant's changes, click Print or "Save as PDF."

NOTE If your accountant subscribes to Intuit's file-transfer service, she may tell you that the file she sent you is available on the Web. In that case, choose File→Accountant's Copy→Import Accountant's Changes from Web to retrieve the file.

---

3. **To make the changes in your company file, click the Incorporate Accountant's Changes button. (If you decide not to import the changes, click Close instead.)**

   QuickBooks backs up your company file and then imports the changes. After you review them, click Close.

Canceling an Accountant's Review Copy

From time to time, you might want to get rid of an accountant's review copy without importing any of the changes. For instance, say you created an accountant's review copy by mistake or your accountant had so few changes that she simply told you what tweaks to make. Unlocking your company file so you can get back to performing any type of task requires nothing more than choosing File→Accountant's Copy→Remove Restrictions. The Remove Restrictions dialog box warns you that you won't be able to import changes from the accountant's review copy if you remove restrictions. To show that you know what you're doing, turn on the "Yes, I want to remove the Accountant's Copy restrictions" checkbox, and then click OK. The words "Accountant's Change Pending" disappear from the QuickBooks window's title bar.

Setting Up an External Accountant User

The *external accountant user* feature lets your accountant peruse your bookkeeping data and make changes while protecting your customers' sensitive financial info. When your accountant logs in as an external accountant user, she can use the Client Data Review tool to look for problems and clean up any she finds. For example, she can look at the changes you've made to lists like the Chart of Accounts and Items List, scan your company file for payments or credits you haven't applied, and find sales taxes or payroll liabilities that you didn't record correctly.

> **NOTE** An external accountant user lets an accountant use the Client Data Review tool from within clients' editions of QuickBooks. When someone logs in as an external accountant user, the Client Data Review item appears in the Company menu in any QuickBooks edition, including Pro and Premier.

Here's how to set up an external accountant user:

1. **Log into your company file as the administrator (page 684).**

   Only an administrator can create an external accountant user (who can perform tasks that even someone with administrator privileges can't, like run the Client Data Review tool).

2. **Choose Company→Set Up Users and Passwords→Set Up Users.**

   After you enter your password, the User List dialog box opens.

3. **Click Add User.**

   The "Set up user password and access" dialog box opens.

4. **In the User Name box, type the name for the external accountant user. In the Password and Confirm Password boxes, type the external accountant user's password and then click Next.**

   The "Access for user" screen appears.

5. **Select the External Accountant option and then click Next.**

   Because the external accountant user is so powerful, QuickBooks asks you to confirm that you want to give that level of access to the person. Click Yes.

6. **Click Finish.**

> **NOTE** You can also change an existing user to an external accountant user. To do that, log into your company file as an administrator and choose Company→Set Up Users and Passwords→Set Up Users. In the User List window that appears, select the person you want to change and then click Edit User. Change the name and password if you want to and then click Next. On the "Access for user" screen, select the External Accountant option, click Next, click Yes, and then click Finish.

▨ 1099s

In QuickBooks, paying independent contractors is no different from paying other vendors: You enter bills from your contractors and then you pay those bills. No messy payroll transactions; no fuss with benefits or other regulatory requirements. But at the end of the year, you have to generate 1099s for your independent workers.

If you set up QuickBooks to track 1099 payments (page 632) and your contractors as 1099 vendors (page 92), generating 1099s is a piece of cake. But before you push a stack of 1099 forms through your printer, it's a good idea to make sure your records are up-to-date and accurate.

> **NOTE** If you turn on the preference for QuickBooks payroll, you can print W-2s for your employees by choosing Employees→Payroll Tax Forms & W-2s→Process Payroll Forms.

Generating 1099 Reports

To review the amounts you've paid to 1099 vendors, choose Reports→Vendors & Payables, and then select either of the following reports:

- **1099 Summary**. This report includes each vendor you've set up as a 1099 vendor and the total amount you've paid each vendor. If any amount looks questionable, double-click it to display that vendor's transactions. Although the report lists only the vendors you set up as eligible for 1099 status, as shown in Figure 18-7, you can modify it to make sure you haven't left any 1099 vendors out. In the first 1099 Options drop-down list, choose "All vendors."

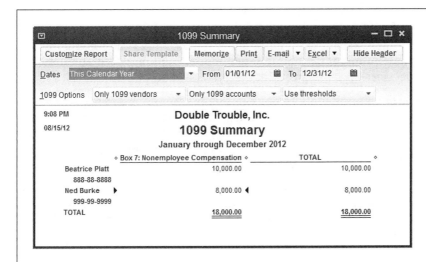

FIGURE 18-7

Regardless of the fiscal year you use for your company, payroll and 1099 tasks run on a calendar year, because your employees and subcontractors pay taxes for each calendar year. That's why the Dates drop-down list for the 1099 Summary report includes calendar-year date ranges.

If the 1099 Summary report is empty, your 1099 account mappings may be missing. In the report window's toolbar, in the middle drop-down list, choose "All allowed accounts" to see payments you made to 1099 vendors regardless of the account. If your vendors leap into view, you need to map your accounts to 1099 boxes, as described on page 632.

> **NOTE** The federal government gives you the tiniest of breaks by setting thresholds for total payments to 1099 vendors. If you pay vendors less than the threshold, you don't have to generate 1099s for them. (For nonemployee compensation, the 2012 threshold is $600.)

In the 1099 Summary report's window, QuickBooks sets the last box in the 1099 Options row to "Use thresholds." This choice filters the vendors in the report to those that exceed the government's threshold. If you want to see *all* your 1099 vendors, regardless of what you paid them, choose "Ignore thresholds" instead.

* **1099 Detail**. If you pay your independent contractors on a regular schedule, this report can pinpoint errors because it shows the transactions that produce the vendor's 1099 amount. If you see a gap in the payment schedule or two transactions in the same month, double-click a transaction amount to open the corresponding window, such as Write Checks.

Printing 1099-MISC Forms

The steps to start printing 1099 forms are simple but, as with any printing task, fraught with niggling details:

1. **Order printable 1099-MISC and 1096 forms or purchase them at your local business supply store.**

   1099-MISC and 1096 forms use special ink so that government agencies can scan them. Intuit sells kits with preprinted 1099 forms. In your web browser, go to *http://intuitmarket.intuit.com*. In that page's horizontal navigation bar, point your cursor at Tax Forms, and then click 1099 Kits.

   You can also order 1099 forms directly from the IRS by going to *www.irs.gov* and clicking the Forms & Pubs heading. On the "Forms and Publications" page, under the Order heading, click "Employer forms and instructions." In the value box for the 1099 MISC form (about halfway down the list), type the quantity of forms you need, and then scroll to the bottom of the page and click "Add to Cart."

> **NOTE** You can print 1099-MISC forms for up to 249 vendors. If you've got more than that, the IRS requires you to file 1099 forms electronically. In that case, bypass printing the forms in QuickBooks and use the government's hopefully easy-to-use system instead.

2. **Load your printer with preprinted 1099-MISC forms.**

   If you use a printer that feeds individual sheets, don't bother placing a Copy 2 form after each Copy 1 form so that you can print multiple copies for each vendor. It's a lot easier to load the Copy 1 sheets and print a set of 1099 forms on those sheets and then load the Copy 2 forms and print a second set of 1099 forms. You then send the Copy 1 sheets to the 1099 vendors, and the Copy 2 sheets to the government in one big batch.

3. **Choose Vendors→Print/E-file 1099s. In the QuickBooks 1099 Wizard window that opens, click Get Started.**

   The QuickBooks 1099 wizard helps verify your 1099 information before you print. After you click Get Started, the "Select your 1099 vendors" screen appears.

4. **To transform a vendor into a 1099 vendor, turn on the checkbox in the vendor's Create Form 1099-MISC Column. Click Continue when all the 1099 vendors are selected.**

   Turn off a vendor's checkbox if you don't need to create a 1099 for them.

5. **In the "Verify your 1099 vendors' information" screen, make any changes to the vendors' tax ID, name, address, and phone number. Click Continue when the information is correct.**

   If required information is missing, the wizard outlines the table cell in red. Simply click the cell and type in the needed info.

6. **In the "Map vendor payment accounts" screen, map the accounts in your chart of accounts to the appropriate box on the 1099 form by clicking the down arrow in the "Apply payments to this 1099 box" cell and choosing the appropriate 1099 box. Click Continue when you're done.**

   Most payments to 1099 vendors are mapped to Box 7: Nonemployee Compensation, which is why this screen includes a "Report all payments in Box 7" checkbox. To map all your 1099 vendors to Box 7, simply turn on this checkbox.

7. **In the "Review payments for exclusions" screen, click View Included Payments to see payments you made to vendors by credit card, debit card, gift card, or PayPal. If any payments made with those payment types appear in the Check Payments Included on Forms 1099-MISC report, double-click the transaction to open the Write Checks window. In the No. field, fill in the payment type, such as Debit, Visa, Giftcard, PayPal, and so on.**

   Beginning with the 2011 tax year, you have to exclude payments you made by credit card, debit card, gift card, or third-party payment networks such as PayPal from Form 1099-MISC because they're reported by the card issuers and third-party payment networks on Form 1099-K. You can click View Excluded Payments to see which payments QuickBooks has excluded from Form 1099-MISC.

If you make a payment in the Write Checks or Pay Bills windows, you can fill in the "No. filed" with the payment type (up to 8 characters) so that QuickBooks can automatically exclude that payment from Form 1099-MISC.

8. **When the Check Payments Included on Forms 1099-MISC report shows only check payments, click Continue.**

   After you edit transactions, click Refresh in the report window to view an updated report.

9. **In the "Confirm your 1099 entries" screen, review the vendors and the compensation to make sure it's correct, and then click Continue.**

10. **In the "Choose a filing method" screen, click Print 1099s to print your forms.**

    If you file more than 249 forms, you have to e-file your 1099s. In that case, you can click "Go to Intuit 1099 E-File Service" to use Intuit's e-file service (which costs extra).

11. **In the "Printing 1099-MISC and 1096 Forms" dialog box, click OK.**

    QuickBooks opens the "Select 1099s to Print" dialog box shown in Figure 18-8, and automatically selects every vendor whose pay exceeds the government threshold (page 498).

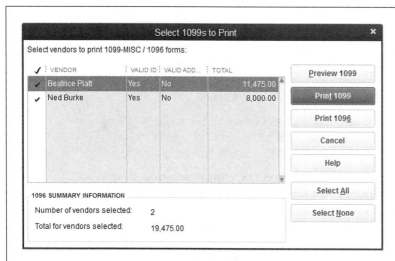

FIGURE 18-8

In addition to columns for the vendor's name and total pay, this table includes the Valid ID and Valid Address columns. If you tend to create vendors on the fly without bothering to enter pesky details like their tax ID numbers or street addresses, scan these columns for the word "No." If you see that in any cell, click Cancel and edit your vendors to add this essential information. Then, repeat steps 7 and 8 and verify that all the Valid ID and Valid Address cells say Yes.

12. **When the Valid ID and Valid Address columns are replete with the word Yes, click Preview 1099 to see the final forms before you print them.**

In the Print Preview window, click Zoom In (if necessary) to verify the information. When you've reviewed the forms, click Close.

13. **Click Print 1099.**

QuickBooks opens the Print 1099 window. If the preprinted forms are waiting in a printer other than the one that the program chose, in the "Printer name" box, choose the printer that holds your preprinted forms.

14. **Click Print.**

> **TIP** Preprinted forms usually include Copy 1 for the vendor and Copy 2 for the government. But you'll also want a copy for your files. Instead of printing a third set of 1099s, run one of the printed sets through your copy machine or printer/scanner/copier.

▌ Closing the Books for the Year

A few months after the end of a fiscal year, when tax returns rest under the gimlet-eyed scrutiny of the tax authorities, most companies close their books for the previous fiscal year. The purpose of closing the books is to lock the transactions that you've already reported on tax returns or in financial results, because the IRS and shareholders alike don't look kindly on changes to the reports they've received.

QuickBooks, on the other hand, doesn't care whether you close the books in your company file. The closing task is mainly to protect you from the consequences of changing the numbers in previous years (like altering the company file so that it no longer matches what you reported to the IRS). But you're free to keep your books open if you're not worried about editing older transactions by mistake.

If you *do* close your books in QuickBooks, you can still edit transactions prior to the closing date. Unlike other bookkeeping programs in which closed means closed, in QuickBooks, folks who know the closing-date password can still change and delete closed transactions to, say, correct an egregious error before you rerun all your end-of-year reports.

Closing the books in QuickBooks takes place in the Preferences dialog box. Switch to single-user mode (page 173). Then, choose Edit→Preferences→Accounting and click the Company Preferences tab. To close the books as of a specific date, click the Set Date/Password button. Figure 18-9 shows what to do next.

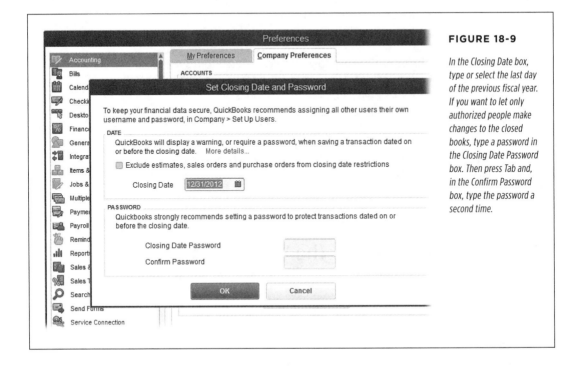

FIGURE 18-9

*In the Closing Date box,
type or select the last day
of the previous fiscal year.
If you want to let only
authorized people make
changes to the closed
books, type a password in
the Closing Date Password
box. Then press Tab and,
in the Confirm Password
box, type the password a
second time.*

TIP Don't cut and paste the password from the Closing Date Password box to the Confirm Password box. These boxes display dots instead of the actual characters, which means you can't see typos. So if you set a password with a typo in it, you'll be unlikely to stumble on the correct password, and your closed books will remain shut as tight as a clam.

After you've set a password for the closing date, you'll have to enter that password whenever you want to modify transactions prior to that date. For example, if you try to edit a check that you wrote before the closing date, QuickBooks opens a message box with a Password field in it. Type the closing-date password, and then click OK to complete your edit.

TIP After you've completed all your year-end activities in QuickBooks, create a backup of your company file (page 175). With all the data that contributed to your financial reports and tax forms in this backup, it wouldn't be overkill to create two copies of this backup: one to keep close by in your office and one stored safely offsite in case of emergency.

Managing Inventory

A s you record inventory purchases and sales in QuickBooks, the program keeps track of your inventory behind the scenes, just as the point-of-service system at the grocery store does when a cashier scans items. This chapter begins by reviewing the setup tasks that make the program work this magic.

Good inventory management means more than just updating the number of items that QuickBooks thinks you have on hand. To keep the right number of items in stock, you also need to know how many you've sold and how many are on order. And to make decisions like how much to charge or which vendor to use, you have to evaluate your purchases and how much you pay for your inventory. QuickBooks' inventory reports and Inventory Center help you look at your inventory items and transactions. In this chapter, you'll learn how to make the most of both these features.

> **NOTE** The Inventory Center is available only in QuickBooks Premier and Enterprise. If you have QuickBooks Pro, you can run inventory reports, but you don't have access to the center.

Another important aspect of inventory is keeping your QuickBooks records in sync with what's sitting on the shelves in your warehouse. Inventory can go missing due to theft or damage, so you might not have as many products in stock as you think you do. QuickBooks can't help with the dusty business of rifling through boxes and counting carafes, coffee mugs, and the occasional centipede. But after the counting is complete, the program *can* help you adjust its records to match the reality in your warehouse. And adjusting inventory is useful for more than just inventory counts. You can also use this process to write off inventory that you have in your warehouse but can't sell because it's dented, dirty, or too darned ugly.

The QuickBooks Inventory Process

Before you look at the inventory-management tools that QuickBooks offers, here's a quick review of how QuickBooks tracks inventory as you buy and sell products.

Setting Up Inventory Items

As you learned in Chapter 5, you set the stage for item tracking when you turn on the QuickBooks inventory preference and create inventory items in your company file. Inventory items in your Item List include purchase costs, sales prices, and accounts, all of which direct the right amount of money into the right income, expense, and cost of goods sold accounts as you buy and sell inventory.

Here are the fields in an item record that QuickBooks uses to track inventory:

- **Cost**. What you pay for one unit of the item.
- **Sales Price**. The price you typically charge for the item (for the same unit size you used in the Cost field).
- **Asset Account**. The account that holds the value of the inventory stored in your warehouse.
- **Income Account**. The account for the income you receive when you sell this item.
- **COGS Account**. The account to which you post the item's cost when you sell it (known as "cost of goods sold").

NOTE As you sell inventory, QuickBooks deducts dollars from the inventory asset account and adds them to the cost of goods sold account. For a refresher on how inventory postings work, see the box on page 237.

When you run low on inventory, it's time to buy more. For products that you keep in stock, knowing how many you have on hand is essential. Happily, QuickBooks keeps a running total of how many units you've purchased and how many you've sold. The difference between these two numbers conveniently tells you how many should be in your warehouse. The running total of inventory quantity on hand stays with the item in your Item List, as Figure 19-1 shows.

Buying and Selling Inventory

Unless you practice just-in-time inventory management, you need inventory in your warehouse to fill customer orders. Here's a quick review of buying and selling inventory:

- **Ordering inventory**. Companies typically create purchase orders for inventory products they buy. These purchase orders don't change the balances of any accounts in your QuickBooks company file (that's why they're called *non-posting transactions*). But they're useful for verifying that the shipments you receive match what you ordered—not unlike opening a pizza box before you leave the parlor to make sure you didn't get an anchovy and garlic pie by mistake. Chapter 9 explains how to order inventory and then pay for the inventory you receive.

- **Purchasing and receiving inventory**. When you receive a shipment, you record it in QuickBooks so you know you have products to sell. The program increases the number of products on hand by the number in the shipment and adds the value of the shipment to the inventory asset account.

FIGURE 19-1

The Total Quantity On Hand value in the Item List (abbreviated to "Total Quantity..." here) shows you how many of each product you have in stock. As you purchase inventory or sell it to customers, QuickBooks updates this value based on the number you bought or sold.

- **Selling Inventory**. Finally, when you sell some of your inventory, the income makes all your bookkeeping seem worthwhile. When you create invoices (Chapter 10), sales receipts, or other sales forms (Chapter 11), QuickBooks deducts the units you sold from each item's Total Quantity On Hand value. The income from the sale posts to an income account, while the cost of the units you sold moves from the inventory asset account to a cost of goods sold account.

  When you sell inventory, QuickBooks also compares the new Total Quantity On Hand value to your reorder point (page 132). When the inventory on hand drops below this number, the program reminds you that it's time to order more. The box below tells you how to shut off reminders for items you aren't selling at the moment.

TROUBLESHOOTING MOMENT

Managing Seasonal Items

The Item List is home to items for every service and product you sell, and it can get really long really fast, especially if you sell different items at different times of the year. For example, if you stock your store with lawn furniture in the spring, you don't want to scroll past dozens of outdoor items or see reminders to reorder them the other nine months of the year.

Fortunately, you can make seasonal items inactive, which temporarily hides them in the Item List and silences the reminders. In the Item List window (choose Lists→Item List to open it), right-click the item and then choose Make Item Inactive from the shortcut menu. Page 146 explains how to reactivate items when a new season rolls around.

Working with the Inventory Center

The Inventory Center (which is only available in QuickBooks Premier and Enterprise) provides information about items you keep in stock. Similar to the Customer Center and Vendor Center, it's a quick way to answer questions like, "How many items do I have on hand to sell?" and, "What purchase orders and sales orders are open?" To open the Inventory Center (shown in Figure 19-2), choose Vendors→Inventory Activities→Inventory Center. Here's how to use the Center to see what's going on with your inventory:

Click this down arrow
to choose an item filter

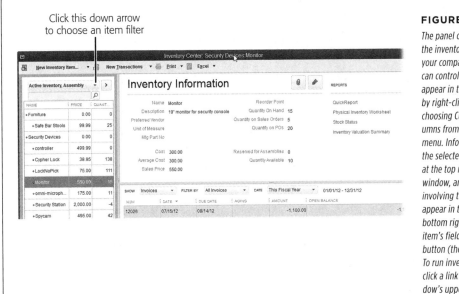

FIGURE 19-2

The panel on the left lists the inventory items in your company file. You can control which fields appear in this panel by right-clicking it and choosing Customize Columns from the shortcut menu. Information about the selected item appears at the top right of the window, and transactions involving that item appear in the table at the bottom right. To edit an item's fields, click the Edit button (the pencil icon). To run inventory reports, click a link in the window's upper right such as Stock Status or Inventory Valuation Summary.

- **Display inventory items**. When you first open the Inventory Center, QuickBooks displays your active inventory items (and assembly items if you use them) in the panel on the left. Then, when you click the name of an inventory item in that panel, the Inventory Information section at the window's top right shows info for that item's record.

- **Filter the list of inventory items**. To narrow the item list to those that fit the criteria you want, such as inventory items that are out of stock, click the down arrow on the right side of the unlabeled filter box that's located immediately below the New Inventory Item entry in the Center's toolbar (see Figure 19-2). In the drop-down list, choose one of the entries, like "QOH < = zero" which is shorthand for "quantity on hand is less than zero."

- **Find an inventory item in the list**. If you have scads of inventory items, you can quickly find the one you want with the find box, which is below the filter box. Simply type part of the item's name and then press Enter or click the Search button, which has a magnifying glass on it.

- **Change the fields that appear in the Center's list**. To display different fields in the list, right-click the panel on the left side of the Center, and then choose Customize Columns. In the Customize Columns dialog box's Available Columns list, select the fields you want to display and then click Add to move them to the Chosen Columns list. To remove a column, select it in the Chosen Columns list and click the Remove button. When the Chosen Columns list includes the fields you want, click OK.

- **Review inventory status**. In the upper-right part of the Inventory Center are several links you can use to see various things about your inventory:

    - Click **QuickReport** to see all transactions for the selected item.

    - Click **Stock Status** to generate a Stock Status report (page 510).

    - Click **Inventory Valuation Summary** to generate this report (page 508).

- **Display transactions for an item**. When you select an item in the list on the left side of the Center, the transactions involving that item appear in the table at the bottom right. To see a specific type of transaction, in the Show drop-down list above the table, choose a type like Invoices or Purchase Orders.

> **TIP** You can filter the transactions shown in the table using the same techniques that work in the Customer Center, which are described on page 29.

Running Inventory Reports

Checking the vital signs of your inventory is the best way to keep it healthy. When products are hot, you have to keep them in stock or you'll lose sales. And if products grow cold, you don't want to get stuck holding the bag (or the lime-green luggage).

For all other temperatures, most companies keep tabs on inventory trends and compare them with what's going on in sales. For example, when the value of your inventory asset account is increasing faster than sales, sales could be poor because your prices are too high, competition is encroaching on your market, or the Salvador Dalí Chia Pets simply didn't catch on.

Good inventory management means keeping enough items in stock to meet your sales, but not so many that your inventory grows obsolete before you can sell it. QuickBooks inventory reports aren't fancy, but they tell you most of what you need to know. You can run any of these reports by choosing Reports→Inventory and then picking the one you want. The following sections describe what each report includes.

How Much Is Inventory Worth?

QuickBooks includes two reports that tell you how much your inventory is worth: Inventory Valuation Summary and Inventory Valuation Detail. Here's what each one does.

■ INVENTORY VALUATION SUMMARY REPORT

The Inventory Valuation Summary report, shown in Figure 19-3, is an overview of the inventory you have on hand, what it's worth as an asset, and what it will be worth when you sell it. (See page 516 to find out what to do if your inventory isn't worth as much as it used to be.)

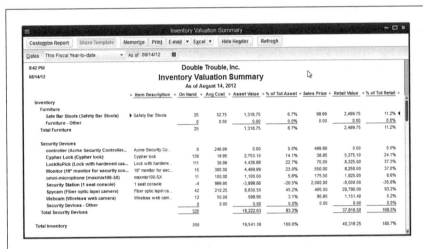

FIGURE 19-3

Because the report is a snapshot of inventory value, month-to-date, quarter-to-date, and year-to-date ranges all produce the same results. But if you want to see the inventory value as of a different date, in the Dates box, choose the date you want.

To run this report, choose Reports→Inventory→Inventory Valuation Summary or (if you have QuickBooks Premier or Enterprise) at the top right of the Inventory Center, click the Inventory Valuation Summary link. QuickBooks initially uses the current month to date as the date range for this report. The first column shows the names of the inventory items from your Item List; subitems appear indented beneath their parent items. Here are the report's other columns and why they are (or aren't so) important to inventory health:

- **Item Description**. This text is the description you entered in the Description on Purchase Transactions box in the item's record. A description doesn't help manage your inventory, but it does identify which item you're looking at, particularly when you use part numbers or abbreviations for item names.

- **On Hand**. To calculate this value, QuickBooks subtracts the number of products you sold and adds the number of products you received. The values in this column can help you quickly check for items that are close to being out of stock. However, because items sell at different rates, the reorder point reminder (page 623) is a better indication that something is perilously close to selling out.

NOTE When you add an out-of-stock item to an invoice, QuickBooks warns that you don't have inventory, but it doesn't prevent you from invoicing for products you don't have. When the On Hand value is negative, you know it's time to order more—and to ask for express shipping.

- **Avg Cost**. Average cost is the only way QuickBooks Pro and Premier value inventory. (QuickBooks Enterprise supports "first in/first out" valuation; see page 518.) To calculate this value, the program uses the price you paid for every unit you've purchased of an inventory item along with any adjustment transactions you've recorded (page 513). If you want to watch price trends so you can adjust your sales prices accordingly, review your most recent bills for inventory purchases.

- **Asset Value**. Asset Value is the item's average cost multiplied by the number on hand. Although changes in asset value over time are more telling, a snapshot of asset value can show trouble brewing. An excessive asset value for one item is a sign that inventory might be obsolete—the item hasn't sold, so you have too many on hand. If you know that the item *is* selling, streamlining your purchasing process can reduce the number you need to keep in the warehouse.

- **% of Tot Asset**. This column shows the percentage of an item's asset value compared with the total asset value of all inventory items. Higher percentages might mean that a product is a significant part of your sales strategy or that it isn't selling well and you have too much in stock. This measurement has meaning only in light of your business strategy and performance.

- **Sales Price**. You set this price in the item's record, but it's meaningless if you regularly change the item's price or charge different prices to different customers. If you didn't set a sales price for an item, you'll see "0.00" in this column.

- **Retail Value**. Because the retail value is the sales price multiplied by the number on hand, this number is useful only if the value in the Sales Price column is the typical sales price for the item.

- **% of Tot Retail**. This percentage is what portion the item's retail value represents of your total inventory's retail value. Different products sell at different profit margins, which you can see when the retail percentage differs from the asset value percentage.

■ INVENTORY VALUATION DETAIL REPORT

The Inventory Valuation Detail report lists every transaction that increases or decreases the number of items you have on hand. Although it can grow lengthy, this report can help you figure out where your inventory went (and perhaps jog your memory about inventory transactions that you forgot to record in QuickBooks). As in other reports, you can double-click a transaction to see its details.

Inventory Stock Status

As you might expect, the Inventory Stock Status by Item report (Reports→Inventory→Inventory Stock Status by Item) tells you where your inventory stands today and how that will change based on your outstanding purchase orders. This report is a great place to see which items you need to reorder, as Figure 19-4 shows.

> **TIP** If you want to use a barcode reader to scan your inventory, go to Intuit's marketplace (*http://marketplace. intuit.com*). In either Search Apps Now box, type *barcode* to find third-party barcode readers.

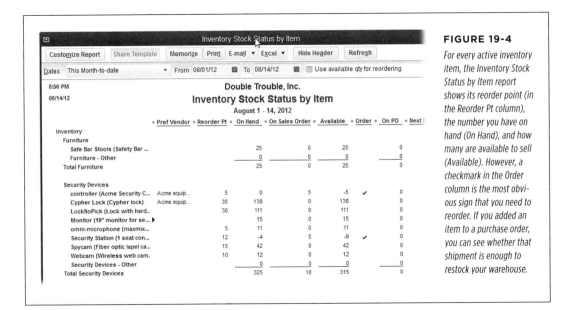

FIGURE 19-4

For every active inventory item, the Inventory Stock Status by Item report shows its reorder point (in the Reorder Pt column), the number you have on hand (On Hand), and how many are available to sell (Available). However, a checkmark in the Order column is the most obvious sign that you need to reorder. If you added an item to a purchase order, you can see whether that shipment is enough to restock your warehouse.

> **NOTE** If you upgrade to QuickBooks Premier or Enterprise, the Inventory Stock Status reports also show how many items you've added to sales orders for future delivery, as shown in the On Sales Order column in Figure 19-4.

You can also run the Inventory Stock Status by Vendor report to see the same information that's in the Inventory Stock Status by Item report, but grouped and subtotaled by vendor. If you seem to run low on products from a particular vendor, you might want to increase the reorder point for those products to fine-tune your lead time.

Viewing One Inventory Item

The Inventory Item QuickReport is a fast yet thorough way to see what's going on with a particular item. To display this report, open the Item List window (Lists→Item List), select the item you want to review, and then press Ctrl+Q or, at the bottom of the window, click Reports→"QuickReport: <item name>." Or, in the Inventory Center, select the item and then click the QuickReport link in the window's upper right.

This report includes purchase and sales transactions for the item, such as bills and invoices (see Figure 19-5). In the On Hand As Of section, invoice transactions represent the sales you've made to customers, so the numbers are negative; bills and item receipts are your purchases from vendors, which increase the number on hand. The On Purchase Order As Of section includes the number of products you've ordered but haven't yet received. At the bottom of the report, the TOTAL As Of figure tells you how many products you'll have in stock when all your purchase orders are filled.

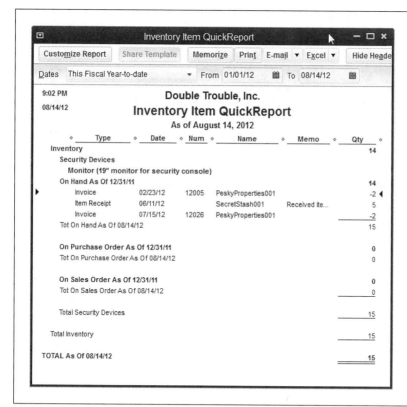

FIGURE 19-5

The Inventory Item QuickReport summarizes how many of an item you have on hand as well as the number that are on order. The headings at the beginning of each section in the Inventory Item QuickReport show the last day of the previous fiscal year, such as "On Hand As Of 12/31/11" as shown here. Then, the report lists the transactions during the current fiscal year which affect a total, such as invoice and item receipts for the On Hand As Of section. The Tot On Hand As Of and TOTAL As Of labels in the report show the actual as-of date for the report along with the final total for the inventory item.

Performing a Physical Inventory

QuickBooks calculates how many products you have on hand based on your purchases and sales, but it has no way of knowing what's actually happening in your warehouse. Employees may help themselves to products; fire can consume some of your inventory; or a burst pipe could turn your India ink sketches into Rorschach tests. Only a physical count of the items in stock can tell you how many units you *really* have to sell.

QuickBooks does the only thing it can to help you count your inventory: provides the Physical Inventory Worksheet report, which lists each inventory item in your Item List and how many units should be on hand. To see it, choose Reports→Inventory→Physical Inventory Worksheet (or click the Physical Inventory Worksheet link in the Inventory Center's upper right.) The Physical Count column has blank lines so you can write in how many you find, as you can see in Figure 19-6. (The box on page 513 explains how to count inventory while business continues to chug along.)

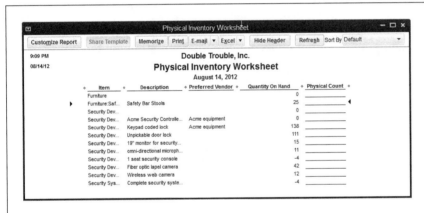

FIGURE 19-6

Your preferred vendor has nothing to do with counting inventory, yet a column with that info appears on this report. To hide that column, click Customize Report in the report window's toolbar. On the Display tab, in the Columns list, click the checkmark to the left of the Preferred Vendor entry to turn it off. If you want to sort the inventory items to list them by the warehouse aisles where they're kept, in the Columns list, turn on the Location field, and then, in the "Sort by" drop-down list, choose Location.

Freezing Inventory While You Count

It's sheer madness to ship customer orders out and receive inventory shipments while you're trying to count the products you have on hand. QuickBooks doesn't have a feature for freezing inventory while you perform the physical count, but you can follow procedures that do the same thing.

Because a physical inventory count disrupts business operations, most companies schedule it during slow periods and off hours. To keep the disruption to a minimum, print the Physical Inventory Worksheet just before you start the count. Then, until the count is complete, do the following to keep your inventory stable:

- **Sales**. In QuickBooks, create invoices for inventory sales as you would normally. After you save each invoice, edit it to mark it as pending (page 305). When you finish the count, edit the pending invoices again to mark them as final, fill the orders, and then send the invoices.

- **Purchases**. If you receive inventory shipments during the count, don't unpack the boxes or use any of QuickBooks' features for receiving inventory (page 233) until you complete the physical count.

Adjusting Inventory in QuickBooks

Your inventory records in QuickBooks may not match your real-world inventory for several reasons:

- **Damage**. Inventory can succumb to breakage or damage from a flood, an out-of-control forklift, or a paintball fight in the warehouse. When these accidents happen, the first thing to do is report the loss to your insurance company. Adjusting the quantity of inventory in QuickBooks should follow close behind.

- **Obsolete products**. If you have several cartons of oh-so-passé women's stirrup pants, the *true* value of that inventory is worthless. Although admitting that you made a mistake is painful, writing off that inventory as unsellable turns the inventory into a business expense, which reduces your net profit and, therefore, the taxes you pay. Adjust the inventory in QuickBooks when you take the products to the recycling center.

- **Theft**. An inventory adjustment is in order after almost every physical inventory count you perform, because the quantities for inventory in the real world rarely match the quantities in QuickBooks. *Shrinkage* is the polite term for the typical cause of these discrepancies. To be blunt, employees, repair people, and passersby attracted by an unlocked door may help themselves to a five-finger discount. And you not only take the hit to your bottom line—you're also stuck adjusting QuickBooks' records to account for the theft.

It's no surprise, then, that QuickBooks has a feature for this multipurpose accounting task. You adjust both the quantity of inventory and its value in the aptly named "Adjust Quantity/Value on Hand" window.

You purchase inventory from vendors, so QuickBooks keeps all inventory features in the same place: the Vendors menu. To open the "Adjust Quantity/Value on Hand" window, choose Vendors→Inventory Activities→"Adjust Quantity/Value on Hand" or, on the Home page, in the Company panel, click Inventory Activities→"Adjust Quantity/Value On Hand."

Adjusting Quantities

You need to adjust quantities when you're updating your company file to reflect the number of items in stock or writing off obsolete inventory. When you adjust inventory quantities, QuickBooks fills in or calculates some of the fields for you. Here are guidelines for filling in the remaining fields of the "Adjust Quantity/Value on Hand" window:

- **Adjustment Type**. To adjust inventory items' quantities to match what's in your warehouse or reflect what you're writing off, choose Quantity from this drop-down menu, as shown in Figure 19-7. QuickBooks uses the average cost of each item to calculate the dollar value that the new quantities represent.

- **Adjustment Date**. QuickBooks puts the current date in this box. If you like to keep your journal entries and other bookkeeping adjustments together at the end of a quarter or year, type the date when you want to record the adjustment.

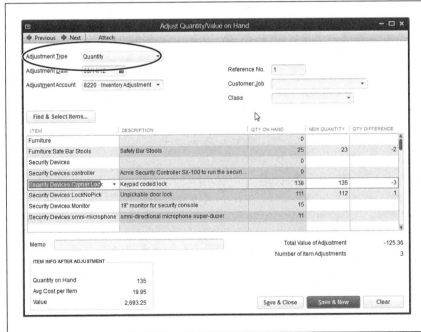

FIGURE 19-7

In this window's table, QuickBooks shades the columns you can't change. When you choose Quantity in the Adjustment Type box, as shown here, the Item, New Quantity, and Qty Difference columns are the only ones you can edit.

- **Adjustment Account**. Choose an expense account you created to track the cost of inventory adjustments. For example, if you adjust an item's quantity to match the physical count, choose an account such as Inventory Adjustment. If you're writing off obsolete or damaged inventory, choose an expense account such as Unsalable Inventory. Because you can assign only one account to each inventory adjustment, adjust the quantity once for physical count changes, and then click Save & New to create a separate adjustment for write-offs.

TIP If the expense account you want to use doesn't exist, at the top of the Adjustment Account drop-down list, choose <Add New> and then fill in the boxes in the Add New Account window. When you click Save & Close, QuickBooks fills in the Adjustment Account box with the account you just created.

- **Reference Number**. You don't have to enter reference numbers, but they come in handy when discussing your books with your accountant. If you don't type anything in this box, QuickBooks increments the number here by one each time you adjust inventory.

- **Customer:Job**. If you want to record products you send to a customer or job at no charge—without adding the items to an invoice—choose that customer or job in this drop-down list. QuickBooks then assigns the cost of the adjustment to that customer or job.

TIP A better way to give products to a customer or job is to add them to an invoice with a price of $0.00. That way, your generosity remains on the record lest your customer forgets.

- **Class**. If you use classes to track sales, choose the appropriate one in the Class box that appears. For example, if one partner handles sales for the item you're adjusting, choose the class for that partner so the expense applies to her.

- **Item**. To adjust a single item, click the first item cell in the table, click the down arrow that appears, and then choose the inventory item you want to adjust. To adjust several items, click the Find & Select Items button above the table. In the Find & Select Items dialog box, turn on the checkmark cells for the items you want to adjust (or click Select All to select all inventory items after a physical count), and then click Add Selected Items.

- **New Quantity/Qty Difference**. When you choose Quantity in the Adjustment Type box, you can type a number in either the New Quantity or the Qty Difference cell. If you're making an adjustment after a physical count, in the New Quantity cell, type the quantity from your physical count worksheet. On the other hand, if you lost four cartons of *Chivalry Today* magazine in a feminist demonstration gone bad, it's easier to type the number you lost as a negative number (such as *-400*) in the Qty Difference cell.

TIP If you're ready to admit that the pet rock fad isn't coming back, you can write off your entire inventory by putting *0* in an item's New Quantity cell. In the Adjustment Account drop-down list, choose an expense account such as Unsalable Inventory.

- **Memo**. To prevent questions from your accountant, in the Memo cell, type the reason for the adjustment, such as "2012 end-of-year physical count."

After you fill in all the boxes, click Save & Close (or Save & New if you want to create a second adjustment for write-offs, say). If you decreased the quantity on hand, QuickBooks decreases the balance in your inventory asset account (using the average cost per item). To keep double-entry bookkeeping principles intact, the decrease in the inventory asset account also shows up as an increase in the expense account you chose. Conversely, if the adjustment increases the quantity or value of your inventory, the inventory asset account's balance increases and the expense account's balance decreases.

Adjusting Quantities and Values

Calculating inventory values by using the items' average cost is convenient—and in QuickBooks Pro and Premier, it's your only option. Using other methods for calculating inventory value, like "first in/first out" (FIFO) and "last in/first out" (LIFO) costing (explained in the box on page 518), quickly turn into a full-time job. But if that's what you want, you can do so manually.

NOTE You can value inventory by using FIFO if you upgrade to QuickBooks Enterprise and subscribe to Advanced Inventory (which costs extra).

Because QuickBooks can handle only average cost for inventory, your sole work-around for achieving LIFO or FIFO costing is to adjust dollar values by hand in the "Adjust Quantity/Value on Hand" window. When you choose Total Value in the window's Adjustment Type box, QuickBooks displays the New Value column. You can then change the asset value of the quantity on hand simply by typing the new value in the New Value cell.

You can also change both quantities *and* values to, for example, make the quantity reflect what's in your warehouse and the value to reflect its poor condition. To do this, in the Adjustment Type box, choose "Quantity and Total Value." QuickBooks then activates the New Quantity, Qty Difference, and New Value columns. To change the number you have, type the value in the New Quantity cell. To adjust the value of one unit of the item, in the New Value column, type the dollar value for a unit.

Mimicking LIFO or FIFO costing takes some effort because you have to review the bills for all your purchases of the inventory item. Here's how to value your inventory using LIFO:

1. **Choose Reports→Purchases→Purchases by Item Detail.**

   QuickBooks generates a report that shows your purchase transactions grouped by inventory item.

2. **For the quantity of the item that you have on hand, add up the prices you paid for your earliest purchases.**

   As shown in Figure 19-8, the Purchases by Item Detail report's Cost Price column shows how much you paid for an item with each purchase. In this example, the first 20 monitors cost $325.00 each and the last 73 cost $300.00 each. So the LIFO value for 80 monitors would be 73 multiplied by $300.00 and 7 multiplied by $325.00, or $24,175.00.

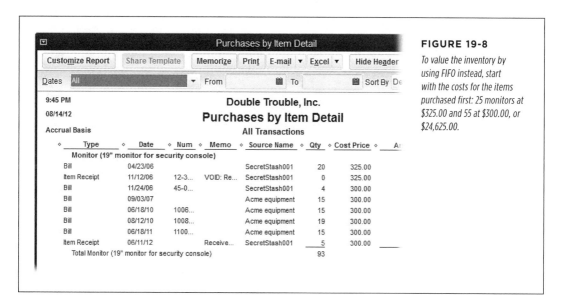

FIGURE 19-8

To value the inventory by using FIFO instead, start with the costs for the items purchased first: 25 monitors at $325.00 and 55 at $300.00, or $24,625.00.

3. **In the "Adjust Quantity/Value on Hand" window (Vendors→Inventory Activities→"Adjust Quantity/Value on Hand"), type the amount you just calculated in the New Value cell.**

   When you click Save & Close, QuickBooks decreases the balance in your inventory asset account using the value in the New Value cell instead of the average cost per item.

FIFO and LIFO Inventory Costing

First in/first out (FIFO) costing means that a company values its inventory as if the first products it receives are the first ones it sells. (Your grocery store always puts the milk closest to its expiration date at the front of the refrigerator, right?)

Last in/first out (LIFO) costing, on the other hand, assumes that the last products in are the first ones sold. This method is like unpacking a moving van: The last valuables you packed are the first ones that come out.

The costing method you use doesn't have to match the order in which you sell products. When you start a business, you can choose whichever costing method you want—but you have to stick with it. For example, when prices are on the rise (as they almost always are), LIFO costing reduces your profit and taxes owed because you're selling the products that cost the most first. However, with the steady decrease in electronics prices, FIFO costing probably produces the least profit. Unless you're sure which method you want to use, you're better off asking your accountant for advice.

Unfortunately, even with the "Adjust Quantity/Value on Hand" window, you can't achieve true LIFO or FIFO costing in QuickBooks Pro or Premier. The program always uses average cost to move money from your inventory asset account to your cost of goods sold account when you add products to an invoice or sales receipt.

Budgeting and Planning

As you've no doubt noticed in business and in life, the activities that cost money almost always seem to outnumber those that bring money in. If you run a small business, you may not need to use a budget. But most companies want to make money and most nonprofits want to do the most with the funds they have, so budgeting and planning are essential business activities.

Like any kind of plan, a budget is an estimate of what's going to happen. Your actual results will never exactly match the numbers you estimate in your budget. (If they do, someone's playing games with your books.) But comparing your actual performance to your budget can tell you that it's time to crack the whip on the sales team, rein in your spending, or both.

Budgeting in QuickBooks is both simple and simplistic. The program handles basic budgets and provides some shortcuts for entering numbers. However, you can't see whether your budget is working as you build it, and playing what-if games with budgets requires some fancy footwork. (The box on page 521 describes one way to create multiple budgets for the same time period.)

The easiest way to handle budgets is to craft them with a spreadsheet program like Excel. You can use all of Excel's commands to massage the numbers and then import your budgetary masterpiece into QuickBooks so you can compare your actual performance to the budget. This chapter explains your budgeting options, teaches you how to import budgets from other programs, and provides an overview of QuickBooks' budget reports.

TIP QuickBooks also includes a Cash Flow Projector (it lives on the Company→Planning & Budgeting submenu). This wizard provides a forecast of cash flow similar to what you can obtain by running a Cash Flow Forecast report (page 481), so it's not covered in this book.

Types of Budgets

To most people, the word "budget" means a profit-and-loss budget—one that estimates what your income and expenses will be over a period of time. QuickBooks profit-and-loss budgets are based on the income and expense accounts in your chart of accounts (see Chapter 3) and typically span your company's fiscal year.

Balance-sheet budgets aren't as common, but you can create them in QuickBooks as well. Balance sheets are snapshots of your assets and liabilities, and balance-sheet budgets follow the same format by showing the ending balances for your asset, liability, and other balance-sheet accounts.

NOTE Most companies plan for major purchases and their accompanying loans outside of the budgeting process. For example, if a company needs an asset to operate, executives usually analyze costs, benefits, payback periods, internal rates of return, and so on before making purchasing decisions. They evaluate cash flow to decide whether to borrow money or use cash generated by operations. But after that, the additional income generated by the asset and the additional interest expense associated with any loans show up in the profit-and-loss budget.

QuickBooks' profit-and-loss budgets come in three flavors, each helpful in its own way:

- **Company profit and loss**. The most common type of budget includes all the income and expenses for your entire company. This is the budget that management strives to follow—whether that's to produce the net profit that keeps shareholders happy or to generate the cash needed to run the company. With QuickBooks' Budget vs. Actual report (page 535), you can compare your actual results to your budget.

- **Customer or job budget**. A customer- or job-based profit-and-loss budget forecasts the income and expenses for a single customer or job. Projects that come with a lot of risk have to offer the potential for lots of profit to be worthwhile. By generating a profit-and-loss budget for a customer or job, you can make sure that the profitability meets your objectives.

- **Class budget**. If you use classes to track income and expenses, you can create profit-and-loss budgets for each class. Class budgets work particularly well when you track income and expenses for independent sections of your company: regions, business units, branches, partners, and so on.

Budgets and Forecasts

If you have QuickBooks Premier or Enterprise, you'll see the Set Up Forecast entry on the Company→Planning & Budgeting submenu. The dialog box that opens when you choose Set Up Forecast is strikingly similar to the Set Up Budgets dialog box. In fact, other than replacing the word "Budgets" with "Forecast," they're identical. So how do you decide whether to use a budget or a forecast?

You can have only one budget for a given period loaded in QuickBooks—for example, a 2013 profit-and-loss budget. A forecast lets you create another set of planning numbers for the same timeframe. So you can create a profit-and-loss budget for 2013 and a separate forecast for the same fiscal year, using the budget to reflect your most likely results and the forecast to show the numbers under more optimistic (or pessimistic) conditions.

QuickBooks has reports that compare your actual performance to budgets and forecasts (Reports→Budgets & Forecasts), so you can use either feature to compare your estimated numbers with your actual performance.

The bottom line: Use budgets unless you want a second set of planning numbers readily available. If you decide to create forecasts instead of—or in addition to—budgets, the instructions in this chapter apply to them, too.

Ways to Build Budgets

If you've just started a business, you may have a business plan that includes estimates of your income and expenses. Or you may have run your business for a while without a budget and now want to create a budget using past performance as a starting point. Either way, there's a method for building a QuickBooks budget. But the easiest approach is to build your budget outside QuickBooks and import the results. Here are your options and what each has to offer:

- **From data in another program**. The best way to build a budget is to create it in a program like Excel and then import it into QuickBooks. Setting up a spreadsheet for your company budget in Excel or some other program offers several advantages. After you set up the Excel file with rows for each account and columns for months and other fields, you can save it as a template for creating future budgets. If you're an Excel wiz, you can use that program's tools to quickly create and fine-tune your budget. You also can copy that file to create what-if scenarios or next year's budget based on the previous year's budget.

- **From previous year's actual results**. If this is your first budget and you have at least a year's worth of data in QuickBooks, you can use that existing data as a starting point (page 523) and edit only the values that change.

- **From scratch**. This method can be tedious because you have to estimate and fill in all the budget numbers (although, as you'll learn on page 530, QuickBooks does offer some data entry shortcuts). Fortunately you only have to use this approach for your first budget. (Page 522 explains how to start from scratch in QuickBooks and page 525 covers starting from scratch with Excel.)

■ Creating Budgets in QuickBooks

The Set Up Budgets wizard is command central for profit-and-loss budgets; balance-sheet budgets; budgets for customers, jobs, and classes; and budgets built from scratch or from previous year's data. Even if you use Excel to build your budgets, the Set Up Budgets wizard can help jumpstart your Excel spreadsheet.

Before you dive into building a budget, you have to perform two setup steps if you want your budgets to work properly:

- **Fiscal year**. QuickBooks uses the first month of your fiscal year as the first month of the budget. To check that you defined your fiscal year correctly, choose Company→Company Information. At the bottom of the Company Information dialog box, make sure that the month in the "First month in your Fiscal Year" box is correct.

- **Active accounts**. QuickBooks budgets cover only the accounts that are active in your chart of accounts. To activate any accounts you want to budget, press Ctrl+A to open the Chart of Accounts window, and then turn on the "Include inactive" checkbox. (If no accounts are inactive, the "Include inactive" checkbox is grayed out.) For any inactive account that you want in your budget, click the X to the left of the account's name to reactivate it.

To start the budget wizard, choose Company→Planning & Budgeting→Set Up Budgets. Depending on whether you already have a budget in QuickBooks, the program displays one of two different wizards. The Create New Budget wizard, shown in Figure 20-1, appears if this is your first budget in this company file.

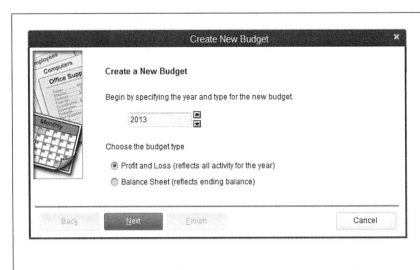

FIGURE 20-1

In the Create New Budget wizard, you first tell Quick-Books about the year and type of budget you want to create. On the second screen, you specify whether the budget works with customers, jobs, or classes.

If you already have at least one budget in your company file, QuickBooks opens the Set Up Budgets wizard instead and displays your most recent budget. To create a new budget in that wizard, click the Create New Budget button to launch the wizard shown here.

The steps for setting up a new budget are the same whether QuickBooks displays the Create New Budget wizard automatically or you click the Create New Budget button in the Set Up Budgets wizard:

1. **On the Create a New Budget screen (Figure 20-1), choose a fiscal year and type for the budget, and then click Next.**

   QuickBooks automatically fills in the next calendar year (perhaps assuming that you're done budgeting for the current year). Click the up and down arrows to the right of the box to choose the fiscal year you're budgeting for.

   Below the year setting, the program automatically selects the Profit and Loss option, because most budgets cover income and expenses for a year. If you want to create a balance-sheet budget instead, select the Balance Sheet option.

NOTE If you create a balance-sheet budget, you don't have to set any additional criteria before you build the budget for your balance-sheet accounts. In the Create New Budget wizard, clicking Next displays a screen that simply tells you to click Finish. When you do, a table containing your balance-sheet accounts appears in the Set Up Budgets window, and you can begin typing ending balances.

---

2. **On the Additional Profit and Loss Budget Criteria screen, select the flavor of profit-and-loss budget you want, and then click Next.**

   QuickBooks automatically selects the "No additional criteria" option, which creates the most common type of budget: a profit-and-loss budget for the entire company. Choose the Customer:Job option to build a budget for a specific customer or job instead. And if you have classes turned on (page 151), you can choose the Class option to build a class-based budget. (The next section explains how to create Customer:Job and Class budgets.)

3. **On the "Choose how you want to create a budget" screen, pick the kind of budget you want to create.**

   Keep the "Create budget from scratch" option selected if you want to create a blank budget. If you go this route, jump to page 524 to learn how to enter data in the Set Up Budgets wizard.

   If you have actual data that you want to use as a foundation for your budget, select "Create budget from previous year's actual data" instead. This option transfers the monthly income and expense account totals from the previous year into the budget.

4. **Click Finish.**

   QuickBooks opens the Set Up Budgets window, which includes a monstrous table. The rows represent each active account in your chart of accounts; each column is one month of the fiscal year. If you opted to create a budget for a customer, job, or class, the window includes either the Current Customer:Job drop-down list containing all your active customers and jobs, or the Class drop-down list containing all your active classes. Before you start entering values for a customer, job, or class budget, choose the customer, job, or class from this list.

The section "Filling in Budget Values" on page 530 explains how to fill in the cells in this table.

NOTE If your monitor's resolution is less than 1024 x 768, the Set Up Budgets window also includes the Show Next 6 Months button, because your screen can't display the entire year. In that case, QuickBooks initially displays January through June. Click Show Next 6 Months to display July through December (the button's label changes to Show Prev 6 Months).

■ Creating Additional Customer: Job or Class Budgets

In QuickBooks, there's no way to store several versions of a fiscal-year budget that covers your entire operation. But you *can* create additional budgets for the same fiscal year for different customers and jobs, or for classes.

After you create your first budget, the Set Up Budgets dialog box opens, displaying the most recent fiscal-year budget. But if you've created at least one budget for a customer or job for a fiscal year (see step 2 below), the Budget drop-down list includes an entry like "FY2013 - Profit & Loss By Account and Customer:Job." Class budgets show up in the Budget drop-down list looking something like "FY2013 - Profit & Loss By Account and Class."

NOTE Class budgets work the way Customer:Job budgets do. In fact, if you replace every instance of "Customer:Job" in the following tutorial with "Class," you'll have the instructions for creating Class budgets.

Here's how to create and save additional Customer:Job or Class budgets:

1. **In the Budget drop-down list, choose the Customer:Job budget for the fiscal year you want to budget.**

   QuickBooks adds the Current Customer:Job box to the Set Up Budgets window between the Budget list and the table.

2. **In the Current Customer:Job drop-down list, choose the customer or job that you want to budget, as shown in Figure 20-2.**

   Any budgetary numbers you've previously entered for the customer or job for the selected fiscal year appear in the budget table.

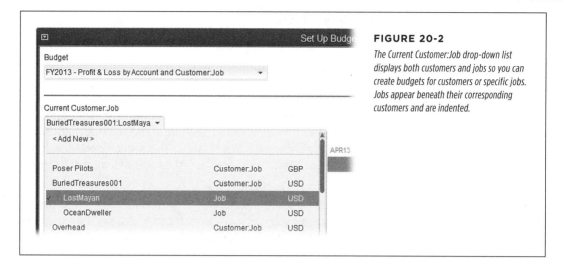

FIGURE 20-2

The Current Customer:Job drop-down list displays both customers and jobs so you can create budgets for customers or specific jobs. Jobs appear beneath their corresponding customers and are indented.

3. **In the budget table, fill in values for the Customer:Job budget.**

Unlike a budget for your entire operation, Customer:Job budgets may have values for only a few accounts. For example, for a job that includes products, services, and reimbursable expenses, your budget may have values only for income accounts and the expense accounts for reimbursable expenses.

4. **When you're finished entering values, click Save.**

If you choose another customer or job without clicking Save, QuickBooks asks if you want to record the budget. In the Recording Budget message box, click Yes.

■ Creating and Copying Budgets with Excel

QuickBooks budget reports can help you plan for the future and evaluate whether your business is going boom or bust. However, the program's tools for building and editing budgets don't compare to what you can do with a program like Excel. QuickBooks keeps only one budget at a time for the same type of budget and time period—for example, the profit-and-loss budget for fiscal year 2013—and it doesn't offer a feature for copying a budget. That's where a spreadsheet program comes in handy. You can easily copy a budget spreadsheet, make the changes you want, and then import the final product into QuickBooks. For example, you might create next year's budget from this year's. Or, you might experiment with what-if scenarios including a bare-bones budget in case a client with shaky finances disappears and a second happy-dance budget if you snag that big new project.

There are three parts to working on budgets with Excel:

1. **Export a budget with the accounts from your company file.**

2. **Edit budget values in Excel.**

3. **Import the final budget into your company file.**

The following sections describe each step in detail.

Exporting Your Budget

Exporting a budget is the quickest way to create an Excel spreadsheet with the accounts from your chart of accounts and the additional information that QuickBooks needs to import the spreadsheet when it's finished. This section begins with the steps for getting the budget ready to export, and then you'll learn how to create the export file.

QuickBooks exports only accounts that contain at least one value. If you have a budget with numbers already, you can skip to the steps for creating the export file (page 527). However, if your budget is blank, you need to add at least one budget value to each account. Here's what you do:

1. **In the Set Up Budgets window (Company→Planning and Budgeting→Set Up Budgets), in the Budget drop-down list, choose the budget you want to add values to.**

   The budget table appears with the accounts in the first column, the annual total in the second column, and columns for each month of the year.

2. **Fill in a value in the cell for January for each account in the budget, as shown in Figure 20-3.**

   Click the first cell in the January column (labeled something like Jan 13) and type _1_ in the cell. Then, fill in the rest of the cells in the column.

3. **When all the cells in the January column contain values, click Save.** Then, click OK to close the Set Up Budgets window.

   That's it! Your budget is ready to export.

NOTE If you have more than one budget in your company file, you can't export only the budget you want to work with—when you export QuickBooks' Budgets list, the export file includes entries for every budget for every fiscal year. So if you created budgets for customers, jobs, and classes, you'll get entries for those, too. When you work on the budgets in a spreadsheet, you can ignore the entries for those other budgets, but the best approach is to delete the extraneous rows so you can focus on one budget at a time.

Here's how to export QuickBooks budgets:

1. **Choose File→Utilities→Export→Lists to IIF Files.**

   QuickBooks opens an Export dialog box with checkboxes for each type of list you can export.

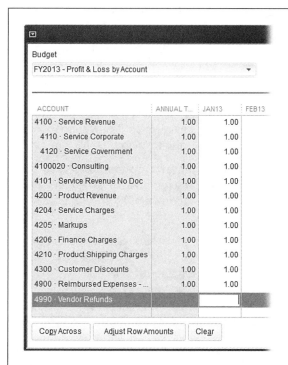

FIGURE 20-3

Using your keyboard is the fastest way to fill in these cells. Click the first cell in the January column and then press the 1 key to enter a placeholder value. Then, press the down arrow to move to the next cell in the column. Press the 1 key again. Rinse and repeat until the entire January column contains values.

2. **In this first Export dialog box, turn on the Budgets checkbox, and then click OK.**

   QuickBooks opens a second Export dialog box, which looks like a Save As dialog box. However, the "Save as type" box is automatically set to "IIF Files (*.IIF)."

3. **In the second Export dialog box, navigate to the folder where you want to save the exported file and, in the "File name" box, replace "*.IIF" with the name for your export file.**

   To keep your files organized, save all your exported files in a single folder called something like *Export_Files*. Name the exported file something like *QBBudgets.iif*.

4. **Click Save to export the budgets.**

   When a QuickBooks Information box appears telling you that the export was successful, click OK to dismiss it.

Working with a Budget in Excel

If your company file contains only one budget, you can open the exported file in Excel and start editing the budget values. On the other hand, if you exported *several* budgets, your work will flow more smoothly if you format the file. Here are the steps for opening and working on a budget in Excel:

1. **In a spreadsheet program like Excel, open the exported file.**

   IIF files are tab-delimited text files (see page 649). To open one in Excel 2010, choose File→Open (in Excel 2007, choose Office→Open). In the Open dialog box, click the down arrow to the right of All Excel Files and choose All Files from the drop-down menu so you can see all the files in your folders (in Excel 2007, head to the "Files of type" box, and then choose All Files). Navigate to the folder that contains the IIF export file and double-click its filename. The Excel Text Import Wizard appears. You don't have to specify any special formats to tell Excel how to read the file; just click Finish to import the file into Excel.

2. **In Excel, to change the order of the budget rows to show budgets by fiscal year, select all the rows below the one that begins with !BUD (Figure 20-4). Then choose Data→Sort and sort the workbook first by start date (START-DATE) and then by account (ACCNT).**

   Before you sort the data, rows for different years' budgets and account names are in no particular order. By sorting the rows first by start date, you can see all the entries for each fiscal year grouped together. (If you have Customer:Job budgets, you can also sort by the CUSTOMER column.) This sort method intersperses income and expense accounts, but because companies typically have fewer income accounts, you can quickly move the rows for income accounts above the expense accounts. Once you do that, you can add subtotals for your income and expenses, and calculate your net profit.

3. **To edit this file to represent only one budget, delete all the rows for budgets that you aren't changing.**

   The STARTDATE column contains the date that the fiscal year for the budget begins. So, for example, if you want to remove all the budgets except the one for fiscal year 2013, delete all the rows that have a date other than 1/1/2013 in the STARTDATE column.

4. **If you want to use an existing budget to create next year's budget, simply change the year in the STARTDATE column.**

   Use Excel's Replace command (press Ctrl+H) to change the year to the new budget (Figure 20-4). For example, the budget entries for 2012 budgets include "1/1/2012" in the STARTDATE column. To create a budget for 2013, change the contents of these cells to "1/1/2013."

   In Excel 2007 and 2010, you can also choose the Home tab and then click Find & Select→Replace (at the right end of the Ribbon); in Excel 2003, choose Edit→Replace.

To modify budget numbers, edit the budget values in the Excel worksheet.

NOTE If you create several what-if budgets in Excel, be sure to copy just the data for your final budget into a file for importing into QuickBooks. Compare the keywords and column headings in the Budget list export file to those in the file you plan to import to make sure that the data imports the way you want. For example, a row that begins with !BUD lists the keywords that identify columns, such as ACCNT for your accounts and AMOUNT for your budget values. (Rows for budget entries have to begin with a cell containing the keyword BUD.) For more on importing and exporting data, see Chapter 24.

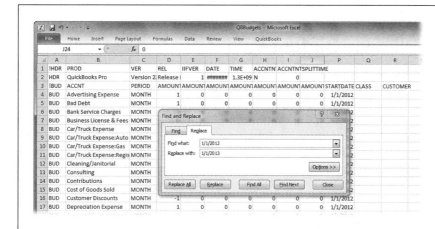

FIGURE 20-4

The entries for 2012 budgets include "1/1/2012" in the STARTDATE column. (Entries for Customer:Job or class budgets include the customer and job name in the CUSTOMER column or the class name in the CLASS column.) To turn an exported 2012 budget into a 2013 budget, change the contents of these cells to "1/1/2013."

5. **In Excel 2010, choose File→Save As. (In Excel 2007, choose Office→Save As.) In the Save As dialog box, save the modified file with a new filename.**

   In the Save As dialog box, leave the file type set to "Text (tab delimited) (*.txt)."

Now you're ready to import the file into QuickBooks.

Importing a Budget into QuickBooks

After you create or edit your budget in Excel, importing the budget is easy. If you're experimenting with several budgets for the same time period, you can import one and then run budget reports to examine it more closely. Just remember to finish by importing the budget you finally decide to use.

Here are the steps for importing a budget file:

1. **To import the modified IIF file into QuickBooks, choose File→Utilities→ Import→IIF Files.**

   QuickBooks opens the Import dialog box and automatically chooses "IIF Files (*.IIF)" in the "Files of type" box. If you don't see your file, in the "Files of type" box, choose "All Files (*.*)" instead.

2. **Double-click the name of the IIF file that contains your edited budget.**

When a QuickBooks Information box appears telling you that the import was successful, click OK to dismiss it.

3. **Choose Company→Planning & Budgeting→Set Up Budgets.**

If you created a budget for a new fiscal year, in the Set Up Budgets window, the Budget drop-down list now contains an entry for that year's budget. If you used a spreadsheet to edit an existing budget, in the Budget drop-down list, choose the entry for that budget to see the updated values in the budget table.

▓ Filling in Budget Values

Regardless of which type of budget you create, the way you fill in and edit values in QuickBooks is the same. To add budget values to an account, in the Set Up Budgets window's Account column, click the account. When you do, QuickBooks automatically selects the cell in the first month column in that row. If you're filling in the entire year's worth of numbers, type the value for the first month, press Tab to move to the next month, and continue until you've entered values for all 12 months. The Annual Total column displays the total for all months, as shown in Figure 20-5. The box below explains what the buttons at the bottom of the Set Up Budgets window do.

Filling in a few budget cells is usually enough to convince you that data entry shortcuts are in order. Luckily, QuickBooks gives you two ways to enter values faster, both described next.

The Set Up Budgets Buttons

In the Set Up Budgets window, several buttons help you manage the work you do on your budgets in QuickBooks. Although you're probably familiar with their functions based on similar buttons in other dialog boxes, here's a quick overview:

- **Clear**. Click this button to delete *all* the values in a budget—for every account and every month. This is the button to click if you want to start over.

- **Save**. When you've added or updated all the values in a budget, click this button to save your work. You can

also click Save so you don't lose the work you've done so far. And don't worry if you forget to click this button: If you click OK or choose another budget, QuickBooks asks whether you want to record the one you've been working on.

- **OK**. Clicking this button records the values you've entered and closes the Set Up Budgets window.

- **Cancel**. Clicking this button closes the window *without* saving your work.

Copy Across Columns

Because budgets are estimates, you don't need extraordinarily detailed or precise values. In the Set Up Budgets window, you can copy a number from one cell in a row to all the cells to its right in the same row, as demonstrated in Figure 20-5.

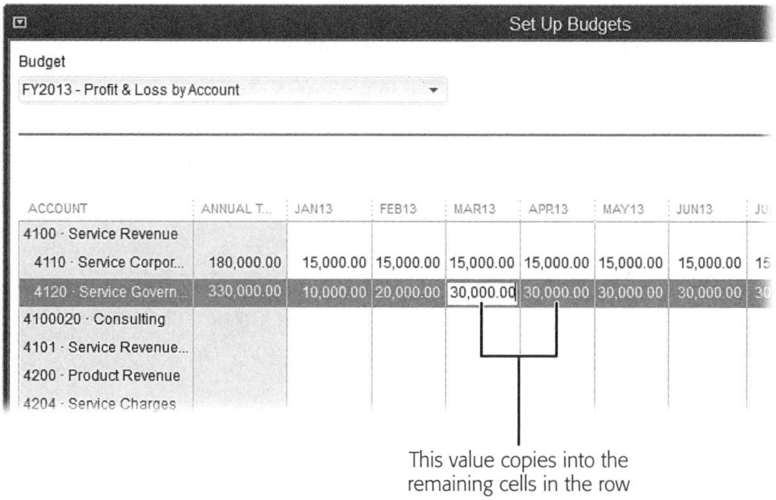

FIGURE 20-5

To copy the value in a cell into the remaining cells in a row, start by selecting the cell, like the cell for Service Government for March 2013 shown here. Then, click Copy Across to make QuickBooks copy "30,000" into the cells for April through December.

This value copies into the remaining cells in the row

TIP If the account names and budget values are hopelessly truncated and you have screen real estate to spare, enlarge the Set Up Budgets window by dragging a corner or maximizing it. The columns show more of the cell contents as you enlarge the window. To resize a specific column to make it wider or narrower, put your cursor over the vertical line to the right of the column's header. When the cursor turns into a two-headed arrow, drag right or left.

This shortcut is fabulous when a monthly expense remains the same throughout the year, like office rent, for example. But it also works if a price changes midyear. For instance, suppose the corporate concierge you've hired to run errands for your employees announces that his rates are going up in May. If your budget contains the old rate in every month, click the cell for May and type the new rate. Then click Copy Across, and QuickBooks lists the new rate for May through December.

TIP If you mistakenly add values to cells that should be blank, Copy Across is the fastest way to empty a row. Clear the first month's cell by selecting its value and then pressing Backspace. Then click Copy Across to have QuickBooks clear all the other cells in that row.

Adjust Row Amounts

The Set Up Budgets window's Adjust Row Amounts button lets you increase or decrease monthly values by a specific dollar amount or percentage. Say you created a budget from the previous year's data, but you want to increase all the values in the current year by 10 percent. Or maybe your company is growing quickly and you want to apply some heat to your sales force by increasing the target income each month. In that case, you can tell QuickBooks to compound the increase, so each month's sales target is a little higher than the previous month's value.

Changing all the cells in a row by a fixed dollar amount isn't as useful as you might think, because Copy Across basically does the same thing in most cases. But when you change budget amounts by percentages or compound increases each month, QuickBooks takes care of the calculations for you. Here's how to adjust row amounts in both of these ways:

1. **Click the row you want to adjust.**

   If you want to start the adjustment in a specific month, click the cell for the starting month.

2. **Click the Adjust Row Amounts button.**

   QuickBooks opens the Adjust Row Amounts dialog box and, in the "Start at" box, automatically selects the option that you chose the last time you opened this dialog box. "1st month" starts adjustments in the first month of the fiscal year. To start with the month you selected instead, choose "Currently selected month" (if you select this option, QuickBooks displays the "Enable compounding" checkbox, which is explained in step 5).

   NOTE The Adjust Row Amunts feature is for adjusting *existing* budget values, not filling in blank cells. For example, when you select the "Increase each remaining monthly amount in this row by this dollar amount or percentage" option and type *100* in the text box, QuickBooks adds 100 to the values in the month cells. So if the January cell is set to 1,000, it increases to 1,100. However, if the remaining months' cells are zero (0), they increase to 100.

3. **Select the appropriate option for how the prices change.**

   QuickBooks automatically selects the "Increase each remaining monthly amount in this row by this dollar amount or percentage" option because prices usually go up. But if prices are decreasing, select the "Decrease each remaining monthly amount..." option instead.

4. **In the text box for the option you selected, type the dollar amount or percentage, and then click OK.**

   If the landlord tells you that rent is going up 5 percent, in the box for the Increase option, type *5%*, and QuickBooks increases the value in all the remaining cells by 5 percent. So if your rent was $5,000 a month, the values in all the remaining months change to $5,250.

To add a dollar amount to the remaining cells instead, type that dollar value. For example, to add $1,000 a month to the Rent cells, in the box for this option, type *1000*. Each subsequent cell in the Rent row increases by 1,000. (Of course, you can do the same thing by typing the new rent amount in the cell for the first month to which it applies, and then clicking Copy Across.)

5. **If you set the "Start at" box to "Currently selected month" in step 2, the "Enable compounding" checkbox appeared; turn it on if you want to adjust each month's value based on the previous month's value.**

    When you compound dollar amounts, QuickBooks adds the dollar amount you specify to the next month's value. For example, if January's value is 25,000 and you change the value by 1,000, February's value becomes 26,000, March's value increases by another 1,000 to 27,000, and so on, as shown in Figure 20-6.

    You can also compound by percentage. If you turn on the "Enable compounding" checkbox and type a percentage in the text box, QuickBooks increases the next month's value by the percentage you specify. If January's value is 25,000 and you increase it by 10 percent, February's value becomes 27,500, March's value increases another 10 percent to 30,250, and so on.

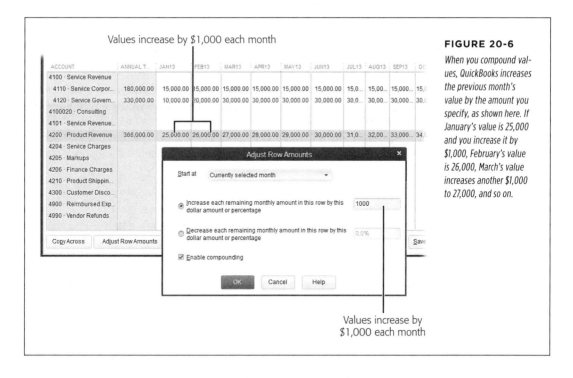

Values increase by $1,000 each month

Values increase by $1,000 each month

FIGURE 20-6

When you compound values, QuickBooks increases the previous month's value by the amount you specify, as shown here. If January's value is 25,000 and you increase it by $1,000, February's value is 26,000, March's value increases another $1,000 to 27,000, and so on.

■ Running Budget Reports

A budget gives you a target to aim for. The Set Up Budgets window lets you type values for income and expense accounts, but it doesn't show you whether your budget results in a net profit or loss. For that, you need a budget report (or your budget exported to a spreadsheet, as described on page 526). And to see how your business is doing compared with your budget, you need a budget report that shows budget and actual numbers side by side. QuickBooks provides four types of budget reports: one to review budgets you've created and three to compare your performance to your plan. This section describes the various reports, what they're useful for, and how to create and format them.

> **NOTE** To learn about *all* the options for customizing any QuickBooks report, see Chapter 21.

The Budget Overview Report

The Set Up Budgets window shows your accounts and the values you enter for each month, but not whether your budget produces a profit or loss. The Budget Overview report shows budget numbers for each account and month, too, but it *also* subtotals values if you use top-level accounts and subaccounts in your chart of accounts, as shown in Figure 20-7. To see whether you earn enough income to cover expenses, at the bottom of the report, look for net income (income minus expenses) for each month and for the entire year.

To run the Budget Overview Report, choose Reports→Budgets→Budget Overview. In the Budget Report dialog box, first choose the budget you want to view and then a layout (explained in a moment). When you click Finish, QuickBooks opens the Budget Overview report window. (The Modify Report dialog box might appear depending on the report settings [page 624] you've chosen. Click Cancel to close that dialog box.)

> **NOTE** The Budget Overview report includes only accounts that have budget values.

■ REPORT LAYOUTS

If you create a report for a profit-and-loss budget for your entire company, the only layout option in the Budget Report dialog box is Account By Month, which lists the accounts in the first column with each subsequent column showing one month of the fiscal year. You can change the columns to different durations in the Profit & Loss Budget Overview window (Figure 20-7).

If you choose a Customer:Job budget in the Budget Report dialog box and then click Next, the Budget Overview Report includes these layout options:

- **Account By Month** lists accounts in the first column and months of the fiscal year in the subsequent columns. The values in the monthly columns represent the totals for *all* the Customer:Job budgets you've created.

- **Account By Customer:Job** lists accounts in the first column and includes additional columns for each customer or job you've budgeted. Each customer and job column shows its annual totals.

- **Customer:Job by Month** adds a row for each customer and additional rows for each job that customer has. The columns are for each month of the fiscal year. The value for a job and month represents the total budgeted value for all accounts.

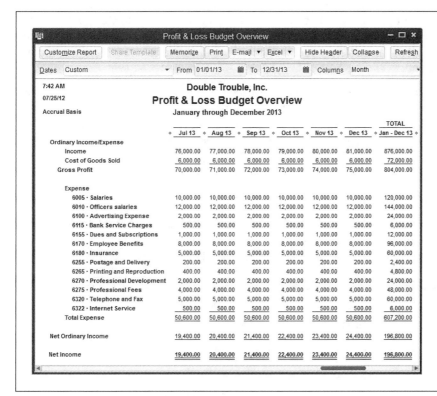

FIGURE 20-7

Although you build budgets month by month, many businesses (particularly ones with shareholders) focus on quarterly performance. To view your budget by quarter instead of by month, in the Columns drop-down list, choose Quarter.

Budget vs. Actual Report

The Budget vs. Actual report (Reports→Budgets→Budget vs. Actual) compares the budget you created to the actual income and expenses your business achieved. Run this report monthly for early warnings that your performance is veering off track. For example, if your income is short of your target, the "% of Budget" column shows percentages less than 100 percent; if you're making more than you planned, this column shows percentages greater than 100 percent. On the other hand, costs greater than 100 percent indicate that expenses are ballooning beyond your budget.

The column with the heading for a month and year (like Jan 13 or, for a quarter, "Jan - Mar 13") is your actual performance. The Budget column includes the budgeted values for the same time period. You can also see the difference between the two values in dollars (in the Over Budget column) and percentage (in the "% of Budget" column).

TIP If the numbers in your report don't seem right, the culprit could be the wrong choice of accrual or cash reporting (page xxiii explains the difference between cash-basis and accrual reporting). Click Customize Report and, on the Display tab, click the Accrual or Cash option to match your reporting style. See page 625 to learn how to change the reporting preference for accrual or cash reporting.

Profit & Loss Budget Performance Report

The Profit & Loss Budget Performance report (Reports→Budgets→Profit & Loss Budget Performance) also compares budgeted and actual values, but initially shows the actual values for the current month so far with the budgeted values for the entire month in the Budget column. Two additional columns show the actual and budgeted values for the year to date. The rightmost column shows the budget for the entire year.

Use this report to check your performance before the end of each month. Because the budget numbers represent the entire month, you shouldn't expect a perfect match between actual and budgeted values. But if your income or expenses are way off the mark, you can take corrective action.

Memorizing Budget Reports

When you generate budget reports, it takes several clicks to specify the budget and layout you want to see. In addition, after the report window opens, you might click Customize Report to change the date range, the columns that appear, and so on. All in all, getting the budget report you really want might require a dozen or more small customizations.

Rather than reapply all these tweaks each time you generate the report, memorize the customized report so you can regenerate it with just one click. Here's how:

1. **In the report's window, click Memorize.** QuickBooks opens the Memorize Report dialog box.

2. **In the Name box, type a name for the customized report,** such as "P&L Budget vs. Actual 2013."

3. **If you want to save the report in a special group, turn on the Save in Memorized Report Group checkbox.** In the drop-down list, choose the group. For example, you might store budget reports in the Company group. If you don't save the report to a special group, QuickBooks adds it to the Memorized Report submenu.

4. **Click OK.**

To run the report, choose Reports→Memorized Reports. If you didn't save the report to a group, choose the report's name on the Memorized Reports submenu. If you *did* save it to a group, in the Memorized Reports submenu, choose the group and then the report's name. To learn how to add this report to your Favorite Reports, see page 544.

Budget vs. Actual Graph

To see a graph comparing your budget to actual performance, choose Reports→Budgets→Budget vs. Actual Graph. Because the report window can't display all the bars at the same time, click Next Group in the window's button bar to display the bars for the next several accounts. This graph displays the differences between your budgeted and actual values in two ways:

- **The upper bar graph** shows the difference between your actual and budgeted net income for each month. When your actual net income exceeds the budgeted value (meaning you made more money than you planned), the bar is blue and appears above the horizontal axis. If the actual net income is less than budgeted, the bar is red and drops below the horizontal axis.

- **The lower bar graph** sorts accounts, customers, or classes (depending on the report you choose by clicking "P&L by Accounts," "P&L by Accounts and Jobs," or "P&L by Accounts and Classes" in the report window's button bar) that are the furthest from your budgeted values (either above or below). For example, if you click "P&L by Accounts and Jobs," the bars show the customers and jobs that exceeded your budget by the largest amount or fell the furthest short.

Working with Reports

Q uickBooks comes with loads of built-in reports that show what's going on with your company's finances. But a dozen report categories with several reports tucked in each category presents a few challenges, particularly if you're new to both business *and* QuickBooks.

The first challenge is knowing what type of report tells you what you need to know. For example, a Profit & Loss (P&L) report tells you how much income and expense you had, but a balance sheet shows how much your company is worth.

The second challenge is finding the report you want within the different report categories. After you decide you want to compare the profit of the items you sell, do you look for the corresponding QuickBooks report in the Customers & Receivables category, Sales category, Inventory category, or "Jobs, Time & Mileage" category? (If you guessed "Jobs, Time & Mileage," you're right.)

The Report Center is a handy way to find the reports you want. But flipping through this book can be even faster, which is why each chapter describes the built-in reports that correspond to the bookkeeping tasks the chapter covers, what they're good for, and where you can find them.

A third challenge—for even the most knowledgeable QuickBooks aficionado—is that the built-in reports might not do exactly what you want. A date range could be off, information that you don't want might be included, or the data could be grouped in ways that don't make sense for your business. After using QuickBooks for a while, most businesses tweak the program's built-in reports. This chapter explains how to customize reports to get what you want. And there's no point in letting that customization go to waste, so you'll also learn how to memorize your customized reports, add them to QuickBooks' menus for fast access, and even how to exchange particularly handy customized reports between company files.

Finding the Right Reports

If you know what kind of report answers your burning business question, finding that report can be as simple as dragging your mouse through the Reports menu to a likely category, and then, on the category's submenu, clicking the name of the report you want. But if you need help figuring out what a report does and what it looks like, the Report Center could be your new best friend.

In the top icon bar or the left icon bar, click Reports (or choose Reports→Report Center). (Page 662 explains how to add this icon to the icon bar if it isn't visible.) The window that appears includes a clickable list of the same report categories and reports listed in the Reports menu. But unlike the menu, the Report Center gives you all sorts of hints for finding the right report. The center also offers several shortcuts for getting to the right report fast, as you can see in Figure 21-1.

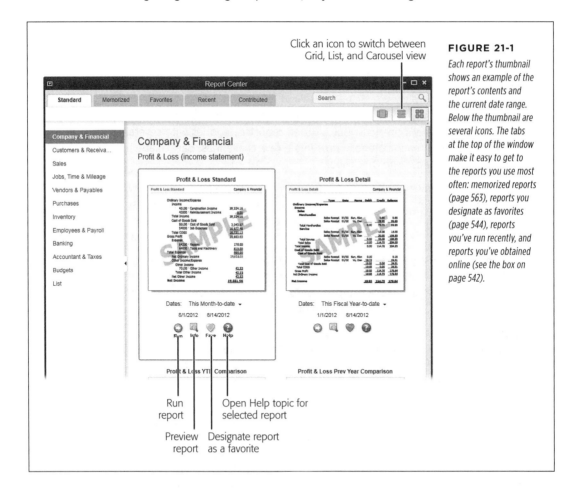

Click an icon to switch between Grid, List, and Carousel view

Run report

Preview report

Open Help topic for selected report

Designate report as a favorite

FIGURE 21-1

Each report's thumbnail shows an example of the report's contents and the current date range. Below the thumbnail are several icons. The tabs at the top of the window make it easy to get to the reports you use most often: memorized reports (page 563), reports you designate as favorites (page 544), reports you've run recently, and reports you've obtained online (see the box on page 542).

On the left side of the Report Center, you'll initially see built-in report categories. (The categories that you see change depending on whether you select the Memorized, Favorites, Recent, or Contributed tab at the top of the center; the categories that these tabs represent are described on page 544.) To see the reports in a category, click the category's name, like Company & Financial, Sales, or Banking. These categories are the same ones you see in the Reports menu (page 544).

Reviewing Reports in the Report Center

The Report Center gives you three ways to view the reports in a category:

- **Grid view**, shown in Figure 21-1, is ideal when you need a little help finding the right report. It displays previews of each type of report in the category selected on the left side of the window. To see more reports in that category, scroll down. Date range and report-related icons appear below each thumbnail. In the upper-right part of the Report Center, click the Grid view icon (which looks like four small boxes in a grid) to display this view.

- **List view** is your best bet when you want brief hints about the right reports and want to get to those reports quickly. Select a category on the left side of the Report Center, and the titles of that category's reports and the questions they answer appear in a space-saving list. To use this view, click the List view icon in the window's upper right, which looks like three horizontal bars.

- **Carousel view** displays a sample report (one that doesn't use your company accounts or data) in the center of the window. In addition to the report's title, the question that it answers appears above the sample, such as "What are my company's total purchases from each vendor?" for the "Purchases by Vendor Summary" report. Below the report, you can change the date range by clicking the arrow to the right of the current range and choosing a new one. To run the report, double-click its preview or click the "Run report" icon (a white arrow inside a green circle).

  Other reports in the category wait in the wings to the left and right of the selected report. To access these reports, either click their preview images or use the slider bar at the bottom of the Report Center window to scroll through them until the one you're looking for appears front and center. To use this view, in the upper-right corner of the Report Center, click the Carousel view icon, which looks like a series of slides (if you use your imagination).

Working with Reports in the Report Center

For each report in the Report Center, its current date range and icons for performing report-related tasks appear below the report preview. Here's what you can do with each one:

- **Date range**. QuickBooks displays the name of the current date range for the report and the dates the range represents, for example, This Fiscal Year and "1/1/2013 12/31/2013." To change the range before you run the report, click the range's name (This Fiscal Year, for example) and then choose a new range from the drop-down list. (See page 553 to learn about the date ranges you can choose from.)

- **Preview a report**. For built-in reports, click the icon that looks like a magnifying glass in front of a piece of paper to see a sample of the report you've selected. (This icon isn't included in Carousel view because the thumbnails act as report previews.) If you click the Report Center's Memorized tab and then click a Preview icon, the samples just say "Memorized Report"; you have to run the report to see what it looks like.

GEM IN THE ROUGH

Sharing Reports with Others

If you don't see the kind of report you want, you may not have to customize a report yourself. The Report Center's Contributed tab makes it easy to grab reports shared by Intuit and others within the online Intuit Community. When you click the Contributed tab, you can filter the list of shared reports by industry and sort it by category. In the View Industry drop-down list, click the industry you want, such as Professional Consulting. Click the Sort By box and choose "Most popular" or "Highly rated" to see the shared reports that others have found helpful. To see recently added reports, choose "Newly shared."

To run a report, put your cursor over the report you're interested in to display its icons. (If you're in Carousel view, the icons will already be visible.) Then click its Display Report icon (the green circle labeled "Run").

If you like, you can rate these shared reports. One of the icons for shared reports is labeled "Rate." When you click it, the "Add

a comment and rate this report" dialog box opens. Comments from others appear in the lower half of the dialog box. Type your comments in the upper box and fill in the Name box with your name or nickname. Then click the number of stars you want to give the report. For example, to give it a five-star rating, click the rightmost star. When you're done, click "Add and Close" to post your review and close the dialog box.

You can also return the favor by sharing your reports with the community. When you click the Memorized tab in the Report Center, each report has an icon labeled Share that looks like two pieces of paper, as shown in Figure 21-2. Click this icon to open the Share Template window. Fill in information about your report, including a title, description, your name, and your email (in case Intuit has a question about the report), and then click Share.

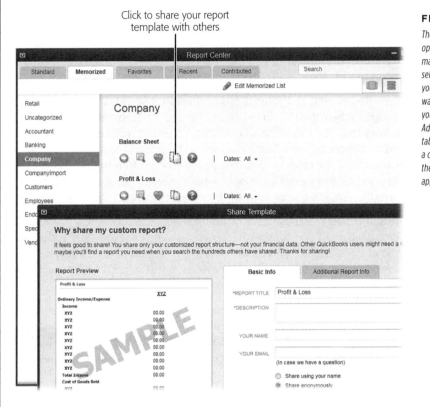

Click to share your report
template with others

FIGURE 21-2

*The "Share anonymously"
option is selected auto-
matically, but you can
select the "Share using
your name" option if you
want some publicity for
your creations. On the
Additional Report Info
tab, you can designate
a category and choose
the industries the report
applies to.*

- **Run a report**. The Display Report icon is a white arrow inside a green circle. When you click this icon, QuickBooks runs the report and displays it in a report window. You can then click Customize Report in the report window's toolbar to make changes (page 551).

> **NOTE** The heart icon lets you designate your favorite reports. You'll learn how to do that in the next section.

- **Learn more**. If you want to know more about a report and how you can cus-tomize it, select the report and then click the "Learn more about this report" icon (the blue circle with a white question mark). QuickBooks opens the Help topic for that report, which gives hints about how to use and customize it. If you click this icon for a memorized report, QuickBooks opens the "Work with memorized reports" Help topic instead.

Finding Frequently Used Reports

The Report Center initially displays its built-in reports and the categories to which they belong. However, the center also offers quick access to reports that you run often:

- **Memorized reports**. If you modify reports to suit your needs, you can memorize them (page 563) and run them again and again with all your customized settings in place. In the Report Center, click the Memorized tab to see your memorized report groups (page 565). Select one to display the reports within it.

- **Favorite reports**. QuickBooks lets you vote for your favorite reports so you can get to them in a jiffy. In the Report Center, the Favorites tab displays all the reports that you designate as favorites. Whenever you select a report in the Report Center, a Fave icon (an orange heart) appears (its tooltip says, "Mark as Favorite"). If the report is one that you run more often than you check email, simply click this icon; QuickBooks adds the report to the Favorites tab and turns the report's heart icon gray to indicate that this is one of your favorites.

- **Recent reports**. You can quickly rerun a report you used lately by clicking the Recent tab and then choosing the report you want. For example, if you produced a Sales by Customer report a few days ago and need to run it again, on the left side of the Recent tab, click the "Last 1-7 days" heading, click the report's name, and then click the Display Report icon.

- **Search**. If you don't know which built-in report you want, you can use keywords to narrow down your choices. For example, if you want to see how much equity you have in your company, in the Search box at the upper right of the Report Center, type *equity* and then press Enter. A Search Results tab appears with a list of reports that include equity, such as Balance Sheet Standard, Net Worth Graph, and Balance Sheet Prev Year Comparison.

NOTE If you type more than one keyword, your search results are likely to grow longer, not shorter, because QuickBooks looks for reports that contain *any* of the keywords you provide, rather than reports that contain all of them.

■ Running Reports

While you're learning about QuickBooks' reports, stick with the Report Center (described in the previous section). Once you're more familiar with what the program's reports do, the Reports menu is the quickest route to running them, as shown in Figure 21-3. Or you can click one of the report links scattered throughout QuickBooks' windows, menus, and centers. (The box on page 546 explains a shortcut you can use when you want to run several reports at the same time.)

TIP Out of the box, QuickBooks automatically opens the report in a report window when you run a report. However, if you find yourself customizing almost every report you run, you can set a preference to tell QuickBooks to open the Modify Report dialog box first (see page 624). That way, you can make the changes you want *before* you see the report.

You can run reports from many locations in QuickBooks. Here's how to run reports depending on which route you choose:

- **Reports menu**. This menu sits in the QuickBooks main menu bar. To run a report, choose Reports, and then select the category you want (such as Memorized Reports, Company & Financial, or Vendors & Payables). On the submenu that appears (Figure 21-3), choose the report you want to run. (If another submenu appears, drag until you can pick the report you want.) A report window opens displaying the report you chose.

- **The Report Center**. Select the report you want to run. If you want to change the date range before you run the report, click the current date range's name and then choose the new range on the drop-down list. To run the report, click the green Run icon, shown in Figure 21-1 (page 540).

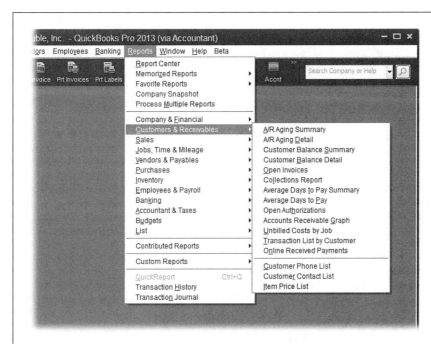

FIGURE 21-3

The Reports menu not only includes built-in QuickBooks reports and reports you memorize; it can also launch the Report Center and the Company Snapshot, and it contains the Process Multiple Reports feature, described in the box on page 546.

- **Favorites menu**. The Favorites menu is on QuickBooks' main menu bar. If you add a report to this menu (page 661), run the report by choosing Favorites→<report name>. If you use the left icon bar, you can click Run Favorite Reports to list the reports you've designated as your favorites. Then, in the Run Favorite Reports section, click the report you want to run.

- **Icon bar**. You can customize QuickBooks' icon bar (page 662) to include your all-time favorite reports or a category of reports. To run a report from the icon bar, simply click the report's icon.

- **List windows**. In a list window, such as the Chart of Accounts window or Item List window, click the Reports button at the bottom of the window and then choose the report you want to run on the drop-down list that appears.

- **Customer, Vendor, Employee, and Inventory Centers**. To run reports about a specific customer, vendor, employee, or inventory item, open the corresponding center. Select the customer, job, vendor, employee, or inventory item to display info about it on the right side of the center's window. Then click one of the report links, like QuickReport or Open Balance. In a center's toolbar, choose Print or Excel to create a hard copy (as explained in the next section) or to export an Excel file (page 549) of a Vendor List, Customer List, Employee List, or Item List report.

GEM IN THE ROUGH

Running Multiple Reports

Perhaps you perform the same tasks every month—calling customers with overdue invoices, checking inventory, and reviewing sales by item, for example—and you need reports to complete each task. Particularly when you print reports, you might sit in front of your computer with nothing but an occasional click to break the monotony, while QuickBooks slowly transforms your data into printed reports one at a time.

But you don't have to do it that way. Tucked away on the Reports menu is the Process Multiple Reports feature, which generates all the reports you choose one after the other. You can stock your printer with paper, make sure the toner cartridge isn't running low, and then use this feature to run dozens of reports while you do something else.

Process Multiple Reports works only with memorized reports, because you don't get the opportunity to customize the reports it runs. So customize each report you run regularly to make sure it includes the correct information and is formatted the way you want, and then memorize each one (page 563).

When you choose Reports→Process Multiple Reports, Quick-Books opens the Process Multiple Reports window. It lists built-in reports along with all your memorized reports in the order that they appear on the Memorized Reports submenu—but doesn't automatically select any, as shown in Figure 21-4.

To include or remove a report from the batch you want to run, click its checkmark cell to toggle the checkmark on or off. The Date Range column shows the period covered by the report. To change the range for this report run, type the dates you want in a report's From and To cells. When all the reports you want to print have checkmarks and the correct date range, click Print. QuickBooks opens the Print Reports dialog box. All you have to do is choose the printer and the number of copies, and then click Print to start pushing reports through the printer. If you want the program to open report windows for each selected report instead, in the Process Multiple Reports window, click Display.

Another way to run multiple reports is to create a report group with all the reports you want to run (see the box on page 565). Call it something like *QuarterlyReports* or *EndofYearReports*. Then you can run the reports by opening the Memorized Reports window (Reports→Memorized Reports→Memorized Reports List). Right-click the report group you want to run and then choose Process Group on the shortcut menu that appears. The Process Multiple Reports dialog box opens with the Select Memorized Reports From box set to the report group you chose and automatically turns on the checkboxes for all the reports in that group. Simply click Print to make QuickBooks print them all.

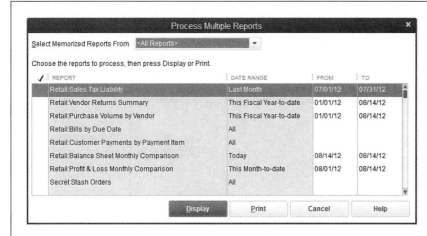

FIGURE 21-4

The Date Range column is grayed out because you can't choose a different date range in the table. However, if you look closely, you'll see that the From and To columns' backgrounds are white, which means you can change the starting and ending dates for reports. After you adjust any dates and turn on the appropriate checkmarks, click Print.

NOTE Some features on reports should remain consistent for every report that a company generates, such as whether you use cash or accrual accounting (page xxiii describes the difference between the two methods). A QuickBooks administrator can set company-wide report preferences to ensure that reports show financial information correctly and consistently. But even without administrator powers, you can still specify a few settings for the reports and graphs you run. See page 624 to learn how to do so.

Some reports take some time to generate because they pull data from every corner of your company file. If you're hunkering down to a report-running session of epic proportions, here are some tips for speeding things up:

- Wait until everyone else has logged out of the company file.

- If possible, log into QuickBooks from the computer that contains the company file. Otherwise, log into the fastest computer that runs QuickBooks on your network.

- Before running the report, switch the file to single-user mode by choosing File→"Switch to Single-user Mode."

Printing and Saving Reports

You can turn any QuickBooks report into either a hard copy or an electronic file. Printing a report is easy: In the toolbar at the top of the report's window, click Print. In the Print Reports dialog box that opens, QuickBooks offers most of the same printing options you find in other programs, as shown in Figure 21-5.

FIGURE 21-5

Select the Printer option and then, in the Printer drop-down list, choose the printer to which you want to send the report. You can print reports in portrait or landscape orientation, and specify the pages you want to print, how many copies to print, where you want page breaks, and whether to print in color. If a report is a bit too wide to fit on one page, turn on the "Fit report to" checkbox, which forces the report onto one (or more) pages.

In the Print Reports dialog box, the Page Breaks section has two checkboxes that control where QuickBooks places page breaks:

- **Smart page breaks (widow/orphan control)**. This checkbox is turned on initially, which tells QuickBooks to insert page breaks in judicious locations to keep associated information on the same page. To stuff as much report as possible onto the fewest pages, turn off this checkbox. When you do, QuickBooks prints to the very last line of a page, even if it means that a single row of a section appears on one page with the rest of the section on another. (The box on page 552 describes another way to squeeze more report onto a page.)

- **Page break after each major grouping**. To add a page break after major sections of the reports, like Income and Expenses in a Profit & Loss report, turn on this checkbox, which appears if a report is more than one page long. When this checkbox is turned off (as it is initially), the report starts a new section on the same page.

Saving Reports as Files

If you save a report as a file, you can feed it to other programs to edit it in ways that you can't do in QuickBooks.

Intuit gives you four places to transform reports into files. The Print Reports dialog box has an option to create three kinds of files: ASCII text files, comma-delimited files, and tab-delimited files. But you can also create comma-delimited files and Excel workbooks by clicking Excel in any report window's button bar. (The comma-delimited files that you create in either place are identical, so you can generate them whichever way you prefer.) You can also print forms and reports as PDF files or create versions to email.

> **TIP** If you plan to import a report into another program, go with a tab- or comma-delimited file, which uses tab characters or commas to separate each value. Many programs can read files in these formats.

Here are the four ways you can create files for reports and the differences among them:

- **Print to file**. In a report's window, click Print to open the Print Reports dialog box. Just below the Printer option is the File option, which has a drop-down list that includes "ASCII text file," "Comma delimited file," and "Tab delimited file." After you choose the File option and select a type of file, click Print and Quick-Books opens the Create Disk File dialog box, which is just a File Save As dialog box where you can specify the filename and where you want to save the file.

> **NOTE** The ASCII text format produces a text file that *looks* like the report, but it uses different fonts and space characters to position values in columns. This type of file isn't suitable for importing into spreadsheets or other programs, but you can use it to store an electronic version of your report.

- **Export to spreadsheet file**. In a report window's button bar, click Excel and then choose Create New Worksheet or Update Existing Worksheet to open the Send Report to Excel dialog box shown in Figure 21-6. There, depending on which entry you chose, QuickBooks selects the "Create new worksheet" or "Update an existing worksheet" option. Click Export to open the report in Excel.

  If you select the "Replace an existing worksheet" option, the "Select workbook" and "Select a sheet" boxes appear. After you specify the workbook and work-sheet that you want to replace and then click Export, QuickBooks replaces the contents of that worksheet with the report.

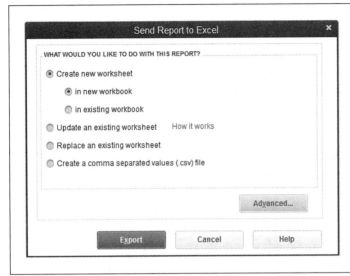

FIGURE 21-6

In a report window's button bar, click Excel→Create New Worksheet or Excel→Update Existing Worksheet to open this dialog box. If you choose the Create New Worksheet option, the dialog box opens with the "Create new worksheet" option selected, but you can choose whichever option you want. If you select the "Create a comma separated values (.csv) file" option, when you click Export, the program opens the Create Disk File dialog box.

TIP QuickBooks is smart about exchanging report information with Excel. When you export a report to an existing worksheet, QuickBooks can update the worksheet while keeping most of the changes you've made to it, such as formulas and formatting.

If you choose the "Create a comma separated values (.csv) file" option and then click Export, QuickBooks opens the Create Disk File dialog box, where you can type a filename and choose where to save the file.

If you want to tell QuickBooks how to set up the Excel spreadsheet, before clicking Export, click Advanced, choose your settings, and then click OK. The Advanced tab has three sections for setting up a report in Excel. The first section focuses on whether to transfer the fonts, colors, and spacing that you set up in your QuickBooks reports to the Excel workbook. The second section provides checkboxes for turning on Excel features such as AutoFit, which makes columns wide enough to display all the data. And the third section lets you decide whether you want the report's header to appear in the Excel header area (which appears at the top of the printed report) or at the top of the worksheet's grid.

- **Save as a PDF file**. To save a report as a PDF (Acrobat) file, run the report and then, with the report window open, choose File→Save As PDF. In the "Save document as PDF" dialog box, navigate to the folder where you want to save the file, type the filename in the "File name" box, and then click Save. (File→Save As PDF also works for saving forms like invoices and sales receipts as PDFs. When you tell QuickBooks to email forms, it automatically creates a PDF file of the form and attaches it to the email message.)

- **Email an Excel file or PDF file**. To email a report, in the report's window, click E-mail and then choose "Send report as Excel" or "Send report as PDF."

Customizing Reports

Report windows are teeming with ways to customize reports. Some tools are easy to spot, like the buttons and drop-down lists at the top of the window. But you can also drag and right-click elements in a report to make smaller changes. This section describes all the techniques you can use to make a report exactly what you want.

Here's where you go to customize a report:

- **Run custom reports from the Reports menu**. If you make it through all of QuickBooks' report categories without finding the report you want, the Reports menu includes two entries for building custom reports from scratch. Choose Reports→Custom Reports and then choose Summary to build a report that displays subtotals by some kinds of categories. For instance, you could customize a summary report to create an income statement for all customers of a particular type. Reports→Custom Reports→Transaction Detail, on the other hand, lets you customize transaction reports to show exactly the fields you want.

  As soon as you choose one of these custom report options, QuickBooks opens both the report window and the Modify Report dialog box—because a custom report needs *some* kind of customization. You can set up the contents and appearance of the report any way you want, as shown in Figure 21-7. For a custom transaction report, the Modify Report dialog box includes a list of fields that you can turn on and off, as well as checkboxes for specifying how you want to sort and total the results.

> **NOTE** The Modify Report dialog box's "Display columns by" drop-down list includes date ranges and the "Total only" option. The Modify Report dialog box for custom reports also includes checkboxes for comparing values to previous periods as well as showing dollar and percentage differences, like Budget vs. Actual reports do.

- **Report window button bar**. The bar across the top of a report window includes the Customize Report button, which opens the all-powerful customization tool—the Modify Report dialog box. This bar also includes other handy customization buttons like Hide Header and Collapse, discussed in the box on page 552.

- **Report window toolbar**. Below the button bar is a customization toolbar where you can choose the date range, the columns to display, and which column to use for sorting the report's contents.

- **Report window**. Hidden within the report itself are a few customization features. For example, by right-clicking text in a report, you can format its appearance. Dragging the small diamonds between column headings changes the column width and, for detailed reports, you can drag columns to new locations.

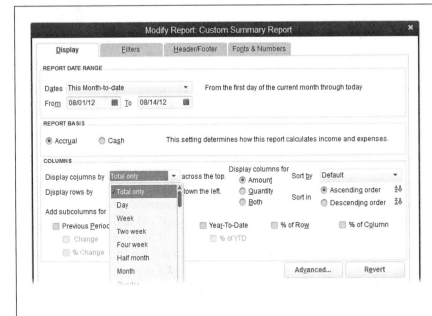

FIGURE 21-7

In addition to date ranges, filters, and other customizations, you can control what QuickBooks displays in a custom report's rows and columns. The entries in the "Display columns by" and "Display rows by" drop-down lists have many of the same choices, so you can set up a report to show your data either across or down. (A report that uses the same category for both columns and rows doesn't make any sense, so be sure to choose different entries for columns and rows.)

Viewing More of a Report

How can I see more of a report on my screen?

If your computer monitor is a closer relative to your mobile phone than to your widescreen TV, you can use several techniques to stuff more of the report onto your screen:

- **Hide Header**. While you're working on a report, you don't need the report's header to tell you which type of report you're viewing, your company's name, or the date range. In the report window's button bar, click Hide Header to hide the report's header and display more content. (The printed report that you send to others still includes the

header.) To redisplay the hidden header, in the button bar, click Show Header.

- **Collapse**. If the report window's button bar has a Collapse button, you can click it to get a high-level view of a report that hides subaccounts, the individual jobs for your customers, and subclasses. QuickBooks totals the results for the subaccounts, jobs, or subclasses under the main account, customer, or class, respectively. Unlike the Hide Header button, the Collapse button affects your onscreen view *and* the printed report. To redisplay the collapsed entries, click Expand.

Date Ranges

Different reports call for different date ranges. Financial statements typically use fiscal periods, such as the last fiscal quarter or the current fiscal year. But many companies manage month by month, so your reports may cover the current month or month to date. Payroll reports span whatever period you use for payroll, whether that's one week, two weeks, or a calendar month. And tax reports depend on the tax periods required by the tax agencies you answer to.

The best place to choose a report's date range depends on how much report modification you have in mind:

- **If the date range is the only thing you want to change**, the report window's toolbar is the way to go. In the Dates drop-down list, choose the range you want, or, in the From and To boxes, pick a starting date and ending date for the report, respectively.

- **If you plan to change more than the date**, in the report window, click the Customize Report button instead. In the Modify Reports dialog box, the Report Date Range section includes the same date-setting features as the report window's toolbar, as well as several additional tabs and sections for every other type of customization.

QuickBooks has two dozen preset date ranges that work based on today's date. For example, if it's December 15, 2013, and your company uses the calendar year as its fiscal year, This Fiscal Year represents January 1 through December 31, 2013, but Today is simply 12/15/2013. And, if none of these date ranges do what you want, in the report window's toolbar, you can set specific start and end dates in the From and To boxes.

The preset date ranges are numerous because they mix and match several types of ranges.

- **Durations**. Some preset periods represent durations, such as Week, Month, Fiscal Quarter, Fiscal Year, and Tax Year. At the extremes, you can pick All to encompass every date in your company file, or Today, which includes only today.

- **This, Last, and Next**. For each duration, you can choose the current period (such as This Fiscal Quarter), the previous period (Last Fiscal Quarter), or the upcoming period (Next Fiscal Quarter).

- **Full and to-date**. You can also pick between a full period and the period up to today's date. For example, on December 15, "This Month" covers December 1 through December 31, and "This Month-to-date" represents December 1 through December 15.

NOTE QuickBooks includes one additional choice, Next 4 Weeks, which many businesses use when checking cash flow.

Subtotals

Many of QuickBooks' built-in reports calculate subtotals. For instance, Profit & Loss summary reports include subtotals by income, cost of goods sold, expenses, and so on. Sales reports by customer subtotal the sales for all the jobs you do for each customer.

When you create a detailed report, such as Sales by Customer Detail, the report shows every relevant transaction, and you can subtotal the results in any way that makes sense for that type of report, as shown in Figure 21-8.

Depending on the report you pick, some choices in the "Total by" drop-down list are more appropriate than others. For example, you might decide to subtotal a sales report by customer type, rep, or account list to see which types of customer provide the most business, which sales rep makes the most sales, or which income account pulls in the most money. If you choose a "Total by" option that doesn't jibe with the report you've run, the report displays a zero balance and no rows of data.

> **TIP** When a selection in the "Total by" drop-down list empties your report, choosing a different field might *not* bring back your report's contents. If that happens, close the report by clicking the report window's Close button (the X in its upper-right corner). In the Memorize Report box that QuickBooks displays, be sure to click No or you'll memorize the empty report. Then run the report anew by choosing it from the appropriate category within the Reports menu.

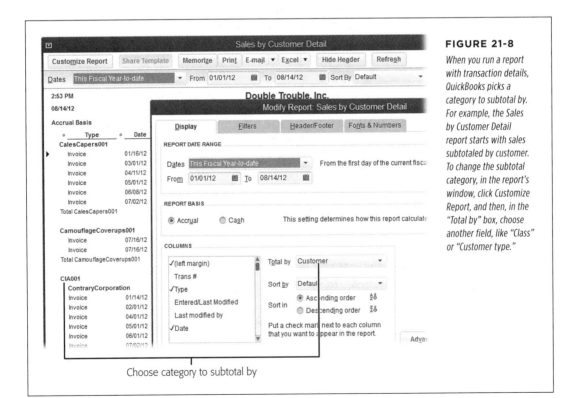

Choose category to subtotal by

FIGURE 21-8

When you run a report with transaction details, QuickBooks picks a category to subtotal by. For example, the Sales by Customer Detail report starts with sales subtotaled by customer. To change the subtotal category, in the report's window, click Customize Report, and then, in the "Total by" box, choose another field, like "Class" or "Customer type."

Customizing the Columns in Reports

Some reports start with only one column, but they don't have to stay that way. Depending on the type of report, you can change the columns that appear in several ways, like showing columns for each time period or choosing fields to display in separate columns. And if you find that your appetite for columns is larger than your computer screen, you can remove, resize, and reorder the columns. This section explains all your options.

■ ADDING AND REMOVING COLUMNS IN SUMMARY REPORTS

As you manage your business, you'll want to see results for different date ranges in the reports you generate. For example, during a year, you might create a Profit & Loss report to show your financial status by month, for each fiscal quarter, and for the entire year. If the report window's toolbar includes a Columns drop-down list (which it does for summary-type reports), choosing an entry there is the quickest way to change the categories that columns represent (see Figure 21-9). You can make the same choices in the Modify Report dialog box by using the "Display columns by" drop-down list.

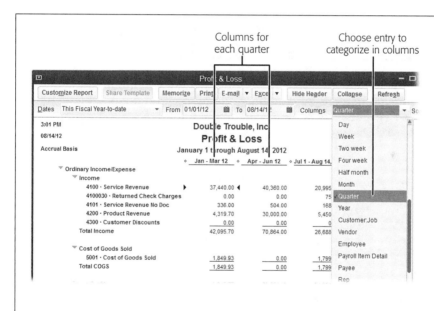

Columns for each quarter

Choose entry to categorize in columns

FIGURE 21-9

In a report window's toolbar, the Columns drop-down list sets the categories for the columns in the report—basically, subtotaling by column. When you choose Quarter, the report changes from a single, yearlong total to columns that subtotal each fiscal quarter (as shown here). In the Columns drop-down list, choose another type of category like Class or Customer:Job to slice results up differently. For example, choosing Class makes QuickBooks include a column for each class you use.

The Modify Report dialog box's Display tab provides different comparison checkboxes for each type of report. For example, when you click the Customize Report button in a Profit & Loss report's window, you'll see checkboxes that let you compare results to the previous period, previous year, or the year to date, *and* show dollar and percentage comparisons. If you want to focus on the percentage difference, then turn off the Change checkbox and turn on the "% Change" checkbox.

The Modify Report dialog box for some reports even includes checkboxes, such as "% of Column," "% of Row," "% of Income," and "% of Expense." If you generate a profit and loss report by quarter and turn on the "% of Row" checkbox, for example, the report shows each quarter's performance as a percentage of the full year's results.

■ ADDING OR REMOVING COLUMNS IN DETAIL REPORTS

Reports that show transaction details, such as Profit & Loss Detail or Inventory Valuation Detail, include columns for data fields like Name, Cost, or Memo. To change the columns that appear in a detail report, in the report's window, click Customize Report, and then choose the columns you want to add or remove, as shown in Figure 21-10.

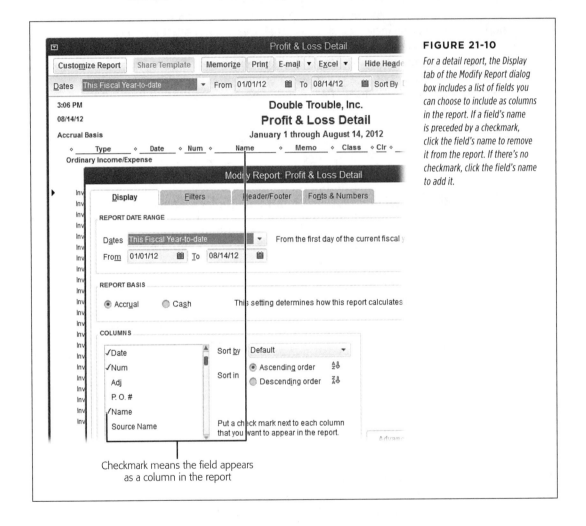

FIGURE 21-10

For a detail report, the Display tab of the Modify Report dialog box includes a list of fields you can choose to include as columns in the report. If a field's name is preceded by a checkmark, click the field's name to remove it from the report. If there's no checkmark, click the field's name to add it.

Checkmark means the field appears
as a column in the report

RESIZING AND MOVING COLUMNS

Some columns seem to use more room than they need, while others truncate their contents. Figure 21-11 shows how to resize columns or rearrange the order in which they appear.

NOTE When you resize columns in some reports, like ones with columns for each month, a Resize Columns dialog box asks if you want to set all the columns to the same size. Click Yes to resize all the columns, or No to resize only the one.

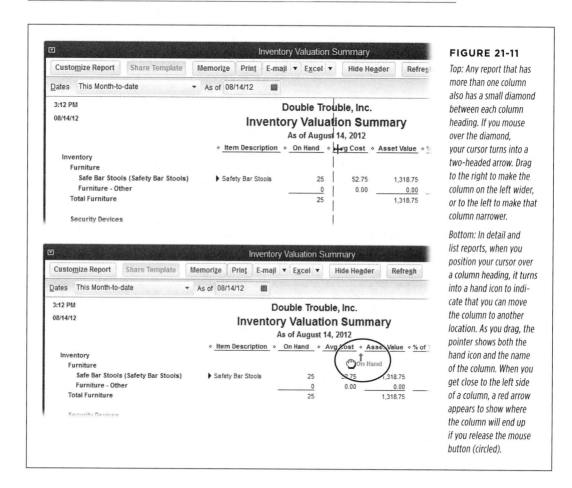

FIGURE 21-11

Top: Any report that has more than one column also has a small diamond between each column heading. If you mouse over the diamond, your cursor turns into a two-headed arrow. Drag to the right to make the column on the left wider, or to the left to make that column narrower.

Bottom: In detail and list reports, when you position your cursor over a column heading, it turns into a hand icon to indicate that you can move the column to another location. As you drag, the pointer shows both the hand icon and the name of the column. When you get close to the left side of a column, a red arrow appears to show where the column will end up if you release the mouse button (circled).

TIP To remove a column from a report, drag the little diamond shown in Figure 21-11 out of the report window.

Sorting Reports

When you first generate a report, the Sort By box is set to Default, which means different things for different reports. For example, if you create a Sales by Customer Detail report, QuickBooks groups transactions by customer, but it sorts each customer's transactions from earliest to most recent. (QuickBooks sorts by only one field at a time.)

If a report is sortable, you'll see the Sort By box in the report window's toolbar. In the Sort By drop-down list, choose the column you want to use to sort the report. As soon as you change the Sort By box to something other than Default, the Ascending/Descending button appears to the right of the Sort By box. (It has the letters A and Z on it along with a blue arrow that points down when the sort order is descending and up when the sort order is ascending.) Clicking this button toggles between sorting in ascending and descending order.

The fields you can use to sort depend on the report. For the Sales by Customer Summary report, the Sort By box lets you choose from only two columns to sort by: Default and Total. Default sorts the report by customer name in alphabetical order. Total sorts the report by the total sales for each customer, from the smallest to largest dollar amount. On the other hand, the Sales by Customer Detail report includes several columns of information, and you can sort by any of them.

> **NOTE** The Modify Report dialog box's Display tab also includes a Sort By drop-down list. In this dialog box, select the Ascending or Descending option to change the sort order.

WORKAROUND WORKSHOP

Fitting More Report onto Each Page

When a report is rife with columns, it's hard to fit everything onto a single piece of paper. QuickBooks automatically prints the columns that don't fit on additional pages, but reports that span multiple pages cause paper rustling and lots of grumbling. Try these approaches for keeping your reports to one page:

- Before you click Print, reduce the width of the columns. In the report's window, drag the diamond to the right of a column heading to make the column narrower, as shown in Figure 21-11, top.

- In the Print Reports dialog box (to open it, click Print in a report's window), turn on the "Fit report to page(s) wide" checkbox and, in the number box, type *1*.

- In the Print Reports dialog box, choose the Landscape option for page orientation. When a report almost fits on an 8.5" × 11" sheet of paper, switching to landscape orientation should do the trick.

- Use legal-size paper (8.5" × 14" inches) if your printer can handle it.

Filtering Reports

Detail reports (the ones that list individual transactions) might show more information than you want. For example, a Purchases by Item Detail report could run page after page, listing your weekly purchases of Turtle Chow. Filtering a report removes transactions that don't meet your criteria, so you can home in on just the Turtle Chow purchases from Myrtle's Turtle Mart.

In QuickBooks, you can apply as many filters as you want at the same time. Each filter adds one more test that a transaction has to pass to appear in your report. For example, when you set the date range for a report, what you're really doing is adding a filter that restricts transactions to the ones that happened between the starting and ending dates. Then, if you want to find the sales for only your corporate customers, you can add a filter based on the Customer Type field.

QuickBooks provides dozens of filters, from the most common—such as dates, items, and transaction types—to those you won't apply very often, such as Workmen's Comp Codes and FOB (that's "free on board," discussed on page 283).

Built-in reports already have filters, but you can customize a built-in report by adding extra filters or editing or removing the existing ones. Here's how:

1. **In the report's window, click Customize Report and then, in the Modify Report dialog box, click the Filters tab.**

   The left side of the tab lets you choose the field you want to filter by and specify the filter's test. The right side of the tab shows all the filters that are applied.

2. **In the Choose Filter list, select the field you want to filter by.**

   Depending on the field you choose, QuickBooks provides different criteria, one example of which is shown in Figure 21-12.

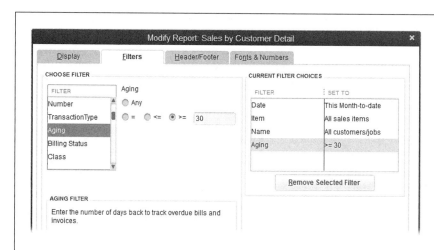

FIGURE 21-12

When you pick a field in the Choose Filter list, the criteria for that field appear. If you're not sure what a field and its criteria settings do, click the "Tell me more" button (not shown) to open the QuickBooks Help window to the topic about that filter.

3. **Using the drop-down lists or options that appear, specify the filter criteria you want to apply.**

For instance, if you filter by account, in the Account drop-down list, you can choose a category such as "All bank accounts," choose "Multiple accounts" and then click each one you want to include, or click a single account. QuickBooks adds the filter to the Current Filter Choices list.

If you choose a numeric field, you can specify a test, like ">=" (greater than or equal to) and then specify the test value. For example, to look for invoices that are late by more than 30 days, choose Aging for the filter, select the ">=" option and then type _30_ in the box, as shown in Figure 21-12.

4. **To remove a filter, select it in the Current Filter Choices list, and then click Remove Selected Filter.**

QuickBooks removes the filter from the list.

5. **To edit a filter, in the Current Filter Choices box, select the filter you want to change. Then, in the Choose Filter section, make the changes you want.**

6. **Click OK to see your report with the new filters applied.**

Report Headers and Footers

You don't have complete control over what appears in report headers and footers, but you can choose from several fields common to all of them. For example, fields like Company Name, Report Title, and Date Prepared are options for headers, and page number is one option for footers. To change the header and footer contents for the report you're working on, in the Modify Report dialog box, click the Header/Footer tab (Figure 21-13).

> **NOTE** To set standards for _all_ report headers and footers, open the Report preferences (page 626) and then set the fields you want.

QuickBooks pulls data from your company file to automatically fill in the header and footer text boxes. For example, if you use a built-in Sales by Customer Detail report, the program fills in the Company Name box with your company's name. If you have a more eloquent title for the report, type it in the Report Title box.

The Show Footer Information section provides the Extra Footer Line box for typing whatever you want. This text isn't associated with any field in QuickBooks, so it's blank unless you type something. Whatever you type here appears in the bottom-left corner of the report page.

The last checkbox in both the Show Header Information and Show Footer Information sections controls the pages on which the headers and footers appear. To conserve paper, turn off the "Print header on pages after first page" checkbox so QuickBooks includes the header on the first page only. If you want to omit the page number from the first page, turn off the "Print footer on first page" checkbox.

The right side of the Header/Footer tab is the Page Layout section, which lets you position header and footer fields to a very limited extent, as explained in Figure 21-13.

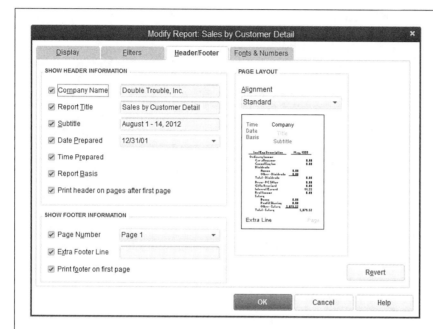

FIGURE 21-13

If you want to realign the header and footer contents, in the Alignment drop-down list, choose Left, Right, Centered, or Standard. QuickBooks chooses Standard automatically, which centers the Company name and title; places the date, time, and report basis (cash or accrual) on the left; and puts the extra line and page number in the left and right corners of the footer.

Fonts and Numbers

The fonts you use and the way you display numbers in reports doesn't change the underlying financial message, but an attractive and easy-to-read report can make a good impression. Just like the fields that appear in the header and footer, you can set QuickBooks' preferences to assign the same font and number formats for all your reports (see page 626). On the other hand, changing fonts directly in a report is quick and has the added advantage of letting you see exactly what the report looks like with the new formatting, as Figure 21-14 shows.

If you already have the Modify Report dialog box open, click the Fonts & Numbers tab. The Fonts section on the left side of the tab lists the different text elements in the report, such as Column Labels, Company Name, and Transactions. To change a font, select an element and then click the Change Font button, which opens the same dialog box you get when you right-click the element in the report.

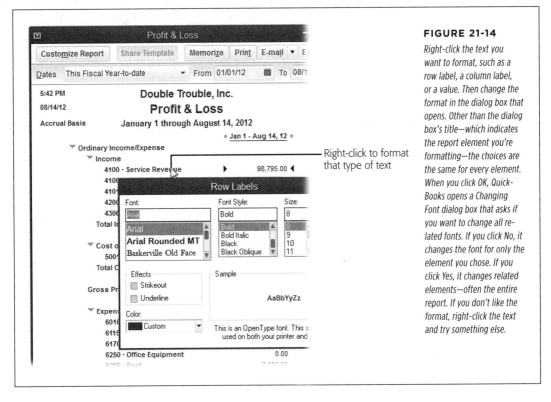

FIGURE 21-14

Right-click the text you want to format, such as a row label, a column label, or a value. Then change the format in the dialog box that opens. Other than the dialog box's title—which indicates the report element you're formatting—the choices are the same for every element. When you click OK, Quick-Books opens a Changing Font dialog box that asks if you want to change all related fonts. If you click No, it changes the font for only the element you chose. If you click Yes, it changes related elements—often the entire report. If you don't like the format, right-click the text and try something else.

The right side of the Fonts & Numbers tab has options for changing the appearance of numbers. Negative numbers are usually something to pay attention to in the financial world, so accountants use several methods to make them stand out. If you're not sure which style of negative number you like, choose an option and then check out the number in the Example area. In QuickBooks, you can choose among three ways of showing negative numbers:

- **Normally**. This option shows negative numbers preceded by a minus sign, like *–1200.00*.

- **In Parentheses**. This option puts negative numbers in parentheses without a minus sign: *(1200)*.

- **With a Trailing Minus**. This option places the minus sign after the number: *1200–*.

TIP If you use a color printer or display reports on your computer screen, make negative numbers even harder to ignore by turning on the In Bright Red checkbox.

To make big numbers easier to read, in the Show All Numbers section, turn on the "Divided by 1000" checkbox. This removes one trio of zeros from numbers in the report—so that $350,000,000 shows up as $350,000—and adds "($ in 1,000's)" to the report's header. And, if a summary report (such as Customer Balance Summary) tends to contain mostly zero values, you can keep it lean by turning on the Except Zero Amounts checkbox. That way, the report omits any rows whose values are zero, such as customers who don't owe you any money. (This checkbox won't appear on the Fonts & Numbers tab for transaction-based reports, such as Customer Balance Detail.) Turn on the Without Cents checkbox to show only whole dollars.

Memorizing Reports

If you take the time to customize a report so it looks just the way you want, it'd be silly to jump through those same hoops every time you run that report. By memorizing modified reports, you can run them again and again with all your customizations just by choosing Reports→Memorized Reports, and then picking the report's name on the appropriate submenu.

When you memorize a report, QuickBooks remembers your settings—like date range and filter criteria—but not the data itself. So if you memorize a report whose date range is set to This Month, the report shows the results for June when you run it in June, and results for December when you run it in December.

Here's how to memorize a report you've customized:

1. **Review the report to make sure it has the information and formatting you want.**

   If you notice later that you missed a setting, you can make that change and memorize the report again.

2. **In the report's window, click the Memorize button.**

   QuickBooks opens the Memorize Report dialog box, which is small and to the point. If you're memorizing a standard report, the dialog box contains a Name box and a checkbox for choosing a memorized report group.

   If you're rememorizing an existing memorized report, the dialog box contains Replace, New, and Cancel buttons. Click Replace to rememorize the existing report with the new settings. Click New to create a new memorized report from the current one.

> **NOTE** You can also share memorized reports with others in the Intuit Community, as described in the box on page 542. To share a memorized report while the Memorize Report dialog box is open, turn on the "Share this report template with others" checkbox.

3. **In the Name box, type a name that indicates what the report shows, like** *Deadbeat Customers*.

4. **If you want to save the report in a special group, turn on the Save in Memorized Report Group checkbox.**

   You can then choose the group. QuickBooks comes with several built-in groups like Accountant, Company, and Customers, which appear on the Memorized Reports submenu shown in Figure 21-15. But you can also create your own groups as the box on the following page explains.

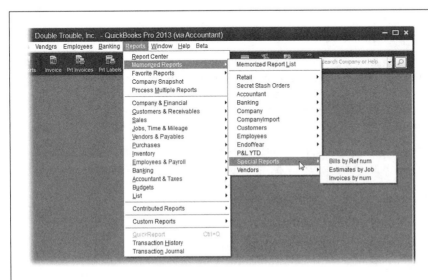

FIGURE 21-15

The Memorized Reports submenu displays QuickBooks' built-in report groups and any report groups you create. To choose a report from a group, put your cursor over the group's name, and then choose the report you want to run. If you don't memorize a report to a group, the report appears above the groups on the submenu, like the Secret Stash Orders report listed here.

5. **Click OK to memorize the report.**

   Voilà—you're done. If you're going to use the report over and over, consider adding it to the Favorites menu (page 661) or to QuickBooks' icon bar (page 662) so you can run it by choosing it from the Favorites menu or clicking its icon, respectively.

> **TIP** The Memorized Report List window comes in handy if you want to edit or delete reports. Choose Reports→Memorized Reports→Memorized Reports List. In the window, select the report you want to work on and then click Memorized Report at the bottom of the window. From the drop-down menu, choose Edit Memorized Report to change the report's name or the group where it's memorized, or choose Delete Memorized Report to obliterate it from the list.

The Memorized Group Doesn't Exist

The Memorize Report dialog box doesn't include a way to create a new memorized group. That's because you have to create a memorized group *before* you can add a report to that group. Here's the secret to creating a memorized group:

1. Choose Reports→Memorized Reports→Memorized Report List. QuickBooks opens the Memorized Report List window, which includes memorized groups and the reports they contain.

2. At the bottom of the window, click Memorized Report→New Group.

3. In the New Memorized Report Group dialog box, type the group's name, and then click OK.

Now, when you memorize a report, the new group appears in the Save in Memorized Report Group drop-down list.

Swapping Reports Between Company Files

Suppose you're one of several business owners who meet to share ideas. Some of your colleagues rave about the QuickBooks reports they've customized, and you'd like to use the reports they've created. If they're willing to share their ideas, you can swap reports by trading *report template* files. Or, if you want to share your reports with a broader audience, you can share them with the whole Intuit Community as described in the box on page 542.

Report templates contain the layouts, filters, and formatting of memorized reports. Someone can export a memorized report as a report template, and someone else can then import that template to save the report in a different company file. For example, if your accountant likes to see information in very specific ways, she can give you a report template file so you can produce the reports she wants to see.

Report templates play well between different editions of QuickBooks (Premier, Pro, and Enterprise) and from version to version (2010, 2013, and so on). However, here are a couple of points to keep in mind:

- If you use QuickBooks Pro, you can only import templates that others create. You need QuickBooks Premier or Enterprise Solutions to *export* report templates.

- QuickBooks patches can affect the compatibility between versions. In that case, you might have to install the most recent QuickBooks update if you want to use someone else's report templates. (QuickBooks displays a warning if there's an update or version incompatibility issue with a report template you try to import.)

Exporting a Report Template

You can only export report templates if you have QuickBooks Premier or Enterprise Solutions. Whether you export one report or an entire group, QuickBooks stores the report settings in a single file with the file extension .qbr (for "QuickBooks report"). Because report templates are meant to move between QuickBooks company files, you don't have to specify any more than the reports you want to export and the file to which you want to export them. Here's the process:

1. **Choose Reports→Memorized Reports→Memorized Report List.**

   QuickBooks opens the Memorized Report List window.

2. **Select the report or memorized group that you want to export.**

   For example, if your customized reports are all memorized in a Special Reports group that you created, select Special Reports.

> **NOTE** In the Memorized Report List, you can select only a single report or a single group; Ctrl-clicking and Shift-clicking don't select several individual reports.

3. **Click Memorized Report and then choose Export Template.**

   QuickBooks opens the Specify Filename for Export dialog box, which is nothing more than a Save As dialog box that automatically sets the file type to "Quick-Books Report Files (*.QBR)." The program also automatically puts the report or group name in the "File name" box. If you want to use a different name, say to add the date you exported the reports, type it in that box.

4. **Navigate to the folder where you want to save the template and then click Save.**

   QuickBooks saves the settings for the report (or reports) to the file. The next section tells you how to *import* a report template.

> **NOTE** QuickBooks won't export memorized reports with filters that reference an account, customer, or other entry specific to your company file, because those report filters won't work in a company file that doesn't contain that account, customer, or entry. If you try to export a template for such a report, a QuickBooks message box opens and suggests that you look for filter settings that wouldn't work in another company file. Click OK to close the message box.

Importing Report Templates

Importing reports from a template file is even easier than exporting report templates. In the Memorized Report List window (Reports→Memorized Reports→Memorized Report List), click Memorized Report→Import Template. QuickBooks opens the Select File to Import dialog box with the "Files of type" box set to "QuickBooks Reports Files (*.QBR)." All you have to do is navigate to the folder that contains the report template file and double-click the filename (or select the filename and then click Open).

Depending on whether you're importing one report or a group, QuickBooks opens a different dialog box:

- **Single report**. QuickBooks opens the Memorize Report dialog box. As you would if you were memorizing a custom report of your own design, in the Name box, type the name you want for the report, and if you wish, choose a memorized report group. Then click OK to save the report template in your company file.

- **Report group**. When you import a report group, the program opens the Import Memorized Reports Group With Name dialog box. QuickBooks fills in the Name box with the group's name from the original company file, but you can type a different name. When you click OK, the program adds the group name to your company file and saves all the imported reports with their original names in that group.

NOTE If you try to import a report or group with the same name as a report or group already in your company file, QuickBooks displays a warning and recommends that you change the name of the report or group that you're importing. Click OK and remember to change the imported report or group's name before you save it.

Online Banking Services

With online banking, you can view your bank balances and transactions anytime, and even download them into your QuickBooks company file. By synchronizing your real bank accounts with the bank accounts in QuickBooks, you'll always know how much cash you have on hand. Before repaying your aunt the start-up money she lent you, you can hop online and check your balance—and avoid an embarrassing family blowout caused by giving her a check that bounces.

Besides managing your cash flow, online banking services are much more convenient than the old paper-based methods of yesteryear. You have a lot of transactions in your account register already (from receiving payments against invoices or making payments to your vendors) and you can easily match these transactions to the ones you download from the bank so you know how much money you *really* have in your account—and whether someone is helping themselves to your money without permission. Or you might be able to transfer money between your money market account and your checking account when you find yourself awake at two in the morning.

If you use online billing, you can pay bills without having to write checks, lick stamps, or walk to the mailbox. After you submit payment transactions online, the billing service either transfers funds from your bank account to the vendors, or generates and mails paper checks. Online billing also lets you set up recurring bills so you can go about your business without worrying about missing a payment.

All this convenience requires some setup. QuickBooks needs to know how to connect to your bank, and your bank needs to know that you want to use its online services. This chapter explains how to apply for and set up online services. With your accounts set up and online services activated, you'll learn how to download transactions and make online payments. If you enter transactions in QuickBooks, you'll learn about matching them with the ones you download—and correcting any discrepancies.

> **NOTE** QuickBooks' Merchant Services and Billing Solution transmit deposits and payments electronically. The note at the bottom of page 574 explains where to learn about and sign up for these services.

◼ Setting Up Your Internet Connection

QuickBooks uses an Internet connection for more than online banking (for example, updating the program, accessing support, and running QuickBooks' add-on services), so chances are the program latched onto your Internet connection during installation. If not, start by choosing Help→Internet Connection Setup.

QuickBooks opens the Internet Connection Setup wizard and automatically selects "Use my computer's Internet connection settings to establish a connection when this application accesses the Internet." That's usually what you want, because this option is for Internet connections that are always available—like a company network, DSL, or cable. Click Next to review the connection that QuickBooks found, and then click Done.

> **NOTE** If you see telephone icons in the Internet Connection Setup wizard's "Use the following connection" box, they represent Internet connections other than always-on connections (dial-up connections, for example). If you dial into the Internet through your Internet service provider, select this option, click the connection you want to use, and then click Done.
>
> If you don't have Internet access, don't bother choosing the third option. The screen that appears tells you what you already know—that you have to sign up with an Internet service provider. Instead, click Cancel and do your homework to find an Internet service provider and get online. When you have an Internet connection, return to this wizard and choose the appropriate option.

TROUBLESHOOTING MOMENT

When Connections Don't Appear

The dial-up connections you've configured for your computer *outside* of QuickBooks should appear in the Internet Connection Setup wizard's "Use the following connection" box. If your dial-up connection isn't listed, click Cancel to close the wizard. Then, use your dial-up connection to access the Internet as if you were planning to check email. While the connection is running, reopen the wizard, which should now list your connection. Choose the connection, and then click Done.

If QuickBooks doesn't recognize your dial-up connection no matter what you do, don't panic. Choose the "Use my computer's Internet connection settings..." option. Then, before you perform any task in QuickBooks that requires Internet access, be sure to dial into the Internet outside of the program.

■ Setting Up Your Accounts for Online Services

Connecting your bank accounts to your accounts in QuickBooks is a lot like running a dating service: You have to prepare each participant for the relationship and then get them together. The services you can subscribe to and the price you pay depend on your financial institution, but the services fall into one of these three categories:

- **Online account access**. This service is usually free. It lets you check transaction status and download transactions into QuickBooks.

- **Online credit card access**. You can download credit card transactions as you do checking transactions, as long as you set up your credit card in QuickBooks as a liability account (page 418) and enter individual credit card charges. Setting up a credit card as a vendor and entering only the monthly bill payment won't work.

- **Online bill paying**. This service usually comes with a fee, but it's often a good deal when you consider the price of stamps and printed checks.

NOTE Although QuickBooks can download transactions in different currencies, the program's online bill payment feature works only with U.S. dollar–based accounts. If you have a bank account that uses a foreign currency, you have to handle your transactions the old-fashioned way.

Applying for Online Services

The first step in linking QuickBooks to your bank accounts is to apply for online banking services with your financial institution. If you use more than one bank, you have to apply to each one separately. If you've already started the application ball rolling, you can skip this section. If you haven't, QuickBooks can help you apply for the services your bank offers.

Choose Banking→Online Banking→Participating Financial Institutions. Peruse the Financial Institution Directory to find your bank and apply for its online services, as shown in Figure 22-1. In the Online Financial Services section, click one of the four buttons to limit the list to institutions providing that service. (QuickBooks automatically selects "Any services," so you see every financial institution that the program works with.) Scroll through the directory to find your financial institution. If your bank doesn't offer the online services you want, check out Intuit's online banking services, described in the note at the bottom of page 574.

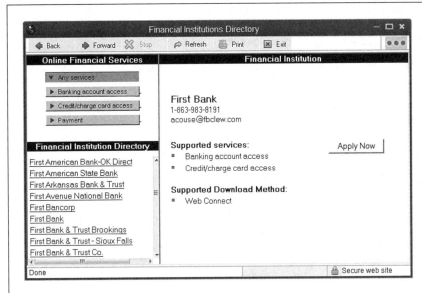

FIGURE 22-1

When you click the link for your bank, you'll see its phone number and email address, the online services it provides, how to connect to it, and any special sign-up offers it has, such as a 30-day trial. An Apply Now button appears if the bank gives you the option of applying online.

When your financial institution processes your application and sends you a confirmation and a PIN (personal identification number) or password, check that the information you received is correct, like the account number. Then you're ready to set up your account for online services.

Activating Online Services for Your QuickBooks Account

When you receive a letter from your bank confirming that your online services are ready to go and you have your customer ID and password (or PIN), all you have to do is set your corresponding account in QuickBooks to use these online services. The Online Banking Setup Interview wizard walks you through the steps:

1. **Choose Banking→Online Banking→Set Up Account for Online Services.**

   In the message box that opens, click Yes to give QuickBooks permission to close any open windows. QuickBooks launches the Set Up Account for Online Services wizard.

   You can also start online setup in the Add New Account window (page 53). If you create a new account and type the account number, when you save the account, the Set Up Online Services message box asks if you want to set up online services. Click Yes to set it up now or No to do it later.

   Yet a third option is to head to the Edit Account window (page 57), and then click the Set Up Online Services button at the bottom of the window to set up the service.

2. **On the Set Up Account for Online Services screen, in the "Select your Quick-Books account" drop-down list, choose the account you want to activate and then click Next.**

   The "Select the Financial Institution for this account" screen shown in Figure 22-2 appears.

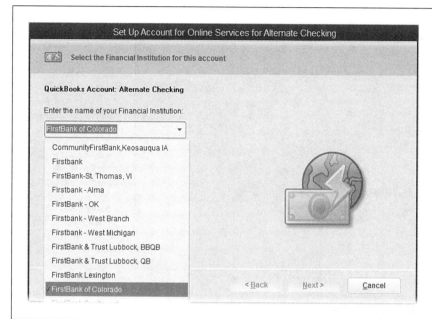

FIGURE 22-2

In the "Enter the name of your Financial Institution" drop-down list, start typing its name. As you type, QuickBooks jumps to the name that matches what you've typed so far. When QuickBooks highlights your bank's name, press Enter to choose it.

3. **In the "Enter the name of your Financial Institution" drop-down list (Figure 22-2), choose your bank, and then click Next.**

   QuickBooks connects to the Internet to download info about your bank. What you see if the program needs more information depends on the type of connection your bank offers. If you see the Account Activation Required screen and you've already signed up for online banking with your financial institution, leave the "Yes, my account has been activated for QuickBooks online services" option selected and then click Next. Otherwise, click Cancel and pick up the phone to call your bank; they can probably help you get your accounts working with QuickBooks. If you see a notification in the Set Up Account for Online Services window that instructs you to download a statement from your bank's website, click the "Go to My Bank's Web site" button at the bottom of the window.

4. **Fill in the Customer ID, Password, and Confirm Password boxes, and then click Sign In.**

   The Customer ID is the ID that the bank assigned to you for online services and should be on the confirmation letter they sent you. If you don't have your ID and password, click Cancel; you can repeat this process after you receive them.

5. **The next screen asks you to select the account at your financial institution. In the table, click the account you want to activate and then click Next.**

QuickBooks and your financial institution start talking. When they're done, you see a screen telling you that the account is set up for online services and how many transactions it downloaded, as shown in Figure 22-3.

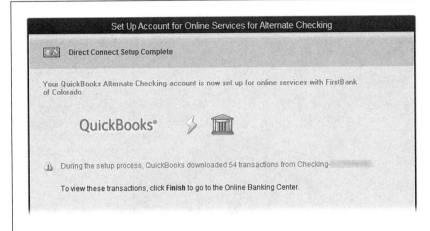

FIGURE 22-3

The Set Up Account for Online Services dialog box shows how many transactions it downloaded during setup. When you click Finish, you may see the Choose Your Online Banking Mode window. If you do, you can choose either Side-by-side mode or Register mode to tell the program how you want to work with downloaded transactions (page 575 explains the two modes).

NOTE If you signed up for online banking with more than one account at the same financial institution, you have to repeat the steps in this section to activate each account at that institution.

6. **Click Finish.**

The Online Banking Center window (explained in the next section) opens and you're ready to bank electronically.

NOTE If your bank is behind the times and doesn't offer online bill payment, Intuit is happy to earn more of your business with its add-on bill-pay service. To learn about it, choose Banking→Learn About Online Bill Payment. A browser window opens to the Intuit QuickBooks Bill Pay Service Web page.

The Intuit website includes information on other services, too. For example, if you're interested in letting your customers pay by credit card, click Payment Processing on the navigation bar. To get Intuit's help paying your employees (page 409), click Payroll Services.

▉ Exchanging Data with Your Bank

Your financial institution takes the lead in controlling how QuickBooks can communicate with it. Your bank can set up this pipeline in two ways:

- **Direct connection** uses a secure Internet connection that links directly to your bank's computers. If your financial institution provides online services, with this type of connection, you can do things like download your bank statements and transactions, transfer funds between accounts, pay bills online, and email your bank. If your bank uses a direct connection, you set up your fund transfers, requests for downloads, online bill payments, and emails *before* you connect.

- **WebConnect** uses a secure connection to your bank's website to download your statement info. With this type of connection, you then have to import the downloaded information into QuickBooks.

> **NOTE** Regardless of the method you use, remember that the online balance usually isn't a true picture of your cash balance, because it doesn't show *all* transactions, such as checks you've written that the bank hasn't received.

Regardless of which type of connection you use, connecting to your financial institution begins in the Online Banking Center (choose Banking→Online Banking→Online Banking Center). The first step in QuickBooks' online banking is exchanging data with your bank. You send any online banking items you've created, like online bill payments or transactions that have cleared at your financial institution. Once you've exchanged data, QuickBooks tries to match the transactions it has with the ones you've downloaded. If it can't match some of the transactions, you step in and tell it what to do. The rest of this chapter explains the whole process.

QuickBooks' Online Banking Modes

The Online Banking Center offers two modes to satisfy everyone's tastes. Side-by-side mode has a lot of nifty features, but you can stick with the old-style Register mode if you like. Here's what each one does:

- **Side-by-side mode**. The best feature of this mode—which is covered in detail beginning on page 579—is that you can match downloaded transactions to any transaction in your company file without leaving the Online Banking Center. For example, you can match a downloaded deposit to an open invoice or a paid invoice where the money is sitting in the Undeposited Funds account (page 618), or simply add the downloaded transaction to QuickBooks. You can also add multiple unmatched transactions to your register or delete downloaded items that you've already taken care of in QuickBooks.

> **NOTE** If you use multiple currencies, Side-by-side mode displays only payees and accounts based in U.S. dollars. To see *all* payees and accounts, use Register mode instead.

Side-by-side mode also automatically creates renaming rules to rename the often inscrutable names that banks give payees. These rules (page 588) are more flexible than the aliases that Register mode sets up. For example, if the payee for a downloaded credit card charge shows up as "Conoco #123-63?#^$&*," you can edit a renaming rule so that the Payee field reads, say, "Conoco" or simply "Gas." From then on, QuickBooks replaces "Conoco #123-63?#^$&*" with "Conoco" or "Gas."

> **TIP** Although you can switch between online banking modes, you're more likely to pick one mode and stick with it. To switch modes, choose Banking→Online Banking→Change Online Banking Mode. QuickBooks opens the Preferences dialog box to the Checking category's Company Preferences tab, so you can choose the Side-by-Side Mode or Register Mode option. When you click OK, QuickBooks closes all open windows to switch modes (and doesn't reopen them when it's done).

- **Register mode**. If you thought that QuickBooks 2008's Online Banking Center was just fine, you can continue to use it by choosing Register mode. This mode lets you see your full account register when you're matching transactions, which is helpful if QuickBooks doesn't find a match. You can scroll through the register and correct a discrepancy that prevented the program from finding a match. In this mode, you can create aliases to rename payees, similar to Side-by-side mode's renaming rules. Register mode is covered in detail starting on page 588.

> **NOTE** Register mode doesn't recognize renaming rules created in Side-by-side mode, nor does Side-by-side mode recognize the aliases you create in Register mode.

Downloading Statements with WebConnect

If your bank communicates via WebConnect, you can download a file of your transactions and import it into QuickBooks. The easiest way to do that is to use your browser to log into your financial institution's website directly. On the website, click the Download to QuickBooks button (or one that creates a file of your transactions). Then you can import that file (choose Banking→Online Banking→Import Web Connect File) to load the recent transactions into your company file.

> **NOTE** You can also access your financial institution's website from within QuickBooks. In the Online Banking Center, choose the financial institution to connect to and then click the Send/Receive Transactions button (its label reads "Receive Transactions" if you don't have any transaction to send, or "Send/Receive" if you're in Register mode). A browser window opens and displays your bank's website; use your customer ID and PIN or password to log in.

Creating Online Items for Direct Connections

Banks that use direct connections can do more than those that use WebConnect. Depending on which services your bank provides, you can do some or all of the following tasks online:

- Receive transactions that cleared in your account

- Pay bills

- Exchange messages with your bank

- Transfer funds between accounts

You don't have to take any action to receive transactions from your accounts. QuickBooks automatically sets up a request for cleared transactions from your bank accounts every time you open the Online Banking Center. This section describes what you have to do in QuickBooks to set up electronic bill payments, messages you want to send to your bank, and online transfers between accounts.

NOTE If you use the Online Banking Center's Side-by-side mode, in the Items Ready To Send section, QuickBooks displays links to create online items for the online services you've signed up for with your financial institution or Intuit (see Figure 22-4 on page 580).

■ PAYING BILLS ONLINE

Whether you use the bill-paying service that your bank provides or subscribe to QuickBooks Bill Pay, you don't have to use any special dialog boxes or windows to make electronic payments. However, changing the payment method in a transaction works only when the bank account associated with payments is activated for online bill payment. Here's how to turn the three ways you make payments into electronic transactions:

- **Pay Bills**. In the Pay Bills window (page 244), in the Method drop-down list, choose Online Bank Pmt.

- **Write Checks**. In the Write Checks window (page 257), turn on the Online Payment checkbox.

- **Account register window**. If you "write" checks by entering a transaction in your checking account's register window (page 259), you can turn a transaction into an online payment by typing *Send* in the Number cell.

When you set up a payment as an online transaction, QuickBooks adds the payment to your list of items to send. Then when you open the Online Banking Center window, you'll see these payments in the Items Ready To Send section (or Items To Send section if you're in Register mode).

When you tell QuickBooks to send transactions (page 575), it sends these electronic payments along with any of your other requests. Once the bill-payment service receives your online payment information, it transfers money from your account to the vendor's account—providing the vendor accepts electronic payments. Otherwise, the bill-payment service generates a paper check and mails it to the vendor.

■ SENDING A MESSAGE TO YOUR BANK

If you have an email address for your bank, you can send messages to them by using your regular old email program. But when you use online banking services, your bank sends you messages that you receive in QuickBooks' Online Banking Center. By sending messages through the center, you can see all the messages that you've exchanged (until you decide to delete them).

Choose Banking→Online Banking→Create Online Banking Message, and QuickBooks opens the Online Banking Message dialog box. If you're addicted to email, you shouldn't have any trouble figuring out what to do in the window's fields:

- In the "Message to" drop-down list, choose the bank you want to send a message to. QuickBooks automatically timestamps the message with the current date and time and puts your company's name in the From box.

- In the Subject box, type a short but informative blurb.

- If you have more than one account enabled for online services, in the Regarding Account drop-down list, choose the appropriate one.

- In the Message box, type your comment or question.

- If you want to keep a hard copy of the message, click Print before you click OK to send it.

■ TRANSFERRING FUNDS BETWEEN ACCOUNTS

If you have two accounts at the same financial institution and they're both set up for online banking, you can set up online funds transfers between them in QuickBooks. Choose Banking→Transfer Funds as you would for a non-electronic transfer (page 424). But in the Transfer Funds window, in addition to filling in the fields, be sure to turn on the Online Funds Transfer checkbox. When you save the transaction, QuickBooks adds the transfer as an item to send to your bank.

NOTE   Online fund transfers using QuickBooks work only with two online-banking-enabled accounts at the same bank. In other words, you can't transfer funds electronically using QuickBooks if the accounts are at different financial institutions or if one of the accounts at your bank is set up for online services but the other isn't.

■ Online Banking Using Side-by-Side Mode

Side-by-side mode makes it easy to see what's going on with your accounts. You can see online balances, downloaded transactions, and the work you have to do to match them to transactions in your company file. You can do everything you need to do to match downloaded transactions to the ones in QuickBooks without leaving the Online Banking Center.

Sending and Receiving Transactions

Every time you go online, QuickBooks automatically requests newly cleared transactions from your financial institution. If you've set up items to send to your bank, going online pushes those along, too. Here's what you do to send requests and receive replies in Side-by-side mode:

1. **Choose Banking→Online Banking→Online Banking Center.**

   The Online Banking Center opens.

2. **If you have online services set up with more than one bank (say, a checking account with one bank and a credit card with another), in the Financial Institution drop-down list, choose the one you want to connect to.**

   To the right of the Financial Institution heading, you see all the accounts you have at the institution you selected. QuickBooks automatically turns on all the Download checkboxes (Figure 22-4) to grab transactions from all your accounts at that financial institution. If you don't want to download transactions for an account, turn off its checkbox.

   As Figure 22-4 shows, the Online Balance column displays your balance according to your financial institution as of the last update. The Last Update column contains the date of that last update.

   If you have any items to send to your bank (like messages you've written or online transfers you've created, as described on page 578), they appear in the Items Ready To Send section. QuickBooks selects all the requests you've set up to send to your bank.

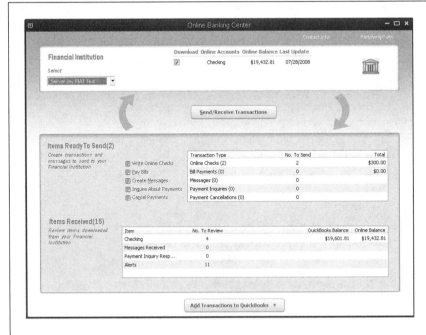

FIGURE 22-4

Side-by-side mode shows the online accounts and balances you have at the institution you connected to. If you've signed up for the corresponding online service with your financial institution or Intuit, you can create online transactions and messages by heading to the window's Items Ready To Send section and clicking the Write Online Checks, Transfer Funds, Pay Bills, or Create Messages links. The transactions, messages, and other items you've downloaded appear in the Items Received section of the window.

3. **If you want to edit or delete any items in the Items Ready To Send section, do that now—*before* you go online. Once you're connected, it's too late.**

   To edit an item like a funds transfer or bill payment you're sending, select the item and then click Edit. Make the changes you want and then click OK. If you want to remove an item like a fund transfer you no longer need, select it and then click Delete.

4. **When the items you want to send are ready, click the Send/Receive Transactions button.**

   If you don't have any items to send, the button's label reads "Receive Transactions" instead. An Update Branding Files message box may appear briefly while QuickBooks and your financial institution talk to each other.

5. **In the "Access to <institution name>" dialog box that appears, type your password or PIN and then click OK.**

   You enter your password or PIN so QuickBooks can communicate with your financial institution. The Online Status dialog box shows the progress QuickBooks is making communicating with your bank. When the two are done talking, the Online Transmission Summary dialog box tells you how many accounts it updated and how many transactions it downloaded.

6. **In the Online Transmission Summary dialog box, click Close.**

The Items Received section shows the number of items QuickBooks received and the balances of your online accounts (see Figure 22-4).

Matching Transactions

Every time you connect to your financial institution, QuickBooks downloads all the transactions that have cleared since the last time you went online. This section describes how to match downloaded transactions using Side-by-side mode.

NOTE The first time you download transactions from an online account, QuickBooks looks at transactions marked as cleared in your account register. For all subsequent downloads, the program tries to match only transactions that haven't already cleared.

After you send and receive transactions (as described in the previous section), the Items Received section displays information about the transactions QuickBooks retrieved, as shown in Figure 22-4, including the number of items received and your current online balances. Here's how you process the items that QuickBooks received:

1. **At the bottom of the Online Banking Center, click the Add Transactions to QuickBooks button and choose the account you want to work on from the drop-down menu.**

QuickBooks opens the Add Transactions To QuickBooks window and tries to match the downloaded transactions to the ones you've already entered in the program. The top of the window's Downloaded Transactions section summarizes how many transactions the program matched on its own, how many new transactions it created, and how many transactions you have to help it with. Initially, only unmatched transactions appear in the list, because those are the ones you have to work on.

2. **If you want to see matched or new transactions in the list, click the Show link to the right of the Matched or New lines.**

In the downloaded transactions list, the status of matched transactions is set to Matched, as shown in Figure 22-5, and you don't have to do anything to them. QuickBooks automatically marks them as cleared in the bank account register (page 429).

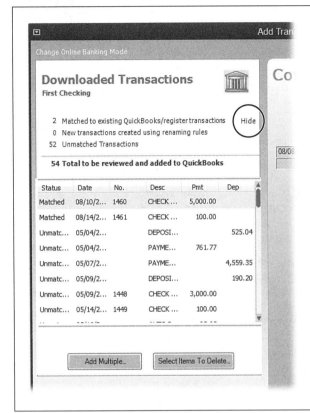

FIGURE 22-5

When you click a Show link to the right of the Matched or New line, QuickBooks displays that type of transaction in the Downloaded Transactions list and changes the link to read "Hide," as shown here (circled). To display only unmatched transactions, click the Hide links to the right of the Matched line and the New line.

Transactions that the program can't match have a status of Unmatched, as you can see in Figure 22-5. The next section tells you how to handle unmatched transactions.

> **NOTE** For transactions without check numbers, QuickBooks matches a downloaded transaction with the oldest transaction of a matching amount. For example, suppose you withdrew $200 from your checking account twice last month. When you download a $200 withdrawal transaction, QuickBooks matches it to the oldest matching transaction in your register.

If QuickBooks matched every transaction, your work is done; if you open the account register (page 414), you'll see a lightning bolt in the Cleared column for every matched transaction. If you're not so lucky, read the next section.

> **NOTE** When you reconcile an account (page 426), the mark in the Cleared column changes from a lightning bolt to a checkmark for transactions that have been reconciled.

Matching Unmatched Transactions

Unsuccessful attempts to match transactions can happen for several reasons, but the source of the problem is *almost* always a mistake or omission in your Quick-Books account register. If you forgot to record a transaction in QuickBooks before you downloaded transactions, this section tells you how to make everything match up. The box on page 586 describes other problems you might encounter and how to correct them.

■ MATCHING DEPOSITS

When you use the Receive Payments window to record check or credit card payments you receive, you might place the payment in your Undeposited Funds account and forget to make the deposit to your bank account using the Make Deposits window (page 397). As shown in Figure 22-6, QuickBooks can match these deposits to payments in your Undeposited Funds account or even to invoices that are still open.

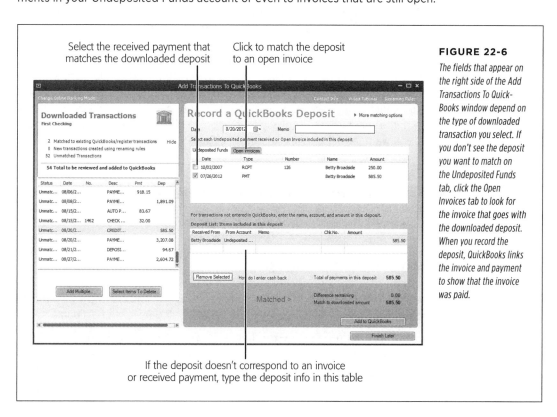

Select the received payment that
matches the downloaded deposit

Click to match the deposit
to an open invoice

If the deposit doesn't correspond to an invoice
or received payment, type the deposit info in this table

FIGURE 22-6

The fields that appear on the right side of the Add Transactions To Quick-Books window depend on the type of downloaded transaction you select. If you don't see the deposit you want to match on the Undeposited Funds tab, click the Open Invoices tab to look for the invoice that goes with the downloaded deposit. When you record the deposit, QuickBooks links the invoice and payment to show that the invoice was paid.

In the Downloaded Transactions list, if a downloaded deposit has a status of Un-matched, select it (the amount is in the Dep column). When you do, the Record a QuickBooks Deposit panel appears on the right side of the window, as shown in Figure 22-6. In QuickBooks, there are three ways to handle deposits. Here's what you do for each:

- **Payments in the Undeposited Funds account**. If you used the Receive Payments window to record a customer payment and the money is sitting in the Undeposited Funds account (page 618), click the Add Transactions To QuickBooks window's Undeposited Funds tab. Turn on the checkbox for the received payment that corresponds to the deposit, and then click the Add to QuickBooks button. If you look at your bank account register, you'll see the deposit with a lightning bolt in the Cleared cell to indicate that it's matched with a transaction downloaded from your bank.

- **Deposits for open invoices**. If you haven't recorded a received payment in QuickBooks, the money is still tied up in an open invoice, which means it's sitting in the Accounts Receivable account. To match a deposit to an open invoice, click the Open Invoices tab labeled in Figure 22-6, turn on the checkbox for the invoice that corresponds to the deposit, and then click Add to QuickBooks.

- **Other deposits**. If you receive some other type of deposit that you haven't recorded in any way in QuickBooks (like an insurance claim refund, say), you can record the deposit's info on the right side of the Add Transactions To QuickBooks window directly in the "Deposit List: Items included in this deposit" table. In the Received From drop-down list, choose the customer or vendor who sent the money, and in the From Account drop-down list, choose the account to which you want to assign the deposit. QuickBooks automatically fills in the Amount cell with the value from the downloaded deposit. Type a memo and check number if you want, and then click Add to QuickBooks.

TIP If your deposit represents several checks from several customers, you can select more than one open invoice or undeposited funds entry, and add more than one item directly in the Deposit List table. Below the Deposit List, the "Difference remaining" value shows the discrepancy between the deposit amount and the items you've selected. When the difference equals 0.00, you're ready to click Add to QuickBooks.

■ MATCHING CHECKS AND EXPENSES

When there's no sign of a check transaction in QuickBooks for the one you downloaded, you may have forgotten to enter the transaction, you created a bill but then forgot to record that you paid it, or someone is stealing from your account.

In the Downloaded Transactions list (Figure 22-4), the amount of a check or bill payment appears in the Pmt column. A value in the No. column tells you the payment is a check; if there's no value in this column, the payment is a bank charge, bank transaction, or electronic payment.

In the Downloaded Transactions list, select the unmatched check or payment that you want to match, and the Record an Expense panel appears on the right side of the window. Here's how to use it to match checks and payments:

- **Checks or charges that aren't bill payments**. These payments include any checks you wrote or electronic payments you made without recording a bill in QuickBooks, or bank charges like monthly service fees and bounced-check charges. To record one of these expenses, in the Record an Expense panel, choose the name of the payee in the Payee drop-down list (or type the payee's name if it isn't in the list), select the account for the expense in the Account drop-down list, and then click Add to QuickBooks.

TIP If you want to add more information about the transaction, like splitting the amount between several accounts or adding a memo, click the "Show splits, memo, date, number" link.

- **Bill payments**. For downloaded transactions that correspond to QuickBooks bill payments, you need to link the payment and the bill so that the bill shows up as paid in QuickBooks. If you didn't record the bill payment in QuickBooks (page 244), at the top right of the Add Transactions To QuickBooks window, click the "More matching options" link. QuickBooks displays three options, shown in Figure 22-7, and the link changes to read, "Hide matching options." Click the "Select open bills to pay in QuickBooks" option. In the Vendor drop-down list, choose the vendor you paid. The "Open Bills for selected vendor" table displays all the open bills for that vendor. Turn on the checkbox for the appropriate open bill and then click Add to QuickBooks.

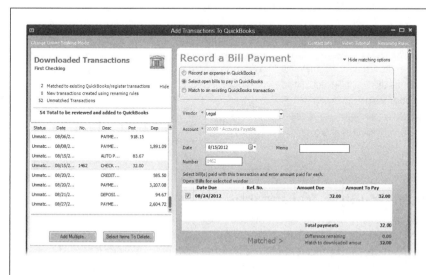

FIGURE 22-7

If you wrote one check to pay several of a vendor's bills, turn on the checkboxes for all the bills that the check covers. As you turn on checkboxes, QuickBooks updates the "Difference remaining" value to show the discrepancy between the downloaded transaction's amount and the total of the bills you selected. When this value equals 0.00, click Add to QuickBooks to save the match.

- **Match an expense manually**. The "Match to an existing QuickBooks transaction" option (click the "More matching options" link at the Add Transactions To QuickBooks window's top right to see it) covers all the other bases. Say QuickBooks doesn't match an ATM withdrawal correctly. When you choose this option, QuickBooks displays the Match to a Register Transaction panel on the right side of the window, and the values for the downloaded transaction appear in the panel. The "Unmatched transactions in QuickBooks" table shows register transactions that haven't yet been matched. For example, if you have two ATM withdrawals, you can pick the one that goes with the downloaded transaction, and then click Confirm Manual Match.

TROUBLESHOOTING MOMENT

Why Transactions Don't Match

If you recorded all your transactions in QuickBooks but your downloaded transactions refuse to match up with what's in your company file, small discrepancies are probably to blame. For example, with downloaded transactions that include check numbers, QuickBooks first looks for a matching check number and, if it finds one, only then does it look at the amount. The program considers check transactions matched only if both the check number and amount match. If the check already exists in QuickBooks, there are two reasons why the program wouldn't be able to match it:

- **The check number in your register is wrong**. For example, if you wrote several checks at the same time, you might have entered them in QuickBooks in a different order than the paper checks you wrote out. Open the account's register window (in the Chart of Accounts window, double-click the name of the account), and then find the transaction and edit its check number. QuickBooks might warn you about duplicate check numbers, but go ahead and use the updated number. After you've edited all the check transactions, you should be back to unique check numbers.

- **The amounts on the checks don't match**. If the amounts disagree, first look at the account register to see if you typed the amount correctly, and correct it if necessary.

If transactions from the bank don't include check numbers, QuickBooks scans transactions without check numbers in your account register for matching amounts. If it doesn't find a match, you might have forgotten to record the transaction in the Pay Bills window (page 244), or the check doesn't link to a bill. If you work in Side-by-side mode, you can rectify these omissions as described on page 583.

If you're *sure* that a check amount you recorded is correct, but the downloaded check amount is different, change the amount in QuickBooks. (Your bank won't go back and edit that transaction.) Then contact your bank and work out the discrepancy. If the bank was at fault, it will issue a separate transaction to correct the error, and you can then download the corrected version.

QuickBooks can't match other types of transactions, like ATM withdrawals or debit card purchases, if the amounts don't match or you haven't recorded the transactions in QuickBooks.

Adding Multiple Transactions

If you write only a few checks and receive a few payments each month, matching each one individually isn't too painful. But you have better things to do than match hundreds of transactions one by one. As long as you don't need to match downloaded transactions to open transactions in QuickBooks or do anything fancy like create splits, you can add several transactions at once with the Add Multiple Transactions dialog box.

In the Add Transactions To QuickBooks window, click Add Multiple. The Add Multiple Transactions to QuickBooks window (Figure 22-8) opens showing renamed, unmatched, and matched transactions. (See the box on page 588 for the scoop on renaming rules.)

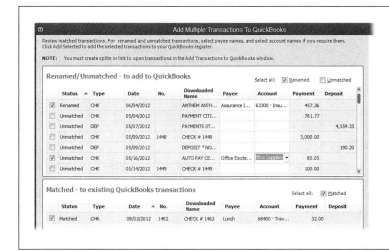

FIGURE 22-8

QuickBooks automatically turns on the checkboxes for transactions that are renamed and matched because they're ready to add to QuickBooks. To turn on all the unmatched checkboxes, click the Unmatched checkbox above the right side of the Renamed/Unmatched table. To turn off all the transaction checkboxes, turn off the appropriate "Select all" checkbox.

To add unmatched transactions to QuickBooks, simply fill in their Payee and Account cells (they have a white background to indicate that they're editable) and turn on their checkboxes. When you're ready to add the transactions to QuickBooks and you've turned on all their checkboxes, click Add Selected.

Deleting Downloaded Transactions

Say you've reconciled your credit card account to your statement. You go online and download transactions only to find that you've downloaded transactions you've already reconciled. You don't have to match the downloaded transactions because your account is already matched up with your bank's records, so you want to delete the downloaded transactions. In the Downloaded Transactions list, click Select Items To Delete; the Select Items To Delete dialog box opens and presents you with two options. Here's how to choose and delete transactions, using each option:

- **Select individual transactions**. QuickBooks picks this option automatically. To select a transaction to delete, turn on its checkbox. After you've done this for all the transactions you want to delete, click Delete Selected.

- **Select all downloaded transactions older than**. This option is perfect if you want to delete transactions that you've already reconciled. Type the cutoff date in the box, and QuickBooks automatically turns on the checkboxes for transactions that occurred before that date. Then just click Delete Selected.

Renaming Downloaded Payees

One drawback to downloading transactions is the crazy payee names that often show up. For example, a gas-station credit card charge downloads with the station's ID number—*Conoco #00092372918027*—or a payment to your favorite office supply store appears as *Internt PMT Have a Great Day 1429AZ#2*. You want payee names that make sense, like *Gasoline*, or that are at least consistent, like *Office Supply Heaven #121*. QuickBooks' renaming rules let you replace downloaded payee names with something short, sweet, and meaningful.

QuickBooks automatically creates renaming rules whenever you change the payee name for a downloaded transaction. Problem is, the renaming rules it creates might be too restrictive. For example, if you change the downloaded payee *Conoco #00092372918027* to *Conoco*, the renaming rule looks for the exact payee name "Conoco #00092372918027" in the future. What you want is a rule that recognizes *any* downloaded payee containing "Conoco" and renames it. Here's how to edit a renaming rule:

1. At the top right of the Add Transactions To QuickBooks window, click Renaming Rules.

2. In the Edit Renaming Rules dialog box, select the payee name stored in QuickBooks ("Conoco," in this example). On the right side of the dialog box, you'll see all the renaming rules that exist for that payee.

3. In the first drop-down list, keep the value set to Contains so that the rule will rename a payee as long as the value you type in the next step appears anywhere in the payee's name.

4. In the second box, type the value that appears in all the downloaded payee names for that vendor, like *Conoco* in this example.

5. Click Save.

If you want to remove one of the existing renaming rules, click the Remove button to the right of the renaming rule boxes. To Edit other renaming rules, repeat steps 2–5.

■ Online Banking Using Register Mode

The Online Banking Center's Register mode lets you see your full account register, which makes it easy to find a matching transaction that QuickBooks doesn't recognize. You can edit transactions in the register to, for example, correct a typo that prevented the program from making a match. This section explains how to do your online banking using Register mode.

Sending and Receiving Items

In Register mode, choose Banking→Online Banking→Online Banking Center to begin connecting to your financial institution. Register mode's Online Banking Center window is more compact than its Side-by-side sibling, as you can see in Figure 22-9.

FIGURE 22-9

If you have online services set up with more than one bank (your checking account with one bank and a credit card with another, say), in the Financial Institution drop-down list, choose one to connect to. QuickBooks automatically selects all requests (like downloading your transactions) in the Items To Send box. If you don't want to send an item, click anywhere in its row to uncheck it. Click Send/Receive to send the selected requests and connect to the bank's website. In the "Access to <your bank>" dialog box that appears, type your password or PIN, and then click OK.

To send requests to your bank, click Send/Receive. After you send your requests, the Online Transmission Summary dialog box tells you how many transactions QuickBooks downloaded from your bank. Click Close, and the Items Received From Financial Institution box shows the balances of your online accounts and any messages that your bank sent you.

Working with Online Items

In the Online Banking Center window, you can make changes to items to send before you go online. After you receive items from your bank, you can view them or delete them. Here's how you use the various buttons in the window:

- **Edit**. Before you go online, you can edit any items other than a request for a statement, like a funds transfer or bill payment you're sending. Simply select the item and then click Edit. Make the changes you want and then click OK.

NOTE   QuickBooks adds a request for a statement to the Items To Send list every time you open the Online Banking Center window (the request is labeled "Download Bank Data for account"). In this context, a *statement* is simply a list of the transactions that cleared in your account since the last time you retrieved information formatted in a way that QuickBooks can import.

- **Delete**. In Register mode, the Online Banking Center window includes two Delete buttons, one for each of the window's two main boxes. Simply click the button to the right of the appropriate box to delete the items you've selected in it. For example, if you set up a fund transfer between accounts that you no longer need or want to remove another type of item, in the Items To Send box, select the item and then click Delete.

  You'll find that your bank is fond of sending you messages about new services or holidays. There's no reason to clutter the Items Received From Financial Institution box with these messages, so simply select them and then click Delete.

- **View**. In the Items Received From Financial Institution box, select an item and then click View to see it in its entirety. When you want to match the transactions in a statement to your QuickBooks bank account transactions, select the statement and then click View; the next section has more details.

Matching Transactions

Every time you connect to your financial institution (by clicking Send/Receive in the Online Banking Center window), QuickBooks requests a statement of all the transactions that have cleared since the last time you went online. After you connect, in the Items Received From Financial Institution box, you'll see an entry for the statement QuickBooks retrieved. To view the downloaded transactions and pull them into your company-file bank account, select this entry and then click View.

When you do, QuickBooks opens the Match Transactions window (Figure 22-10) and tries to match the downloaded transactions to the ones you've already entered in the program. If QuickBooks automatically matches transactions, the Results of Automatic Transaction Matching dialog box tells you how many it paired up. Click OK to close the dialog box. At the bottom of the Match Transactions window, on the Downloaded Transactions tab, the status for those transactions is set to Matched and you don't have to do anything to them; QuickBooks automatically marks them as cleared in the register. Transactions that the program *can't* match have a status of Unmatched, as shown in Figure 22-10.

FIGURE 22-10

If you dutifully enter all your transactions before you download your statement, seeing dozens of unmatched transactions might make you nervous. To make QuickBooks compare the downloaded transactions to the ones in your account register, turn on the Show Register checkbox near the top of this window.

NOTE The first time you download transactions from an online account, QuickBooks looks at transactions marked as cleared in your account register. For all subsequent downloads, the program tries to match only transactions that haven't previously cleared.

If QuickBooks matches every transaction, your work is done. In the account register's Cleared column, you'll see a lightning bolt for every matched transaction. If you're not so lucky, here's how to deal with the unmatched items:

- **Unmatched checks**. For checks that are payments for bills, you first have to use the Pay Bills window to enter the transaction (page 244) so that your bills in QuickBooks show up as paid. For checks that aren't linked to bills or refunds, select the check that you didn't enter in QuickBooks and then click Add One to Register. In the Account box, choose the account to which you want to post the expense and then click Record.

- **Unmatched deposits**. When you use Register mode, you have to record all your customer payments in QuickBooks and move deposits from the Undeposited Funds account into your bank account in your company file *before* you download transactions from your bank. If you have a deposit that doesn't link to a customer payment, such as an insurance claim check, you can add the transaction to the register from the Match Transactions window. In the list of downloaded transactions, select the deposit, and then click Add One to Register. In the Account box, choose the account to post the deposit to and then click Record.

- **Bank charges**. For charges including monthly service fees, bounced check charges, and so on, in the list of downloaded transactions, select the transaction and then click Add One to Register. In the Account box, choose the appropriate account for the charge and then click Record.

Adding Multiple Transactions

If you have several unmatched transactions that you want to add to the register, in the Match Transactions window, click Add Multiple. The "Add Multiple Transactions to the Register" window opens and lists all the unmatched transactions. As you can see in Figure 22-11, the top half of the window lists transactions that are either ready to go or are missing an account. After you choose accounts for the transactions that don't have them, click Record.

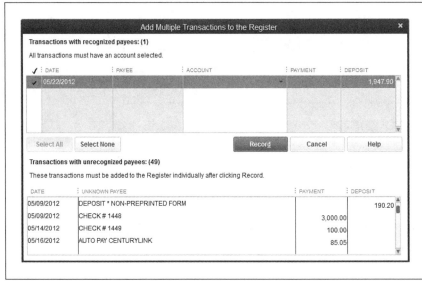

FIGURE 22-11

In this window, you can't do anything with the transactions listed at the bottom of the window that have unrecognized payees. To correct those transactions, close this window and, back in the Match Transactions window, select each one individually and then click Add One to Register. You can then edit the payee name in the register.

Deleting Downloaded Transactions

Register mode doesn't give you a way to delete transactions on the Match Trans-actions window's Downloaded Transactions tab. If you've already reconciled your account and then downloaded the transactions, you might think you have to live with those unmatched transactions forever. But with some fancy footwork, you can get rid of those downloaded orphans. Here's what you do:

1. **Scroll in the register at the top of the Match Transactions window to find the reconciled transaction that pairs with an unmatched transaction.**

   An asterisk in the cleared cell (the one in the column whose heading is a checkmark) means the transaction is cleared; a checkmark indicates that it's reconciled.

2. **Keep clicking its cleared cell until the cell is blank.**

   As soon as the cleared cell is blank, QuickBooks automatically matches the register transaction and the downloaded transaction. You'll see a lightning bolt in the cleared cell to indicate the match, and the downloaded transaction disappears from the Downloaded Transaction tab.

3. **Click the cleared cell again until you see a checkmark.**

   The register transaction is back to being reconciled, and the downloaded transaction is gone forever.

Configuring Preferences to Fit Your Company

An organization's approach to accounting often depends on the type of business it is and its objectives, policies, procedures, and industry. For example, maybe you want inventory tracking and payroll—but maybe you don't. The way you and your accountant like to work also influences your organization's accounting practices. For instance, you might prefer the simplicity of cash accounting to the more intimate pairing of income and expenses that accrual accounting offers (see page xxiii).

Enter QuickBooks, which has the Herculean task of satisfying every nuance of business operation and personal proclivity. The program's *preferences* are configurable settings that accommodate different business approaches and personal tastes. During installation, QuickBooks picks the settings likely to work for a majority of organizations. And if you set up your company file by using the QuickBooks Setup feature (page 6), you might already have most preferences set the way you want.

But you can change the program's preferences to match the way you work, such as whether you create estimates for jobs you go after and how you calculate the amount of inventory that's available. Preferences also let you turn on QuickBooks' features, such as estimates, sales tax, inventory, and payroll. Using QuickBooks for a while can make it clear which preferences you need to change. This chapter presents all the program's preferences and helps you determine which settings are appropriate for you and your organization.

> **NOTE** You can toggle most preferences at any time, but you can't turn the preference for multiple currencies off once you turn it on. Before you change any preferences, back up your company file. Then feel free to tweak and tinker with your preferences.

Preferences: The Basics

You can't complain that QuickBooks 2013 doesn't offer enough preference settings—the program gives you 23 categories of preferences that control the program's behavior. Each preference category has several settings, so finding the ones that do what you want is the biggest challenge. To view and set preferences, open the Preferences dialog box by choosing Edit→Preferences.

On the left side of the dialog box is a pane that lists each preference category, as shown in Figure 23-1. To display the preferences within a category, click the appropriate entry in the pane. QuickBooks highlights the icon you click to indicate that it's selected.

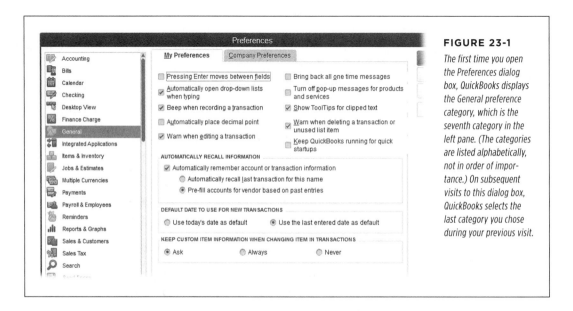

FIGURE 23-1

The first time you open the Preferences dialog box, QuickBooks displays the General preference category, which is the seventh category in the left pane. (The categories are listed alphabetically, not in order of importance.) On subsequent visits to this dialog box, QuickBooks selects the last category you chose during your previous visit.

> **TIP** On the right side of the Preferences dialog box, the Also See list identifies other preference categories that affect the one you're currently viewing.

To accommodate both company-wide and personal preferences, QuickBooks includes two tabs for each category:

- **My Preferences**. As you might expect, this tab contains options that people who log into QuickBooks can set for their QuickBooks sessions alone. For example, in the Desktop View preference category, you can choose options to determine whether you see multiple windows and whether QuickBooks saves the desktop when you close the company file without forcing your tastes on everyone else.

- **Company Preferences**. Some preferences have to remain consistent for everyone in an organization. For example, the IRS won't tolerate some financial reports produced using cash accounting and others using accrual accounting (see page xxiii for the pros and cons of each method). The settings on this tab ensure consistency because they're applied to everyone who logs into your company file. To make sure company preferences are set properly, only folks who log in as QuickBooks administrators (page 684) can change the settings on this tab.

> **NOTE** If you're puzzled by QuickBooks' habit of opening the Preferences dialog box to a My Preferences tab that has no preferences, rest assured that Intuit has its reasons. Because only QuickBooks administrators can change settings on the Company Preferences tab, QuickBooks displays the My Preferences tab to avoid taunting the majority of people who log into the company file by showing them preferences they can't modify.

When you click OK to close the Preferences dialog box, QuickBooks saves the changes you made in the current category. But what if you're on an energetic mission to reset preferences in several categories? If you change preferences in one category and then click the icon for another category, QuickBooks asks you whether you want to save the changes in the category you're about to leave. Make sure you save what you want by selecting one of the following options:

- Click **Yes** to save the changes in the current category before switching to the category whose icon you clicked.

- Click **No** to discard your changes and move on to the category whose icon you clicked.

- Click **Cancel** to discard your changes and remain in the current category so you can make other choices.

The rest of this chapter explains each set of preferences. They're listed here in alphabetical order, just as they are in the Preferences dialog box. You'll also find preferences mentioned throughout this book where they apply to specific bookkeeping tasks.

Accounting

These preferences control key accounting practices, such as requiring accounts assigned to transactions and closing the books at the end of a fiscal year. Accounting practices stay the same throughout a company, so the preferences in the Accounting category all reside on the Company Preferences tab. Here's what they do:

> **NOTE** For QuickBooks Premier and Enterprise, the My Preferences tab has one preference: the "Autofill memo in general journal entry" checkbox. You can keep the debit and credit sides of general journal entries linked by adding memos to the lines of the entries. Leave this checkbox on if you want QuickBooks to copy the memo you enter in the first line of a journal entry to every subsequent line of the entry.

- **Use account numbers**. If you follow a numbering standard for your accounts (page 48 shows a common one), turn on this checkbox so you can assign a number, in addition to a name, to each account you create.

TIP When you assign an account to a transaction, such as applying your rent check to the Rent expense account, you can locate the account in the Account drop-down list by typing either its number *or* the first few letters of its name.

- **Require accounts**. If remembering details isn't your strong suit, keeping this checkbox turned on forces you to assign an account to every item and transaction you create, which, in turn, creates a trail that you, your accountant, and the IRS can follow. With this checkbox turned on, when you click Record without an assigned account, QuickBooks informs you that you have to enter an account. To record the transaction, in the Warning message box, click OK. Then choose the account in the transaction's Account field. Then, when you click Record again, QuickBooks completes the transaction.

  If you turn this checkbox off and record transactions without assigned accounts, QuickBooks assigns the transaction amounts to either the Uncategorized Income or Uncategorized Expense account. For example, if you receive a payment from a customer and don't assign an account to the deposit, that income posts to the Uncategorized Income account.

WARNING If the IRS decides to audit your tax returns, you'll have to go back and move your uncategorized income and expenses into the right accounts to prove that you paid the right amount of taxes. And, if you happened to pay too little, the IRS will charge you penalties and interest.

- **Show lowest subaccount only**. If you use only top-level accounts in your chart of accounts, you have no need for this behavior. And if you don't use account numbers, this checkbox is grayed out. But if your chart of accounts is a hierarchy of accounts and subaccounts, as described in the box on page 55, turn on this checkbox so Account fields show only the subaccount number and name instead of the full account path from the top-level account to the lowest subaccount.

- **Use class tracking**. If you want to track your business in more ways than accounts, items, customer types, and job types can offer, you can use classes (page 150) to add another level of categorization to your reports. For example, you can create classes to track business units' income and expenses, regardless of which types of customers they support or the type of work they do. To activate the Class feature, turn on this checkbox, which adds a Class field to every transaction window.

- **Prompt to assign classes**. If you turn on the Class feature, reports organized by class won't accurately reflect your business performance unless you assign classes to *all* your class-related transactions. If most or all of your transactions are class-related, turn on this checkbox so that QuickBooks reminds you when you forget to enter a class assignment for a transaction.

- **Automatically assign general journal entry number**. Journal entries get their name from the traditional approach to accounting, in which accountants assign credits and debits to accounts in paper-based journals. There's no reason to turn this checkbox off. With it on, QuickBooks makes sure that each general journal entry has a unique number. When you create a new general journal entry, QuickBooks increments the previous journal entry number by one, as shown in Figure 23-2, which makes it easier for you and your accountant to refer to the correct journal entries.

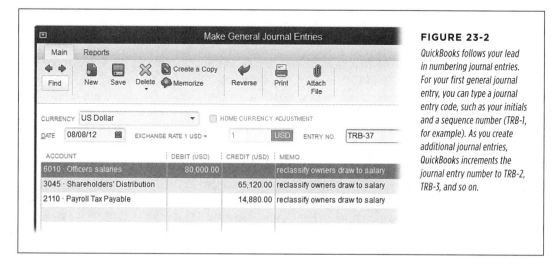

FIGURE 23-2

QuickBooks follows your lead in numbering journal entries. For your first general journal entry, you can type a journal entry code, such as your initials and a sequence number (TRB-1, for example). As you create additional journal entries, QuickBooks increments the journal entry number to TRB-2, TRB-3, and so on.

NOTE If the previous entry number is blank, QuickBooks won't automatically assign a number to the next entry. So if you notice that QuickBooks has begun to shirk its automatic numbering duties, look for a blank entry number. Add numbers to any existing journal entries that don't have them. After that, when you add a new journal entry, QuickBooks will number the next entry as it should.

- **Warn when posting a transaction to Retained Earnings**. QuickBooks automatically turns on this checkbox, and it's a good idea to leave it that way. The program creates a Retained Earnings account to track past profits that you've retained in the company's coffers. For example, if your company earned $50,000 in 2013 and didn't distribute that money to the owners or as profit-sharing bonuses to employees, the money becomes Retained Earnings once your fiscal year 2014 begins. QuickBooks updates the balance in the account automatically at the beginning of a new fiscal year by transferring the previous year's net profit into it. With this preference turned on, QuickBooks warns you when you try to post a transfer directly to the Retained Earning account and inadvertently create inaccurate records. (See the box on page 487 to learn how to differentiate your most recent year's retained earnings from earlier retained earnings.)

- **Date warnings**. If your books are up-to-date, then very old or very prescient dates are usually mistakes. To receive warnings for dates too far in the past or future, leave the "Warn if transactions are _ day(s) in the past" checkbox and its companion, the "Warn if transactions are _ day(s) in the future" checkbox, turned on. The boxes are initially set to 90 for past dates and 30 for future dates, but you can change them.

- **Closing date**. After producing the financial reports for a fiscal year and paying corporate income taxes, most companies *close their books*, which means locking the transactions so no one can change anything. By closing the books, you ensure that your past transactions continue to match what you submitted to your accountant, reported to the IRS, and communicated to your shareholders.

  When you use QuickBooks, your QuickBooks company file is synonymous with your "books." Therefore, you close your books by clicking Set Date/Password here and then choosing a date in the "Set Closing Date and Password" dialog box. For example, if you run your company on a calendar year and just reported and paid taxes for 2012, type or choose *12/31/2012*.

  You can assign a password so that you can edit, delete, or create transactions that alter account balances in closed books. In the "Set Closing Date and Password" dialog box, type the password in the Closing Date Password and Confirm Password boxes, and then click OK. That way, if you have to edit a transaction prior to the closing date, you'll first have to type the password to tell QuickBooks you mean it.

Bills

The Bills category lets you specify how you want to handle bills that vendors send you. The My Preferences tab is empty, so these settings all appear on the Company Preferences tab:

- **Bills are due _ days after receipt**. The first time you access Bills preferences, you'll find that QuickBooks has set this preference so that bills you enter show a due date 10 days after the date of the bill. For instance, if you receive a bill dated June 15 and you enter that date in the Enter Bills window's Date field, QuickBooks automatically changes the Bill Due field to June 25. This value is fine in most cases. If a bill arrives that's due in a different number of days, you can simply change its due date in the Enter Bills window's Bill Due field.

- **Warn about duplicate bill numbers from same vendor**. Surely you don't want to pay the same bill twice, so be sure to leave this checkbox turned on so QuickBooks warns you that you're entering a bill with the same number as one you already entered from the same vendor.

- **Paying bills**. If you want QuickBooks to automatically apply to your bills any credits and discounts to which you're entitled, turn on the "Automatically use credits" and "Automatically use discounts" checkboxes. For example, if you typically receive a 15 percent discount on all purchases and also have a $100 credit, QuickBooks applies these adjustments to your bill before calculating the total. When you turn on the "Automatically use discounts" checkbox, in the Default Discount Account drop-down list, choose the account to which you usually post the discounts you take, such as an expense account specifically for vendor discounts.

Calendar

The QuickBooks calendar (page 33) shows you when transactions and to-dos are due, so you can be sure to perform the tasks you're supposed to, such as paying bills or following up on open invoices. Calendar preferences are all on the My Preferences tab, so that each person who works in the company file can choose what they see:

- **Calendar settings**. The preferences in this section control the calendar's appearance. You can see one day, one week, or month at a time. For the weekly view, you can specify whether you want to see Monday through Friday or the entire week. Initially, the preference is set to show all transactions, but you can change it to Transactions Due or choose a specific type of transaction, such as Invoice, Received Payment, or Bill.

- **Upcoming & past due settings**. On the right side of the Calendar is a pane that lists to-dos and transactions that are coming up or overdue. You can tell QuickBooks to show or hide this pane, or better yet, show the pane only if there are upcoming or past due items. Initially, the Calendar shows what's coming up in the next 7 days and what was due in the past 60 days. You can change the period in the future to up to 31 days, while the past due period can shrink to as few as 14 days.

Checking

Checking preferences let you adjust company-wide settings to control the appearance of the checks your company prints through QuickBooks. On the My Preferences tab for this category, you can tell QuickBooks which accounts to select automatically for several types of financial transactions, as shown in Figure 23-3.

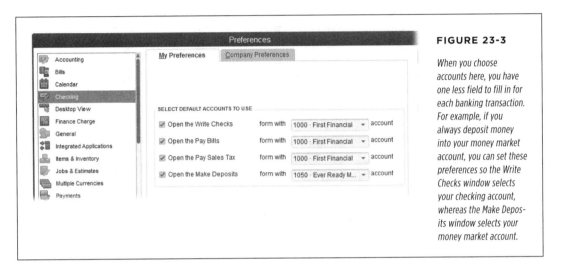

FIGURE 23-3

When you choose accounts here, you have one less field to fill in for each banking transaction. For example, if you always deposit money into your money market account, you can set these preferences so the Write Checks window selects your checking account, whereas the Make Deposits window selects your money market account.

Choosing the Bank Accounts You Use

If you have only one bank account, you can ignore the preferences for default accounts and QuickBooks will automatically choose your checking account for writing checks, paying bills, paying sales tax, and making deposits. But suppose your company has stores in several states and each store has its own checking account. By setting the options on the My Preferences tab, each person who logs into QuickBooks can choose her store's bank accounts for financial transactions. For example, the person in Miami wants the Florida checking account to appear in the Write Checks window, but the person in New York wants to see the Manhattan checking account. To save some time (and prevent folks from selecting the wrong account in a drop-down list), set your accounts according to the following guidelines:

- **Open the Write Checks form with _ account**. In this drop-down list, choose the account you typically use to write checks. That way, when you open the Write Checks window, QuickBooks automatically fills in the Bank Account field with the account you specify here.

- **Open the Pay Bills form with _ account**. For this preference, choose the account you typically use to pay bills, which is often the same checking account that you chose in the "Open the Write Checks form with" preference. When you open the Pay Bills window, QuickBooks automatically fills in the Account field at the bottom right of the window with the account you specify here.

- **Open the Pay Sales Tax form with _ account**. If you collect sales tax from your customers (see page 140), you have to remit the taxes you collect to the appropriate tax authority, such as the state where your business is located. When it's time to send the taxes in, you open the Pay Sales Tax dialog box and create a payment. This preference sets the account that QuickBooks uses in the Pay From Account field.

- **Open the Make Deposits form with _ account**. Unlike the other options on the My Preferences tab, this preference sets up the account you typically use when you *deposit* money. For many small businesses, the deposit account and the checking account are one and the same. But some businesses deposit money into an account that pays interest, and then transfer money into a checking account only when it's time to pay bills. After you choose the account you use to deposit money, the Make Deposits window automatically puts it in the Deposit To field.

Settings for Company Checks

Although a company might have several checking accounts, QuickBooks assumes that company checks should look the same no matter who prints them. Most preferences on the Company Preferences tab let you set the company standard for printing checks from QuickBooks. (If you use preprinted checks and write them out by hand, you can skip some of these options.) Here's what these preferences do:

- **Print account names on voucher**. If the checks you print include check stubs, you might as well turn on this checkbox. When you do, QuickBooks prints the name of the account you used to pay the check on the stub. If you use only one bank account, printing the account name might not seem all that useful. But with this preferences turned on, QuickBooks also prints the payroll item on the stub for payroll checks, and for checks used to purchase inventory, it prints the name of the inventory item you purchased—both of which can help you keep track of where your money is going.

NOTE Regardless of how you set the "Print account names on voucher" preference, QuickBooks always prints the payee, date, memo, amount, and total amount on check stubs.

- **Change check date when non-cleared check is printed**. When you turn on this checkbox, QuickBooks inserts the date that you *print* checks as the check date, which is just fine in most situations. You can then enter checks into QuickBooks over several days, but date all the checks with the day you print them. Leave this checkbox turned off if you want to control the check dates, for example, to defer payments for a few days by post-dating checks with the date the payees receive them.

- **Start with payee field on check**. If you always write checks from the same account, or you use the "Open the Write Checks form with" preference to specify an account (page 602), pressing Tab in the Write Checks window to skip the Bank Account field for each check transaction gets old quickly. When you turn on this checkbox, you can save one pesky keystroke each time you write a check. Turning on this preference also makes it so that the Enter Credit Card Charges window opens with the cursor in the Purchased From box.

- **Warn about duplicate check numbers**. Not surprisingly, when this checkbox is turned on, QuickBooks warns you if you're trying to record a check with the same number as one you already entered.

- **Autofill payee account number in check memo**. Just as you assign account numbers to your customers, the vendors you do business with assign your company an account number, too. Printing account numbers on the checks you write helps vendors credit your account, even if the check gets separated from its accompanying payment slip. If you enter your company's account number in each Vendor record in QuickBooks (page 92), be sure to leave this checkbox on to print these account numbers on your checks.

Choosing Company-Wide Payroll Accounts

If you don't use QuickBooks' payroll features, don't bother with these preferences. If you *do* use Intuit Payroll Services (page 409), the two settings in the Select Default Accounts To Use section of the Company Preferences tab let you set the accounts you use for payroll. You might think QuickBooks is jumping the gun by offering company-wide settings for the accounts used for payroll and payroll liabilities, but most companies centralize payroll no matter how regional other operations are. Here are your options:

- **Open the Create Paychecks form with _ account**. In this drop-down list, choose the account you use to write payroll checks. If you use QuickBooks payroll, when you open the Create Paychecks window, the program automatically fills in the Bank Account field with the account you specify here.

- **Open the Pay Payroll Liabilities form with _ account**. In this drop-down list, choose the account you use to pay payroll taxes.

> **TIP** A separate bank account for payroll simplifies reconciling your regular checking account, particularly if your company has numerous employees and weekly paychecks. Otherwise, you'll have to reconcile dozens or even hundreds of paychecks each month in addition to the other checks you write.

Selecting an Online Banking Mode

QuickBooks lets you choose between two versions of the Online Banking Center (one from QuickBooks 2008 and earlier and another introduced in QuickBooks 2009). The Side-by-side mode is more flexible, but you can switch between the two modes any time by selecting an option. Page 575 explains how the two modes work.

Desktop View

Each person can customize her own QuickBooks desktop with the preferences on the My Preferences tab—your choices don't affect anybody else who logs into QuickBooks. On the other hand, the Company Preferences tab includes preferences that control what appears on the QuickBooks Home page for everyone who uses this company file.

Window Preferences

You can keep your desktop neat with only one window at a time, or you can view multiple windows:

- **One Window**. If you're not good at multitasking or you prefer full-size windows, choose this option so that QuickBooks displays only one full-size window at a time. Although you can still open multiple windows, they're stacked on top of each other so you see only the top one. With this approach, you can switch windows by choosing windows in the Open Window List (choose View→Open Window List to display it) or on the program's main menu bar, choose Window and then select the name of the window you want to display.

> **NOTE** You can switch between one and multiple windows by choosing View→One Window and View→Multiple Windows, respectively.

- **Multiple Windows**. If you like to view several windows at once or want to size windows based on how much information they display, as shown in Figure 23-4, choose this option. When you do, the Window menu includes entries for arranging windows such as Cascade and Tile Vertically.

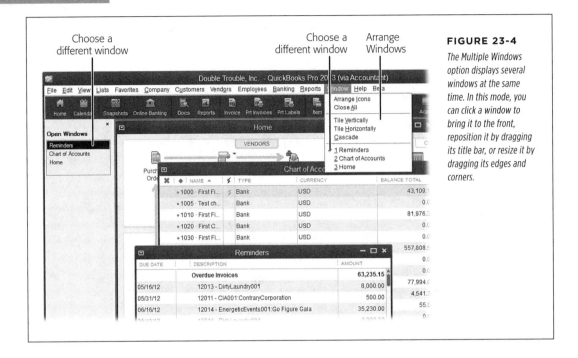

Choose a different window   Choose a different window   Arrange Windows

FIGURE 23-4

The Multiple Windows option displays several windows at the same time. In this mode, you can click a window to bring it to the front, reposition it by dragging its title bar, or resize it by dragging its edges and corners.

NOTE In QuickBooks 2013, you can no longer choose a color scheme.

Preferences for Saving the Desktop

The My Preferences tab in the Desktop category includes four choices for what QuickBooks does with the windows that are open when you exit the program, as well as an option related to the Home page. For example, if you have the windows arranged just the way you like, you can save your QuickBooks desktop so the windows open in exactly the same arrangement the next time you log in. Here's the lowdown on why you might choose each option:

- **Save when closing company**. If you typically continue bookkeeping tasks from one QuickBooks session to the next, this option saves the open windows and their positions when you exit the program. The next time you log in, QuickBooks opens the same windows and positions them where they were last time so you can finish entering the remaining 300 checks you have to write.

- **Save current desktop**. If you have a favorite arrangement of windows that works well for the bulk of your efforts in QuickBooks, you can save that arrangement and display it every time you log in. To do so, first open the windows you want and position them. Then open the Preferences dialog box, choose this option, and then click OK. After that, the next time you open the Preferences dialog box, QuickBooks adds the "Keep previously saved desktop" option (explained below) to the My Preferences tab.

- **Don't save the desktop**. Choosing this option displays a desktop with only the menu bar, the icon bar, the Home page, and the Reminders window. This makes QuickBooks open faster, and the Home page gives you fast access to the windows and dialog boxes you use regularly.

- **Keep previously saved desktop**. Once you've saved a desktop you like, this option appears on the My Preferences tab of the Desktop View category. In fact, once you choose "Save current desktop" and click OK to close the Preferences dialog box, QuickBooks automatically selects this option the next time you open the dialog box. With this option selected, QuickBooks opens with the desktop as it was when you selected "Save current desktop," regardless of which windows you've opened since then or how you've rearranged them.

- **Show Home page when opening a company file**. The Home page shows the entire workflow of your accounting tasks, as well as links to oft-opened windows like the Chart of Accounts. Keep this checkbox turned on to see the Home page each time you log in.

NOTE The Windows Settings section at the bottom of the My Preferences tab has two buttons: Display and Sounds. These buttons take you to the appropriate category of the Windows Control Panel to change your Windows settings, where any changes you make affect every program on your computer, not just QuickBooks.

Customizing the Home Page

This window lets you access almost any accounting task. The Home page has three horizontal panels for tasks related to vendors, customers, and employees (Figure 23-5 shows the Vendors and Customers panels). The Company Preferences tab of the Desktop View category is where you can customize what appears there.

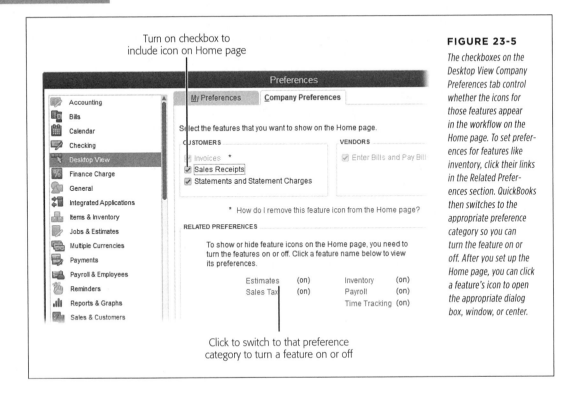

Turn on checkbox to
include icon on Home page

FIGURE 23-5

The checkboxes on the Desktop View Company Preferences tab control whether the icons for those features appear in the workflow on the Home page. To set preferences for features like inventory, click their links in the Related Preferences section. QuickBooks then switches to the appropriate preference category so you can turn the feature on or off. After you set up the Home page, you can click a feature's icon to open the appropriate dialog box, window, or center.

Click to switch to that preference
category to turn a feature on or off

NOTE If the checkboxes for invoices or bill-payment tasks are dimmed and you want to remove those tasks from the Home page, you first need to turn off other preferences. For example, for invoices, you have to turn off the Estimate and Sales Orders preferences (in the Jobs & Estimates and Sales & Customers preference categories, respectively). Click the "How do I remove this feature icon from the Home page?" link to read a Help topic that lists the settings you need to change.

Finance Charge

If you're lucky enough to have customers who always pay on time or if you run a nonprofit organization that graciously accepts donations, you can bypass the finance charge preference category. But if you want to add an incentive for customers to pay on time, these preferences determine your level of persuasion.

Because you probably want a consistent policy for charging customers for late payments, all the preferences in the Finance Charge category appear on the Company Preferences tab. That means only someone logged into QuickBooks as an administrator can change these settings. To learn how to add the finance charges configured here to the invoices you create, see page 335.

Here are the finance charge preferences you can set and what they mean to your customers:

- **Annual Interest Rate (%)**. Type the interest rate that you charge per year for overdue payments. For example, if you charge 18 percent per year, type *18* in this box. QuickBooks then calculates the finance charge due by prorating the annual interest date to the number of days that the payment is late.

- **Minimum Finance Charge**. If you charge a minimum finance charge no matter how inconsequential the overdue amount, type that value in this box. For example, to charge at least $20, type *20*. If you work with more than one currency, you still specify your minimum finance charge in your home currency. QuickBooks then converts the amount to the customer's currency when you apply finance charges.

- **Grace Period (days)**. Just like the grace period that you probably appreciate on your mortgage, the grace period in QuickBooks is the number of days that a payment can be late before finance charges kick in. In this box, type the number of days of grace you're willing to extend to your customers.

- **Finance Charge Account**. Choose the account you use to track finance charges you collect. Most companies create an Other Income account (page 469) to track these charges, which are interest income.

- **Assess finance charges on overdue finance charges**. If a customer goes AWOL and doesn't pay the bill *or* the finance charges, you can get tough and levy finance charges on the finance charges that the customer already owes. If your customer owes $100 in finance charges and you assess an 18 percent finance charge, turning on this checkbox would result in an additional $18 the first year on the outstanding charges alone.

- **Calculate charges from**. You can calculate finance charges from two different dates, depending on how painful you want the finance charge penalty to be. Choosing the "due date" option here is the more lenient approach; it tells QuickBooks to assess finance charges only on the days that an invoice is paid past its due date. For example, if the customer pays 10 days late, QuickBooks calculates the finance charges for 10 days. If you want to assess finance charges from the date on the invoice, choose the "invoice/billed date" option instead.

In that case, if the customer pays 10 days late on a Net 30 invoice (meaning payment is due within 30 days after the invoice date), QuickBooks calculates finance charges based on 40 days—the 30 days until the invoice was due and the 10 days that the payment was late.

- **Mark finance charge invoices "To be printed."** If you want QuickBooks to remind you to print invoices with finance charges, turn on this checkbox. Invoices that you haven't printed yet then appear as alerts in the Reminders window.

General

QuickBooks selects the General preferences category the very first time you open the Preferences dialog box. Most of the General preferences appear on the My Preferences tab, so you can make QuickBooks work the way you do, but a few preferences apply to everyone who works on the company file.

Tuning QuickBooks to Your Liking

The following settings on the My Preferences tab can help you fine-tune QuickBooks' behavior:

- **Pressing Enter moves between fields**. In the Windows world, pressing the Enter key usually activates the default button in a dialog box, while the Tab key advances the cursor to the next field. If you press Enter in QuickBooks and find that a dialog box or window closes unexpectedly, this checkbox can provide some relief. When you turn it on, pressing Enter moves the cursor between fields in a dialog box or window rather than closing it. However, because Enter no longer closes dialog boxes and windows, you have to press Ctrl+Enter or click a button—such as OK, Record, Save & Close, or Save & New (depending on the dialog box or window)—to do so.

- **Automatically open drop-down lists when typing**. This setting makes drop-down menus spring open as soon as you type a letter in a field. You can then click the entry you want, as shown in Figure 23-6.

- **Beep when recording a transaction**. If you like auditory assurance that your software is working, leave this checkbox turned on to have QuickBooks beep when it records a transaction. (Remember, you'll hear the beeps only if you haven't muted the audio on your computer.) If you decide you prefer peace and quiet, simply turn off this setting.

- **Automatically place decimal point**. When you turn on this checkbox, QuickBooks places decimals so that the last two numbers you type represent cents. For example, typing *19995* automatically becomes 199.95. (If you want to enter a whole dollar, type a period at the end of the number.) Having QuickBooks place decimal points in numbers for you can be quite addictive once you get used to it, particularly if you haven't graduated to rapid-fire entry on your computer's numeric keypad—or if you work on a laptop and haven't realized that your keyboard *has* a numeric keypad.

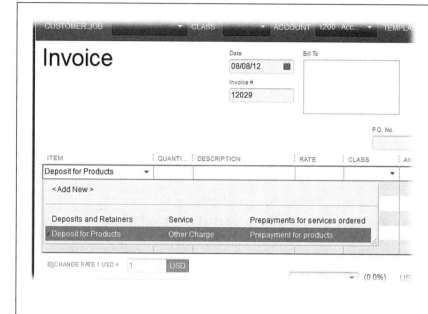

FIGURE 23-6

With the "Automatically open drop-down lists when typing" preference turned on, drop-down lists appear as soon as you begin typing an entry in a field, so you can simply keep typing or click an entry. The list narrows down to the choices that match the letters you've typed so far (showing "Deposits and Retainers" and "Deposit for Products" if you've typed "dep," for example). You can also adjust the width of the drop-down list by dragging its bottom-right corner to show as much or as little information as you want.

- **Warn when editing a transaction**. QuickBooks turns on this checkbox automatically, which means that the program displays a warning if you edit a transaction and attempt to leave it (for instance, by clicking another transaction) without explicitly recording the change. If you inadvertently modify a transaction, like a check or invoice, this warning gives you a chance to save the changes or exit without saving.

  If you decide to turn off this feature, QuickBooks automatically records transactions that aren't linked to other transactions. However, if a transaction has links—such as a payment that links to a customer invoice—you need to record it after you change it regardless of how you've set this preference.

- **Bring back all one time messages**. One-time messages instruct beginners in the ways of QuickBooks, but for experienced folks, dismissing these messages simply consumes valuable time. If you were overly enthusiastic about hiding one-time messages and find yourself in need of QuickBooks' mentoring, turn this checkbox on.

- **Turn off pop-up messages for products and services**. Initially, QuickBooks displays pop-up messages about other products and services that Intuit offers. If you're content with what QuickBooks offers out of the box, turn this checkbox on.

- **Show ToolTips for clipped text**. Text in QuickBooks fields is often longer than what you can see onscreen. For example, if you see the text "Make sure you always" in a text box, you'll want to read the rest of the message. This checkbox, which is turned on initially, tells QuickBooks to display the entire contents of a field when you position your cursor over it.

- **Warn when deleting a transaction or unused list item**. QuickBooks turns this checkbox on automatically, so you have to confirm that you want to delete a transaction, such as a deposit or a check, or a list item that's never been used in a transaction. Caution is a watchword in the financial world, so although QuickBooks lets you delete transactions, it's a good idea to leave this setting on to make sure you're deleting what you want. If you turn off this checkbox, you can delete a transaction or unused list item without confirmation.

> **NOTE** Regardless of how this preference is set, QuickBooks won't let you delete a list item, such as a customer type or shipping method, if it's been used in even one transaction. Page 167 explains how to delete or inactivate list items.

- **Keep QuickBooks running for quick startups**. If you fire up QuickBooks frequently, turn on this checkbox so the program launches faster (because it stays running in the background). In fact, QuickBooks launches in the background when you reboot your computer. If you turn off this checkbox, QuickBooks doesn't run in the background or use your computer's memory, so it takes longer to start up.

- **Automatically remember account or transaction information**. Say you write checks each month to the same vendor, for the same amount, and post them to the same account. Out of the box, QuickBooks turns on the "Pre-fill accounts for vendor based on past entries" option in this section, which means that the program automatically fills in the accounts you use consistently for vendor transactions. But since you can set up pre-fill accounts for vendors with other QuickBooks features (page 93), the "Automatically recall last transaction for this name" option gives you more bang for the buck. With that option selected, when you type a name in a transaction, QuickBooks fills in the rest of the fields with the values you used in the last transaction for that name.

  However, AutoRecall has a couple of limitations: It can't recall a transaction in one account if the previous transaction was in another account, and it can recall transactions for bills, checks, and credit card charges only. For other transactions—such as purchase orders, invoices, sales receipts, and credit memos—you have to fill in all the fields or use a memorized transaction.

- **Default date to use for new transactions**. In this section of the My Preferences tab, choose the "Use today's date as default" option if you want QuickBooks to put the current date in the Date field of every new transaction you create.

  If you create invoices over the course of several days but want each one to reflect the first day of the month, choose the "Use the last entered date as default" option instead. Then, in the first invoice you create, type the date you want for all your invoices. For subsequent invoices, QuickBooks fills in the Date field with the date you entered on the previous invoice. When you want to use a new date (after all the month's invoices are complete), simply type it in your next transaction.

TIP When the "Use the last entered date as default" option is selected, be sure to check the Date box in a transaction window (like Create Invoices) to make sure it's the one you want.

- **Keep custom item information when changing item in transactions**. This setting determines how QuickBooks responds when you change an item in a transaction after customizing its description. Say you add an item to an invoice, edit the description in the invoice, and *then* realize that you added the wrong item. When you choose a new item to replace it, if you've selected the Ask option for this setting, QuickBooks asks whether you want to use the edited description for the new item. The Always option automatically applies the edited description to the new item. And with the Never option, QuickBooks discards the edited description and uses the description from the new item's record.

Company-Wide General Preferences

The Company Preferences tab includes four preferences, shown in Figure 23-7. Remember, only a QuickBooks administrator can change these settings. Here's what they do:

- **Time format**. You can enter hours as decimal numbers that represent hours and fractions of hours, or as hours and minutes separated by a colon, as you can see in Figure 23-7. This preference tells QuickBooks which way to display time values.

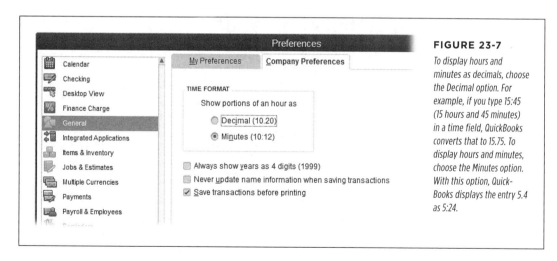

FIGURE 23-7

To display hours and minutes as decimals, choose the Decimal option. For example, if you type 15:45 (15 hours and 45 minutes) in a time field, QuickBooks converts that to 15.75. To display hours and minutes, choose the Minutes option. With this option, Quick-Books displays the entry 5.4 as 5:24.

- **Always show years as 4 digits (1999)**. This setting tells QuickBooks to display all four digits of the year whether you type two digits or four. For example, if you type *09*, then QuickBooks displays 2009. Turning off this checkbox makes the program display years as two digits. When you type a two-digit number for a year, QuickBooks translates numbers from 00 through 41 as years 2000 through 2041; 42 through 99 become 1942 through 1999.

> **TIP** If you turn off the "Always show years as 4 digits" checkbox, QuickBooks does as it's told and displays only two digits for the year. If a date field shows 40 and you want to see whether that stands for 1940 or 2040, in the date field, click the Calendar icon. The Calendar shows both the month and the full four-digit year.

- **Never update name information when saving transactions**. QuickBooks initially turns this checkbox off so that, when you edit the name of a customer or vendor, for example, the program asks if you want to replicate that change back in the original record—on the Customer:Job List or Vendor List. The only situation where you might want to change this behavior (by turning on this checkbox) is if you use generic names, such as Donor or Member. If you receive donations and your donors want receipts with their names and addresses filled in, you don't want the names and addresses you enter on sales receipts to alter your generic donor record.

- **Save transactions before printing**. QuickBooks turns this checkbox on initially, and it's a good idea to leave it that way. It tells the program to save transactions before you print them so that the transactions in QuickBooks are the same as the ones you print. If you turn this checkbox off, you could print the transaction with one set of data and then close the dialog box or window without saving that data, thus making your QuickBooks records different from your paper records.

Integrated Applications

As you'll learn in more detail in Chapter 24, QuickBooks plays well with other programs, like Microsoft Excel and Word, and oodles of third-party applications. For example, by integrating Microsoft Outlook with QuickBooks, you can easily keep your contact information synchronized in both programs. And other software companies create all sorts of programs that integrate with QuickBooks for tasks like inventory tracking, project tracking, creating bar codes, and so on. If you're a QuickBooks administrator, the Integrated Applications preferences category is where you control which programs can interact with QuickBooks and the extent of their interaction. For example, you can use another program to produce estimates and then transfer the completed estimates into QuickBooks to fill out invoices and other forms.

To access these preferences, choose Edit→Preferences and click the Integrated Applications icon. Here's a guide to adjusting the settings on the Company Preferences tab to allow or restrict other programs' access to your QuickBooks company file:

- **Don't allow any applications to access this company file**. The quickest way to keep other programs from using a QuickBooks company file is to turn on this checkbox. When you do so, QuickBooks prevents integrated programs from accessing the file and stops displaying screens that allow people to authorize access. If you want QuickBooks to display access screens, leave this checkbox off. (Others can authorize access only if a QuickBooks administrator sets up their accounts to do so, as discussed on page 691.)

- **Notify the user before running any application whose certificate has expired**. The most security conscious of administrators might turn on this checkbox to see a warning if a program trying to access the QuickBooks company file has an expired certificate. But an expired certificate doesn't mean that the program has changed or has morphed into malicious code—only that the certificate has expired. For most administrators, leaving this checkbox off is preferable.

- **Applications that have previously requested access to this company file**. When programs request access to a company file, QuickBooks displays an access screen to the QuickBooks administrator who has to approve or deny access. Programs that have received approval to access your company file appear in this list. To deny access to one of these programs, click its checkmark in the Allow Access column, or select the program and then click Remove.

Items & Inventory

The Items & Inventory preferences apply mainly to what QuickBooks does when you create purchase orders or invoices for inventory. The first setting on the Company Preferences tab is the most important: You tell QuickBooks that you want to track inventory by turning on the "Inventory and purchase orders are active" checkbox, which activates the program's inventory-related features (Chapter 19) and adds icons like Purchase Orders and Receive Inventory to the Home page. If you turn inventory tracking on, here are the settings you may want to adjust:

- **Warn about duplicate purchase order numbers**. Leave this checkbox on if you want QuickBooks to alert you when you're creating a purchase order with the same number as one you already entered.

- **Warn if not enough inventory quantity on hand (QOH) to sell**. In QuickBooks Pro, you can turn this checkbox on so QuickBooks will warn you if you prepare an invoice to sell more doodads than you have in stock. Suppose you sell 500 quarts of sesame soy swirl frozen yogurt, but you have only 400 quarts in stock. When you attempt to save the invoice for the 500-quart order, QuickBooks displays a message box informing you of the shortage. But QuickBooks doesn't go any further than that. You can save the invoice, but it's up to you to order more inventory. Besides giving you a heads-up that inventory is low, this setting helps you keep your customers happy, since you can ask them if they want to wait for a backorder to be filled. The box on page 616 describes the inventory preferences you can set if you use QuickBooks Premier or Enterprise.

■ Jobs & Estimates

If you create estimates or document job progress in QuickBooks, head to the Jobs & Estimates preferences category to set up your progress terminology and estimating features. QuickBooks includes five job-status fields: "Pending," "Awarded," "In progress," "Closed," and "Not awarded." Despite the fields' names, you can type any term you want in any of the five boxes. You can type *Waiting* in the Pending box, *Whoopie!* in the Awarded box, and *Finally!* in the Closed box, for example. Then, when you edit a job and display the Job Status drop-down list, you can choose from these terms.

Advanced Inventory Settings

Unless you use QuickBooks Enterprise, the Advanced Inventory Settings button (on the Items & Inventory Company Preferences tab) is grayed out. To see if these settings are worth the cost of upgrading, click the "Learn about serial #/lots, FIFO and multi-location inventory" link.

If you don't opt for QuickBooks Enterprise, you can obtain a few additional inventory preferences by upgrading from QuickBooks Pro to QuickBooks Premier:

- **When calculating Quantity Available for my inventory, deduct**. QuickBooks Premier tracks two quantities for inventory items. Quantity On Hand is the actual number of items sitting in inventory. Quantity Available can equal Quantity On Hand, but you can also tell QuickBooks to remove the number of items on sales orders or used in pending builds (when you build products out of components) from the Quantity Available number. If you use sales orders (page 307) to track orders that haven't been invoiced, QuickBooks automatically turns on the "Quantity on Sales Order" checkbox here. With this setting selected, QuickBooks calculates the number of inventory items available by deducting the number of items on sales orders from the number of items on hand, which helps prevent you from accidentally selling out-of-stock items. If you turn this checkbox off, the quantity available reflects only the inventory that's been invoiced and shipped, so you won't know that your inventory is low until you start filling the sales orders you created.

- **Warn if not enough inventory to sell**. In QuickBooks Premier, you can specify whether you want the program to warn you when the quantity being sold is greater than the quantity on hand or the quantity available. Because quantity available is equal to or less than the quantity on hand, choosing that option is the safest route.

- **Unit of measure**. In QuickBooks Enterprise and some QuickBooks Premier editions (Accountant, Contractor, and Manufacturing & Wholesale), you can specify more than one unit of measure for inventory items, in case you sell wine by the bottle, by the case, and by the vat, for example. To do this, in the Unit of Measure section, click the Enable button and then select Single U/M Per Item or Multiple U/M Per Item.

You define units of measure in the Create Item or Edit Item window (page 130). In either of those windows, to open the Unit of Measure dialog box to the "Select a Unit of Measure Type" screen, in the Unit of Measure box, click the down arrow. To use one of the built-in units, like count, length, weight, volume, area, or time, select the corresponding option and then click Next. On the Select a Unit of Measure screen, choose a measure. For example, if you select the Length option as the unit of measure, you can choose Foot, Inch, Yard, Mile, Millimeter, Meter, or Other. If you select Other on the Select a Unit of Measure Type screen and then click Next, you can type a name and abbreviation for the measure, like Space Warp Area or SWArea.

Choose any or all of the following preferences on the Company Preferences tab to set up estimates and progress invoicing:

- **Do you create estimates?** Choose the Yes option only if you want to create estimates *in QuickBooks*, as described on page 310, so the program adds the Estimates icon to the Home page. If you create estimates in a program other than QuickBooks, choose the No option.

- **Do you do progress invoicing?** Also known as "partial billing," progress invoicing means that you invoice your customer for work as you go instead of billing for the entire job at the end. For example, if you're building a shopping mall, you don't want to carry the costs of construction until shoppers walk in the front door—you want to charge your client as you meet milestones. To create invoices for portions of your estimates, choose the Yes option. That way, you can invoice for part of an estimate and show how much you billed previously, as described in detail on page 315.

NOTE If you choose the No option, you can still create progress invoices from your entire estimate. After you bring the whole estimate into your invoice, remove entries until the invoice includes only what you want to bill. The flaw in this approach is that you can't show previous totals billed or compare the billed and remaining amounts to your estimate.

- **Warn about duplicate estimate numbers**. Leave this checkbox on if you want QuickBooks to alert you if you're creating an estimate with the same number as one you already entered.

- **Don't print items that have zero amount**. This checkbox is grayed out unless you select Yes in the "Do you do progress invoicing?" section. If you do use progress invoicing, you might not charge for every estimated item on every progress invoice. To keep your progress invoices tidy, suppress the items that you're not charging for by leaving this checkbox turned on.

Multiple Currencies

If you use only one currency, you can skip these preferences, because QuickBooks automatically selects the "No, I use only one currency" option. But if you have customers who pay you in other currencies or vendors who want to be paid in their countries' currencies, turn on the multiple currency preference. Just know that once you turn this setting on, it's on for good. If you stop doing business with foreign-currency customers and vendors, you can simply skip the currency boxes in QuickBooks' windows and dialog boxes (the program automatically fills them in with your home currency, as shown in Figure 23-8).

To turn on multiple currencies, choose Edit→Preferences→Multiple Currencies, and then click the Company Preferences tab. Select the "Yes, I use more than one currency" option and, in the "Select the home currency you use in transactions" drop-down list, choose your native currency.

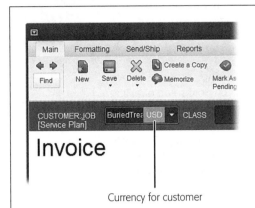

FIGURE 23-8

QuickBooks initially sets the home currency to US Dollar, but you can change that in the "Select the home currency you use in transactions" drop-down list. In transaction windows and dialog boxes, QuickBooks initially fills in the Currency box with your home currency, as shown here. However, after you set up a customer or vendor to use a foreign currency, QuickBooks automatically uses that currency instead. See page 617 for more on using multiple currencies.

Currency for customer

▇ Payments

The Receive Payments section of the Company Preferences tab in this category lets you set the following options:

- **Automatically apply payments**. You'll probably want to turn this checkbox off so that you can choose the customer invoices to which you want to apply payments you receive. With this checkbox on, QuickBooks applies customer payments to invoices for you. If a payment doesn't match any of the invoice amounts, QuickBooks applies the payment to the oldest invoices first, which could mask the fact that a payment wasn't received or that a customer's check was for the wrong amount.

- **Automatically calculate payments**. This preference, on the other hand, is one you'll want to keep turned on. When you receive a payment from a customer, in the Receive Payments window's Amount box, you typically type the amount that the customer sent. Then, as you choose the invoices to apply the payment to, QuickBooks calculates the payment for you. If the customer underpaid, QuickBooks asks if you want to keep the underpayment or write off the amount that the customer didn't pay. When this checkbox is off, as you choose invoices, you also have to enter the amount of the payment to allocate to each invoice.

- **Use Undeposited Funds as a default deposit to account**. If you typically collect a few payments before heading to the bank to deposit them, leave this checkbox turned on so QuickBooks automatically adds payments you receive to the Undeposited Funds account. With this setting turned on, QuickBooks doesn't show the "Deposit to" box in the Receive Payments window, so payments automatically get stowed in the Undeposited Funds account. If you want a say in whether to deposit payments right away, turn this checkbox off. That way, in the Receive Payments window's Deposit To field, you can choose a bank account to deposit funds immediately, or you can choose Undeposited Funds to collect several payments before you make a deposit.

NOTE The rest of the Payments category's Company Preferences tab has options for accepting payments via Intuit's PaymentNetwork, which allows you to send and receive payments online. See page 577 for the full scoop on online payments.

Payroll & Employees

Perhaps the most annoying thing about employees is their insistence on being paid. Sad to say, but using QuickBooks for payroll doesn't eliminate the need to pay your employees, and it can only simplify the task so much. If you choose one of the QuickBooks payroll service options, the Payroll & Employees preference category is command central for configuring your payroll service and how it operates. Payroll and employee preferences appear on the Company Preferences tab, so only QuickBooks administrators can set them.

TIP If you'd rather someone else incur brain damage figuring out government payroll requirements, on the QuickBooks menu bar, choose Employees→Payroll→Turn on Payroll in QuickBooks. In the web browser window that appears, the Intuit QuickBooks Payroll Services screen displays options you can choose to learn more. If you like what you see, you can then sign up for one of Intuit's payroll services.

The QuickBooks Payroll Features section gives you three options for choosing a payroll service. Here's some info that can help you determine which one to choose:

- **Full payroll**. This is the option you want if you plan to calculate payroll yourself and use QuickBooks' features to produce the documents, or if you use QF-FuickBooks Basic Payroll, Enhanced Payroll, or Assisted Payroll to figure out payroll amounts. With this option selected, you can produce documents such as paychecks; payroll reports; and payroll forms, including 940s (employer federal unemployment taxes), 941s (employer quarterly federal taxes), W-2s (employee wage and tax statement), and W-3s (transmittal of W-2s).

TIP If you want to allocate wages and payroll taxes to jobs, you have two choices. If you use a third-party payroll service, you can select the No Payroll option and then use journal entries to reassign payroll and payroll taxes to jobs. The alternative is to choose the Full Payroll option and use QuickBooks' payroll features to assign payroll and payroll taxes to jobs. See page 409 to learn about Intuit's payroll services.

- **No payroll**. Choose this option if you don't run payroll in any way or you use a third-party payroll service. So if you're a sole proprietor and pay yourself by taking owner's draws, or if you use an outside payroll service, such as Paychex or ADP, and have no need to print payroll documents or assign payroll costs to jobs, choose this option. With this option selected, you don't see payroll-related features on the Employees menu or in the Employee Center.

> **NOTE** If you have transactions from prior payrolls and switch to using an outside payroll service, the past payroll data remains in your QuickBooks file.

- **Online Payroll**. If you use Intuit Online Payroll, choose this option. When you use this service, you can also run payroll without QuickBooks.

The Payroll & Employees preference category has plenty of additional settings that are intimately linked to payroll. For example, you can specify the deductions and payroll items that affect every employee, and control the fields that appear on paychecks and paycheck stubs.

Whether you run payroll or not, here's the lowdown on the remaining preferences that *don't* relate to payroll:

- **Display employee list by**. If your company employs only a few people, you can choose the First Name option so that QuickBooks sorts the Employee List by first names. However, if you have hundreds of employees, choose the Last Name option. Regardless of which option you choose, QuickBooks prints paychecks with employee first names first and last names last.

- **Mark new employees as sales reps**. If only a few of your employees act as customer contacts and receive commissions, you can reserve the Sales Rep List for them by leaving this checkbox off and adding names to the list manually (page 157). But if you consider every employee a potential sales rep, turn on this checkbox so that QuickBooks automatically adds every employee you create to the Sales Rep List, saving you a five-step process each time.

- **Display employee social security numbers in headers on reports**. QuickBooks automatically turns off this checkbox, which is preferable if you want to protect your employees' financial privacy.

◼ Reminders

QuickBooks reminds you when to perform many accounting and business tasks, so you can save your brain cells for remembering more important things—like your employees' names. Even if your brain is the size of a small planet, you're likely to rely on QuickBooks' reminders to nudge you when it's time to print checks or reorder inventory. And when you turn on reminders for To Do Notes, the program can give you hints about any task that you don't want to forget, whether it's for a customer, vendor, employee, or yourself.

Reminders on the My Preferences Tab

In the Reminders preference category, the My Preferences tab has only one setting, but it can render all of the settings on the Company Preferences tab useless. If your short-term memory is mere nanoseconds, turn on the "Show Reminders List when opening a Company file" checkbox. That way, QuickBooks displays the Reminders list window (Figure 23-9) whenever you open your company file, and the window stays open unless you close it.

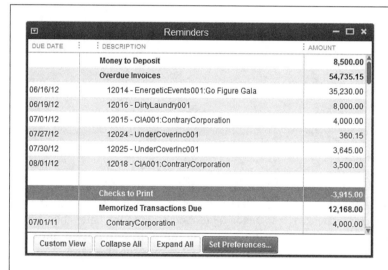

FIGURE 23-9

The way information is displayed in this window depends on what settings you choose on the Reminders Company Preferences tab. The Show Summary options tell QuickBooks to display a single reminder and the total amount of money in the Reminders window, like the "Checks to Print" row here. The Show List options display each transaction on a separate line instead, as shown below the Overdue Invoices heading. QuickBooks displays one line with the total for overdue invoices, followed by a line showing each overdue invoice.

Reminders for Everyone

The Company Preferences tab lists a plethora of different types of reminders, which are available only if you've turned on the corresponding feature. For example, if you don't use QuickBooks inventory, the Inventory to Reorder reminder is dimmed. Figure 23-9 explains the difference between the Show Summary and Show List options for each reminder. As shown in Figure 23-10, you can specify the level of detail for each type of reminder and, in some cases, when you want QuickBooks to remind you.

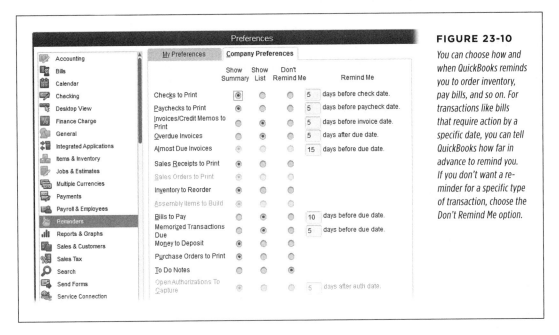

FIGURE 23-10

You can choose how and when QuickBooks reminds you to order inventory, pay bills, and so on. For transactions like bills that require action by a specific date, you can tell QuickBooks how far in advance to remind you. If you don't want a reminder for a specific type of transaction, choose the Don't Remind Me option.

QuickBooks can generate reminders for the following transactions:

- **Checks to Print**. This reminder tells you that you've got checks queued up to print (you add checks to the queue by turning on the Print Later checkbox in the Write Checks window [page 257]). You can also specify how many days' notice you want before the date you entered to print the checks.

- **Paychecks to Print**. This reminder tells you that paychecks are waiting to be printed. You can specify how many days' notice you want before the payroll date you entered.

- **Invoices/Credit Memos to Print**. To print invoices or credit memos in batches, as described on page 346, in the Create Invoices window, turn on the Print Later checkbox. This reminder notifies you about unprinted invoices or credit memos. You can specify how many days' notice you want before the invoice or credit memo date you entered.

- **Overdue Invoices**. This reminder warns you about invoices that have passed their due dates with no payment from the customer. You can specify how many days overdue an invoice needs to be before QuickBooks reminds you.

- **Almost Due Invoices**. This reminder tells you about invoices that are due soon. The Show Summary option is selected for this reminder, and you can't change it. However, you can change the number of days before the due date.

- **Sales Receipts to Print**. If you queued up sales receipts to print as a batch (page 346), this is the reminder about printing them. QuickBooks reminds you as soon as you have any sales receipts to print.

- **Sales Orders to Print**. This preference is available only if you use QuickBooks Premier or Enterprise, and it reminds you to print sales orders you've queued up.

- **Inventory to Reorder**. When you create Inventory Part items in QuickBooks, you can set a reminder for when you need to reorder inventory. This reminder warns you when a sales form you create reduces the number of items on hand below your reorder point. (The program generates a reminder immediately.)

- **Assembly Items to Build**. This preference is available only if you use QuickBooks Premier or Enterprise. It warns you when the quantity of assembled items drops below your build point (page 131).

- **Bills to Pay**. This reminder nudges you about bills you have to pay. (Entering bills is described on page 219.) You can specify how many days' notice you want before the date the bills are due.

- **Memorized Transactions Due**. When you memorize transactions, you can specify a date for the next occurrence (page 354). This reminder tells you about recurring memorized transactions. You can specify how many days' notice you want before the next scheduled occurrence.

- **Money to Deposit**. When you receive payments, you can group them with other undeposited funds so you aren't running to the bank every 5 minutes as checks pour in. If you want to put your money to work as soon as possible, turn on this checkbox to receive a reminder as soon as you have any funds to deposit.

- **Purchase Orders to Print**. This reminder gives you a prod about purchase orders you haven't yet printed.

- **To Do Notes**. To-do items that you associate with customers can include dates, as described on page 108. This reminder shows you when to-do items are due.

> **NOTE** The Open Authorizations To Capture setting is grayed out unless you use QuickBooks Enterprise.

Reports and Graphs

Each person who logs into QuickBooks can specify a few preferences for the reports and graphs she generates. And QuickBooks administrators can modify settings that apply to every report and graph their company produces.

Preferences for the Reports You Generate

Here's a guide to the personal preferences shown in Figure 23-11 and the effects they have:

- **Prompt me to modify report options before opening a report**. The reports you want usually require small tweaks—a different date range perhaps—so turning on this checkbox works for most people. With this checkbox turned on, QuickBooks automatically opens the Modify Report window when you generate a report so you can make any changes you want. (Click OK to view the results.) If you leave this checkbox turned off, in a report window, click Customize Report to make changes.

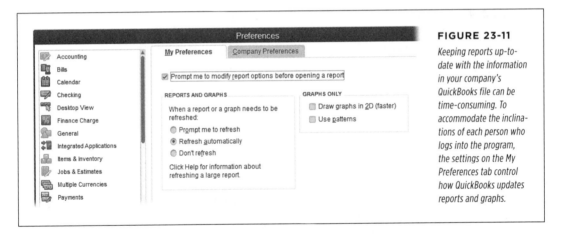

FIGURE 23-11

Keeping reports up-to-date with the information in your company's QuickBooks file can be time-consuming. To accommodate the inclinations of each person who logs into the program, the settings on the My Preferences tab control how QuickBooks updates reports and graphs.

- **Reports and graphs.** This set of preferences lets you decide what QuickBooks should do when a report or graph needs to be refreshed because the data within it has changed. You can choose one of the following options (QuickBooks automatically selects the first option unless you change it):

  - **Prompt me to refresh**. If your QuickBooks file changes frequently and you don't want to wait while the program refreshes every report you have open, choose this option. When you do, QuickBooks reminds you to refresh reports when you've changed data that affects them. For example, suppose you generated a Profit & Loss report and then created a new invoice for a customer; with this setting selected, QuickBooks would prompt you to refresh the report. When you're ready to refresh a report or graph, in the report's window, simply click Refresh.

- **Refresh automatically**. If numerous people are frantically changing data in the company file, as is often true as year-end approaches, this option can slow your work. However, if it's critical that your reports and graphs are always accurate, choose this option so QuickBooks automatically refreshes reports and graphs whenever the underlying data changes.

- **Don't refresh**. If you find yourself distracted by refreshes or even prompts about refreshing, choose this option. That way, QuickBooks won't refresh your reports and graphs or remind you—no matter how significant the changes to the underlying data. When you've finished your report and graph customizations, click Refresh to generate the report with the current data.

- **Draw graphs in 2D (faster)**. If you care about time more than fancy graphics, turn on this checkbox. QuickBooks then displays graphs in two dimensions, which is faster than drawing the 3-D graphs that appear if you leave this checkbox off.

- **Use patterns**. When you turn on this checkbox, QuickBooks uses black-and-white patterns instead of colors to differentiate areas on graphs. If you leave this checkbox off, QuickBooks displays colors on color monitors and shades of gray on black-and-white monitors.

Company-Wide Report Preferences

The Company Preferences tab has several preferences for the reports and graphs you generate for your company. If you're a QuickBooks administrator, use the following preferences to format reports and graphs:

- **Summary reports basis**. Nothing starts adrenaline flowing like financial reports that aren't what you expect, particularly when IRS auditors are dropping by to peruse your company's books. Be sure to choose the correct option here—Cash or Accrual (page xxiii explains the difference)—so that the reports you generate accurately reflect your financial performance.

NOTE In most cases, when your accountant recommends cash or accrual accounting, you can choose the appropriate option here and then forget about it. But if you upgrade or reinstall QuickBooks, make sure that the program didn't reset your Summary Reports Basis choice.

- **Aging reports**. You can control how QuickBooks calculates age for invoices, statements, and bills. If you choose the "Age from due date" option, the program shows the number of days between the due date and the current date. If you choose "Age from transaction date" instead, QuickBooks shows the number of overdue days from the date of the transaction to the current date. For example, suppose an invoice is dated September 1 with a due date of October 1. On October 10, the "Age from due date" option shows the invoice's age as 10 days, whereas the "Age from transaction date" option shows the invoice's age as 40 days.

- **Reports – Show items by**. Reports initially list items by name and description, but you choose a different option here to show only name or only description.

- **Reports – Show accounts by**. Reports typically list accounts by name. If you use especially short account names, you can use the account descriptions in reports instead. You can also show both names *and* descriptions.

- **Statement of cash flows**. Although QuickBooks does a great job of associating your accounts with the Operating, Investing, and Financing categories of the Statement of Cash Flows report, some companies are bound to require a customized cash flow report. In that case, click Classify Cash here to open the Classify Cash dialog box. (See page 478 to learn how to generate and customize a cash flow statement for your company.)

- **Format**. Click this button to set up standards for all your reports. For example, you can choose the information that you want to appear in headers and footers, and whether they're aligned to the left, right, or center of the page.

Sales & Customers

The Sales & Customers preferences, shown in Figure 23-12, control how QuickBooks handles sales you make to your customers, including the shipping method you use and whether the program notifies you that you've created a duplicate invoice number.

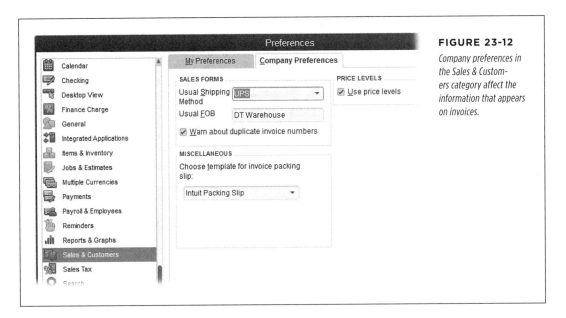

FIGURE 23-12

Company preferences in the Sales & Customers category affect the information that appears on invoices.

The My Preferences tab has options that tell the program what to do about outstanding billable time and expenses. Here's what each one does:

- **Prompt for time/costs to add**. If you typically bill for time and expenses, select this option. That way, the Choose Billable Time and Costs dialog box (Figure 10-14 on page 300) opens automatically when you create an invoice for a customer who has outstanding billable time charges or expenses.

- **Don't add any**. Select this option if you rarely have time or expenses to invoice and don't want to see the Choose Billable Time and Costs dialog box or receive a reminder that outstanding time and expenses exist.

- **Ask what to do**. This option merely adds an additional step to what the "Prompt for time/costs to add" option does because you have to tell QuickBooks whether or not to open the Choose Billable Time and Costs dialog box. Selecting the "Prompt for time/costs to add" option instead is your best bet.

Here's a guide to the Sales & Customers preferences on the Company Preferences tab, all of which only QuickBooks administrators can change:

- **Usual Shipping Method**. If you negotiate a sweet deal with a shipping company and use them whenever possible, choose that company in this drop-down list. When you do, QuickBooks automatically selects this method in sales forms' Ship Via (or Via) fields. If the method you want to use isn't on the list, choose <Add New> to open the New Ship Method dialog box (page 162).

- **Usual FOB**. FOB stands for "free on board" and represents the location at which the customer becomes responsible for the products you ship. For example, suppose you ship products from your warehouse in Severance, Colorado, and you use Severance as your FOB location. As soon as your shipments leave Severance, the customer becomes the official owner of the products and is responsible for them if they get lost, damaged, or stolen in transit. Type a brief description of your FOB location in this box, and QuickBooks then puts this info in the FOB field on invoices and other sales forms.

- **Warn about duplicate invoice numbers**. Turn on this checkbox if you want QuickBooks to alert you when you create an invoice with the same number as one you already entered.

- **Choose template for invoice packing slip**. If you ship products to customers, you can print a packing slip from QuickBooks to include in your shipments. To specify the packing slip you want the program to use, choose it in this drop-down list. From then on, when you create an invoice and choose Print→Packing Slip (page 348), QuickBooks automatically uses the template you selected. QuickBooks initially selects its predefined packing slip (Intuit Packing Slip) here, but you can create your own, as described on page 669.

- **Use price levels**. You can set multiple prices for the items you sell by using price levels. To do so, first turn on this checkbox. Then refer to pages 153 and 155 to learn how to define and apply price levels.

- **Sales orders**. To use sales orders (QuickBooks Premier and Enterprise only) to record customer orders before you create invoices, turn on the Enable Sales Orders checkbox. With it turned on, you can tell QuickBooks to warn you when you create a sales order with duplicate numbers, and to leave off any items with zero amounts when you convert the sales order into an invoice.

Sales Tax

Charging sales tax can be a complicated business, as the number of preferences on the Sales Tax Company Preferences tab indicates. If you don't charge sales tax, in the "Do You Charge Sales Tax?" area, simply leave the No option selected and move on to more important endeavors. If you do charge sales tax, you'll learn how to adjust the rest of these preferences as you set up Sales Tax items (page 142), charge sales tax, and pay sales tax to the appropriate authorities (page 264).

Search

The Search box (which is located at the top of the left icon bar, or the right end of the top icon bar) lets you search your company file to find customers, vendors, and other names; transactions like invoices and bills; amounts; dates; or text within memos, notes, and descriptions. If you use the top icon bar, in the My Preferences tab, the "Show Search Box in the Icon Bar" checkbox is turned on automatically, which makes the Search box easy to access at all times. If you turn this checkbox off, you can access the search feature by choosing Edit→Search. If you use the left icon bar or hide both icon bars, these preferences are grayed out.

Sometimes, you want to find things in your company file, like an invoice number or an inventory item. Other times, you want to search QuickBooks help files to find out how to do something in the program. Out of the box, QuickBooks sets the "Choose where to search by default" setting to "Let me choose where I search each time." That way, when you type in the Search box in the top or left icon bar, you can choose "Search company file" or "Help" from the box's drop-down menu. However, if you're a wiz at QuickBooks, you can choose the "Search my company file" option instead, so that QuickBooks automatically searches your company file for what you type in the Search box. If you usually need help on using QuickBooks, select the "Search QuickBooks help" option instead.

QuickBooks always searches your company file when you choose Edit→Search.

The Company Preferences tab contains settings that control how often QuickBooks updates the data it uses to search. Because these updates make the program run a little slower, you have to compromise between performance and up-to-date informa-tion. QuickBooks initially turns on the "Update automatically" checkbox, and that's usually what you want. In the "Update every" drop-down list, choose a frequency for the automatic updates. In most cases, 30 or 60 minutes works well. If you want to update search info now, click Update Now. If you turn this checkbox off, QuickBooks might run a little faster, but you then have to click the Update Now button to be sure that you're searching up-to-date info in your company file.

Send Forms

As you've learned throughout this book, you can include a cover note when you send invoices, purchase orders, and other business forms via email. For example, if you email a purchase order, you can include details about the delivery in the note. Or you can include a cover note along with an invoice to add some personal interaction with your customer. When you email an invoice or other form, QuickBooks opens the Send Invoice dialog box (or the dialog box corresponding to the form you're sending) with your note filled in. The program attaches your invoice or other sales form to the email as an Adobe PDF file.

Setting Your Send Preferences

On the My Preferences tab, QuickBooks automatically turns on the "Auto-check the 'Email Later' checkbox if customer's Preferred Send Method is e-mail" checkbox. That way, you don't have to remember whether customers prefer to receive paperwork by email or snail mail.

If you want to send QuickBooks email using Microsoft Outlook, select the Outlook option. (This option is available only if Outlook is installed on your computer.) If you use a Web-based email service, select the Web Mail option, as shown in Figure 23-13, and then click Add to tell QuickBooks about your email service. In the Add Email Info dialog box, fill in your email address and select your email provider (Gmail, Yahoo, or Hotmail, for example). QuickBooks then fills in the server name and the port with the typical settings for the provider you specified. If you use an email provider other than the ones on the list, you have to fill in the server name and port manually. See page 351 to learn about the QuickBooks E-mail option.

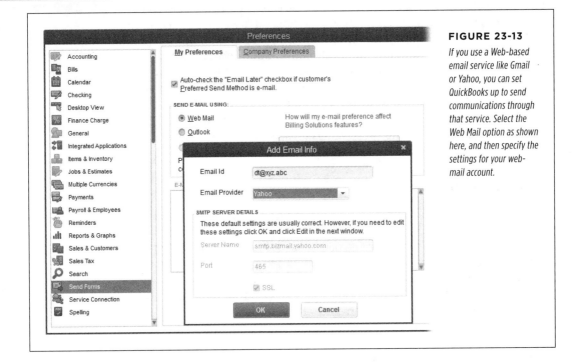

FIGURE 23-13

If you use a Web-based email service like Gmail or Yahoo, you can set QuickBooks up to send communications through that service. Select the Web Mail option as shown here, and then specify the settings for your web-mail account.

Customizing Messages

QuickBooks includes standard messages for each type of form you send via email. If you want to customize the messages you send out, any QuickBooks administrator can change them. You can create standard notes for invoices, estimates, statements, sales orders, sales receipts, credit memos, purchase orders, reports, pay stubs, overdue invoices, and almost-due invoices. If your company has standard letters on file, you can simply copy and paste the contents of those letters from another program, such as Microsoft Word, into QuickBooks as explained below.

To configure a standard note for a particular type of form, follow these steps.

1. **In the "Change default for" drop-down list, choose the form you want to customize.**

   For example, if you want to set up a cover letter to go with your invoices, choose Invoices in the list.

2. **To specify the salutation you want, choose one from the drop-down list.**

   Your choices are "Dear" or the impersonal "To."

3. **To specify the format for the recipient's name, choose it from the format drop-down list.**

   Depending on how formal or chummy you like to be, you can display the person's first name only, their first and last name, or a title and their last name. For example, if you choose <First>, your note begins with something like "To Dana" or "Dear Dana." For more formal notes, choose <Mr./Miss/Ms.> <Last> to begin with "Dear Ms. Dvorak."

4. **Edit the content of the note using typical editing techniques.**

   For instance, click in the text to position the cursor where you want to add text, drag your cursor to select text you want to replace, or double-click a word to select it. To use a standard letter that's stored in another program, open the letter in that program and copy the text, and then paste it into QuickBooks by pressing Ctrl+V.

   To make sure everything is spelled correctly, click Spelling below the text box and QuickBooks alerts you to any suspect words in the Subject line or body of your letter.

5. **To save the changes to your notes and close the Preferences dialog box, click OK.**

   If you make changes to notes and then click another preference icon, QuickBooks displays a Save Changes dialog box. To save the changes you made, click Yes.

▉ Spelling

QuickBooks' spell checker helps you find common misspellings in most text fields. Spell checking is a personal preference: Each person who logs into a company file can choose whether to use spell checking by leaving the "Always check spelling before printing, saving, or sending supported forms" checkbox on or turning it off.

If you leave spell checking on, you can choose words that you want the spell checker to ignore. For example, you can ignore Internet addresses, words that contain numbers, words that begin with a capital letter, words that are in all uppercase letters, and words with a mixture of upper- and lowercase letters.

When QuickBooks checks spelling in transactions you record, such as item descriptions in invoices, you can click Add to add custom words to the QuickBooks dictionary so that the program won't flag those unusual spellings in future transactions. You'll see the custom words you've added in the Word table on the My Preferences tab. To remove a custom word from the dictionary, click its "Delete?" cell to add a checkmark.

■ Tax: 1099

The Company Preferences tab in the Tax: 1099 preference category begins with the most important 1099 question: "Do you file 1099-MISC forms?" If you don't use 1099 vendors, such as self-employed subcontractors, or you delegate 1099 generation to your accountant, simply choose the No option and ignore the rest of the preferences in this category. If you do file 1099-MISC forms, you can specify the accounts you use to track 1099 vendor payments and the minimum amount you have to report to the IRS. To learn how to generate 1099s and set these preferences, refer to page 497.

POWER USERS' CLINIC

Service Connection Preferences

If your company uses QuickBooks' services, such as online banking, QuickBooks administrators can control how people log into those services. The easiest way to learn about or sign up for these services is to choose Help→Add QuickBooks Services, and then click the Learn More button or link for the one you want.

Each person who uses QuickBooks services can control the behavior of online sessions, but security is a company-wide issue, so the options for whether to prompt for a password appear on the Company Preferences tab. Here are the service connection preferences that administrators can set and when you might want to use them:

- **Automatically connect without asking for a password**. Choosing this option automatically logs people into the QuickBooks Business Services network without a login name or password. This option is appropriate if you're the only person who accesses the network or you aren't concerned about security.

- **Always ask for a password before connecting**. Choose this option if you want your employees to provide a login name and password each time they access QuickBooks Business Services. This option is handy if several people access the services or different people have different privileges with the services you use.

- **Allow background downloading of service messages**. If you want QuickBooks to check for messages and updates when your Internet connection isn't tied up with other work, leave this checkbox turned on. QuickBooks then checks the Intuit website periodically and downloads updates or messages. If you turn this checkbox off, you can check for updates at a convenient time by choosing Help→Update QuickBooks.

If you aren't a QuickBooks administrator, you can still make some choices about your connection to QuickBooks Business Services. On the My Preferences tab, the "Give me the option of saving a file whenever I download Web Connect data" checkbox lets you decide when to process downloaded transactions. If you want QuickBooks to ask you whether to process downloaded transactions immediately or save them to a file, leave this checkbox on. If you turn it off, QuickBooks automatically processes downloaded transactions immediately.

You can launch QuickBooks by downloading WebConnect data or by double-clicking a QuickBooks file that contains WebConnect data you downloaded previously. When you open the program this way, you often want to continue working in QuickBooks after you process the downloaded transactions. To keep QuickBooks open after it processes transactions, leave the "If QuickBooks is run by my browser, don't close it after WebConnect is done" checkbox turned on.

▇ Time & Expenses

The first setting in this category (on the Company Preferences tab) tells QuickBooks whether you track time at all. If you do, select the Yes option. Then you can choose the first day of the work week that appears if you use weekly timesheets in QuickBooks (see page 203). The "Mark all time entries as billable" checkbox is new in QuickBooks 2013 and is initially turned on, which means QuickBooks automatically marks time records as billable. If you bill only some of your time, turn this checkbox off. That way, you can turn on the Billable checkbox or cell to designate time as billable.

The Invoicing Options section has settings related to how you handle billable time and expenses on invoices:

- **Create invoices from a list of time and expenses**. If you turn this checkbox on (it appears only in QuickBooks Premier and Enterprise), the Customer menu includes the Invoice for Time & Expenses feature. With this setting, you can view a list of all your unbilled time and expenses and select the customers you want to bill, as described on page 274.

- **Track reimbursed expenses as income**. Companies differ in their approach to reimbursed expenses, as explained on page 240. Some assign reimbursed expenses as income and then deduct the expenses as costs. The method you choose doesn't affect the profit you earn—the reason for tracking reimbursable expenses as income is to charge sales tax on those expenses. If you want to post reimbursed expenses to an income account, turn this checkbox on.

- **Mark all expenses as billable**. This checkbox is new in QuickBooks 2013 and is initially turned on, which means QuickBooks automatically marks all your expenses as billable. If only some of your expenses are billable to your customers, turn this checkbox off so you can turn on the Billable checkbox or cell to designate specific expenses as billable to a customer or job.

- **Default Markup Percentage**. Suppose you're an interior decorator and you mark up the furniture and bric-a-brac you sell by a standard percentage. When you specify your markup percentage in this box and then create a new item (page 121), QuickBooks calculates the item's sales price based on its cost. For example, if you create an inventory part for a black leather sofa and enter its cost as $10,000, a 20 percent markup results in a sales price of $12,000. If you charge a different markup on a few of the things you sell, then simply modify the sales price that QuickBooks calculates.

- **Default Markup Account**. To assign the income from your markup percentage to a specific account, select it in this drop-down list. You can choose an account dedicated to markup income or simply assign markup to your product-related income account.

Integrating QuickBooks with Other Programs

Most businesses use other programs in addition to QuickBooks to keep things running smoothly. You can use QuickBooks data in other programs to study your company's financial ratios, calculate employee bonuses based on hours worked and services sold, send special sales letters to customers on their birthdays, and so on. Similarly, other programs may contain data that would be useful to pull into QuickBooks. For example, if you use an estimating program that has all the products and services you sell in its database, there's no reason to manually enter those in QuickBooks.

QuickBooks doesn't share its most intimate details with just any program. It reserves its data for a few select programs—or the ones you tell it to play nicely with. For example, you can set up letters in QuickBooks to send to customers, and the program automatically opens Microsoft Word with your customer data merged into form letters and envelopes. If you use Outlook (not Outlook Express) as your contact-management tool, keeping records up-to-date is easy. By synchronizing your QuickBooks company file and your contact database, you enter changes in one place and the programs automatically copy data from one file to the other.

Programs that can read a QuickBooks company file still have to ask permission to grab QuickBooks data. The QuickBooks administrator (or other QuickBooks users that the administrator anoints) can say whether another program can have access and how much. For software that can't read a company file directly but *can* provide valuable assistance processing your financial data (such as Excel, whose spreadsheets can calculate financial ratios that QuickBooks can't), you can export and import data between programs (page 649).

This chapter describes how to integrate QuickBooks at whatever level of trust you prefer. It also tells you about add-on services that Intuit provides and how to find third-party programs that work with QuickBooks.

Mail Merge to a Word Document

Business communications are the perfect marriage of QuickBooks data and word processing. You can generate letters and envelopes in no time by combining QuickBooks' customer contact info and other data with Microsoft Word mail-merge documents. QuickBooks includes dozens of ready-to-mail letters as Word documents that cover the most common business communications, from customer thank-you notes to less-friendly denials of requests for credit. If nothing less than Pulitzer-prize quality will do for your business letters, you can modify the built-in letters and envelopes in Word or write your own.

The best place to start when you want to prepare letters in QuickBooks is by choosing Company→"Prepare Letters with Envelopes," which displays a submenu with the following entries:

- **Collection Letters** include the invoices or statements that are overdue, and remind customers to pay up. QuickBooks automatically pulls the overdue balance and overdue invoices from your company file.

- **Customer Letters** pull only the customer's contact and address information from QuickBooks to address the letter and envelope. The rest of the letter is boilerplate for situations such as thanking customers for their business, apologizing for a mistake, or sending a contract.

- **Vendor Letters** include credit requests, disputed charges, payments on your account, and two blank templates for sending mail or a fax to a vendor.

- **Employee Letters** cover birthdays, sick time, vacations, and general communications.

- **Letters to Other Names** cover a hodgepodge of different recipients, so QuickBooks doesn't even try to guess what you need. The only template in this category is a blank letter with basic mail merge fields.

- **Customize Letter Templates** is a feature that helps you create a brand-new template, convert a Word document into a template, edit an existing template, or organize the templates you already have, as described in the box on the next page.

Customizing Letter Templates

To create, edit, or otherwise manage customized letter templates, choose Company→Prepare Letters with Envelopes→Customize Letter Templates. (The first time you choose this entry, QuickBooks may tell you it can't find the preinstalled letter templates in your company file folder. In that case, it asks if you want to copy its built-in templates. Click Copy to create copies of the built-in templates in the folder with your company file. If you store letter templates in another folder on your computer, click Browse to choose that folder.) Then, in the Letters and Envelopes wizard, choose one of these options:

- **Create a New Letter Template From Scratch**. You can specify the type of letter you want to create and the name of the template. QuickBooks sends a blank letter template to Word along with the toolbar shown in Figure 24-1. In addition to writing the content of the letter, you can add fields from QuickBooks to automatically fill in your company and customer (or other recipient) info.

- **Convert an Existing Microsoft Word Document to a Letter Template**. This option lets you use an existing Word document as the basis for a new template. Then, once you specify the type of letter, you can add more text or QuickBooks fields to the document as if you were creating a new template from scratch.

- **View or Edit Existing Letter Templates**. You can open and edit any existing template.

- **Organize Existing Letter Templates**. When you choose this option, you can navigate through each template category, choose a template, and then delete, duplicate, rename, or move it to a different category.

QuickBooks stores the Word documents for letter templates in a document folder. In Windows Vista and Windows 7, the templates are in *C:\Users\Public\Public Documents\Intuit\ QuickBooks\Company Files\QuickBooks Letter Templates*. In Windows XP, they're in *C:\Documents and Settings\All Users\ Shared Documents\Intuit\QuickBooks\Company Files\Quick- Books Letter Templates*. There's a subfolder for each category of template (Collections Letters, Customer Letters, and so on).

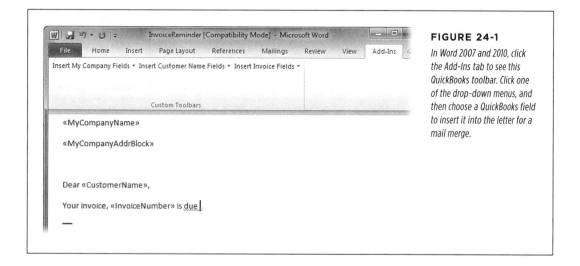

FIGURE 24-1

In Word 2007 and 2010, click the Add-Ins tab to see this QuickBooks toolbar. Click one of the drop-down menus, and then choose a QuickBooks field to insert it into the letter for a mail merge.

Creating Letters and Envelopes in QuickBooks

Preparing any kind of letter with QuickBooks' letter wizard takes no more than a few clicks, and the collection letter wizard has some extra smarts. For most letters, you can tell QuickBooks whether you want to include active and inactive names and then select recipients. The collection letter wizard can also filter the customer list by how late payments are.

Here are the steps for creating letters and envelopes using a collection letter as an example:

1. **Choose Company→Prepare Letters with Envelopes→Collection Letters.**

   QuickBooks opens the "Letters and Envelopes" wizard and shows the recipient options for collection letters.

2. **Choose options to filter who you send letters to (Figure 24-2).**

   QuickBooks remembers the options you choose and selects them automatically the next time you launch the wizard.

NOTE For non-collection letters, you still choose active or inactive customers (or both) and whether to send letters to each customer or each job, but those are your only choices. For a recall notice, for example, choose the Both option to send the letter to active and inactive customers alike. (The first screen you see for letters to vendors, employees, and people on the Other Names List combines the list of selected names and the options for filtering names.)

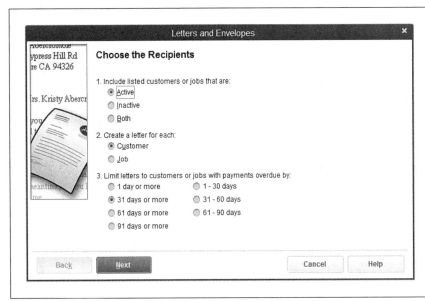

FIGURE 24-2

For collection letters, on the "Choose the Recipients" screen, QuickBooks initially selects the Both option to include active and inactive customers. The next set of options on the screen lets you choose whether to send a letter to each customer or to the contact person for each job a customer hires you to do. For collection letters, the third set of options asks you to specify how late the payment has to be before you send a letter.

3. **Click Next to display the "Review and Edit Recipients" screen.**

For collection letters, QuickBooks displays a message if any customers have unapplied credits or payments. Rather than embarrassing yourself by sending a collection letter to a customer whose payments are up-to-date, you're better off clicking OK to close the message box, and then clicking Cancel to exit the wizard so you can apply credits and payments before preparing collection letters. (The box on page 641 explains how to check for customer credits and payments.)

If there are no unapplied credits or payments, QuickBooks automatically selects all the names that match the criteria you specified on the previous screen.

4. **If you've already talked to some customers and want to remove them from the list, click the checkmarks in front of their names to turn them off.**

You can click Mark All or Unmark All to select or clear every name. If you want only a few names, it's faster to click Unmark All and then click each name you want. The list is initially sorted by name but, for collection letters, you can also select the Amount option to sort by the amount that's overdue if you want to send letters only to customers whose balances are greater than $100, for instance.

5. **When you've selected the customers you want to send letters to, click Next.**

QuickBooks displays the Choose a Letter Template screen.

6. **Select the collection letter template that you want to send, and then click Next.**

QuickBooks includes three types of collection letters. The formal one is a straightforward request for payment, the friendly one assumes the customer simply forgot, and the harsh one includes the threat of turning the account over to a collection agency. The friendly and formal letters can't do any harm, but if you're considering sending harsh letters, you might want to create your own template for that communication.

To use a different template entirely, select the "Create or Edit a letter template" option. When you click Next, you can choose one of the options described in the box on page 637 (create a new template, convert a Word document, or edit an existing template).

7. **In the "Enter a Name and Title" screen's Name box, type the name you want to include in the letter's signature block. In the Title box, type the signer's title.**

When you click Next, QuickBooks sends the information to Microsoft Word, as shown in Figure 24-3. Depending on how many letters you're sending, you might have to wait a few minutes before Word launches with your letters.

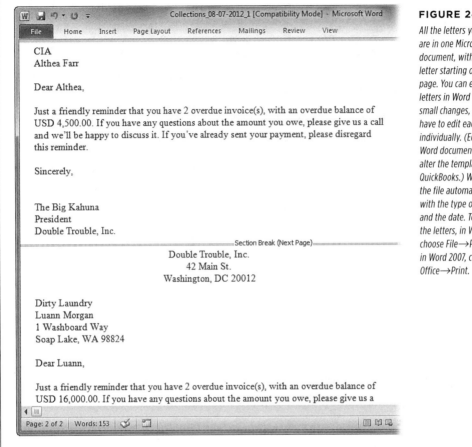

FIGURE 24-3

All the letters you create are in one Microsoft Word document, with each letter starting on a new page. You can edit the letters in Word to make small changes, but you have to edit each letter individually. (Editing the Word document doesn't alter the template in QuickBooks.) Word names the file automatically with the type of letter and the date. To print the letters, in Word 2010, choose File→Print; in Word 2007, choose Office→Print.

NOTE QuickBooks warns you if there's any info missing, like the recipient's address. If there is, you can either fill in the missing info in Word or close the Word document, add the missing info to QuickBooks, and then redo the steps in this section.

8. **After you print the letters from Word, go back to QuickBooks.**

   The "Print Letters and Envelopes" screen appears.

9. **Click Next if you want to print envelopes that go with the letters you just printed in Word.**

   If you don't want to print envelopes, click Cancel. The wizard closes and you're done.

10. **If you clicked Next to print envelopes, QuickBooks opens the Envelope Options dialog box.** In the Envelope Size drop-down list, choose the type of envelope you use.

    If your envelopes already include your return address, turn off the "Print return address" checkbox. When you click OK, you'll see a preview of the envelopes in Word.

11. **When you've got envelopes in your printer, click OK.**

    QuickBooks starts printing your envelopes.

UP TO SPEED

Reviewing Customer Credits and Payments

The Open Invoices report shows unapplied credits and payments as well as open invoices, but you can modify this report to show only the payments and unapplied credits that are available. After you run this report, skip to pages 371 and 375 to learn how to apply those payments and credits to your customers' balances. Then, when you create collection letters, QuickBooks selects only the customers with overdue balances.

Here's how to produce a report of payments and unapplied credits:

1. Choose Reports→Customers & Receivables→Open Invoices.

2. To see only unapplied credits and payments, in the report window's toolbar, click Customize Report, and then click the Filters tab. (If the Modify Report dialog box opens automatically, simply click the Filters tab.)

3. In the Filter list, choose Transaction Type (you may have to scroll down to see this option).

4. In the Transaction Type drop-down list, choose Multiple Transaction Types.

5. In the Select Transaction Types dialog box, click Payment and then click Credit Memo.

6. Click OK to close the Select Transaction Types dialog box and then click OK once more to update the report to show only unapplied credit memos and payments.

For a quick view of one customer's transactions, open the Customer Center (on the Home page, click Customers) and select the customer on the Customers & Jobs tab. Then, at the top right of the Customer Information panel, click the QuickReport link.

■ Synchronizing Contacts

If you keep information about contacts in Microsoft Outlook (2002 through 2010)—*not* Outlook Express—you can synchronize those records with your QuickBooks contact data. In addition to saving time by not duplicating data entry, synchronizing your contact info helps reduce errors. As long as you enter an update correctly in one program, you're sure to get the right info in your other contact database. Regardless of which program you update contact info in, you can transfer any changes to the other database.

NOTE The only time synchronizing doesn't apply is when you delete contacts. So if you delete contacts in Outlook, QuickBooks *doesn't* delete the corresponding records in your company file. (If you really want those records gone, make them inactive, as described on page 88.) On the other hand, if you delete a contact in QuickBooks but don't delete it in Outlook, it'll reappear in QuickBooks unless you tell Contact Sync to ignore it (see step 11 on page 644).

Using QuickBooks Contact Sync for Outlook

If you use QuickBooks 2007 or later (and Outlook 2002 or later), you use QuickBooks' Contact Sync for Outlook tool to synchronize contact data. Although the entry to synchronize is already on the File→Utilities menu, you have to install Contact Sync before you get started. Here's how to download this tool and put it to work:

1. **Choose File→Utilities→Synchronize Contacts.**

   If Contact Sync isn't installed, a message box tells you that you have to download and install it. Click OK to do just that. QuickBooks opens a web browser to the QuickBooks Contact Sync for Outlook page (*http://support.quickbooks. intuit.com/support/tools/contact_sync*). Type the email address you used when you registered QuickBooks (page 702), and then click Continue To Download. You can save the installation file (click Save) or run it immediately (click Run) to install the software.

   Installing is easy. First, be sure to close Outlook. Then, run the installation wizard as you do for other programs. Accept the license agreement, choose a destination folder, and then click Next, and the installation begins.

2. **After you install Contact Sync, launch Outlook.**

   Log into QuickBooks as the administrator and open the company file you want to synchronize.

   In Outlook, the Contact Sync Setup Assistant appears, offering to help you import contacts from QuickBooks. After you click Get Started, a Connecting To QuickBooks message box appears briefly while Outlook and QuickBooks talk to each other. Then, the QuickBooks Contact Sync dialog box opens and selects the company file that's open in QuickBooks.

NOTE If you want to import contacts from a different company file, click Cancel and then, in QuickBooks, open the company file with the contacts you want to import.

3. **In the QuickBooks Contact Sync dialog box, click Setup to begin the setup in earnest.**

   The Select An Outlook Folder screen appears. If you're like most people, you have only one folder for contacts, named something like *Personal Folders*\ *Contacts* or *Outlook**Contacts*, which the wizard selects automatically.

4. **If you want to synchronize to a different Outlook folder, choose it, and then click Next.**

   The Select QuickBooks List Types To Synchronize screen appears.

5. **To synchronize all contacts, turn on the Customer, Include Customer Jobs, and Vendor checkboxes, and then click Next.**

   For each checkbox you turn on, the Setup Assistant creates a subfolder in the Outlook Contacts folder.

6. **On the Exclude Contacts From Synchronization screen, turn on the checkboxes for the types of names you *don't* want to transfer back and forth, and then click Next.**

   When you turn on these checkboxes, names assigned to Outlook's Personal category or marked as Private won't transfer to QuickBooks.

7. **On the "Mapping Customer Fields (Part 1 of 2)" screen, change the mapping of any QuickBooks field that doesn't point to the right Outlook field, as shown in Figure 24-4. Click Next when the mappings are the way you want them.**

   The Mapping Customer Fields screen displays the QuickBooks contact fields on the left, and its guesses about what Outlook fields they're equivalent to on the right.

8. **If you turned on the checkboxes to import jobs and vendors, repeat step 7 to map job and vendor fields to the corresponding Outlook fields.**

   Chances are you'll make the same changes for jobs and vendors as you did for customer fields.

9. **On the Set Conflict Action screen, select how you want Contact Sync to resolve discrepancies between Outlook and QuickBooks, and then click Save.**

   Contact Sync automatically selects the "Let me decide each case" option, which means you get to tell QuickBooks what to do if the contact info in Outlook differs from the data in QuickBooks. If you usually update contacts in Outlook, select the Outlook Data Wins option. If you usually update contacts in QuickBooks, select the QuickBooks Data Wins option instead.

10. **On the "Change Settings or Synchronize Now" screen, if you want to change any settings, click Setup (you'll retrace your steps until you're back at the "Change Settings or Synchronize Now" screen). If you're ready to synchronize, click Sync Now.**

    The Contact Sync screen keeps you updated on the progress it's making. When the synchronization is done, the Contact Overview Complete screen appears, showing you how many customers and vendors it found and either matched or added to Outlook.

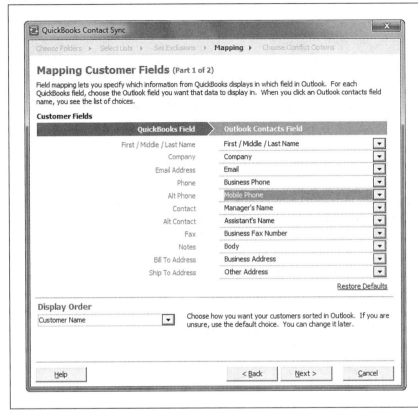

FIGURE 24-4

The Setup Assistant makes some astute guesses about which Outlook fields match up with which QuickBooks fields. However, if the selected field isn't what you want, click the down arrow to the right of the Outlook field's name, and then choose the correct field.

11. **When the Contact Overview Complete screen appears, click Next.**

If contacts that already existed in Outlook don't match up to a QuickBooks list (like Customer or Vendor), the "Select Categories for QuickBooks" screen appears. You can add an Outlook contact to a QuickBooks list by selecting the contact, choosing the appropriate QuickBooks list in the "Select list for contact" drop-down menu, and then clicking Apply.

If the contacts don't match up to a QuickBooks list because they aren't business contacts, you can tell Contact Sync to ignore them. Click the first contact and Shift-click the last contact to select them all. Then, in the "Select list for contact" drop-down menu, choose Ignore, and then click Apply.

After you've selected the QuickBooks lists for your Outlook contacts, click Next.

12. **On the Accept Changes screen, review the changes that will occur in Outlook and QuickBooks. If you don't want to make the changes, click Cancel. If the changes are OK, click Accept.**

A progress box shows you where Contact Sync is in transferring data. The Synchronization Complete message box appears when your info is synchronized. Click OK and you're done.

From now on, you can update contact information with just one click. In Outlook 2010, on the Add-Ins tab, click Synchronize Contacts to make Contact Sync analyze the changes in the two programs and update both as necessary.

Working with Third-Party Programs

Because QuickBooks is so popular with small businesses, plenty of companies besides Intuit offer programs to fill the niches that QuickBooks doesn't handle—or doesn't handle the way you want. For example, QuickBooks' inventory-tracking feature only offers average cost inventory (page 115), so many users turn to third-party inventory applications for LIFO (last in, first out) and FIFO (first in, first out) costing. Estimating is another example, and there are a gazillion more. Third-party developers can build products that integrate with QuickBooks by using Intuit's Software Development Kit (SDK). And Intuit offers quite a few add-ons of its own, as described in the box below. This section describes how you can find applications that meet your needs and how to set them up to play nicely with QuickBooks.

GEM IN THE ROUGH

QuickBooks' Add-on Services

Intuit offers scads of business services you can subscribe to for a fee. The price might be worthwhile when you take into account the cost of your employees' time or—far more valuable—you being able to relax on weekends instead of catching up on company paperwork.

When you perform a task that relates to one of QuickBooks' add-on services, the program promotes the services that might be of interest. For example, click Receive Payments on the QuickBooks Home page, and the ribbon in the Receive Payments window displays an icon labeled Add Credit Card Processing. And the Payments tab in the Receive Payments window includes Add Credit Card Processing and Add eCheck Processing icons.

At the bottom of the left icon bar (page 36), the section labeled "Do More with QuickBooks" lists several Intuit services, including payroll, credit card processing, ordering supplies, and mobile access. If you want to review all of Intuit's business services, in the bar's middle section, click My Apps, and then, in the My Apps list, click App Center. (You have to be signed in to your Intuit account to do this; if you're not, click the Sign In link at the top of the icon bar.) You can also access Intuit's offerings by choosing Help→Add QuickBooks Services, or Help→App Center: Find More Business Solutions.

Finding Third-Party Programs

The Intuit Marketplace website (*http://marketplace.intuit.com*) is one place to look for third-party programs, most of which offer free trials that last from 30 to 90 days. Programs listed in the Marketplace share data with QuickBooks but target different industries or services. Sure, QuickBooks has Premier editions for a few industries (see page xx); but the Marketplace offers additional software for those industries, as well as customized accounting solutions for industries like agriculture, hotels and restaurants, transportation, and utilities. For example, the Construction/Contractors section has programs that produce estimates and that generate documents that conform to industry association standards—while still sharing data with your QuickBooks company file.

Intuit lists third-party programs in two ways: by industry and by business function. For example, if you're looking for contact-management software, you don't have to navigate every industry link looking for programs. Below the Find Apps heading, click Search By Business Need and then, in the list that appears, click Customer Management (CRM).

You can also refine your search for applications that are compatible with your edition of QuickBooks. After you select a category you're interested in on the main Marketplace page, below the list of industries or business needs, click the down arrow to the right of the Check Product Compatibility box, and then choose the edition you use: Pro, Premier, Enterprise, Canada, and so on.

The Marketplace doesn't list *every* third-party program that integrates with QuickBooks. If you use Google to search for basic terms like "QuickBooks third-party application," you'll get tons more results. Of course, if you focus your search (by adding "medical office," for example) you can narrow the results. And, if you use all of the 10 keywords that you can enter in a Google search to describe the QuickBooks add-ons you seek, you might get a few dozen links worth investigating.

If you're familiar with websites like Download.com (*www.download.com*), try using "QuickBooks" as a keyword for a search there. Download.com has dozens of programs that work with QuickBooks, some of which aren't industry-based at all but are still incredibly valuable. For example, you can download a database driver so you can access data in your QuickBooks company file from your database-management program.

TIP Before you let a third-party application loose on your QuickBooks company file, you need to check it out. Does it work with your computer's operating system and your network? Does it have the features you need? Is it easy to use? Does it come with helpful documentation? Back up your company file and any ancillary files (they use the same filename as the company file but have different file types, such as .tlg and .nd). Store the backup on a CD, DVD, or thumb drive, so you can't overwrite it by mistake. Then, make a copy of your company file specifically for your test. If the program doesn't pass the test, you can uninstall it and go back to using your regular company file.

Setting Up an Integrated Application

Integrated applications don't read data from exported text files; they actually access your company file to get info. To protect your data from programs that *shouldn't* read your company file, you have to tell QuickBooks which programs you *do* want digging into your financial data.

Letting programs access your data is something you set up with preferences. In QuickBooks, choose Edit→Preferences→Integrated Applications, and then click the Company Preferences tab, shown in Figure 24-5. There, you can turn on the "Don't allow any applications to access this company file" checkbox to keep all programs out. But if you're reading this section, you probably want at least one program to access your QuickBooks data.

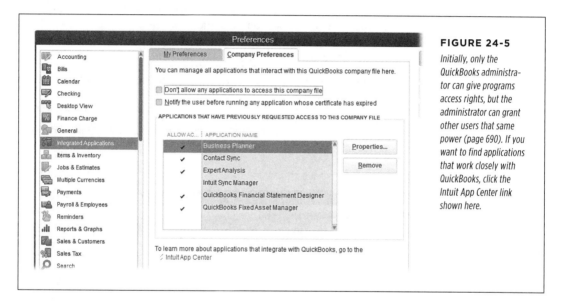

FIGURE 24-5

Initially, only the QuickBooks administrator can give programs access rights, but the administrator can grant other users that same power (page 690). If you want to find applications that work closely with QuickBooks, click the Intuit App Center link shown here.

As long as the "Don't allow any applications to access this company file" checkbox is turned off, when a program tries to access your company file, QuickBooks displays an Application Certificate dialog box. If you're the QuickBooks administrator or have permission to dole out file access, choose one of the dialog box's options to set the program's access to the company file. Obviously, choosing No keeps the program out. But you have three options when you want to let the program in:

- **Yes, prompt each time**. When you're letting another program access your data, this is the safest option. The program can get in only when someone with the rights to approve access says so—a small obstacle that prevents the wrong person from running the program after breaking in after hours. If someone who can approve access isn't available to say yes, the integrated application (or the person who's running it) is out of luck.

- **Yes, whenever this QuickBooks company file is open**. This option is a bit more trusting. As long as someone is working on the company file, the integrated application can access the file without asking permission.

- **Yes, always allow access even if QuickBooks is not running**. This is by far the most lenient choice. The integrated program can help itself to your financial data even if no one with a QuickBooks login is working on the file. This option is exactly what you need if the integrated application is a resource hog that you run at night.

When you choose this option, you can specify that the application be a Quick-Books user and that it must log in. Rather than use one of your employee's logins, create a separate QuickBooks user (page 689) specifically for that integrated application. That way, you can control the type of data the program can access without affecting anyone else's login and the Audit Trail report (page 694) shows the changes the application makes.

> **TIP** Name the user after the third-party application. For example, call the user Fishbowl if you're setting it up for the Fishbowl inventory app.

After a program has accessed your company file, you can change its access rights in the Properties dialog box, as shown in Figure 24-6.

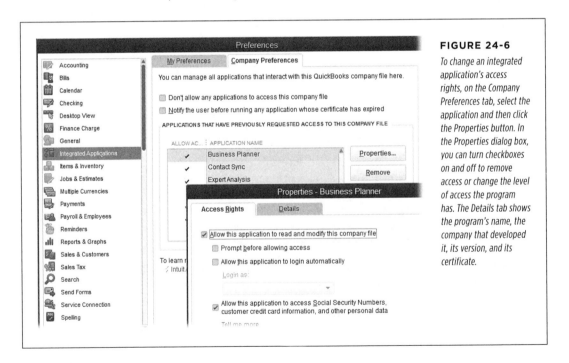

FIGURE 24-6

To change an integrated application's access rights, on the Company Preferences tab, select the application and then click the Properties button. In the Properties dialog box, you can turn checkboxes on and off to remove access or change the level of access the program has. The Details tab shows the program's name, the company that developed it, its version, and its certificate.

▇ Exporting QuickBooks Data

Programs that don't integrate with QuickBooks can still do things that QuickBooks can't. For example, you can export a report to Excel and take advantage of that program's wider range of calculations and formatting options. To get data out of your QuickBooks company file and into another program, you have three choices:

- **Export file**. You can create a *delimited text file* (that is, a file that separates each field with a delimiter like a comma or a tab) that contains data from your QuickBooks file. For example, you can generate export files for QuickBooks lists, such as the Item List. For records with contacts in QuickBooks like your Customer:Job and Vendor lists, you can produce export files that contain all your contact info or only address information.

- **Report file**. You can export any QuickBooks report to a file that you can use in another program. Compared to exporting a list in its entirety, this option gives you more control over how much information you export. If you want to export data from specific customers, specific data from several lists, from transactions, or from specific fields, exporting reports is your *only* choice.

- **Excel file**. Throughout QuickBooks, you can get to the same Export dialog box that you see when you export reports. For example, at the bottom of the Item List window, click Excel→Export All Items. In the Customer Center's menu bar, click Excel, and then choose either Export Customer List or Export Transactions. (The Vendor Center and the Employee Center have similar feature.)

Exporting Lists and Addresses

When you export QuickBooks lists as delimited text files, the export file (called an IIF file because of its .iif file extension) contains values from all the fields associated with those lists. Creating export files is easy—the only choice you have to make is which list(s) to export. If you export several lists, the IIF file that QuickBooks creates contains every field for every list you chose.

▇ EXPORTING LISTS TO A TEXT FILE

Exporting one or more lists to a delimited text file involves only a few quick steps:

1. **Choose File→Utilities→Export→Lists to IIF Files.**

   QuickBooks opens an Export dialog box that contains checkboxes for each list in QuickBooks, as shown in Figure 24-7.

2. **Turn on the checkbox for every list you want to export into the same file, and then click OK.**

   If you want to export lists into *separate* files, repeat these steps for each export file you want to create. For example, if you want to export your Customer List and your Item List to two different files, repeat these steps twice through.

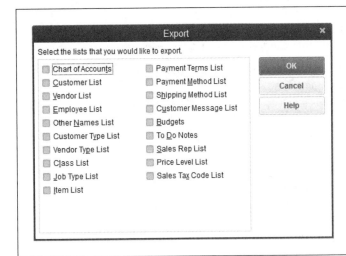

FIGURE 24-7

Turning on a checkbox tells QuickBooks that you want to export all the records in that list. If you turn on more than one checkbox, the data for every list you choose ends up in a single export file.

3. **In the second Export dialog box (which is basically a Save As dialog box), navigate to the folder where you want to save the export file and, in the "File name" box, type a name for the file.**

   Your export files are easier to find if you create a folder specifically for them. For example, you could create a subfolder called Export_Files within the folder that holds your company files.

4. **Click Save to create the file.**

   When the QuickBooks Information message box tells you that your data was exported successfully, click OK to close the message box. Now you're ready to import the file into Microsoft Excel or another program, as described later in this chapter (page 657).

> **TIP** Exporting QuickBooks data can help you learn the format you need to *import* data into your company file. For instance, once you've entered a customer type or two (using the manual process described on page 158), you can export them. Then, in the export file, create the rest of your codes by using the same format, and then import that file back into QuickBooks.

■ EXPORTING ADDRESSES

With QuickBooks features to generate mail-merge letters, export contact list reports, and synchronize your company file with Outlook, you may not need the tab-delimited address files that QuickBooks produces. However, if you need a text file of names and addresses to import into another program, here's what you do:

1. **Choose File→Utilities→Export→Addresses to Text File.**

   The Select Names for Export Addresses dialog box opens.

2. **In the "Select Names to be exported to your Address data file" box, choose the category of names you want to export, and then click OK.**

   Initially, QuickBooks chooses "All names" to export all the names in your company file. You can also choose categories of names, like "All vendors." To select individual names, choose "Multiple names," and then pick the ones you want.

3. **In the Save Address Data File dialog box, select a folder where you want to save the exported file, type a filename in the "File name" box, and then click Save.**

   QuickBooks automatically assigns a .txt extension to the file. You can now import it into any program that can handle tab-delimited addresses.

Exporting Reports

As you learned in Chapter 21, you can customize reports to contain just the information you want, presented just the way you want. When you want to export only *some* QuickBooks data or export it in a specific way, your best bet is customizing a report and then exporting it.

If the program you want to import the report data into is fussy about data formats, export the report to Excel, where it's easier to make changes than in a text-editing tool such as Windows Notepad. You can also export a report to a comma-delimited file if that's what another program needs. Exporting reports is an effective way to extract some QuickBooks lists like the Item List, Customer List, Vendor List, and Employee List. Here are the different ways you can use this technique:

- **Running a report**. Start by running the report you want to export (page 544). In the report window, click Excel→Create New Worksheet. The "Send Report to Excel" dialog box lets you choose the file and options for the export, as shown in Figure 24-8.

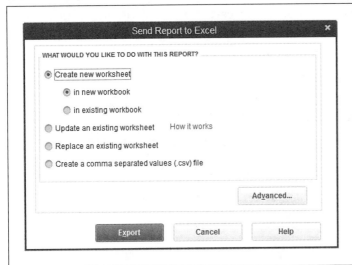

FIGURE 24-8

When you create an Excel workbook by exporting a report, QuickBooks automatically includes a worksheet in it with tips for working with the resulting Excel worksheet. If you don't need help with Excel, click the Advanced button shown here. In the Advanced Excel Options dialog box, turn off the "Include QuickBooks Export Guide worksheet with helpful advice" checkbox.

- **From the Item List window**. Open the Item List window (on the Home page, click the Items & Services icon) and then, at the bottom of the list window, click Excel→Export All Items. QuickBooks opens the Export dialog box, which has similar options to the ones you see when you export a report (Figure 24-8).

- **From a QuickBooks center**. In the Customer Center's menu bar, click Excel, and then choose Export Customer List or Export Transactions. In the Vendor Center and Employee Center, choose Export Vendor List or Export Employee List, respectively.

Regardless of whether the Export dialog box or the "Send Report to Excel" dialog box opens, you can choose the same basic options for where you want to save the exported report:

- The **Create new worksheet** option creates a brand-new Excel worksheet for the report. If you choose Excel→Create New Worksheet in a report window, the "Create new worksheet" and "in new workbook" options are selected, which means QuickBooks will create a new Excel workbook with a worksheet for the exported data, as shown in Figure 24-9. If you export a list and the Export dialog box appears, selecting the "Create new worksheet" option also displays the "in new workbook" and "in existing workbook" options so you can create a new worksheet in an existing file or a brand-new one.

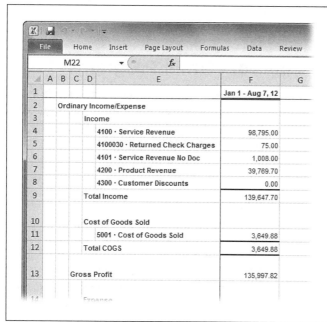

FIGURE 24-9

QuickBooks reports have headers, columns, and rows. When you export a report to Excel, the data in the report's columns and rows transfer into columns and rows in the worksheet. But exporting a report to a workbook isn't a mindless transfer of values: First, the subtotals in the workbook actually use Excel's SUM function to add up the workbook cells that make up the subtotal. Second, if you choose the "Update an existing worksheet" option, QuickBooks can update values in an existing worksheet without overwriting most of the edits you've made.

- The **Update an existing worksheet** option exports the report to an existing worksheet in an existing file. This option is ideal if you're planning to calculate ratios and want your most recent financial statements in the same workbook as statements for previous periods. If you export to an existing file, you can also choose options to create a new worksheet for the report or add the report to a sheet already in the workbook. If you choose Excel→Update Existing Worksheet in a report window, the "Send Report to Excel" dialog box opens with this option selected, which displays the "Select workbook" box so you can choose the file and worksheet you want to update.

- The **Replace an existing worksheet** option exports the report to an existing worksheet but replaces the contents of that worksheet. In the "Select workbook" box, choose the file and then specify the worksheet you want to replace.

- The **Create a comma separated values (.csv) file** option creates a comma-delimited file that you can use with programs that can read files formatted that way.

TIP The Advanced button in the Export and "Send Report to Excel" dialog boxes opens the Advanced Excel Options dialog box, which lets you set the formatting you want to transfer from QuickBooks to Excel, which Excel features you want the workbook to use (like AutoFit to size the columns to display all the data), and where you want the report's header information displayed.

After you've selected the type of export file and other options, click Export. Quick-Books launches Excel and copies the data in the report to the Excel workbook you specified, placing the data from the report's columns into the worksheet's columns, as shown in Figure 24-9.

Importing Data from Other Programs

Importing data from other programs comes in handy mostly for generating lists in QuickBooks. However, you can also import data to generate your chart of accounts (page 44) or to load different versions of your company budget (page 525). The biggest requirement for importing data is that the files have to be either Excel workbooks (.xls or .xlsx files) or delimited text files, which separate each piece of information with commas or tabs.

Importing an Excel Spreadsheet

If you're familiar with importing Excel spreadsheets into other programs, importing them into QuickBooks is a snap. In fact, QuickBooks includes several Excel import templates that walk you through getting your Excel data for customers, vendors, and items into the format that QuickBooks requires. (If you have a file that's already formatted to work with QuickBooks, skip to the box on page 656, which explains how to import a preformatted file.) Here's how to use QuickBooks' Excel import templates:

1. **Choose File→Utilities→Import→Excel Files.**

   QuickBooks opens the "Add Your Excel Data to QuickBooks" wizard. (If you see the Add/Edit Multiple List Entries dialog box, click No to proceed to the wizard. If you don't want to see this message again, turn on the "Do not display" checkbox.)

2. **Click the button for the type of data you want to import: Customers, Vendors, or Products I Sell.**

   You see a message warning that you can't undo the import and recommending that you back up your company file first. If you want to create a backup, click No, create the backup, and then begin with step 1 again. If you're ready to import data, click Yes to close the message box.

   QuickBooks opens an Excel template for the type of data you're importing, as shown in Figure 24-10.

3. **Copy your data into the template.**

   Open the Excel spreadsheet whose info you want to get into QuickBooks, select the data you want to copy, and then press Ctrl+C. Next, switch to the Excel template QuickBooks created and press Ctrl+V to paste the data. (If you need help, click the template's Show Detailed Instructions button.)

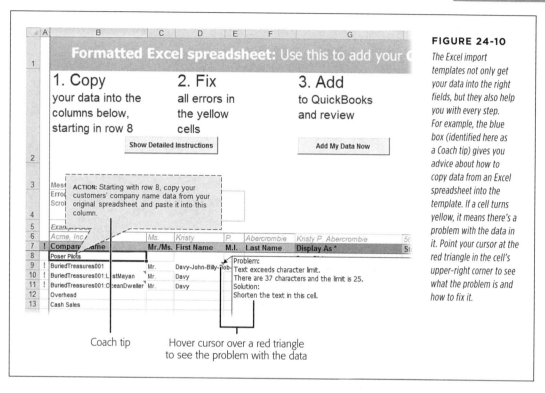

Coach tip

Hover cursor over a red triangle
to see the problem with the data

FIGURE 24-10

*The Excel import
templates not only get
your data into the right
fields, but they also help
you with every step.
For example, the blue
box (identified here as
a Coach tip) gives you
advice about how to
copy data from an Excel
spreadsheet into the
template. If a cell turns
yellow, it means there's a
problem with the data in
it. Point your cursor at the
red triangle in the cell's
upper-right corner to see
what the problem is and
how to fix it.*

4. **After you've copied all the data from your spreadsheet into the Excel template and none of the template's cells are yellow, save the template.**

   In Excel 2010, choose File→Save. In Excel 2007, choose Office→Save.

5. **In the Excel template, click Add My Data Now.**

   QuickBooks resumes control, and the "Add Your Excel Data to QuickBooks" wizard shows the progress of the import. When it's done, it places green checkmarks to the left of all three steps and shows you how many records it imported. You can click the button that says "View <type of imported info>" to see the list you imported, or click Close and view your lists as you usually do. For example, to see your Customer List, click Customer Center on the Home page.

Importing Formatted Excel Files

QuickBooks veterans often amass all sorts of tools that they've built over the years, like Excel files set up to import information. Although QuickBooks has a wizard that shows you exactly where to put what kind of info in an Excel file, you can skip the handholding by following these steps:

1. Back up your company file in case you run into a problem with the import.

2. Choose File→Utilities→Import→Excel Files.

3. In the "Add Your Excel Data to QuickBooks" wizard, click the Advanced Import button.

4. In the "Import a file" dialog box, on the Set Up Import tab, click Browse and select the Excel file you want to import. (QuickBooks 2012 can import workbooks from Excel 2000 through Excel 2010.)

5. QuickBooks fills in the "Choose a sheet in this Excel workbook" drop-down list with the worksheets from the workbook you selected. Choose the worksheet you want to import.

6. QuickBooks automatically turns on the "This data file has header rows" checkbox, which is the perfect choice when the first row of the Excel workbook contains text labels for the columns.

7. In the "Choose a mapping" drop-down list, choose <Add New>. Then, in the "Mapping name" box, type a name for the set of correspondences between fields and columns you're about to choose. (Once you've set up a mapping,

you can reuse it by clicking Mappings and selecting it.)

8. If you're defining a mapping, in the "Import type" drop-down list, choose the data you're importing: Customer, Vendor, Item, or Account.

9. For each QuickBooks field listed in the left column, in the "Import data" column, choose the corresponding Excel header or column name, as shown in Figure 24-11.

10. After you've mapped all the columns you want to import to QuickBooks fields, click Save.

11. On the "Import a file" dialog box's Preferences tab, tell QuickBooks how to handle errors and duplicate records. QuickBooks sets the Duplicate Handling option to "Prompt me and let me decide," so you're in complete control unless you choose another option.

12. To review the data you're about to import, click Preview. In the Preview dialog box, in the "In data preview show" drop-down list, choose "only errors" to see rows of data that contain errors. When you select an incorrect entry, the "Details for" table shows the values you're trying to import and what the problem is so you can correct it. You can also select options to skip importing rows with errors or import records and leave error fields blank. Click OK to close the Preview dialog box.

13. In the "Import a file" dialog box, click Import. Click Yes to complete the import (as long as you backed up your company file in step 1).

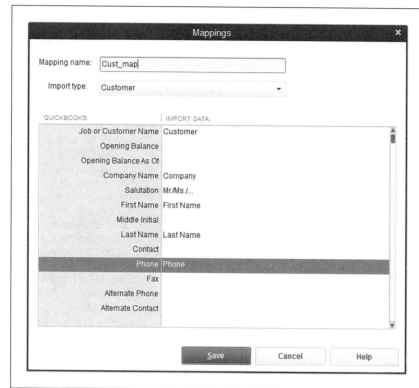

FIGURE 24-11

*The correct column is easy
to pick when the Excel
workbook contains column
headers in the first row.
Otherwise, you're left to
guess what kind of information Column A and Column
B hold.*

Importing a Delimited File

If you're importing a Customer List, Vendor List, or Item List, don't even think about importing it as a delimited file. It's much easier to open that kind of file in Excel and then use the wizard described in the previous section. But if you want to import other kinds of lists or a budget, using a delimited file works just fine.

QuickBooks needs to know the *kind* of data you're importing—and it learns that from special *keywords* for row and column headers. (Keywords are strings of characters in a delimited text file that identify QuickBooks' records and fields.) Before you import data from another program into a QuickBooks list, you need to know the correct keywords for the fields you're importing. The easiest way to see the keywords for a list is to export that list from QuickBooks and examine the keywords at the beginning of the rows and at the tops of the columns.

Deciphering keywords requires a smattering of computerese. For example, when you see the column heading "Billing Address," you know instantly what kind of information you're looking at. But the only way QuickBooks recognizes the first line of a billing address is from the keyword BADDR1. Figure 24-12 explains all (it shows the delimited file in an Excel spreadsheet to make the fields easier to read).

FIGURE 24-12

1: In the first cell in the first row of a list, an exclamation point in front of the keyword tells QuickBooks that the data in the rows that follow are for that list. For example, !CUST represents data for the Customer List.

2: Keywords in the other cells of the same row specify the QuickBooks field names. In cell B36, the keyword NAME identifies the values in that column as the name of each customer. In cell G36, BADDR3 identifies the third part of the billing address.

3: A keyword is the first text in the row. Each row that begins with CUST in the first cell represents a separate customer record.

4: The other cells in a row contain the values that QuickBooks imports into the designated fields.

When you have an IIF file with the correct keywords, here's how to import it into QuickBooks:

1. **Choose File→Utilities→Import→IIF Files.**

   QuickBooks opens the Import dialog box with the "Files of type" box set to "IIF Files (*.IIF)."

2. **Navigate to the folder where the file you want to import is saved, and then double-click the filename.**

   QuickBooks displays a message box telling you that it imported the data successfully. (If you didn't set up the keywords correctly or QuickBooks ran into other problems with the data in the file, it tells you that it *didn't* import the data successfully.)

Customizing QuickBooks

L aid out like the workflow you use when you're bookkeeping, the QuickBooks Home page provides instant access to all the accounting tasks you perform. You can take your pick of helpful shortcuts to your favorite features from the QuickBooks top icon bar, the new left icon bar, or from within the centers for vendors, customers, and employees.

But your business isn't like anyone else's. If you run a strictly cash-sales business, you couldn't care less about customer lists and invoices; making deposits, though, is a daily event. Fortunately, you don't have to accept QuickBooks' initial take on convenience. The Home page and the icon bars come with a set of popular shortcuts, but you can add, remove, rearrange, and otherwise edit which features appear there. You can also add your favorite features, windows, and reports to the Favorites menu. This chapter covers all your options.

In addition to tweaking QuickBooks' layout, you can also customize the program's forms. QuickBooks helps you get up and running with built-in business form templates. They'll do if you have to blast out some invoices. But when you finally find a few spare minutes, you can create templates that show the information you want, formatted the way you want, and laid out to work with your letterhead. Create as many versions as you want. For example, you can make one invoice template to print on your letterhead and another that includes your logo and company name and address for creating electronic invoices to email. This chapter describes the most efficient ways to create forms: using QuickBooks' form designs or built-in templates as a basis for your own. In Appendix E (online at *www.missingmanuals.com/cds*), you can learn how to fine-tune forms with advanced customization techniques and even create templates from scratch.

Customizing the Desktop

Each person who uses QuickBooks can make the program's desktop look the way they want (choose Edit→Preferences→Desktop View to open the My Preferences tab). Page 605 gives the full scoop on how you set preferences to customize the desktop, but here are the different ways you can make the desktop your own:

- **One window or several**. You can focus on one window at a time with the One Window option. The Multiple Windows option lets you see several windows at once.

- **Show Home page when opening a company file**. The Home page shows the entire workflow of your accounting tasks, along with shortcuts to popular windows and tasks like the Chart of Accounts window and writing checks.

NOTE Unlike previous versions, QuickBooks 2013 doesn't let you choose a color scheme.

Customizing the Home Page

You can adjust the QuickBooks Home page so that it fits your business's workflow. The program incorporates the answers you gave during QuickBooks Setup with your companywide Desktop View preferences, as shown in Figure 25-1, but you can change these settings. For example, if you don't have inventory, turn off the inventory feature and the icons for buying, receiving, and paying for inventory won't appear on your Home page. And if you don't have employees, the employee panel disappears. See page 607 for the full scoop on changing the icons on your Home page.

Fast Access to Favorite Features

In addition to the Home page, QuickBooks gives you two other ways to access your favorite features fast: the Favorites menu and the icon bar. Out of the box, the Favorites menu is nearly empty, waiting for you to add your preferred features and reports. On the other hand, icons for QuickBooks' centers and other popular features fill up the icon bar from the get-go, but depending on how you like to work, those icons may languish unclicked. This section describes how to add entries to the Favorites menu and modify the icon bar to display only the features you want.

Building Your Favorites Menu

The Favorites menu, which appears to the right of the Lists menu on the QuickBooks menu bar, initially has only one entry: Customize Favorites, which opens the Customize Your Menus dialog box where you can add almost any feature or report to the Favorites menu. Here's how:

1. **Choose Favorites→Customize Favorites.**

   The Customize Your Menus dialog box opens. The Available Menu Items list is a directory of every feature QuickBooks has to offer—every entry on every menu and submenu on the QuickBooks' menu bar appears in this list. The top-level menu bar entries are aligned with the left side of the list box, menu entries are indented, and submenu entries indented even more. Even the Reports section leaves nothing out—you can choose any built-in, customized, or memorized report in your company file.

2. **Select the feature you want to add in the Available Menu Items list and then click Add.**

   The feature appears in the Chosen Menu Items list, as shown in Figure 25-2.

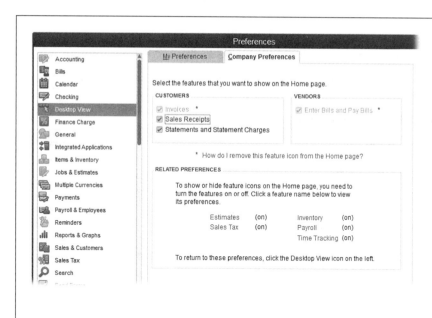

FIGURE 25-1

The Edit→Preferences→ Desktop View→Company Preferences tab is where you customize your Home page. Display or hide icons on the Home page by turning their checkboxes on or off here. For example, if you don't send statements to customers, turn off the "Statements and Statement Charges" checkbox. To show or hide the icons that appear on the Home page (like Estimates and Payroll), simply click the links for the features in the bottom part of the tab, and QuickBooks jumps to the corresponding preference section so you can turn the feature on or off.

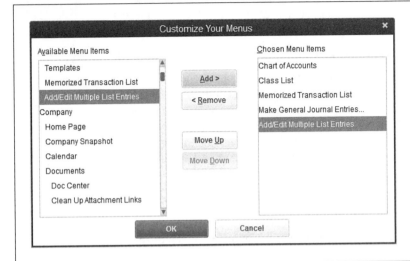

FIGURE 25-2

To remove an entry from the Favorites menu, select it in the Chosen Menu Items list, and then click Remove. To change the order of the entries, select the entry you want to move, and then click Move Up or Move Down until the entry is where you want it.

3. **If you want to rearrange the entries, select one and then click Move Up or Move Down until it's in the position you want.**

   You can't indent entries or add any kind of separator to help you find the ones you want.

4. **Click OK to close the dialog box.**

Now when you click the Favorites menu, it displays all the features you added to it.

Customizing the Icon Bar

The QuickBooks icon bar initially includes icons that open some of the program's popular features, like the various centers, the Home page, and others, depending on which edition of the program you use. If the Home page always seems to be hidden behind several open windows, you can use the icon bar to access your favorite features, memorized reports, or windows you open often. You can customize the icon bar to include just the entries you want and change its appearance in several ways. The following sections show you how.

NOTE In QuickBooks 2013, you can position the icon bar at the top of the QuickBooks main window or down the left side. (To specify which location you want, from the View menu, select Top Icon Bar or Left Icon Bar, respectively.) The top icon bar takes up less screen real estate, but the left icon bar makes features easy to find because you can see both their icons and their full text labels. The My Shortcuts section of the left icon bar offers several other handy features. For the full story, see page 36.

Here are the basic steps for customizing the icon bar:

1. **Choose View→Customize Icon Bar.**

   If the top icon bar is visible, you can right-click it and choose Customize Icon Bar. If you use the left icon bar, the easiest way to customize the icon bar is to choose View→Customize Icon Bar. (If the My Shortcuts section is displayed at the top of the left icon bar, you can also right-click within that section and then choose Customize Shortcuts.)

NOTE The icon bar has to be visible before you can customize it. If you open the View menu when the icon bar is hidden, the Customize Icon Bar entry is dimmed. Choose View→Top Icon Bar or View→Left Icon Bar to turn the bar back on, and *then* choose View→Customize Icon Bar.

2. **In the Customize Icon Bar dialog box (Figure 25-3), add shortcuts to the icon bar, remove icons for features you don't want, and edit or change the order in which they appear, as described in the following sections.**

   The icon bar immediately reflects the changes you make in the Customize Icon Bar dialog box.

3. **To save your changes, in the Customize Icon Bar dialog box, click OK.**

■ ADDING AND REMOVING ICONS

If you know which icons you want and don't want, you can make those changes in one marathon session. First, open the Customize Icon Bar dialog box by right-clicking the icon bar and choosing Customize Icon Bar (or Customize Shortcuts for the My Shortcuts section of the left icon bar). Here's what you do then:

1. **In the Customize Icon Bar dialog box, select the entry that you want to be to the left of or above the new icon you insert (depending on whether you use the top icon bar or the left icon bar).**

   In the Icon Bar Content list, the entries appear one below the other, even though the icons appear from left to right on the top icon bar. If you use the left icon bar instead, the icons appear in the same order as in the Icon Bar Content list. When you select an entry in the list and add an icon, QuickBooks inserts the new icon below the selected entry in the Icon Bar Content list, so it appears to the right of the selected icon on the top icon bar, or below the selected icon on the left icon bar.

2. **Click Add.**

   The Add Icon Bar Item dialog box shown in Figure 25-4 opens.

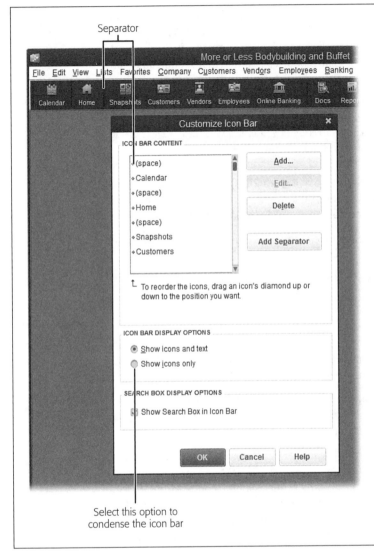

Separator

FIGURE 25-3

You can add separators to organize the top icon bar. To do that, select the entry to the right of which you want to insert the separator and then click Add Separator. In the Icon Bar Content list, the separator appears below the entry you selected and shows up as "(space)". (The left icon bar doesn't display separators, so you can't add them while the left icon bar is visible.)

If screen real estate is at a premium, you can reduce the height of the top icon bar by removing icon labels. Simply select the "Show icons only" option. Without labels to identify what the icons represent, you can see a hint by pointing your cursor at the icon to display its tooltip description.

Select this option to
condense the icon bar

3. **In the list on the left, click the window or feature you want to add, like Chart of Accounts to open the Chart of Accounts window.**

QuickBooks automatically selects an icon in the list of graphics and fills in the Label and Description boxes. If you like, click a different graphic and/or edit the text in these boxes to change the label that appears on the icon bar or the description that appears as a tooltip.

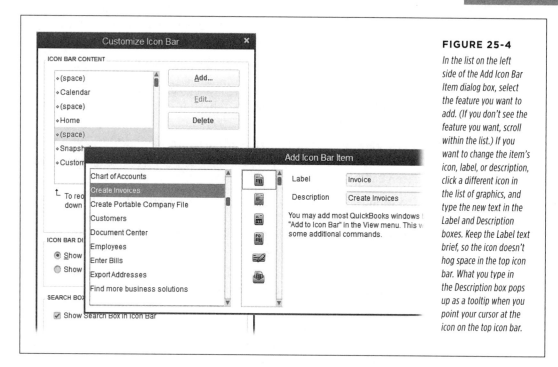

FIGURE 25-4

In the list on the left side of the Add Icon Bar Item dialog box, select the feature you want to add. (If you don't see the feature you want, scroll within the list.) If you want to change the item's icon, label, or description, click a different icon in the list of graphics, and type the new text in the Label and Description boxes. Keep the Label text brief, so the icon doesn't hog space in the top icon bar. What you type in the Description box pops up as a tooltip when you point your cursor at the icon on the top icon bar.

TIP See page 66 to learn how to add almost *any* QuickBooks window to the icon bar, even if it doesn't appear in the Add Icon Bar Item list.

4. **Click OK to add the item to the icon bar.**

   You don't have to close the Customize Icon Bar dialog box to see your changes—QuickBooks makes them right away.

5. **Repeat steps 2–4 to add more icons to the bar.**

   Back in the Customize Icon Bar dialog box, you can rearrange or edit the entries as explained in the following pages.

6. **To remove an icon from the bar, simply select its entry in the Customize Icon Bar dialog box, and then click Delete.**

   When you're done customizing the icon bar, click OK to close the Customize Icon Bar dialog box.

ADDING WINDOWS TO THE ICON BAR

The Add Icon Bar Item dialog box doesn't list every QuickBooks window, but that doesn't prevent you from adding windows to the icon bar. Once you realize that you open the same window again and again, you can add an icon for it to the icon bar without even opening the Customize Icon Bar dialog box. Here's how:

1. **Open the window for the feature or report you want to add to the icon bar.**

   For example, you can add a window for a memorized report that you've created (an Accounts Receivable Aging Detail report, say) since reports open in their own windows.

2. **Choose View→"Add '<window name>' to Icon Bar," where <window name> is the name of the window you just opened, as in "Add 'A/R Aging Detail' to Icon Bar."**

   If the wrong window name appears in the entry name, be sure to activate the window you want before choosing the entry on the View menu. When you choose View→"Add '<window name>' to Icon Bar," QuickBooks opens the Add Window to Icon Bar dialog box.

3. **In the Add Window to Icon Bar dialog box, click the icon you want to use and, in the Label and Description boxes, type the text you want for the icon's label and description.**

   In the icon bar, the text in the Description box appears as a tooltip when you position your cursor over the icon. Keep the Label short and use the Description to elaborate on the window or report's contents.

4. **Click OK to add the window to the icon bar.**

   QuickBooks plunks the window at the right end of the top icon bar or, if you're using the left icon bar, at the bottom of the My Shortcuts section. If you want the icon somewhere else, choose View→Customize Icon Bar, and then reposition the window in the list (page 667).

CHANGING AN ICON'S APPEARANCE

To change an icon or its associated text, in the Customize Icon Bar dialog box, click the icon's entry, and then click Edit. QuickBooks opens the Edit Icon Bar Item dialog box, which lets you change three features of each icon:

- **Icon.** In the icon list, select the graphic you want to appear on the icon bar. You can't design your own icons, and QuickBooks doesn't care whether you choose an icon that fits the feature you're adding. For instance, an icon with a checkbook register and pen might be good for Writing Checks, but you could choose the faucet with a drop of water if you prefer.

- **Label.** If you want to shorten the label to condense the top icon bar, in the Label box, type your own.

- **Description.** To change the text that appears as a tooltip for the icon, in the Description box, type your own.

■ CHANGING THE ORDER OF ICONS

If you want to group related icons, you can change the order of the items in the icon bar. And, as explained in Figure 25-3, you can add separators to make the groups stand out in the top icon bar. Open the Customize Icon Bar dialog box to make these changes (choose View→Customize Icon Bar). Figure 25-5 shows how to rearrange icons.

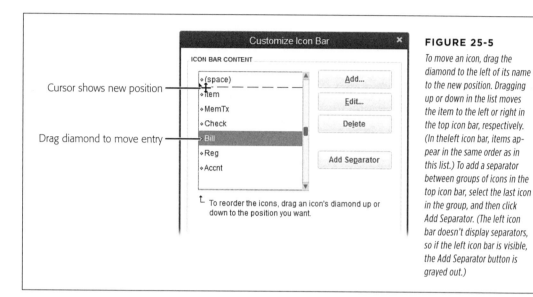

FIGURE 25-5

To move an icon, drag the diamond to the left of its name to the new position. Dragging up or down in the list moves the item to the left or right in the top icon bar, respectively. (In the left icon bar, items appear in the same order as in this list.) To add a separator between groups of icons in the top icon bar, select the last icon in the group, and then click Add Separator. (The left icon bar doesn't display separators, so if the left icon bar is visible, the Add Separator button is grayed out.)

■ Customizing the Company Snapshot

The Company Snapshot (page 32) displays key statistics about your business in one convenient dashboard window. It has three tabs so you can choose from almost two dozen different views of financial status, like income and expense trends, account balances, customers who owe money, invoice payment status, receivables reports, and so on.

To change the views that appear in the Company Snapshot window, first open the window by choosing Company→Company Snapshot. Next, click the Company, Payments, or Customer tab, and then click Add Content near the top-left corner of the window. The "Add content to your <tab name> Snapshot" panel appears with the name and a thumbnail of each view you can choose, as shown in Figure 25-6. Here's how you customize the Company Snapshot:

- **Add a view.** Click the Add button to the right of the view you want, and Quick-Books adds it to the body of the Company Snapshot.

- **Remove a view.** Click the Close button (the X) at its top-right corner.

- **Reposition a view.** Put your cursor over the view's header and, when the cursor changes to a four-headed arrow, drag the view to its new location in the Company Snapshot window.

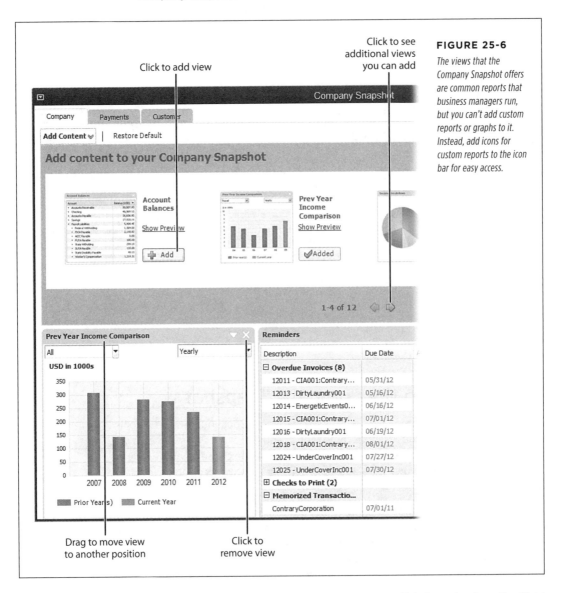

Click to see
additional views
you can add

Click to add view

FIGURE 25-6

The views that the Company Snapshot offers are common reports that business managers run, but you can't add custom reports or graphs to it. Instead, add icons for custom reports to the icon bar for easy access.

Drag to move view
to another position

Click to
remove view

When the Company Snapshot shows what you want, click Done to close the "Add content to your <tab name> Snapshot" panel. If you want to undo the changes you've made, click Restore Default below the tabs at the top of the window.

■ Customizing Forms

Everything you do says *something* about your business—even the forms you use. If you run a small company and don't have a spare second to customize forms, the built-in QuickBooks invoices and other form templates work just fine. But if you want business forms that convey your sense of style and attention to detail, customized form templates are the way to go. A *form template* controls the appearance of a specific type of form, such as a purchase order, invoice, or credit memo; you can specify what fields appear on the form, how the fields are formatted, and how they're laid out.

In QuickBooks, the customization you can apply to form templates comes in several shapes and sizes, described in detail in the sections that follow:

- **Basic customization.** You can add a logo to forms or turn company information fields on or off, depending on what your letterhead includes. Aesthetics like the color scheme and fonts are also at your command.

- **Changing fields.** To notch the customization up, you can choose the fields that appear in forms: the header, footer, and columns. You can also specify some printing options, whether to print trailing zeroes, and the minimum number of decimal places if you display trailing zeroes. To learn all these tricks, see "Additional Customization" on page 674.

- **Designing form layout.** The ultimate in form customization, QuickBooks' Layout Designer gives you full control over form design. You can add fields and images, plunk them where you want, and format them as you please. For example, you can resize and reposition fields to emphasize the balance due. To learn how to fine-tune forms and build them from scratch, see Appendix E on this book's Missing CD page at *www.missingmanuals.com/cds*.

- **Form designs.** The QuickBooks Forms Customization online tool helps you produce consistent, professional-looking business forms by creating a *form design* for your company file. Unlike a form *template*, the QuickBooks Form Customization tool helps you create a form *design* that specifies the appearance—including the background (like a watermark), logo, colors, fonts, and the format of the grid that holds your data—of *any* form. Because a form design applies to any form, it only specifies form formatting, not the fields contained in a form or where fields are located. Using the online tool is a step-by-step process that's easy to follow, and when you're done, you can save the design and apply it to *all* the forms in your QuickBooks company file in one fell swoop. From then on, you choose the forms you want to use as you would normally (page 280).

  Although you can use the designs you create as long as you like, once you apply a design to a company file, you have only 30 days to edit your design, create new ones, and apply them to your forms. After that, you'll pay $4.99 to apply a new design to your forms or apply your original design to new forms. Each time you pay $4.99, you start a 60-day period in which you can edit your design and apply it to any form.

NOTE Don't expect miracles from form designs. The formatting you can choose is limited. If you want to get fancy, use the customization tools within QuickBooks, which are described in the following sections and in online Appendix E (*www.missingmanuals.com/cds*).

Editing an Existing Template in QuickBooks

One way to build your own forms is to start with a template that QuickBooks provides or use another customized template that you've put together. Whether you plan to make minor adjustments or major revisions, you won't have to start from scratch. (To learn how to customize a template while you're in the middle of a task like creating an invoice, see the box on the next page.)

Here's how to edit an existing template:

1. **Choose Lists→Templates.**

   QuickBooks opens the Templates window, which displays built-in templates and any that you've created. If you're looking for a specific type of form to start with, look in the Type column, which displays labels such as Invoice and Credit Memo.

2. **In the Name column, click the template you want to edit, and then press Ctrl+E to open the Basic Customization dialog box (Figure 25-8).**

   You can also click the template's name and then click Templates→Edit Template.

3. **In the Basic Customization dialog box, click Manage Templates so you can make a copy of the form.**

   In the Manage Templates dialog box, QuickBooks automatically selects the name of the template you're editing. Click Copy, and QuickBooks automatically fills in the Template Name box on the right side of the dialog box with "Copy of: <form>." Type over this text to name the form something meaningful, and then click OK to return to the Basic Customization dialog box. This way, you can keep the edited form or go back to the original.

4. **In the Basic Customization dialog box, make the changes you want.**

   For basic customization instructions, see the next section. To learn about changing the fields on a form, see page 674. And, for full layout instructions, see Appendix E at *www.missingmanuals.com/cds*.

5. **When the form looks the way you want, in the Basic Customization dialog box, click OK.**